Introduction to Law in Canada

SECOND EDITION

John Fairlie & Philip Sworden

emond ▪ Toronto, Canada ▪ 2019

Emond Montgomery Publications Limited
1 Eglinton Avenue E., Suite 600
Toronto ON M4P 3A1
http://www.emond.ca/highered

Printed in Canada.
Reprinted November 2020.

We acknowledge the financial support of the Government of Canada.   **Canadä**

Emond Montgomery Publications has no responsibility for the persistence or accuracy of URLs for external or third-party Internet websites referred to in this publication, and does not guarantee that any content on such websites is, or will remain, accurate or appropriate.

Vice president, publishing: Anthony Rezek
Publisher: Mike Thompson
Director, development and production: Kelly Dickson
Developmental editor: Sarah Downey
Production supervisor: Laura Bast
Production editor: Natalie Berchem
Permissions editor: Karen Hunter
Copy editor: Rebecca Russell
Typesetter: Transforma
Text designer: Tara Agnerian
Proofreader: Ann Lau
Indexer: Andrew Little
Cover image: Gunter Marx/Alamy Stock Photo

Library and Archives Canada Cataloguing in Publication

Title: Introduction to law in Canada / John Fairlie, Philip Sworden.
Names: Fairlie, John, author. | Sworden, Philip James, 1950- author.
Description: Second edition. | Includes bibliographical references and index.
Identifiers: Canadiana 20190054409 | ISBN 9781772554687 (softcover)
Subjects: LCSH: Law—Canada—Textbooks. | LCGFT: Textbooks.
Classification: LCC KE444 .F35 2019 | LCC KF385.ZA2 F33 2019 kfmod | DDC 349.71—dc23

For my wife, Christine
—JF

To my grandsons, Lachlan and William
—PS

Brief Contents

Contents

PART I
Theory and Context

Table of Cases

Table of Statutes

Preface

Our objective in writing the second edition of *Introduction to Law in Canada* is, like the first edition, to provide a theoretical basis for understanding the law and its development in the Canadian context, and to examine the key features of our legal system.

We have tried to be inclusive, imagining how readers from, or interested in, all parts of Canada would interpret the book's relevance. When citing statutory or case law, for example, we have represented as many regions as possible. And in our discussion of the division of powers under the Constitution, the territories are included alongside the provinces in our explanations of the relevant principles.

We also wanted to reflect Canada's social and multicultural diversity. For example: we describe not only how we are a bijural nation primarily influenced by the common law and civil law traditions, but also how other legal traditions play a significant role in other countries, and how we are placed in the larger international context; we look at how Indigenous peoples have contributed, and continue to contribute, to our legal heritage; and we examine how the *Canadian Charter of Rights and Freedoms* has shaped equality and other rights.

At the same time, we have been mindful that law is a tool for the regulation of individuals and societies and has a very practical side. As well as introducing the law in a way that is accessible, we have attempted to describe it in sufficient detail to be useful and, for this edition, have incorporated recent changes to the law and legal practice.

Part I covers theory and context. Part II examines the Canadian Constitution, including: how legislative power is divided between our federal, provincial, and territorial governments; how executive power is used to administer the law; how judicial power is distributed through our system of courts; and, finally, how civil liberties and the guarantee of rights and freedoms under the Charter influence our laws. In Part III, we consider an array of subject areas—including tort law, contract law, property law, family law, administrative law, criminal law, and international law—allowing readers to take the next steps in their studies and providing them with a firm legal grounding wherever their future career paths may take them. Part IV concludes the book by looking at legal professionals and their ethical obligations to the public and others, and by examining access to justice and law reform.

It is our hope that this text will serve as a useful guide for all students studying the law—including those in legal programs (law, paralegal, notary, law clerk, legal assistant, and related areas), justice studies, criminology, security and policing, border services, social work, history, business, and political science—and for anyone else who is interested in learning how the law operates in Canada.

Our thanks to the following reviewers for providing their helpful feedback and suggestions during the development of this edition: Kandace Bond Wileman, Durham College; Sirvan Karimi, York University; Jason Kohn, Humber College; Jennifer Northcote, Centennial College; Stacey Pipicelli, Fanshawe College; and Sarah Sheaves, Mohawk College.

Finally, we would like to thank the staff at Emond Publishing for helping us put this book together, and in particular: Sarah Downey, who worked on the initial drafts; Rebecca Russell and Ann Lau, for their thoughts and contributions during the galley stages; Natalie Berchem and Karen Hunter, who provided editorial assistance throughout; and Kelly Dickson and Mike Thompson for their unwavering support and encouragement. Our gratitude goes out to them all.

John Fairlie
Vancouver, British Columbia

Philip Sworden
Sydney, Australia

In Memoriam—A Special Dedication

In 2016, Philip Sworden retired from teaching and moved to Australia with his wife to spend more time with his son and grandchildren. Sadly, he passed away unexpectedly in 2018. Philip had a passion for teaching law, Canadian history, and celebrating the diversity of his students and Canada's peoples. His passions are reflected in this book. Philip was also an accomplished painter, inspired by Tom Thomson and the Group of Seven. He will be greatly missed, and this edition is dedicated to his memory.

John, Sarah, and the Emond team

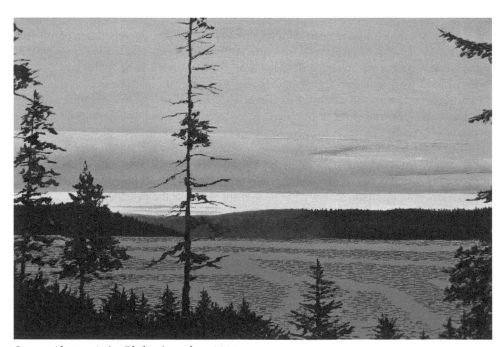

Serene Algonquin by Philip Sworden, 2011.

About the Authors

John Fairlie, BMus, LLB, LLM, is chair of the School of Legal Studies at Capilano University in North Vancouver. He was the lead developer of Capilano's Bachelor of Legal Studies (Paralegal) degree, which launched in 2010. He has taught a range of law courses, including introduction to law, jurisprudence, torts, contracts, property, family, company, business, criminal, evidence, and legal research.

He has also lectured at Simon Fraser University in the School of Criminology, and at the British Columbia Institute of Technology in the School of Business. His other pursuits have included working as a legal writer and co-running a small importing business.

In addition to this book, John is the author of *How to Find Canadian Law*, a guide to legal research published in 1999, and a co-author of *A Brief Introduction to Law in Canada*, published by Emond in 2017.

Philip Sworden, BA, MA, LLB, PhD, was a professor in the Business School at Humber College Institute of Technology and Advanced Learning in Toronto and a former coordinator of Humber's Paralegal Education Diploma Program. He was instrumental in the development of Humber's Bachelor of Applied Arts (Paralegal Studies) degree program and he co-designed its four-year curriculum.

Philip's publications include *A Brief Introduction to Law in Canada* (2017) and *Dimensions of Law: Canadian and International Law in the 21st Century* (2004), both with Emond. His interest in history inspired an essay in *Inside the Law: Canadian Law Firms in Historical Perspective* (volume 7, 1996) as well as legal history articles in *Business History Review*, *Research in Economic History*, and the Law Society of Ontario's *Gazette*.

During his teaching career, Philip taught at McMaster University, Osgoode Hall Law School, Nipissing University, and Laurentian University. He was a co-recipient of the College Innovation of the Year Award and a recipient of Humber College's Distinguished Faculty Award.

PART I
Theory and Context

1 What Is Law?

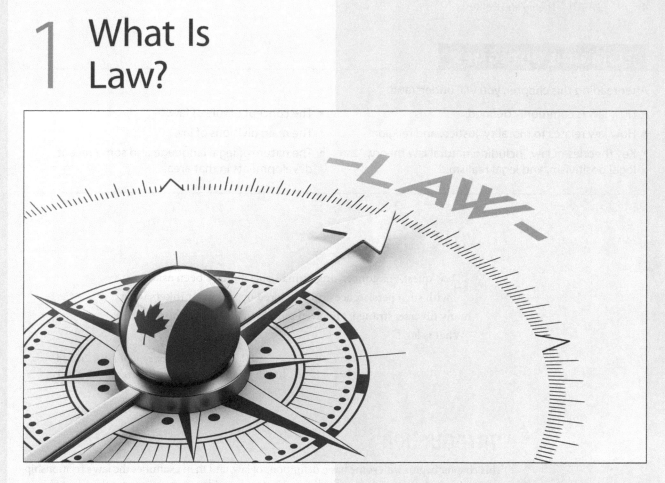

After reading this chapter, you will understand:

- How law is commonly defined.
- How law relates to morality, justice, and religion.
- Key theories of law, including natural law theory, legal positivism, and legal realism.

- The concept of rule of law.
- The main divisions of law.
- The nature of legal language and some recent developments in that area.

Few questions concerning human society have been asked with such persistence and answered by serious thinkers in so many diverse, strange, and even paradoxical ways as the question "What is law?"

HLA Hart, *The Concept of Law*, 2nd ed
(Oxford: Oxford University Press, 1994) at 1

Introduction

This chapter begins with some basic definitions of law, and then examines the law's relationship to morality and ethics, justice, and religion. Next, we consider some prominent theories of law—including natural law theory, legal positivism, and legal realism—and the concept of rule of law. In the final sections, we look at the divisions of law and at some of the challenges and developments associated with legal terminology.

Exploring these concepts will raise questions that cannot always be answered. Absolutes and certainties are sometimes unavailable, and accepting the limitations of the law can be challenging. However, despite its imperfections, the law is an endlessly rich and fascinating field with the potential to engage you for a lifetime.

How Law Is Commonly Defined

Is the law simply what we say it is? Or is there more to it than that? Is it subject to higher standards? And do our legal rules have to meet these standards in order to qualify as law? For example, if our Parliament passed a law providing that all green-eyed babies must be given up for medical stem cell research, would that law be valid? Why or why not?

We will return to these questions later in the chapter, in connection with various conceptions of justice and theories of law. For now, though, we need a basic definition of law to help us get our bearings. There are many definitions available (see Box 1.1). For our purposes, the law can be defined as *a system of enforceable rules that governs the relationship between the individual members of a society and between those members and the society itself*. The law allows us to live in communities safely and to balance the needs of the individual with the needs of the community.

BOX 1.1

Definitions of Law

The more laws and restrictions there are, the poorer people become. ... The more rules and regulations, the more thieves and robbers.

Laozi (ca. 6th century BCE),
Tao Te Ching

[L]aws were invented for the safety of citizens, the preservation of States, and the tranquility and happiness of human life.

Marcus Tullius Cicero (106-43 BCE),
De Legibus, or *On the Laws*

Law ... is nothing else than an ordinance of reason for the common good, made by him who has care of the community, and promulgated.

Thomas Aquinas (1225-1274),
Summa Theologica

Law ... is the perfection of reason.

Edward Coke (1552-1634),
Institutes of the Laws of England

No enactment of man can be considered law unless it conforms to the law of God.

William Blackstone (1723-1780),
Commentaries on the Laws of England

[L]aw [may be thought of] as a set of rules which are generally obeyed and enforced within a politically organized society.

Peter Shears & Graham Stephenson,
James' Introduction to English Law, 13th ed
(London: Butterworths, 1996) at 6

Types of Rules

The *rules* that make up the law can be divided into many categories. A good place to start is to say that there are three types of rules:

1. *General norms or standards of behaviour*. These rules usually prohibit certain activities, such as murder or careless driving.
2. *Condition rules*. These rules establish conditions or requirements that must be met before certain activities can be carried out. Licensing requirements for conducting a business, for getting married, or for driving a car are examples of these rules.
3. *Power-conferring rules*. These rules allow you to define your own legal relationship within certain contexts. The main examples of power-conferring rules are those relating to the law of contract—they allow you to set the terms and conditions that govern your relationship with another person, such as when purchasing or selling property, and in business transactions generally. Other examples of power-conferring rules include those relating to wills, which allow you to control how your property is distributed after you die.

Structure of Rules

Whatever the type of rule involved, the *form* of the rules is relatively standard:

If A, B, and/or C, then X

A, B, and C are elements (or conditions) that must be present for X (the legal result) to occur. Many legal rules involve three elements: A, B, and C. But some rules may have more elements, some fewer. And more complex rules may involve sub-elements.

If the elements are joined by *and* (A, B, *and* C), it is called a *conjunctive* list. This means that all elements must be satisfied or proved in order for the legal result to occur. If the elements are joined by *or* (A, B, *or* C), it is a *disjunctive* list. In this case, only one of the elements must be satisfied or proved in order for the legal result to occur. (Sometimes the elements may be part of a hybrid list, part conjunctive and part disjunctive.)

The crime of murder, simply defined, is structured in the conjunctive form. If an accused engages in behaviour (element A: the *actus reus* element) that causes the death of the victim (element B: the causation element), and if the accused means to cause the death (element C: the *mens rea* element), then the accused is guilty of murder and subject to punishment (X: the legal result).

Now let's look at a motor vehicle accident liability case. Again, simply defined, it is also based on a conjunctive list of elements. If a defendant's driving falls below the standard of a "reasonable motorist" (element A: the standard of care element), and this causes a loss to the plaintiff (element B: the causation element), and the loss is a compensable form of injury (element C: the damages element), then the defendant is liable in negligence and obliged to pay damages to the plaintiff (X: the legal result).

Legal claims are based on these underlying rules, regardless of their type or precise form. To succeed with a claim—that is, to obtain a legal result—you must establish all the required elements and sub-elements of the case. This is true whether you are a prosecutor in a criminal case or a plaintiff in a civil case.

How Law Relates to Other Rules

One thing that distinguishes the law from other kinds of rules is its enforceability. This enforcement occurs by way of state-sanctioned mechanisms or institutions such as the following: police forces, regulatory agencies (such as those that license certain activities), and court systems. The state does not enforce other kinds of rules—ethical or religious codes, abstract principles of justice—until they have been incorporated into or recognized as law.

Law, Morality, and Ethics

Most of us have a sense of right and wrong. And many of us are in general agreement about what is moral or immoral, ethical or unethical. Despite this common ground, ethical and moral disagreements frequently arise. What seems immoral to one person may be acceptable to another. For example, when is it acceptable to lie? Never? Sometimes, depending on the circumstances? Always?

morality
standards of right and wrong, often associated with personal character

We can define **morality** as a system of values or principles concerning what is right or wrong with respect to human behaviour. Morality can be viewed from two perspectives:

1. descriptive, or
2. normative.

When we consider morality from a *descriptive* perspective, we are simply observing what a particular community believes to be right or wrong. We are offering no judgments or endorsements of these beliefs. We are describing things as they are.

When we approach a moral system from a *normative* perspective, we believe it to have an objective truth, or to set an ideal standard. We accept it and are invested in it. A moral code viewed in this light tells us how we should behave. Conduct that offends the code is considered immoral.

Ethics also deals with standards of human behaviour—with what is right or wrong, good or bad. And ethics, like morality, can be approached from either a descriptive or a normative point of view. There are many branches and sub-branches of ethics. One of these is *meta-ethics*. This area deals with basic questions such as how we determine what is good or bad and the nature of behavioural standards.

There is no generally accepted distinction between morality and ethics. One view is that morality focuses on personal character and behaviour, whereas ethics focuses on standards of behaviour in defined social settings. The word *ethics* is frequently used in professional contexts to describe standards of conduct. Most professions, including the legal profession, have codes of ethics. Members who offend these codes may be disciplined by their governing bodies. We will examine codes of ethics in the legal profession in more detail in Chapter 16.

Concerning the relationship between law and ethics, Earl Warren (1891-1974), a former American chief justice, said the following: "In civilized life, law floats in a sea of ethics."[1] In other words, a civilized society contains many ethical rules and standards; they vary according to context and do not have the status of law. They do, however, underlie the society's laws, which are applicable to everyone and are enforceable by the state. And both the law and the myriad ethical rules and standards are rooted in a common value system.

ethics

standards of right and wrong often applied to specific groups—for example, professions

Law and Justice

A Roman statesman once said the following regarding justice: "Let justice be done, though the heavens fall." This view posits that justice must prevail regardless of the consequences. But what is justice? Where does it come from? Are conceptions of justice fixed or can they change? The answer to these questions depends, of course, on how we define justice (see Box 1.2).

BOX 1.2

Definitions of Justice

What I say is that "just" or "right" means nothing but what is in the interest of the stronger party.

Plato (429-347 BCE),
The Republic

Revenge is a kind of wild justice; which the more man's nature runs to, the more ought law to weed it out.

Francis Bacon (1561-1626),
"Of Revenge" from *Essays* (1625)

Justice is truth in action.

Benjamin Disraeli (1804-1881),
House of Commons speech, 1851

Injustice anywhere is a threat to justice everywhere.

Martin Luther King (1929-1968),
Letter from Birmingham Jail, Alabama, 1963

Overcoming poverty is not a gesture of charity. It is an act of justice. It is the protection of a fundamental human right, the right to dignity and a decent life.

Nelson Mandela (1918-2013)
Speech at Trafalgar Square in London, England, 2005

Everyone knows that law is not the same thing as justice.

SM Waddams,
Introduction to the Study of Law, 8th ed (Toronto: Carswell, 2016) at 4

---

1 Earl Warren, "Address" (Speech delivered at the Louis Marshall Award Dinner of the Jewish Theological Seminary, Americana Hotel, New York City, 11 November 1962).

Justice is often associated with criminal law. A person might ask, "Where's the justice?" when a person commits a serious crime and is freed on a technicality. Or, "Where's the justice?" when a person commits murder but only serves jail time. Such questions, often raised during news coverage of criminal trials, reflect the view that our criminal laws place too much emphasis on the rights of criminals and process and that sentencing is generally too lenient. But theories of justice can transcend criminal law and apply to other areas of the law, too.

Justice can be considered in two ways:

1. as an end itself, or
2. as an instrument, or a means to an end.

deontological
theories that focus on the inherent rightness or wrongness of behaviour, without regard to the behaviour's consequences or outcomes

Proponents of justice as an end in itself take what is called a **deontological** (from the Greek *deon*, meaning "obligation, duty") approach. This approach is non-consequentialist and rule-based; it holds that certain rights and responsibilities are fundamental and universal and that justice consists in upholding them. These standards are objectively good and true and require no analysis of social consequences or outcomes for their justification; they are an end in themselves.

instrumentalist
theories that focus on something—for example, justice or the law—as a means to an end

Proponents of justice as a means to an end (an instrument) take what we call the **instrumentalist** approach. A desired social end might be, for example, a safer community or the reduction of poverty. A method of regulation would be a just one, according to this view, if it succeeded in making the community safer or in reducing poverty. This distinction— between deontological and instrumentalist conceptions of justice—offers us a general organizing principle and a context in which to discuss three established and commonly cited models of justice: corrective justice, retributive justice, and distributive justice.

Corrective Justice

corrective justice
theory of justice according to which (1) a person has a moral responsibility for harm caused to another, and (2) the latter's loss must be rectified or corrected

The concept of justice most closely attached to the deontological approach—that is, taking justice as an end in itself—is **corrective justice**. Central to the notion of corrective justice is the belief that a person has a moral responsibility for the harm he causes another and that the loss must be rectified or corrected, usually in the form of compensation. (Corrective justice is also known as *rectificatory justice*.) Responsibility here is defined by the relationship between the causer and the injured, and there is no regard to consequences beyond the required rectification. The rectification (or correction) itself represents justice.

An early exposition of corrective justice appears in the *Nicomachean Ethics* by Aristotle (384-322 BCE).[2] Aristotle's theory addresses the imbalance that occurs when one person injures another; corrective justice restores the *status quo*, which his theory presumes to be good. The parties to an injury (the injurer and the injured) are assumed to be in a position of material equality before the injury. The theory holds that the injurer removes a benefit from the injured party and gains an equivalent benefit herself (regardless of whether she *actually* derives any benefit from her action). Justice seeks to restore equality by compensating the injured party at the injurer's expense; it requires the return of the victim's original benefit in order to restore the balance.

Certain parts of Aristotle's theory raise doubts and questions. For example, why should we presume that the injurer and the injured start from a position of equality, or that the

---

2   See Aristotle, *Nicomachean Ethics*, translated by David Ross and revised by JL Ackrill & JO Urmson (Oxford: Oxford University Press, 1998) book V at 4, 8; Jonathan Barnes, *Aristotle: A Very Short Introduction* (Oxford: Oxford University Press, 2000) at 4-5.

injurer always receives a benefit equivalent to the injured party's loss? While this may occur in the case of a theft, what about in a case involving physical injury? And how does the degree of culpability affect responsibility? For example, does corrective justice apply where an injury is caused indirectly, or to losses caused by a failure to act (nonfeasance), such as failing to help a person whose life is in danger where there is little or no risk to yourself in helping? Enlightenment and modern philosophers have developed, refined, and supplemented Aristotle's ideas about corrective justice, but there is still no consensus about the extent of its application or its limitations.

Despite these uncertainties, corrective justice theory is still relevant today. Recently, a Supreme Court of Canada (SCC) judge remarked that private law—and, certainly, tort law (a specific area of private law)—can be "viewed primarily as a mechanism of compensation. Its underlying organizing structure remains grounded in the principle of corrective justice."[3] As the judge's words suggest, corrective justice underlies private law disputes. But it also applies to criminal cases, where *restitutionary orders*—based on principles of corrective justice—are possible. For example, a person who physically or mentally injures a victim or damages his property in the course of committing a crime and is convicted of the crime may be ordered, at the time of sentencing, to compensate the victim directly for these losses.[4]

BOX 1.3

The Image of Justice

The personification of justice as a woman, blindfolded,* and holding scales and a sword is based on ancient iconography. Her earliest incarnations were the Egyptian goddesses Maat and Isis. Later, in the classical era, she appeared as the Greek goddess Themis, and then as the Roman equivalent of Themis: Justitia.

In the modern context, the personification of justice is often referred to as Lady Justice. Her statues are seen outside courthouses, government buildings, universities, and other buildings where order and fairness are central ideals. The blindfold represents impartiality. Her scales signify that she will weigh opposing claims and conflicting evidence. And the sword represents the power she has to enforce her judgments. This icon of justice is associated with the law in general.

* The statue of Lady Justice atop the dome above the Old Bailey courthouse in London, pictured here, does not include a blindfold. Courthouse pamphlets explain that this is because Lady Justice originally did not wear one. The blindfold did not become standard until the 16th century.

Retributive Justice

retributive justice
theory of justice based on *lex talionis*, or the law of retaliation

If corrective justice is more relevant to private law disputes, then **retributive justice** relates more to criminal law and to the perceived need for punishment. Does it reflect a *deontological*

---

3   See LeBel J in *Whiten v Pilot Insurance Co*, 2002 SCC 18 at para 152.

4   See the *Criminal Code*, RSC 1985, c C-46, ss 718, 738.

or an *instrumentalist* approach? Retribution can be viewed either as an end in itself—that is, as a self-evidently appropriate response to morally wrong behaviour—or as the means to socially worthwhile objectives, such as public safety or appeasement. To the extent that one accepts both views, it is a hybrid theory, with both deontological and instrumentalist aspects.

The law of retaliation, or *lex talionis*, is often cited as the guiding principle of retributive justice. We are all familiar with such phrases as *an eye for an eye, measure for measure*, and *let the punishment fit the crime*. These expressions are based on the idea that the response should be proportional to the wrong. Retaliation, which is linked to revenge, has always been part of human behaviour. Some of the oldest recorded references to *lex talionis* are in the *Code of Hammurabi*, a collection of Babylonian laws compiled around 1750 BCE.

When it comes to administering retributive justice, we are faced with questions of balance and measure. At first glance, it appears that retribution is based on the ideal of an equal response—an eye for an eye. In practice, however, retributive codes seem to depart from this ideal. In the *Code of Hammurabi*, for example, the punishment for striking your father is not to be struck yourself, but to lose your hand. Also, the eye for an eye rule varied in Babylon according to the social status of the participants. Crimes against those of lesser status called for lesser punishments. Other ancient legal codes, too, seem to depart from the ideal of an equal response. To the modern mind, some of the punishments prescribed by the Old Testament—for example, stoning to death a person who swears—seem to exceed the limits of reasonable retaliation.

The law of retaliation therefore raises questions about how it should be applied in modern legal systems. When is an equal response the right one? When are greater or lesser consequences appropriate? Whatever the answers, most people today would agree that the Babylonian practice of reducing the penalty because of the victim's "low" social standing is unacceptable. As an instrument for social order, retributive justice also raises questions of cause and effect. When it comes to public safety or crime reduction, are harsh penalties or lenient penalties more effective? Will new penalty regimes result in unintended consequences?

While retributive justice is most relevant to criminal law, it can play a role in private law disputes—for example, in tort and breach of contract cases. This doesn't happen often, because such disputes rarely involve behaviour worthy of punishment. And yet Canadian courts have awarded punitive damages—that is, damages over and above compensatory damages and designed as a form of punishment—in cases where a defendant's behaviour has been particularly offensive. Such awards have both a moral end-in-itself (deontological) purpose and an instrumentalist purpose, as the SCC has made clear. They "give a defendant his or her just desert (retribution)," but they also "deter the defendant and others from similar misconduct in the future (deterrence)," and they "mark the community's collective condemnation (denunciation) of what has happened."[5]

What is the principle that courts use when determining punitive damages? The SCC has dictated that proportionality, based on a number of factors, must be the guiding principle. Key factors include the following:

- the blameworthiness of the defendant's conduct,
- the vulnerability of the plaintiff,
- the harm caused,
- the need for deterrence, and
- whether the defendant has been guilty of the conduct in the past.[6]

---

5   *Whiten v Pilot Insurance Co, supra* note 3 at para 94.

6   *Ibid* at paras 111-26.

In most civil cases, the SCC's model of reasoned proportionality results in relatively modest punitive damage awards. This contrasts with US courts, which have sometimes allowed extremely large punitive damage awards.

Distributive Justice

The third form of justice, **distributive justice**, is concerned with the way assets and entitlements are shared among members of a society. In his *Nicomachean Ethics*, Aristotle also described distributive justice. His model of distributive justice provides for the distribution of a state's bounty (property and honours, for example) according to merit.

One of the most significant modern commentators on the subject of distributive justice, and on the subject of justice generally, is John Rawls. In *A Theory of Justice*, he expresses his general conception of justice as follows:

> All social values [or social primary goods]—liberty and opportunity, income and wealth, and the social bases of self-respect—are to be distributed equally unless an unequal distribution of any, or all, of these values is to everyone's advantage.[7]

Injustice, then, according to Rawls, becomes "inequalities that are not for the benefit of all."[8]

Today, debates about distributive justice can arise in the context of, for example, automobile insurance and workers' compensation programs. The debates concern whether and how to "distribute" the cost of injuries. Should all members of a group pay premiums or fees for the sake of the smaller number of members who will suffer injuries? If all members of the group contribute to the fund, then the few unlucky enough to suffer injuries will not have to bear the full weight of medical costs themselves. Outside of this type of context, however, distributive justice plays only a small role in Canadian private law.

Distributive justice is more concerned with public law matters than with private law. For instance, a government initiative may involve raising taxes to pay for new programs to assist a minority community. In other words, the cost of the new program, which would benefit only a portion of the population, would be distributed among all taxpayers.

distributive justice
theory of justice concerned with appropriate distributions of entitlements, such as wealth and power, in a society

---

BOX 1.4

Pierre Trudeau's Just Society

The phrase *just society* was coined by former Canadian Prime Minister Pierre Elliott Trudeau (1919-2000) during his bid to win the 1968 Liberal Party leadership campaign. It has become part of Canada's political terminology.

Trudeau meant the phrase to apply not to any specific policy, but to his entire platform. In the years that followed, he applied it to all his policies: official bilingualism; decriminalizing sexual matters involving consenting adults; and his crowning achievement, the patriation of the Canadian Constitution and the enactment of the *Canadian Charter of Rights and Freedoms.** Equality was a central theme of the just society.

*   *Canadian Charter of Rights and Freedoms*, Part I of the *Constitution Act, 1982*, being Schedule B to the *Canada Act 1982* (UK), 1982, c 11.

---

7   John Rawls, *A Theory of Justice*, revised ed (Cambridge, Mass: Harvard University Press, 1999) at 54.

8   *Ibid.*

Law and Religion

In most of the world, there is now a separation between church and state. But that is a relatively recent phenomenon. In the West, the Christian religion has certainly influenced the law. For example, in one of the most important common law court decisions ever handed down, Lord Atkin formulated his neighbour principle. This principle deals with a person's obligation to take care when engaging in an activity—any activity—that might affect other people. In describing this principle, Atkin draws directly from the Biblical parable of the Good Samaritan:

> The rule that you are to love your neighbour becomes in law, you must not injure your neighbour; and the lawyer's question, Who is my neighbour? receives a restricted reply. You must take reasonable care to avoid acts or omissions which you can reasonably foresee would be likely to injure your neighbour. Who, then, in law is my neighbour? The answer seems to be—persons who are so closely and directly affected by my act that I ought reasonably to have them in contemplation as being so affected when I am directing my mind to the acts or omissions which are called in question.[9]

Atkin's decision and the principle it expresses continue to shape the law of torts in Canada today. Whenever the Canadian courts are asked to recognize new duties of care, they almost invariably refer to Lord Atkin's neighbour principle as a starting point for their analysis.

Our Constitution also reflects the influence of religion. The preamble to the *Canadian Charter of Rights and Freedoms* (often simply referred to as the Charter) reads as follows: "Whereas Canada is founded upon principles that recognize the supremacy of God and the rule of law." This reference to God is slightly paradoxical, in the Canadian context; the Charter's guarantee of religious freedom (s 2) in our multicultural society has made references to specific religious influences—such as Atkin's reference to the parable of the Good Samaritan—less acceptable in recent years.

Theories of Law: "Ought" and "Is"

jurisprudence
also known as
philosophy of law or
science of law; concerns
theories that are used
to describe, explain,
or criticize the law

Jurisprudence—the philosophy or science of law—and the theories that compose it are our concern in this section. There are many theoretical approaches to the law, and there is some overlap with justice theories. A common way of classifying theories of law is to divide them into two main categories: *analytic* and *normative*. Analytic theories are concerned with what the law *is*, while normative theories are concerned with what the law *ought* to be. The two are not mutually exclusive. There are hybrid theories—such as feminist legal theory—and other theories—such as legal realism—that seem to challenge or subvert the distinction between analytic and normative.

Analytic jurisprudence generally concerns critical, explanatory, and value-free assessments of the law. It may involve, for example, examining the internal logic of a system of rules. Sometimes the investigations are more empirical in nature—that is, concerned with experience or observation rather than with theory. The common thread between analytic

---

9   *M'Alister (or Donoghue) v Stevenson*, [1932] AC 562 at 580 (HL).

theories of law is that they do not involve value judgments. They are concerned with what law *is*, not what it *ought to be*.

Normative jurisprudence, on the other hand, generally concerns the rightness or wrongness of the law based on various conceptions of justice, fairness, and morality. It involves making value judgments; it is evaluative, not explanatory. Because there are no objective, universally accepted standards of right and wrong, normative legal analysis depends less on logic and empiricism than analytic jurisprudence does.

The following is a brief overview of three well-established fields of jurisprudence: natural law theory, legal positivism, and legal realism.

Natural Law Theory

The idea of a "higher power" or source that guides our behaviour or offers us an ideal standard is likely as old as civilization itself. A person who believes this to be the case—who believes such external standards exist—believes that human-made or *positive* law is subject or subordinate to this higher or **natural law**.

What is the source of natural law? Is it virtue, divine law, reason, human nature, morality, or some invisible wellspring? And how do we come to know it? How do we evaluate the standards that are to guide us? Do we base these standards on the beneficial results they promote, or do we base them on unchangeable notions of what is right, independent of the consequences they produce? Or is it sometimes a combination of these? Natural law theorists have offered different answers to these questions.

The Greek philosopher Plato's ideas about justice and just laws are among the most ancient expressions of natural law. One of the starting points of Platonic thought is that there are eternal, immutable ideas of good—what he called the world of the Forms. These ideals, according to Plato, are more "real," in a sense, than the material world of change and sensation. In *The Republic*, Plato envisages a utopia governed by philosopher rulers whom the ordinary citizens trust to know these Forms and to rule by their light. Plato's student Aristotle, whom some consider the father of natural law theory, saw natural law as being based on virtue and the golden mean (that is, the idea that everything should be done in moderation). Aristotle developed these ideas in his *Nicomachean Ethics*, along with his theories of justice mentioned above.

In the Middle Ages, the theologian Thomas Aquinas (1225-1274) reworked Aristotle's ideas about natural law into a Christian context. Natural law was associated with God's will or divine law, and this was identified, in turn, with reason. According to Aquinas, when we correctly use our abilities to reason, we are participating in or identifying with God's reasoning.

Hugo Grotius (1583-1645) was a Dutch jurist who contributed to the natural law debate primarily by secularizing it, or removing its religious basis. He believed that natural law would still exist even if God didn't. He grounded natural law in human nature itself, arguing that the natural law was discoverable through the use of right reason, which is a human faculty rather than a divine one.

Connected to this secularizing shift was the development of social contract theory. This is the theory that human existence in earliest times was not ideal—or as Thomas Hobbes (1588-1679) wrote in *Leviathan,* it was "nasty, brutish, and short"—and that, to secure our safety and happiness, we surrendered our absolute freedom and agreed to be governed by rulers through a "contract." The English philosopher John Locke (1632-1704) believed that this contract was based on natural law, which he identified with human or natural reason. French philosopher and writer Jean-Jacques Rousseau (1712-1778) had similar ideas (see Box 1.5).

natural law
theory that there is a source of law that is higher than man-made law, with which man-made law must try to comply

Jean-Jacques Rousseau (1712-1778).

Natural Law and the US Declaration of Independence

The works of Locke and Rousseau, among others, provided a philosophical basis for the American Revolution in the late 1700s, in which 13 colonies fought a war to break free from British rule. According to Locke, natural law teaches us that we are all equal and have certain natural rights to life, health, liberty, and possessions. Locke also maintained that no government has the authority to deny its people these rights. If it does, it is placing its subjects in a state of nature, and war is justified.

Rousseau's most famous work is *The Social Contract* (1762). It begins as follows: "Man was born free, yet everywhere he is in chains. One man thinks himself the master of others, but remains more of a slave than they."

The second sentence of the Declaration reads as follows: "We hold these truths to be self-evident, that all men are created equal, that they are endowed by their Creator with certain unalienable Rights, that among these are Life, Liberty and the pursuit of Happiness."

These words constitute the philosophical justification for the American Revolution.

An important modern exponent of natural law was the Harvard law professor Lon Fuller (1902-1978). In *The Morality of Law* (1964), Fuller wrote about the connection between morality and law and described "eight ways to fail to make law." They are as follows:

1. *Deciding issues on an ad hoc basis, without laws.* This is the most obvious kind of failure: simply failing to make laws at all, necessitating decision making that is unpredictable. Laws must be made, despite the apparent difficulty in crafting them.

2. *Failing to publicize laws or make them available to the affected party.* The unfairness here is obvious. How can laws be effective if they are unknown?

3. *The abuse of retroactive legislation.* As a general rule, laws must be prospective. Retroactive legislation is legislation that applies to past behaviour. Without advance notice that such legislation will be passed, it cannot be a guide to conduct (unless you have the power of foresight), and if the power to make it is inappropriately used, it will undercut the integrity of prospective rules. Why follow an existing rule today if your now "legal" behaviour could be punished by a contrary law passed tomorrow, with retroactive effect?

4. *Failing to make rules understandable.* Rules that are too complex serve little purpose and suffer from the same failing as laws that are not publicized.

5. *The enactment of contradictory rules.* The only outcome here, for the person trying to obey the law, is failure. No matter which rule a person follows, she will be breaking another rule.

6. *Enacting rules with which the parties affected lack power to comply.* Rules that cannot be complied with cannot be a guide to action.

7. *Making frequent changes to law.* This challenges the stability of the legal system. If the law changes frequently, it becomes difficult if not impossible to plan ahead effectively.

8. *Announcing rules and then failing to enforce them.* If people come to believe that laws will not be enforced, they will not respect them and may not abide by them. Fear of negative consequences motivates many to follow the rules.[10]

---

10   Lon L Fuller, "The Morality That Makes Law Possible" in *The Morality of Law*, revised ed (New Haven, Conn: Yale University Press, 1965) ch 2.

Fuller maintains that we need to avoid these pitfalls in order to achieve a legal system that is just and consistent. Unlike earlier natural law thinkers, Fuller does not believe that we discover natural law through external absolutes based on religion or reason. He believes that we find "natural" moral standards through analyzing social behaviour and human nature. However, he doesn't elaborate on what those moral standards are.

The work of Margaret Mead (1901-1978), an American cultural anthropologist, points to some interesting possibilities concerning natural moral standards—natural laws grounded in human nature itself that appear across cultures. Her study of human populations revealed common standards of behaviour and common rules relating to such things as justified and unjustified killing, the prohibition of incest, and—in many cases—the right to own private property.[11]

Ronald Dworkin (1931-2013), a student of Fuller, does not count himself as a natural law theorist, but he does believe in agreed-upon communal principles such as justice and fairness.[12] He believes these principles must inform the law and be used to resolve gaps and inconsistencies in it. The law, according to Dworkin, is a "seamless web" connected by these principles, dictating the correct answer to any legal problem.

Systems founded on natural law supply us with ideals. But they also raise many questions:

- What is the basis of natural law—virtue, religion, reason, or human nature?
- How do we determine what its rules are?
- Whom do we authorize to determine these rules?
- How do we resolve contradictions between natural law and positive (that is, human-made) law?

Legal Positivism

Natural law's main opposition as a legal theory is **legal positivism**. On the scale of *ought* and *is* (that is, normative versus analytic jurisprudence), legal positivism tends more toward the analytic. It evaluates laws and legal systems without, for the most part, placing value judgments on them. As legal theories go, it is a relatively recent development.

Legal positivism's first real proponent was John Austin (1790-1859), a professor of jurisprudence at the University of London (now University College). He was a utilitarian, believing the goal of legislation to be "the greatest happiness of the greatest number." But he was better known for his analytic method and his use of precise terminology to define positivist thinking. His greatest work is the *Province of Jurisprudence Determined*.[13] The core positivist beliefs, according to Austin, are as follows:

1. All commands of the sovereign are valid and enforceable.
2. *Commands* means **positive law**—that is, human-made rules.

legal positivism
theory that the only valid source of law is the principles, rules, and regulations expressly enacted by the institutions or persons within a society that are generally recognized as having the power to enact them

positive law
man-made law, as opposed to a higher law (natural law) that transcends persons or institutions

11   Margaret Mead, "Some Anthropological Considerations Concerning Natural Law (1961)" in Michael DA Freeman, ed, *Lloyd's Introduction to Jurisprudence*, 8th ed (London, UK: Sweet & Maxwell, 2008) 185 at 225.

12   His most famous works are Ronald M Dworkin, *Taking Rights Seriously* (Cambridge, Mass: Harvard University Press, 1977) and *Law's Empire* (Cambridge, Mass: Harvard University Press, 1986).

13   John Austin, *The Province of Jurisprudence Determined* (London, UK: John Murray, 1832).

3. *The sovereign* refers to the person or agency who receives habitual obedience in a given society.

4. Laws made in accordance with the society's existing formalized and recognized process are valid, regardless of so-called natural law, morality, or any external standard.

More recently, professors HLA Hart (1907-1992) and Joseph Raz (1939-) have continued the positivist tradition. They have made the point that a person's holding positivist beliefs does not prevent the person from either having moral standards or advocating for their legal recognition. However, law and morality are separate, and the validity of the former is not tied to the latter.

Hart also writes about the frailty of language with respect to the law. There will be gaps and inconsistencies in the laws we make, however hard we try to avoid them. Gaps can be filled by judicial discretion, but at some point, Hart argues, the law simply breaks down. (Dworkin's response to this idea, in keeping with his natural law premises, is that justice and fairness fill these gaps.)

It is fair to say that the Anglo-Canadian legal tradition has a positivist basis. The principle of parliamentary sovereignty (which we discuss in more detail in Chapter 4) means that laws made in accordance with the recognized process are valid without reference to external standards. The Charter provides for self-imposed standards based on a kind of natural law, but legislators may disregard them in making law (by invoking s 33 of the Charter, the notwithstanding clause; see Chapter 7).

In times of political stability, when governments follow commonly accepted standards and the existing order is acceptable to the majority of people in the society, legal positivism is effective as an underlying theory. It endorses the validity of what *is*. But during times of war or oppressive regimes, people begin to question the validity or fairness of existing laws and to measure them against external standards. According to legal positivism, a bad law properly constituted under a cruel regime is a valid law. To many people, this might seem a shortcoming in the theory.

Legal Realism

legal realism
a theory, developed in the US and Scandinavian countries, that encouraged a more thoroughly empirical study of the process by which laws are made and applied

Legal realism is a field of jurisprudence that arose in the 20th century. It was largely a response to the emphasis on logic that dominated British positivist theory in the 1800s. The first writers of legal realist theory were American (see Box 1.6). But Scandinavian countries, too, saw a strong theoretical movement in this direction. The adherents in both countries shared the positivist view that law is a human invention. But they also advocated a more intensely empirical study of the process by which laws are made and applied, and they argued that law is subject to many of the flaws and weaknesses of other human activities.

Legal realism accepts that law does not operate in a vacuum; it is one of many parts in the whole social machine. It follows from this premise that an interdisciplinary approach to the study of law offers advantages. For instance, the study of non-legal fields such as history and economics will help us better understand the legal system. Legal realism also holds that law should be seen as an instrument to further desired social objectives.

Several legal realists focus on the judicial process—a single part of the overall legal system—and, specifically, on how judges make their decisions. In theory, the primary role of judges is to make decisions by applying rules to specific fact situations (in other words, the cases appearing before them). Many of us believe, or would like to think, that certainty and objectivity surround this process: in go the facts and out comes the unerring, inevitable decision. But most experienced litigators, who are veterans of legal proceedings, believe the process works otherwise. If litigators often advise their clients to settle, it is to avoid the uncertainty of going to court.

BOX 1.6

Legal Realism and Oliver Wendell Holmes (1841-1935)

Oliver Wendell Holmes was born in Boston, Massachusetts and fought in the American Civil War on the Union side. He studied law at Harvard and practised law for 15 years before becoming, first, a legal editor, then a professor at Harvard Law School, and, finally, a judge of the Supreme Judicial Court of Massachusetts. He was appointed to the United States Supreme Court in 1902 and retired from the court in 1932 at age 90, the oldest judge ever to serve on the court. He left a legacy of ideas that are still relevant today.

Holmes was an early leading light in a new way of thinking about law. He is noted for many famous pithy sayings,

including the following: "The life of the law has not been logic; it has been experience."* With this statement, Holmes was not denying that logic plays an important role in the law; he was merely affirming his belief that practical experience is a more important factor in the law than pure reason is. Opposed to the doctrine of natural law, he took a pragmatic approach to the study of law and felt it was largely about predicting what courts would decide. He is considered by some to be the father of legal realism in America.

* Oliver Wendell Holmes, *The Common Law* (Boston: Little, Brown and Company, 1881) at 1.

A legal realist would argue that many factors can contribute to judges' decisions, including the following:

- how credible they find the witnesses,
- how much weight they give to documentary and other real evidence,
- how they approach the synthesis of complex and conflicting legal principles,
- how they go about applying general principles to specific fact situations, and
- how far they are able to recognize and deal with uncertainties in the rules themselves and in the facts to which these rules are applied.

The intellectual ability, personality, morality, biases, and proclivities of the judge in question are therefore relevant. Also, individual judges are likely to be inconsistent themselves from time to time, affected by their changing and personal circumstances. For instance, what tensions or conflicts is the judge who is hearing the case experiencing outside the courtroom, in her personal life? How rested and prepared is she for the case? One American jurist, Jerome Frank, remarked that a judicial decision might be determined by what the judge had for breakfast.

The study of legal realism has waned since the 1980s. It was a theory that pointed out some weaknesses in legal systems, but it did not come up with solutions. Other kinds of legal theories have arisen during this period, but most bear the influence of legal realism's empiricism, pragmatism, and openness to other disciplines.

Other Legal Theories

We have described three important theories of law, but there are many others—too many to describe in detail here. However, a brief mention of some of them will give you an idea of the vast scope of jurisprudential study.

Utilitarianism is an ethical philosophy (mentioned above in connection with John Austin and legal positivism). It originated with Jeremy Bentham (1748-1832), and it measures the utility or worth of actions in terms of the overall happiness they generate. It is instrumentalist (or consequentialist)—taking the law as a means to an end—and it underlies any current theory of law that considers the law to be a tool for social change.

The *law and economics* movement (also referred to as the economic analysis of law) espouses one such utilitarian theory; it measures a law's worth in terms of its capacity to increase social wealth. This theory substitutes wealth for the "happiness" of the utilitarian standard, happiness being difficult to measure. A prominent exponent of this legal theory is the American jurist Richard Posner (1939-). The law and economics movement has not had the same influence in Canada that it has had in the United States.

Another theory of law is the so-called *pure theory of law*, which owes its name to a book of the same name by the Czech legal scholar Hans Kelsen (1881-1973).[14] It is an outgrowth of legal positivism but acknowledges its "normative" aspects more openly than traditional positivism does. One interesting aspect of this theory is that it posits the existence of a basic norm called a *Grundnorm*, from which all others can be derived. This basic norm is to be chosen based on a principle of efficiency. A principle is considered "efficient" if people in general can be shown to follow it independently of any legal rules requiring them to do so. However, the theory does not tell us what this basic norm is.

The **law and society** and **sociology of law** disciplines are related in that they look at law from a broad social, interdisciplinary perspective. The difference between these two theories is that the first identifies most closely with legal studies, and the second with sociology. One important issue debated in both is whether laws come about through consensus or through conflict within a society.

Marxist theories of law are based on the writings of Karl Marx (1818-1883), Friedrich Engels (1820-1895), and other advocates of communist policies. Such policies address the distribution of wealth and class structure within a society. These kinds of legal theories are compatible with distributive justice thinking, which, as we have seen, is also concerned with the distribution of wealth (among other benefits) in a society.

Feminist theories of law cover a wide range of issues and can be seen as an outgrowth of the women's movement in the 1960s and 1970s, and as having connections with critical legal studies (described next). While works on women's rights are not new—for example, the seminal work *A Vindication of the Rights of Women* (1792) by Mary Wollstonecraft (1759-1797)—feminist jurisprudence arguably did not establish itself until the 1970s. The modern literature in this field is far-reaching and diverse, and goes well beyond issues concerning reproductive rights, violence against women, equal pay for equal work, and sex discrimination more generally. Feminist legal theories also examine such areas as how gender roles and women's subordination are perpetuated and concealed by the law's assumptions, language, and structure; how patriarchal interests are supported by the law; and what legal reforms are necessary to improve the position of women in society.

As a theory, **critical legal studies** (also known as *CLS* or *Crit*) is an outgrowth of American legal realism. Forged as an independent theory in the late 1970s, it is largely concerned with exposing law as an instrument of the rich and powerful. Its adherents have suggested many legal reforms. Emerging from CLS is **critical race theory** (also known by

---

law and society
a kind of legal study that looks at law from a broadly social, interdisciplinary perspective

sociology of law
a kind of sociological study that looks at law from a broadly social, interdisciplinary perspective

Marxist theories of law
legal theories, based on the writing of the communist philosopher Karl Marx, that are concerned with the distribution of wealth in a society; related to distributive justice theories

feminist theories of law
theories of law that generally concern the legal, social, and economic rights of and improving opportunities for women

critical legal studies
theory of law largely concerned with exposing law as an instrument of the rich and powerful

critical race theory
theory of law that focuses on race-based inequities; an offshoot of critical legal studies

---

14   Hans Kelsen, *Pure Theory of Law*, translated by Max Knight (Berkeley: University of California Press, 1960).

its acronym, CRT), a kindred theory of feminist jurisprudence. The difference between feminist legal theory and critical race theory is that the latter focuses on race-based inequities in place of gender-related issues.

There are various other areas and sub-areas of legal study, as well as non-legal movements that touch on the law—for example, postmodernism, post-structuralism, deconstruction theory, and discourse analysis. All of these non-legal movements deal in some way with whether objective truth is ascertainable and with the logic of language systems and their hidden assumptions. Common to many current theories is a belief in the value of multi- and interdisciplinary study, and in the artificiality of trying to isolate any process, such as law, given that it is just one part of a complex social system.

Rule of Law

The term **rule of law** concerns fairness in the administration of the law. Its central tenets are that

1. everyone in a society, regardless of their social or political position, should be treated equally before the law; and
2. power under the law should not be used arbitrarily.

The rule of law is one of the cornerstones of the Canadian legal system and is expressly referred to in the Charter.

rule of law
a key legal concept whose central tenets are that everyone is equal before the law and that power under the law should not be used arbitrarily

Origins

Principles related to the rule of law appear in the legal culture of the Greeks and Romans. Cicero, a famous orator who lived in an era of Roman democracy, is quoted as saying the following: "[We] are servants of the law, that we all may be free."

The concept of the rule of law was generally not recognized in the next phase of Western history, the Dark Ages. It resurfaced in the Middle Ages, when King John of England (1167-1216), after enjoying supreme power for much of his reign, was suddenly faced with a revolt by his barons. He capitulated by executing one of the most famous legal documents in the democratic world, the *Magna Carta* (1215). (See Box 1.7.) In this document, he agreed to give up some of his power and to recognize some of his barons' liberties. The seeds of the rule of law were planted with the *Magna Carta*. Some of its provisions are still in force today in England and in Canada.

Basic Principles

In the modern era, rule-of-law doctrine was given prominence through the work of AV Dicey, who is widely recognized as one of the fathers of modern English constitutional law. He popularized the phrase *rule of law* in his most influential work, *An Introduction to the Study of the Law of the Constitution* (London, 1885). We may summarize Dicey's three core rule-of-law principles as follows:

1. The law must trump the influence of arbitrary power. It follows from this that no one can be punished except for breach of an established law as determined through an established process before the courts.

2. No one is above the law, whatever his place in society—or, to put it another way, the law applies equally to everyone. And, again, it is recognized judicial process that will make the rulings to ensure this occurs.

3. Personal rights and liberties must be protected by giving every person the ability to apply to the courts for a remedy should any of those rights and liberties be denied.

Dicey's first principle recognizes that the arbitrary application of state power will lead to discontent. Rules must be in place and then enforced according to a set process. Otherwise, punishment for their infringement will not be seen as fair. (See Box 1.8.)

Adherence to the second principle is a key feature of true democracies; it distinguishes them from autocracies, where rulers have absolute power, and from societies where the law applies to people differently depending on their status. Equal application of the law promotes respect for the legal system.

Dicey's third principle highlights the idea that the courts are instrumental in protecting our rights and liberties. How effective that protection is depends directly on how free our courts are from political interference. (The separation of powers between the legislative, executive, and judicial branches of government is discussed in Part II of this book.)

BOX 1.7

The Magna Carta: The Great Charter of English Liberties

In the early feudal era, when English kings were first establishing a strong, centralized kingdom in England, their powerful nobles resisted giving them total power. When King John raised taxes to help finance his wars in France, the nobles rebelled and forced him to agree to the *Magna Carta*, which placed limits on royal powers. One notable limit on royal power was described in clause 39 of this document:

> No free man shall be taken or imprisoned or disseised [stripped of his rights or possessions] or outlawed or exiled or in any way ruined, nor will we go or send against him, except by the lawful judgement of his peers or by the law of the land.*

Arthur Hogue explains how the *Magna Carta* introduced the concept of the rule of law:

> In effect, each confirmation of the Charter became a solemn assurance to the realm that the king would act with a regard for the welfare of all subjects. It was an assurance, moreover, that the king would act according to clearly established procedure; in short, the king, like all of his subjects, was under the law.†

This idea—namely, that the same law applies equally to everyone and that a person's legal rights cannot be taken away from them except by the law of the land—is one of the great legal legacies that Canadians have inherited from English law.

King John agreeing to the *Magna Carta* at Runnymede, June 1215. (Many representations, like this one, show him signing it; in fact, he affixed his royal seal.)

* James C Holt, *Magna Carta*, 3rd ed (Cambridge, UK: Cambridge University Press, 2015) at 389.

† Arthur R Hogue, *Origins of the Common Law* (Bloomington, Ind: Indiana University Press, 1966) at 50-51.

BOX 1.8

Roncarelli v Duplessis

The SCC's decision in *Roncarelli v Duplessis** is one of Canada's defining decisions on abuse of power. It illustrates all three of Dicey's rule-of-law principles, but in particular highlights how the arbitrary use of discretionary power violates the rule of law.

Roncarelli was a Jehovah's Witness and a successful restaurateur in Montreal. During this period, in the mid-20th century, Quebec was trying to control the distribution of religious literature. A number of Jehovah's Witnesses were arrested for contravening local by-laws that prohibited peddling without a licence. Roncarelli provided bail for many of those arrested. To prevent his further involvement, Maurice Duplessis, who was then the premier and attorney general of Quebec, ordered the province's liquor commissioner to permanently revoke Roncarelli's liquor licence, which had been issued under the *Liquor Act*.[†] Roncarelli sued for damages.

A majority of the SCC found in favour of Roncarelli and ordered Duplessis to pay damages. Justice Rand's judgment, one of two majority judgments, is a classic from our country's highest court. Justice Rand reasoned that legislative discretion given to government administrators must be exercised in accordance with the general policies underlying the legislation itself. Extraneous factors such as different religious beliefs or opposing political views, which are wholly unconnected to the purpose of the legislation (here, the regulation of the sale of alcohol in the public interest), must not influence the use of the discretion.

Justice Rand stated the following:

> In public regulation of this sort there is no such thing as absolute and untrammelled "discretion," that is, that action can be taken on any ground or for any reason that can be suggested to the mind of the administrator. ... "Discretion" necessarily implies good faith in discharging public duty; there is always

a perspective within which a statute is intended to operate; and any clear departure from its lines or objects is just as objectionable as fraud or corruption. Could an applicant be refused a permit because he had been born in another province, or because of the colour of his hair? The ordinary language of the legislature cannot be so distorted. [‡]

Justice Rand also said the following:

> To deny or revoke a permit because a citizen exercises an unchallengeable right totally irrelevant to the sale of liquor in a restaurant is equally beyond the scope of the discretion conferred. ... [W]hat could be more malicious than to punish this licensee for having done what he had an absolute right to do in a matter utterly irrelevant to the *Liquor Act*? Malice in the proper sense is simply acting for a reason and purpose knowingly foreign to the administration, to which was added here the element of intentional punishment by what was virtually vocation outlawry. [§]

Justice Rand intimated that arbitrary power might be exercisable only if there were express statutory language authorizing such an action. He states the following:

> [N]o legislative Act can, *without express language*, be taken to contemplate an unlimited arbitrary power exercisable for any purpose, however capricious or irrelevant, regardless of the nature or purpose of the statute.[#]

*   [1959] SCR 121, 1959 CanLII 50.

†   *Alcoholic Liquor Act*, RSQ 1941, c 255.

‡   *Ibid* at 140.

§   *Ibid* at 141.

Ibid at 140 (emphasis added).

It has been frequently observed that Dicey's conception of the rule of law relates more to *procedural* fairness than to *substantive* fairness. In other words, it deals with when and how laws are applied (procedural) rather than with the fairness of the laws themselves (substantive). Dicey does not propose any general guidelines for determining whether laws themselves are fair.

Most modern definitions of the rule of law follow Dicey's approach; they leave substantive fairness issues to be dealt with in official bills of rights and human rights documents at both the national and international levels. This disregard for substantive fairness issues has interesting implications. For example, an established law permitting torture would not offend the idea of the rule of law so long as that law were clearly and equally applied through a recognized court process. But it might well violate whatever human rights document that society subscribes to.

No agreed-upon set of principles underlies the concept of the rule of law. There are principles other than Dicey's. For example, Joseph Raz has listed the following eight:

1. All laws should be prospective, open, and clear.
2. Laws should be relatively stable.
3. The making of particular laws (particular legal orders) should be guided by open, stable, clear, and general rules.
4. The independence of the judiciary must be guaranteed.
5. The principles of natural justice must be observed.
6. The courts should have review powers over the implementation of the other principles.
7. The courts should be easily accessible.
8. Crime-prevention agencies should not be allowed to pervert the law at their discretion.[15]

Raz's first three principles relate to the laws themselves. The clearer and more certain our laws are, the better they will guide us, and the less scope there will be for arbitrary power. The remaining five principles relate to fairness in the enforcement process, primarily through the court system but also through the police and other crime-prevention arms of government. You may notice that many of these rule-of-law principles are similar if not identical to Lon Fuller's "eight ways to fail to make law," discussed above in "Natural Law Theory."

Other legal scholars have suggested other requirements for the rule of law:

- The independence of the legal profession ("the bar") must be secure.
- Lawyer–client confidentiality must be guaranteed.
- Legal services must be affordable for the average person.

The principles above relate to the public's access to legal services generally and to the quality and integrity of those services. The legal system is complex, and most lay persons are not able to navigate their way successfully through its maze; most of us recognize the need for legally trained professionals to help us. And in Western societies, we recognize the need for an independent bench to uphold and apply the law. The need for an independent bar seems to be less obvious. In recent years, some countries have enacted laws changing the regulatory structure of the legal profession. The legal professions in these countries have gone from being largely self-regulatory (in other words, lawyers regulating themselves through law societies) to being subject to government control. What usually happens is that government representatives are appointed to a newly created body charged with regulating the legal profession.

The arguments for these changes resemble arguments for government regulation of police forces and other professional bodies. People suspect that professional organizations that discipline their own members are inclined to be lenient. Members of the "club" will

15   Joseph Raz, "The Rule of Law and Its Virtue" (1977) 93 Law Q Rev 195 at 198-202.

receive special treatment. The main arguments in support of self-regulation are that the professions undertake this responsibility seriously; there is no evidence that it is abused.

With respect to the legal profession, there is a need for it to be free from political control so that cases can be effectively argued before the courts. This is especially true of cases where rights and liberties are at issue. And there are options other than government control. So long as the self-regulatory process is open, measures can be taken to ensure that it is effective. For example, one could appoint an ombudsman who would have the power to embarrass through public exposure any law society that was lax in controlling its members.

Concerning lawyer-client privilege, this privilege of confidentiality is necessary to ensure that the client and his or her lawyer have the security they need to properly defend charges, to advance claims, and to seek and give advice.

Finally, if legal services are not affordable, then the existence of laws designed to assist or protect us will be of little use. One of the ways that the overall cost of legal services can be reduced is through the increased use of para-professionals, such as paralegals and notaries public (see also Chapter 17 and the discussion of access to justice).

Rule of Law in the International Context

Rule of law is not just an English or Western idea anymore. It has a global influence. The United Nations, established in 1945 and now with 193 member states, has made the rule of law a standing agenda item for its General Assembly since 1992. The Security Council has focused on this issue on a number of occasions, emphasizing the need to adhere to rule-of-law principles in times of conflict.[16]

The United Nations has defined the rule of law as follows:

> For the United Nations, the rule of law refers to a principle of governance in which all persons, institutions and entities, public and private, including the State itself, are accountable to laws that are publicly promulgated, equally enforced and independently adjudicated, and which are consistent with international human rights norms and standards. It requires, as well, measures to ensure adherence to the principles of supremacy of law, equality before the law, accountability to the law, fairness in the application of the law, separation of powers, participation in decision making, legal certainty, avoidance of arbitrariness and procedural and legal transparency.[17]

Canada follows the rule of law, and all member states of the UN profess to do so. A number of organizations collect and summarize data that offer a snapshot of the rule of law around the world on an annual basis. Among them are the World Bank, which measures adherence to the rule of law in over 200 economies as one of its six governance indicators, and the World Justice Project, whose *Rule of Law Index* provides detailed data on 113 countries.[18]

---

16 See United Nations, "United Nations and the Rule of Law," online: <http://www.un.org/ruleoflaw>.

17 Secretary-General, *Report of the Secretary-General on the Rule of Law and Transitional Justice in Conflict and Post-Conflict Societies*, UNSC, 2004, UN Doc S/2004/616.

18 To view data maps and tables illustrating countries' rankings according to various factors, visit <http://info.worldbank.org/governance/wgi/index.aspx> and <https://worldjusticeproject.org/our-work/wjp-rule-law-index/>.

Some countries' interpretation of and adherence to the principles of rule of law vary dramatically. For example, according to the World Justice Project's *Rule of Law Index 2017-2018*, Denmark ranks first (1) and Venezuela last (113). The rankings were based on

- constraints on government powers,
- fundamental rights (looking at the absence of discrimination, right to life and security, due process, freedom of expression and religion, and other indicia),
- order and security, and
- criminal justice.

Both Denmark and Venezuela are members of the United Nations and profess to follow the rule of law. However, the evidence indicates that the recent (at the time of writing) political and economic crises in Venezuela have markedly and negatively affected its rule-of-law markers compared with more politically and economically stable countries, such as Denmark.

Divisions of Law

substantive laws
laws that deal with core rights and obligations

procedural law
law relating to the process by which core rights and obligations are determined and enforced

practice norms
ethical standards and legal skills that legal practitioners must follow and possess to deliver legal services effectively

domestic law
the law of a particular state or society

public international law (or international law)
the law relating to international treaties and customs, to inter-state relationships, and to the relationship between states and non-nationals

The law can be divided into many different subject areas (see Figure 1.1). However, not all of these areas are discrete and self-contained. For example, insurance law overlaps with contract law (many issues in insurance turn on the interpretation of insurance policies, which are usually based on a contract). Further, some areas of the law are really amalgams, or combinations, of other areas: sports law, for instance, can involve contracts, torts, criminal law, labour law, and even civil liberties. Also, and quite commonly, a single fact situation may give rise to claims in different areas. For example, if one person physically assaults another person, that could lead to a private law tort claim for battery *and* a criminal law charge of assault.

Canada's Constitution—as we will see in Chapters 3 and 4—divides the power to make and regulate the law in the various areas between the federal Parliament and the provincial legislatures. And just as there is overlap between some areas of the law, the *jurisdiction* over some areas overlaps and is shared by Parliament (federal) and the legislatures (provincial). The area of family law, for example and as we shall see in Chapter 9, is partly regulated by Parliament and partly by the legislatures.

In the top box of Figure 1.1 is law in general—the whole concept, which includes positive law as well as natural law. Figure 1.1 further subdivides positive law according to whether the laws deal with core rights and obligations (**substantive law**) or with the processes for determining and enforcing those rights and obligations (**procedural law**). Running parallel to these two basic types of law are **practice norms**, which influence the law's application when the legal profession is involved (which is frequently the case in more complex legal matters). These norms are not always legally binding and, when they are not, they are not "law" in the strict sense. However, legal professionals' adherence to high standards in practice—whether they are legally enforceable or not—is critical in any system of law that is effective and fair.

Note how these three broad categories (that is, substantive law, procedural law, and practice norms) feed into both **domestic law**—in other words, the law of a particular state—and **public international law** and its branches, which deal primarily with the treaties, customs, and other legal sources that govern inter-state relationships. Both domestic law and public international law have substantive *and* procedural law aspects to them, and often require the intercession of the legal profession.

FIGURE 1.1 Divisions of Law

(Figure 1.1 is concluded on the next page.)

FIGURE 1.1 Divisions of Law   concluded

PUBLIC LAW	PRIVATE LAW
Governs relationships between persons and the state, and between the various organs of the state	Governs relationships between persons

PUBLIC LAW

CONSTITUTIONAL — Concerns governmental powers and structures and civil liberties

CRIMINAL — Regulates behaviour deemed particularly socially offensive

ADMINISTRATIVE — Deals with the relationship between government agencies and persons

ABORIGINAL — Involves rights, land claims, and other legal issues relating to Indigenous peoples in Canada

IMMIGRATION — Governs immigration into and deportation from Canada (often broadly defined to include matters relating to citizenship)

TAX — Concerns various forms of government taxation

OTHER — E.g., municipal, competition (antitrust) and public safety

PRIVATE LAW

TORTS — Consists of a broad range of civil wrongs not covered by other areas

CONTRACTS — Governs the making and enforcing of binding agreements

PROPERTY — Regulates ownership and the use of real, personal, and intellectual property

FAMILY — Defines rights and obligations within family relationships

COMPANY — Relates to corporations and their structures and dealings

EQUITY — Concerns trusts, fiduciary relationships and obligations, and equitable remedies

SUCCESSION — Concerns wills and estates and the transmission of property after death

LABOUR AND EMPLOYMENT — Deals with rights and obligations in unionized and non-unionized work environments

INSURANCE — Pertains to insurable interests, insurance policies, and claims

OTHER — E.g., commercial transactions, secured transactions, real estate transactions, conveyancing, landlord and tenant, professional malpractice, creditors' remedies, and conflict of laws

HYBRID AREAS: PUBLIC LAW *AND* PRIVATE LAW ASPECTS

E.g., business and consumer, bankruptcy and insolvency, securities, sports, entertainment, elder law, animal law, environmental, natural resources, fisheries, admiralty (or maritime) law

public law
law dealing with the legal relationship between a state and individual members of the state

private law
law that concerns the relationships between persons

Domestic law is divided into public law, private law, and military law. **Public law** deals with the legal relationship between persons and the state, and between the various organs of the state. It can be divided into a number of different areas, many of which are set out in Figure 1.1 and some of which are covered elsewhere in this book: Chapters 4 to 7 (constitutional law), Chapter 11 (administrative law), and Chapter 12 (criminal law). **Private law**, which concerns the relationships between persons, can be subdivided into many areas. The more common ones are set out in Figure 1.1, and a few of these will be examined in Chapters 8 and 9. Chapter 10 (business and consumer law) concerns a hybrid area with public law and private law aspects, and Chapter 14 surveys a number of areas not covered in detail elsewhere in the book.

Military law is a special area, a constitutionally separate and largely self-contained system of law regulating the Canadian Forces. It governs the armed forces during times of conflict and in peacetime, at home and abroad.

Finally, note that there are many hybrid areas of law—areas that defy easy classification and that cross broad subdivisions in the law. This is reflected in the boxes linking domestic law and public international law, and public law and private law. Note also that military law, though usually classed as a separate area of domestic law, has public law and private law aspects, as well as a public international law aspect.

military law
a constitutionally separate and relatively self-contained system of law regulating the Canadian Forces

Legal Terminology

Law is expressed through language. Over the centuries, the language of the law has developed a separate life of its own. In fact, most students of law feel like they are learning a whole new language when they begin reading cases and legislation. It's not just that some of the words—particularly the Latin ones—are unfamiliar; it's also the way the words are used and how legal arguments are structured.

HLA Hart has referred to a shadow of uncertainty surrounding legal rules. As an example, earlier in this chapter, in our discussion of the structure of rules, we referred to the negligence rule in the context of motor vehicle accidents and noted that the standard of care used to determine negligence was based on the "reasonable motorist." But who is the reasonable motorist? What does this phrase mean, exactly? How well does the reasonable motorist drive? Does it matter if it's dark and raining or if she's rushing to the hospital because her child is sick at the time of the accident? These are the kinds of uncertainties that the language of the law is often unable to avoid. What fills these shadows or grey areas of uncertainty around the legal rules? According to Hart, it is discretion (that is, the discretion of judges when interpreting the law).

Apart from the uncertainty it involves, legal language is very specialized. Its language is so unfamiliar that it may sometimes seem to you that the legal profession has conspired to make the law more difficult than it is. Recently, there has been a reaction against such specialized, deliberately obscure professional language. This has been a positive development for students and legal practitioners, as well as the public. Expressions such as *hereinafter*, *aforesaid*, *notwithstanding the generality of the foregoing*, and *the said party of the first part* are no longer considered to be impressive.

A plain-language movement in business and law started in the 1970s. This change is often attributed to banks' wishing to simplify their contracts for consumers to prevent unnecessary litigation. The benefits of this measure were soon clear to all, and the plain-language movement has continued to the present day. Nowadays, in most jurisdictions, legislative counsel responsible for drafting legislation are directed to use plain language in writing or rewriting legislation; they are given lists of "difficult" words and told to replace them with clear ones. Newly appointed judges in many jurisdictions are now required to go to "judge school" for training, which includes sessions on how to write clear, structured judgments.

Despite these developments, legal language remains a challenge to new law students. To help you navigate the language of the law, there are resources that you can use alongside your other course materials. These include dictionaries and collections of legal words and phrases. (See the list of dictionary resources under Further Reading at the end of this chapter.) Also, be sure to use the glossaries in this and other law books. Finally, pay close attention to context when reading legal materials; there are many expressions, such as *common law* and *civil law*, that have multiple meanings within the law (see Chapter 2). The context in which they are used should help you with the intended meaning.

CHAPTER SUMMARY

Law is not easily or simply defined. We have seen that, at a basic level, it relates to the regulation of human activity by way of rules. The broad categories of rules and their forms are relatively standard, but the content of rules varies greatly. In many societies, especially liberal democracies of the West, the law is distinguished from other types of rules, such as those based on morality, justice, or religion.

There are numerous theories concerning the law and its development. Some of these theories are analytic in nature, describing what the law *is*. Others are normative in nature, describing what the law *ought to be*. Some theories have both analytic and normative elements. Many countries, including Canada, have a positivist and analytic bias.

The concept of rule of law informs the law in most countries around the world, including Canada, although the degree to which its core tenets are adhered to varies. Rule of law concerns fairness in the administration of the law. Equality in the application of the law and balance in the use of power are key principles.

Law has many divisions and subdivisions, particularly within the domestic law category, and also many areas of overlap between these divisions. As you continue your legal studies, you will become more familiar with these specific areas, as well as with the legal terminology used to describe them. With that familiarity will come a greater comfort with the whole area of the law.

KEY TERMS

corrective justice, 8

critical legal studies, 18

critical race theory, 18

deontological, 8

distributive justice, 11

domestic law, 24

ethics, 7

feminist theories of law, 18

instrumentalist, 8

jurisprudence, 12

law and society, 18

legal positivism, 15

legal realism, 16

Marxist theories of law, 18

military law, 27

morality, 6

natural law, 13

positive law, 15

practice norms, 24

private law, 26

procedural law, 24

public international law
   (or international law), 24

public law, 26

retributive justice, 9

rule of law, 19

sociology of law, 18

substantive laws, 24

FURTHER READING

BOOKS AND ARTICLES

Arlidge, Anthony & Igor Judge. *Magna Carta Uncovered* (Oxford: Hart, 2014).

Black's Law Dictionary, 10th ed (West Group, 2014) and the abridged version *Black's Law Dictionary, Abridged*, 10th ed (West Group, 2014).

Culver, Keith C, ed. *Readings in the Philosophy of Law*, 3rd ed (Peterborough, Ont: Broadview Press, 2017).

The Dictionary of Canadian Law, 4th ed (Toronto: Carswell, 2011) and the abridged version, the *Pocket Dictionary of Canadian Law*, 5th ed (Toronto: Carswell, 2011).

Freeman, Michael DA. *Lloyd's Introduction to Jurisprudence*, 9th ed (London, UK: Sweet & Maxwell, 2014).

Fuller, Lon L. "The Case of the Speluncean Explorers" (1949) 62 Harv L Rev 616.

Fuller, Lon L. *The Morality of Law*, revised ed (New Haven, Conn: Yale University Press, 1965).

Harris, Phil. *An Introduction to Law*, 8th ed (Cambridge, UK: Cambridge University Press, 2016) ch 1.

Hart, HLA. *The Concept of Law*, 2nd ed (Oxford: Oxford University Press, 1994).

Holt, James C. *Magna Carta*, 3rd ed (Cambridge, UK: Cambridge University Press, 2015).

Waddams, SM. *Introduction to the Study of Law*, 8th ed (Toronto: Carswell, 2016) chs 1, 3.

WEBSITES

Irwin Law, *Canadian Online Legal Dictionary*: <http://www.irwinlaw.com/cold>.

United Nations and the Rule of Law: <http://www.un.org/en/ruleoflaw/index.shtml>.

REVIEW QUESTIONS

1. Describe the basic structure(s) of legal rules.

2. What is one way to differentiate morality from ethics?

3. Is a lie ever justified in your opinion? Include in your answer the correct use of the words *deontological* and *instrumentalist*.

4. Compare corrective justice with retributive justice, including the areas of law to which they most clearly apply.

5. Briefly describe the relationship between the law and religion.

6. Describe natural law in your own words.

7. Describe legal realism in your own words.

8. What is the rule of law and what are some of its basic principles?

9. What is the difference between substantive law and procedural law?

10. Briefly describe the plain-language movement and its application to legal terminology today.

EXERCISES

1. Choose a definition of law that, in your opinion, has both strengths and weaknesses. Describe the strengths and weaknesses and then rewrite the definition to remove the weaknesses.

2. Locate and read two speeches or articles by or about Pierre Elliott Trudeau and his *just society*. Next, describe in your own words what you think a just society is.

3. In your view, does the law of retaliation reflect an innate need or a learned response? Provide reasons to support your view.

4. What is the basic difference between analytic and normative theories of law? If you had to write a paper on one or the other, which would you choose and why?

5. Using the United Nations and the Rule of Law website, locate, read, and summarize two UN documents dealing with the rule of law.

2 Common Law, Civil Law, and Other Legal Systems

The Bayeux Tapestry celebrates the events leading to and culminating in the Norman Conquest of England in 1066 by William the Conqueror and dates to the late 11th century. The French-speaking Norman king came from mainland Europe (in what is now the Normandy region of France) where the civil law system was developing and now predominates. William's legal reforms in England led to the establishment of another great legal tradition: the common law system.

After reading this chapter, you will understand:

- The common law's origins and defining characteristics.
- The civil law's origins and defining characteristics.
- How the common law and civil law systems compare and their relevance in the Canadian context.

- Some of the measures taken in Canada to harmonize the common law and civil law systems.
- The role that religion and customary law play in some legal systems, and the prevalence of hybrid or mixed legal systems around the world.

Canadian bijuralism is an integral part of our legal heritage.

Anne McLellan, former minister of justice, quoted in M Brunet, *Out of the Shadows: The Civil Law Tradition in the Department of Justice Canada, 1868-2000* (Ottawa: Queen's Printer, 2000) at ii

Introduction

bijural
term describing the operation of two legal systems in one jurisdiction, such as the common law and civil law systems in Canada

common law
system of law, based on the English legal tradition, that relies on precedent rather than on codified rules; may also refer to (1) decisions by courts exercising their common law jurisdiction as opposed to their equitable juris-diction based on broad principles of fairness, or (2) case law generally as opposed to legislation

civil law
system of law based on codified rules; may also refer to private law

The legal systems, or traditions, that exist in the world today reflect the diverse and some-times complex histories of the world's peoples. Canada is a **bijural** nation. This means that it has two legal systems. All regions in Canada, except Quebec, employ the **common law** system. Quebec, where roughly one-quarter of our population lives, is bijural—the **civil law** applies in respect of private law matters and the common law in respect of public law mat-ters (primarily federal areas, including criminal law). Quebec's bijuralism is what makes Canada a bijural nation.

It is important to be aware of the existence and basic structure of other legal systems be-sides our own for several reasons, including:

1. *Multiculturalism.* Canada is a multicultural society made up of people from all around the world. To understand something about the traditions of our fellow Canadians can only be a benefit.
2. *Trade.* International trade is necessary for a healthy economy. Knowing how our trading partners in other countries with different systems of law view legal rights and obligations will improve our business relations.
3. *Globalization.* The world has become a "smaller" place because of technology. The interconnectedness of all peoples is more apparent now than ever, making it increasingly important for us to understand our "neighbours" in other parts of the world.

Comparative law is the study of different legal systems. It is a relatively new field of legal study, and there is some debate about how best to classify the different systems of law. At least five categories exist, as follows:

1. common law,
2. civil law,

3. religious law,
4. customary law, and
5. mixed or hybrid systems.[1]

Roughly half of the world's nations are monosystems using one of the first four legal systems, while the other nations, including Canada, employ a mix of systems. The focus of this chapter is on the first two systems: common law and civil law. Most legal issues in Canada involve one or both of these systems. Following our discussion of common law and civil law, we will briefly examine religious law and customary law, and the range of mixed or hybrid systems. Appendix 2.1 illustrates how the various legal systems are distributed around the world.

Common Law

The common law system arose from circumstances unique to England. The system's defining feature is that judges follow precedent. The precedents that are the basis of the system originated with judges who sat in royal courts of justice. These courts were established by early English kings following the Norman invasion of England in 1066 CE.

Law in Pre-Norman England: Romans and Anglo-Saxons

The Roman era in England lasted from 43 CE, when the Romans conquered the island, until the fifth century CE, when they abandoned it. During this 400-year period, the Romans introduced their legal system to Britain. However, this system did not take root in England as it had in continental Europe, and little remained of it after the Roman departure.[2]

Other invaders succeeded the Romans in England. Germanic tribes—the Angles, Saxons, Jutes, and Danes—established the Anglo-Saxon era in Britain, which lasted from the fifth century until the Norman invasion of 1066. These tribes established separate kingdoms across southern England. Each had its own system of Germanic laws based on tribal customs and principles of communal justice. Initially, their codes of justice were not written; they were transmitted orally. In time, some Anglo-Saxon kings had their tribes' legal codes compiled in written form. But each tribe's legal code applied only to its specific territory, and there was no centralized nationwide justice system. This changed with the invasion of the island by the Norman king William the Conqueror in 1066.

Origins of Common Law

William the Conqueror (1028-1087), unlike the Anglo-Saxon invaders before him, proceeded to establish a centralized royal kingdom in most of southern England. One way he accomplished this was by introducing a political structure called **feudalism**. Under this system, William claimed ownership of all land on the island. He then distributed large areas of it to favoured nobles in return for their promises of loyalty and military support. And the nobles, in turn, granted portions of land to their subjects, known as vassals, in return for their oaths of allegiance. This new socio-political arrangement, with its hierarchical system

feudalism
socio-political system in medieval Europe based on relationships of obligation and allegiance among king, nobles, and subjects, with land given to subordinates in return for loyalty and military support

---

1   For a global overview of legal systems by continent, and for data on individual countries, visit JuriGlobe's website at <http://www.juriglobe.ca/eng>. JuriGlobe is a research group affiliated with the Faculty of Law at the University of Ottawa.

2   George W Keeton, *The Norman Conquest and the Common Law* (London, UK: Ernest Benn, 1966).

of obligation and allegiance, helped unify the island under a single monarch. This centralization of authority contributed greatly to the formation of the common law system.

Another way that William gained control over his English domain was to set up a centralized government administration. He and the kings who succeeded him established something called the *curia regis*. This was a group of nobles who advised the king on governing the country. They helped him in the following areas, in particular:

Chancery
department of state established by English monarchs to assist with legal matters and to issue writs

- overseeing departments of state—for example, the **Chancery** for legal matters and the Exchequer for the king's finances;
- securing royal control throughout the island by issuing royal documents, such as charters, to establish new towns and villages; and
- creating administrative officers, such as sheriffs, who were responsible, within their respective regions of the country, for maintaining the king's powers and privileges.

A further centralizing measure that William introduced was the expansion of the island's legal system through royal courts of justice. These courts were particularly crucial to the emergence of the common law.[3]

Development of a Royal Court System

king's peace
the ideal peace and well-being of a nation that the English monarch was obliged to uphold and protect

The Anglo-Norman kings, unlike their Anglo-Saxon predecessors, viewed justice as a royal obligation and believed that, as kings of England, they were responsible for the **king's peace**. This meant that an English king had the right and the duty to preserve public order and to punish anyone who disturbed the well-being of English subjects. A system of criminal law was initiated in the name of the king. In each county, the king appointed justices of the peace to keep order, and he established the grand jury to seek out suspected wrongdoers and bring them to his judges' attention. Through these measures, which were implemented across most of England, English law began to derive its authority directly from the king.[4]

The royal courts of justice evolved over time. English monarchs such as Henry I (1100-1135) and Henry II (1154-1189) appointed royal judges from the *curia regis* and sent them out on a circuit of the outlying counties, away from the London capital, to preside over the courts. The courts presided over by these travelling judges were known as *assizes*. Representing the monarch, these royal judges dealt with local offenders who had contravened the king's peace, and they helped to settle local disputes.

Court of King's (or Queen's) Bench
English court that decided criminal matters

English monarchs set up three separate royal courts of justice—the Court of Common Pleas, the **Court of King's (or Queen's) Bench**, and the Exchequer Court—to decide legal disputes. The Court of Common Pleas decided civil and landholding disputes. The Court of King's (or Queen's) Bench decided criminal matters. The Exchequer Court decided revenue matters involving the king. The English people favoured these three royal courts. They appreciated the judges' expertise and other features of the courts, including the following:

- their power to summon witnesses;
- their use of juries rather than older modes of trial, such as ordeal or combat (which were physical tests that did not accurately measure the truth of asserted claims);

---

3 Raoul C Van Caenegem, *The Birth of the English Common Law* (Cambridge, UK: Cambridge University Press, 1988).

4 William R Cornish, *The Jury* (Harmondsworth, UK: Penguin, 1968).

- their use of written records (which promoted certainty and consistency in decision-making); and
- their power to enforce their judgments.[5]

The Writ System

The royal courts were popular, but they did involve one problematic feature: the writ system of civil procedure. A person—known as the *plaintiff*—who started a civil or non-criminal action in these royal courts first had to purchase from the king a specific document called a **writ**. A writ was a written order to a defendant. It came not from the plaintiff but from the king. It was affixed with a royal seal, notifying a defendant that the plaintiff had a particular complaint or cause of action against him, such as breach of contract, trespass, or assault. It also stated that if the defendant wished to challenge the plaintiff's court action, he must precisely follow the procedures prescribed by the writ.

The problem with this system arose in the following way. The king could not issue all writs personally; they were too numerous. So the practice arose of having the chancellor, who headed the king's Chancery, issue them instead. Over the course of several centuries, many different writs developed for specific disputes, and each writ had its own formal procedures. The plaintiff's choice of writ became crucial. If plaintiffs chose the wrong writ for their cause of action, later amendment was impossible. At the same time, if no writ was appropriate for the plaintiff's cause of action, then no remedy was available from the royal courts. To overcome these formal, rigid, and increasingly technical pleading rules, litigants began to appeal to the king, who was seen as the fountainhead of justice, to intervene on their behalf.[6] Their appeals were heard by the chancellor, who was the king's representative.

writ
court document, obtained by a plaintiff, by which the defendant was informed that a particular type of action had been started against him

Chancery Separates from Common Law

Over time, chancellors established a royal court that was separate from the three other royal courts of justice. It was called the **Court of Chancery**, and its purpose was to grant relief on grounds of equitable justice and to adjudicate petitions from plaintiffs appealing outside the writ system. While the other royal courts of justice used the common law, the Court of Chancery created a parallel system of law consisting of its own separate body of maxims or rules, called **equity**.

For example, the common law courts interpreted contracts, and particularly contracts involving land, very strictly. If a person who had mortgaged his land (the mortgagor) missed a payment, the mortgagee (or lender) was permitted to exercise his contractual right to take the land in satisfaction. In many cases this would be unfair, especially if the mortgagor had paid off most of the debt. (The relevant maxim here is *equity abhors a forfeiture*.) In such a case, the Court of Chancery could step in and give the mortgagor some extra time (a redemption period) to pay back the lender.

Another special feature of the Court of Chancery was that it could hear disputes informally and quickly, without a jury, and could provide a plaintiff with remedies—for example, specific performance, or rectification of a contract, or an injunction—other than monetary damages. These remedies were not available in the three other royal courts.

Court of Chancery
English court, existing separate from common law courts, established to provide equity

equity
discretionary legal decisions offered by judges in the Court of Chancery, based on fairness and providing relief from the rigid procedures that had evolved under common law courts

---

5 Arthur R Hogue, *Origins of the Common Law* (Bloomington, Ind: Indiana University Press, 1966).

6 John H Baker, *An Introduction to English Legal History*, 4th ed (London, UK: Butterworths, 2002).

Judicature Acts

The existence of two completely separate court systems—the royal courts (using common law rules) on the one hand, and the Court of Chancery (using equitable rules) on the other—created certain difficulties. These were not resolved until 1873, when the English Parliament passed a series of statutes, the *Judicature Acts*, unifying the courts under one court system. This system was made up of the High Court of Justice (with five specialized divisions) and the Court of Appeal. The system allowed for a further right of appeal to the House of Lords. Both common law and equitable rules could now be administered under one court system. This measure simplified court procedure considerably.

In Canada, each province has its own unified high (or superior) court system with a trial level and an appeal level. These courts—except in Quebec, which employs the civil law system—apply both common law and equitable rules. Generally, the maxim *equity follows the law* governs the relationship between the two sets of rules. This means that the role of equity is to add to or fill in the gaps left by the common law, based on principles of fairness, but not to change the common law. However, in limited situations where there is a conflict between the two sets of rules, most provincial "judicature" statutes provide, as do the English *Judicature Acts*, that equity prevails.

Chief Features of Common Law

stare decisis
Latin phrase ("to stand by decided matters") referring to the common law principle that a precedent is binding on lower courts in the same jurisdiction

The distinguishing features of the common law system are the reliance on precedent, the principle of **stare decisis**, and the use of an adversarial process in court.

Use of Precedents

Inns of Court
professional associations for lawyers in England and Wales, with supervisory and disciplinary functions over their members and authority to call law students to the bar; the four Inns of Court today are Inner Temple, Middle Temple, Lincoln's Inn, and Gray's Inn

English common law was a product of centuries of evolution. This process began with the development of the royal courts during the medieval period, as described above. The itinerant royal judges, on returning to London from their county assizes, would meet and dine with their fellow judges at the **Inns of Court**. This collegial process promoted respect for and attention to one another's judgments. Court reporting began in 1283, with the Year Books. Two centuries later, the invention of the printing press made it even easier for English judges to critically examine one another's judgments. From there, it was a short distance to the practice of following **precedent**. In other words, a judge would apply an earlier judicial decision to the case before him if the facts and the law were similar.[7]

This practice became institutionalized when royal judges formally accepted the principle known as *stare decisis* ("to stand by decided matters"). According to this principle, cases that are alike should be treated alike. What this meant for English law, practically speaking, was that royal judges on the county circuit would decide cases by following precedents rather than by following local customs. As a result of this practice, there arose one cohesive system of judicial rules and practices common to England. This became known as the common law.

precedent
court decision that, under the doctrine of *stare decisis*, is binding on lower courts in the same jurisdiction

PRECEDENT AND STARE DECISIS IN A COURT HIERARCHY

Over time, changes in the English court system affected the operation of *stare decisis*. In the 16th century, the English court structure was eventually reorganized into a hierarchy, with trial courts at the bottom and superior appellate courts at the top. After this, a user of the system was required to enter first through a trial court, where one judge would decide on the matter.

---

7   Alan Harding, *The Law Courts of Medieval England* (London, UK: Allen and Unwin, 1973).

Those wanting to dispute the trial judge's decision were then required to appeal the judgment upward, to a higher appellate court at Westminster. At this upper level, a panel of appellate judges (usually three) would hear the trial judgment and decide whether it was correct in law.

The reorganization of the courts affected the principle of *stare decisis*; it was expanded to include the rule that a decision made by a higher appellate court is **binding**. In other words, the higher court's decision must be followed by a lower court in the same judicial hierarchy if the facts and the ***ratio decidendi*** ("reason for the decision") or principle of law in both cases are substantially similar.

The principle of *stare decisis* is very rational, but it has limitations. In 1966, the House of Lords issued the *Practice Statement*. This was a formal recognition that "too rigid adherence to precedent may lead to injustice in a particular case and also unduly restrict the proper development of the law."[8] It gave the House of Lords the power to *overrule itself* and to depart from precedent to achieve justice. Since then, most courts in other common law jurisdictions have recognized a similar power to overrule themselves in appropriate circumstances. However, there has to be a good reason for a court to exercise this power. This development has had no effect on lower courts, which continue to be bound by higher court decisions in the same jurisdiction.

Even in the lower courts, the doctrine of precedent is not as absolute as it first appears. For example, lawyers and judges wishing *not* to follow an apparently binding precedent from a higher appellate court have certain arguments open to them. They might argue, for example, that there are material factual differences between the preceding case and the one under consideration. Such a precedent is said to be **distinguishable**. Other arguments can be made against an apparently binding precedent. You might argue, for example, that a precedent

- has been overruled by an even higher court,
- is no longer applicable because of changed social circumstances,
- was poorly reasoned and has lost its reputation as good law, or
- has been reinterpreted differently by other judges.

Any one of these arguments, if made successfully, could render a precedent non-binding. One English judge wrote the following in this regard: "The common law evolves not merely by breeding new principles but also, when they are fully grown, by burying their ancestors."[9]

Circumstances may arise where there is no binding precedent. In this case, a judge or lawyer may also want to use a precedent from another jurisdiction that is directly on point. Such a precedent, taken from another province or from another common law country, is said to be **persuasive**. Today in Canada, a lawyer trying to "persuade" a judge to examine such a precedent would have to convince her that there was no relevant precedent from the judge's own province or from the Supreme Court of Canada (SCC).

Figure 2.1 shows the flow of precedent downward in the Canadian court system, with the SCC at the top. Each province is considered a separate jurisdiction; decisions from other provinces are therefore not binding but can be persuasive. How persuasive a decision is depends on a number of factors, including the level of the other court, the judge who wrote

binding
term used to describe a higher court decision that a lower court in the same jurisdiction must follow according to the principle of *stare decisis*

ratio or ***ratio decidendi***
Latin phrase ("the reason for the decision") referring to the governing rule in a case or the way it was applied to the facts

distinguishable
term given to a precedent from a higher court that a lower court decides not to follow, usually on the grounds that the facts in the cases differ

persuasive
describes a precedent that a court is persuaded to give some weight to but is not bound to follow, because the precedent is from another jurisdiction or is otherwise not binding

---

8   See *Practice Statement*, [1966] 3 All ER 77 (HL). Prior to 1966, the House of Lords had considered itself bound by its own decisions under the principle of *stare decisis*: see *London Street Tramways Co v London City Council*, [1898] AC 375 (HL). See also Gordon Bale, "Casting Off the Mooring Ropes of Precedent" (1980) 58 Can Bar Rev 255.

9   *Hong Kong Fir Shipping Co Ltd v Kawasaki Kisen Kaisha Ltd*, [1962] 1 All ER 474 at 488 (CA), Lord Diplock.

the decision, the quality of the reasoning, and the date of the decision. The same standard applies to decisions from other countries.

FIGURE 2.1 Flow of Precedent in Canada

In Chapter 6, we will look at Canada's court system in more detail, including the federal court system's place in it, as well as how lower courts and administrative tribunals form part of the hierarchy.

DEVELOPING NEW PRECEDENTS

If there is neither a binding precedent applicable to a case nor a persuasive precedent from another jurisdiction, litigants may call on the court to develop a new precedent (see Box 2.1). Under what circumstances would there be no binding precedent? The case might involve, for example, a novel issue, or it might be an old issue in a modern social context.

If a court feels that establishing a new precedent might be too contentious or radical a step, it can leave the matter for elected representatives to address through legislation. If the court is feeling bold or believes that a new precedent would represent a reasonable, incremental change to the common law, it may articulate the new precedent itself.

There are three important factors that a court may take into consideration when establishing a new precedent:

1. the existence of *similar* cases,
2. the approach taken in other jurisdictions, and
3. policy considerations.

In considering similar cases, the court might see a common thread that connects them all; these cases may reveal a common direction in which the law is moving. Under these circumstances, the new precedent established by the court's decision will simply be a logical extension of the decisions made in these similar cases.

A second factor that courts might consider is the approach that other courts, in other jurisdictions, have taken to the issue at hand. Such comparative analysis has become increasingly important in the last few decades, owing to globalization. More and more often, our courts ask the following question: How have courts elsewhere—in other provinces, other countries, even (on occasion) countries with other legal systems—treated a particular issue? If other jurisdictions have taken a consistent or reasoned approach to a particular problem, our courts might take a similar approach.[10]

Applying Law Versus Making Law

Where an established rule (from an earlier precedent) seems relevant to a judge's decision in a case, she will *apply* that rule to the facts of the case. In a typical motor vehicle accident case involving liability, for example, the judge's decision will hinge on whether the defendant exercised reasonable care in all the circumstances (the standard of care element in a negligence action). Did the defendant breach any of the rules of the road by speeding or by not stopping at a stop sign or by not yielding at a courtesy corner? Was he impaired? Was he distracted by his cellphone? The judge will apply the reasonable care rule to the specific circumstances of the case and reach a conclusion.

The situation is different in cases where the judge or court is asked to articulate a new rule and opts to do so. The *Donoghue v Stevenson** case (referred to in Chapter 1) was famous for a couple of reasons. First, Lord Atkin proposed something no one had proposed before—that people have a general legal obligation to take care where other people are concerned (the neighbour principle). Second, Lord Atkin narrowed this general principle to fit in a particular context, holding that manufacturers have a specific obligation or duty to ensure that their products are reasonably safe for consumers even though the manufacturer has no contractual relationship with the consumer. By establishing this new precedent, did the court *make* law?

What precisely is the role of judges and courts in the common law world? Historically, common law judges were tasked with "finding the law." In other words, they were supposed to determine what the existing law was according to common customs and then apply it to the facts before them. They were not charged with "making law," which was seen as too activist and not within their bailiwick. If a new law was required, Parliament or the Crown (during the period when the king or queen could make laws) was supposed to step in. But in cases where a matter was pressing, waiting for a legislative response was not always satisfactory. Under these circumstances, judges have sometimes taken the bold step of establishing a new precedent.

Still, some judges and commentators have argued that courts always *find* rather than *make* new law. This argument goes as follows. When judges recognize a new rule, they do so in a rational manner, by searching for common threads in existing laws, by furthering established policies, and by effecting incremental change. A process of legal reasoning dictates the result. People who make this argument are reluctant to acknowledge the courts' power to make law. Their reluctance stems from the historical ideal of how the law was supposed to work. Judges were supposed to apply existing law, not create new laws. A greater creative authority on the part of judges could lead to uncontrolled change and instability.

Whether we characterize the recognition of a new rule as *making* law or *finding* it, the crucial element in the process seems to be the quality of the analytical reasoning that generates it.

* *M'Alister (or Donoghue) v Stevenson*, [1932] AC 562 at 580 (HL).

Policy is the third factor the courts might consider when deciding whether or not to recognize a new precedent. A court might consider the possibility, for example, that a new rule would benefit society by providing a useful deterrent to some problematic behaviour. On the other hand, the court would shy away from creating a new precedent if it foresaw that the new rule might lead to negative economic consequences or to a flood of cases clogging up the courts (a policy argument known as the *floodgates argument*).

Adversarial System

In the common law system, the government appoints judges from among members of the legal profession—lawyers who have practised for a certain number of years. These judges preside over an **adversarial system** of justice. The adversarial system is based on the idea that truth

adversarial system
system, used in common law courts, whereby the primary responsibility for the presentation of cases lies with the opposing litigants and their counsel, not with the judge presiding over the case

---

10 For example, in *Whiten v Pilot Insurance Co*, 2002 SCC 18, referred to in Chapter 1 under "Retributive Justice," the SCC looked at how other common law countries (England, Australia, New Zealand, Ireland, and the United States) had dealt with the question of punitive damages before developing a rule for our country.

will best be determined when lawyers oppose each other in the courtroom and present their respective cases without interference from the trial judge. Judges can ask questions to seek clarification and can do their own independent research, but the adversarial approach ensures that the *primary* responsibility for the presentation of cases lies with the opposing litigants and their counsel. At the end of the case, judges render their decisions based on the factual and legal material before them. As noted, this is one other key feature of the common law system.

Sources of Law

Bill of Rights (1689)
English statute that formally ended the power of the Crown to legislate without the consent of Parliament

Besides judge-made rules, other written laws have at various times been recognized as binding in England. Before 1689, the monarch was able to legislate by decree. This ended with the Glorious Revolution of 1688, when Parliament completely took over the Crown's power to legislate. The English **Bill of Rights (1689)** formally declared that the "pretended" power of the Crown to legislate without the consent of Parliament was illegal.

Since that time, jurisdictions that follow the common law tradition have recognized two primary sources of law:

1. legislation, and
2. case law (the decisions of the courts).

The doctrine of parliamentary sovereignty dictates that where there is a conflict between case law and legislation, the latter prevails. In Chapter 4, we examine this doctrine in more detail.

Common Law: A Summary

The distinguishing features of the common law, which developed over many centuries of English legal history, are as follows:

- It arose from the English kings' efforts, after the Norman invasion of 1066, to centralize their authority over the island through the use of royal courts of justice with experienced judges who travelled to and held court in the outlying counties. To begin with, these judges applied local customs in deciding their cases.
- Over time, judges of the royal courts of justice began the practice of following one another's precedents to decide cases. They did this when the facts and legal issues of a later case were the same as or similar to those of an earlier case (or precedent).
- Once the courts were organized in a hierarchy, in the 16th century, the requirement to follow precedents became institutionalized in the legal principle of *stare decisis*.
- The court process is based on an adversarial approach, with lawyers opposing each other in the courtroom and presenting their respective cases without interference from the trial judge.
- The legal rules in common law jurisdictions are not set out in one central document or code.
- Judge-made rules are one of two main sources of law. The other is legislation.

Evolving over many centuries, with its own particular legal doctrines, courts, practices, and institutions, the common law system was unique to England and was too strong—too complex and well established—to be overcome by the civil law system used on the European continent. It was this common law legal system, carried to the New World by English settlers, that was received in Canada as well as in other countries that began as English colonies, including the United States, Australia, New Zealand, Jamaica, and Belize.

Civil Law

The civil law system evolved in continental Europe. Under this system, the civil code is the primary source of private law and is more important than judicial decisions. A **civil code**, according to *Black's Law Dictionary*, is a "comprehensive and systematic legislative pronouncement of the whole private, non-commercial law in a legal system of the continental civil law tradition."[11]

The civil law system's methods and techniques of analyzing legal issues are different from those of the common law system. When dealing with private law matters, judges must consult the civil code and decide the cases in accordance with the code's general principles and laws. Judicial precedents are used in the civil law system, but they do not have the same binding nature as they do in the common law system, under the principle of *stare decisis*.

civil code
authoritative legislative encoding of a country's private law

Origins of Civil Law

The most ancient legal code that has survived in its entirety is the *Code of Hammurabi* (see Figure 2.2), referred to briefly in Chapter 1. Other codes preceded it, such as the *Code of Ur-Nammu*, which dates from around 2050 BCE, but these earlier codes are not complete. The *Code of Hammurabi* was written around 1750 BCE, during the reign of the Babylonian king Hammurabi, in the Akkadian language. Archaeologists unearthed the most famous copy of it in 1901, in Susa (now the modern Iranian town of Shush).

The following are some of the 282 laws from the *Code of Hammurabi*:

> 5. If a judge try a case, reach a decision, and present his judgment in writing; if later error shall appear in his decision, and it be through his own fault, then he shall pay twelve times the fine set by him in the case, and he shall be publicly removed from the judge's bench, and never again shall he sit there to render judgment. ...
>
> 22. If anyone is committing a robbery and is caught, then he shall be put to death. ...
>
> 59. If any man, without the knowledge of the owner of a garden, fell a tree in a garden he shall pay half a mina in money. ...
>
> 132. If the "finger is pointed" at a man's wife about another man, but she is not caught sleeping with the other man, she shall jump into the river for her husband. ...
>
> 196. If a man put out the eye of another man, his eye shall be put out. ...
>
> 229. If a builder build a house for someone, and does not construct it properly, and the house which he built fall in and kill its owner, then that builder shall be put to death. ...
>
> 252. If [a man] kill [another] man's slave, he shall pay one-third of a mina. ...
>
> 282. If a slave say to his master: "You are not my master," if they convict him his master shall cut off his ear. ...[12]

FIGURE 2.2 Code of Hammurabi
In a relief on the upper part of this stela, which is 2.25 metres tall, Hammurabi (standing, left) is shown receiving the royal insignia from the god Shamash (seated, at right). The laws are carved into the stone below.

---

11 *Black's Law Dictionary*, 10th ed, *sub verbo* "civil code."

12 The complete text is available through the Avalon Project at Yale Law School, online: <http://avalon.law.yale.edu>.

The laws in the *Code of Hammurabi* bear little resemblance to those in modern civil law jurisdictions. But any modern civil code, like the ancient Babylonian one, is essentially an authoritative statement of rules regulating conduct in a particular society.

Roman Era

Romans began keeping records of their laws as early as 450 BCE, with their *Law of the Twelve Tables*. This was not a comprehensive statement of all Roman law; it provided definitions of various private rights and obligations.

Rome's first conquests and settlements beyond the Italian peninsula began in the third century BCE. In the centuries that followed, during the time of the late Republic and early Empire, the Romans expanded across Europe and brought their legal system with them. A common body of laws, developed by Roman legal scholars over many centuries, was imposed on this increasingly vast territory.

In 534 CE, almost 1,000 years after the *Law of the Twelve Tables*, the emperor Justinian produced a comprehensive codification of Roman law in his monumental work **Corpus Juris Civilis**.[13] Also referred to as the *Justinian Code*, it is a compilation of the strongest features and principles of Roman law then in existence.

Corpus Juris Civilis
comprehensive codification of Roman civil law, compiled by the emperor Justinian (483-565 CE)

Justinian's work was an authoritative restatement of Roman legal scholarship and law concerning Roman citizens' private rights and obligations. It addressed, for example, the rights and obligations among family members, the rules about making contracts, and citizens' rights to acquire and dispose of property. The *Justinian Code* included four main parts:

1. the Codex, containing a collection of imperial edicts on private law matters;
2. the Digest, containing Roman jurists' commentary on these laws;
3. the Institutes, providing a textbook portion for Roman law students; and
4. the Novels, detailing new laws applicable to this area.

It was intended as a source of private law for all Roman citizens and as a reference work for Roman legal scholars and for Roman judges deciding cases.

Dark Ages

The Roman legal system did not entirely disappear in Europe, as it did in England, with the fall of the Roman Empire in the 5th century CE. The Germanic tribes that succeeded the Romans and settled the southern parts of Europe based many of their tribal customs and traditions on Roman laws.

This was not the case with the Germanic tribes in northern Europe. During the Dark Ages after Rome's collapse, these northern tribes—the Franks, Burgundians, and Visigoths, for example—established diverse regional kingdoms, each with its own customs and its own system of communal justice. Some of the Frankish (or French) kings summoned certain members of their council of noble advisers (the *curia regis*) to form a judicial assembly known as a *parlement*. A *parlement* compiled written accounts of local tribal customs, called *coutumes*. During the medieval period, many different French *parlements* developed many different *coutumes*, with the *coutume de Paris* being one of the most important.[14]

---

13   Alan Watson, *The Law of the Ancient Romans* (Dallas: Southern Methodist University Press, 1970).

14   René David & Henry P de Vries, *The French Legal System* (New York: Oceana, 1958).

French law in the medieval era was not transformed, as English law was, by the centralizing ambitions of a foreign invader. No French king did what William the Conqueror had done in England, creating royal courts that applied a uniform law across the country. French law was changed by a different event: the Renaissance.

The Law in Post-Renaissance Europe

The Dark Ages in Europe gave way to the Renaissance in the late 12th and 13th centuries. During this period, there was a great revival of classical learning; people turned their attention to Greek and Roman art, medicine, literature, philosophy, and theology. A renewed interest in Roman law was part of this revival. Renaissance scholars at Italy's influential University of Bologna developed a special interest in the Roman law and in its formal codifications, such as the *Justinian Code*. Academics from across Europe who attended this university rediscovered the universal appeal of classical Roman law. They discussed how improved laws, based on the Roman model, could help European society.

Renaissance legal scholars realized that if classical Roman law were to be reapplied across modern Europe, it would need to be updated. Some sought to adapt classical Roman law to the new circumstances in modern Europe. Others felt the need of an entirely new legal system that would address contemporary European concerns related to human rights, justice, morality, order, and security. There was a long-standing debate between those who revered the old Roman law and those who believed that new systems were needed. This debate continued for several centuries. Over time, many European states established their own civil codes of law.[15]

It is also significant that, in the development of the civil law system, legislated codes (and other statutes) were considered the only primary source of law. Judicial decisions were *not* considered a source of law. While earlier cases could be consulted for interpretive purposes, they were not considered binding in later cases.

In Canada, France's *Code Civil*, established in 1804 by Napoleon (it is commonly called the *Napoleonic Code*), was very influential. This influence is evident in Quebec's first code (enacted in 1866) and its current code, the *Civil Code of Quebec*,[16] which replaced the first one in 1994 (see Box 2.2; see also the discussion of Quebec's codes in Chapter 3). The *Napoleonic Code*, like Justinian's *Corpus Juris Civilis*, was designed to be an authoritative and universal statement of private law areas. It also combined the following: (1) the laws and customs based on Roman influences that had remained the basis of law in southern France, and (2) the diverse Germanic-based laws and customs of northern France's *coutumes*. Other European countries followed the French lead and established their own civil codes. England was the main exception.[17] The civil law system has been adopted by many countries and is now the most commonly used system worldwide, extending well beyond mainland Europe and its colonial spheres of influence.

---

15 John H Merryman & Rogelio Pérez-Perdomo, *The Civil Law Tradition: An Introduction to the Legal Systems of Europe and Latin America*, 3rd ed (Stanford, Cal: Stanford University Press, 2007); and Peter Shears & Graham Stephenson, *James' Introduction to English Law*, 13th ed (Oxford: Oxford University Press, 2005).

16 CQLR, c CCQ-1991.

17 Alan Katz, "France" in *Legal Traditions and Systems: An International Handbook* (New York: Greenwood, 1986) ch 6.

BOX 2.2

The Civil Code of Quebec

The *Civil Code of Quebec* became law on January 1, 1994. It was designed to reflect contemporary Quebec society's social realities and modern attitudes to, among other things, marriage, children, human rights, and parental equality rights. The *Civil Code of Quebec* comprises ten books covering private law in Quebec. The topics, by book, are as follows:

1. persons,
2. the family,
3. succession,
4. property,
5. obligations,
6. prior claims and hypothecs [mortgages],
7. evidence,
8. prescription,
9. publication of rights, and
10. private international law.

As the foregoing account makes clear, the civil law system has a long and historical evolution on the European continent. It has been shaped by Roman law more than English common law was. It also differs from the common law in that judges play a more active role in the judicial process (such as in the questioning of witnesses and marshalling of evidence), in what is referred to as an **inquisitorial system**. Further, the interpretation of civil codes is more influenced by legal scholars than by judges.

inquisitorial system feature of civil law proceedings whereby trial judges actively assist lawyers in presenting their cases and are free to call and question witnesses and to order investigations into other evidentiary matters; contrasts with the adversarial system used in common law courts

Civil Law: A Summary

The history of the civil law system is much older than that of the common law. Its antecedents go back thousands of years to when the first attempts to codify laws were made. Some of its key distinguishing features include the following:

- Authoritative law is set out in comprehensive legislative documents called *codes*.
- Judicial decisions are not binding, and there is no formal recognition of precedent or the doctrine of *stare decisis*.
- The court process is based on an inquisitorial system.
- Scholarly writing can have significant weight when interpreting civil codes.

The certainty—and to a degree the simplicity—of having a central legislated document setting out core principles of the law may explain the importance of this system around the world today.

Comparison of the Common Law and Civil Law Systems

Both the civil law system and the common law system strive for certainty, stability, and predictability. The civil law achieves these things through a comprehensive civil code, with laws set out for all to see, understand, and follow. The common law achieves them chiefly by the legal principle of *stare decisis*, with judges following precedents based on the idea that similar cases should be treated in similar ways. Clearly, one of the key differences between the two systems is the different role each assigns to previous judicial decisions.

BOX 2.3

Common Law and Civil Law: Alternate Meanings

As we have seen, some legal expressions have different meanings in different contexts. It addition to referring to legal *systems*, the phrases *common law* and *civil law* can have other meanings, too.

The phrase *civil law* is sometimes used as a synonym for *private law*—in other words, laws governing the relationship between persons (as opposed to *public law*, which deals with the legal relationship between a state and its individual members). Private and public law are generally recognized distinctions in both common law and civil law systems (except perhaps in some socialist countries). Therefore, somewhat confusingly, there could be a reference to civil law (where the context means private law) and its application in a common law jurisdiction. Adding to the

confusion is the fact that in many civil law countries, their civil codes are primarily concerned with private, or civil, law matters as opposed to public law ones. Criminal law and other areas of public law are frequently dealt with in other "non-code" statutes. However, the key features of civil law systems—such as the inquisitorial approach of judges and the lack of precedent—usually apply to these legislated areas as well.

The phrase *common law*, apart from its reference to the legal system that originated in England, can also refer to decisions by courts exercising their common law jurisdiction (used in contradistinction to decisions by courts exercising their equitable jurisdiction) and to case law generally (used in contradistinction to legislation, or enacted laws).

Despite this fundamental difference between these two major legal systems, in practice they have much in common. Judges in both systems consult prior decisions and legal scholarship when trying to resolve the issues before them. And in both systems, statutes are a source of law. The biggest challenge for newcomers to a common law jurisdiction is researching and analyzing the stand-alone judge-made rules that apply to their particular case. For newcomers to a civil law jurisdiction, the biggest adjustment tends to come in a litigation context, where judges play a more active role in an inquisitorial system. Table 2.1 summarizes some of the key differences between the civil law and common law systems.

In the practice of law in common law Canada, it is still important to understand how the civil law system works, because it may apply whenever a legal problem involves a connection with Quebec. To resolve social or business issues in our bijural nation, both legal systems are sometimes needed. Another good reason to learn about the civil law system is that, as mentioned above, it is the most common system worldwide. It is used in most of South and Central America, including Mexico, and in Continental Europe, including Russia.[18] Also, many Asian countries (China and Japan, for example) and some Middle Eastern countries employ a civil law system, sometimes in combination with other systems (customary law, religious law, or even common law).

---

18 The legal systems in socialist countries that use the civil law system—such as Russia, China, and North Korea—have some features that distinguish them from most other civil law systems. For example, the role that doctrine (that is, academic commentary) plays in socialist countries varies with the government; authoritarian regimes tend not to permit academic criticism that is political or value-based. In such cases, academic commentary on existing laws will be confined to explanation and analysis.

TABLE 2.1   Comparison of Civil Law and Common Law

CHARACTERISTICS	CIVIL LAW SYSTEM	COMMON LAW SYSTEM
Judicial Decisions	*Not Authoritative* • not a primary or authoritative source of law; only legislation (civil code and other statutes) is binding • regard for precedent is informal (however, previous cases may be persuasive, along with academic commentary, as noted below)	*Authoritative* • a primary and authoritative source of law, along with legislation • judges are bound by precedent following the principle of *stare decisis*
Role of Judges in Dispute Resolution Process	*Inquisitorial System* • judges are appointed from a special school for judges in many civil law jurisdictions—prior experience as a lawyer not required • judges conscious of being part of civil service—i.e., representatives of government • courtroom process is based on the idea that judges should actively assist lawyers in presenting their case—truth is best determined this way • judges are free to call and question witnesses, and order investigations into other evidentiary matters	*Adversarial System* • judges are appointed from the legal profession, after years of practice as lawyer or law professor • judges are conscious of being independent of the government that appoints them • courtroom process is based on the idea that truth is best determined by lawyers presenting their respective cases, unhindered by interference from the trial judge
Academic Commentary	*Important Interpretive Role* • academic commentary is one of the foundations of the civil law system and is called *doctrine* • scholarly texts and articles about the civil code play a significant role overall in helping judges decide cases	*Persuasive* • academic commentary is a type of secondary source and assists in the finding or interpretation of primary sources (judicial decisions and legislation) • texts and articles about the law have varying degrees of persuasiveness in cases in which they are cited, depending on the type of case and the author of the commentary
Juries	Generally not used	Can be used

Harmonizing Common Law and Civil Law in Canada

To avoid having a legal divide between the common and civil law systems, the Government of Canada must ensure that federal laws are compatible with the civil law system in Quebec. The following are some examples of government departments, institutions, and other organizations that assist in harmonizing Canada's two legal systems:

- *Federal Department of Justice.* This department was first created in 1868. A civil law section was established in 1952 and a new civil code section in 1993. The department's legislative bijuralism section is concerned with, among other things, developing proposals and programs that will harmonize federal areas of legislative control—which operate under the common law system—with the terms and concepts of Quebec's new civil code, in force as of January 1, 1994.

- *The Supreme Court of Canada.* Canada's highest court is composed of nine judges. By law, under the *Supreme Court Act*, three of these nine judges must come from Quebec.[19] Thus, if a case involving Quebec's civil law comes before the court, there are French civilian judges on the court to help decide the appeal based on Quebec's civil law legal system. As well, the choice of who becomes chief justice of Canada has usually alternated between an anglophone and a francophone judge.
- *Law faculties.* Some law faculties—for example, the University of Ottawa and McGill University—offer both civil law and common law degrees. The University of Ottawa and the University of Moncton also offer a common law program in French, and McGill offers a civil law program in English.
- *The Canadian Bar Association.* This national organization, which represents Canada's legal community, has for some time sponsored events and seminars to promote a better understanding of Canada's two different legal systems among civilian and common law lawyers.

In Chapter 3, we examine more specifically how and when the common law and civil law systems were received into the various regions of Canada.

Other Legal Systems

In this final section, we examine three other legal systems: religious law, customary law, and hybrid or mixed systems. Despite the importance of the common law and civil law systems in the Canadian context, these other systems have relevance here, too.

Religious Law

Historically, many countries had a close connection between church and state. In classical Greece, for example, state power, law, and religion were closely intertwined, and the same was true in ancient Israel. Hindu law played a significant role in ancient India, and it continues to do so in India today.[20]

However, most nations today separate church and state—in other words, religion and law. In the West, the idea that the two should be separated can be traced to John Locke and his social contract theory. One of the tenets of this theory was that the government should not interfere in matters of individual conscience, including religion. The specific phrase *separation of church and state* is often credited to US President Thomas Jefferson (1743-1826), one of the framers of the US Constitution. While the US Constitution does not formally refer to the separation of church and state, the First Amendment guarantees religious freedom. Section 2 of Canada's Charter[21] does the same thing (despite the preamble's reference to the "supremacy of God"). Judicial decisions in England, the United States, and Canada have also explicitly recognized this separation—between politics and law on the one hand and religion on the other.

19 RSC 1985, c S-26, s 6.

20 Robert Parker, "Law and Religion" in Michael Gagarin & David Cohen, eds, *The Cambridge Companion to Ancient Greek Law* (Cambridge, UK: Cambridge University Press, 2005).

21 *Canadian Charter of Rights and Freedoms*, Part I of the *Constitution Act, 1982*, being Schedule B to the *Canada Act 1982* (UK), 1982, c 11.

As we saw in Chapter 1, however, viewing religion and the law as belonging to different spheres does not mean that religion plays a limited role in the law. When a significant portion of the population holds similar religious views, they inevitably *influence* matters of state, including the state's laws. Lord Denning, a very religious man and perhaps the most famous English judge in the last 100 years, had this to say about the interplay between religion and the law:

> Although religion, law and morals can be separated, they are nevertheless still very much dependent on one another. Without religion, there can be no morality, there can be no law. … I will try to indicate how they [important legal principles] are challenged by a changing world which knows no religion, or which at best treats religion as something which is of no moment in practical affairs.[22]

Despite the prevalence of a formal separation between law and religion in the world today, some states still acknowledge an official connection between the two, at least in part (and even when they also recognize religious freedom). In Israel, for instance, freedom of religion is protected under the country's Basic Law, and Judaism, the predominant religion, is not formally designated as the state religion. At the same time, however, religious law (Halacha) and state law converge in a number of areas, including marriage and divorce.[23] Israel seems to fall somewhere between countries that declare a separation of church and state, and countries that acknowledge a significant connection between the state, its laws, and religion, such as many Islamic states.

Legal systems based on Islamic law, also known as sharia (the "way to follow") or sharia law, are the leading examples of religion-based legal systems today. In countries that follow Islamic law, it is seen not as a branch of state regulation but as part of the Islamic religion (the part prescribing rules of behaviour). (See Box 2.4.)

Most Muslim states today are not governed exclusively by sharia. Instead, they blend Islamic law with other forms of law. Only three states today are Islamic law *monosystems*—meaning that they base their legal systems almost entirely on Islamic law. The three states are Afghanistan, the Maldives (or Maldive Islands), and Saudi Arabia.

For example, Saudi Arabia's constitution (adopted in 1992) declares that the country is an Islamic state and recognizes the primacy of sharia in legal matters. It includes the following provisions:

1. Government in Saudi Arabia derives power from the Holy Quran and the Prophet's tradition (article 7).
2. The state protects Islam; it implements its Shariah; it orders people to do right and shun evil; it fulfills the duty regarding God's call (article 23).

It should be noted that even these so-called Islamic monosystems employ non-sharia law in some contexts. Positive, man-made laws, based on legislation and custom, have been added to deal with administrative and other practical matters that lie outside the scope of Islamic law.

---

22 Lord Denning, *The Influence of Religion on Law* (Calgary: Canadian Institute for Law, Theology & Public, 1997) [reprint of an address given to the UK Lawyers' Christian Fellowship in 1952].

23 Other nations that recognize a religious law component in their legal systems include Bhutan, a mountain nation in the Himalayas (Buddhist law), and India (Hindu law).

BOX 2.4

Sharia

Sharia in Islamic States

Most predominantly Muslim countries incorporate sharia into their legal systems, although the level of integration varies depending on the state. From the perspective of individuals used to political traditions based on the separation of church and state, the rules prescribed by sharia appear to blend legal rules with seemingly non-legal requirements. For example:

- Five times daily, Muslims are required to pray while facing Mecca.
- Affluent Muslims are required to pay an annual poor tax to indigent Muslims as part of a purification process and as an obligation to their community.
- Among sharia's complex laws concerning inheritance is a rule that if a man and a woman (a brother and sister, for example) both stand to inherit money or other property, the female's share generally will be half that of the male's share.
- Fasting between dawn and sunset is required daily during the month of Ramadan.

Disputes are heard in courts with judges (or *qadis*) and lawyers trained in sharia law.

There are three main sources of sharia. The first source, the Quran, is a collection of Muhammad's revelations, while the second, the *sunna*, is a collection of traditions (*hadīth*) based on the acts and sayings of Muhammad. These two sources are considered fundamental or primary, but they do not cover all situations; there are legislative gaps. Legal scholars are authorized, based on specific verses in the Quran, to fill in these gaps through interpreting the Quran and the *sunna*. If these scholars agree about an interpretation of this kind, it becomes a binding secondary authority and part of the *ijmā* (or consensus)—the third main source of sharia law.

A fourth source of sharia law, less central than the three listed above, is *qiyās*, or analogical deduction. It is also a secondary source. This source is based on analogies to situations covered by the Quran. Like consensus (*ijmā*), it was developed to deal with circumstances not covered by the primary sources. Analogical deduction is accepted by Sunnis but not by Shiites, who replace it with *aql* or reason, which is based on intellect or logic. The difference between *qiyās* and *aql* is a matter of debate among sharia scholars.

While there is basic agreement in Muslim countries about the nature of these sources, the precise interpretation and application of sharia varies from country to country and among modernists, traditionalists, and fundamentalists.

Sharia in Canada

Canada recognizes a separation between law and religion, but it also guarantees religious freedom under the Charter. It attempts to accommodate faiths—Judaism, Islam, Hinduism, or Buddhism, for example—that involve special practices, so long as these practices do not violate Canadian law. And it attempts to accommodate the religion-based laws of certain communities, provided that these laws do not offend the Charter.

In 1991, Ontario amended its *Arbitration Act** to allow for "faith-based arbitration" in family law matters. Tribunals were set up so that adherents of Judaism and Catholicism could resolve their family law disputes according to their religious beliefs: Jews according to Halacha, Catholics according to their version of the Christian faith. Use of the new system was optional for Jewish and Catholic participants. But once they had agreed to use it, its decisions were binding.

In 2004, Muslims argued that they too ought to be entitled to faith-based arbitration in family law matters. In their case, the tribunals would be based on sharia law. The Ontario government reviewed the matter and concluded that the arbitration process could be expanded to include religious groups beyond Jews and Catholics, provided that Charter rights and freedoms were maintained.

Controversy ensued. Women's groups voiced their strong opposition to sharia-based decisions. Other organizations, too, argued that women are not accorded equal rights and protections under sharia. Religious groups newly entitled to faith-based arbitration responded to Muslim charges of inequity by agreeing to give up their own new-found rights under the *Arbitration Act* amendments.

Faced with this controversy, the Ontario government decided to repeal its faith-based arbitration procedures altogether.

*   SO 1991, c 17.

Customary Law

customary law
system of law based on rules of conduct considered binding either at a local or an international level, with no formalized process in place for making, changing, or recording them

What is **customary law**? Lon Fuller defines it very broadly as follows: "Customary law is not the product of official enactment, but owes its force to the fact that it has found direct expression in the conduct of men toward one another."[24] In other words, customary law is made up of rules that have not been officially recognized or enacted but have become conventional or habitual within a society. For such rules to be considered customary *law*, the society's members must accept them as legally binding.

The term *customary law* is often applied to Indigenous laws and to the laws of subgroups within a state—that is, laws that the subgroup considers binding but that differ from state-sanctioned positive laws.[25] Such laws are often based on oral tradition; there may only be a fragmentary written record of them. States will sometimes recognize them in some way, and customary law has in some cases influenced official systems. But customary law plays a much-reduced role in the legal systems of the modern world. Only very rarely today does it operate as a major source of law at the state level.

The term *customary law* also refers to a source of international law—rules that are based on conventional, habitual practices in the relations between states. These rules may concern peaceful transactions between states or they may concern wartime conventions. What defines them as law in either case is that they are recognized as binding. We examine international law later in this text, in Chapter 13.

Customary law, whether at the local or at the international level, raises two basic questions. First, how widespread does a practice have to be before we regard it as customary? There is no precise test for determining when a tradition is sufficiently widespread to qualify as a tribal custom or a customary international law. Second, how do you define exactly what the custom is, in the absence of a formalized process for making, changing, or recording such practices? While there is definitional certainty in some local traditions, in many contexts this question has no clear answer.

Other questions about customary law, related to these two basic ones, concern the following:

- the length of the tradition on which the rules are based (for example, one generation or five generations?),
- the regularity with which the rules are followed (which reflects the degree of consensus about the rules),
- dispute resolution mechanisms and enforcement methods, and
- the way in which customs are preserved (for example, by the memory of community elders or by written records).

The following sections briefly describe the three ways that customary practices *within* states may come to have legal significance. They may be

1. recognized and applied by subgroups within a state,
2. incorporated into a mainstream system, or
3. adopted as the state system.

24　Lon Fuller, "Human Interaction and the Law" (1969) 14 Am J Juris 1 at 1.

25　Marianne Constable, *Just Silences: The Limits and Possibilities of Modern Law* (Princeton, NJ: Princeton University Press, 2005).

Customary Law at the Sub-State Level

The world contains many instances of subgroups that adhere to their own legal systems within their multicultural societies. This can happen in various ways. In some cases, the subgroup exists outside the effective control of the state. Today, certain minority groups in Afghanistan fit into this category, as do some Amazonian tribes in Brazil.

In other cases, the state may not officially recognize the subgroup's legal system, but may tolerate it for political or other reasons. The state has the power to impose its own system but chooses not to. Some tribes in sub-Saharan African nations fall into this category. These tribes have not fully submitted to state control and have continued to maintain their own customary practices.

In other cases, a state may decide to officially recognize a subgroup's right to follow its own customary legal practices (see Box 2.5). Or the state may go further still and recognize an "enclave system" within the main state system—in other words, a legal system within a legal system. Some First Nations groups in British Columbia have negotiated such arrangements. For example, the Nisga'a Treaty provides for self-government by the Nisga'a Nation within a defined region of British Columbia (see the discussion in Chapter 3).

BOX 2.5

Aboriginal Rights Within the Canadian Legal System

Section 35(1) of the *Constitution Act, 1982* provides that the "existing [A]boriginal ... rights of the [A]boriginal peoples of Canada are hereby recognized and affirmed." Among the existing rights affirmed by this provision and as determined by the courts is the right of the Sault Ste Marie Métis to hunt without a licence. In the *Powley* case,* the SCC had to decide whether section 35(1) protected a father and son who were charged with hunting a moose without a licence and who claimed to be members of the Sault Ste Marie Métis community. Subsection (2) states that "'[A]boriginal peoples of Canada' includes the Indian, Inuit and Métis peoples of Canada."

Among other things the court had to determine was whether the accused were in fact members of this Métis community. The word *Métis* is not expressly defined in the Constitution. Generally speaking, Métis people are considered to be people who have a mixed First Nations and European heritage. The court set out a non-exclusive list of criteria to help it determine whether the father and son were in fact Métis. The court decided that, to qualify as Métis, a person must:

1. "self-identify" as Métis,
2. be able to prove their "ancestral connection" with the Métis community, and
3. be "accepted by the modern community" (that is, the modern Métis community).

Concerning the third factor, the court stated the following: "The core of community acceptance is past and ongoing participation in a shared culture, in the *customs* and traditions that constitute a Métis community's identity and distinguish it from other groups."†

In the case of the accused father and son, the court accepted that they qualified as Métis according to the criteria above. They were acquitted of the charge of unlawfully hunting without a licence. This case illustrates how the customs of Indigenous groups can be recognized within the broader context of a state's legal system.

* *R v Powley*, 2003 SCC 43.

† *Ibid* at para 33 (emphasis added).

Customary Law Incorporated into Civil Law and Common Law Systems

We distinguish between formally recognized positive law systems and customary law. But formal systems are ultimately derived from customary law. Ancient and modern codifications in the civil law tradition, from the *Code of Hammurabi* to the *Civil Code of Quebec*, preserve and formalize common (that is, customary) rules and practices. The preamble to the latter code states the following: "The [Quebec] Civil Code comprises a body of rules which, in all matters within the letter, spirit or object of its provisions, lays down the *jus commune*, expressly or by implication."[26] The phrase *jus commune* refers to the society's customary law—the law commonly accepted by a society.

Customary practice was the basis of the common law system, too. In medieval England, the itinerant judges of the royal courts derived principles from the established practices they encountered on their travels through the English counties. And custom continues to play a role in the common law. In modern negligence actions, for example, when courts are trying to determine whether a defendant has behaved "unreasonably," they may look to local customs within the community. If the defendant was simply following accepted practice, her behaviour may be considered reasonable in the circumstances.[27]

Finally, in Canada, constitutional conventions (or customs) regulate the behaviour of government institutions and officials, such as the Senate and the governor general, and also the relations between the provinces and the federal government. We will consider constitutional conventions when we look at executive power in Chapter 5.

Customary Law at the State Level

Independent customary legal systems were numerous before the modern era. Examples include pre-colonial sub-Saharan Africa tribal law, early Germanic law, Celtic law, and Indigenous law in Australia. Modern examples of purely customary systems are hard to find, however.

According to JuriGlobe,[28] only three customary monosystems exist in the world today: the small nation of Andorra in the Pyrenees, and the two Channel Island UK dependencies, Guernsey and Jersey.

Other nations with customary systems have mixed them in varying combinations with common law, civil law, or Islamic law systems (see Appendix 2.1).

Hybrid or Mixed Systems

There are 195 countries in the world today. Roughly half of these have monosystems based on one tradition, while the other half have hybrid systems—various mixes of common law, civil law, Islamic law, and customary law systems. We cannot describe all of these hybrid systems here, but we discuss the key ones below.

Common Law and Civil Law

Canada, the United Kingdom, and the United States are often said to have legal systems based on the common law tradition. But that is only partly true. All three of these countries contain regions—Quebec, Scotland, and Lousiana, respectively—in which civil law and common law systems are mixed (see Figures 2.3 and 2.4 in Appendix 2.1). The civil codes

---

26 SQ 1991, c 64.

27 For example, see *Waldick v Malcolm*, [1991] 2 SCR 456, 1991 CanLII 71, a slip-and-fall case. Here, the SCC was asked to determine whether there was a local custom of *not* salting or sanding icy walkways—a custom that might excuse the defendant for not doing so herself. The court found that there was no such local custom, and the defendant was held liable in negligence.

28 *Supra* note 1.

in these jurisdictions apply to certain areas of the law, and the common law system applies to others. A mix of two traditions is known as *bijuralism*, as noted at the beginning of this chapter.

In Chapter 3, we will look at how law was received into Canada, including Quebec. The **Civil Code of Quebec** covers much of the private law in that province.

The United Kingdom is a unique state because it comprises four other countries: England, Scotland, Wales, and Northern Ireland are countries within a country. England, Wales, and Northern Ireland have common law monosystems. Scotland, however, owing to its historical allegiances and connections with France, has a dual system based on civil law and common law. The US state of Louisiana, because it was formerly a French colony, has, like Quebec, a dual system.

This mix of systems has enriched the development of the law in these countries. For instance, the *Donoghue v Stevenson* case (referred to in Box 2.1 and in Chapter 1) is in fact a civil law case, arising as it did in Scotland. Lord Atkin wrote the following:

> The case has to be determined in accordance with Scots law; but it has been a
> matter of agreement between the experienced counsel who argued this case … that
> for the purposes of determining this problem the laws of Scotland and of England
> are the same.[29]

The decision in this case, which concerns the tort of negligence, has become one of the most influential ever made in the common law world.

In Canada, the *Roncarelli* decision, also mentioned in Chapter 1, was a Quebec case decided under article 1053 of the *Civil Code of Quebec*, as it then was. It is still the leading case in Canada on abuse of power, and it has been cited repeatedly as a binding authority in the common law provinces as well as in Quebec.

Other Hybrid Systems

Some countries—former colonies of England—have maintained England's common law system after becoming independent but have added or revived other systems in the process. In India, for instance, the common law system applies generally throughout the country. On the local level, however, customary law, Hindu law, and Islamic law sometimes apply, depending on the region and the religion involved.

The legal systems in some countries mix civil law with customary law. This is true of China (not including Hong Kong and Macau), Taiwan, North and South Korea, and Japan. China and North Korea have socialist versions of civil law, and the degree to which local customary law plays a role is a matter of debate, at least in China. (The less tolerant the socialist system, the less influence a competing system will have.)

Many nations have a strong Islamic law base with other systems mixed in. Syria, Iraq, and Iran, for instance, combine Islamic law with civil law. Other countries based primarily on Islamic law contain elements of three or four systems. The legal system in Indonesia, for example, incorporates Islamic, civil law, and customary law. And there are four states—Bahrain, Qatar, Somalia, and Yemen—that have elements of all four legal systems (Islamic law, common law, civil law, and customary law). The majority of countries in Africa combine two or more legal systems.

Figures 2.5, 2.6, 2.7, and 2.8 in Appendix 2.1 detail four regions with the most complex mixes of legal systems: Africa, the Middle East, Southeast Asia, and Asia, respectively.

Civil Code of Quebec (Code Civil du Québec)
Quebec's current civil code, which came into effect on January 1, 1994, and which replaced the *Civil Code of Lower Canada* that had been in force since 1866

---

29   *M'Alister (or Donoghue) v Stevenson*, [1932] AC 562 at 579 (HL).

Appendix 2.1   Legal Systems Around the World

The following figures are a graphical representation of the different legal systems as distributed in a number of areas around the world.

For a global overview of legal systems by continent, and for data on individual countries, visit JuriGlobe's website at <http://www.juriglobe.ca/eng>.

FIGURE 2.3   North America

FIGURE 2.4   The United Kingdom

FIGURE 2.5 Africa

Legend:
- Civil law
- Common law
- Customary law
- Muslim law

FIGURE 2.6 The Middle East

FIGURE 2.7 Southeast Asia

FIGURE 2.8 Asia

CHAPTER SUMMARY

There are four major legal system groups in the world today: common law, civil law, religious law, and customary law. Roughly half of the world's nations are monosystems, using predominantly one of these traditions. The other nations, including Canada, use a mix of traditions.

In Canada, the two most significant legal systems are the common law and the civil law systems. The common law developed in England over many centuries. It was brought to Canada by English settlers and became the legal system in all provinces and territories except for the province of Quebec. The key features of the common law system are the reliance on precedent and the principle of *stare decisis*. Another key feature of this system is the use of an adversarial process in the courtroom, with lawyers opposing each other and presenting their respective cases with (generally speaking) little interference from the trial judge.

The civil law system can be traced to ancient Rome and to societies even more ancient. Where Canada is concerned, the most important civil code is the *Napoleonic Code* of 1804; it strongly influenced Quebec's first code, which came into effect in the 1800s, and its current code, the *Civil Code of Quebec*, enacted in 1994. Codes of this kind play a central role in the civil law system and are more important than previous judicial decisions. Other distinguishing features of the civil law system are the inquisitorial nature of the decision-making process (with judges playing a much more active role than they do in the common law system) and the importance of academic commentary.

Religion has influenced most political and legal structures, but legal traditions with a *significant* religious component today are found principally in nations with a substantial Muslim population. Sharia (or Islamic) law can be thought of as the "legal" part of Islam; however, civil law and other legal systems often play a role in states that follow sharia. There are only a few Muslim nations whose legal systems are based almost exclusively on Islamic law.

We commonly associate customary law with local oral traditions and with international law. In the early stages of their development, however, all legal traditions were indebted to customary law. And yet few legal systems in the world today are based predominantly on customary law.

The need for an awareness of all legal systems is greater now than ever, as our world continues to become more interconnected and we find ourselves interacting with people from all parts of the globe. In Canada, knowledge of both the common law and civil law systems is particularly important because we are a bijural nation based on these two systems.

KEY TERMS

adversarial system, 39

bijural, 32

Bill of Rights (1689), 40

binding, 37

Chancery, 34

civil code, 41

Civil Code of Quebec
  (Code Civil du Québec), 53

civil law, 32

common law, 32

Corpus Juris Civilis, 42

Court of Chancery, 35

Court of King's (or Queen's) Bench, 34

customary law, 50

distinguishable, 37

equity, 35

feudalism, 33

Inns of Court, 36

inquisitorial system, 44

king's peace, 34

persuasive, 37

precedent, 36

ratio or *ratio decidendi*, 37

stare decisis, 36

writ, 35

FURTHER READING

BOOKS

Baker, John H. *An Introduction to English Legal History*, 4th ed (London, UK: Butterworths, 2002).

Cross, Rupert & James W Harris. *Precedent in English Law*, 4th ed (Oxford: Clarendon Press, 1991).

David, René & John EC Brierley. *Major Legal Systems in the World Today: An Introduction to the Comparative Study of Law*, 3rd ed (London, UK: Stevens & Sons, 1985).

Glenn, H Patrick. *Legal Traditions of the World*, 5th ed (Oxford: Oxford University Press, 2014).

Shears, Peter & Graham Stephenson. *James' Introduction to English Law*, 13th ed (Oxford: Oxford University Press, 2005).

WEBSITES

JuriGlobe: <http://www.juriglobe.ca/eng>.

Yale Law School, The Avalon Project: Documents in Law, History and Diplomacy: <http://avalon.law.yale.edu>.

REVIEW QUESTIONS

1. What is meant by the term *bijural nation*?

2. Why is it important to be aware of legal traditions other than our own? Give at least three reasons.

3. Explain how the common law developed in England.

4. Briefly describe the role of the English Court of Chancery.

5. What is the principle of *stare decisis*? Under what circumstances is a precedent found to be either (a) binding, (b) distinguishable, or (c) persuasive?

6. What are the benefits of the common law system's practice of following precedent?

7. Briefly describe how the civil law system in Europe was indebted to Roman law.

8. What are some of the main features of civil law?

9. What is meant when we say that courts in civil law jurisdictions use an inquisitorial system?

10. What are three differences between the common law and civil law systems?

11. Describe three ways in which Canada has tried to harmonize the common law and civil law legal systems in this country.

12. Why is it difficult to find examples of customary law operating at the state level in the world today?

13. How is customary law inevitably part of the common law and civil law systems?

EXERCISES

1. When a common law judge recognizes a new precedent, is she *finding* new law or *making* new law? Explain why you think there is—or is not—a difference between these two processes within the common law system.

2. Consider one way in which the civil law is different from the common law and describe a situation where you think that difference might affect the outcome of a case.

3. How is Canadian bijuralism an asset when it comes to Canadians doing business with other countries?

In your answer, consider two of Canada's trading partners and their legal systems.

4. Do you believe there is a significant difference between a legal system that is *influenced by* religious beliefs and one that is *based on* religious beliefs? Support your answer with specific reasons and examples.

5. Choose an Indigenous nation in Canada and research how it applies its own customary laws.

3 From the Reception of English and French Law into Canada to the Charter

The *Canadian Charter of Rights and Freedoms*, bearing the signature of Pierre Trudeau in the bottom right corner.

LEARNING OUTCOMES

After reading this chapter, you will understand:

- General rules governing the reception of law into England's colonies.

- How and when the various regions of Canada received English (or French) law and how and when they joined Confederation.

- The events leading to the enactment of the *British North America Act, 1867* and the nature of the union it created.

- Some important post-Confederation issues, such as those relating to the absence of an amending formula in the Constitution and the role of the courts in shaping Canadian federalism.

- The rise of Canadian nationalism, and the activism of Indigenous peoples and women with respect to the development of the Constitution and the *Canadian Charter of Rights and Freedoms.*

- The patriation of the Constitution and the Charter.

With the advent of the Charter, the principles on which the rights and freedoms of Canadians are based have the status of constitutional law. … The fundamental principle underlying this dimension of our most basic law is that there are some phases of Canadian life which should normally be beyond the reach of any majority, save by constitutional amendment.

The Hon Brian Dickson, "The Canadian Charter of Rights and Freedoms: Context and Evolution" in Errol Mendes & Stéphane Beaulac, eds, *Canadian Charter of Rights and Freedoms*, 5th ed (Toronto: LexisNexis, 2013) at 3

Introduction

Canada's legal history from its early colonial period to the present day is interesting and unique. This chapter outlines how and when the various regions of British North America received the English common law and, in the case of Quebec, the French civil law. It also describes the unification process and some key events leading to Confederation in 1867, which resulted in the Canada we know today. Next, the chapter examines some post-Confederation issues, including those related to omissions in our Constitution and the shaping of Canadian federalism. Following this is a consideration of some of the legal and social issues behind the movement to patriate the Constitution and adopt the *Canadian Charter of Rights and Freedoms*[1] (the Charter) in the 1980s. It concludes with an overview of some of the key changes brought about by our new Constitution.

Common Law Rules of Reception of English Law

When the first European settlers from France and England arrived in Canada, they found that it was already occupied by Indigenous[2] peoples, who had their own cultures and legal

---

1 Part I of the *Constitution Act, 1982*, being Schedule B to the *Canada Act 1982* (UK), 1982, c 11.

2 In this book, we use *Indigenous* generally when describing the first inhabitants of Canada—First Nations (or Indians, as the government called them, based on a geographical mistake made by

systems. How Aboriginal rights, including title to land, came to be gradually recognized within our current legal structure is described in this and later chapters (for example, see Box 3.1 on Indigenous legal systems and Box 3.5 on Aboriginal land claims). The settlers mainly arrived in eastern Canada, and European expansion moved westward and northward; despite the uneasy relationship that developed between the new settlers and Indigenous peoples, colonization was rapid.

BOX 3.1

Indigenous Legal Systems

Canada's Aboriginal peoples had their own legal systems before contact with Europeans. [They] did not write their laws down … but transmitted them orally from generation to generation. This tradition was one of the responsibilities of the elders in each nation's community. Sometimes the tribal laws were transmitted in the form of legends or stories to make them easier to remember and to inspire the listener with respect for the law.

The Iroquois Confederacy, located south of Lake Ontario, was one of the most powerful groups of Aboriginal peoples. Originally it consisted of five nations: the Mohawk, Seneca, Oneida, Onondaga, and Cayuga. The Confederacy was established by two great chiefs, Dekanawida and Hiawatha, around 1142 CE. According to their oral history, it took them 40 years to convince the tribes to form a union bound together by a

formal constitution. This constitution was called the *Gayanashagowa*, Iroquois for "great binding law." It provided a system of checks and balances by giving every man and woman in the Confederacy a voice in tribal affairs. The powers of the war chiefs were held in check by those of the peace chiefs. All chiefs were appointed by the clan mothers, who also had the power to remove any chief who did not act in the interests of the people. At some point in the 18th century, the leaders of the Iroquois Confederacy agreed to write down their Great Binding Law. The framers of both the US constitution and the *Charter of the United Nations* referred to the Iroquois Great Binding Law in drawing up their own legal documents.

Source: Reproduced from George Alexandrowicz et al, *Dimensions of Law: Canadian and International Law in the 21st Century* (Toronto: Emond Montgomery, 2004) at 39-40.

General common law colonization rules determined how English law was received into its colonies.[3] These rules were designed to provide new colonies with a legal structure from the outset and avoid the negative consequences of beginning their colonies in a "legal vacuum." How a particular territory was acquired by England often determined what rule was followed.

A discussion of all of the reception rules is beyond the scope of this text. The following sections describe only the three most relevant to Canada: settlement, conquest or cession, and adoption.

European colonists), Inuit, and Métis—and their laws. We also use *Aboriginal* synonymously when it seems appropriate based on context, such as when quoting other sources that use the term or when discussing Constitutional rights (*Aboriginal* is the term used in the *Constitution Act, 1982*—referred to later in this chapter and described in more detail in Chapter 4). Of the two terms, *Indigenous* has become more accepted in recent years, likely in part because of the United Nations Declaration on the Rights of Indigenous Peoples (UNDRIP), adopted by the UN General Assembly in 2007 (see also Chapter 13 under the heading "International Human Rights Law"). Our intention is to be accurate and respectful; however, we recognize that some Indigenous people may prefer another term or identify only with their own nation or tribe.

3 See Peter W Hogg, "Reception" in *Constitutional Law of Canada*, 2018 student ed (Toronto: Carswell, 2018) ch 2; JE Cote, "The Reception of English Law" (1977) 15 Alta L Rev 29.

Settlement

When England colonized a territory and sent English subjects there to settle it, that colony received English law then in force, including common law (that is, judge-made rules) and statute law. These became the colony's first laws. This practice prevailed even though the territory was already inhabited; First Nations' legal systems were simply disregarded. Colonial courts in Canada decided that the reception date—that is, the date on which the colony specifically received English laws—would be the same as the date on which a colony first established its own local legislature.

The reception of English law into its colonies as they were settled was subject to some limitations. Only those laws of general application that were suitable, taking into consideration the colonial environment, were received. If a law—whether it was a common law precedent or legislated—was inapplicable in light of the local circumstances, it did not become part of the law of the colony. The laws that were received could be amended or abolished by the colonial legislature at a later date, as required by changing circumstances. The only laws that could *not* be changed were English **imperial statutes**. These were statutes that the English Parliament enacted specifically for its overseas colonies—over which England reserved ultimate legal control.

imperial statute
law passed by the English Parliament applying specifically to an overseas English colony

Conquest or Cession

cession
the transfer of a colony from one country to another

If England acquired an overseas colony by conquest (or by transfer or **cession** from another country, pursuant to a treaty), a second common law colonization rule held that laws already existing in the colony continued in force until such time as they were specifically changed by the English government. Provided that no local legislature existed in the colony, English law could be imposed on the colony by the English monarch, exercising his or her prerogative power, or by England's imperial Parliament.

Adoption

A third way English law could be received into a British colony was by adoption. In this instance, a colony's legislature would pass a reception statute that adopted English law as of a certain date. From that time, English law would be received and in force in the colony. This might occur to clarify any uncertainty surrounding the reception date or to change the laws already in place in the colony.

Reception of English and French Law into Canada's Provinces and Territories

The following is an overview of how and when English or French law was received in each Canadian province and territory, and the date on which each one joined Confederation. For the five provinces from Quebec east to Newfoundland, English and French laws were introduced by settlement or cession, the first two methods. For the five provinces from Ontario west and the territories, English laws were adopted by reception statutes, the third method. Table 3.1 provides a summary.

TABLE 3.1   Reception Dates for Receiving English and French Law and Entering Confederation for Each Canadian Province and Territory

PROVINCE/TERRITORY	RECEPTION OF LAW	ENTERED CONFEDERATION
Alberta	1870	September 1, 1905
British Columbia	1858	July 20, 1871
Manitoba	1870	July 15, 1870
New Brunswick	1758 (or possibly 1660)	July 1, 1867
Newfoundland and Labrador	1832	March 31, 1949
Northwest Territories	1870	July 15, 1870
Nova Scotia	1758	July 1, 1867
Nunavut	1870	April 1, 1999
Ontario	1792	July 1, 1867
Prince Edward Island	1758 (or possibly 1773)	July 1, 1873
Quebec	French civil law restored in 1774	July 1, 1867
Saskatchewan	1870	September 1, 1905
Yukon	1870	June 13, 1898

Newfoundland and Labrador

Newfoundland was England's first Canadian colony. British fishing fleets, along with others from Spain, France, and Portugal, sailed to the island as early as the 1500s to catch fish on the Grand Banks. In time, some members of the fishing crews began to spend the winter there, cutting wood and preparing for the fishing fleet's return the next spring. Generally speaking, fishing took priority over settlement in this early period.

In 1583, Sir Humphrey Gilbert claimed the island for England, and several British settlements were founded on the island's east coast. Settlers later came under the governance of the admiral of the English naval squadron that arrived each year to guard the fishing fleet. As a result of these developments, the island was considered a settled colony of England. Its first Legislative Assembly was held at St. John's in 1832, and this date became the reception date for English law in the colony.[4]

Although Newfoundland was England's first Canadian colony, it was actually the last to join **Confederation** and the last to be admitted to Canada, which occurred on March 31, 1949.

Confederation
the coming together of the three British North American colonies of Nova Scotia, New Brunswick, and the Province of Canada (Ontario and Quebec) to form the Dominion of Canada in 1867; the term later included all the provinces and territories that have joined Canada since that date

---

4   C English, "From Fishing Schooner to Colony: The Legal Development of Newfoundland, 1791-1832" in LA Knafla & SWS Binnie, eds, *Law, Society, and the State: Essays in Modern Legal History* (Toronto: University of Toronto Press, 1995) 73; J Bannister, *The Rule of the Admirals: Law, Custom, and Naval Government in Newfoundland, 1699-1832* (Toronto: University of Toronto Press, 2003).

Nova Scotia

The reception of English law into Nova Scotia was complicated by the fact that this colony was originally part of French Acadia, that part of New France located in Canada's Atlantic region. French colonists first settled this area in the 1600s, and it was under French control until 1713. In that year, under the terms of the *Treaty of Utrecht*, France ceded Acadia to England.

Given that England acquired Nova Scotia by cession, French law ought to have continued there until England changed it. But things did not proceed according to this common law reception rule. In effect, once England established a colonial administration in Nova Scotia after the *Treaty of Utrecht*, and once Edward Cornwallis set up a seat of government and military base at Halifax in 1749, the colony was treated instead as having been acquired by settlement. The colony convened its first Legislative Assembly in 1758, and this was established as its reception date for English law.

In the next century, Nova Scotia was one of the original three colonies to join Confederation, doing so on July 1, 1867.

BOX 3.2

Difficulties Involving the Reception of English Law into Canada

Beamish Murdoch (1800-1876; pictured at right) was a Nova Scotia lawyer and author whose work *Epitome of the Laws of Nova Scotia* was an important early study of Nova Scotia law. Murdoch recognized that some circumstances in a young colony such as Nova Scotia were different from those in England, and he suggested that colonial Canadian judges could use two criteria to determine whether English statutes should apply to local conditions. Murdoch suggested that English statutes, if they were to be binding on Canada, must be "applicable to our social condition" and "suitable to our local wants."*

The following case from Murdoch's lifetime shows Murdoch's criteria being applied:

> In the 1841 case of *Dillingham v Wilson*, a farmer apprenticed his son to a cabinet maker. The son complained to his father of some mistreatment and the father ended the apprenticeship. The plaintiff cabinet maker sued the defendant father under the terms of their apprenticeship agreement for failing to complete its terms. The issue was whether an old English apprenticeship statute, dating back to the 16th-century reign of Elizabeth I, applied to Upper Canada [Ontario]. Justice Sherwood held that it did not, saying that the court considered the statute

> "a local act which was probably adapted to the state of society in England three hundred years ago, but is not now, and never was adapted to the population of a colony, and was never in force here."†

*   "'Nova Scotia's Blackstone' on the Origins of Nova Scotia Law. [Lecture by Beamish Murdoch, QC, 29 August 1863]" in Peter B Waite, Sandra Oxner & Thomas Barnes, eds, *Law in a Colonial Society: The Nova Scotia Experience* (Toronto: Carswell, 1984) 187 at 190.

†   *Dillingham v Wilson* (1841), 6 UCQB (OS) 85 at 86-87.

Prince Edward Island

The reception of English law in Prince Edward Island was linked to its reception in Nova Scotia. The island was originally settled by France, and, under the 1713 *Treaty of Utrecht*, France kept it. However, in 1763, France ceded the island to England by the *Treaty of Paris*. Then, by the English Royal Proclamation of 1763, the island was annexed to Nova Scotia. Shortly afterward, in 1769, the island became a separate colony, and its first elected Assembly was held there in 1773.

As with Nova Scotia, England apparently acquired the island by cession. However, the reception of English law in Prince Edward Island was consistent with the island's being acquired by settlement. The probable date (legal scholars are not all in agreement about this) for its receiving English law may not be 1773 (the date of its own first elected Assembly) but 1758—the date of the first Legislative Assembly in Nova Scotia.[5]

Interestingly, though Charlottetown was the location of Canada's first meeting, in 1864, to discuss Confederation (see below), the colony did not enter Confederation for another nine years; it was admitted to Canada on July 1, 1873.

New Brunswick

Like Nova Scotia and Prince Edward Island, New Brunswick was originally settled by French colonists and was also part of French Acadia. Like those colonies, it was ceded or transferred by France to England. Parts of it were ceded in 1713, by the *Treaty of Utrecht*, and the remainder by the *Treaty of Paris*, in 1763. In 1763, like Prince Edward Island, it was annexed to Nova Scotia, but subsequently (again like Prince Edward Island), it separated from Nova Scotia and became a separate colony. That was in 1784.

New Brunswick was also like the other two maritime colonies in that the reception of English law there was deemed to be by settlement and not by cession. However, the actual date for the reception of English law in the colony is unclear. Some legal scholars consider that New Brunswick's case is similar to Prince Edward Island's. In other words, though the province had its first Legislative Assembly in 1786, its being previously annexed to Nova Scotia makes Nova Scotia's reception date of 1758 applicable to New Brunswick. Other commentators on this matter, including the New Brunswick courts, have held 1660 as the reception date. According to Peter Hogg, this date was chosen because it was the year in which Charles II was restored to the English throne.[6]

New Brunswick was, like Nova Scotia, one of the three original colonies to join Confederation and was admitted to Canada on July 1, 1867.

Quebec

In contrast to Canada's maritime colonies, Quebec's status as a colony was always clear. England acquired it from France by conquest and later by cession.

---

5   See Hogg, *supra* note 3 at 2-15; JD Whyte & WR Lederman, "The Extension of Governmental Institutions and Legal Systems to British North America in the Colonial Period" in WR Lederman, ed, *Continuing Canadian Constitutional Dilemmas* (Toronto: Butterworths, 1981) 70.

6   See DG Bell, "A Note on the Reception of English Statutes in New Brunswick" (1979) 28 UNBLJ 195 at 196-200; Hogg, *supra* note 3 at 2-3.

FIGURE 3.1 Anglo-American painter Benjamin West famously captured the death of General Wolfe on the Plains of Abraham. The French general, Montcalm, was also killed in the battle, which followed a three-month siege by the British and lasted only 15 minutes.

French colonists first settled Quebec in the early 1600s, and it thus became a French overseas colony, known as *la Nouvelle-France*. As such, the colony received French civil law for its legal system. However, the British general James Wolfe defeated the French general Marquis de Montcalm at the battle of the Plains of Abraham, also called the Battle of Quebec, near Quebec City, in 1759 (see Figure 3.1). Subsequently, in 1763, France ceded Quebec to England under the terms of the *Treaty of Paris*. What followed was the *Royal Proclamation of 1763*. Exercising his royal prerogative power, King George III of England declared that Quebec would have English law imposed there in place of French civil law.

This uneasy shift of affairs, with Quebec slated to receive English law, did not last long. The English government was influenced to change things by two early civilian governors there, Murray and Carleton, who were both conciliatory to the French *Canadiens* and who were sensitive to the uncertain state of the legal system in Quebec in the wake of the *Royal Proclamation*. As a result, the English government passed the *Quebec Act, 1774*, a statute that restored French civil law there. Section 8 of the *Quebec Act* stated that "in all Matters of Controversy, relative to Property and Civil Rights, Resort shall be had to the Laws of Canada, as the Rule for the Decision of the same."[7] This provision restored pre-conquest French civil law to Quebec, although English criminal law was retained there, making 1774 the date for receiving (or restoring) civil law in the province.

One related effect of this Act was also important. At that time, the territory of Quebec extended beyond its current western boundary (the Ottawa River) into what is now southern Ontario. After the American Revolution in 1776, many American settlers, still loyal to England, left their country and re-established themselves in present-day Ontario (at that time part of

---

7   *Quebec Act, 1774* (UK), 14 Geo III, c 83.

western Quebec). These United Empire Loyalists soon petitioned the English monarch to have the western part of Quebec, where they had relocated, separated from the older, eastern part. They were successful. In response to their demands, the English government passed the *Constitutional Act, 1791*.[8] This Act separated Quebec into two colonies, called Upper Canada (present-day Ontario) and Lower Canada (present-day Quebec) relative to their geographic location along the Great Lakes-St. Lawrence River watershed.

Quebec continued in this way until the *Union Act, 1840*,[9] by which England once again reunited Lower Canada with Upper Canada into the new Province of Canada (see the discussion below). Under this Act, Quebec was then called Canada East and Ontario was then called Canada West. This united province lasted from 1841, when the *Union Act* took effect, until 1867, when the Province of Canada became one of the original colonies to enter Confederation. At this point, the province was once again divided into Quebec and Ontario. Quebec joined Confederation on July 1, 1867.

The Civil Code of Quebec

During the union period (that is, when Ontario and Quebec composed the Province of Canada), Quebec was undergoing a great economic transition; it was changing from an agrarian and rural society into a modern one, industrial, capitalist, and urban. The practical demands of this transformation—which involved, for example, the rapid expansion of canals, roads, railways, banks, insurance companies, milling, and lumbering—in combination with an increased influx of British immigration, created the need for a less confusing legal system in the province, especially for commercial law. Uncertainty also arose over which legal system—the common law or the civil law—applied to diverse legal matters needing to be addressed.

The demands for more certainty forced politicians to act. George-Étienne Cartier, Quebec's attorney general, established a three-person Codification Commission in 1857 to revise existing laws in Quebec and consolidate them into a comprehensive civil code (see Figure 3.2). Its efforts resulted in the *Civil Code of Lower Canada*,[10] or *Code civil du Bas Canada*, which took effect in 1866, the year before Confederation. The Code was in force from 1866 until December 31, 1993. By the 1950s, it was increasingly felt that many of the Code's provisions were out of step with modern living conditions in Quebec. As a result, Quebec's Civil Code Revision Office, created in 1955, helped the government reform and modernize the Code. On January 1, 1994, a revised and newly comprehensive *Civil Code of Quebec*,[11] designed to reflect contemporary society's new social realities and modern attitudes, became law (see Box 2.2 in Chapter 2).

The 1866 Code and the 1994 Code have served to protect Quebec law against encroachments by the common law system practised in all other Canadian provinces. Generally speaking, these codes have helped preserve Quebec's separate civil law in predominantly common law North America.[12] (As mentioned in Chapter 2, Quebec is not fully regulated by the civil law system; the common law system pertains to its public law, including criminal law.)

Civil Code of Quebec (Code Civil du Québec) Quebec's current civil code, which came into effect on January 1, 1994, and which replaced the *Civil Code of Lower Canada*, which had been in force since 1866

---

8   *Constitutional Act, 1791* (UK), 31 Geo III, c 31.

9   (UK), 3 & 4 Vict, c 35.

10   (UK), 29 Vict, c 41, (1865).

11   CQLR, c CCQ-1991.

12   B Young, *George-Étienne Cartier: Montreal Bourgeois* (Montreal and Kingston, Ont: McGill-Queen's University Press, 1981); FP Eliadis, "The Legal System in Québec" in GL Gall, ed, *The Canadian Legal System*, 5th ed (Toronto: Thomson, 2004) 263.

FIGURE 3.2 The Codification Commission at work, in their offices in Quebec City, about 1865. The three judges on the Commission were Charles Dewey Day (second from left), Augustin-Norbert Morin (second from right), and René-Édouard Caron (centre). Their secretaries are on the far left and right.

Ontario

As we have noted, present-day Ontario originated when the *Constitutional Act, 1791*[13] divided Quebec, and the western part became Upper Canada. However, the Act also provided, under section 33, that the laws of Quebec (that is, the civil law) were to continue in force in Upper and Lower Canada until such time as they were changed by the respective assemblies of each new colony.

Quebec retained its civil law unchanged, but Upper Canada did not. At the first Legislative Assembly for Upper Canada, in Newark (now Niagara-on-the-Lake) in 1792, the first statute passed was a reception act regarding English law. Section III of this act provided that "in all matters of controversy relative to property and civil rights, resort shall be had to the Laws of England as the rule for the decision of the same." As a result of this Act, the legislature of Upper Canada adopted English law as of 1792. This is recognized as the date for the reception of English laws into the province of Ontario.

Upper Canada continued in this way until the *Union Act, 1840*, when, as noted earlier, the colony was reunited with Lower Canada (Quebec), and the Province of Canada was created. Ontario joined Confederation on July 1, 1867, separating from Quebec at the same time.

Manitoba

At the time Ontario entered Confederation in 1867, the area on its western border, stretching west to the Rocky Mountains, was divided between the Hudson's Bay Company's Rupert's Land and the North-Western Territory (see Figure 3.3).

---

13   (UK), 31 Geo III, c 31.

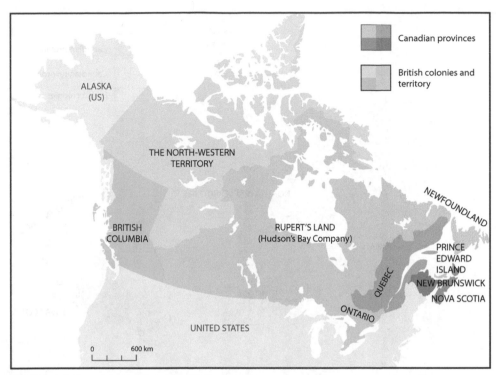

FIGURE 3.3 Dominion of Canada, 1867
Note the vast territory comprising Rupert's Land and the North-Western Territory.

For the newly formed Dominion of Canada, this western area was highly coveted; possession of it was crucial if Canada was to extend its borders "from sea to sea." Canada's first prime minister, John A Macdonald, soon entered into negotiations with the Hudson's Bay Company to purchase its western landholdings with the help of the British government. Terms were reached in 1869, and the area was transferred to Canada in 1870. That same year, the federal Parliament created the province of Manitoba out of part of Rupert's Land, and created the Northwest Territories, as this area was renamed, out of the remainder of Rupert's Land and out of the former North-Western Territory. By statute, the reception date for English law into Manitoba was 1870. The actual date for Manitoba's joining Confederation, the fifth province to do so, was July 15, 1870.

Saskatchewan

This province, like Alberta and the three northern Canadian territories, was also created out of the vast Northwest Territories west and north of the province of Manitoba. Saskatchewan joined Confederation on September 1, 1905, and its reception date for English law was 1870. (See Figure 3.4.)

Alberta

Like Saskatchewan, this province too was created out of the Northwest Territories, and it joined Confederation at the same time as Saskatchewan, on September 1, 1905. The date of reception for English law there was the same as for Saskatchewan—that is, 1870. (See Figure 3.4.)

FIGURE 3.4 Map of Canada, 1895

The district boundaries of Saskatchewan, Manitoba, Alberta, and the Yukon are shown. Alberta and Saskatchewan had expanded to their northern boundaries by 1905 (into the area marked District of Athabasca), and Manitoba expanded northward in 1912.

British Columbia

British Columbia was England's Pacific coast colony. Originally there were two of them: Vancouver Island, created in 1849, and British Columbia on the mainland, created in 1858. When England united these two separate colonies in 1866 and called the new territory British Columbia, the governor declared 1858 (later confirmed by its Legislative Council) as the reception date for English law. British Columbia joined Confederation on July 20, 1871, becoming Canada's sixth province (see Figure 3.5).

Yukon

The gold rush of 1898 was the primary reason for Yukon's being created as a separate territory. Mainly as a result of this event, Yukon was created out of the Northwest Territories and became a separate territory on June 13, 1898. The reception date for English law there, as in the three other western provinces created out of the Northwest Territories, was 1870.

Northwest Territories

The Northwest Territories, to the east of Yukon, has retained its original name, which dates from 1870. Its present area is of course smaller than it was originally; since 1870, as we have seen, the area has been divided into various other provinces and territories: Alberta, Saskatchewan, Yukon, and, most recently, the territory of Nunavut. The reception date for English law in the Northwest Territories was 1870, the year it originally entered Confederation.

Nunavut

Nunavut is Canada's newest territory. It was officially created out of the eastern half of the Northwest Territories on April 1, 1999, though its boundaries had been established in 1993. The Inuit are the majority population in this territory, and the word *Nunavut* means "our land" in Inuktitut, the Inuit language. The date for the reception of English law there, as in the two other arctic territories, is 1870.

FIGURE 3.5 This photoengraving, originally printed in the May 11, 1872 edition of the *Canadian Illustrated News,* shows the BC representatives presenting the terms of BC's entry into Confederation to Sir John A Macdonald.

Prelude to Confederation in 1867

The idea of uniting some or all of Britain's six separate Canadian colonies—Newfoundland, Nova Scotia, Prince Edward Island, New Brunswick, the Province of Canada (Canada West and Canada East), and British Columbia—began in the early 1800s. The unification movement gained further momentum when, in 1864, politicians from the Atlantic region met at Charlottetown, Prince Edward Island, to discuss the possibility of a maritime union of Britain's Atlantic colonies (see Figure 3.6). They were joined there by politicians from the Province of Canada, led by John A Macdonald and George-Étienne Cartier, who put forward an ambitious plan to unite more of Britain's Canadian colonies. Many of these politicians reconvened to discuss this idea further at two subsequent conferences—one in Quebec City, later that same year, and another in London, England, in 1866.

These conferences led to three of these colonies—Nova Scotia, New Brunswick, and the Province of Canada (Ontario and Quebec)—uniting into the new Dominion of Canada, in 1867. They did so under an imperial statute of the British Parliament called the *British North America Act, 1867*[14] (also referred to as the BNA Act, and now renamed the *Constitution Act, 1867*). Note that the colonies were called *Provinces* in the preamble to the Act.

---

14   SS 1867, c 3.

FIGURE 3.6 Delegates to the Charlottetown Conference, 1864
The delegates discussed the idea for a union of Britain's separate North American colonies into a new Canadian federal state, achieved in 1867.

Canadian historians and political scientists have examined several key factors leading to Canadian Confederation in 1867 and ascertained important political, military, economic, and imperial forces behind this development.[15] Principal among these were the following:

1. Political stalemate in the Province of Canada caused by a number of issues, including the split legal system (the common law in Canada West [Upper Canada] and the civil law in Canada East [Lower Canada]), regional rivalries (Canada West and Canada East were divided on many issues by language, cultural, and religious differences), and the unsettled location of the Legislative Assembly before Queen Victoria chose Ottawa as the capital in 1859.

2. The influence of the United States (including worries about the possibility of an invasion and its westward expansion to the Pacific coast based on an ideology called *manifest destiny*—the belief that the United States "was destined by the will of Heaven to become a country of political and territorial eminence").[16]

3. Expansion of railways across British North America.

4. Hopes for a larger domestic market for manufactured goods (union could result in a continental economy).

5. British support and approval for Confederation (Britain was encouraging greater independence for its colonies in British North America for economic reasons).

---

15 See PB Waite, *The Life and Times of Confederation, 1864-1867* (Toronto: University of Toronto Press, 1962); R Cook, C Brown & C Berger, eds, *Confederation* (Toronto: University of Toronto Press, 1967); Patrick Malcolmson & Richard Myers, *The Canadian Regime: An Introduction to Parliamentary Government in Canada*, 3rd ed (Peterborough, Ont: Broadview Press, 2005); and Roger Gibbins, *Conflict and Unity: An Introduction to Canadian Political Life*, 3rd ed (Scarborough, Ont: Nelson, 1994).

16 Norman A Graebner, "Introduction" in *Manifest Destiny* (Indianapolis, Ind: Bobbs-Merrill, 1968) at xv.

As mentioned, the last pre-Confederation conference was in London in 1866. Here, delegates made final revisions to their union plan, and on March 29, 1867, the British Parliament passed the BNA Act. The Act was proclaimed in force on July 1, 1867, and the newly completed Parliament buildings in Ottawa were set to host Canada's first national government.

Canada Is Born

The government structure eventually adopted by the framers of the BNA Act was **federalism**. This was something new to British constitutional history and was different from Britain's own unitary system of government. Federalism was an American, not an English, political idea, and was reflected in the BNA Act's division of powers between the new Canadian federal government in Ottawa and the provinces. Interestingly, the federal structure that was the basis of the Iroquois Confederacy pre-dated both the American and the Canadian unions (see Box 3.1).

federalism
in Canada, the division of state powers between the federal Parliament in Ottawa and the legislatures of the provinces and territories

Why did Canadian politicians end up adopting a federal system of government? It was not the first choice of Macdonald, our country's first prime minister. Macdonald desired a **unitary government** like Britain's, whereby all legislative authority would be centred in one governing body for all of Canada. But he realized this would not be possible. A unitary government was unacceptable in two quarters: the maritime provinces and Quebec.

unitary government
a form of government whereby one supreme authority governs the whole country

The inhabitants of the maritime provinces, though enticed by the prospect of a railway connection to central Canada that would reduce their geographic and economic isolation, feared that a unitary structure would undermine their distinctive political culture. A federal political union would better safeguard their local interests. The same was true for Quebec, which had, in addition, deep-seated cultural and language concerns. Quebec politicians saw the need for a French-controlled provincial government to legislate over areas such as language, schools, their civil law, religion, and political institutions.

Political deadlock in the Province of Canada was, as noted above, a leading underlying factor in the push for federal union. But the system that created this political frustration was also, ironically, a key to the future success of Canadian federalism. From 1841 to 1867, the Province of Canada already had an unacknowledged federal form of government. Its civil service and government departments were already *dual*; they operated in both English and French. It was governed under dual French–English premierships—for example, Baldwin and LaFontaine, Brown and Dorion, and Macdonald and Cartier. For legislation to pass, a double majority of votes was needed—in other words, a majority from representatives of both parts of the province. Though problematic, this political arrangement respected the regional and linguistic rights of the Province of Canada's two entities. As well, the later use of French and English in the province's Legislative Assembly showed that a bilingual Parliament could work in Canada.

John A Macdonald and the New Federal Government

The framers of the BNA Act were aware of American federalism and borrowed some ideas from it. At the same time, however, Macdonald was wary of some negative aspects of American federalism. For one thing, he felt that the American Constitution gave too much power to individual states, at the expense of their federal government in Washington.

Such a perceived weakness in the American system helped convince Macdonald that Canada's new federal government had to be stronger than the provinces. This was reflected in the division of powers between the provinces and the federal government. Macdonald's vision was that "all the great questions which affect the general interests of the Confederacy as a whole, are confided to the Federal Parliament, while the local interests and local laws of each section are preserved intact, and entrusted to the care of the local bodies."[17]

Section 91 of the BNA Act lists a number of matters of national importance under the Parliament of Canada's areas of control, including the following:

- The Regulation of Trade and Commerce (s 91(2));
- The Raising of Money by any Mode or System of Taxation (s 91(3));
- Militia, Military and Naval Service, and Defence (s 91(7));
- Currency and Coinage (s 91(14));
- Indians, and Lands reserved for the Indians (s 91(24)); and
- Criminal Law (s 91(27)).

Section 91 also states that the Parliament of Canada has residual power "to make Laws for the Peace, Order, and good Government of Canada, in relation to all Matters not coming within the Classes of Subjects by this Act assigned exclusively to the Legislatures of the Provinces."

Other sections of the BNA Act assign further powers to the federal Parliament's control. For example, section 24 gives it the exclusive power to appoint senators; and section 58, the power to appoint the provinces' lieutenant governors. Section 92(10) gives the Parliament of Canada the power to declare some provincial works "to be for the general Advantage of Canada" and thus to come under federal control. Section 96 authorizes the federal government to appoint judges to the highest courts in each province. Finally, section 101 provides for the Parliament of Canada to establish a "General Court of Appeal for Canada." (The division of powers between Parliament and the provinces is explored in more detail in Chapter 4.)

Post-Confederation Problems

A number of problems emerged following Confederation—principally, those stemming from omissions in the BNA Act and the role the Privy Council played in interpreting the Constitution.

Omissions in the BNA Act

The BNA Act was a crucial development in Canada's political history. However, it later proved problematic in various ways. First, it was an imperial statute of the English Parliament, not of the Canadian Parliament, and it lacked a formula enabling Canadians to amend it themselves. "In constitutional and legal terms this was a major blunder," law professor Edward McWhinney noted, "and undoubtedly stemmed from the ignorance of British constitutional lawyers with the problems of written constitutions and the practical necessity of having amendment formulae built in."[18]

The BNA Act's omission of a domestic amending formula was not a problem in 1867. However, it later emerged as a problem in the 1960s and 1970s, when Canadian nationalism became more pronounced. Many Canadians were getting frustrated at being unable to amend the Constitution by themselves, without Britain's approval.

---

17   John A Macdonald, "Confederation Debates, Legislative Assembly, Feb 6, 1865" in PB Waite, ed, *The Confederation Debates in the Province of Canada, 1865* (Toronto: McClelland & Stewart, 1963) at 45.

18   Edward McWhinney, *Canada and the Constitution, 1979-1982* (Toronto: University of Toronto Press, 1982) at 65.

A second problem with the BNA Act over time was that it did not contain an entrenched bill (or charter) of rights for Canadian citizens. In this respect, it differed markedly from the American Constitution, whose first ten amendments are known as the *Bill of Rights*. The preamble to the BNA Act stated that Canada's Constitution was to be "similar in Principle to that of the United Kingdom." However, the United Kingdom's Constitution did not have anything similar to the American Constitution's Bill of Rights.

Britain's Constitution itself came from various sources. Its measures for protecting the civil liberties of English subjects were found, for example, in the 1689 *Bill of Rights* and written documents such as the *Magna Carta*; they were also based on common law court decisions, customs, political practices, public support for democracy, and remedies such as *habeas corpus*.

BOX 3.3

Chief Dan George, "Lament for Confederation," July 1, 1967

How long have I known you, Oh Canada? A hundred years? Yes, a hundred years. And many, many years more. And today, when you celebrate your hundred years, Oh Canada, I am sad for all the Indian people throughout the land.

For I have known you when your forests were mine; when they gave me my meat and my clothing. I have known you in your streams and rivers where your fish splashed and danced in the sun, where the waters said, "Come, come and eat of my abundance." I have known you in the freedom of the winds. And my spirit, like the winds, once roamed your good lands.

But in the long hundred years since the white man came, I have seen my freedom disappear like the salmon going mysteriously out to sea. The white man's strange customs, which I could not understand, pressed down upon me until I could no longer breathe. When I fought to protect my land and my home, I was called a savage. When I neither understood nor welcomed his way of life, I was called lazy. When I tried to rule my people, I was stripped of my authority.

My nation was ignored in your history textbooks—they were little more important in the history of Canada than the buffalo that ranged the plains. I was ridiculed in your plays and motion pictures, and when I drank your fire-water, I got drunk—very, very drunk. And I forgot.

Oh Canada, how can I celebrate with you this Centenary, this hundred years? Shall I thank you for the reserves that are left to me of my beautiful forests? For the canned fish of my rivers? For the loss of my pride and authority, even among my own people? For the lack of my will to fight back? No! I must forget what's past and gone.

Oh God in Heaven! Give me back the courage of the olden chiefs. Let me wrestle with my surroundings. Let me again, as in the days of old, dominate my environment. Let me humbly accept this new culture and through it rise up and go on.

Oh God! Like the thunderbird of old I shall rise again out of the sea; I shall grab the instruments of the white man's success—his education, his skills—and with these new tools I shall build my race into the proudest segment of your society.

Before I follow the great chiefs that have gone before us, Oh Canada, I shall see these things come to pass. I shall see our young braves and our chiefs sitting in the house of law and government, ruling and being ruled by the knowledge and freedom of our great land.

So shall we shatter the barriers of our isolation. So shall the next hundred years be the greatest in the proud history of our tribes and nations.

Source: Reproduced from Cheryl Patten, "Chief Dan George acclaimed actor, gentle soul" (2003) 21:3 Windspeaker Publication 30, online: <https://ammsa.com/publications/windspeaker/chief-dan-george-acclaimed-actor-gentle-soul>

The aim of making Canada's Constitution "similar in principle" to England's meant that Canada inherited Britain's varied civil liberties and legal inheritance, which contrasted with the American approach of protecting its citizens' civil rights in one central, entrenched document that could be changed only by a constitutional amendment.

A third problem with the BNA Act, as later events would reveal, was that it was formulated without consulting the first peoples to inhabit the land now called Canada: the Indigenous population of Canada. On the 100th anniversary of Confederation, Chief Dan George of the Tsleil-Waututh Nation, a Coast Salish band in North Vancouver, delivered his "Lament for Confederation" in Vancouver's Empire Stadium, offering a poignant reflection on the meaning of this centenary from a First Nations perspective (see Box 3.3).

Lastly, though Macdonald thought it "wise and expedient" to empower the Parliament of Canada, under section 101 of the BNA Act, to establish a General Court of Appeal for Canada, this section did not directly state whether this court would be the final Supreme Court of Appeal for Canada. Nor did the BNA Act indicate who would resolve future disputes likely to arise over the division of powers between the new federal government and the provinces.

Interpreting the Constitution: The Role of the Privy Council

Using section 101 of the BNA Act, the federal government (under the Liberal administration of Prime Minister Alexander Mackenzie) passed the *Supreme Court Act*[19] in 1875. This Act established the Supreme Court of Canada (SCC) as this country's "General Court of Appeal for Canada." However, a problem that later emerged with this court, as indicated above, was that it was not then the *final* appellate court for Canada. Litigants could still appeal a decision from the SCC to the **Judicial Committee of the Privy Council** (or simply, Privy Council) in London, England. The Privy Council, established in 1833, was then the highest appeal authority for the British Empire. Litigants could even bypass the SCC altogether, taking their appeal from a lower provincial court of appeal directly to the Privy Council.

This was significant for a number of reasons, but perhaps none was more important than the influence this would have on the interpretation of the Constitution. Beginning shortly after Confederation, the courts in Canada would be called upon to decide the precise meaning of the areas of jurisdiction assigned to Parliament under section 91 of the BNA Act, and to the provincial legislatures under section 92. Section 91, as already noted, tended to list matters of national importance, and, as we will see in the next chapter, section 92 listed matters of local importance, such as hospitals, municipal institutions, and property and civil rights. A generous or restrictive interpretation of the various areas of jurisdiction could change the balance of power one way or the other.

In addition, the Canadian courts would be asked from time to time to decide the *constitutionality* of legislation based on a *division-of-powers* argument (see Box 3.4). This is sometimes referred to as **judicial review on federalism grounds**. Today, if one level of government tries to pass legislation in an area assigned to the other level, the courts can strike down the legislation because it offends the Constitution. For instance, if the provinces try to pass legislation that deals with criminal law, an area assigned to Parliament, the legislation could be declared *ultra vires* (that is, outside the jurisdiction of the enacting authority). This power of the courts to strike down legislation was not clearly addressed in the BNA Act, and was developed as a necessary implication of having split legislative jurisdiction in a federal system.

Judicial Committee of the Privy Council
the highest appeal authority for colonies in the British Empire; exercised final appeal for Canada until 1949

judicial review on federalism grounds
process by which a court reviews the constitutionality of legislation based on a division-of-powers analysis, that is, by determining whether one level of government has attempted to enact legislation in an area assigned to the other level under the Constitution

---

19 RSC 1985, c S-26.

BOX 3.4

The Queen v Chandler (1869), 12 NBR 556 (SC)

This case is widely regarded as the first Canadian case dealing with judicial review on federalism grounds.

In its division of powers between the new federal Parliament and provincial governments, the BNA Act gave the federal Parliament, under section 91(21), exclusive jurisdiction over "Bankruptcy and Insolvency." In 1868, shortly after the Act came into effect, the New Brunswick provincial legislature passed an amendment to its *Insolvent Confined Debtors Act*. This amendment allowed a debtor confined in jail to apply to a county court judge for a discharge. Taking advantage of this amendment, a man named Hazelton, in jail in Saint John for debt, applied to a county court judge (Chandler) to be discharged from his debts.

The issue was whether the New Brunswick government had the power to make a provincial statute concerning insolvency—a legislative area over which the BNA Act gave the federal Parliament exclusive jurisdiction.

Chief Justice Ritchie of New Brunswick held that New Brunswick's 1868 amendment to the *Insolvent Confined Debtors Act*, because it dealt with insolvency, was in "undoubted conflict" with section 91(21) of the BNA Act. His view was that the New Brunswick provincial legislature had "exceeded its powers" with this statute, and he issued an order prohibiting judge Chandler from proceeding under it.

Source: G Bale, *Chief Justice William Johnstone Ritchie: Responsible Government and Judicial Review* (Ottawa: Carleton University Press, 1991).

For reasons that are not entirely clear, the Privy Council, hearing appeals from the Canadian courts, tended to favour an expansive interpretation of provincial powers (particularly the power over property and civil rights, which was interpreted to cover almost all trade within provincial boundaries) and a restrictive interpretation of federal powers (for example, the trade and commerce power was interpreted to cover trade only *across provincial or national boundaries*). More federal legislation was narrowly interpreted or struck down than was provincial legislation. Arguably, the intent of the drafters of the Constitution was to create a strong federal government, but these decisions by the Privy Council did not favour centralization.

The SCC did not become Canada's final court of appeal until 1949, when appeals to the Privy Council finally ended. Until then, this English body was both the final appeal court for Canadian legal matters generally *and* the final authority when it came to constitutional issues. In other words, the SCC was a subordinate court to the Privy Council. Though not all cases with constitutional issues were (and are) appealed (such as *The Queen v Chandler*; see Box 3.4), many were. As a result, many of the initial decisions interpreting the BNA Act—decisions that shaped the early evolution of Canadian federalism—came from the Privy Council, not from the SCC. This also meant that the SCC had a difficult beginning developing a distinctive Canadian jurisprudence for this country. (The power of the courts to interpret the Constitution, including striking down legislation, is examined in more detail in Part II.)

The Movement to Patriate the Constitution and Adopt a Charter of Rights

The post-Confederation problems reviewed above were not the only ones causing Canadians to believe a change in the country's Constitution was needed. A concern among Canadians in the decades after the Second World War was protecting human rights. Many Canadians, aware of wartime atrocities that came to light after the war, worried about the inadequacy of Canada's human rights legislation. They feared that the human rights of individuals—particularly visible minorities coming to Canada in increasing numbers after the war—were inadequately protected against racial, religious, and ethnic discrimination in such areas as housing and employment.

A growing number of civil liberties activists articulated an argument for, and hoped to entrench, a formal bill of rights in Canada's Constitution. They also wanted Canadian courts to have a more active role in protecting civil liberties. They were heartened by the theory of an *implied* bill of rights used by the courts to help protect individuals against misuse of government power (see Chapter 7). However, many realized that, in the end, a concerted federal effort would be needed to achieve their goal. Here they found an ally in then Prime Minister PE Trudeau.[20]

Pierre Trudeau and the Quest for a Domestic Amending Formula and Charter of Rights

In his *Memoirs*, Pierre Trudeau noted that one of the main reasons he entered federal politics was the issue of "national unity and the place of Quebec within Canada."[21] During Trudeau's first period as prime minister (1968-1979), Canadian nationalism was on the rise. The 1960s saw the nation adopt a new maple-leaf flag, introduce the Canada Pension Plan, experience a glorious centennial in 1967, and welcome the world at Expo '67. This growing feeling of national pride helped weaken long-standing colonial ties to Britain. A corollary to this national pride was a desire to **patriate** Canada's Constitution from England so that amendments to it could be made by Canadians alone, without needing British approval.

patriate
remove a nation's legislation or constitution from the control of the mother country and bring it under the control of the nation itself

Trudeau supported the idea of patriation and the idea of securing, through further constitutional reform, a domestic amending formula for Canada's Constitution, though he knew that previous prime ministers who had tried to do this had been unsuccessful. However, he had an added incentive in his pursuit of these goals. Quebec nationalism was rising alongside Canadian nationalism in the 1960s and 70s and was part of Quebec's "Quiet Revolution." In 1976, Quebec elected its first Parti Québécois government under René Lévesque. In 1980, the party held a referendum on sovereignty association regarding Quebec's future relationship with the rest of Canada. Trudeau, returning as prime minister in 1980 after losing the 1979 election, was determined to oppose Quebec separatists.

Including a charter to his patriation plan and opposition to separatism were important to Trudeau for several reasons. Such accomplishments would be a cornerstone of the *just society* he was trying to achieve in Canada. (See also Box 1.4 in Chapter 1.) Later, looking back on this period, Trudeau wrote that the Charter expressed his long-held view that "the subject of law must be the individual human being ... [who] has certain basic rights that cannot be taken away by any government."[22] Trudeau also recognized that the Charter would help promote Canadian identity and—since a majority of Canadians favoured the

---

20   B Dickson, "The Canadian Charter of Rights and Freedoms: Context and Evolution" in Errol Mendes & Stéphane Beaulac, eds, *Canadian Charter of Rights and Freedoms*, 5th ed (Toronto: LexisNexis, 2013) at 3.

21   Pierre Elliott Trudeau, *Memoirs* (Toronto: McClelland & Stewart, 1993) at 228.

22   *Ibid* at 322.

idea of having an entrenched charter of rights—that it would increase public support for his efforts in the patriation process. Strong public support could help him counter provincial opposition to his patriation process, help counter Quebec separatism, and be an instrument of national unity.[23]

When the federalist "no" side defeated the separatist "yes" side in Quebec's 1980 referendum on sovereignty association, Trudeau continued his commitment for a "renewed federalism" and continued to shepherd his patriation plan through to completion. He met with Canada's premiers, but found that they continued to add—as the price of their support—their own provincial demands to his undertaking. In response, a seemingly frustrated Trudeau decided to see if he could, as prime minister, patriate the Constitution unilaterally, amending the BNA Act without provincial consent. Though Ontario and New Brunswick supported him, he met strong opposition from the other eight provinces. They argued that such an important change to Canada's constitutional framework also required provincial approval. The question whether Trudeau could act unilaterally in this regard was put to the SCC. The SCC held that Trudeau's unilateral action to seek a proposed amendment to the BNA Act was legal, but that, under the circumstances, a substantial measure of provincial consent was necessary by constitutional convention for Trudeau to proceed further. (See Chapter 5 for a discussion of constitutional conventions.)

Faced with this judgment, in 1981 Trudeau once again met with provincial premiers to try to obtain their consent. At this stage, however, the patriation process was opened up for public input, and two interest groups in particular—Indigenous peoples and women—came forward and pressed their proposals for reforms to members of Parliament. Both groups had been following the patriation process closely and did not want to be excluded from it.

Indigenous Peoples and the Patriation Process

Canada's Indigenous peoples were keenly aware of Trudeau's patriation plan for their own constitutional status and treaty rights. Having had their interests and treaty rights left out of the original BNA Act, they were determined not to be disregarded a second time.

By the mid-20th century, Indigenous peoples had experienced many decades of economic, social, and cultural hardship, and suffered serious damage caused by the residential school system. As the Royal Commission on Aboriginal Peoples summarized:

> The assimilation process enforced by the federal government severely disrupted family relationships in [Aboriginal] communities. Residential schools caused the greatest damage; the [widespread physical, emotional, sexual, and spiritual/cultural] abuse left the children with serious emotional scars. Those who escaped the worst abuse still suffered loss of both language and family relationships. Some were unable to develop healthy relationships with their own children.
>
> As the residential system wound down in the 1960s, a new form of family dislocation occurred: the child welfare system. Cross-cultural adoptions and foster placements were so common that many communities lost almost an entire generation of children. ...

---

23   Malcolmson & Myers, *supra* note 15 at 37; Ian Greene, *The Charter of Rights* (Toronto: Lorimer, 1980); Stephen Clarkson & Christina McCall, *Trudeau and Our Times: The Magnificent Obsession* (Toronto: McClelland & Stewart, 1990) vol 1; Michael Mandel, *The Charter of Rights & the Legalization of Politics in Canada*, revised ed (Toronto: Thompson, 1994).

> Loss of land through the colonization process and economic collapse in Aboriginal communities led to extreme poverty and economic reliance on the Canadian government. At the conclusion of the era of colonization—an era that arguably continues to this day—Aboriginal people endured "ill health, run-down and overcrowded housing, polluted water, inadequate schools, poverty and family breakdown/violence at rates found more often in developing countries than in Canada."[24]

Indigenous people wanted to improve their situation, a sentiment expressed by Chief Dan George in his "Lament for Confederation" (see Box 3.3), and they recognized the importance of organizing themselves politically and developing an infrastructure for activism. But it was not easy to accomplish this. They faced various difficulties, including poor communication among Indigenous groups (as a result of isolation, vast geographical distances, and language differences); lack of funds for travel and other expenses; hostility from the federal Department of Indian Affairs; and a lack of experience with such mobilization efforts.[25]

Yet Indigenous organizations had slowly begun to form, first at the provincial level and later, in the 1960s, at the national level. They began to inform Canadians about the difficulties Indigenous peoples experienced in trying to preserve their distinctive culture, about the hardships of life on reserves, and about the many problems they experienced in the areas of health, education, and unemployment. They pressured the Canadian government to change its policies toward Indigenous peoples, and their efforts began to meet with some success. For example, the government lifted its ban on the potlatch ceremony, gave all status Indians the right to vote in federal elections, and phased out residential schools. Two events in particular proved critical in bringing Indigenous demands into the public's awareness during Trudeau's constitutional patriation process: the federal government's 1969 white paper on Aboriginal peoples, and the SCC's recognition in 1973 of Aboriginal title to land in a case involving the Nisga'a in British Columbia (see Box 3.5).

Having achieved considerable unity and political organization, Indigenous groups became alarmed when it appeared that Trudeau and many of the provincial premiers negotiating patriating the Constitution were once again ignoring them. In 1981, organizations representing the First Nations, Métis, and Inuit people of Canada—the National Indian Brotherhood, the Native Council of Canada, and Inuit *Tapirisat* of Canada—put pressure on these politicians to allow them to participate in the constitutional amending process. They had long-standing concerns about such issues as land claims, self-government, maintaining their special legal status,[26] and obtaining constitutional recognition from the Crown

---

24   Royal Commission on Aboriginal Peoples, *People to People, Nation to Nation: Highlights from the Report of the Royal Commission on Aboriginal Peoples* (Ottawa: Supply and Services Canada, 1996) <http://www.aadnc-aandc.gc.ca/eng/1100100014597/1100100014637>. For additional discussion, see also John Roberts, Darion Boyington & Shahé S Kazarian, "Current Socio-economic Issues" in *Diversity and First Nations Issues in Canada*, 2nd ed (Toronto: Emond Montgomery, 2012) ch 10.

25   See Harold Cardinal, *The Unjust Society: The Tragedy of Canada's Indians* (Edmonton: Hurtig, 1969); DE Sanders, "The Indian Lobby" in Keith Banting & Richard Simeon, eds, *And No One Cheered: Federalism, Democracy and the Constitution Act* (Toronto: Methuen, 1983) 301; D Sanders, "Aboriginal Rights in Canada: An Overview" in Olive Patricia Dickason, ed, *The Native Imprint: The Contribution of First Peoples to Canada's Character*, vol 2, *From 1915* (Athabasca: Athabasca University Educational Enterprises, 1996) 518.

26   "[T]he doctrine of [A]boriginal rights exists … because of one simple fact: when Europeans arrived in North America, [A]boriginal peoples were already here, living in communities on the land, and participating in distinctive cultures, as they had done for centuries. It is this fact … above all others, which separates [A]boriginal peoples from all other minority groups in Canadian society and which mandates their special legal … status" (*R v Van der Peet*, [1996] 2 SCR 507, 1996 CanLII 216).

of their Aboriginal and treaty rights. They argued that Indigenous peoples were key stake-holders in Trudeau's constitutional reform process.

Indigenous organizations and their leaders soon realized that they needed to become even more active politically. They began speaking to Canadians with a unified voice, making skillful use of the media, and mobilizing across Canada to put pressure on the government to give more consideration to their interests. They even sent representatives to England to express their concerns before the British Parliament, using their historic treaty relationship with the English Crown. A key document in this relationship is the *Royal Proclamation*, issued by Britain in 1763; as we shall see, its importance is highlighted in provisions of the *Constitution Act, 1982* (ss 25 and 35).[27]

BOX 3.5

The White Paper and Land Claims: Increasing Awareness of Indigenous Issues

In 1969, Prime Minister Trudeau and his minister of Indian affairs, Jean Chrétien, unveiled a white paper that set out the government's new policy for Indigenous peoples. This white paper was issued in response to a government-commissioned report that concluded that Indigenous peoples were Canada's most marginalized and disadvantaged population.* The government proposed measures including repealing the controversial *Indian Act*[†] (the federal legislation that has regulated registered Indians and reserves since 1876 and that was part of the larger government agenda to absorb Indigenous people into mainstream Canadian culture), dissolving the Department of Indian Affairs, eliminating Indian status, converting reserves to private property that could be sold by bands or their members, transferring responsibility for Indigenous affairs to the provinces, and appointing a commissioner to address outstanding land claims, thereby terminating existing treaties over time.

The Indigenous response to the white paper was one of fierce opposition. For one thing, the policy did not take into account the many concerns Indigenous peoples had raised in their consultations with the government prior to the paper's release. As well, although the *Indian Act* severely compromised Indigenous independence, it also secured important rights—namely, reserve lands and a special status within the country. If the *Indian Act* were simply abolished, Indigenous people imagined that whatever legislation replaced it would likely be worse. As well, the government's plan to transfer its responsibility for Indigenous affairs to the provinces was viewed as an effort to evade historic obligations. So angry was the Indigenous reaction that the government withdrew the white paper shortly after it was issued.

Around the same time, a landmark Supreme Court case involving land claims in British Columbia underscored another key issue. In its 1973 decision *Calder v British Columbia (AG)*,[‡] the SCC affirmed the position of the Nisga'a people of BC that Aboriginal title to land, based on traditional occupancy, survived later European settlement and the Crown's assumption of sovereignty. In recognizing Aboriginal title, the court weakened the federal and provincial governments' reluctance to negotiate land claims in parts of Canada not covered by existing treaties. In 1975, in Quebec, the Cree and Inuit were successful in securing the James Bay and Northern Quebec Agreement, which compensated Indigenous peoples in that region for Quebec's building of power operations on their land. In 1977, Justice Thomas Berger, who had been appointed to head a royal commission tasked with studying and making recommendations on the effects of a proposed gas pipeline through the Mackenzie Valley, issued a report opposing any construction until Aboriginal land claims in the areas in question had been settled.

*   H Hawthorne, "A Survey of the Contemporary Indians of Canada: Economic, Political, Educational Needs and Policies," October 1966 and 1967.

†   RSC 1985, c I-5.

‡   [1973] SCR 313, 1973 CanLII 4.

---

27   *Constitution Act*, 1982, Schedule B to the *Canada Act* 1982 (UK), 1982, c 11; The *Royal Proclamation* was issued by King George III to delineate British and Indian land in North America. It was the first public recognition of Aboriginal rights to lands and title. The Proclamation also stated that Indian lands could be purchased only by the Crown. It is the cornerstone of Aboriginal land claims today.

In the end, the government acceded to the pressure from Indigenous peoples to have their rights entrenched in and guaranteed by the new Constitution. The long-term impact of the resulting provisions remains to be seen.

Women and the Patriation Process

Women's groups were also aware of the importance of Trudeau's patriation plan for a new Constitution and were similarly anxious not to be excluded from it. In Canada as elsewhere, women had traditionally been denied many political rights granted to men. They obtained the right to vote long after men: not until 1918 could they vote in federal elections, and not until 1951 could they vote in all provinces and territories. In 1917, the first woman was elected to provincial office, in Alberta, and in 1921 the first woman was elected to the federal Parliament. However, as late as 1929, women were still not considered "persons" eligible to become Canadian senators (see Box 3.6).

Since the end of the 19th century, volunteer women's groups, clubs, and organizations have been advocating for equal rights. In the 1960s and 1970s, the agenda of the women's movement broadened. These decades saw the rise of women's liberation and a greater number of women entering the workforce and pursuing post-secondary education. Many in the women's movement began to lobby governments over concerns such as pay equity; access to good, affordable daycare; violence against women; sexual harassment; reproductive rights; family law reform; pension reform; and education. One of the women's movement's greatest victories during this pre-Charter period came in 1967, when the federal government appointed the Royal Commission on the Status of Women to examine women's concerns in a wide range of equality-related matters, including employment outside the home, child care, affirmative action, and discrimination.[28]

BOX 3.6

The Privy Council and the "Persons" Case

Emily Murphy of Edmonton, appointed in 1916 as the first female judge in the British Empire, initiated a drive to become a Canadian senator. But the federal government believed, based on section 24 of the BNA Act, that she was not a "qualified person" to become a senator. Murphy came up with a strategy. She petitioned the federal government to direct a reference—that is, a formal request for a tribunal's opinion about a certain matter—to the SCC concerning section 24 and the question whether the phrase "qualified persons" could be interpreted to include female persons. She invited four other women to sign the petition with her.

Prime Minister King accepted their petition. His government then referred the matter to the SCC, which ruled against the "famous five," as these women became known. However, King's government agreed to support their appeal to the UK's Judicial Committee of the Privy Council, where Lord Sankey declared that women were "persons" and were eligible to be appointed to the Canadian Senate.

Sources: *Edwards v Canada (AG)*, [1930] AC 124 (JCPC); RJ Sharpe & PI McMahon, *The Persons Case: The Origins and Legacy of the Fight for Legal Personhood* (Toronto: University of Toronto Press, 2007).

---

28   See C Hosek, "Women and Constitutional Process" in Banting & Simeon, *supra* note 25, 280; P LeClerc, "Women's Issues" in Patrick James & Mark Kasoff, eds, *Canadian Studies in the New Millennium* (Toronto: University of Toronto Press, 2008) 185; Lise Gotell, *The Canadian Women's Movement, Equality Rights, and the Charter* (Ottawa: Canadian Research Institute for the Advancement of Women, 1990).

Despite this success, women continued to have major concerns about equality rights in Canada. Some of their dissatisfaction centred on former Prime Minister John Diefenbaker's *Canadian Bill of Rights*[29] (1960) and its provision in section 1(b) regarding "the right of the individual to equality before the law and the protection of the law." Women were concerned that this section was not worded strongly enough to protect equality rights. Experience had shown that, in cases involving women's equality rights, courts tended to interpret this provision narrowly, to the disadvantage of women.

One of these cases was the 1974 *Lavell* case. It involved two Aboriginal women who married non-Aboriginal men, and it raised the question of whether these women's Indian status ought to be affected by their marriage.[30] If a male status Indian married a non-Aboriginal person, he would not lose his Indian status. However, section 12(1)(b) of the *Indian Act* denied Indian status to an Aboriginal woman who married a non-Aboriginal man. There was obvious inequality here. The issue was whether this section of the *Indian Act*, by discriminating on the basis of sex, violated the equality-before-the-law section 1(b) of the *Canadian Bill of Rights*. The SCC held that it did not.

In the wake of this and other SCC decisions, and with Trudeau's possible new Charter on the horizon, women from across Canada attended a conference in 1981 to discuss their concerns. Patrice LeClerc summarized these as follows:

> The consensus of the conference was that gender equality rights had to be in the Charter. Specific points were made, especially by the cadre of feminist lawyers: the use of the word "persons," which was familiar in Canadian law after the *Persons* case, should be used throughout. All points in the Charter were to apply equally to male and female persons. It was agreed that equality under the law must be stated as broadly as possible and that as many protections for this as necessary must be written in to cover eventualities. There was an enhanced emphasis on collective rights, on the rights of women as a group.[31]

As noted below, one measure taken by women's groups "to cover eventualities" was to have the framers of the Charter add another specific guarantee of equality rights. This, however, required further vigorous lobbying.

Patriation and a Revived Constitution

Prime Minister Trudeau's patriation efforts culminated in the *Canada Act 1982*,[32] enacted by the UK Parliament on March 29, 1982. Schedule B of the Act included the *Constitution Act, 1982*. The *Canada Act 1982* came into force on March 29, and the *Constitution Act, 1982* some two weeks later. The reason for the delay in the case of the latter statute was that section 58 of the *Constitution Act, 1982* specified that the Act "shall come into force on a day to be fixed by proclamation issued by the Queen or the Governor General under the Great Seal of Canada." In a public ceremony in Ottawa on April 17, 1982, Queen Elizabeth

---

29 SC 1960, c 44.

30 *Canada (AG) v Lavell* [1974] SCR 1349, 1973 CanLII 175. See also *Bliss v Canada (AG)*, [1979] 1 SCR 183, 1978 CanLII 25.

31 LeClerc, *supra* note 28 at 203. See also Sherene Razack, *Canadian Feminism and the Law: The Women's Legal Education and Action Fund and the Pursuit of Equality* (Toronto: Second Story, 1991) at 34.

32 (UK), 1982, c 11.

herself signed the proclamation, bringing it into force (see the opening photo of this chapter). It was the culmination of much hard work by many Canadians.

The *Canada Act 1982* and its Schedule B, the *Constitution Act, 1982*, provided solutions to many of the difficulties the BNA Act had created for Canada. For example, section 2 of the *Canada Act 1982* states the following: "No Act of the Parliament of the United Kingdom passed after the *Constitution Act, 1982* comes into force shall extend to Canada as part of its law." This provision, ending the authority of the English Parliament to legislate for Canada, satisfied this country's growing nationalist impulse. So did part V of the *Constitution Act, 1982*, which sets out the general procedure by which Canadians could amend their own Constitution, without Britain's involvement. In another nod to Canadian nationalism, the *British North America Act, 1867* was renamed the *Constitution Act, 1867*.[33] Part I of the *Constitution Act, 1982* also contains the *Canadian Charter of Rights and Freedoms*—which was something else many Canadians keenly wanted.

The Charter guarantees a range of rights and freedoms, including religious freedom, the right to vote, legal rights on arrest, and—some might argue, most importantly—procedural *and* substantive rights of equality. This last right is set out in section 15 of the Charter. The push by women's groups to have gender equality enshrined in the Charter, as discussed above, was a significant contributing factor to the resulting broad-based protection against discrimination that section 15 affords. It goes beyond discrimination on the basis of sex and includes other listed (and analogous unlisted) grounds such as race, religion, age, and disability. However, to further protect gender equality, section 28 was also included in the Charter. This section makes it clear that not only is there to be equality before and under the law generally (per s 15), but also that the Charter rights and freedoms themselves are to be guaranteed equally to male and female persons.

Indigenous groups, too, saw results stemming from their lobbying efforts. Section 25 provides that any Aboriginal and treaty rights already in place—including those recognized by the Royal Proclamation of 1763 and under land claims agreements—would not be affected by the Charter. The *Royal Proclamation of 1763* was an important document in relation to Aboriginal title, as noted above (see also Box 9.1 in Chapter 9). Further, in part II of the *Constitution Act, 1982*, entitled "Rights of the Aboriginal Peoples of Canada," section 35 formally recognizes and affirms the existing rights of Aboriginal peoples referred to in section 25.

Charter rights and freedoms are examined in more detail in Chapter 7.

In general, the patriation process and the British legislation it generated breathed new life into the Constitution. Our Constitution now provides for formal independence from Great Britain, it entrenches our rights and freedoms, and it creates a legal structure that will inform Canadian society for many years to come.

A country's constitution and its legal underpinnings play an important role in the determination of the nation's collective identity, and Canada is no exception to this influence. Peter Hogg defines **constitutional law** as follows:

constitutional law
law dealing with the distribution of governmental powers under Canada's Constitution

> Constitutional law is the law prescribing the exercise of power by the organs of a State. It explains which organs can exercise legislative power (making new laws), executive power (implementing the laws) and judicial power (adjudicating disputes), and what the limitations on those powers are. In a federal state, the allocation of governmental powers (legislative, executive and judicial) among central and regional (state or provincial) authorities is a basic concern. The rules of

---

33   (UK), 30 & 31 Vict, c 3, reprinted in RSC 1985, Appendix II, No 5.

federalism are especially significant in Canada because they protect the cultural, linguistic and regional diversity of the nation. Civil liberties are also part of constitutional law, because civil liberties may be created by the rules that limit the exercise of governmental power over individuals. A constitution has been described as "a mirror reflecting the national soul": it must recognize and protect the values of a nation.[34]

The chapters that follow in Part II describe our constitutional law in more detail. Chapter 4 provides an overview of the key constitutional statutes and describes the processes by which new legislation is enacted. Chapter 5 explores the responsibility of the executive branch for administering and implementing our laws, and Chapter 6 examines judicial power and its role in resolving legal disputes. Finally, Chapter 7 considers how Canadian civil liberties place important limits on private sector behaviour and the power of governments.

---

34 Hogg, *supra* note 3 at 1-1.

CHAPTER SUMMARY

Canada is a bijural nation: Quebec uses the civil law system (in particular for private law matters), and the rest of Canada uses the common law system. Both legal systems have deep roots in this country and have undergone unique developments since the early colonial influences of France and England. Quebec, originally a colony of France, received French civil law, while the rest of Canada's provinces and territories were originally English colonies (or later came under England's jurisdiction) and received English common law.

Common law rules of reception dictated how different regions of Canada received English law. These rules varied in part according to how the region came to be an English colony. If colonization came about through settlement, the mother country's laws—both judge-made law and statute law—were received upon settlement, generally agreed to be the date when the colonial legislature first met. If England acquired the territory by conquest (or cession), the region's pre-existing legal system continued until the English monarch or imperial Parliament formally imposed English law there. Alternatively, and regardless of method of colonization, the colonial legislature could pass a reception statute adopting the laws of England as of a certain date. Each province and territory has a unique history concerning its reception of English (or French) law.

The transformation of a collection of independent colonies into a united Canada was the culmination of a long, difficult reform process. There were strong political, military, and economic reasons for the enactment of the BNA Act, the imperial statute that created our country and federal system of government. But the BNA Act left certain things unresolved. It lacked, for example, a domestic amending formula and a bill of rights. Its framers disregarded the interests and rights of Indigenous peoples. It did not adequately address the role of the SCC as a final court of appeal or clearly define the power of the courts to review the constitutionality of legislation in disputes regarding the division of powers between the new federal government and the provinces.

As Canadian society became more multicultural and diverse, particularly after the Second World War, various political movements sought to reform the BNA Act. Canadian nationalism became more pronounced in the 1960s, and an initiative arose, led by Prime Minister Pierre Trudeau, to patriate the Constitution from Britain so that Canadians could amend the Constitution without recourse to the British Parliament. Along with this initiative, there was a corollary movement to add an entrenched charter of rights to our Constitution. Indigenous people mobilized politically to ensure that their special status and treaty rights were protected by the new Constitution, and women lobbied to have the proposed new Charter contain strongly worded equality rights. The result was the passage of the *Canada Act 1982*, which includes the *Constitution Act, 1982* and the Charter. With our revitalized Constitution, we now have legal independence from Britain, the power to amend our Constitution, and the Charter to protect our legal rights and freedoms, together with other reforms, all of which will guide us into the foreseeable future.

KEY TERMS

cession, 62

Civil Code of Quebec (Code Civil du Québec), 67

Confederation, 63

constitutional law, 84

federalism, 73

imperial statute, 62

Judicial Committee of the Privy Council, 76

judicial review on federalism grounds, 76

patriate, 78

unitary government, 73

FURTHER READING

BOOKS

Berger, Thomas R. *A Long and Terrible Shadow: White Values, Native Rights in the Americas, 1492-1992* (Vancouver/Toronto: Douglas & McIntyre, 1991).

Castel, J-G. *The Civil Law System of the Province of Quebec* (Toronto: Butterworths, 1962).

Davenport, Paul & Richard H Leach, eds. *Reshaping Confederation: The 1982 Reform of the Canadian Constitution* (Durham, NC: Duke University Press, 1984).

Frideres, James S & René R Gadacz. *Aboriginal Peoples in Canada*, 9th ed (Toronto: Pearson, 2012).

Girard, P & J Phillips, eds. *Essays in the History of Canadian Law*, vol 3, *Nova Scotia* (Toronto: Osgoode Society/University of Toronto Press, 1990).

Guth, DeLloyd & W Wesley Pue, eds. *Canada's Legal Inheritances* (Winnipeg: Canadian Legal History Project, Faculty of Law, University of Manitoba, 2001).

James, Patrick & Mark Kasoff, eds. *Canadian Studies in the New Millennium* (Toronto: University of Toronto Press, 2008).

Knafla, LA & J Swainger, eds. *Laws and Societies in the Canadian Prairie West, 1670-1940* (Vancouver: University of British Columbia Press, 2005).

Reesor, Bayard. *The Canadian Constitution in Historical Perspective* (Scarborough, Ont: Prentice Hall, 1992).

Reynolds, James I. *Aboriginal Peoples and the Law: A Critical Introduction* (Vancouver: Purich Books, an imprint of UBC Press, 2018).

Saywell, John T. *The Lawmakers: Judicial Power and the Shaping of Canadian Federalism* (Toronto: University of Toronto Press, 2002).

Sharpe, Robert J & Kent Roach. *The Charter of Rights and Freedoms*, 5th ed (Toronto: Irwin Law, 2013).

Strayer, Barry L. *Canada's Constitutional Revolution* (Edmonton: University of Alberta Press, 2013).

Waite, PB. *The Life and Times of Confederation, 1864-1867* (Toronto: University of Toronto Press, 1962).

WEBSITES

Indigenous Bar Association: <http://www.indigenousbar.ca>.

McCord Museum, Montreal Social History Museum: <http://www.mccord-museum.qc.ca/en>.

Osgoode Society for Canadian Legal History: <http://www.osgoodesociety.ca>.

REVIEW QUESTIONS

1. How did the reception of English law in an overseas colony differ depending on whether England had acquired the colony by settlement or by conquest?

2. List five key factors leading to Confederation.

3. Why did Canadian politicians end up adopting a federal system of government in the BNA Act?

4. List five areas of laws assigned to the federal government under section 91 of the BNA Act.

5. List four problems with the BNA Act that later proved to be problematic in Canada.

6. What difficulties did Indigenous people encounter in organizing themselves politically and developing an infrastructure for activism?

7. Explain how sections 15 and 28 of the Charter, respectively, are important for protecting women's equality rights.

EXERCISES

1. What circumstances unique to Canada in our colonial past might have made applying English case law unsuitable here?

2. Consider ways in which having a separate civil law legal system is a benefit to the province of Quebec. Do you think that bijuralism is a good attribute for the nation as a whole? Explain.

3. Why do you think the BNA Act did not originally have a charter of rights in it?

4. Find and read a recent court case that addresses Aboriginal rights. Identify the issue, explain the arguments of each side, and state the court's decision. What implications could this decision have for other Indigenous groups in Canada and for the public?

5. Look at the website for the Women's Legal Education and Action Fund (LEAF) (<http://www.leaf.ca>) and review materials on this public interest group. Why do you think LEAF has been so effective in supporting women's legal rights in Canada?

PART II
Law and the Canadian Constitution

4 The Legislature: The First Branch of Government

The Centre, East, and West Blocks of the Parliament buildings, in Ottawa, were begun in 1859. The original Centre Block was destroyed by fire in 1916 and reopened in 1922. The new design and elements reflected the sense of Canadian identity that emerged from the First World War. The Centre Block (pictured) closed in 2018 as part of a restoration and modernization project and is not expected to reopen for 10 years. During construction, the House of Commons has moved to the West Block, and the Senate to the Government Conference Centre (renamed, in 2018, the Senate of Canada Building).

After reading this chapter, you will understand:

- The nature of legislative power in Canada.
- The different types of statute law and the process by which statutes are enacted.
- The nature of subordinate legislation.

- The concept of parliamentary sovereignty.
- The basics of reading and understanding legislation.

One of the pillars of the Canadian federal system is the explicit distribution of law-making or "legislative powers" between Parliament and each of the provincial legislatures. Part VI of the *Constitution Act, 1867* (which includes ss. 91 to 95) fulfills this purpose largely by assigning responsibility over "matters" coming within different "classes of subjects" to the Parliament and the provincial legislatures.

Bernard W Funston & Eugene Meehan, *Canada's Constitutional Law in a Nutshell*, 4th ed (Toronto: Carswell, 2013) at 58

Introduction

separation-of-powers doctrine
doctrine according to which separate powers are assigned to the legislative, executive, and judicial branches of government

As we noted in the previous chapter, constitutional law is largely concerned with a nation's legislative, executive, and judicial powers. These three powers are sometimes referred to as the three branches or pillars of government. The **separation-of-powers doctrine** deals with the relationship between them. We can summarize this relationship as follows: the legislature makes the law; the executive implements the law; and the judiciary applies and interprets the law.

In this chapter, we look at the legislative branch, which, in Canada, despite the separation-of-powers doctrine, is closely connected to the executive branch—this connection is a consequence of our system of responsible government.

legislature
representative assembly charged under a constitution with making laws for a particular region or state

Legislative Power

The legislative branch is the most powerful of the three branches, with ultimate control over the other two. It operates through a legislative body called a **legislature**. A legislature is a representative assembly charged under a constitution with making laws for a particular region or state. Legislatures go by various names, such as *parliament, congress,* or *legislative assembly.* The members are usually elected, but they can be appointed in other ways, depending on the political system. Legislatures have a settled number of members or seats. This number may be changed periodically in response to population changes and other factors.

unicameral
legislature with one house involved in the passage of legislation

bicameral
legislature with two houses involved in the passage of legislation

Most legislatures are either **unicameral** or **bicameral**. A unicameral legislature has only one body. A bicameral legislature has two, with lower houses (having names such as *House of Commons* or *House of Representatives*) and upper houses (for example, *Senate* or *House of Lords*). Canada's Parliament, like the British or United Kingdom (UK) Parliament and the US Congress, has a bicameral structure. A bicameral legislature may be partly elected and partly appointed, as are the UK and Canadian Parliaments, with their elected House of Commons and their appointed House of Lords and Senate, respectively. Alternatively, both houses of a bicameral legislature can be elected. This is the case with the US Congress. Members of both the House of Representatives and the Senate are elected.

In unitary states, such as Britain, legislative power is not constitutionally divided between central and regional authorities (although regions may have revocable power delegated to them); there is just one supreme legislative body. In federal states such as Canada, the US, and Australia, legislative jurisdiction is divided between central and regional authorities. Depending on how many regions the nation contains, its legislative power can be vested in a large number of separate legislative bodies.

Legislation refers to written laws made by legislative assemblies. The following section examines the main form of legislation (statutes), legislative bodies, and the process by which statutes are enacted. The next section briefly considers subordinate legislation, a form of legislation passed under delegated authority granted by enabling statutes, as well as quasi-legislative rules, which—though not legislated—operate analogously. This is followed by a discussion of the limits of legislative power and the doctrine of parliamentary sovereignty in the Canadian context. The final section covers the essentials of reading, understanding, and citing legislation.

legislation
written laws made by legislative assemblies

Statutes

Statutes are the primary form of legislation. In Canada, which is a federal state, the power to make statutes is divided between the federal Parliament and the provincial legislatures. Most Canadian statutes are therefore either federal or provincial statutes.

statutes
the primary form of legislation

However, our most important *constitutional* statutes are British. As described in Chapter 3, Canada before 1867 was a collection of separate British colonies. Therefore, our transition to nationhood required the cooperation of the UK Parliament. The principal constitutional statutes, including the *Constitution Act, 1867*[1] itself (formerly called the *British North America Act, 1867*, or BNA Act), were written by and passed at the request of Canadians. But they were British statutes; the UK Parliament had to pass them. It was not until 1982 and the patriation of our Constitution that there existed a Canadian legislative formula or power for amending the Constitution without Britain's involvement.

There are four types of statutes, distinguished according to type or jurisdiction:

1. constitutionally entrenched statutes, which are mainly British;
2. federal statutes;
3. provincial statutes; and
4. territorial statutes.

We will discuss the four types of statutes in the following sections.

Constitutionally Entrenched Statutes

Canadian constitutional statutes are statutes that concern this country's governmental powers as well as important civil liberties matters. They include federal and provincial statutes, and statutes from the UK. Many federal and provincial statutes relating to government

---

1   (UK), 30 & 31 Vict, c 3, reprinted in RSC 1985, Appendix II, No 5.

powers and civil liberties are not entrenched; they can be changed via the usual legislative process.

Our **constitutionally entrenched** statutes are ones that cannot be changed by ordinary federal or provincial legislation. Generally speaking, a statute is *entrenched* if it requires a special process to change it. Specifically, a statute is constitutionally entrenched if it is part of the Constitution of Canada as set out in section 52 of the *Constitution Act, 1982*.[2] The relevant subsections of section 52 are as follows:

> 52(2) The Constitution of Canada includes
>> (a) the *Canada Act 1982*, including this Act [that is, the *Constitution Act, 1982*];
>> (b) the Acts and orders referred to in the schedule; and
>> (c) any amendment to any Act or order referred to in paragraph (a) or (b).
>
> (3) Amendments to the Constitution of Canada shall be made only in accordance with the authority contained in the Constitution of Canada.

This provision tells us that the Constitution of Canada includes not only the *Canada Act 1982*[3] and the *Constitution Act, 1982* (which includes the Charter),[4] but also the 30 statutes and orders listed in the Schedule to the *Constitution Act, 1982* (see Appendix B). These include the *Constitution Act, 1867*; the *Parliament of Canada Act, 1875*;[5] the *Statute of Westminster, 1931*; a number of statutes and orders creating and/or admitting new provinces and territories into Canada; and various amending statutes. The list comprises the main parts of the Constitution of Canada. However, because of the use of the word *includes*, it is not exhaustive. The Supreme Court of Canada (SCC) has held that other laws may be included in the Constitution of Canada.

Section 52(3) states that the statutes, laws, and orders included in the Constitution can be changed only through the use of the special constitutional amendment procedure set out in part V of the *Constitution Act, 1982* (see the discussion below).

Key Constitutional Statutes

Canada's key constitutional statutes are the following:

- *Constitution Act, 1867*;
- *Statute of Westminster, 1931*;
- *Canada Act 1982*; and
- *Constitution Act, 1982*.

They are briefly described next.

CONSTITUTION ACT, 1867

Before the enactment of the *Constitution Act, 1867*, what is now Canada (or then British North America) was a collection of British colonies and territories. As we saw in the last

---

2 Schedule B to the *Canada Act 1982* (UK), 1982, c 11.

3 (UK), 1982, c 11.

4 *Canadian Charter of Rights and Freedoms*, Part I of the *Constitution Act, 1982*, being Schedule B to the *Canada Act 1982* (UK), *1982*, c 11.

5 RSC 1985, c P-1.

chapter, this statute brought together three of those colonies—New Brunswick, Nova Scotia, and the Province of Canada (which would become Ontario and Quebec)—and created the new country of Canada in 1867. The new country was in the form of a federation, with government power divided between a central authority and the former colonies, now called *provinces*.

The *Constitution Act, 1867* is divided into 11 parts. Parts II-VIII and XI are the key ones:

- Part II, entitled "Union," united the three colonies mentioned above to form the new country.
- Part III outlines federal executive power.
- Sections 58-68 in part V, headed "Provincial Constitutions," outline provincial executive power.
- Legislative power is covered in parts IV, V (ss 69-90), and VI. The cornerstone sections are sections 91-92 in part VI, which divide the power or **jurisdiction** to make laws between the federal Parliament and the provincial legislatures. Sections 93-95 are also important, however; they deal with jurisdiction over such things as natural resources, education, and immigration.
- Part VII is entitled "Judicature" and deals with the federal power to appoint judges and create new courts. It complements a parallel jurisdiction over courts and judges given to the provinces in section 92 (see Chapter 6).
- Part VIII deals with taxation and money issues and supplements the coverage given these areas in sections 91-92.
- Part XI, entitled "Admission of Other Colonies," gave the government special powers to admit new colonies. It is owing to part XI that Canada now consists not of three but ten provinces and three territories (see Chapter 3).

jurisdiction
refers (in the context of legislative power under the Constitution) to the specific subject areas over which the federal Parliament and the provincial legislatures have been assigned authority

Key excerpts from the *Constitution Act, 1867* are reproduced in Appendix A.

STATUTE OF WESTMINSTER, 1931

The *Statute of Westminster, 1931* can be thought of as Canada's second step toward full legislative independence from Britain. The first step was the *Colonial Laws Validity Act, 1865*. This earlier Act provided that British colonies—including those in British North America (and the soon-to-be-formed country of Canada)—could enact laws contrary to English laws "of general application" that had been received by the colonies upon formation. They could not, however, enact laws contrary to British imperial statutes that were intended to extend to the colony in question. Laws of general application were English laws that weren't specifically directed at the colonies but had been received from England to avoid a legal vacuum when the colonies were established. Until the *Colonial Laws Validity Act, 1865* was passed, there was some doubt about the power of the colonies to change these laws. This Act made it clear they could.

The *Statute of Westminster, 1931* repealed the *Colonial Laws Validity Act, 1865*. It took colonial independence one step further. Not only did it confirm Canada's legislative autonomy, it also recognized Canada's legislative equality with Britain. However, Britain did reserve the power to amend key constitutional statutes such as the *British North America Act* (now the *Constitution Act, 1867*).

This reservation of power was due less to paternalism on Britain's part than to the fact that the federal government and the provinces were unable at the time to agree on a constitutional amending formula. Because of this disagreement, the UK Parliament still needed to be involved in Canada's constitutional amendments. Britain was always accepting of Canada's requests for such amendments, invariably passing them.

CANADA ACT 1982

In 1982, the UK Parliament, at the request of the federal government, passed the *Canada Act 1982*, giving up all legislative power over Canada. This was Canada's third and final step toward legislative independence from Britain. Section 2 of the Act provides as follows:

> 2. No Act of the Parliament of the United Kingdom passed after the *Constitution Act, 1982* comes into force shall extend to Canada as part of its law.

Schedule B of the *Canada Act 1982* is the *Constitution Act, 1982*. The amending formula it sets out in part V empowered Canadians, for the first time, to make changes to their own Constitution. The Canadian Constitution had finally been patriated. Canada had achieved full legislative autonomy.

CONSTITUTION ACT, 1982

The *Constitution Act, 1982* is divided into seven parts and is set out in Appendix B. Part I is the *Canadian Charter of Rights and Freedoms* (the Charter), which is arguably the most significant legacy of the patriation process. It guarantees certain rights and freedoms and has become the main basis of Canadian civil liberties (see Chapter 7 of this text).

Part II of the Act addresses Aboriginal rights, while part III concerns the joint federal and provincial commitment to equal opportunities for Canadians regardless of regional disparities in wealth, as well as the federal commitment to equalization payments for the less wealthy provinces. Parts IV and IV.I, now both repealed, dealt with constitutional conferences.

Part V sets out the amendment procedure for the Constitution of Canada. Part VI contains amendments concerning provincial power over natural resources, forestry resources, and electrical energy.

Part VII of the Act is entitled "General" and covers miscellaneous matters such as minor amendments, English and French versions of the legislation, commencement dates for certain provisions, and citation protocols. Significantly, it also includes section 52(1), the **supremacy clause**, which provides the following:

> 52(1) The Constitution of Canada is the supreme law of Canada, and any law that is inconsistent with the provisions of the Constitution is, to the extent of the inconsistency, of no force or effect.

If a federal or provincial statute offends or is inconsistent with the Constitution, section 52(1) states that the law is "of no force or effect." This may seem clear, but precisely what remedial responses are available when dealing with unconstitutional legislation is not always so clear. The courts have interpreted their power to deal with unconstitutional legislation broadly, using section 52(1) and, sometimes, also section 24 of the Charter (see Box 7.4 in Chapter 7). A range of responses are possible, including the following:

1. *striking down* the legislation altogether and declaring it invalid (this is the most extreme response);
2. *severance* of a portion of the legislation (if only part of the statute contravenes the Constitution—for example, a particular section—the court can declare that just that part is invalid and sever it from the rest of the legislation);

supremacy clause
section 52(1) of the *Constitution Act, 1982,* which provides that the Constitution is the supreme law of Canada and empowers the courts to find that laws that are inconsistent with the Constitution are of no force and effect

3. *reading down* (with this remedy, the courts narrowly interpret the legislation to ensure conformity with the Constitution);

4. *reading in* (this remedy is a little more activist and involves adding language to the legislation to ensure conformity with the Constitution—for example, adding a new class of persons covered by the legislation, or adding a new and unlisted ground of discrimination (see Box 7.4);

5. a *constitutional exemption* (with this rarely used remedy, and so far never used by the SCC, the court does not declare the legislation invalid, but finds that it doesn't apply to a particular person or class of persons); and

6. the *temporary suspension* of an order declaring the legislation or part of it invalid (this gives Parliament or the legislature the opportunity to enact new, valid legislation within a set period of time—see Box 12.1 in Chapter 12 as an example).

Prior to patriation, the main ground for challenging the constitutionality of legislation in court was based on a **division-of-powers** argument, where it is argued that one level of government has tried to pass legislation in an area assigned to the other level (see the discussion of *judicial review on federalism grounds* in Chapter 3). With the passage of the *Constitution Act, 1982*, another important ground has emerged: challenging the constitutionality of legislation on the basis that it infringes the Charter, sometimes referred to as **judicial review on Charter grounds**, or simply a *Charter challenge* (see Chapter 7 for more on the scope of the Charter).[6]

division of powers refers to the divided jurisdiction—between Parliament, on one hand, and the provinces, on the other hand—to make legislation in a federal state such as Canada

Constitutional Amendments

The making or changing of constitutionally entrenched statutes requires a special process. Section 52(3) states that "[a]mendments to the Constitution of Canada shall be made only in accordance with the authority contained in the Constitution of Canada."

Part V of the *Constitution Act, 1982* sets out the amendment procedures. Typically, an amendment will require the agreement of Parliament and of two-thirds of the provinces, with the support of at least 50 percent of the general population. This is known as the *general procedure* for amendment. The particular requirements are set out in section 38 of the Act. Currently, given the number of Canadian provinces and the way the population is distributed across the country, an amendment following the general procedure would need the support of seven provinces, and one of them would have to be either Ontario or Quebec.

judicial review on Charter grounds (or Charter challenge) process by which a court reviews the constitutionality of legislation on the basis that it infringes the Charter

There are certain kinds of amendments that require the *unanimous* agreement of Parliament and the provinces (see s 41 of the *Constitution Act, 1982*). These amendments include:

- changes to the office of the Queen,
- the use of the English or French language when dealing with federal institutions,
- the composition of the SCC, and
- any changes to the amendment procedure itself.

---

6 It should be noted that this power to deal with unconstitutional legislation can also extend to common law rules. This could occur, for example, if the government or agent of the government (such as a police officer or Crown prosecutor) were involved in a dispute and were relying on a common law rule that offended the Charter. This power does not extend, however, to common law rules being applied in private sector disputes not involving the government.

Part V of the Act also provides for simpler amendment procedures if the proposed change affects only one or two provinces or the federal government alone (see ss 43-45 of the *Constitution Act, 1982*). For instance, provinces can change their boundaries without the consent or agreement of provinces that are not affected by the change. Only Parliament and the provinces directly affected by the boundary change need agree to it. Similarly, the provinces—with parliamentary approval—can also independently make amendments concerning the use of either official language within the province (except, as noted above, where this use pertains to federal institutions). See Box 4.1.

Federal Statutes

Federal statutes are enacted by the Parliament of Canada. Because our Parliament is bicameral, there are two houses involved in the making of statutes. At the time of writing, the House of Commons, which is elected, has 338 seats; the Senate, which is appointed, has 105.

BOX 4.1

Constitutional Amendments Since Patriation

Since 1982, there have been 11 amendments to the Constitution of Canada using the amending procedures set out in part V of the *Constitution Act, 1982*.

The *general procedure* pursuant to section 38 requires the consent of two-thirds of the provinces, with at least 50 percent of the population (the so-called 7/50 procedure). One amendment has occurred using this procedure (the *Constitution Amendment Proclamation, 1983*). It followed the constitutional conference mandated by section 37, which considered Aboriginal peoples and their constitutional rights. Aboriginal rights were strengthened through changes to sections 25 and 35, which made it clear that past *and future* rights acquired under land claims agreements were protected. The amendment also ensured that Aboriginal and treaty rights are guaranteed equally to male and female persons.

After the 1983 amendment, there were two significant attempts at constitutional change using the general procedure. One was the Meech Lake Accord of 1987, which aimed to encourage Quebec to endorse the 1982 constitutional changes (Quebec had been the only province not to give its consent when Canada approached England with the patriation proposal in 1982). The Accord included recognition of Quebec as a "distinct society," and it gave all provinces the power to veto constitutional amendments. But consensus was never reached, and the Meech Lake Accord was never ratified.

The second attempt at constitutional change using the general procedure was the Charlottetown Accord, negotiated in 1992 by the federal and provincial governments. Proposing changes to the division of legislative powers, it gave the provinces exclusive jurisdiction in several contentious areas where jurisdiction is divided, including natural resources and cultural policy. The Charlottetown proposal also included a social charter that promoted health care, welfare, education, and environmental protection, and that formally recognized, by way of the "Canada Clause," certain "Canadian" values such as equality, diversity, and Quebec's status as a "distinct society." The Charlottetown Accord also proposed a number of institutional changes to the SCC, to Parliament, and to the consultation process between the federal, provincial, and territorial governments. Following a national referendum in which the majority voted against the Accord, the Charlottetown Accord was abandoned. It remains to be seen whether we will be able to agree on any broad-based changes in the future as a nation, such as changes modifying the distribution of powers between Parliament and the provinces.

There have been no amendments using the procedure requiring unanimous consent of Parliament and the provinces under section 41. The remaining 10 amendments, made pursuant to sections 43 and 44 and of more limited scope, covered such matters as modifying the method for apportioning seats in the House of Commons, replacing ferry service to Prince Edward Island with the Confederation Bridge (amending Prince Edward Island's constitutional guarantee of "efficient steam service"), education rights within a province, and language rights within a province (in 1993, New Brunswick succeeded in amending the Charter through the addition of a new section—section 16.1—guaranteeing the equal status of the English and French languages in that province).

Constitutional convention dictates that the House of Commons, as an elected body, takes the lead in making new legislation. See Figures 4.1 and 4.2.

New statutes can be passed only while Parliament is in session. Each new session commences with a formal state opening at which the governor general (or occasionally the British monarch) reads the Speech from the Throne. Each session is formally brought to a close when it is **prorogued**. Most sessions are one to two years in length, sometimes with lengthy adjournments during that time. Under section 4 of the Charter, an election must be called at least once every five years. This means that, after each election, the governing party has five years in which to advance its legislative agenda through Parliament.

prorogue
the formal closing of a legislative session

Federal Jurisdiction

The principal sections of the Constitution that give power to Parliament are section 91 (many subject areas), section 94A (old age pensions), and section 95 (agriculture and immigration, though these areas are shared with the provinces). Any new legislation proposed by Parliament must be authorized by a section in the Constitution.

Section 91 is the source of most federal power. It lists 30 specific subject areas over which Parliament has exclusive jurisdiction. It also gives the federal government a general power to make laws for the "Peace, Order and good Government of Canada," in areas over which the provinces are not assigned exclusive jurisdiction.

FIGURE 4.1   Canada's 338 ridings are represented in the lower house by members of Parliament. The primary colour used (green) is the same colour used in Britain's House of Commons for more than 300 years. The home of the House of Commons in the Centre Block, pictured above, has temporarily moved during renovations, as has the home of the Senate, pictured in Figure 4.2.

POGG POWER

This general power to make laws for the peace, order, and good government of Canada is often referred to as **POGG power**. The POGG power clause in section 91 appears to give Parliament a general *residuary power*—that is, jurisdiction in any area that the Constitution

POGG power
the general residuary power given to Parliament—in other words, the power to fill in the gaps left by the specifically enumerated areas of jurisdiction assigned to the two levels of government

does not explicitly assign to either level of government. In other words, section 91 gives Parliament the power to fill the legislative gaps. This reflects the fact that the framers of the Constitution aimed to build a strong federal authority. In this respect, Canada contrasts with other federations, such as the US and Australia, where the residuary power is given to the regional or state legislatures.

FIGURE 4.2 The Speech from the Throne is given in the Senate chamber. Canada adopted this custom from Britain, where neither the unelected members of the upper house (Senate) nor the sovereign are permitted to enter the House of Commons.

Besides recognizing POGG power as a means to fill legislative gaps in the assigned areas of jurisdiction, the courts have interpreted POGG power as justifying federal laws to regulate matters of national concern (such as marine pollution, aeronautics, and nuclear power) and to deal temporarily with serious emergencies (for example, during times of war, insurrection, or economic turbulence).

SPECIFIC AREAS OF FEDERAL JURISDICTION

The list of subject areas in section 91 is extensive. According to this provision's introductory words, Parliament's authority "extends to all Matters coming within the Classes of Subjects" listed. Given that each area listed is a "class of subjects" and that federal jurisdiction is over "all matters" within those classes, the federal power to legislate appears to be quite far-reaching. For a full listing of the areas that fall under federal jurisdiction according to section 91 of the *Constitution Act, 1867*, see Table 4.1.

To help determine whether a statute is within a legislature's jurisdiction, the courts try to determine what the "matter" of the law is. The courts are looking for the statute's essence here. Various phrases have been used to refer to a law's essence—for example, its *true meaning*, its *true nature and character*, and, most often, its *pith and substance*.

TABLE 4.1   Federal Powers Under Section 91 by Category

CATEGORY	RELATED SUBSECTION(S) OF SECTION 91	NOTES
Taxation, money, and public assets	1A. The Public Debt and Property 3. The Raising of Money by any Mode or System of Taxation 4. The Borrowing of Money on the Public Credit 14. Currency and Coinage 15. Banking, Incorporation of Banks, and the Issue of Paper Money 16. Savings Banks 18. Bills of Exchange and Promissory Notes 19. Interest 20. Legal Tender 21. Bankruptcy and Insolvency	The framers of the *Constitution Act, 1867* saw this category as important. Putting it under Parliament's jurisdiction was a means of creating a strong and effective central government. These powers are supplemented by part VIII.
Trade and employment	2. The Regulation of Trade and Commerce 2A. Unemployment Insurance 17. Weights and Measures	The trade and commerce power was interpreted narrowly soon after Confederation by the Privy Council as only applying to interprovincial and international trade and commerce, not intraprovincial trade and commerce, which was held to be a matter within provincial jurisdiction under s 92(13).*
Intellectual property	22. Patents of Invention and Discovery 23. Copyrights	The law in this area, which involves an intangible form of property without specific geographical context or connection, requires consistent rules across wide-ranging boundaries. It is also affected by international relations and agreements.
First Nations	24. Indians, and Lands reserved for the Indians	The reason for including this area under s 91 was apparently to protect First Nations against European expansion and to have a consistent set of policies across Canada.†
Immigration and citizenship	25. Naturalization and Aliens	In Canada, as in most countries, immigration and citizenship is primarily a national priority. However, the federal government collaborates with the provinces in establishing goals and policies in this area.
Marriage and divorce	26. Marriage and Divorce	Family law is also regulated by the provinces, which have some shared jurisdiction with Parliament (e.g., spousal support and child custody) and some exclusive jurisdiction (division of family assets).

* *Citizens' Insurance Co of Canada v Parsons* (1881), 7 App Cas 96 (PC).
† Peter W Hogg, *Constitutional Law of Canada*, 2018 student ed (Toronto: Carswell, 2018) at 28-2.

(*Table 4.1 is continued on the next page.*)

TABLE 4.1   Federal Powers Under Section 91 by Category   concluded

CATEGORY	RELATED SUBSECTION(S) OF SECTION 91	NOTES
Transportation and communication	13. Ferries between a Province and any British or Foreign Country or between Two Provinces 29. Such Classes of Subjects as are expressly excepted in the Enumeration of the Classes of Subjects by this Act assigned exclusively to the Legislatures of the Provinces [Section 91(29) must be read together with s 92(10): 10. Local Works and Undertakings other than such as are of the following Classes: (a) Lines of Steam or other Ships, Railways, Canals, Telegraphs, and other Works and Undertakings connecting the Province with any other or others of the Provinces, or extending beyond the Limits of the Province: (b) Lines of Steam Ships between the Province and any British or Foreign Country: (c) Such Works as, although wholly situate within the Province, are before or after their Execution declared by the Parliament of Canada to be for the general Advantage of Canada or for the Advantage of Two or more of the Provinces.]	These areas are of national importance.
Water matters: coasts, shipping, and fishing	9. Beacons, Buoys, Lighthouses, and Sable Island 10. Navigation and Shipping 11. Quarantine and the Establishment and Maintenance of Marine Hospitals 12. Sea Coast and Inland Fisheries	With so much water and coastline, federal jurisdiction was needed for reasons of safety, security, and uniformity.
Criminal law	27. The Criminal Law, except the Constitution of Courts of Criminal Jurisdiction, but including the Procedure in Criminal Matters 28. The Establishment, Maintenance, and Management of Penitentiaries	Parliament's jurisdiction over criminal law has been used to enact a variety of criminal statutes, including the *Criminal Code* and *Youth Criminal Justice Act*. Not all federations have a national criminal law system. In the US, for instance, criminal law jurisdiction rests with the individual states.
National defence	7. Militia, Military and Naval Service, and Defence	The need for a national armed services is clear.
Miscellaneous	5. Postal Service 6. The Census and Statistics 8. The fixing of and providing for the Salaries and Allowances of Civil and other Officers of the Government of Canada	National regulation in these areas was thought to be in the country's best interests.

BOX 4.2

Assisted Human Reproduction Act, SC 2004, c 2

In 1989, Parliament established the Royal Commission on New Reproductive Technologies (the "Baird Commission"). In its report, the Baird Commission recommended that legislation be enacted to regulate what it and many others considered to be unethical practices. In 2004, after extensive consultations with the provinces, the territories, and various interest groups, Parliament passed the *Assisted Human Reproduction Act*. It prohibited human cloning and required licensing for certain "controlled activities." These activities included (1) manipulating human reproductive material or *in vitro* embryos, (2) transgenic engineering, and (3) paying for expenses of donors and surrogate mothers.

In a reference—that is, a formal request for a tribunal's opinion about a certain matter—to the Quebec Court of Appeal, the attorney general of Quebec conceded the constitutional validity of some provisions in the Act, such as the prohibition against human cloning. But the attorney general also argued that many sections in the Act, especially the ones dealing with "controlled activities," were an attempt by the federal government to regulate matters—the practice of medicine, and research related to assisted reproduction—that properly fall within provincial jurisdiction. In response, the attorney general of Canada argued that the entire Act was authorized by Parliament's jurisdiction over criminal law, a power given it by section 91(27) of the *Constitution Act, 1867*. The Quebec Court of Appeal held that the impugned provisions in question—the ones dealing with "controlled activities"—were invalid, and the attorney general of Canada appealed to the SCC.*

The SCC analyzed the legislation to determine its matter, or "pith and substance." The court held that the dominant purpose and effect of the statutory scheme was to prohibit practices that would undercut moral values, generate public health evils, and threaten the security of people involved in assisted reproduction. These were criminal law matters, even though they touched on provincial jurisdiction over medical research and practice.

However, despite the *overall* characterization of the statute as criminal law, the SCC also found that the Act contained certain provisions whose dominant purpose and effect concerned provincial areas of jurisdiction. These included provisions dealing with the manipulation of human reproductive material to create embryos, keeping and handling gametes and embryos, combining human and non-human genes, and certain privacy of information rules that were not criminal in nature.

These provisions, according to the SCC, represented an attempt to regulate the medical profession in the field of assisted reproduction and did not address a criminal concern. The field of assisted reproduction was judged to be an area of provincial rather than federal jurisdiction, coming under the provincial powers over property and civil rights (s 92(13)) and matters of a merely local or private nature (s 92(16)). Hence these provisions were struck down as unconstitutional.

* *Reference re Assisted Human Reproduction Act*, 2010 SCC 61.

Determining the statute's pith and substance requires looking at its dominant purpose and effect. If the courts find that the dominant purpose and effect address an appropriate area—that is, an area that falls within the jurisdiction of the legislature that made the statute—the statute will pass the division-of-powers test and will be accepted as constitutional. On the other hand, the new legislation may not pass this test. For instance, if a provincial legislature enacts a statute whose dominant effect and purpose relate to criminal law, which is a federal area, the law will be declared unconstitutional (see Box 4.2).

OVERLAPPING JURISDICTION

Determining a law's *pith and substance* is sometimes complicated by the fact that a law has multiple purposes and effects. A law can relate to more than one jurisdictional area. If the areas overlapping in this way are either all federal areas or all provincial ones, there is no constitutional problem. However, if the law involves complete overlap between a federal subject area and a provincial one—that is, if it falls fully within the jurisdiction of each—the law is said to have a *double aspect*.

FIGURE 4.3 Double-Aspect Law

| Criminal Law: Section 91(27) | | Property and Civil Rights: Section 92(13) |

double-aspect law
a law whose subject matter falls within a federal subject area *and* a provincial one

A **double-aspect law** can be enacted by either legislative body—either by Parliament or by a provincial legislature. For example, many laws dealing with traffic offences have a double aspect, covered both by the federal criminal law power (s 91(27)) and by the provincial power over property and civil rights (s 92(13)). (See Figure 4.3.) A law that falls fully within an area that belongs to one level of government, but that merely touches on an area belonging to the other, is not a true double-aspect law. For these kinds of laws, only the level of government with complete jurisdiction over the area can pass them.

As we have mentioned, either Parliament or the provinces can enact double-aspect laws. But what happens if both levels of government pass laws in a shared jurisdictional area and the laws conflict with one another? To deal with this situation, the courts have developed the **federal paramountcy doctrine**, according to which, in the event of conflict, the federal law prevails over the provincial one.[7]

federal paramountcy doctrine
doctrine according to which, in the event of conflict between a federal law and a provincial law in an area over which both levels of government have jurisdiction, the federal law governs and overrides the provincial one

How Parliament Makes Statutes

New laws or amendments to old ones are usually a response to a perceived need for regulation in a particular area. They may be preceded by public hearings, commissions, or other forms of study, depending on the complexity of the issue addressed by the proposed legislation. The responsibility for drafting proposed legislation falls to legislative counsel employed by Parliament. With Canada's bicameral federal Parliament, both the House of Commons and the Senate are involved in making statutes.

INTRODUCING A BILL

bill
the draft version of a proposed new statute

A proposed statute is first introduced as a **bill** either in the House of Commons (as a Commons bill) or in the Senate (as a Senate bill). Most bills are first introduced in the House of Commons; on occasion, however, they are initiated by the Senate. There are two types of bills: *public bills* and *private bills*.

---

7 For a detailed discussion of federal paramountcy, see Peter W Hogg, "Paramountcy" in *Constitutional Law of Canada*, 2018 student ed (Toronto: Carswell, 2018) ch 16.

A **public bill** can belong to one of two categories, the first being the most common:

1. *Government bills.* Most of these bills deal with matters of public policy. They are usually introduced by a minister in the House of Commons, after being reviewed and approved by the federal Cabinet. In a formal written notice, the minister responsible for the bill asks the clerk of the House for leave to introduce it, and the minister gives it a title at this point. Leave to introduce the bill is granted without debate, questions, or amendments. Government bills are occasionally introduced not in the House but in the Senate. If they originate in the House of Commons, they are numbered consecutively, from C–1 to C–200, in the order in which they are introduced. Senate bills are numbered from S–1 upward, also in their order of introduction.
2. *Private members' bills.* These bills, also dealing with matters of public policy, are introduced by individual MPs, who are usually members of the opposition. They are numbered C–201 to C–1000.

A **private bill** is one that is introduced and sponsored by a government, opposition, or Senate member and that deals with a private matter—for example, a matter relating to a particular individual, corporation, or charity. Private bills introduced in the Commons are numbered C-1001 upward. Those introduced in the Senate are numbered S-1 upward as they are introduced, and are numbered together with, not separate from, public bills.

public bill
a bill dealing with a matter of public policy

private bill
a bill dealing with a private matter that relates, for example, to a particular individual, corporation, or charity

PASSAGE THROUGH PARLIAMENT

A bill's passage through Parliament, whether it is a public or a private bill, follows a set process. Parliamentary standing orders provide, among other things, the various procedural stages that all bills must pass through in order to become statutes. A federal bill requires six **readings**, three in the Commons and three in the Senate, followed by **royal assent**.

On a motion by its initiator, the bill is read for the first time in the House. At this stage, the House passes the motion without debate and makes no amendments to the bill. A date is then set for second reading. The bill is given an alphanumeric order number and printed in French and English. It is then distributed to all members of Parliament.

On the date fixed for the second reading of the bill, members of the House debate the bill's general principle and main features. Amendments are still not permitted. If the bill is approved for second reading, it is referred to a House of Commons committee. If the matter is urgent and the bill has been approved with unanimous consent or is a money bill, this committee may be a committee of the whole House. If not referred to a committee of the whole House, the bill will be referred to one of the House's standing, special, joint, or legislative committees. The committee examines the bill clause by clause and can make amendments at this point. Ministers and public servants may be called for explanations, and public input is sometimes invited.

Once a legislative committee has examined the bill, the committee reports its findings back to the House, with or without amendments. The House can either concur with the committee's recommendations or suggest (move) further amendments. A motion is then brought for the bill to be adopted and to proceed to the third reading.

The bill is read a third time. Debate is limited at this stage. A House vote is then held. If passed by the House of Commons, the bill goes to the Senate for approval.

reading
a bill's formal presentation to the legislature before it becomes a statute

royal assent
formal approval of a bill by the Queen's representative

BOX 4.3

Royal Assent

The ceremony of Royal Assent is one of the oldest of all parliamentary proceedings and brings all three elements of Parliament together (the Crown, the Senate and the House of Commons). Royal Assent is the stage that a bill must complete before officially becoming an Act of Parliament. A bill will not be given Royal Assent unless it has gone through all of the stages of the legislative process and been passed by both Houses in identical form [as shown in Figure 4.4].

Royal Assent may be granted in one of two ways: (1) through a written procedure, and (2) through the traditional ceremony, where Members of the House of Commons join with their Senate colleagues in the Senate Chamber.

The written procedure involves the Clerk of the Parliaments (the Clerk of the Senate), or his or her Deputy, meeting with the Governor General, or his or her Deputy, to present the bills with a letter indicating that they have been passed by both Houses and requesting that the bills be assented to.

An Act that has been given Royal Assent in written form is considered assented to on the day on which the two Houses of Parliament have been notified of the declaration. The *Royal Assent Act* preserves the traditional ceremony by requiring that it be used at least twice in each calendar year, including for the first bill in each session that authorizes government spending.

The traditional procedure for Royal Assent involves a formal ceremony that takes place in the Senate Chamber. When the House is sitting, it suspends its proceedings in order that its Members may proceed to the Senate Chamber, where the Governor General or his or her Deputy grants Royal Assent.

Once a bill has been granted Royal Assent, it becomes law and comes into force either on that date or at a date provided for within the Act or specified by an order of the Governor in Council.

Source: Reproduced from Parliament of Canada, "Compendium of Procedure: House of Commons Procedure Online," <http://www.parl.gc.ca/About/House/compendium/web-content/c_g_legislativeprocess-e.htm#2i>.

The bill must now pass through a similar process in the Senate. Bills that are first introduced in the Senate (less common than those introduced in the House of Commons) follow the same steps as those introduced in the House, except that the starting points are reversed: the first three readings are in the Senate, followed by three more in the House of Commons.

Once the final reading has been given to the bill, a motion is made for it to be given royal assent. After receiving royal assent, the bill becomes a statute. The pomp and pageantry of the royal assent ceremony is described in Box 4.3.

If a bill does not receive all required readings and royal assent before the end of the legislative session in which it was introduced (in other words, before the session *prorogues*), it "dies on the order paper." However, it can be reintroduced in the next session if the opposition consents.

Assuming all six readings and royal assent occur before the end of the session, the newly enacted statute is assigned a chapter number and is published in the *Canada Gazette* part III and, later, in annual statute volumes. The federal government also publishes electronic versions of its legislation. These were recently given official status alongside the print versions.

A bill becomes a statute once it receives royal assent, but it may not come into *effect* at this point. If a statute is silent on the question of when it comes into force, it is effective upon receiving royal assent. It may, however, specify some future date on which it comes into force, or it may indicate that it will come into force on a day to be fixed by **proclamation**. Or (very rarely) it may provide for retroactive effect, specifying a date prior to royal assent on which it is deemed to have come into force. With complicated statutes, different portions may come into force at different times and in different ways—some portions on receiving royal assent, some on specified dates, and others upon proclamation.

Figure 4.4 summarizes the statutory enactment process.

proclamation
a special government order bringing a statute into force

FIGURE 4.4 Federal Statutory Enactment Process

1. CANADIAN SOCIETY
Values, beliefs, politics, economics, wealth, capital, income, environmental issues, global events

2. PRE-PARLIAMENTARY RESPONSE
Consensus or conflict (public hearings, commissions, study papers, reports)

3. PARLIAMENTARY RESPONSE

HOUSE OF COMMONS OR SENATE	
1st Reading	• Bill is introduced on a motion • No debates or amendments
2nd Reading	• Bill is debated on its general principles and main features • Still no amendments are permitted
Committee Review	• Bill referred to committee after second reading • Committee examines proposed legislation, section by section, and can recommend amendments
3rd Reading	• Bill is read again with any recommended changes • Members vote

SENATE OR HOUSE OF COMMONS
For bills that begin in the House of Commons (C-bills, the majority of bills), the process above will be repeated in the Senate. For bills that begin in the Senate (S-bills), the process above will be repeated in the House of Commons. Federal bills, therefore, receive a total of six readings.

GOVERNOR GENERAL	
Royal Assent	• Bill is approved by governor general or representative • Formal ceremony

4. IMPLEMENTATION
• Proclamation (if statute requires)
• Regulations passed pursuant to statute (if required and statute authorizes)

Provincial Statutes

Provincial statutes are enacted by the provincial legislatures in each of the ten provinces. All provincial legislatures in Canada are elected bodies and are unicameral, with a single house involved in the legislative process.

With each provincial election, there is said to be a new "Parliament," even though the provincial bodies are called *assemblies* or *legislatures*. Like federal statutes, provincial statutes can be passed only while the legislature is in session, with sessions lasting one to two years on average but permitted, under section 4 of the Charter, to continue for as many as five years, at which point an election must be called. The Charter also requires that provincial elections be called at least once every five years. Thus, governing parties have as many as five years to advance their legislative agendas.

FIGURE 4.5 Federal/Provincial Legislature Standard Seating Arrangement

Provincial Jurisdiction

The principal sections of the *Constitution Act, 1867* that distribute power to the provincial assemblies are

- section 92 (many subject areas),
- section 92A (natural resources, forestry, and electrical energy),
- section 93 (education), and
- section 95 (agriculture and immigration—though the provinces share jurisdiction in these areas with the federal level of government).

Provincial laws, like federal laws, must be authorized under the Constitution to be valid.

Section 92 is the source of most provincial power. Although the provinces have no general residuary power comparable to federal POGG power, there is a reasonable balance of power between the provincial and federal levels of government. This is because a few areas deemed to be under provincial jurisdiction—for example, property and civil rights, and matters of a merely local or private nature—have been broadly interpreted. For a full account of the subject areas listed in section 92, see Table 4.2.

How Provincial Legislatures Make Statutes

The process of making provincial statutes is generally the same in each province. It is very similar to the federal process, with committee review between the second and third readings. Provincial bills, too, can be public or private; the vast majority are public government bills. One important difference between the federal and provincial processes is that provincial bills require only three readings, because there is only one chamber involved (there is no Senate). Royal assent follows the third reading.

After a bill receives three readings and royal assent, it becomes a statute. It is assigned a chapter number and is later published in print and electronic versions. Regarding when the statute comes into force, the same rules that apply to federal statutes apply to provincial ones. If the statute is silent about when it comes into force, it is effective upon royal assent. Alternatively, it may specify a date upon which it comes into force, or it may leave the date open, to be fixed by proclamation.

As with a federal bill, if a provincial bill does not receive all of the required readings and royal assent before the legislative session prorogues, it "dies on the order paper." If this happens, a provincial bill (like a federal one) can, with the opposition's consent, be reintroduced in the next session.

Territorial Statutes

Territorial statutes are enacted by the legislative assemblies in each of Canada's three territories: Yukon, the Northwest Territories, and Nunavut. All territorial assemblies in Canada are elected bodies and are unicameral, with just one house involved in the legislative process.

After each territorial election there is a new assembly. As with federal and provincial statutes, territorial statutes can be passed only while the assembly is in session. As with Parliament and the provincial legislatures, these sessions may last up to five years, as prescribed by the Charter (ss 4 and 30).

The Yukon assembly is party-based, as the provinces and Parliament are, but the Northwest Territories and Nunavut have a consensus style of government. These are the only two jurisdictions in Canada with Indigenous majorities, and the consensus style reflects the traditional decision-making customs of First Nations and Inuit peoples.

TABLE 4.2 Provincial Powers Under Section 92 by Category

CATEGORY	RELATED SUBSECTION(S) OF SECTION 92	NOTES
Taxation, money, and public assets	2. Direct Taxation within the Province in order to the raising of a Revenue for Provincial Purposes 3. The borrowing of Money on the sole Credit of the Province 5. The Management and Sale of the Public Lands belonging to the Province and of the Timber and Wood thereon 9. Shop, Saloon, Tavern, Auctioneer, and other Licences in order to the raising of a Revenue for Provincial, Local, or Municipal Purposes	The power of the provinces in this area, though more limited than Parliament's, is still significant. It is supplemented by part VIII of the *Constitution Act, 1867*. Forestry and natural resources are also covered by section 92A.
Property and civil rights	13. Property and Civil Rights in the Province	This category is a very important one for the provinces and has been interpreted to cover many specific areas, such as intraprovincial trade and commerce (business) (see also (11)), employment, regulation of the professions, contracts, torts, property, family law (see also (12)), civil liberties in the private sector, and many others.
Local matters	10. Local Works and Undertakings (subject to exceptions listed in the federal table, Table 4.1) 16. Generally all Matters of a merely local or private Nature in the Province	The scope of property and civil rights has relegated these headings to the role of "backup" jurisdiction in many instances.
Health care	7. The Establishment, Maintenance, and Management of Hospitals, Asylums, Charities, and Eleemosynary Institutions in and for the Province, other than Marine Hospitals	Health care is mainly provincial and comes under a number of different heads of power, including property and civil rights (13), local matters (16), and the power over hospitals ("Establishment, Maintenance, and Management") set out here (7). Parliament has jurisdiction over health matters under POGG power if they become serious enough to have national dimensions or to be classed as an emergency. Parliament also controls health care through substantial payments to the provinces. If a province wants to receive federal funding for health care, it must comply with national standards set out in the *Canada Health Act*.
"Provincial" crime and punishment	6. The Establishment, Maintenance, and Management of Public and Reformatory Prisons in and for the Province 15. The Imposition of Punishment by Fine, Penalty, or Imprisonment for enforcing any Law of the Province made in relation to any Matter coming within any of the Classes of Subjects enumerated in this Section	"True" crime is a federal jurisdiction, but the provinces have the power to proscribe and punish lesser offences, such as traffic and regulatory offences.
Courts	14. The Administration of Justice in the Province, including the Constitution, Maintenance, and Organization of Provincial Courts, both of Civil and of Criminal Jurisdiction, and including Procedure in Civil Matters in those Courts	Each province has jurisdiction generally over its own courts but it is partly a shared jurisdiction (see Chapter 6).
Miscellaneous	4. The Establishment and Tenure of Provincial Offices and the Appointment and Payment of Provincial Officers 8. Municipal Institutions in the Province 11. The Incorporation of Companies with Provincial Objects 12. The Solemnization of Marriage in the Province	At the time of Confederation, regional regulation in these areas was considered most efficient.

In both territories, members of the legislative assembly are elected as independent candidates, and there are no political parties. Unanimity is often achieved, though it is not required for decisions, such as the passage of motions or legislation. A majority vote often suffices.

Territorial Jurisdiction

The territories do not have an equivalent to section 92 of the *Constitution Act, 1867* assigning them areas of legislative jurisdiction. Each territory is under the control of Parliament, and the source of each territory's power is a federal statute that grants provincial-like legislative power to each of them. These statutes are the *Yukon Act*, the *Northwest Territories Act*, and the *Nunavut Act*.[8] They are not constitutionally entrenched and can be legally changed by Parliament at any time, despite legislated and political promises not to do so without first consulting the territories.

The organizational arrangement between Parliament and the territories is one of **devolution**. This is the name for a legislative arrangement whereby a central authority grants power to regional authorities that are subordinate to it. The organization of the UK, with subordinate regional elected assemblies in Scotland, Wales, and Northern Ireland, is an example of devolution. Another example is the provinces' delegating authority to municipalities to make by-laws.

devolution
the legislative arrangement whereby a central authority grants power to regional authorities that are subordinate to the central authority

Devolution involves the delegation of legislative authority, which occurs any time a legislature gives power to another body to make legislation on the legislature's behalf. The most common form of delegation is a statute's enabling another body to make regulations. (Regulations are described in the next section, "Subordinate Legislation.")

The legislative power that Parliament has granted the territories in their constituting statutes is similar to the power it has given the provinces. For example, section 18 of the *Yukon Act* states the following:

Legislative powers
    18(1) The Legislature may make laws in relation to the following classes of subjects in respect of Yukon:
        [(a)-(c), (g), (m), (n), (q), (r), (u)-(v) omitted]
        (d) the establishment and tenure of public offices in Yukon and the appointment, conditions of employment and payment of office-holders;
        (e) municipal and local institutions;
        (f) direct taxation and licensing in order to raise revenue for territorial, municipal or local purposes;
        (h) the incorporation of companies with territorial objects, other than railway, steamship, air transport, canal, telegraph or telephone companies, but including street railway companies;
        (i) the solemnization of marriage;
        (j) property and civil rights;
        (k) the administration of justice, including the constitution, maintenance and organization of territorial courts, both of civil and of criminal jurisdiction, and including procedure in civil matters in those courts;
        (l) the establishment, maintenance and management of prisons, jails or lock-ups;
        (o) education [clauses (i)-(ii) omitted]
        (p) immigration;
        (s) hospitals and charities;

---

8   Respectively, SC 2002, c 7; SC 2014, c 2, s 2; and SC 1993, c 28.

(t) agriculture;

(x) generally, all matters of a merely local or private nature;

(y) the imposition of fines, penalties, imprisonment or other punishments in respect of the contravention of the provisions of a law of the Legislature; and

(z) any other matter that may be designated by order of the Governor in Council.

Using the legislative powers granted them, the territorial assemblies have passed statutes equivalent to provincial statutes, such as taxation acts, motor vehicle acts, and human rights acts.

One constitutional question where the territories are concerned is whether Parliament actually has the power to delegate legislative jurisdiction to them in all the areas it has done. These are areas assigned to the provinces under the *Constitution Act, 1867* and not to Parliament. The specific source of Parliament's power to delegate authority to the territories is section 4 of the *Constitution Act, 1871*:

4. The Parliament of Canada may from time to time make provision for the administration, peace, order, and good government of any territory not for the time being included in any Province.[9]

The question is whether this statute—one of the statutes composing Canada's Constitution—gives Parliament the jurisdiction to delegate to the territories as it has done. So far, Parliament's power in this regard has not been challenged.

With their delegated power and their lack of constitutional entrenchment, the territories are legally analogous to municipalities. At the same time, the nature of their power, their geographical size, and their position on the national stage make them politically closer to provinces.

How Territorial Legislatures Make Statutes

Statute making in the territories is modelled on—and very close to—the provincial system. A public or private territorial bill becomes a statute after three readings, with a committee review between the second and third readings, followed by assent. Assent comes from a federal appointee to each territory, called a *commissioner*. When it comes to approving a bill, the commissioner's role in the territories is similar to that of the lieutenant governor in the provinces.

With respect to enactment, assent, and coming into force, territorial bills are like provincial or federal ones. The enactment process must be complete before the session prorogues, or the bill "dies on the order paper." Assuming it passes in time, the bill is reborn as a statute, is assigned a chapter number, and is later published in print and electronic versions. Territorial statutes, like other statutes, come into force on assent. Alternatively, a statute may specify a date upon which it comes into force, or it may leave the date open, to be fixed by proclamation. Or a territorial statute may come into force through a combination of these methods.

subordinate (or delegated) legislation
legislation passed pursuant to a statute whereby the principal lawmaking power has *delegated* authority to another body to make laws

Subordinate Legislation

Primary legislative bodies (in Canada, Parliament or the provincial legislatures) have the power to delegate their powers to subordinate bodies (see Chapter 11 for a more detailed discussion of delegated power). **Subordinate (or delegated) legislation** in Canada is legislation passed pursuant to federal or provincial statutes that authorize the delegation of power to

9   (UK), 34 & 35 Vict, c 28.

some entity to make subordinate legislation. This kind of legislation is made not by the principal law-making power but by the subordinate body to which the former has *delegated* authority to make laws.

TABLE 4.3   Provincial and Territorial Legislatures

PROVINCE/TERRITORY	NAME OF ASSEMBLY	MEMBER DESIGNATION*	SEATS
Alberta	Legislative Assembly of Alberta	MLA	83
British Columbia	Legislative Assembly of British Columbia	MLA	85
Manitoba	Legislative Assembly of Manitoba	MLA	57
New Brunswick	Legislative Assembly of New Brunswick	MLA	56
Newfoundland and Labrador	House of Assembly of Newfoundland and Labrador	MHA	48
Northwest Territories	Legislative Assembly of the Northwest Territories	MLA	18
Nova Scotia	Nova Scotia Legislature	MHA	52
Nunavut	Legislative Assembly of Nunavut	MLA	19
Ontario	Legislative Assembly of Ontario	MPP	107
Prince Edward Island	Legislative Assembly of Prince Edward Island	MLA	27
Quebec	National Assembly of Quebec	MNA	125
Saskatchewan	Legislative Assembly of Saskatchewan	MLA	58
Yukon	Yukon Legislative Assembly	MLA	18

* MLA = Member of the Legislative Assembly; MHA = Member of the House of Assembly
MPP = Member of the Provincial Parliament; MNA = Member of the National Assembly

There are two important limits on the primary legislator's power to delegate. They are as follows:

1. the primary legislator cannot give away its power to legislate completely, and
2. the primary legislator can delegate only powers within its jurisdiction.

Another general constitutional law principle relevant to this area is that of ***delegatus non potest delegare***. This means that the person or body to whom power is delegated cannot subdelegate it.

The main types of subordinate legislation are regulations and municipal by-laws.

Regulations

Regulations are closely related to statutes. They can be made only under the authority of a particular statute and are always associated with that statute. The section of the statute that delegates to another body—usually to the government Cabinet—the power to make regulations

delegates non potest delegare
principle that a person or body to whom power is delegated cannot subdelegate that power (Latin: "one to whom power is delegated cannot himself further delegate that power")

regulations
form of subordinate legislation passed by a person or body (frequently the government Cabinet) to expand on or fill out a statute's legislative scheme

is the *enabling section*. Not all statutes have regulations. Those that do are usually longer, more complex statutes.

Regulations are passed differently from statutes. They are not passed by means of a series of readings, followed by royal assent. To become law, they are simply drafted and approved by the relevant body, filed with a government registrar or clerk (federally, with the clerk of the Privy Council), and then published in the relevant *Gazette* (federally, *Canada Gazette* part II). Regulations are sometimes republished periodically in bound consolidations, like statutes. Almost all jurisdictions now publish ongoing loose-leaf and electronic versions of their regulations.

Regulations belong to one of two main categories:

1. "ordinary" regulations, and
2. rules of practice.

Ordinary regulations are simply referred to as *regulations*. They are passed under statutes for the purpose of filling in the details of a statutory regime. Because regulations are much easier to make, amend, or repeal than statutes, they are a more appropriate place to include legislative details (for example, procedural rules or fees) that are changed frequently. For example, the federal *Access to Information Regulations* were passed under the *Access to Information Act*.[10]

Rules of practice set out the procedure or practices to follow when pursuing particular types of claims, or when pursuing any kind of claim before particular courts or tribunals. Some examples of federal regulations that are rules of practice include the *Bankruptcy and Insolvency General Rules*, the *Rules of the Supreme Court of Canada*, and the *Federal Court Immigration Rules*.

When dealing with regulations, you should be aware not only of the statute authorizing a particular regulation but of the *general regulations statute* for the jurisdiction in question. This is a special Act that sets out the precise rules for the making and publishing of regulations. Regulations can be challenged if they fail to follow the procedure set out in the relevant regulations statute or if they exceed the mandate outlined in the enabling section.

Municipal By-Laws

municipal by-laws
form of subordinate
legislation passed
by municipalities

Municipal by-laws are like regulations in that they exist only in relation to a statute. Under section 92 of the *Constitution Act, 1867*, the provinces have power over municipalities. The federal government has likewise given power to the territorial assemblies to regulate municipalities. Municipal by-laws are created pursuant to provincial or territorial statutes and can be thought of as a special type of provincial or territorial regulation. The authorizing legislation for these by-laws can be a general municipal statute or a special charter for an individual city.

By-laws cover many topics. Some of the more familiar ones include property taxes, health and safety (for example, no-smoking areas), animals (for example, dog licensing and on-leash areas), structures and property maintenance (for example, clearance of snowy walkways), and business licensing.

---

10 RSC 1985, c A-1.

Quasi-Legislative Materials

Quasi-legislative materials are non-legislated written rules. Strictly speaking, they are not subordinate legislation, or in fact legislation at all, and as such they are not legally binding. However, they play an important role in some areas of the law. You must follow, observe, and consider these rules as you do legislated rules. If not, you risk having applications or documents rejected by the relevant authorities, delaying a legal process, or misunderstanding a related piece of legislation. Quasi-legislative materials relate to many different areas of the law. Examples of quasi-legislative materials include government policy statements (for example, policy statements or guidelines issued by tax departments or securities commissions explaining how they interpret certain legislative provisions), court directions (usually in the form of practice directives clarifying legislated procedural rules), and certain kinds of agreements (such as trade arrangements between different governments).

> **quasi-legislative materials**
> non-legislated written rules that relate to and affect a legal process

Parliamentary Sovereignty

The doctrine of **parliamentary sovereignty** holds that Parliament has total power. It is a doctrine that became entrenched in 17th-century England, as parliamentary power superseded that of the Crown. Thus Parliament, rather than the monarch, became recognized as the country's supreme legislative authority. Parliamentary sovereignty implies at least three principles:

> **parliamentary sovereignty**
> doctrine that Parliament has ultimate and complete power to pass any law

1. Parliament can make or unmake any law;
2. Parliament cannot bind itself against using its power in the future; and
3. a procedurally valid Act of Parliament cannot be questioned by the courts.[11]

In theory, these principles have been transplanted to Canada—part of the English political system we have inherited. In the Canadian context, however, the theory of parliamentary sovereignty is complicated by certain factors.

There are three features of the Canadian system that appear to qualify the notion of Parliament's "total power." First, we are a federation, with legislative power split between two levels of government, the federal and the regional. Second, we have an entrenched Charter (see Chapter 7) that limits the power of our legislators. Third, the power to amend the Constitution lies outside the sole jurisdiction either of Parliament or of the provinces.

Federalism and Parliamentary Power

As we have seen, Canada is a federal state, with split jurisdiction. This means that no legislative body in Canada has total power, as the UK Parliament does. However, it is accepted that we have modelled our system on the British one, which means that between the two levels of government (federal and provincial), there is no power vacuum—between them, there exists law-making power over *all* subject areas. They have the combined power to enact any law.

---

11   Hogg, *supra* note 7 at 12-1ff.

In *Reference re Same-Sex Marriage*,[12] the SCC affirmed this principle. As Hogg summarizes:

> The Supreme Court of Canada reaffirmed "the principle of exhaustiveness," which it described as "an essential characteristic of the federal distribution of powers." A "legislative void is precluded." It followed that "legislative competence over same-sex marriage must be vested in either Parliament or the Legislatures," and the most apt home for the matter was s 91(26) [federal].[13]

The conclusion we can draw from this is that, in our federal system, there are no limits on the *combined* power of the federal and provincial legislatures. Parliamentary sovereignty—of a kind—exists.

The Charter and Parliamentary Power

The next challenge to the notion of parliamentary sovereignty in Canada comes from the Charter. As an entrenched statute, it places limits on the powers of Parliament and the provincial and territorial legislatures to pass laws that offend the Charter's guaranteed rights and freedoms. These limits are qualified, however, by the notwithstanding or *override* clause (s 33), which allows legislators to pass legislation that would otherwise infringe many, though not all, of the Charter's provisions (see Chapter 7). To the extent that legislatures can override the Charter, parliamentary sovereignty remains *theoretically* intact; in practice, this clause is rarely invoked.

Constitutional Amendment and Parliamentary Power

Finally, we must address the fact that the power to amend the Canadian Constitution lies outside the unilateral jurisdiction of either Parliament or the provinces. This also seems a challenge to the doctrine of parliamentary sovereignty in this country. The answer to this is as follows. While it is true that, subject to a few limited exceptions, neither Parliament nor the provinces can amend the Constitution *unilaterally*, there is no "legislative void" here, either. Provided the two levels of government cooperate according to the legislative process established in part V of the *Constitution Act, 1982*, they can make any amendment to the Constitution, including to the Charter. Though they have yet to exercise this power successfully, it is available to them.

When we consider legislative authority in Canada as a collective of federal and provincial power, we see that the principle of parliamentary sovereignty applies in this country as it does in Britain. The English system has, at least theoretically, been transplanted onto Canadian soil. Of the three branches of government—legislative, executive, and judicial—the legislative branch is supreme. The executive and judicial branches are ultimately subject to its control.

Reading and Understanding Legislation

When looking at a piece of legislation, knowing a little about its structure and some basic rules of interpretation can help in the search for meaning. And knowing how legislation is

---

12 2004 SCC 79.

13 Hogg, *supra* note 7 at 12-5.

cited when referred to in legal writing is helpful when trying to locate it in the first place and to properly reference it. The following discussion of legislative structure, interpretation, and citation focuses on statute law, but most of it also applies similarly to subordinate legislation.

Structure of Statutes

All Canadian statutes have many structural components and features in common regardless of jurisdiction. The main elements of a statute are as follows (although not all elements—for example, tables of contents, schedules, and bilingual text—are present in every statute):

- title,
- chapter number or citation,
- table of contents,
- preamble,
- parts,
- sections,
- sectional endnotes (legislative history),
- marginal notes or headnotes,
- schedules, and
- bilingual text.

Title

Many statutes have lengthy titles that include the purpose of and reason for the legislation. In this case, the statute will usually contain, either at its beginning or its end, a section that provides a short title for the statute, and the statute will state that it can be cited by its **short title**. For example, Canada's criminal law is contained in a statute whose long title is *An Act Respecting the Criminal Law*. However, section 1 of this statute states that it may be cited as the *Criminal Code*. If no short title is provided, the statute is cited by its long title.

short title
abbreviated version of the full statute title

Chapter Number or Citation

The **chapter number** is usually set out just before or after the title. Sometimes the full citation is set out here, too. It identifies the statute's location in the relevant statute volume based on the legislative session or year in which it was passed or on the revision in which it was republished.

chapter number
the number assigned to a statute when it is first passed or when it is republished in a statutory revision—refers to the chronological position of the statute within a particular legislative session, year, or revision

Table of Contents

A table of contents at the beginning of a statute used to be uncommon. Tables of contents are becoming more common, however, owing to the recent emphasis on plain language and clarity of expression in legislation. A table of contents allows the reader to quickly scan the contents of the entire statute and pinpoint the section he is looking for. In many jurisdictions now, all statutes, long or short, complex or simple, have tables of contents.

Preamble

A statute may have a **preamble**—an introductory sentence or two that succinctly states the statute's key purpose. For example, the preamble to the *Constitution Act, 1867* states that Canada is to have a "Constitution similar in Principle to that of the United Kingdom." The preamble to the *Canadian Charter of Rights and Freedoms* states the following: "Whereas Canada is founded upon principles that recognize the supremacy of God and the rule of law." The preamble is an official part of a statute and can help courts interpret it. (Statutory interpretation is examined in the next section.)

Parts

Lengthy statutes are usually divided into large divisions, called *parts*, that are numbered consecutively. Each part contains the law pertaining to a specific subject area in the statute. For example, part XII of the *Criminal Code* pertains to offences relating to currency.

Sections

The basic "unit" of a statute is a **section**, also referred to as a *provision*. The body of a statute is made up of consecutively numbered sections. Depending on its level of complexity, a section may be subdivided further into subsections, paragraphs, and subparagraphs (and, if necessary, clauses and subclauses).

The sections of a statute typically include *definition sections, enabling sections, consequential amendment sections*, and *commencement sections*. A **definition section**, usually found at the beginning of a statute or part of a statute, defines words intended to have a specific meaning in the statute. For example, section 2 of the *Criminal Code* lists definitions for terms such as *bank note, day, explosive substance, motor vehicle*, and *weapon*. Apart from the definition section, the beginning of the statute may include other introductory sections that indicate the scope of the statute's application and how it is administered.

Some statutes require regulations to flesh out their legislative policy. For this to happen, the statute must authorize the passing of such regulations. The section in a statute that sets out this authority is called the **enabling section**. When researching statutes, always look for this possibility.

New statutes often affect existing legislation. A new statute may introduce a completely new set of laws in a particular area and by doing so amend existing legislation consequentially. Or the sole purpose of the statute may be to amend existing legislation. Usually the title of this latter type of statute has the word *amendment* in it, making its purpose clear—for example, *An Act to Amend the Controlled Drugs and Substances Act (methamphetamine and ecstasy)*.

To reconcile existing legislation with a new statute, the new statute will amend older statutes by way of a **consequential amendment section** or sections, usually located near the end of the statute. Often the changes are minor. For instance, if a new statute changes the name of a government department, all references to the old name in earlier statutes will have to be changed.

Some statutes have a **commencement (or coming-into-force) section**—a section that details when or how a statute comes into effect. As we have seen, the usual method of bringing statutes into force is to do so by proclamation at some unspecified time in the future. Other statutes, silent about when they come into force, do so upon receiving royal assent. But the coming into force of statutes is often delayed to allow governments time to make administrative adjustments to accommodate the new legislation. On occasion, too, statutes come into force retroactively. Such statutes will include a commencement (or coming-into-force) section.[14] This section will specify a date on which the statute or particular sections of it come or came into effect.

Sectional Endnotes (Legislative History)

Only consolidated or revised statutes include sectional endnotes. Placed at the end of each section of a revised statute, these endnotes give the reader details about the statute's legislative history. When a statute is first passed, there will be no sectional endnotes because the statute has no history at this point. In the case of a consolidated or revised statute, the reader may need to find out when the statute was first passed—to determine, for example, when particular legal rights granted by the statute accrued for the first time.

This information tells the reader when the section first appeared or if it appeared in a previous revision or consolidation. The first number is the year, session, or revision in which it first or previously appeared. The chapter number is next. The final detail is the section number or other pinpoint information. Some jurisdictions no longer include legislative history information in revisions or consolidations in the form of endnotes. Instead, they publish separate tables with this information.

Marginal Notes or Headnotes

In the margin beside sections of a statute are brief words or **marginal notes**, which summarize the contents of each section. For example, beside a section on definitions will be found the marginal note *Definitions*. The marginal notes are for guidance and ease of reference only. They do not qualify as part of the formal statute and cannot be used in interpretations of it. In some jurisdictions, the practice is to place the summaries *above* each section, in which case they are called **headnotes**.

marginal notes
notes in the margin beside a section briefly summarizing its contents

headnotes
notes immediately above a section briefly summarizing its contents, serving the same purpose as marginal notes

Schedules

Some statutes have schedules. Schedules set out information in the form of lists or tables, for the reader's convenience. For example, sometimes a lengthy list of consequential amendments is set out in a schedule. If a statute has a schedule, one or more sections will refer you to it. The schedule itself will likewise indicate what the referring section(s) is.

Schedules are part of the statute and should be read carefully if they concern the issue that you are researching. They can contain very important information. The most famous example is the *Canadian Charter of Rights and Freedoms*. As we have seen, the Charter is part of the *Constitution Act, 1982*, which is a schedule to another Act—the *Canada Act 1982*.

Bilingual Text

Federal and territorial statutes are bilingual. (Nunavut publishes its statutes in Inuktitut, too.) Among the provinces, Ontario, Quebec, Manitoba, and New Brunswick publish their statutes in both official languages. A few provinces—Saskatchewan, for example—publish certain statutes in both languages. The other provinces publish their statutes in English only. See Figure 4.6 for examples of some of these structural features.

---

14 Some jurisdictions, such as British Columbia, have recently started the practice of including a commencement section even when the statute or part comes into force on assent. Presumably this is for the sake of clarity and because most lay readers would be unfamiliar with the silence rule.

FIGURE 4.6   Structure of a Statute

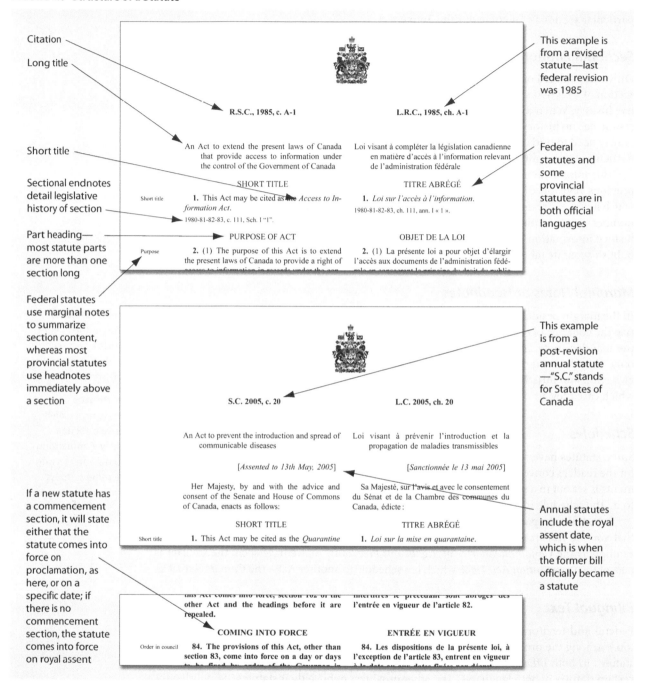

Citation

Long title

Short title

Sectional endnotes detail legislative history of section

Part heading—most statute parts are more than one section long

Federal statutes use marginal notes to summarize section content, whereas most provincial statutes use headnotes immediately above a section

If a new statute has a commencement section, it will state either that the statute comes into force on proclamation, as here, or on a specific date; if there is no commencement section, the statute comes into force on royal assent

This example is from a revised statute—last federal revision was 1985

Federal statutes and some provincial statutes are in both official languages

This example is from a post-revision annual statute —"S.C." stands for Statutes of Canada

Annual statutes include the royal assent date, which is when the former bill officially became a statute

Statutory Interpretation

Varying degrees of ambiguity inevitably exist in statutes, despite legislative counsels' best efforts to make them clear and consistent. Many statutes contain wording and phrasing that is unclear. When they are called upon, the responsibility falls to the courts to resolve the ambiguity.

Courts faced with such ambiguity must engage in **statutory interpretation**. To help with this process, the courts have developed common law rules over hundreds of years, and these rules have been supplemented with various legislated rules regarding interpretation. Ultimately, what the courts are trying to establish in these cases is **legislative intent**.

In Canada today, there are three main contexts in which courts are called upon to interpret statutes:

1. cases where the search is for jurisdictional meaning—that is, whether the legislation is within the authority of the enacting legislature (for example, when there is a division-of-powers issue);
2. cases concerned with whether the statute offends one or more of the rights and freedoms guaranteed by the Charter; and
3. cases where the search is for basic meaning—that is, there is no concern about the legislation's validity.

The following is an overview of the rules and interpretive guides the courts can draw on when construing legislation.

General Rules of Statutory Interpretation

The courts have developed a number of general rules regarding statutory interpretation. The first three—the mischief rule, the literal rule (or plain meaning rule), and the golden rule—are traditional common law rules that evolved over many centuries. The fourth one, the modern principle, borrows parts of these earlier rules, adds to them, and creates a single all-encompassing principle. The SCC has cited this latter principle with approval, and it is *the* approach to follow today.

MISCHIEF RULE

Using this rule, which was derived from a 1584 English precedent called *Heydon's Case*, a judge looks at more than just the statute's words. She examines Parliament's objective or purpose in enacting a statute in relation to the "mischief" or deficiency that the statute was intended to remedy or correct, and interprets the statute in accordance with this view.[15]

LITERAL RULE

Using this rule, which is sometimes called the *plain meaning rule* or *ordinary meaning rule*, a judge will not consider why the legislature passed a statute. The judge examines only the words and phrases of the statute itself—nothing more—and considers their ordinary sense or plain meaning. This rule entails a further consideration. When using it, a judge must interpret the legislation according to the meaning the words had at the time the statute was first enacted—that is, according to their original meaning and not to what their meaning may have become over time. These words and their ordinary plain—and original—meaning are followed, even if doing so leads to some injustice, difficulty, or absurdity. According to this rule, a judge must not assume that the legislature intended anything other than what is contained in the words of the statute itself.

statutory interpretation
process of interpreting legislation to resolve any ambiguities regarding its meaning or effect

legislative intent
a legislature's express or implied intent in passing a statute

---

15   Edmund Kwaw, *The Guide to Legal Analysis, Legal Methodology, and Legal Writing* (Toronto: Emond Montgomery, 1992).

GOLDEN RULE

This rule, based on the 1857 English case of *Grey v Pearson*, modifies the literal or plain meaning rule. The court in the *Grey* case stated that the ordinary sense or literal meaning of a statute's words are to be adhered to unless doing so "would lead to some absurdity, or some repugnance or inconsistency with the rest of the instrument, in which case the grammatical and ordinary sense of the words may be modified, so as to avoid the absurdity and inconsistency, but no farther."[16] Using this rule, a judge will modify only the problematic words of a statute. For example, a court could read a statute's *and* as an *or* under circumstances where a conjunctive set of conditions (as established by the *and*) would lead to an absurd result.

MODERN PRINCIPLE

In modern times, attempts have been made to unify the general rules. For example, Parliament enacted section 12 of the *Interpretation Act*, which provides as follows: "Every enactment is deemed remedial, and shall be given such fair, large and liberal construction and interpretation as best ensures the attainment of its objects."[17] The provinces and territories have similar provisions in their interpretation acts.

Elmer Driedger, summing up the modern principle (as he called it) in his seminal book on statutory interpretation, wrote the following:

> Today, there is only one principle or approach, namely, the words of an Act are to be read in their entire context and in their grammatical and ordinary sense harmoniously with the scheme of the Act, the object of the Act, and the intention of Parliament.[18]

Driedger's summary captures the spirit of the *Interpretation Act* provision and of the modern principle. See Box 4.4.

BOX 4.4

The Modern Principle: An Illustration

To illustrate how the modern principle might apply, assume that a province passed a traffic safety statute that contained a provision making it an offence for a "motorized vehicle" to "park on a road in a travelling lane." Assume further that the statute also included provisions dealing with speeding, obeying traffic signs, littering, and various other matters concerning the safe use of roads. If a propeller-driven light-sport airplane made an emergency landing on a road and came to a stop straddling the centre line, would a "parking" offence have been committed? The words describing the offence cover this situation in a literal sense (that is, a "motorized vehicle" has parked in the manner described), but, reading the offence provision in context and harmoniously with the object of the legislation, a court might conclude that the offence only covered vehicles designed to travel on roads and not aircraft landing on roads in cases of emergency.

---

16   *Ibid* at 126.

17   *Interpretation Act*, RSC 1985, c I-21, s 12.

18   Elmer A Driedger, *Construction of Statutes* (Toronto: Butterworths, 1974) at 67. Professor Driedger's text continues to be published, but with the fifth edition, his name has been dropped. See Ruth Sullivan, *Sullivan on the Construction of Statutes*, 5th ed (Toronto: LexisNexis, 2008).

The SCC has cited the modern principle with approval in a number of its decisions. In 2011, in the *Celgene* case, the court was called upon to interpret some provisions in the *Patent Act*. Abella J, writing for the court, stated the following:

> The parties both relied on the approach used in *Canada Trustco Mortgage Co. v. Canada*, 2005 SCC 54, [2005] 2 S.C.R. 601, at para. 10, which confirmed that statutory interpretation involves a consideration of the ordinary meaning of the words used and the statutory context in which they are found:
>
> > It has been long established as a matter of statutory interpretation that "*the words of an Act are to be read in their entire context and in their grammatical and ordinary sense harmoniously with the scheme of the Act, the object of the Act, and the intention of Parliament*": see *65302 British Columbia Ltd. v. Canada*, [1999] 3 S.C.R. 804, at para. 50. The interpretation of a statutory provision must be made according to a textual, contextual and purposive analysis to find a meaning that is harmonious with the Act as a whole. When the words of a provision are precise and unequivocal, the ordinary meaning of the words plays a dominant role in the interpretive process. On the other hand, where the words can support more than one reasonable meaning, the ordinary meaning of the words plays a lesser role. The relative effects of ordinary meaning, context and purpose on the interpretive process may vary, but in all cases the court must seek to read the provisions of an Act as a harmonious whole.
>
> The words, if clear, will dominate; if not, they yield to an interpretation that best meets the overriding purpose of the statute.[19]

In all statutory interpretation cases, then, a "textual, contextual, and purposive analysis" is nowadays the approach to take. We might sum up this approach as follows:

- *textual analysis* focuses on the meaning of the words read by themselves,
- *contextual analysis* focuses on the meaning of the words in the context of the whole statute, and
- *purposive analysis* focuses on the meaning of the words in light of the underlying purpose or object of the Act.

Driedger's principle refers to all of these things. What the SCC appears to be adding to his principle is the dominance of the words themselves—provided they are clear—in the interpretive process.

In his classic 1938 article on statutory interpretation, John Willis, after describing the traditional common law rules concerning interpretation, wrote as follows:

> Having inquired into the difference between the three familiar approaches and discussed the manner in which each is applied, we are now in a position to ask the final question which was posed at the beginning. … [W]hich of these approaches does a court prefer and when? … A court invokes whichever of the rules produces a result that satisfies its sense of justice in the case before it.[20]

---

19   *Celgene Corp v Canada (AG)*, 2011 SCC 1 at para 21 (emphasis added).

20   John Willis, "Statute Interpretation in a Nutshell" (1938) 16 Can Bar Rev 1.

Today, courts may and still do refer to the spirit of one or more of the three traditional common law rules—the mischief rule, the literal rule (or plain meaning rule), and the golden rule. However, given the position now taken by the SCC on statutory interpretation, the courts' guide in the final analysis must now be the modern principle.

Grammatical Rules

In addition to general rules of interpretation, the courts have developed some specific rules to help them construe grammatical patterns commonly found in statutes. These rules and patterns are as follows:

- *ejusdem generis,*
- *noscitur a sociis,*
- *expressio unius est exclusio alterius,*
- and/or,
- means/includes, and
- must/may.

EJUSDEM GENERIS

The *ejusdem generis* rule ("of the same kind or class") dictates that where two or more specific words (or phrases) in a statute belong to the same class and are followed by general words, the general words should be interpreted to be of the same type or class as the specific words preceding them. For example, if a statute states that "no dogs, cats, or other animals may wander in public places without being controlled by means of a leash," how should "other animals" be interpreted? According to the *ejusdem generis* rule, in this example "the specific words preceding the general phrase refer to the class of domestic animals, hence squirrels and rabbits would not fall within the provision."[21]

NOSCITUR A SOCIIS

The second grammatical rule is known as *noscitur a sociis* ("it is known by its associates"). Here, a general word in a statute can be interpreted as referring to things that are in the same class as other things specifically referred to in the same context. For example, if a statute states that "no vehicles, bicycles, skateboards, or scooters can enter this park," the general word *vehicles* could be interpreted as referring to a vehicle in the same class as bicycles, skateboards, or scooters—in other words, a recreational vehicle. This means that someone might be permitted to enter the park in a wheelchair—a non-recreational vehicle.

EXPRESSIO UNIUS EST EXCLUSIO ALTERIUS

The third grammatical rule is known as *expressio unius est exclusio alterius* ("to express one thing is to exclude another"). What this rule means is that if something was left out of a statute, it was meant to be left out. For example, as one commentator has said, "[a] by-law that applies to owners of orange, blue, red, green, black, and yellow cars would not, it could be argued, apply to owners of brown cars."[22]

---

21 Kwaw, *supra* note 15 at 130.

22 Ted Tjaden, *Legal Research and Writing* (Toronto: Irwin Law, 2001) at 76.

AND/OR

Many statutes list elements or conditions that relate to a definition or rule. Sometimes these lists are conjunctive, and sometimes they are disjunctive. With a conjunctive list, the last two items are connected by an *and*. In this case, *all* elements or conditions must be present to satisfy the definition or rule. If the last two items are connected by an *or*, it is a disjunctive list, and *only one* element or condition needs to be present to satisfy the definition or rule.

The definition of the Constitution of Canada, as described earlier, is an illustration of a conjunctive list. Section 52 of the *Constitution Act, 1982* states the following:

> 52(2) The Constitution of Canada includes
>> (a) the *Canada Act 1982*, including this Act;
>> (b) the Acts and orders referred to in the schedule; *and*
>> (c) any amendment to any Act or order referred to in paragraph (a) or (b).
> [Emphasis added.]

This is a *conjunctive* list, and all the items listed are part of the definition.

The definition of culpable homicide in criminal law gives us an example of a *disjunctive* list. Homicide, of course, is when a person causes the death of another human being. Culpable homicide can be murder, manslaughter, or infanticide, and is defined in the *Criminal Code* as follows:

> 222(5) A person commits culpable homicide when he causes the death of a human being,
>> (a) by means of an unlawful act;
>> (b) by criminal negligence;
>> (c) by causing that human being, by threats or fear of violence or by deception, to do anything that causes his death; *or*
>> (d) by wilfully frightening that human being, in the case of a child or sick person.[23]

According to the and/or rule of statutory interpretation, the homicide is culpable if any one of the conditions listed above is present.

These examples are relatively straightforward. In more complex provisions, there can be lists within lists. For example, each paragraph could have a list of subparagraphs joined disjunctively or conjunctively. A reading of these provisions that takes careful note of the *ands* and *ors* will help determine the various relationships.

MEANS/INCLUDES

Statutes often refer to general concepts or tests. Then, to provide greater clarity, they go on to provide specific examples. When the word *means* precedes the examples, it indicates that the definition is complete and the list exhaustive. Conversely, the word *includes* or *including* before a list indicates an open definition and a non-exhaustive list.[24]

Again, section 52 of the *Constitution Act, 1982* provides an illustration:

> 52(2) The Constitution of Canada *includes*
>> (a) the *Canada Act 1982*, including this Act;
>> (b) the Acts and orders referred to in the schedule; and
>> (c) any amendment to any Act or order referred to in paragraph (a) or (b).
> [Emphasis added.]

---

23 RSC 1985, c C-46, s 222(5) (emphasis added).

24 Donald J Gifford, Kenneth H Gifford & Michael I Jeffery, *How to Understand Statutes and By-Laws* (Toronto: Carswell, 1996) at 66-68.

The SCC has held that the word *includes* in section 52(2) permits an expansive interpretation; in other words, this list of the Constitution's contents is not an exhaustive one. In the *New Brunswick Broadcasting* case, accordingly, the SCC found that the unwritten doctrine of parliamentary privilege was included in the Constitution of Canada even though it was not listed in the definition.[25]

MUST/MAY

The word *must* is commonly used today to signify mandatory action or inaction; it implies a duty and the absence of discretion. The word *shall* was used to the same effect in older legislation and is still used in some jurisdictions. The word *may*, on the other hand, signifies discretionary rather than mandatory action; it confers the power to do something, but does not make it a duty. The following section from BC's *Motor Vehicle Act* illustrates the use of both *must* and *may*. Generally, drivers have a duty to stop at an intersection if there is a red light. However, bus drivers have a limited power to enter intersections on a red light:

> 129(1) Subject to subsection (2), when a red light alone is exhibited at an intersection by a traffic control signal, the driver of a vehicle approaching the intersection and facing the red light *must* cause it to stop … before entering the intersection. …
>
> (2) The driver of a bus approaching an intersection and facing a red light and a prescribed white rectangular indicator *may* cause the bus to proceed through the intersection.[26]

Internal Aids to Interpretation

Definition sections, usually located at the beginning of a statute or the part of the statute to which they relate, define specific words used in the legislation and should always be consulted. Words may have a special or unusual meaning within the statute.

The long or short titles of a statute, along with part headings, can be used to help determine the statute's purpose and scope. This can help, in turn, with the interpretation of the wording of a specific provision. The same applies to the preamble.

Marginal notes, headnotes, and endnotes can be helpful, but they are for ease of reference only and should not be used as the basis for interpretation. Section 14 of the federal *Interpretation Act* states the following: "Marginal notes and references to former enactments that appear after the end of a section or other division in an enactment form no part of the enactment, but are inserted for convenience of reference only."[27]

External Aids to Interpretation

DICTIONARIES

Judges sometimes consult legal dictionaries for assistance in defining a word. *Black's Law Dictionary*, a respected American reference text, is one example. Canadian legal dictionaries include Yogis's *Canadian Law Dictionary* and Dukelow's *Dictionary of Canadian Law*.

---

25 See *New Brunswick Broadcasting Co v Nova Scotia (Speaker of the House of Assembly)*, [1993] 1 SCR 319, 1993 CanLII 153. See also Hogg, *supra* note 7 at 1-9.

26 *Motor Vehicle Act*, RSBC 1996, c 318, s 129 (emphasis added).

27 *Interpretation Act*, RSC 1985, c I-21, s 14. See also the provincial and territorial equivalents.

WORDS AND PHRASES REFERENCE SETS

There are legal reference works dealing specifically with words and legal phrases whose meanings have been considered by judges in previous cases. Carswell's *The Canadian Abridgment: Words & Phrases Judicially Defined in Canadian Courts and Tribunals* is one of the most comprehensive Canadian sets. Carswell also publishes *Sanagan's Encyclopedia of Words and Phrases, Legal Maxims*, which also focuses exclusively on interpretations from Canadian courts and tribunals.

INTERPRETATION ACTS

The federal, provincial, and territorial *Interpretation Acts* also define words that are intended to have a specific meaning whenever they are used in legislation.[28] However, the definitions provided by these general statutes are always subject to contrary definitions in particular statutes. When reading a statute, you must consult both the statute's definition section(s) and the relevant jurisdiction's *Interpretation Act* if you have doubts about the meaning of particular words.

HANSARD

Hansard, the common name for legislative debates, is the written record of parliamentary proceedings. Judges sometimes refer to it, especially for the purpose of determining Parliament's intent in passing a specific statute. However, judges have disagreed on whether *Hansard* can or cannot be used in all instances to help interpret a statute.[29]

Interpreting Bilingual Statutes

As noted earlier, federal and territorial statutes are published in both official languages, as are the statutes of Ontario, Quebec, Manitoba, and New Brunswick. A few provinces, such as Saskatchewan, publish select statutes in both languages, and the other provinces publish their statutes in English only. Where statutes are published in both languages, the English and French versions are usually arranged in columns side by side. Depending on the precise wording in a particular bilingual statute, there may be subtle differences in meaning between the two versions.

According to various constitutional provisions (including s 133 of the *Constitution Act, 1867*, s 23 of the *Manitoba Act, 1870*, and s 18 of the Charter), as well as the SCC's interpretation of these provisions, federal and territorial statutes—as well as the statutes of Quebec, Manitoba, and New Brunswick—must be enacted in both official languages, and both versions must be considered equally authoritative. One version is not paramount over the other; both have equal status when it comes to their application.

The shared meaning rule dictates the primary approach to interpreting bilingual statutes from these jurisdictions. Under this rule, both the French and English versions must be read together, and "the meaning that is shared by the French and English versions is presumed to be the meaning intended by the legislature."[30] In other words, recognizing that translations may

---

28 See for example *Interpretation Act, ibid*; *Interpretation Act*, RSA 2000, c I-8; *Interpretation Act*, RSBC 1996, c 238; *Interpretation Act*, RSNS 1989, c 235; *Legislation Act*, SO 2006, c 21, Schedule F (Part VI); *Interpretation Act*, RSY 2002, c 125.

29 See Gifford, Gifford & Jeffery, *supra* note 24, ch 27.

30 Ruth Sullivan, *Statutory Interpretation*, 3rd ed (Toronto: Irwin Law, 2016) at 98.

not always be able to provide an exact equivalency, to the extent that both the English and the French texts share a meaning, that is considered to be what is intended. Interpreting bilingual legislation is a matter of getting at this common meaning.

Citation of Legislation

Canadian legislation, like cases and other legal sources, are cited according to specialized rules. There are many such rules, too many to discuss comprehensively here; below, we offer only the basic ones. See the *Canadian Guide to Uniform Legal Citation* (or "McGill Guide," for short) for more in-depth coverage.[31]

Proper citation of legal sources is expected in legal writing and provides information necessary to locate the exact source referred to. Members of the legal community are not in complete agreement about what the rules for citation should be. In Canada, however, courts, law schools, law offices, and legal publications are increasingly adopting the rules set out in the McGill Guide. That is the guide we follow in this text. The following is a look at the basic rules for citing the two most common forms of legislation: statutes and regulations.

STATUTES

The citation for a statute generally consists of the following components: title, jurisdiction and year, chapter, and section.

TITLE

The title or name of the statute is cited first. As noted above, a statute often has a long title. If the title is long, and if the statute also has a short title, the statute is cited by its short title. The title is italicized.

JURISDICTION AND YEAR

The next part of the citation refers to the statute's jurisdiction and year. Abbreviations are always used to indicate which jurisdiction enacted the statute and the year it was enacted or, for older statutes, the most recent revision in which it appeared. For example, a federal statute enacted in 2012 would be published in the *Statutes of Canada* 2012 volume, which is abbreviated *SC 2012*. For older statutes appearing in the *Revised Statutes of Canada* 1985—the most recent federal revision—the abbreviation is *RSC 1985*.

Statutes are published in hardbound volumes at the end of the year in which they are enacted. Federal statutes are also published every three months in a softcover volume of the *Canada Gazette* part III. This ensures that a print version of all federal statutes is available soon after they are enacted. The hardbound volumes in which they are published are called *annual* or *sessional* volumes. Today, statutes are also published electronically.

revised statutes
republished, revised collection of all public statutes for a jurisdiction, providing a comprehensive statutory "snapshot" as of the revision date

Periodically, print versions of a jurisdiction's entire catalogue of public statutes are re-published in hardbound **revised statutes** volumes. A statute revision is a "snapshot" of all public statutes in a jurisdiction as of the revision date. All amendments or changes to the statutes are incorporated into the revised versions of the statutes. Repealed statutes are not included in the revision. Most jurisdictions also publish ongoing loose-leaf revisions and online consolidations.

---

31 McGill Law Journal, *Canadian Guide to Uniform Legal Citation*, 9th ed (Toronto: Carswell, 2018).

FIGURE 4.7 Components of a Statutory Citation

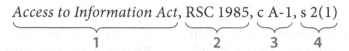

Access to Information Act, RSC 1985, c A-1, s 2(1)

1   2   3   4

1   Title
The title is italicized, followed by a comma (not italicized) and a space.

2   Jurisdiction and Year
The jurisdictional reference is abbreviated, then a space and the year, followed by a comma and another space. In this example of a federal revised statute, "R" is for revised, "S" is for statutes, and "C" is for Canada. If it were an annual statute it would be just "SC". Each province and territory has its own abbreviation—for example, "A" for Alberta, "BC" for British Columbia, and "M" for Manitoba. When citing provincial or territorial statutes, "RS" or "S" would precede the relevant jurisdictional abbreviation. The *Canadian Guide to Uniform Legal Citation* has a comprehensive listing of abbreviations used in legal citations of all types.

3   Chapter
Chapter is abbreviated to "c". Then comes a space and the numeric or alphanumeric designation ("A-1"), followed by a comma and another space if there is a section reference.

4   Section
Section is abbreviated to "s". Then comes a space and the number along with any subdivisions, which are placed in parentheses with no spaces in between. Regardless of the particular level or sublevel being referred to, when written as part of a full citation, it always begins with the abbreviation for section, "s". When spoken, the level is noted. For example, at the third level, you would say, "section 2, subsection 1, paragraph b."

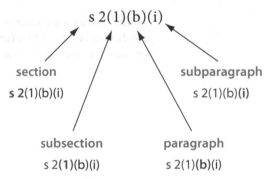

The Subdivisions of a Section

s 2(1)(b)(i)

section
s 2(1)(b)(i)

subparagraph
s 2(1)(b)(**i**)

subsection
s 2(**1**)(b)(i)

paragraph
s 2(1)(**b**)(i)

CHAPTER

As soon as a bill becomes a statute, it is assigned a chapter number. From that point on, it is properly referred to by its statute citation rather than its bill number. (Sometimes we find the news media continuing to use the bill number in cases where the bill has achieved some notoriety.) *Chapter* is abbreviated as a lowercase *c*. Statutes in the annual or sessional statute volumes are ordered according to their chapter numbers (numeric).

When statutes are republished in a revision, they are assigned new chapter numbers (sometimes numeric and sometimes alphanumeric) to correspond with their position in the consolidation. For example, when the *Access to Information Act* was first enacted in the 1980-1983 federal legislative session, it was cited as *Access to Information Act*, SC 1980-81-82-83, c 111. When it was republished in the 1985 revision, it was given a new citation: *Access to Information Act*, RSC 1985, c A-1.

SECTION

You will often need to refer to a specific section(s) of a statute. If so, the abbreviations used are *s* for *section* and *ss* for *sections* (with no periods, according to the McGill Guide rules). Sections can be broken down into subdivisions (called *subsections*), paragraphs, and subparagraphs (and sometimes further still, into clauses and subclauses), depending on their complexity.

Regulations

Regulations are cited, much like statutes, according to their chapter or other number in a consolidation or according to the year in which they were made and to their chronological number for that year. Including the title is optional. Older federal regulations that appear in the 1978 consolidation (the most recent one) are abbreviated *CRC* for "Consolidated Regulations of Canada." If they are more recent, they are abbreviated *SOR* for "Statutory Orders and Regulations." Provincial regulations are usually abbreviated by province, and *regulation* is shortened to *Reg*. Older Ontario regulations appearing in the 1990 revision are cited as *RRO* ("revised regulations of Ontario").

The following are some sample citations from federal and provincial regulations:

- *Coastal Fisheries Protection Regulations*, CRC, c 413, s 12;
- *Citizenship Regulations*, SOR/93-246;
- *Federal Court Immigration Rules*, r 10;
- *Clean and Renewable Resource Regulation*, BC Reg 291/2010, s 2; and
- *Critical Defects of Commercial Motor Vehicle Regulation*, O Reg 512/97, s 1.

The citations for rules of practice are simpler than those for ordinary regulations. The jurisdiction is set out first (unless it's clear from the title), followed by the title, which is not optional, and then the rule number. *Rule* is abbreviated *r*. The regulation number is omitted.

CHAPTER SUMMARY

There are three branches of government: the legislative branch, the executive branch, and the judicial branch. The legislative branch is the most powerful of the three, with ultimate control over the other two.

The legislative branch is the supreme law-making authority. The doctrine of parliamentary sovereignty holds that our legislatures, collectively, can make or unmake any law. The divided jurisdiction between federal and provincial levels of government can in theory be brought together to make law in any area, including changes to the Constitution. Also, some provisions in the Charter can be overridden by the different levels of government on their own, in respect of their laws, through a special procedure. *Total* legislative power—including the power to amend our Constitution—has resided in Canada only since the patriation of our Constitution in 1982 (before then, legislative power was shared in part with the British Parliament).

In our federal union, the power to make legislation is divided more or less equally between Parliament and the provinces. Broadly speaking, Parliament has jurisdiction over matters of national importance, and the provinces have jurisdiction over private law and local matters. Parliament has devolved, or delegated, province-like jurisdictional authority to the territories.

Making statute law in this country follows set procedures whereby a bill is introduced into the legislative chamber, and after a number of readings, followed by royal assent, it becomes a statute. Also, pursuant to some statutes, authority is delegated to other bodies to make subordinate legislation, such as regulations and municipal by-laws. As well, we are subject to certain non-legislated rules, such as policy statements, issued by various government agencies. Collectively, this growing mass of regulation touches on almost every aspect of our lives.

Knowing about the structure of legislation and relevant interpretative approaches is helpful in determining the intended meaning of legislation. Regardless of the enacting jurisdiction, Canadian statutes and regulations are structured similarly. Common elements include a title; a body of text divided into sections; and schedules, which provide information best conveyed in the form of lists or tables. When interpreting ambiguous wording in legislation, the courts employ various rules (such as the modern principle, which focuses on the ordinary meaning of words read in context and considering the object of the legislation) and interpretive aids (such as legal dictionaries). Finally, understanding the basics of legal citation protocols can help law professionals and researchers locate and reference relevant legislation accurately. Citations provide the reader with details such as the enacting jurisdiction and the year of enactment (or publication).

KEY TERMS

bicameral, 92

bill, 104

chapter number, 117

commencement (or coming-into-force) section, 118

consequential amendment section, 118

constitutionally entrenched, 94

definition section, 118

delegates non potest delegare, 113

devolution, 111

division of powers, 97

double-aspect law, 104

enabling section, 118

federal paramountcy doctrine, 104

headnotes, 119

judicial review on Charter grounds (or Charter challenge), 97

jurisdiction, 95

legislation, 93

legislative intent, 121

legislature, 92

marginal notes, 119

municipal by-laws, 114

parliamentary sovereignty, 115

POGG power, 99

preamble, 118

private bill, 105

proclamation, 106

prorogue, 99

public bill, 105

quasi-legislative materials, 115

reading, 105

regulations, 113

revised statutes, 128

royal assent, 105

section, 118

separation-of-powers doctrine, 92

short title, 117

statutes, 93

statutory interpretation, 121

subordinate (or delegated) legislation, 112

supremacy clause, 96

unicameral, 92

FURTHER READING

BOOKS

Funston, W Bernard & Eugene Meehan. *Canada's Constitutional Law in a Nutshell*, 4th ed (Toronto: Carswell, 2013).

Gifford, Donald J, Kenneth H Gifford & Michael I Jeffery. *How to Understand Statutes and By-Laws* (Toronto: Carswell, 1996).

Hogg, Peter W. *Constitutional Law of Canada*, 2018 student ed (Toronto: Carswell, 2018).

McGill Law Journal. *Canadian Guide to Uniform Legal Citation*, 9th ed (Toronto: Carswell, 2018).

Monahan, Patrick J, Byron Shaw & Padraic Ryan. *Constitutional Law*, 5th ed (Toronto: Irwin Law, 2017).

Régimbald, Guy & Dwight Newman. *The Law of the Canadian Constitution*, 2nd ed (Toronto: LexisNexis, 2017).

Sullivan, Ruth. *Statutory Interpretation*, 3rd ed (Toronto: Irwin Law, 2016)

Sullivan, Ruth. *Sullivan on the Construction of Statutes*, 6th ed (Toronto: LexisNexis, 2014).

The Constitutional Law Group. *Canadian Constitutional Law*, 5th ed (Toronto: Emond, 2016).

WEBSITES

Gateway Site for Canadian Legal Databases

Canadian Legal Information Institute (CanLII): <http://www.canlii.org>.

Canadian Legislature and Legislation Databases

Federal

Parliament of Canada: <http://www.parl.ca>.

Justice Laws Website: <http://laws.justice.gc.ca/eng/>.

Alberta

Legislative Assembly of Alberta: <http://www.assembly.ab.ca>.

Alberta Laws: <http://www.qp.alberta.ca/Laws_Online.cfm>.

British Columbia

Legislative Assembly of British Columbia: <http://www.leg.bc.ca>.

British Columbia Laws: <http://www.bclaws.ca>.

Manitoba

Legislative Assembly of Manitoba: <http://www.gov.mb.ca/legislature>.

Manitoba Laws: <http://web2.gov.mb.ca/laws>.

New Brunswick

Legislative Assembly of New Brunswick: <http://www.gnb.ca/legis>.

New Brunswick Laws: <http://www2.gnb.ca/content/gnb/en/departments/attorney_general/acts_regulations.html>.

Newfoundland and Labrador

House of Assembly of Newfoundland and Labrador: <http://www.assembly.nl.ca>.

Newfoundland and Labrador Laws: <http://www.assembly.nl.ca/legislation>.

Nova Scotia

Nova Scotia Legislature: <http://nslegislature.ca>.

Nova Scotia Laws: <http://www.gov.ns.ca/just/acts.asp>.

Ontario

Legislative Assembly of Ontario: <http://www.ontla.on.ca>.

Ontario Laws: <http://www.e-laws.gov.on.ca>.

Prince Edward Island

Legislative Assembly of Prince Edward Island: <http://www.assembly.pe.ca>.

Prince Edward Island Laws: <https://www.princeedwardisland.ca/en/legislation/all/all/a>.

Quebec

Assemblée Nationale Québec: <http://www.assnat.qc.ca/fr/index.html>.

Québec Laws: <http://www.justice.gouv.qc.ca/english/sites/lois/quebec-a.htm>.

Saskatchewan

Legislative Assembly of Saskatchewan: <http://www.legassembly.sk.ca>.

Saskatchewan Laws: <http://www.qp.gov.sk.ca>.

Northwest Territories

Legislative Assembly of the Northwest Territories: <http://www.assembly.gov.nt.ca>.

Northwest Territories Laws: <http://www.justice.gov.nt.ca/en/legislation/>.

Nunavut

Legislative Assembly of Nunavut: <http://www.assembly.nu.ca>.

Nunavut Laws: <http://www.nunavutlegislation.ca/>.

Yukon

Legislative Assembly of the Yukon: <http://www.legassembly.gov.yk.ca/>.

Yukon Laws: <http://www.justice.gov.yk.ca/legislation/index.html>.

REVIEW QUESTIONS

1. What are the three branches of government in Canada, and what is the function of each?

2. List the four types of statutes in Canada.

3. Describe the process for enacting a federal statute, from the introduction of a new bill to the statute's coming into force.

4. What does it mean to say that a statute is "constitutionally entrenched"? Name and briefly describe two entrenched statutes under the Canadian Constitution.

5. What is POGG power?

6. What is a double-aspect law? How is conflict between federal and provincial double-aspect laws resolved?

7. What is the source of territorial power to make statutes?

8. What are the two main types of regulations? Briefly explain each.

9. Name two types of quasi-legislative materials and explain why it is important to have a working knowledge of them.

10. Describe the doctrine of parliamentary sovereignty and its relation to the separation-of-powers doctrine as applied in Canada.

11. Describe the modern principle of statutory interpretation.

EXERCISES

1. Research the website for the legislative assembly in your province or territory. Find and read all available information about the assembly's location, its members, and the legislative process it follows.

2. Go to the Supreme Court of Canada judgments website (<http://scc-csc.lexum.com>) and type "division of powers" (in quotation marks) in the Decisions search field. Scan through the judgments to find one of interest to you, and then read the case to determine how the SCC resolved the argument about which level of government had jurisdiction to enact the challenged legislation.

3. Visit the federal Justice Laws website (<http://laws-lois.justice.gc.ca>). Click the Consolidated Acts link under the Laws sidebar heading. Search through the alphabetical listing of statutes and choose one of

interest to you. Locate as many of the structural features of statutes discussed in Appendix 4.1 (for example, the title, preamble, part headings, and different types of sections) as you can.

4. Consider the idea of parliamentary sovereignty in the context of Canadian Confederation, and discuss whether you believe that legislative power considered in its totality *should* be limited (and if so, how any limits could be imposed). If not, consider whether legislative power is, in practical terms, sufficiently limited or too limited. Provide specific examples and reasons for your opinion.

5. Locate the following statutes online and provide full citations according to the format outlined in the final section of this chapter:
   - *Identification of Criminals Act* (federal)
   - *Gaming and Liquor Act* (Alberta)
   - *Sale of Goods Act* (Ontario)
   - *Official Tree Act* (Nova Scotia)
   - *Legal Profession Act* (Yukon)

5 The Executive: The Second Branch of Government

Canada's longest-serving prime minister, William Lyon Mackenzie King (centre), at a meeting with his Cabinet ministers in the Privy Council Chamber in the East Block of Parliament (1930).

After reading this chapter, you will understand:

- The nature of executive power.
- The Canadian system of responsible government.
- The key sources of executive power in Canada.

- The concept of Crown immunity.
- The basic limits of executive power.

---

executive
the branch of government that is responsible for administering or implementing the laws in Canada and whose authority, in this country, is divided between the federal, provincial, and territorial governments based on the division of legislative authority under the Constitution

responsible government
system of government in which the members of the executive branch are drawn from the elected members of the legislative branch and in which their power continues only so long as they enjoy the support of the majority in the legislature

There is no [clear] separation of legislative and executive functions in the Canadian context. The key members of the executive, the prime minister and the Cabinet, must hold seats in Parliament. The government also has the power to control and direct the affairs of the House of Commons. In part, this control is derived from the fact that, in accordance with the principles of responsible government, the government controls a majority of seats in the House of Commons. It can therefore be assured that most of its legislative proposals will be adopted by [Parliament].

Patrick J Monahan, Byron Shaw & Padraic Ryan, *Constitutional Law*,
5th ed (Toronto: Irwin Law, 2017) at 102

Introduction

In this chapter, we explore the second branch of government, the **executive**, which is responsible for administering and implementing our laws. In Canada, it is common to refer to the executive branch simply as *the government*, although it is, technically, only one of the three branches of government.[1] As noted in the quotation above and in the introduction to the previous chapter, in Canada there is no clear separation between the first two branches of government: the executive branch, while it enjoys the support of the majority in the legislature, controls the legislative branch.

In this section, we look at our system of responsible government, the various sources of executive power, and some of the limits of executive power.

Responsible Government

Our system of government evolved in the UK over hundreds of years and is known as **responsible government**. This system was formally recognized and named in Great Britain

---

1   In the US, it is more common to refer to the executive as *the administration*, particularly in reference to the federal executive branch.

in 1835. In 1848, Nova Scotia became the first colony in the British Empire to adopt the system. In 1867, with Confederation, responsible government became the system for the new country of Canada.

Three main features distinguish the system of responsible government:

1. a dual executive;
2. elected office (that is, members of the political executive must have elected seats in the legislature); and
3. reliance on **convention** (that is, agreed-upon customary practice).

Dual Executive

Peter Hogg describes the system of responsible government in the Canadian context as follows:

> In a system of responsible government, there is a "dual executive," consisting of a formal head of state and a political head of state. The *formal* head of state for Canada is the Queen, but she is represented in Canada by the Governor General of Canada and the Lieutenant Governors of the provinces. ... The *political* head of state for Canada is the Prime Minister, who is the leader of the party that commands a majority in the elected House of Commons. In each province, the equivalent of the Prime Minister is the Premier, who is the leader of the party that commands a majority in the elected Legislative Assembly.[2]

The formal head of state and chief executive in Canada, then, is the British monarch—that is, the **Crown**. At the time of Confederation, this was Queen Victoria. Since 1952, it has been Queen Elizabeth II. The Queen "reigns" in Canada through her representatives: the governor general at the federal level, and the lieutenant governors at the provincial level. Legally, according to the Constitution, the Queen and her representatives wield executive power in Canada.

As we will see, however, this legal power has passed, by convention, to the Queen's representatives in council—that is, the federal and provincial Cabinets, who hold the *real* executive power. Most people examining our Constitution for the first time find it confusing that formal executive power, as spelled out in the *Constitution Act, 1867*,[3] is so divorced from political reality, and that the Constitution contains no mention of the prime minister of Canada or the provincial premiers.

Elected Office

The second distinctive feature of the Canadian system of responsible government is that the members of the political executive must have elected seats in the legislature. (In rare instances, non-elected members may be appointed to Cabinet, but they are

convention
established and traditional "rules" on which our system of responsible government is based and which qualify many of the rules of government set out in constitutional legislation, such as the *Constitution Act, 1867*, but which are not, technically, legally binding

Crown
the sovereign (currently the Queen), whose authority in Canada has been formally delegated to the governor general (federally) and to the lieutenant governor (provincially), but is actually exercised by the executive branch of government

FIGURE 5.1 Under the Constitution, Queen Elizabeth II, as the reigning British monarch, is the formal head of the executive government in Canada. Here, she is seen meeting with Governor General Julie Payette, her federal representative, in the library at Balmoral Castle in Scotland in 2017.

---

2   Peter W Hogg, *Constitutional Law of Canada*, 2018 student ed (Toronto: Carswell, 2018) at 9-2 (emphasis in original).

3   (UK), 30 & 31 Vict, c 3, reprinted in RSC 1985, Appendix II, No 5.

required to seek election within a reasonable time after appointment.) The members of the political executive are "responsible" to the legislature in the sense that they must enjoy the confidence of the majority of the assembly. And the elected members of the assembly must, in turn, have the support of the people or risk losing their seats in the next election. In the US system, by contrast, the members of the president's Cabinet need not be elected.

The classic model of government from which ours is derived requires a clear separation of powers between the legislative, executive, and judicial branches. However, our system of responsible government, with its (by and large) elected Cabinet, significantly modifies this classic model. In Canada, as we have seen, the executive exercises significant control over the legislature. At the same time, the executive maintains its authority only while it has the support of the majority of the elected assembly. In the US, by contrast, the administration, federally and at the state level, is not part of the legislative branch. If there is a political divide between the two branches—if, for example, the administration is Democratic and the legislative branch is predominantly Republican—the administration will simply have less say in the legislative agenda.

Convention

Perhaps the most surprising aspect of responsible government is that, as Peter Hogg has said, "the rules which govern it are almost entirely 'conventional,' that is to say, they are not to be found in the ordinary legal sources of statute or decided cases."[4] When we say that the rules are "conventional," we mean that they are based on tradition and past practice rather than on principles set out in formal documents. While there may be political consequences for not following these practices, the Supreme Court of Canada has ruled that conventions are not legally binding.[5] Again, the US model serves as a contrast to the Canadian system of responsible government; in the US, the national system of government is clearly spelled out in its written Constitution.

It should be noted that, despite the ruling of the SCC, it is the view of some commentators that responsible government does—or at least should—have "legal" constitutional status in Canada. Their view is based on the preamble clause to the *Constitution Act, 1867*, which states that we have "a Constitution similar in Principle to that of the United Kingdom." They interpret the preamble clause to mean that the rules of responsible government (though they may have been merely conventional in the UK) have become constitutionally entrenched in Canada.

Sources of Executive Power

What are the sources of executive power in Canada? Our constitutional legislation is one source, especially the *Constitution Act, 1867*. But this legislation does not fully define the extent of executive power in the Canadian government. Convention, too, plays an essential

---

4 Hogg, *supra* note 2 at 9-5.

5 See *Reference re a Resolution to amend the Constitution*, [1981] 1 SCR 753, 1981 CanLII 25. This case dealt with whether the federal executive could, without the unanimous consent of all provinces, approach the UK Parliament to request an amendment to the *Constitution Act, 1867* that would affect provincial powers. There was a convention that such consent was required. The SCC held that because conventions are not legally binding, the federal government could ignore past practice without offending the law. In other words, it is not the role of the courts to enforce constitutional conventions. Whether there would be political consequences if such conventions were breached was another matter.

role in this area. Also relevant are certain common law and statutory (federal, provincial, and territorial) rules. We examine all of these sources of executive power in this section.

Constitutional Basis

The *Constitution Act, 1867* contains many of the key constitutional provisions dealing with formal executive power in Canada. These provisions include the following: all of part III (ss 9-16), relating to federal executive power, and sections of part V (ss 58-68), concerning provincial executive power.

Peter Hogg summarizes these provisions as follows:

> [Section] 9 provides that the "executive government" of Canada is vested in "the Queen"; s. 10 contemplates that the Queen's powers may be exercised by a "Governor General"; and s. 11 establishes a "Queen's Privy Council for Canada" whose function is "to aid and advise in the government of Canada" and whose members are to be appointed and removed by the Governor General. ...
>
> In each province, there is a "Lieutenant Governor" and an "Executive Council" with powers similar to those of the Governor General and Privy Council [ss. 58-68]. The Lieutenant Governors are appointed by the Governor General in Council (s. 58).[6]

The *Constitution Act, 1867* does not make it expressly clear who is responsible for appointing the **governor general**, but by implication it is the reigning British monarch, and this is the practice that is followed. By convention, however, the British monarch appoints the governor general on the advice of the prime minister. Similarly, the Governor General in Council (often shortened to **Governor in Council**), that is, the federal Cabinet, appoints the provincial lieutenant governors on the advice of the prime minister.

Early in our history, there was a question about the nature of the power of the **lieutenant governor**, given that he was an appointee of the federal Cabinet. Did he, like the governor general, represent the Crown, or was he a delegate of the Governor in Council? The answer to this question was significant. If the lieutenant governor represented the Crown, he would be vested with all the executive powers and prerogatives of the Crown in relation to provincial matters. However, if he were merely a delegate of the federal Governor in Council, his power would be limited to whatever that committee expressly delegated to him. In the latter case, all executive power in Canada would be federally controlled. The Judicial Committee of the Privy Council (that is, the British appeal court, not to be confused with Queen's Privy Council for Canada) ruled in 1892 that lieutenant governors are representatives of the Crown, not delegates of the federal Cabinet.

The governor general and lieutenant governors also play a part in the legislative process. Under sections 17 and 55 of the *Constitution Act, 1867*, the governor general (it could also be the Queen) is required to sign federal bills as a final formal step before they become law. Similarly, the lieutenant governors are required to sign provincial bills into law (s 90). This last step of the legislative process, as described in Chapter 4, is known as royal assent; it is another example of how the Canadian system of government has modified the separation-of-powers doctrine with respect to the executive and legislative branches.

The *Constitution Act, 1982*[7] includes an important constitutional provision relating to executive power. Section 44 of the Act provides that Parliament "may exclusively make laws

governor general
Queen's representative in Canada, formally authorized to exercise her powers as head of the executive government in Canada, but who, by convention, exercises these powers only on the advice of the prime minister and federal Cabinet

Governor in Council
official name for the federal Cabinet

lieutenant governor
formal head of the provincial executive government who, by convention, exercises executive power on the advice of the provincial premier and Cabinet

---

6   Hogg, *supra* note 2 at 9-6.
7   Schedule B to the *Canada Act 1982* (UK), 1982, c 11.

amending the Constitution of Canada in relation to the executive government of Canada." So far, this amendment power has not been used.

On the surface, then, it looks like formal executive power in Canada resides with the British monarch and her representatives, with few restrictions on their power. For instance, a literal reading of section 55 of the *Constitution Act, 1867* would suggest that the Queen has unlimited discretion to refuse to sign into law any legislation she doesn't like and thereby to bring the law-making process in Canada to a halt.

Conventional Practice

As mentioned, responsible government in Canada is primarily based on convention rather than on principles explicitly set out in the Constitution. Knowing the conventional practice in this area is important because it qualifies—that is, modifies—the rules explicitly set out in the Constitution.

Are there any situations where the governor general or lieutenant governor (or the Queen, for that matter) could—acting independently, without the advice of Cabinet ministers appointed by the prime minister—exercise the legal power vested in them under the Constitution without offending conventional practice? When might this option seem compelling? Possibilities include where confidence conventions are being rejected or ignored—for example, where

- a government refuses to resign after losing the confidence of the majority of members in the legislature;
- a prime minister or premier refuses to resign after losing an election; or
- a prime minister or premier wants to call an election immediately after one had just taken place, with the aim of increasing her party's number of seats.

Faced with these situations, the governor general or lieutenant governor (or the Queen) could, in theory, exercise the legal powers granted by the Constitution legal powers in opposition to the political executive. In other words, if the political executive government were ignoring the conventional constraints on its power, the Queen's representative—the governor general or the lieutenant governor—could use his legal power to override the government. She could force a government to resign, call an election, or refuse to call an election. Has this ever happened?

There have been instances in our history where governors general and lieutenant governors have independently exercised their legal powers of reservation and disallowance (essentially refusing to grant royal assent) to prevent bills from becoming statutes. Their power to do so is set out in sections 55-57 and section 90 of the *Constitution Act, 1867*. But they have not exercised this power in over 50 years. Most likely, a modern convention has developed according to which the Queen's representatives are never to use these powers. This means that if a government wants to push through a truly objectionable law, it can do so, but then must answer for it not to the Queen's representatives but to the electorate alone (and perhaps to the courts if the new law offends the Charter).

Key Conventions

prime minister
the political head of
state in Canada who
leads the party with
control of the majority in
the House of Commons

The following are some important conventional practices relating to the federal executive:

- *Prime minister.* The political executive is headed by the leader of the political party that controls the majority of Parliament (either by way of an outright party majority or, in the case of a minority government, by way of a coalition with other parties)—namely, the **prime minister**.

- *Cabinet*. Section 11 of the *Constitution Act, 1867* provides that the governor general has the aid and advice of the **Queen's Privy Council for Canada**, referred to more informally as the Privy Council. By convention, the key members of the Privy Council are the Cabinet ministers appointed by the prime minister, with appointments made on a representative basis (with at least one Cabinet minister from each province, if possible). The Cabinet (or Governor in Council) is the part of the Privy Council that, under the direction of the prime minister, has members who currently sit as members of Parliament. There are other members of the Privy Council, including former ministers of government, whose status is nominal rather than practical; they have no real influence. It is extremely rare for the entire Privy Council to meet, and when it does it is usually for ceremonial purposes. As noted above, *Governor General in Council* is generally taken to refer to the federal Cabinet and is often shortened to *Governor in Council*. When legislation refers to the Governor General in Council or Governor in Council, it means the federal Cabinet.

- *Political and legislative agenda*. The prime minister takes the lead in setting the government's agenda as well as the composition, organization, and procedures of Cabinet. Cabinet ministers also play a role in policy development, particularly within their portfolios.

- *Ministerial responsibility*. Although the government stands or falls as one, individual ministers are responsible in the sense that they are the executive heads of their portfolios and must take responsibility not only for their own actions but for those of their subordinates within the ministry as well. Ministers are also required to answer to Cabinet and to Parliament for their activities within the Ministry.

- *Confidence convention*. Arguably, the most important convention of all is the **confidence convention**. If the government loses the support of the majority of the elected representatives in the House of Commons, the confidence convention requires the government to resign, and, if a new government cannot be formed, it must call an election.

Most of these conventions apply, with certain modifications, to the provinces (see Figure 5.2). The political head provincially is the **premier**. The lieutenant governor is appointed by the governor general under the Constitution, but, by convention, the governor general follows the recommendation of the premier. The **Lieutenant Governor in Council** is the official name for the provincial Cabinet. The provincial Executive Councils, as they are referred to in part V of the *Constitution Act, 1867*, are made up exclusively of current Cabinet ministers; there are no "outsiders" as there are with the federal Privy Council.

Similar conventions apply in Yukon and the Northwest Territories. Although, as we saw in Chapter 4, the territories are federal dependencies, their executive governments operate much as the provincial ones do. The federal government appoints a **commissioner** who acts as the formal head of the territorial executive government. The **Commissioner in Executive Council** is the official name for a territorial Cabinet. The system is different in Nunavut; it operates according to a system of consensus democracy, not responsible government, and it has no political parties.

The political reality, then, concerning executive power is that it differs significantly from the legal reality spelled out in the Constitution. Does it matter that our administration operates according to a set of rules that are not legally enforceable? Does it matter that those with legal power—namely, the governor general and the lieutenant governors—are expected not to use it except as directed by political leaders? Perhaps not, as long as everyone involved respects and accepts the system. So far, this has been the case in Canada. But

Queen's Privy Council for Canada
formal advisory council of the governor general, the active portion of which is the federal Cabinet

confidence convention
convention requiring the government to resign if it loses the support of the majority of the elected representatives in the House of Commons and, if a new government cannot be formed, to call an election

premier
the political head of a provincial or territorial government who leads the party with control of the majority in the Legislative Assembly (in Nunavut, there are no political parties, but the premier must command the support of the majority in the Assembly)

Lieutenant Governor in Council
official name for a provincial Cabinet

commissioner
federally appointed official who is the formal head of the territorial executive government

Commissioner in Executive Council
official name for a territorial Cabinet

there is no guarantee that it will always be the case. Arguably, in times of extreme political uncertainty, rules based on convention are less stable than those enshrined in law.

FIGURE 5.2   Executive and Legislative Government in Canada

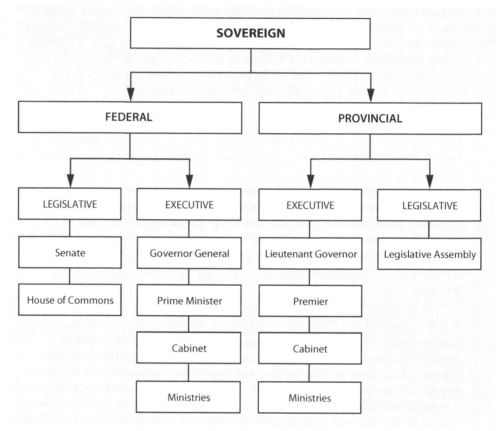

Common Law and Royal Prerogative

royal prerogative
powers and privileges given by the common law to the Crown; a source of limited executive power

The power of the British Crown to legislate by decree or otherwise was limited by the *Magna Carta* (see Box 1.7 in Chapter 1.) and was finally taken over completely by Parliament when the English *Bill of Rights* (1689) was passed (see "Sources of Law" in Chapter 2.) Similarly, the Crown lost the right to adjudicate disputes, criminal and civil, early in its legal history. This was confirmed in the 1607 *Case of Prohibitions*, in which Chief Justice Edward Coke stated the following for the court: "[No] King after the Conquest assumed to himself to give any judgment in any cause whatsoever, which concerned the administration of justice within this realm, but these were solely determined in the Courts of Justice."[8]

royal proclamation
public announcement of a formal order concerning some executive action based on royal prerogative, such as a declaration of war

However, the Crown had long exercised *executive* authority. The expression **royal prerogative** refers to one of the sources of the Crown's executive authority. Royal prerogative is exercised through various kinds of orders, which have different names depending on the context. One of them is the **royal proclamation**. This is a formal order concerning some executive action, such as declaring war, and it announces this action to subjects of the realm. For example, the *Royal Proclamation of 1763*, issued by King George III after the end

---

8   See *Prohibitions Del Roy*, [1607] EWHC KB J23, 12 Co Rep 63, 77 ER 1342.

of the Seven Years' War, was meant to organize Great Britain's new North American empire and to stabilize relations with North American Indigenous peoples.

Another class of order, expressing the royal prerogative in a more limited way, consists of **letters patent**. These are usually orders that establish rights, titles, or offices of particular persons or corporations. In 1947, for example, King George VI officially constituted the office of the governor general in Canada by letters patent—although the office had already been constituted, by implication, under the terms of the *Constitution Act, 1867*.

The Crown's ability to *independently* exercise prerogative power survived much longer than its adjudicative and legislative powers. But this independent prerogative power, too, came to be curtailed as responsible government took hold in the 1700s. Since then, it has been exercised only on the advice of the prime minister and Cabinet (with a few exceptions, as in matters relating to the royal family itself).

The common law courts have defined the exact nature and extent of the Crown's prerogative. It is therefore a part of the common law and not a separate source of law. As Peter Hogg writes,

> The royal prerogative consists of the powers and privileges accorded by the common law to the Crown. Dicey described it as "the residue of discretionary or arbitrary authority, which at any given time is left in the hands of the Crown." The prerogative is a branch of the common law, because it is the decisions of the courts which have determined its existence and extent.[9]

In Canada, royal prerogative survives and is exercised by the federal and provincial Cabinets, or—to give these bodies their more formal titles—by the Governor General in Council (or Governor in Council) and the Lieutenant Governors in Council. As mentioned, even though the lieutenant governors are appointed by the governor general, they are also representatives of the Crown. Because we are a federation, the Crown's executive authority is split between

1. the federal Crown (or Crown in right of Canada), which exercises prerogative in relation to matters under its legislative authority; and
2. the provincial Crown (or Crown in right of Alberta and other provinces), which exercises prerogative in relation to matters under its legislative authority.

Prerogative Power Today

Many executive actions that were at one time authorized by prerogative power are now authorized by statute. For example, the power to confer honours such as the Queen's Counsel (QC) designation on lawyers (usually conferred by the provincial Crown) is now based on legislation. The *Queen's Counsel Act* in BC, for example, contains the following provision:

> 2(1) On the recommendation of the Attorney General, the Lieutenant Governor in Council, by letters patent under the Great Seal, may appoint, from among the members of the Bar of British Columbia, Provincial officers under the names of Her Majesty's Counsel learned in the law for the Province of British Columbia.[10]

letters patent
orders, based on royal prerogative, that establish rights, titles, or offices of particular persons or corporations

---

9   Hogg, *supra* note 2 at 1-18.

10   *Queen's Counsel Act*, RSBC 1996, c 393, s 2(1).

Examples of Prerogative Power

A well-known example of prerogative power is the federal Crown's power to grant mercy in criminal cases. The *Criminal Code* provides that nothing in it "in any manner limits or affects Her Majesty's royal prerogative of mercy."* Although its exact bounds are not entirely clear, the royal prerogative of mercy (RPM) is considered a far-reaching power that includes all forms of clemency, from free pardons (total expungement of a conviction together with its record) to conditional pardons (expungement, but with the record kept) to the remission or reduction of sentences. The RPM is traditionally associated with the commutation of a death sentence to prison time—an instance of RPM that no longer applies in Canada because we abolished the death penalty in 1976.

Some other areas where prerogative power is exercised, as Hogg has noted, include the following:

- conduct of foreign affairs, including making treaties;
- declarations of war;
- appointment of the prime minister and other ministers;
- issuance of passports; and
- creation of Indian reserves.[†]

The power to appoint provincial premiers and ministers is an example of the provincial Crown's prerogative power.

*   *Criminal Code*, RSC 1985, c C-46, s 749.

†   Peter W Hogg, *Constitutional Law of Canada*, 2018 student ed (Toronto: Carswell, 2018) at 1-21.

This general trend toward statutory authority has reduced the actual scope of prerogative power. Even where a general prerogative power continues to exist, as in the case of the royal prerogative of mercy (confirmed in s 749 of the *Criminal Code*), statutes may provide authority in the same area. For example, sections 748 and 748.1 of the *Criminal Code* deal with pardons and remissions of fines and forfeitures. Such legislative duplication reduces the need to resort to prerogative power.

The nature of royal prerogative—as well as executive authority that was once based on royal prerogative but is now legislated—can be characterized as either authorizing or *restricting* conduct, depending on the particular prerogative in question. For example, royal prerogative sometimes authorizes conduct or action by the Crown (such as the power to make treaties or declare war). But royal prerogative also includes a restrictive aspect, by imposing limits on the Crown's responsibilities in certain circumstances. In particular, the courts have developed rules relating to Crown immunity (see the next section). For examples of prerogative power, see Box 5.1, above.

Statute

The main source of executive power today is statutory law. Federal, provincial, and territorial statutes assign specific executive powers to their respective governments.

Most ministries or departments have their own statutes that define, among other things, the powers and duties of the responsible minister. For example, the *Department of Health Act*[11] and the *Department of the Environment Act*[12] grant the federal minister of health and the minister of the environment, respectively, specific executive authority. The pattern is the same at the provincial and territorial levels. For example, Ontario's *Ministry of Energy Act*[13] grants specific administrative powers to the Ontario minister of energy; Saskatchewan's

---

11   SC 1996, c 8.

12   RSC 1985, c E-10.

13   SO 2011, c 9, Schedule 25.

Department of Social Services Amendment Act[14] gives such powers to the Saskatchewan minister of social services; and the Yukon *Education Act*[15] empowers the Yukon minister of education. There are many statutes of this kind.

The various powers granted to ministers by these various federal, provincial, and territorial statutes include the authority

- to enter into contracts to facilitate ministry business,
- to hire and manage staff, and
- to pursue actions to enforce the liabilities of others.

Sometimes, when it comes to particular matters over which the responsible minister has general administrative control, the legislation will grant executive power to the entire Cabinet or impose a Cabinet approval requirement. In BC, for example, the *Ministry of Environment Act* requires the minister of the environment to gain Cabinet approval before entering into agreements with other provincial governments or with the federal government.[16]

There are many statutes creating institutions under the control of the executive government. For example, there are statutes that authorize

- setting up and regulating the armed forces and the national security service (the Canadian Security Intelligence Service, or CSIS);
- setting up and regulating law enforcement agencies (such as the Royal Canadian Mounted Police, or RCMP, and the Canada Border Services Agency, or CBSA); and
- setting up administrative boards and tribunals to regulate almost every area of society, from energy to human rights to transportation.

Finally, where statutes come into force by proclamation, the Cabinet is almost always given the power to fix the date of their coming into force. This makes sense, given that the Cabinet is well informed about new legislation and receives regular reports about it. The proclamation language for federal statutes states that the act comes into force "by order of the Governor in Council."

The proclamation language for provincial and territorial statutes is less settled. It might say that the act commences "by order of the Lieutenant Governor in Council," "by regulation of the Lieutenant Governor in Council," or "by proclamation." Yukon legislation states that legislation comes into force on dates fixed "by the Commissioner in Executive Council." In the Northwest Territories and Nunavut, the commissioner for the territory, not Cabinet, is assigned the administrative power to proclaim statutes in force.

Again, in modern times, statutory law has become the main source of executive authority. In other words, most day-to-day executive power finds its basis in legislation that confers authority on Cabinets and individual ministers.

Crown Immunity

Crown immunity is sometimes seen as part of the law of royal prerogative. It includes the Crown's immunity from liability as well as any privileges and presumptions that operate in favour of the Crown. It is a complicated area, and a detailed examination of all the issues

Crown immunity covering term for the various protections afforded the Crown, including Crown privilege, the presumptions of legislation not applying to the Crown, and (formerly) immunity from tortious liability

---

14 SS 1996, c 13.

15 RSY 2002, c 61.

16 *Ministry of Environment Act*, RSBC 1996, c 299, s 6.

involved in it is beyond the scope of this text (for example, we do not discuss Crown immunity from criminal liability and its limits). However, a basic awareness of the area is important.

To Whom It Applies

Crown immunity in Canada today, when it does apply, applies to the federal Crown, to the provincial Crown (that is, the federal and provincial Cabinets), and also to agents of the Crown. Not all government bodies or organizations are "agents" of the Crown. There are three factors determining which of them meet this qualification:

1. the legislation that constitutes (and defines) them,
2. the degree of authority granted to the organization by Cabinet, and
3. the degree of Cabinet's control over the organization.

Generally speaking, the more closely the organization is associated with and controlled by Cabinet, the more likely it is to qualify as a Crown agency and to be afforded the same protections as the Crown. But there are many government agencies that operate at arm's length from the executive, are not considered agents of the Crown, and are not accorded the same privileges.[17]

There are three main forms of Crown immunity:

1. Crown privilege,
2. the presumption against legislation applying to the Crown, and
3. Crown immunity in civil cases.

Crown Privilege

Crown privilege
aspect of Crown immunity that permits the Crown to claim that evidence is privileged on the ground that its disclosure would adversely affect some matter of public interest

Crown privilege, also known as "public interest immunity," is an evidentiary rule that originates in common law. It permits the Crown to claim that evidence relevant to the case at hand—evidence that ordinarily would have to be disclosed—is privileged on the ground that its disclosure would adversely affect some matter of public interest. Such privileged areas might include, for example, matters of national security or defence, and certain Cabinet communications.

Federally, the *Canada Evidence Act*[18] now codifies the rules relating to public interest immunity, so Crown privilege no longer needs to be claimed at common law.[19] At the provincial level, Crown privilege exists, but it is qualified according to the common law, statutory rules, and combinations of the two. Both under the common law and statutory rules, Crown privilege is restricted and involves a balancing of interests—on the one hand, the interest of

---

17 It should also be noted that Crown corporations are not necessarily Crown *agents*. At the federal level, for example, Atomic Energy of Canada Limited, Canada Post Corporation, the Canadian Broadcasting Corporation, and the Royal Canadian Mint—along with over 20 other Crown corporations—*are* Crown agents. But the Bank of Canada, the Canada Pension Plan Investment Board, and VIA Rail, among others, are not. Each year, the Treasury Board's *Annual Report to Parliament: Crown Corporations and Other Corporate Interests of Canada* details the operations of the various federal corporations and organizations, and it includes their Crown agency status. Similarly, at the provincial and territorial levels, government corporations and institutions may or may not have Crown agency status.

18 RSC 1985, c C-5.

19 RSC 1985, c C-5, ss 37-39.

resolving disputes fairly through full disclosure, and, on the other hand, the interest of protecting the state from undue harm by disclosure.

Presumption Against Legislation Applying to the Crown

At common law, there is a presumption against legislation applying to the Crown. This presumption exists unless the legislation itself expresses or clearly implies that it does in fact apply to the Crown. This common law presumption has been confirmed by section 17 of the federal *Interpretation Act*, which states the following: "No enactment is binding on Her Majesty or affects Her Majesty or Her Majesty's rights or prerogatives in any manner, except as mentioned or referred to in the enactment."[20] Most provinces contain statutes with equivalent provisions. The two exceptions are British Columbia and Prince Edward Island, which have removed the presumption, thus putting the government in these provinces on an equal footing with other persons generally.[21] In other words, legislation in British Columbia and Prince Edward Island is presumed to apply to the government unless the legislation states otherwise.

Crown Immunity in Civil Cases

The Crown has always been able to enter into contracts itself and to appoint agents to do so on its behalf. The general rules of contract apply to the Crown; when it enters into a contract, it is subject to the same rights and liabilities as an ordinary person.

However, at common law, while the Crown could sue others in tort, in the past it was immune from tortious liability to others. Federal and provincial legislation has now removed this common law immunity. The federal and provincial governments—in other words, the federal Crown and the Crown "in right of all the provinces"—can now be sued in tort. However, the relevant legislation needs to be examined carefully because there are still some limitations on the Crown's liability, particularly in the area of remedies. Often, for instance, it is not possible to get injunctive relief against the Crown—that is, an order requiring the Crown to perform or refrain from performing a certain act (other than an order to pay a judgment for money).

Limits of Executive Influence

As noted in the discussion of responsible government, the separation-of-powers doctrine is modified under the Anglo-Canadian system. The modification consists in the fact that, in our system, the executive branch is made up of elected members of the legislature who exert control over the majority of members. The executive in our system therefore controls the legislature with its majority.

It is important to remember, however, that if the executive loses majority control the reverse becomes true; the legislature controls the executive. Majority control can be lost if a minority government loses the support of its coalition partners, or if a party with a majority loses control of its own members. In these situations, the legislature exercises its ultimate control, and the government, by convention, must resign.

Assuming, however, that the executive branch has clear control of the legislature, there are still limits to its power. In this section, we look at the two main kinds of limits.

---

20 RSC 1985, c I-21, s 17.

21 See *Interpretation Act*, RSBC 1996, c 238, s 14, and *Interpretation Act*, RSPEI 1988, c I-8, s 14.

Separation-of-Powers Limits

The separation of the legislative and executive branches of government is, as we have seen, not absolute in Canada; it is qualified. Nonetheless, there are boundaries that cannot be crossed. For instance, legislators—that is, elected representatives—cannot act as administrators unless they have been given the authority to do so. And members of the executive cannot overstep the bounds of their appointed executive authority. A minister, for example, who, under a statute, has been assigned executive authority in relation to a particular matter must not exceed the stated bounds of that authority.

The separation of powers between the legislative and executive branches may be murky at times in the Canadian system. But the separation between the executive and judicial branches is clear. It becomes especially clear when a government official attempts to directly influence the outcome of a case before the courts. Politicians who do this risk ending their careers. Perhaps the most famous example of such political interference is the so-called Judges Affair (see Box 5.2).

BOX 5.2

The Judges Affair of 1976

In December 1975, a federal Cabinet minister in the Trudeau government, André Ouellet, was cited by Justice Kenneth Mackay of the Quebec Superior Court for contempt when Ouellet criticized Justice Mackay for acquitting three companies that had been charged with price fixing. In the months that followed the citation, other instances of interference with the judicial process came to light, and material in support was placed before the House of Commons in March 1976. Three occurrences were noted:

- In 1969, Marc Lalonde, who was at the time an official with the Prime Minister's Office, called on Justice Mackay at his home concerning the trial of three persons from Trinidad who had been charged with property damage at a university. Lalonde had received information from the High Commission for Canada in Trinidad and was concerned that a conviction could lead to riots in Trinidad.
- 1n 1971, Jean Chrétien, then minister of Indian Affairs and Northern Development, telephoned Justice Aronovitch about a bankruptcy case in his constituency on behalf of some unemployed persons who were affected by the proceedings.
- Bud Drury, minister of public works, telephoned Justice Hugessen of the Quebec Superior Court, who was hearing the Ouellet contempt proceedings, to ask if an apology from Ouellet would end the proceedings.

Justice Hugessen refused to make any commitments on that point, and in the end Ouellet's contempt citation was upheld.

No firings or resignations actually resulted from these three disclosures. Bud Drury did offer his resignation but Trudeau refused it. Ouellet resigned but gave reasons other than the contempt citation.

In March 1976, however, Prime Minister Trudeau issued the following statement in the House of Commons:

> In future no member of the Cabinet may communicate with members of the judiciary concerning any matter which they have before them in the judicial capacities, except through the minister of justice, his duly authorized officials, or counsel acting for him.

This whole affair came to be known as the Judges Affair. After Trudeau issued this statement, other statements, similar in spirit, were issued in provincial assemblies. In the time since this affair, a number of ministers have been forced to resign where there was evidence of their communicating directly with judges concerning cases before them.

Source: Peter Russell, *The Judiciary in Canada: The Third Branch of Government* (Toronto: McGraw-Hill Ryerson, 1987) at 78-81.

According to Peter Russell, the **principle of non-interference** is a principle based on convention; therefore, it is a principle of political rather than legal consequence.[22] However, the fact that a minister who attempts to influence a judge might be cited for contempt of court suggests that the legal consequences for violating the principle of non-interference are real. This principle is an aspect of judicial independence; it concerns the administrative independence of the courts. And the SCC has held that judicial independence has become legally entrenched by way of the preamble clause to the *Constitution Act, 1867*, which states that we have "a Constitution similar in Principle to that of the United Kingdom." Judicial independence and its constitutional protection are described in more detail in Chapter 6.

Although the existence of the principle of non-interference is clear, its exact *scope*—and that of judicial independence generally—is not. Certain forms of interference clearly offend the principle. For example, politicians must not communicate with judges concerning matters before them. But other forms of interference are not so clear. For instance, it was at one time considered unacceptable for a politician to criticize court judgments publicly. As seen in Box 5.2, André Ouellet was cited for contempt after publicly criticizing Justice Mackay's decision. Since then, however, there have been no similar contempt citations despite several instances of politicians' criticisms of judgments and the judicial process.

The Canadian judicial system's increased tolerance for public criticism by politicians has several possible causes. Legal scholars have cited the following:

- the rise of the "rights culture,"
- the value placed on freedom of expression,
- the increasing involvement of the courts in social policy by way of Charter decisions (and the invitation to criticism that comes with such involvement),
- the "rise of neo-conservative (and often populist) ideology" and the "decline of deference" within society toward traditional institutions.[23]

As a final point, it should be noted that the federal and provincial governments recognize the non-interference principle as applying not only to courts but also to administrative tribunals that are exercising quasi-judicial functions. A recent guide for ministers contained the following directive concerning tribunals of this sort:

> Parliament's intention to lessen or remove political influence in decision making in such areas underlies the principle that Ministers should not intervene with administrative or "quasi-judicial" tribunals on any matter that requires a decision *in their quasi-judicial capacity*.[24]

Civil Liberties Limits

The area of civil liberties is the subject of Chapter 7, but we mention it here briefly concerning its relationship to executive power and the limits on that power.

principle of non-interference
the convention prohibiting direct interference by politicians with court proceedings

---

22 Peter Russell, *The Judiciary in Canada: The Third Branch of Government* (Toronto: McGraw-Hill Ryerson, 1987) at 78.

23 See Lori Hausegger, Matthew Hennigar & Troy Riddell, *Canadian Courts: Law, Politics, and Process* (Toronto: Oxford University Press, 2009) at 204, and Neil Nevitte, *The Decline of Deference: Canadian Value Change in Cross National Perspective* (Peterborough, Ont: Broadview Press, 1996).

24 Library and Archives Canada Cataloguing in Publication, *Accountable Government: A Guide for Ministers and Ministers of State 2011*, Annex H (Ottawa: Privy Council Office, 2011) at 67 (emphasis in original).

At common law, the starting point is that basic freedoms, such as freedom of expression and freedom of movement, exist until they are taken away by law. The doctrine of parliamentary sovereignty allows the legislative branch to restrict or eliminate these freedoms. But the executive branch in itself has no power, except under legislative authority, to restrict these freedoms.

With the increasing regulation of society, more administrative power has been given to governments. The common law has responded by developing rules that protect civil liberties where they haven't been clearly taken away by law. Two examples will serve to illustrate this, the first related to police power and the second to administrative agencies.

Police forces are agents of the executive branch and have various powers to arrest individuals. At common law (and now by ordinary legislation and the Charter), the police are required to give individuals reasons for their being arrested. This requirement helps to protect the individual against the arbitrary use of power.

In the area of administrative agencies, the common law has responded similarly. The *Roncarelli*[25] case, which we discussed in Chapter 1, showed how the courts would not permit discretionary executive power to be used arbitrarily. They determined that the discretion to grant or refuse to grant a liquor licence could be based only on the legislative policies set out in the relevant statute and not on extraneous factors. And, more generally, the courts have held that any administrative action affecting a person's interests is reviewable if it doesn't satisfy certain rules of fairness, which at the very least means that the person be told the case to be met and be given an opportunity to respond.[26]

In addition to common law rules, there is legislation—most notably, the *Canadian Bill of Rights* and the constitutionally entrenched Charter—to curtail executive action and protect civil liberties. These statutes and others are examined in Chapter 7.

---

25 *Roncarelli v Duplessis*, [1959] SCR 121, 1959 CanLII 50.

26 See Sara Blake, *Administrative Law in Canada*, 6th ed (Toronto: LexisNexis Canada, 2017) at 11, and *Nicholson v Haldimand-Norfolk Regional Police Commissioners*, [1979] 1 SCR 311, 1978 CanLII 24. In Canada, duties of fairness in this context are also sometimes referred to as *natural justice*. *Due process* is a more common expression in the US.

CHAPTER SUMMARY

The formal head of state in Canada is the British monarch, currently Queen Elizabeth II. Her official representative at the federal level is the governor general and, at the provincial level, the lieutenant governors. By convention, her representatives in council, the Governor in Council (the federal Cabinet) and the Lieutenant Governors in Council (the provincial Cabinets), exercise the executive power that is formally vested in her under the Constitution.

The executive branch of government is charged with implementing and enforcing the law. Under the classic separation-of-powers doctrine, the executive branch would operate independently of the legislative branch, as it does in the United States. But under the Anglo-Canadian system of responsible government, the executive branch is composed of elected members of the legislature. Federally, the political party that controls the majority of the House of Commons chooses its leader. This leader becomes the prime minister of Canada and in turn chooses his or her Cabinet, primarily from the House of Commons. Provincially, the political party that controls the majority of the Legislative Assembly chooses its leader, who becomes the premier of the province and who similarly chooses a Cabinet. Executive governments that lose the support of the majority of the relevant legislature must resign. In that sense, the prime minister or premier and his or her Cabinets are accountable or "responsible" to the elected assembly.

Executive power comes from a variety of sources: constitutional rules, convention, common law and royal prerogative, and statutory law. Most of the constitutional rules are located in the *Constitution Act, 1867*, and most of them are followed in form only. The *real* basis of executive power is political and democratic convention—that is, agreed-upon customary tradition. It is the federal Cabinet ("the Crown in right of Canada") and the provincial Cabinets ("the Crown

in right of the provinces") who hold that power as "advisors" to Her Majesty's representatives. The federal Cabinet administers federal law and the provincial Cabinets administer provincial law.

Royal prerogative, rooted in the common law, is also a source of some executive power. Examples of royal prerogative are the power to conduct foreign affairs and the power to issue passports. Most of the surviving instances of royal prerogative relate to matters within the jurisdiction of the federal Crown. The main source of executive power is statutory law. Federal and provincial statutes define many of the day-to-day powers and duties of executive government.

Because of the Crown's special status and because of the power and responsibility it must continuously exercise, the common law has developed a number of immunities to protect the Crown and its agents (that is, the executive government). These immunities have traditionally included the following: a Crown privilege to hold back evidence that would harm the public interest; a presumption in the Crown's favour that legislation does not apply to it unless the legislation contains a clear indication otherwise; and, most importantly, immunity from liability in tort. This last immunity has been significantly modified by statute. Today, in fact, the federal government and all the provincial governments have given up this protection to varying degrees.

Finally, the Crown's practical need to maintain its status and power—things that it needs in order to govern effectively—justifies the principle of Crown immunity (to the extent that it still exists). And it is the potential for abuse *by* the Crown that justifies the various limits that have been placed on its power. Two of the most important of these limits today are the requirements that executive governments not interfere with judicial proceedings and that they adhere to various standards prescribed by law relating to civil liberties.

KEY TERMS

commissioner, 141

Commissioner in Executive Council, 141

confidence convention, 141

convention, 137

Crown, 137

Crown immunity, 145

Crown privilege, 146

executive, 136

governor general, 139

Governor in Council, 139

letters patent, 143

lieutenant governor, 139

Lieutenant Governor in Council, 141

premier, 141

prime minister, 140

principle of non-interference, 149

Queen's Privy Council for Canada, 141

responsible government, 136

royal prerogative, 142

royal proclamation, 142

FURTHER READING

BOOKS

Aucoin, Peter, Jennifer Smith & Geoff Dinsdale. *Responsible Government: Clarifying Essentials, Dispelling Myths and Exploring Change* (Ottawa: Canadian Centre for Management Development, 2004). <http://publications.gc.ca/collections/Collection/SC94-107-2004E.pdf>.

Bernier, Luc, Keith Brownsey & Michael Howlett, eds. *Executive Styles in Canada: Cabinet Structures and Leadership Practices in Canadian Government* (Toronto: University of Toronto Press, 2005).

Government of Canada. *Accountable Government: A Guide for Ministers and Ministers of State 2011* (Ottawa: Privy Council Office, 2011). <http://publications.gc.ca/collections/collection_2011/bcp-pco/CP1-3-2011-eng.pdf ht>.

Heard, Andrew. *Canadian Constitutional Conventions: The Marriage of Law and Politics*, 2nd ed (Don Mills, Ont: Oxford University Press, 2014).

Hogg, Peter W. *Constitutional Law of Canada*, 2018 student ed (Toronto: Carswell, 2018).

MacKinnon, Frank. *The Crown in Canada* (Calgary: McClelland & Stewart West, 1976).

Saywell, John T. *The Office of Lieutenant-Governor* (Toronto: Copp Clark Pitman, 1986).

Seidle, FL & Louis Massicotte, eds. *Taking Stock of 150 Years of Responsible Government in Canada* (Ottawa: Canadian Study of Parliament Group, 1999).

WEBSITES

Gateway Site for Canadian Legal Databases
Canadian Legal Information Institute (CanLII): <http://www.canlii.org>.

Canadian Government Databases
Federal Government: <http://www.canada.gc.ca>.
Alberta Government: <http://alberta.ca/index.aspx>.
British Columbia Government: <http://www2.gov.bc.ca>.
Manitoba Government: <http://www.gov.mb.ca>.
New Brunswick Government: <http://www2.gnb.ca>.
Newfoundland and Labrador Government: <http://www.gov.nl.ca>.

Northwest Territories Government: <http://www.gov.nt.ca>.
Nova Scotia Government: <http://www.gov.ns.ca>.
Nunavut Government: <http://www.gov.nu.ca>.
Ontario Government: <http://www.ontario.ca>.
Prince Edward Island Government: <https://www.princeedwardisland.ca/en>.
Quebec Government: <http://www.quebec.ca>.
Saskatchewan Government: <http://www.saskatchewan.ca>.
Yukon Government: <http://www.gov.yk.ca>.

REVIEW QUESTIONS

1. What is the role of the executive branch of government?
2. Who is the formal head of state in Canada?
3. Briefly describe how our system of responsible government modifies the classic separation-of-powers model.
4. Why is it important to read the provisions of the *Constitution Act, 1867* in light of convention? Describe at least three specific situations to support your answer.
5. Name three instances where the federal Crown could invoke royal prerogative as the basis of executive action.
6. What is the source of power for most executive authority in Canada today?
7. How is executive authority divided between the federal and provincial governments?
8. What is Crown immunity? Briefly describe three forms.
9. What is a Crown agent? Provide an example.
10. Name and describe two limits on executive power.

EXERCISES

1. In your opinion, is having a *dual* executive, with a formal and a political head of state, a good system or a bad system? Support your answer with specific reasons. If you think the system should be changed, indicate how.

2. For your province or territory, find the statute that assigns specific executive authority to the provincial or territorial minister of health. Use the websites listed under Further Reading.

3. Although executive (and legislative) power is divided in Canada, there are certain areas—for example, education, the environment, and tourism—in which the federal and provincial/territorial governments cooperate in implementing laws, either because of jurisdictional overlap or because of the availability of federal funding. Choose one of the areas in which such cooperation occurs and research *how* the federal government and your regional government have together implemented the program that has resulted from this collaboration. Consider, for example, the funding and administrative structures that have been used.

4. Prepare an argument setting out why you think the protection afforded the Crown under existing Crown immunity rules is adequate or inadequate. Provide at least three reasons to support your argument.

5. While it is clear that politicians cannot interfere directly with the judicial process, it is less clear whether they can criticize judges and judgments after proceedings have been concluded. Do you believe that politicians should be able to call into question the judicial process in this way? Should it depend on what type of case is involved? In your answer, refer to the separation-of-powers doctrine and provide specific reasons and examples (hypothetical or real) for your position.

6 The Judiciary: The Third Branch of Government

The Supreme Court Building in Ottawa, designed by Ernest Cormier, is a national landmark and a symbol of the Canadian justice system. Begun in 1938, it is constructed from granite and includes a chateau-style copper roof.

After reading this chapter, you will understand:

- The role of the judiciary in Canada.
- The constitutional basis of the Canadian court system.
- How the Canadian court system is organized and how the different types and levels of courts function, from the Supreme Court of Canada to the military courts.

- How the doctrine of precedent operates within the Canadian court system.
- How judges are appointed to the various types of courts.
- The open court principle and the principle of judicial independence.
- The basics of reading and understanding case law.

Courts are the operating rooms of the legal system: theatres where preparation and expertise are brought to bear in critical moments of questioning and arguing, where decisions sometimes have to be made on the fly, where blood sometimes flows—at least metaphorically … underlying [this] is the framework upon which our modern courts operate: the adversarial system, which contemplates that a court hearing is generally a contest between two opponents who have come together to do battle with each other over some specific issue, one seeking to blame the other for some form of misdeed in the past.

Jessie J Horner, *Canadian Law and the Canadian Legal System*
(Toronto: Pearson, 2007) at 238

Introduction

court
state-sanctioned forum where disputes between opposing litigants are formally adjudicated

The third branch of government is the judiciary. Judges exercise their power by rendering decisions in our country's courts. A **court** is a state-sanctioned forum where disputes between opposing litigants are formally adjudicated. As we will see, the Canadian court system is complex. This is largely because, under the Constitution, the authority over the courts themselves and over the appointment of judges is divided between Parliament and the provinces.

Most courts in Canada are so-called *inferior* courts. (*Inferior* here is not a pejorative term. It refers not to the quality or value of these courts, but to their level in the overall hierarchy of the court system.) All such courts are courts of first instance—that is, trial courts—that hear matters for the first time and have a single judge. The provincial inferior courts are the main point of entry for most people when they interact with the justice system. They deal with less serious criminal matters and matters related to traffic, family, and small claims. Inferior courts do not hear appeals.

Other courts in Canada are *superior* courts. Some superior courts are courts of first instance—that is, trial courts. These courts have a general (or inherent) jurisdiction to deal with most legal cases but are most often used for important matters such as civil disputes involving large sums of money or serious criminal cases—murder, for example. Other superior courts are appellate courts. These courts hear appeals from courts of first instance and have more than one judge (and sometimes as many as nine).

It is important for anyone involved with the court system to understand each court's jurisdictional limitations and its place in the overall hierarchy. Such understanding will, for example, guide litigants to the right forum and help them determine routes of appeal.

This chapter begins with a general overview of the Canadian court system. We consider the role of the judiciary and the constitutional basis for the different types of courts in Canada. Then we look more closely at the organization and function of the various courts— the Supreme Court of Canada (SCC), the provincial court systems, the territorial court systems, the federal court systems, and the military courts. We next explain the flow of precedent within the Canadian court system. Then we consider how judges are appointed and discuss the two overarching principles of the Canadian judicial system: the open court principle and the principle of judicial independence.

In the last part of the chapter, we discuss how the decisions of the courts are recorded and reported. We also outline the conventions for briefing and citing cases.

Role of the Judiciary

A court's judgment or decision is the final outcome of the dispute heard before it. In cases where the court provides reasons for its decision, the record of those reasons becomes part of our law and—depending on the court's position in the hierarchy—may bind later courts under the doctrine of precedent (see Chapter 2, as well as the discussion of precedent and *stare decisis* later in this chapter). Canadian courts make decisions that affect all aspects of our public and private lives.

In the common law provinces (in other words, all provinces except Quebec) and in the territories, judge-made rules play an important if diminishing role in the whole body of the law. Statutes, which are made by legislatures, play an increasing role as the state regulation of society expands. Despite this trend, the judiciary's role is as significant as ever in Canada.

As we saw in Chapter 4, judges add to legislated rules by interpreting statutes. Specifically, they establish the basic meanings of statutory provisions; they determine the jurisdictional validity of statutes; and they decide whether a particular statute offends the *Canadian Charter of Rights and Freedoms*.[1] Once judges have interpreted a statute, the statute will, from that point on, have to be read in light of that interpretation.

On occasion, judges perform a fourth interpretive exercise with respect to statutes; they may be asked to decide if a statute has superseded a common law rule. According to the principle of parliamentary sovereignty, statutes, which are made by legislators, take precedence over judge-made common law rules in the event that they conflict with one another. Sometimes the conflict is clear, and may even be express (that is, definitely stated rather than implied—for example, where a statute states that "the common law rule concerning XYZ is abolished"). Sometimes, however, the conflict is less clear. Where uncertainty exists, judges may be called upon to rule in this regard.

---

1 Part I of the *Constitution Act, 1982*, being Schedule B to the *Canada Act 1982* (UK), 1982, c 11.

Canadian Courts: Constitutional Basis

The *Constitution Act, 1867* sets out the power over courts and judicial appointments. The key provisions are the following:

92. In each Province the Legislature may exclusively make Laws in relation to Matters coming within the Classes of Subject next hereinafter enumerated; that is to say, …

4. The Establishment and Tenure of Provincial Offices and the Appointment and Payment of Provincial Officers. …

14. The Administration of Justice in the Province, including *the Constitution, Maintenance, and Organization of Provincial Courts, both of Civil and of Criminal Jurisdiction*, and including Procedure in Civil Matters in those Courts. …

96. The *Governor General shall appoint the Judges of the Superior, District, and County Courts in each Province*, except those of the Courts of Probate in Nova Scotia and New Brunswick. …

99.(1) Subject to subsection (2) of this section, the judges of the superior courts shall hold office during good behaviour, but shall be removable by the Governor General on address of the Senate and House of Commons.

(2) A judge of a superior court … shall cease to hold office upon attaining the age of seventy-five years. …

101. *The Parliament of Canada may*, notwithstanding anything in this Act, from Time to Time *provide for the Constitution, Maintenance, and Organization of a General Court of Appeal for Canada, and for the Establishment of any additional Courts for the better Administration of the Laws of Canada.* [2]

Since Confederation, Parliament and the provinces have used their constitutional powers to create three types of court:

1. inferior courts,
2. superior courts, and
3. the Supreme Court of Canada.

They have also used their powers to create a fourth related institution, the administrative tribunal (discussed in Chapter 11).

Inferior Courts

inferior courts
provincial and territorial courts whose jurisdiction is limited to the less serious criminal matters, family and youth matters, and small claims disputes; the federal courts martial, part of the military court system, are also inferior courts

The inferior courts fall into two categories: provincial/territorial and federal.

Provincial and Territorial

The main **inferior courts** are the provincial and territorial ones. Their jurisdiction typically is over the following:

-   criminal matters (but not the most serious crimes, such as murder and treason, which go before the provincial superior courts),
-   family and youth matters, and
-   small claims disputes.

_____

2   (UK), 30 & 31 Vict, c 3 (emphasis added).

BOX 6.1

Terminology: Provincial and Territorial Courts

The nomenclature applied to the provincial courts, inferior and superior, is inconsistent. For example, provincial superior courts are known variously as Superior Courts, Superior Courts of Justice, Supreme Courts, or Courts of Queen's Bench.

The provincial inferior courts are often simply referred to as the *provincial courts*. However, the phrase *provincial courts* sometimes refers to the provincial *superior* courts, and at other times to all provincially constituted courts, superior and inferior. The context should make the intended meaning clear. There is a similar ambiguity with territorial inferior courts. They are often referred to as the *territorial courts*. But this name may also refer to the territorial superior courts or to all of the territorial courts, both superior and inferior. Again, the context should make the reference clear.

The provincial inferior courts, as noted above, are constituted under section 92(14) of the *Constitution Act, 1867*, with provincially appointed judges under section 92(4). Parallel provisions exist in the various federal statutes devolving legislative powers to the territories—that is, provisions that set out the power to establish inferior courts and appoint territorial judges.[3] These inferior courts, provincial and territorial, are the workhorses of the court system, and they are where most Canadians are likely to experience their "day in court."

Federal

Apart from the provincial inferior courts, there is also a very specialized set of *federal* inferior courts—namely, the military courts martial. These include the General Court Martial and the Standing Court Martial, and they have jurisdiction over armed forces personnel who commit service offences.

Superior Courts

Like the inferior courts, the superior courts fall into two categories: provincial/territorial and federal.

Provincial and Territorial

The **provincial superior courts**, as noted, are constituted under section 92(14) of the *Constitution Act, 1867*, with their judges appointed *federally* under section 96 of the Act. Because of this they are sometimes referred to as **section 96 courts**. Why are the judges in these provincial courts appointed federally? Though these are provincial courts, they can, under section 92(14), hear not only matters falling under provincial legislative power (for example, motor vehicle accident cases) but also some matters falling under federal legislative power (for example, bankruptcy cases). (See Chapter 4 for a discussion of how legislative power is divided under Canada's Constitution.) The fact that the judges in these provincial superior courts are federally appointed ensures balance. Balance is needed because of the power these provincial courts have to adjudicate certain federal matters.

It should also be noted that it would be unconstitutional for the provinces to assign to provincial inferior courts (with provincially appointed judges) matters that historically—at

provincial superior courts
provincially constituted courts with inherent jurisdiction to hear all matters (unless taken away by legislation); two levels—a trial level and an appeal level; sometimes refers just to the trial level

section 96 courts
provincial superior courts, so called because their judges are federally appointed under section 96 of the *Constitution Act, 1867*

---

3   See the *Yukon Act*, SC 2002, c 7 and the *Northwest Territories Act*, SC 2014, c 2, s 2. Nunavut is an exception, however. It has a unified superior and territorial court called the Nunavut Court of Justice, which has the combined jurisdiction of an inferior and a superior court. It is the only jurisdiction with such an arrangement.

the time of Confederation—were adjudicated by superior courts. Such matters must be heard by section 96 courts, with their federally appointed judges.[4]

The provincial superior courts—that is, section 96 courts—have two levels: a trial level and an appeal level. The provincial courts of appeal are the highest level of court in the provinces.

territorial superior courts
federally constituted superior courts with jurisdiction in the territories

The **territorial superior courts** are very similar, in terms of their function, to the provincial superior courts, and they likewise have federally appointed judges. They differ, however, in that they are constituted under federal legislation. The source of Parliament's jurisdiction over the territorial courts, superior and inferior, is section 4 of the *Constitution Act, 1871*,[5] an imperial statute that is part of our Constitution.

Federal

federal superior courts (or federal courts)
the Federal Court, the Federal Court of Appeal, the Tax Court of Canada, and the Court Martial Appeal Court

The **federal superior courts** (sometimes just called **federal courts**) are:

- the Federal Court,
- the Federal Court of Appeal,
- the Tax Court of Canada, and
- the Court Martial Appeal Court.

These courts are constituted under federal legislation, with federally appointed judges. Parliament's authority over these courts flows from the second leg of section 101 of the *Constitution Act, 1867*, which gives Parliament the power to create "additional Courts for the better Administration of the Laws of Canada." The phrase *Laws of Canada* in section 101 has been interpreted as limiting the jurisdiction of these courts to disputes involving federal (as opposed to provincial) laws.

The Federal Court and the Federal Court of Appeal have jurisdiction throughout Canada. The authority of these courts overlaps with that of the provincial superior courts, and this has given rise to a number of jurisdictional disputes. The Tax Court of Canada has jurisdiction throughout Canada, but only in the area of tax law. The jurisdiction of the Court Martial Appeal Court is limited to appeals from the courts martial.

The Supreme Court of Canada

Supreme Court of Canada
Canada's highest court and final court of appeal

The **Supreme Court of Canada** is also a federal superior court. But it has a special status and occupies its own category. Parliament's authority over this court flows from the first leg of section 101, which gives Parliament the power to create a "General Court of Appeal for Canada." The SCC has been Canada's "general Court of Appeal" since 1875 and its final Court of Appeal since 1949.

Canadian Courts: Organization and Function

Figure 6.1 shows how the three types or categories of courts in Canada are organized. Administrative tribunals sit just below the fourth level. (For more on administrative tribunals, see Chapter 11.)

---

4 See *Toronto v York*, 1938 CanLII 252, [1938] AC 415 (UKJCPC).

5 (UK), 34 & 35 Vict, c 28.

FIGURE 6.1 Overview of the Canadian Court System

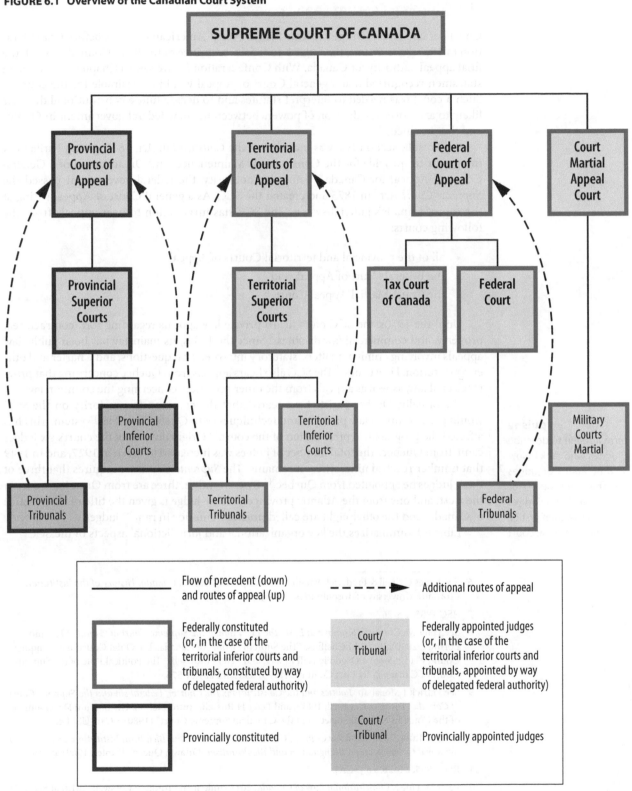

The Supreme Court of Canada

Courts of law existed in the separate British North American colonies before Confederation in 1867. At that time, the English Judicial Committee of the Privy Council was still the final appeal authority for Canada. With Confederation (as we saw in Chapter 3), Canadian statesmen recognized that a general Court of Appeal would be desirable for the country. Such a court was needed to interpret statutes and to decide future constitutional disputes likely to arise over the division of powers between the new federal government in Ottawa and the provinces.[6]

As a result, section 101 was included in the *Constitution Act, 1867*, giving Parliament the power to "provide for the Constitution, Maintenance, and Organization of a General Court of Appeal for Canada." Using this authority, the federal government passed the *Supreme Court Act*[7] in 1875 and created the SCC. As a general Court of Appeal sitting at the top of Canada's judicial system, the SCC has jurisdiction to hear appeals from the following courts:

- all of the provincial and territorial Courts of Appeal,
- the Federal Court of Appeal, and
- the Court Martial Appeal Court.

Until the 1970s, the SCC often heard private law appeals regarding tort, contract, real property, and commercial law disputes.[8] Since the 1980s, its mainstay has been public law appeals involving criminal matters, statutory interpretation questions, and Charter and other constitutional law issues.[9] The SCC also hears appeals from Quebec concerning that province's civil law, as well as appeals from the other provinces concerning the common law.

Historically, Quebec jurists have feared that the common law majority on the SCC would graft common law precepts and techniques onto Quebec's civil law system. This has affected the geographic representation of the court.[10] Originally, two of the court's six judges came from Quebec. The total number of judges was increased to seven in 1927, and in 1949 that number reached nine, where it remains. The *Supreme Court Act* requires that three of these judges be appointed from Quebec.[11] By convention, three are from Ontario, two from the west, and one from the Atlantic provinces.[12] One judge is given the title of chief justice of Canada, and the other eight are called **puisne** ("inferior in rank") judges.

Table 6.1 summarizes the key organizational and jurisdictional aspects of the SCC.

puisne
term applied to describe judges who rank below another judge or judges on the same court—for example, the judges below the chief justice on an appeal court

---

6   See James G Snell & Frederick Vaughan, *The Supreme Court of Canada: History of the Institution* (Toronto: University of Toronto Press, 1985).

7   RSC 1985, c S-26.

8   See Peter McCormick, *Supreme at Last: The Evolution of the Supreme Court of Canada* (Toronto: Lorimer, 2000); Ronald I Cheffins, "The Supreme Court of Canada: The Quiet Court in an Unquiet Country" (1965-66) 4 Osgoode Hall LJ 259; and Peter H Russell, "The Political Role of the Supreme Court of Canada in Its First Century" (1975) 53 Can Bar Rev 576.

9   See Patrick J Monahan, *Politics and the Constitution: The Charter, Federalism and the Supreme Court of Canada* (Toronto: Carswell, 1987); and Peter H Russell, "Introduction: History and Development of the Court in National Society and the Canadian Supreme Court" (1980) 3 Can-USLJ 4.

10 Peter H Russell, *The Supreme Court of Canada as a Bilingual and Bicultural Institution: Documents of the Royal Commission on Bilingualism and Biculturalism* (Ottawa: Queen's Printer, 1969) at 215.

11 RSC 1985, c S-26, s 6 [SCA].

12 Peter W Hogg, *Constitutional Law of Canada*, 2018 student ed (Toronto: Carswell, 2018) at 8-29.

TABLE 6.1 SCC: Key Facts and Features

Name	Supreme Court of Canada (1875)
Constitutional Authority	Section 101, *Constitution Act, 1867*
Act	*Supreme Court Act*, RSC 1985, c S-26
Rules	*Rules of the Supreme Court of Canada*
Judges	• 1 chief justice of Canada • 8 puisne judges • Quorum: 5-9 judges
Key Jurisdictional Features	• Hears appeals in criminal and non-criminal cases (if the case concerns a matter of public importance or significant legal question) • Leave to appeal is required in some instances • Hears appeals in criminal cases involving indictable offences where the court of appeal upholds a conviction but with a dissenting opinion • Hears appeals in criminal cases where the court of appeal substitutes a guilty verdict for an acquittal • Hears references

How Cases Come Before the SCC

Cases come before the SCC in one of three ways: (1) leave to appeal, (2) appeal as of right, or (3) on a reference.

LEAVE TO APPEAL

This occurs when a court grants a party leave to appeal his case to the SCC. It is the most common way for non-criminal cases to come before the SCC. In some instances, a provincial Court of Appeal or the Federal Court of Appeal can grant such leave. However, most parties who want to appeal their cases to the SCC must get permission or leave to appeal from the court itself.

Applicants must file written submissions with the court. In most cases, these submissions are considered by one of three panels (each composed of three SCC judges) that have been selected by the chief justice of Canada. Either the panel will grant leave or it will not, and it does not provide reasons either way.

Section 40(1) of the *Supreme Court Act* sets out the main criteria the court considers when deciding whether to grant a party leave to appeal. Under this section, the SCC may grant leave if it is of the opinion that the case involves

- a matter of public importance,
- a significant legal question, or
- any other matter the court believes warrants its attention.

Cases involving constitutional issues (including civil liberties) or Aboriginal rights, or important matters dealing with criminal law, administrative law, or private law, stand the greatest chance of success on a leave application. Cases that are purely factual or that involve matters that are specific to a particular province or territory are less likely to succeed.

APPEAL AS OF RIGHT

With certain kinds of criminal cases, there is a right of appeal to the SCC without the need for prior leave. Section 691 of the *Criminal Code* identifies these cases. Circumstances under which an *appeal as of right* exists for an accused person include the following:

1. The person is convicted of an indictable offence at trial and the conviction is upheld by the Court of Appeal, but one of the appeal court judges dissents on a question of law.
2. The person is acquitted of an indictable offence, but the Court of Appeal sets aside the acquittal and substitutes a guilty verdict.

If there is no prescribed right of appeal under section 691, an accused can still apply for leave to appeal, just as parties in *non-criminal* cases can. (See the discussion of leave to appeal, above.)

ON A REFERENCE

reference
special case in which the executive branch of government refers a question of law to a court of appeal, usually a question concerning the constitutionality of a statute or course of action the government is considering

Section 53 of the *Supreme Court Act* provides a third way for a matter to come before the SCC. Unlike the two preceding ways, this one is not dependent on an existing legal action in a lower court. Under this section, the Governor in Council (the federal Cabinet) may refer important questions of law or fact to the SCC for an advisory opinion. Typically, these questions would concern the constitutionality of a proposed statute or of a course of action the government is considering.

These questions don't originate only with the federal Cabinet. A provincial Cabinet might direct a **reference** question to its own provincial Court of Appeal. That court's decision regarding the reference question can be appealed as of right (by the provincial Cabinet) to the SCC.[13]

BOX 6.2

The Supreme Court: From 1875 to the Present

For a long time, the SCC was not well understood by Canadians. Few grasped its role in the nation. The court was created in 1875, but, as we have noted elsewhere, it was not Canada's final court until 1949, when all appeals to the Judicial Committee of the Privy Council ended. Until then, it was "a captive court" (as former Chief Justice Laskin noted), with little opportunity to develop any jurisprudence "distinctively its own."* Indeed, for the court's first sitting on January 17, 1876, it had literally no work to do.

The situation is different now. Today, the SCC is an active player in the political and legal life of this country. Its decisions have a major impact on the lives of all Canadians, who see and read about the court frequently on television and in newspaper accounts. Its docket is now increasingly concerned with criminal cases, civil liberty matters, statutory interpretation, and constitutional law cases. The court's pivotal role for Canadian law has expanded even more since the introduction of the *Canadian Charter of Rights and Freedoms*.

* Bora Laskin, "The Supreme Court of Canada: A Final Court of and for Canadians" (1951) 29 Can Bar Rev 1038 at 1075; see also Bora Laskin, "The Supreme Court of Canada, the First One Hundred Years: A Capsule Institutional History" (1975) 53 Can Bar Rev 459.

---

13 *Ibid* at 8-15ff.

Hearings

Before an appeal is heard, the parties must file with the Supreme Court registrar all of the documents, in both paper and electronic versions, that the Supreme Court judges need in order to prepare for the appeal. These documents include the following:

- the trial transcripts;
- the **facta** of all parties, which contain the written legal arguments to be presented on the appeal; and
- a book of authorities containing copies of all precedent cases, statutes, and secondary sources, such as excerpts from books and articles.

facta (sing. *factum*)
written legal arguments to be presented on an appeal

The Supreme Court registrar then schedules a date for the hearing of the appeal. At the hearing, the parties may appear before a panel consisting of five, seven, or all nine Supreme Court judges. The chief justice determines the size of the panel, with five judges constituting a quorum—that is, a minimum number of members. The modern practice is generally for all nine judges to hear the appeal.[14]

The Supreme Court judges hear the appeal from a semicircular bench (see Figure 6.2). The chief justice sits in the middle, flanked by the puisne judges, who range outward from the chief justice in order of seniority. Judges are normally gowned in black silk robes, but they wear red ones for ceremonial occasions (see Figure 6.3). The courtroom is open to the public. Oral argument is permitted at the appeal hearing, but with strict time limits imposed. Hearings are conducted in either English or French. The judges can (and often do) ask the lawyers questions, and they can also hear from intervenors—persons or groups who are not parties to the lawsuit but who can participate in the hearing with the court's permission.

FIGURE 6.2 The nine judges' benches in the main courtroom at the SCC.

Judgments

After the appeal hearing concludes, the judges move directly to a conference room for initial discussion of the case. Though the judges can return from this discussion and give the

---

14 See McCormick, *supra* note 8, and Bora Laskin, "The Supreme Court of Canada: A Final Court of and for Canadians" (1951) 29 Can Bar Rev 1038 at 1075.

reserve
postpone rendering its decision, after a hearing has concluded, so the court can carefully prepare the reasons for its judgment

court's judgment directly from the bench, the usual practice is to **reserve** their decision. This means that they reserve for themselves a period of time in which to reflect further on the case, to do more research, possibly to review how other common law courts in other countries might have decided a similar matter, and to allow themselves more time to write the reasons for their decision.[15]

In the conference room immediately after the hearing, during the judges' initial discussion of the case (which is presided over by the chief justice), the most junior member appointed to the court first gives his opinion. The other judges follow, in reverse order of seniority.[16] The main aim of this formalized, private preliminary conference is not just to canvass initial views but also to determine in a collegial way who will write the court's judgment.

majority
refers (in the context of a split decision on appeal) to the group of justices who form the majority and whose decision becomes the decision of the court

Writing a judgment is labour-intensive and time-consuming. Judges often confer with their clerks and develop a draft judgment, which may require further research at the court's own library. The draft is then circulated among the other panel judges for comments until a consensus is (ideally) reached and a final judgment is completed. The court's judgment on an appeal is decided by a **majority** and need not be unanimous. Unanimity is preferred, however, because it signals most forcefully the court's position regarding the appeal, and this kind of clarity is helpful to the legal profession. A judge may also concur (or agree) with the court's decision and be part of the majority, but write different reasons. Another judge may **dissent**, or disagree with the majority, and write the reasons for her dissent. Dissenting judgments may later become influential if shown to be better reasoned than the majority decision.

dissent
refers (in the context of a split decision on appeal) to the judgment of one or more justices in the minority

Once made, the decision is deposited with the Supreme Court registrar, who releases it in both English and French. It is then published in print form in the Supreme Court Reports and online on the court's website (it will also be reproduced in other report series and in other electronic databases).

Provincial Court Systems

A plaintiff in a civil or non-criminal matter, or an accused in a criminal matter, enters a specific level of the Canadian court system in accordance with pre-established criteria—for example, the monetary amount involved in the plaintiff's civil action or the nature of the accused's criminal charge. Serious criminal charges, such as murder or treason, are tried in a provincial superior trial court, while civil claims lower than a specified amount ($25,000 in most provinces) involve trials in small claims court, at the lowest level of the judicial hierarchy.

Most provinces structure their court systems as described earlier in this chapter (see Figure 6.1). In all provinces, there are two levels of superior court—a trial-level superior court and, above it, a provincial Court of Appeal. The chief justice of the latter is usually the chief justice of the province. Beneath the trial-level superior courts are the inferior courts. Cousins to the inferior courts, but beneath them in the overall system of justice, are the many provincial administrative tribunals.

Not all cases can move up the judicial hierarchy from lower-level trial courts to the SCC. Parties must have solid grounds in law to appeal decisions made by a trial judge. Trial cases first must reach the provincial superior Court of Appeal—in other words, the top court in

---

15   Michael J Herman, "Law Clerking at the Supreme Court of Canada" (1975) 13 Osgoode Hall LJ 279; Jack Batten, "The Supreme Court of Canada" in *Judges* (Toronto: Macmillan, 1986); Ian Greene et al, *Final Appeal: Decision-Making in Canadian Courts of Appeal* (Toronto: Lorimer, 1998).

16   Antonio Lamer, "A Brief History of the Court" in *The Supreme Court of Canada and Its Justices, 1875-2000: A Commemorative Book* (Toronto: Dundurn Group, 2000) at 23-25.

each province—and this court decides whether an appeal is warranted. A case can proceed from the provincial superior Court of Appeal to the SCC only if certain appeal criteria are met, as described above in our discussion of the SCC.

Provincial Superior Courts

The provincial superior courts are historically related to the English royal courts of justice (see Chapter 2) and have inherent jurisdiction over *all* civil and criminal law disputes in their respective provinces. This absolute jurisdiction is granted by the common law and is limited only where some aspect of it has been exclusively assigned, by clear and constitutionally valid legislation, to another court or tribunal (such as a provincial inferior court).

The provincial superior court's jurisdiction very often overlaps with that of the inferior court. In most provinces, for instance, a small claims court has been created to adjudicate civil claims below a specified dollar value (in most provinces, between $25,000 and $50,000). However, the provincial superior court, with its inherent jurisdiction over all civil and criminal disputes in the province, is still authorized to hear such claims.

Why would a plaintiff choose to go to a higher court for resolution of a dispute involving a small amount of money? After all, costs are less and procedures simpler in small claims court. The rationale for going to the provincial superior court, under these circumstances, might be that the higher court's decision will have greater precedential value. For example, the plaintiff might be an insurance company suing to recover moneys it paid out on the basis of a misinterpretation of contract language. If the insurance company is successful, the superior court's decision could subsequently serve as a precedent for similar cases. Each claim might be small, but the cumulative effect could be large, and the insurance company stands to benefit a great deal from the higher court's authoritative decision.

The higher provincial courts are not required to hear all claims brought before them. In certain circumstances, the superior court can transfer such cases to the lower court on its own initiative. For example, if the court's docket were backlogged, or the matter were insignificant and of concern only to the particular parties, the court could refer the case down.

The superior courts also have an inherent jurisdiction, as modified by legislation, to review the decisions of the inferior courts and administrative tribunals, as well as the right to hear appeals from these courts and tribunals if permitted by the superior courts' constituting statutes. (See Chapter 11.) The provincial superior courts' wide-ranging adjudicative power means they have the largest share of overall judicial power in Canada.

Table 6.2 summarizes the key organizational and jurisdictional aspects of the provincial superior courts.

TABLE 6.2   Provincial Superior Courts: Key Facts and Features

Constitutional Authority	Sections 92(14) and 96, *Constitution Act, 1867*
Key Jurisdictional Features at the Appeal Level	• Is the general court of appeal for the province in both civil and criminal matters • Hears appeals from the provincial superior trial level • Hears some appeals from provincial court decisions • Hears some appeals from provincial administrative tribunal decisions
Key Jurisdictional Features at the Trial Level	• Has inherent jurisdiction in all cases arising in the province • Hears some appeals from provincial court decisions (e.g., from small claims court) • Hears some appeals from provincial administrative tribunal decisions • Hears applications for judicial review of some provincial administrative tribunal decisions

FAMILY LAW IN THE PROVINCIAL COURT SYSTEMS

We should also note that a number of provinces have modified their court systems in the area of family law. Traditionally, family law disputes are heard in either the provincial inferior or superior courts—or in both, depending on the issues. (Constitutional jurisdiction over family law is split between Parliament and the provinces.) Family breakups are emotionally and financially trying enough without the added stress of having to deal with complicated jurisdictional divisions within the court system. To help with this, initiatives in seven provinces—Manitoba, New Brunswick, Newfoundland and Labrador, Nova Scotia, Ontario, Prince Edward Island, and Saskatchewan—have resulted in **unified family courts** (UFCs).

unified family courts
special divisions of the trial level of a provincial superior court with complete jurisdiction over family law matters, including matters that would otherwise be heard in a provincial inferior court

UFCs are special divisions of the trial level of the superior court, and they have complete jurisdiction over family law matters. Judges with special training or expertise oversee these disputes, and the parties are encouraged to use non-adversarial approaches to resolve their claims. The objective is to make the process less onerous. Should the court be called upon to finally adjudicate any issues, there is, at least, only one court involved. The UFCs operate only in select cities and venues within the province, so parties not able or willing to go to these locations must follow the traditional route.

Provincial Inferior Courts

Most provinces have one provincial inferior court with multiple divisions. The following divisions are typical:

- criminal,
- youth (young offender matters),
- traffic,
- family, and
- small claims (civil claims, generally between $25,000 and $50,000).

These divisions vary among the provinces. For example, Nova Scotia has multiple provincial courts with separate constituting legislation for each, and Manitoba's small claims disputes are handled by a division of its superior court, the Manitoba Court of Queen's Bench.

Regardless of the precise organizational setup, it is important to understand that the provincial inferior courts are the main point of entry for most people when they interact with the justice system. These courts handle the vast majority of criminal and civil cases in Canada.

Provincial inferior courts are creatures of statute and have no inherent jurisdiction as the provincial superior courts do. In other words, inferior courts can exercise only powers given to them by legislation. (The source of the inherent jurisdiction of the superior courts, as we mentioned above, is the common law.)

Each division within a provincial inferior court—or, in Nova Scotia, each separate specialized provincial court—must look to its constituting provincial statute to determine the criminal, quasi-criminal, or civil matters over which it has jurisdiction. In the case of jurisdiction over criminal matters, the *Criminal Code* must also be considered; it requires that certain serious offences, such as murder and treason, be tried by a superior court. The provincial inferior courts also have rules of practice governing procedure in all areas over which they have jurisdiction. In civil matters particularly, their court procedures are generally set up to be simpler, faster, and less expensive than those of the superior courts.

As mentioned, the superior courts have an inherent power to review the provincial inferior courts' decisions. This power is generally confined to reviewing the procedural fairness of the lower court's decision, and this power can be modified by statute. Also, the legislation constituting most provincial inferior courts provides for a general right of appeal to the superior court, which allows the superior court to assess the merits of the lower court's decisions, a much broader power than judicial review. (The basic principles of judicial review and rights of appeal as they apply to administrative decisions are described in Chapter 11. These principles also apply to inferior courts.)

Territorial Court Systems

Most of what we have said about the provincial court systems applies to the territorial court systems. Perhaps the most significant difference between the two systems is their constitutional basis. As we have seen, the territorial systems are not rooted in a constitutionally entrenched statute, as the provincial ones are, but in federal statutes that can be changed unilaterally by Parliament.[17]

We may assume, however, that this lack of constitutional protection for the territorial court systems is mostly a matter of legal theory. The political and practical difficulties involved in unilaterally changing them would be significant. In terms of functionality and jurisdiction, the territorial court systems are very similar to the provincial ones.

Territorial Superior Courts

Yukon and the Northwest Territories structure their superior courts as set out in Figure 6.1. There are two superior court levels, with jurisdiction similar to that of the provincial superior courts.

In Yukon, the Court of Appeal of the Yukon Territory is the top court and hears appeals from the Supreme Court of Yukon and the Territorial Court. The Court of Appeal is made up of justices from British Columbia, Yukon, the Northwest Territories, and Nunavut. This court's small case load is the reason for its not having a full complement of resident justices. It sits for only one week each year in Whitehorse; at other times, it sits in Vancouver, from which the court "borrows" some of its judges.

Similarly, the Court of Appeal for the Northwest Territories hears appeals from the Supreme Court of the Northwest Territories and the Territorial Court. It sits regularly in Yellowknife (occasionally it sits in other territorial locations and in Alberta) and is made up of justices from Alberta, Saskatchewan, and the Northwest Territories.

Nunavut is unique. It has a unified court, the Nunavut Court of Justice, which combines the jurisdiction of an inferior court with the jurisdiction of the trial level of a superior court. It is like a unified family court except that it covers not just family law but all jurisdictional areas. There is a single court for Nunavut because its population is very small—30,000 to 40,000 people, spread over a region roughly the size of Western Europe. There is a separate Court of Appeal, however. The Court of Appeal of Nunavut sits mainly in the territorial capital, Iqaluit, and is composed of justices from Alberta, Yukon, the Northwest Territories, and Nunavut.

Territorial Inferior Courts

Yukon and the Northwest Territories each have a territorial inferior court (in each territory, simply called the Territorial Court) that is organized along the lines of the provincial

---

17 *Yukon Act*, SC 2002, c 7; *Northwest Territories Act*, SC 2014, c 2, s 2; and *Nunavut Act*, SC 1993, c 28.

inferior courts. The territorial courts are creatures of the territorial assemblies, which exercise provincial-like statutory power under the federal statutes that devolve power to them. Nunavut is an exception to this, as mentioned above.

Federal Court System

As we have seen, the federal court system includes the SCC and four other superior courts (the Federal Court, the Federal Court of Appeal, the Tax Court of Canada, and the Court Martial Appeal Court). Additionally, it includes the two military courts martial (the General Court Martial and the Standing Court Martial), which qualify as federal inferior courts. The SCC, discussed above, has been the main focus of our discussion because of its relative importance.

Federal Court and Federal Court of Appeal

In 1971, Parliament created the Federal Court of Canada under the *Federal Courts Act*.[18] This court replaced the Exchequer Court of Canada. The jurisdiction of the Federal Court of Canada was increased to include not only the matters formerly under the Exchequer Court's jurisdiction—revenue matters, disputes involving the federal government, and other types of claims concerned with copyright, trademarks, and patents—but also (among other things) the review of federal boards and tribunals. The Federal Court of Canada had two divisions: the trial division and the appeal division.

In 2003, the new *Courts Administration Service Act*[19] came into force, amending a number of federal statutes involving the administration of justice, including the *Federal Courts Act*. The *Courts Administration Service Act* reconstituted the Federal Court of Canada, converting its two divisions (the trial division and the appeal division) into two separate courts: (1) the Federal Court and (2) the Federal Court of Canada. The *Federal Court Act* was renamed the *Federal Courts Act*. One of the main purposes of the new *Courts Administration Service Act* was to "facilitate coordination and cooperation among the Federal Court of Appeal, the Federal Court, the Court Martial Appeal Court and the Tax Court of Canada for the purpose of ensuring the effective and efficient provision of administrative services to those courts."[20]

The Federal Court and Federal Court of Appeal are both itinerant courts, with hearing locations in major cities across Canada. Judges from both courts travel to hear disputes according to a set schedule. The key features of the two courts are summarized in Table 6.3.

Tax Court of Canada

The Tax Court of Canada used to be characterized as an inferior court or administrative tribunal but is now considered a superior court. It was created in 1983 pursuant to the *Tax Court of Canada Act*.[21] It has a chief justice and an associate chief justice and numerous puisne judges. Like the Federal Court and Federal Court of Appeal, the Tax Court of Canada is an itinerant court with hearing locations in cities across Canada and regular sittings in those locations.

---

18   RSC 1985, c F-7.

19   SC 2002, c 8 [CASA].

20   CASA, s 2.

21   RSC 1985, c T-2.

TABLE 6.3 Federal Court and Federal Court of Appeal: Key Facts and Features

	FEDERAL COURT	FEDERAL COURT OF APPEAL
Name	• Federal Court (1971-)	• Federal Court of Appeal (1971-)
Constitutional Authority	• Section 101, *Constitution Act, 1867*	• Section 101, *Constitution Act, 1867*
Act	• *Federal Courts Act*, RSC 1985, c F-7	• *Federal Courts Act*, RSC 1985, c F-7
Rules	• *Federal Courts Rules* • *Federal Courts Immigration and Refugee Protection Rules*	• *Federal Courts Rules* • *Federal Courts Immigration and Refugee Protection Rules*
Judges	• 1 chief justice of the Federal Court • Numerous itinerant judges and deputy judges • Quorum: 1 judge	• 1 chief justice of the Federal Court of Appeal • 12 puisne judges • Quorum: usually 3-5 judges
Key Jurisdictional Features	• Has *exclusive jurisdiction* in the following areas: (1) reviewing decisions of most federal boards and tribunals, with the exception of those assigned to the Federal Court of Appeal; (2) hearing copyright, trademark, patent, and industrial design matters; hearing citizenship appeals; hearing certain armed forces matters • Has *concurrent jurisdiction* with provincial superior courts in certain disputes (e.g., those involving bills of exchange and promissory notes, aeronautics, and interprovincial works and undertakings) • Has *residuary jurisdiction* to hear matters over which no other court has jurisdiction	• Hears appeals from the Federal Court • Hears appeals from the Tax Court of Canada • Has exclusive jurisdiction to review decisions of certain federal boards and tribunals as specified in the *Federal Courts Act* (e.g., the Canadian Radio-television and Telecommunications Commission, the National Energy Board, and the Copyright Board)

The court has jurisdiction to hear appeals from individuals and corporations concerning matters arising out of a number of federal statutes, including the *Income Tax Act*,[22] the *Employment Insurance Act*,[23] the *Excise Tax Act*[24] (GST), the *Canada Pension Plan*, and the *Old Age Security Act*.[25] It is an independent court and not an instrument of the Canada Revenue Agency or other government departments.

Military Court System

Military law is a specialized area and something of which most Canadians who are not in the military have only a vague understanding. Section 91(7) of the *Constitution Act, 1867*

22 RSC 1985, c 1 (5th Supp).

23 SC 1996, c 23.

24 RSC 1985, c E-15.

25 RSC 1985 c O-9.

gives Parliament jurisdiction over "Militia, Military and Naval Service, and Defence." The *National Defence Act*[26] passed pursuant to this authority is the governing statute for the armed forces. The Office of the Judge Advocate General is responsible for the prosecution and defence functions of the military justice system, which is parallel to but separate from the regular justice system.

As mentioned above, the courts martial (the General Court Martial and Standing Court Martial) are a very specialized set of *federal* inferior courts with jurisdiction over armed forces personnel who commit service offences. These courts are constituted under the *National Defence Act* and are analogous to the provincial and territorial inferior courts that have jurisdiction over criminal cases. However, unlike the provincial and territorial inferior courts, they also have jurisdiction over serious offences and are vested with the same powers as superior courts. Parliament's constitutional jurisdiction over these courts is based on either section 91(7) or section 101 of the *Constitution Act, 1867*.

The Court Martial Appeal Court hears appeals from the courts martial. It is a superior court and is also constituted under the *National Defence Act*. Parliament's jurisdiction over this court is clearly based on section 101.

Precedent and Stare Decisis in the Canadian Court System

In order to research the law effectively and to assess the binding or persuasive value of earlier decisions properly, you need some familiarity with the hierarchical structure of the courts and their jurisdiction. In Chapter 2, we described the doctrine of *stare decisis*. According to this doctrine, the decision in an earlier court case (in other words, a **precedent**) binds lower level courts *in the same jurisdiction*. It does so in cases where the facts and applicable legal principle (sometimes referred to as *ratio decidendi*, or simply *ratio*) in the later case are materially similar to those in the earlier one.

precedent
court decision that, under the doctrine of *stare decisis*, is binding on lower courts in the same jurisdiction

What is meant by *jurisdiction* in this context? And more specifically, what does it mean in the context of the Canadian court system? Each of the four pathways (or court systems) leading up to the SCC, as shown in Figure 6.1, is considered a separate jurisdiction or jurisdictional grouping. The federal court system is considered a separate jurisdiction, as is the system of courts martial (the military courts). The provincial and territorial court systems are the two other jurisdictional groupings—each province and territory is its own jurisdiction within the general provincial and territorial court pathways. For example, a decision by a court in one province would not bind a court in another province. Precedent flows only downward and only within the jurisdiction in which the decision was made. Decisions of the SCC, however, as Canada's highest court and "general Court of Appeal," are binding on all courts across Canada.

Cases from the same level of court within the same jurisdiction aren't, strictly speaking, binding on each other (for example, an earlier decision from the Manitoba Court of Appeal isn't technically binding on a later decision by that same court), but the principle of comity   that is, respect for the decisions of fellow judges at the same level—requires that they be followed, unless there is a good reason not to follow them. A judge might choose not to follow an earlier decision if it involved, for example, a missed precedent or a missed statutory provision.

---

26 RSC 1985, c N-5.

Legal researchers start by looking for **binding** authority from the decisions of higher courts. For example, if researching a matter within the jurisdiction of the provincial superior or inferior court system, they would start by looking for SCC decisions. Then they would look for Court of Appeal decisions from the relevant province, then for decisions of the provincial superior court (trial level). Finally, they would look for decisions from provincial inferior courts and, possibly, from administrative tribunals.

If no binding authority is found—and sometimes even if it is—researchers may find it helpful to search for **persuasive** authority from other jurisdictions. A person researching a matter within the provincial court systems would look at decisions from other provinces or territories, from the federal courts (if there is joint authority over the matter in question), and possibly also from other countries with common law traditions, such as England, Australia, and the United States (generally in that order of preference). The higher the level of court from the other jurisdiction, the more persuasive the decision. Intangibles, such as the reputation of the particular judge who rendered the decision, may also influence the weight given to a particular decision.

As a general rule, the more recent the authority, the better. It should also be noted that decisions that initially appear to be binding or persuasive may seem less so (in other words, they may be *distinguishable*) upon careful examination. A precedent may be distinguishable for a variety of reasons (see Chapter 2).

binding
term used to describe a higher court decision that a lower court in the same jurisdiction must follow according to the principle of *stare decisis*

persuasive
describes a precedent that a court is persuaded to give some weight to but is not bound to follow, because the precedent is from another jurisdiction or is otherwise not binding

Judicial Appointments

There is essentially one appointment process for superior court judges—that is, provincial and territorial superior court judges, Federal Court and Federal Court of Appeal judges, and judges of the SCC. All are federally appointed (but see the discussion below regarding the process for SCC appointments). The provinces and territories each have separate but parallel appointment processes for provincially and territorially appointed judges (that is, judges in the inferior courts).

Superior Court Judges

In the following sections we will look at the appointment authority, appointment process, and the qualifications of superior court judges.

Appointment Authority

The appointment power set out in section 96 of the *Constitution Act, 1867* states that the governor general shall appoint the provincial superior court judges. By constitutional convention, this means that the Governor in Council (that is, the federal Cabinet) makes the appointments.

Section 96 says nothing, however, about the Cabinet's appointing *federal* superior court judges. In their case, the federal Cabinet's appointment power comes from section 101. This provision, as we have seen, states that Parliament may from time to time "provide for the Constitution, Maintenance, and Organization of a General Court of Appeal for Canada, and for the Establishment of any additional Courts for the better Administration of the Laws of Canada." This provision

FIGURE 6.3 Justice Bertha Wilson, who in 1982 became the first woman appointed to the Supreme Court, wearing the red ceremonial robe.

has been interpreted as giving the federal Cabinet the executive power to appoint federal superior court judges, including SCC judges. The *Federal Courts Act* and the *Supreme Court Act* have since expressly given the federal Cabinet this power.

The appointment of territorial superior court judges follows the same process as that of provincial superior court judges.

Appointment Process

There are many judicial appointments, and the federal Cabinet cannot be closely involved with all of them. To deal with the volume, a special federal office called the Office of the Commissioner for Federal Judicial Affairs Canada (FJA) was created under the *Judges Act*.[27] Since 1988, the FJA has played a major role in vetting proposed appointments. To assist it in this process, the FJA has overseen the creation of judicial advisory committees in the ten provinces and three territories. Most provinces have one such committee, but Ontario and Quebec, because of their size, have multiple committees (three and two, respectively).

Potential judges now have to apply for the position and go through background checks by the advisory committee. The advisory committee puts forward a list of names, which is then reviewed by the federal minister of justice and the FJA. From this list and following this review, recommendations are made to Cabinet. One of the main purposes in setting up the appointment process this way was to eliminate patronage (that is, appointments based on political connections rather than merit). The advisory committees have members from all corners of the legal profession, so no one person on the committee can dominate the selection process. This diversity inhibits patronage. Patronage may still exist in some degree, but these measures have helped reduce it.

The FJA process is used for all federally appointed superior court judges except SCC judges. In 2016, Prime Minister Justin Trudeau introduced a new appointment procedure for Canada's highest court. Any qualified judge or lawyer can apply to the FJA for appointment to the SCC. The candidate's application will then be reviewed by a seven-member advisory board, which will be free from political influence and which will use publicly available assessment criteria. The prime minister will choose a nominee from a short list of three to five applicants. Before the nominee is appointed, Parliament will discuss the selection process, and the nominee will appear before an all-party committee for questioning. The first justice appointed under this new process was Malcolm Rowe (he is also the first judge from Newfoundland and Labrador to sit on the SCC).

By convention, the prime minister decides who will be the chief justice of the SCC. There is also a decades-old tradition, which may have reached the status of a constitutional convention, that the position of chief justice alternates between a francophone justice from Quebec and an anglophone justice from elsewhere in Canada. In 2017, Beverley McLachlin retired (see Box 6.3), and Prime Minister Justin Trudeau appointed Richard Wagner, a civil law lawyer from Quebec who had been appointed to the court in 2012, as her successor.

---

27 RSC 1985, c J-1.

BOX 6.3

The Right Honourable Beverley McLachlin

Beverley McLachlin was born in Alberta and went to law school at the University of Alberta, graduating first in her class. She practised law for six years before joining the Faculty of Law at the University of British Columbia. In 1980, while still a professor, she was appointed to the bench. She quickly rose through the BC courts and in 1989, after four years on the BC Court of Appeal, was appointed to the SCC. In 2000, she was appointed chief justice of Canada by Prime Minister Jean Chrétien.

As chief justice, she strengthened her reputation for fairness and consensus building (more unanimous judgments were issued by the court under her tenure than ever before). And the judgments that she authored were respected for their clarity and depth of research—her judgments covered the full range of subject areas, from complex civil matters involving economic loss to pressing constitutional issues involving the Charter.

In December 2017, she retired from the court as required by section 99(2) of the *Constitution Act, 1867*, which stipulates that a judge of a superior court shall cease to hold office at the age of 75 years. She had been a SCC justice for 28 years, and for almost 18 years she had been the court's chief justice. She was the first woman to hold the position and is the court's longest-serving chief justice.

While Beverley McLachlin may have retired from the SCC, she continues to be very active as she moves "into the next chapter of her life."* After her retirement from Canada's top court, she accepted part-time appointments to the Hong Kong Court of Final Appeal and the Commercial Court of Singapore. She also published a novel, a legal thriller called *Full Disclosure*.

* Karen Dickson, "The Rt Hon Beverley McLachlin, PC" (2018) 76:3 Advocate 339 at 344.

Qualifications

To qualify for appointment as a provincial superior court judge, a candidate must

1. be a barrister or advocate of at least ten years standing at the bar of any province, or
2. have had a total of at least ten years in which the candidate (a) was a barrister or advocate at the bar of any province and then (b) served full-time as a member of a body that performed duties of a judicial nature.[28]

Qualifications for the Federal Court and Federal Court of Appeal are identical, except that a candidate must also be or have been "a judge of a superior, county or district court in Canada."[29]

---

28 *Judges Act*, s 3.

29 *Federal Courts Act*, s 5.3.

The required qualifications for the SCC judges are the following:

1. prior appointment as a judge of a superior court of a province, or
2. being a barrister of at least ten years standing at the bar of a province.[30]

Inferior Court Judges

In the following sections we will look at the appointment authority, appointment process, and qualifications for provincial/territorial and federal court judges.

Provincial

APPOINTMENT AUTHORITY AND PROCESS

The constitutional jurisdiction for the appointment of judges to the provincial inferior courts flows from sections 92(4) and (14) of the *Constitution Act, 1867.* Jurisdiction over these appointments belongs to the provincial legislatures. Each provincial legislature has in turn delegated this power, by way of its provincial courts legislation, to the Lieutenant Governor in Council (that is, the provincial Cabinet). The provincial executive branch, therefore, is responsible for appointing judges to this level of court.

BOX 6.4

The National Judicial Institute

Who educates and trains the judges? How confident are you that a judge will really know the law and the context within which a dispute has arisen?

Judges in Canada are appointed from the practising bar and, sometimes, from the academic world. This means that the usual preparation for a career as a judge is a law practice or an academic position. These experiences don't necessarily give someone a wide experience of the law. New judges often face areas of the law that are relatively unfamiliar to them. For example, a lawyer whose practice has been confined to personal injury disputes may, once she becomes a judge, have to deal with family disputes or criminal law cases.

New judges face two significant challenges. First, they must learn about areas of the law in which they have no previous experience. A second challenge has to do with achieving objectivity. Most lawyers are professional advocates. Lawyers who have spent long careers practising advocacy must, once they become judges, move beyond the advocacy mindset of many years and make themselves sensitive to the circumstances of both parties in a case.

This second requirement is especially challenging. How does a judge fully understand, for example, the social and economic obstacles facing a single mother charged with welfare fraud? How does a judge make sense of the cultural aspects of a case involving a First Nations person charged with hunting out of season? How do judges make themselves sensitive to the social, cultural, and power elements of a case? Where do they obtain the necessary sensitivity training?

In 1988, the National Judicial Institute (NJI) was formed. It is an independent non-profit organization that serves the Canadian judiciary by planning, coordinating, and delivering judicial education concerning the law, the craft of judging, and the social context in which legal disputes arise.

The NJI's mandate is to "engender a high level of social awareness, ethical sensitivity, and pride of excellence within an independent judiciary." For example, new judges are encouraged to attend a four-and-a-half-day seminar that focuses on the craft of judging and the role of judges in the social context. The program includes such topics as:

---

30 SCA, s 5.

- judicial independence,
- judicial ethics,
- equality issues in the courtroom,
- Aboriginal law,
- persons with disabilities and the judicial system, and
- introduction to judicial dispute resolution.

The seminars are conducted by experienced judges, legal academics, and other experts.

Canada is widely regarded as having one of the finest judiciaries in the world. The NJI's seminars and workshops, together with training and educational programs from other organizations, play a large part in ensuring that Canada's judiciary lives up to its reputation.

Source: Reproduced from George Alexandrowicz et al, *Dimensions of Law: Canadian and International Law in the 21st Century* (Toronto: Emond Montgomery, 2004) at 54.

The appointment process varies slightly from province to province, but all provinces now have judicial councils created under their respective provincial courts legislation. These provincial councils recruit, screen, and recommend potential candidates for judgeships. Their purpose is to accomplish at the provincial level what the FJA accomplishes at the federal level—that is, to promote quality in judicial appointments and eliminate patronage. The provincial Cabinet still makes the final decision on appointments.

QUALIFICATIONS

The basic qualification for judicial appointment to a provincial inferior court is five years' practice as a lawyer in good standing with the provincial bar, or other legal or judicial experience considered satisfactory to the council. The experience requirement, in other words, is half what it is for superior court judges. Close to 50 percent of all Canadian judges are appointed to provincial inferior courts.

Territorial

The appointment process for the territorial inferior courts operates in much the same way as for the provincial ones. The territorial assemblies have, using the power delegated to them by Parliament, passed legislation creating their own territorial courts as well as their own territorial judicial councils—equivalent to the provincial councils—to assist with the appointment process. In Yukon, for example, the statute that accomplishes this is the *Territorial Court Act*.

Federal

The *National Defence Act* sets out the process for appointing judges to the federal courts martial, which are the only federal inferior courts. It gives the power of appointment to the federal Cabinet. However, the FJA process does not apply to these judges. The basic qualification level is ten years' practice as a lawyer at a provincial bar.

Public Proceedings

The **open court principle** is generally taken for granted today in Canada. In the context of criminal charges, it is guaranteed under the Charter, subject to reasonable limits.[31] In Jeremy

open court principle
principle that judicial proceedings should be administered in public

---

31 See ss 1 and 11(d) of the Charter. Some of the limits that have been recognized include cases involving vulnerable victims (for example, children and individuals who have been sexually abused) and national security issues. In these cases the court may protect a person's identity from being disclosed or may even close the court to the public altogether.

Bentham's words, publicity is the "security of securities." We expect to be able to observe our justice system at work and to ensure that it is fair.

Courts have not always been open in this way. In England in the 1600s, the Star Chamber abuses highlighted the importance of having open courts. The Star Chamber was a special court set up alongside the well-established common law and equity courts (see Chapter 2). Its jurisdiction was to hear cases considered too important to be handled by the ordinary courts. Its proceedings were secret, and in its final days it became a political instrument used by the Stuart monarchy to punish those who opposed them. After a number of cases of unfair treatment involving prominent political and religious activists, it was abolished by an act of Parliament, the *Habeas Corpus Act* of 1640, just before the English Civil War.

The open court principle has been called "the best security for the pure, impartial, and efficient administration of justice, the best means of winning for it public confidence and respect."[32] What this means is that public proceedings are a check against the injustices that can flourish in private or secret proceedings. Where power is not scrutinized, civil liberties tend to suffer. The English historian Henry Hallam cited public proceedings—the "open administration of justice"—as among the most important safeguards of civil liberty:

> Civil liberty in this kingdom has two direct guarantees; the open administration of justice according to known laws truly interpreted, and fair constructions of evidence; and the right of Parliament, without let or interruption, to inquire into, and obtain redress of, public grievances. Of these, the first is by far most indispensable; nor can the subjects of any State be reckoned to enjoy a real freedom, where this condition is not found both in its judicial institutions and in their constant exercises.[33]

Judicial Independence

judicial independence
principle that judges should be free to make decisions based on the law and free from outside interference

According to the principle of **judicial independence**, judges should be free to make decisions based on the law without threat of negative consequences should their decisions be unpopular. Also, the public needs to see such independence in order to have confidence in the justice system. The idea that the judicial arm of government should be independent of the other branches is related to the rule-of-law doctrine described in Chapter 1, and to the separation-of-powers doctrine that provides a framework for constitutional law (see Box 5.2 on the Judges Affair).

In Canada, there are recognized to be three main aspects of judicial independence:

1. security of tenure,
2. financial security, and
3. administrative independence.[34]

Security of tenure ensures that judges can render decisions without fear of losing their positions if their decisions are not well received. Financial security ensures that any temptation

---

32   *Scott v Scott*, [1913] AC 417 at 463 (HL).

33   *Ibid* at 477.

34   Lori Hausegger, Matthew Hennigar & Troy Riddell, "Judicial Process and Alternative Dispute Resolution" in *Canadian Courts: Law, Politics, and Process*, 2nd ed (Toronto: Oxford University Press, 2015) ch 6.

to accept bribes will be minimized. And administrative independence ensures that the running of the courts is by the judges themselves and not by outside parties who may subject the judges to external biases.

Constitutional protection for the independence of the judiciary comes from a number of sources, most notably the following:

- The preamble clause to the *Constitution Act, 1867*. The preamble clause provides implied protection by stating that we in Canada have "a Constitution similar in Principle to that of the United Kingdom."[35] Protection is *implied* because, although it exists under the Constitution of the UK, protection is not expressly referred to in the preamble clause.

- Section 99 of the *Constitution Act, 1867*. This section provides that superior court judges "hold office during good behaviour" and that they are "removable by the Governor General on address of the Senate and House of Commons." (Security of tenure consists in the fact they cannot be removed otherwise.)

- Section 11(d) of the Charter. This section provides that any person charged with an offence has the right to a "public hearing by an independent and impartial tribunal."[36] The terms *independent* and *impartial* indicate a general standard for the judiciary in Canada.

Judicial independence finds protection as well in various federal, provincial, and territorial statutes.[37] Their provisions recognize judicial independence through salary guarantees and institutional structures. Also, the "good behaviour" tenure provision in section 99 of the *Constitution Act, 1867*, a provision directed at provincial superior court judges, is echoed in provisions directed at federal superior court judges and at provincial and territorial inferior court judges.

Good behaviour tenure means that judges can only be removed from office if their behaviour falls below a certain standard, into what could be termed "bad behaviour." There is no generally accepted common law or statutory definition of bad behaviour or misconduct. Section 65 of the federal *Judges Act* sets up the Canadian Judicial Council, which can investigate a superior court judge if she becomes "incapacitated or disabled from the due execution of the office" owing to age or infirmity, misconduct, incompetence, or to "having been placed, by her conduct or otherwise, in a position incompatible with the due execution of that office." This provision goes some way toward defining bad behaviour. After an investigation, the Council can recommend that a judge be removed for misconduct. The provinces and territories have constituted similar judicial councils with similar powers in relation to provincially and territorially appointed judges.

Since Confederation, six attempts have been made to remove superior court judges (including four recommendations for removal from office by the Canadian Judicial Council), but none of these attempts have progressed to the required joint address process set out in

---

35 In *Reference re Remuneration of Judges of the Provincial Court (PEI)*, [1997] 3 SCR 3, 1997 CanLII 317, the SCC stated that judicial independence is an unwritten norm, constitutionally entrenched by virtue of the preamble clause to the *Constitution Act, 1867*. Further, this "norm" is not restricted to superior courts but applies to all courts, including inferior courts.

36 Although this Charter guarantee of an independent tribunal applies only to courts and tribunals exercising criminal jurisdiction, it is clear that judicial independence applies to all courts regardless of the nature of the claim. The protection provided by the preamble clause is not qualified, while the Charter guarantee is.

37 Federally, for example, see the *Judges Act*, the *Federal Courts Act*, and the *Supreme Court Act*.

section 99 of the *Constitution Act, 1867*. The judges in question have so far retired or resigned before that stage. A handful of lower court judges have been removed, however, through less stringent processes.[38]

Judicial independence finds further support in the common law doctrine of judicial immunity (now also legislated in many jurisdictions). This immunity protects judges in courts at all levels from civil liability in lawsuits instigated by dissatisfied litigants or accused persons.

Judicial independence, in its many facets, plays a key role in supporting the freedoms we enjoy in Canadian society.

Reading and Understanding Case Law

In this final section, we discuss how the decisions of the courts are recorded and reported, and review the conventions for briefing and citing cases.

The term *case law* refers to decisions of the courts. There are hundreds of thousands of Canadian cases, covering a vast array of issues. They range from complex constitutional law appeal cases with multiple judgments hundreds of pages long to simple one-paragraph oral decisions; from clearly written, well-reasoned, and well-researched judgments that have become leading precedents to poorly written and reasoned decisions that are soon forgotten.

It is not possible for anyone, legal professional or lay person, to master all the case law in Canada. There is too much of it, and it is always growing and changing. But you can learn to analyze judicial decisions effectively, and once you have acquired this skill, you can narrow your focus by reading the cases most relevant to the issue you are facing.

Knowing a little about how judgments are reported and how to summarize (or "brief") cases can help you understand their significance. And knowing how cases are cited can help you locate them easily and reference them accurately. The following is a brief introduction to the analysis of case law, beginning with a preliminary point about terminology.

Terminology: Judgment, Decision, and Case

judgment
final outcome or disposition of the dispute heard before the court, or, when the court provides reasons for its judgment, the entire set of reasons

decision
depending on context, refers to the outcome or disposition of a case, to the holding in the case, or (where the court provides them) to the entire set of reasons the court gives for its judgment

case
depending on context, refers to the reasons for judgment (where the court provides them), to the court process more generally, or to the entire dispute from beginning to end

The words **judgment**, **decision**, and **case** are sometimes used interchangeably to refer to the *entire set of reasons* the court provides to explain how it has resolved a dispute. It is in this sense that we use these words here. In the court file for the matter in question, this set of reasons is usually one of the last documents in the paper or electronic folder.

Unfortunately, these words have alternate meanings, and it is important to pay close attention to the context in which they appear. Both *judgment* and *decision*, for example, can simply refer to the disposition or outcome of the case, as in "judgment for the plaintiff." The word *case* is similarly prone to ambiguity. To the parties and the court, it can mean the entire proceedings before the court. To the lawyer, paralegals, and others who worked on the file, it can mean the whole process, starting with the client interview and proceeding through to trial, then to the appeal (if there is one), and ending with the final judgment (or possibly settlement). Again, context should help you determine the sense in which the words are used.

Law Reports

Many cases are reported in print volumes (referred to variously as *law reports*, *case reports*, *report series*, and *reporters*) or their online equivalents. The editors don't simply reproduce

---

38 Hausegger, Hennigar & Riddell, *supra* note 34 at 187-89.

the judgment from the court file, however. They add features to help the reader understand the decision, like summaries of the decision called *headnotes*, and lists of cases and statutes referred to in the judgment.

Note also that even if a case is unreported (that is, it hasn't been independently published), it is still possible to locate the full text of the judgment in various places, such as in the court's registry file for the matter in question, or the court's online judgment database (many courts have such databases now), or a third-party database that provides access to unreported judgments (the Canadian Legal Information Institute, or CanLII, for example—see under Further Reading at the end of this chapter). Locating an unreported judgment in this way means you will generally have only the text of the judgment at your disposal, however, and not the value-added features that come with reported cases.

Format of Law Reports

Cases published in print law reports contain several standard structural components in addition to the actual reasons for judgment written by the court. The law report publisher prepares this additional information and sets it out, together with the court's reasons for judgment, in a particular format. Online versions generally follow the same format. For an illustration of the format of a case report, see Figure 6.4, following the sample case brief near the end of this chapter.

NAMES OF PARTIES

A report or record of a court's decision normally begins with the names of the parties on opposite sides of the legal dispute. In civil disputes, the individual, corporation, or other entity who initiates the lawsuit is called the **plaintiff**. The plaintiff's name is listed first. The abbreviation *v* (meaning "versus") separates the plaintiff's name from that of the individual, corporation, or other entity being sued, who is called the **defendant**. In criminal cases, there is no plaintiff. The government initiates cases in the name of the Queen. For this reason, almost all Canadian criminal cases begin with *R*. This is an abbreviation for *regina* (or *rex*), which is the Latin word for queen (or king). It is followed by *v* and the name of the defendant or accused.

On an appeal, the individual, corporation, or other entity who lost at trial and who initiates an appeal to a higher court is called the **appellant**. The other party is called the **respondent**. In such instances, the name of the appellant is generally placed first, followed by *v* and then the name of the respondent.

Other terms found in case names are *Re* and *Ex parte*. The first means "in the matter of" and precedes a named party. It is used in cases where someone is applying to the court for an interpretation of someone's rights. Cases in this category include bankruptcy, adoption, and certain estate matters. *Ex parte*, meaning "on the application of one party," is used when only one side is before the court. This might occur, for example, where, prior to trial, one party is applying to the court for an order to prevent the other party from dissipating certain assets. (Generally, these kinds of applications involve some kind of urgency.)

There are other terms used in case names to describe the parties or to qualify the nature of the proceedings, but these are the most common ones.

DATE OF DECISION

After the names of the parties, the law report lists the date of the court's decision. Be aware of the date. An old case can sometimes stand the test of time, but changes in the law or context may mean it is no longer a reliable precedent.

plaintiff
individual, corporation, or other entity who initiates a non-criminal lawsuit

defendant
individual, corporation, or other entity who defends a non-criminal lawsuit initiated by the plaintiff

appellant
individual, corporation, or other entity who lost at trial and who initiates an appeal to a higher court

respondent
individual, corporation, or other entity who won at trial and who is responding to the appellant on an appeal to a higher court

COURT AND JUDGES

After the date of the court's decision, the law report notes the court that decided the case, along with the judge or judges involved. It could list either a single judge, if the case involves a trial, or a panel of judges, if the case is heard on appeal.

HEADNOTE

headnote
concise summary of reasons for judgment, located near the beginning of a reported version of the case

A **headnote** is a concise summary of the entire case. The headnote is prepared by the editor of the law report, not by the judge or judges who wrote the decision. It is placed before the reasons for judgment, enabling the reader to quickly obtain an overview of the facts, issues, and reasons for the court's decision. It also lists the cases, legislation, and other secondary sources that the court examined in making its judgment. These features of the headnote make it an invaluable source for further research in the area. Note, however, that it is there only to assist the researcher and is not part of the judgment—it is not something you would rely on in court when making a legal argument, for instance.

NATURE OF THE PROCEEDINGS AND COUNSEL

Before reporting the actual decision, the law report generally states the purpose or nature of the proceeding—for example, "an appeal from a decision of Justice Smith"—and provides the names of the lawyers (counsel) representing each side of the dispute.

REASONS FOR JUDGMENT

This part of the law report contains the actual decision by the court. A student of case law will soon discover that individual judges have their own unique writing style. Generally, most judges adhere to the following format and order of presentation:

1. the nature of the proceedings,
2. the relevant facts of the case,
3. the legal issue(s) that must be resolved,
4. the argument of both lawyers at trial or on appeal,
5. the legal rule(s) pertaining to the issue(s),
6. the application of the rule(s), and
7. the court's conclusion(s).

obiter dicta **or** *obiter*
(sing. *obiter dictum***)**
statements made by the court in its reasons for judgment that may be of interest but that are inessential to the decision and therefore have no binding authority

The *ratio* of the case usually refers to the governing legal rule. It can also refer to the way in which a rule is applied to a given set of facts. Isolating the rule and the key facts to which it relates takes practice, and being able to determine the *ratio* of a case is the mark of a good legal researcher. Judicial statements about the law that may be of interest but that are not necessary to the decision in the case are called ***obiter dicta*** (sometimes shortened to ***obiter***). This is Latin for "statements said in passing."

Multiple Judgments

In the preceding discussion, we have been assuming a single judgment in the case. This will always be the case for trial judgments, because they involve a single judge. On appeals, however, there will be more than one judge. Provincial and territorial courts of appeal can have as many as five judges hearing the appeal. In the SCC, it can be up to nine. If the judges are unanimous on an appeal, there will be a single judgment. But often they are not unanimous, and two or more of the judges write their own reasons or judgments. Although the court *as a whole* will have disposed of the case in one way, there are multiple judgments.

The difficulty with multiple judgments is figuring out which judgment represents the judgment of the court. What is the governing rule or *ratio* in the case? Sometimes it is easy to answer this question, sometimes not. In cases where there are two or three judgments, you must first note which judges are agreeing with which judgment. (The names of the concurring judges are usually in brackets next to the name of the judge writing the judgment.) The number of concurring judges plus one (that is, the writer) gives the weight of the judgment in relation to the total number of judges hearing the appeal.

The following examples, all with a quorum of nine, illustrate some of the possibilities.

First, consider this example:

Disposition A (majority)	Disposition B (dissent)
Judgment X (5)	Judgment Y (4)

This is a simple case where there are only two judgments and there is a clear majority—a five/four split (four judges agreed with one writer's judgment and three agreed with the other writer's judgment). In this case, judgment X is the judgment of the court and is binding.

Now consider the following example:

Disposition A (majority)	Disposition B (dissent)
Judgment X (4)	Judgment Z (3)
Judgment Y (2)	

Here, there is a majority for Disposition A, but there is division within this majority with respect to reasons. Judgment X has the support of only four of the six judges agreeing with Disposition A. This means that, in the court as a whole, five judges do not agree with Judgment X. In other words, Judgment X is not the majority judgment of the whole court, only of the "majority of the majority." In practice, in cases of this type, Judgment X is generally followed by later courts because its weight exceeds Judgment Z. Strictly speaking, however, it is not binding because it does not have the support of the majority of the court.

Now consider the following example:

Disposition A (majority)	Disposition B (dissent)
Judgment X (3)	Judgment Z (4)
Judgment Y (2)	

Again, we have a split majority, but this time the number in dissent actually exceeds Judgment X. While Disposition A has gained a majority, it is arguable that no binding rule or holding (the court's answer to a legal issue) emerges from a case like this.

When briefing multiple-judgment cases (see the discussion of case briefs below), isolate the most important judgment—in the examples above, Judgment X—and do a case brief of it. In a note following the brief, summarize the differences between that judgment and the others. Were different rules applied? Or were the same rules applied but with a different conclusion or holding?

DISPOSITION

After the reasons for judgment, and at the end of the case, the formal order of the court is given. It could be, for example, "motion dismissed," "judgment for the plaintiff," or "appeal dismissed." Where there are multiple judgments, the disposition represents the decision of the majority.

Case Briefs

An effective technique for learning how to analyze legal problems is not just to read court decisions. Going one step further, by summarizing—or briefing—judgments, can help intensify the learning process. A **case brief** follows a defined pattern, with the constituent parts of the court's judgment summarized in a set order (key parts include the legal issues and the governing rules). The brief also provides a concise, easy-to-remember overview of the case.

There is no one way to brief a case, and different names may be used for the parts of the summary. What is important is that you understand what you are summarizing and how it relates to the overall process of reaching a reasoned legal decision.

case brief
summary of a case, with the constituent parts of the court's reasons for judgment arranged in a set order

Format of Case Briefs

Summarizing a case with the headings and components described below will help you understand and remember it and will help you become more proficient at legal analysis.

With some cases it is easy to find these elements because the judgment has headings similar or identical to those we use in this discussion. The use of headings is more common in recent judgments—newly appointed judges now receive training in judgment writing, among other things. In older judgments, headings were rarely used. Another challenge for the researcher who is trying to isolate the various parts of a judgment is ambiguous writing. Ambiguity is the result of hastily written reasons and sometimes, one suspects, of the judge's fear of committing to a clear position.

The ease with which the researcher or student will be able to break down a judgment depends on his level of experience and training. It is difficult for most people at first but gets easier with practice.

A sample case and the brief that was created from it are included following this discussion.

STYLE OF CAUSE

It is useful to begin with the name of the case.

FACTS

The facts make up the context that has given rise to the legal question(s) or issue(s) in a particular case. Sometimes the facts are complex, sometimes simple, and often the judgment includes more facts than are necessary to understand the issues. Only include the facts that are necessary in this regard. (Some rare cases—cases where purely legal questions are referred to the court—have no facts.)

PROCEEDINGS

This is where you describe the claim (who is suing whom for what) and, if the case is on appeal, the result in the lower court(s) and the grounds for appeal and cross-appeal (if there is one). This section is sometimes referred to as the *procedural history*. Note also that another way to format a case brief is to put the proceedings or procedural history information at the end of the facts section, combining these two sections.

ISSUE(S)

There may be one or more issues that arise from a given set of facts. Issues fall into two broad categories or types:

1. issues concerned with defining what the rules are, and
2. issues concerned with how the rules should be applied to the facts.

Most issues that arise in everyday cases are of the second type. The first type arises where the law is unclear or complex and the court needs to or is asked to sort it out. Both types may be found in the same judgment.

HOLDING(S)

For every issue there must be a holding. A holding is the court's answer to an issue. If the issue is of the first type, the holding will be a statement of the rule. If it is of the second type, the holding will concern how the rule is applied to the facts. If there is just one main rule relevant to the disposition of the case, this heading is sometimes named *ratio decidendi* or *ratio* for short (as described earlier in the chapter).

REASONING/REASONS

The reasoning is the court's explanation and justification for its holding(s). The court may refer to policy reasons for adopting or not adopting a particular rule—for example, a concern that it will flood the courts with litigation (the floodgates argument) or that it will cost the government or industry too much money ("indeterminate liability"). At other times, the court may apply or not apply an established rule based on a simple assessment of the facts, or because it feels bound by precedent. Note that some other case brief formats combine the holdings and reasons under one heading.

DISPOSITION/JUDGMENT

As noted, the disposition is the result of the case (for example, "judgment for the plaintiff," "appeal granted," or "new trial ordered") and is usually found at the end of a court's decision. And again, the word *judgment* here refers to the disposition of the case, but it can also refer to the entire set of reasons. Context should make the meaning clear.

Sample Case and Case Brief

CASE: *MATTHEWS V MACLAREN* (1969), 4 DLR (3D) 557 (ONT H CT J)

The *Matthews* case was based on a claim in negligence, an area of tort law that generates more litigation than any other type of claim (see Chapter 8, which includes an overview of the law of negligence). The argument in *Matthews* focused on the limited duty of a person to rescue another in distress. Two fatalities resulted from a boating mishap, and the estates of both victims, Matthews and Horsley, sued the boat owner. As explained in the case, the Matthews claim was actually one-half of the two combined claims. Only the portion of the judgment dealing with liability in the Matthews claim is set out.

REASONS FOR JUDGMENT

LACOURCIERE J.: - These two actions under the *Fatal Accidents Act*, R.S.O. 1960, c. 138, were tried together, and involve the claim of the widows and children respectively of the late Roland Edgar Matthews and the late John Albert Horsley, both of whom lost their lives in a tragedy on Lake Ontario on May 7, 1966. The defendant Kenneth MacLaren was at the material time the owner and operator of an Owens, Empress 30-foot six inch cabin cruiser known as the "Ogopogo" powered by two inboard 100 h.p. engines driving two propellers or twin screws. At the opening of trial, on consent, the action was discontinued against the defendant, Richard J. Jones, on terms. Any reference to the defendant hereafter will be to the defendant MacLaren only. A Halton County jury listened to the evidence during five days of the trial, and on January 24th defence counsel renewed a motion, which had been dismissed at the opening of trial, to strike out the jury notice; plaintiffs' counsel agreed and the jury was dismissed by me with regret.

On the day of the fatal accident, the late Roland Edgar Matthews and the late John Albert Horsley were gratuitous passengers, or invited guests, of the defendant on this boat, which left Port Credit Yacht Club at approximately 6:30 p.m. for the return voyage to Oakville. The weather at that time was starting to cool and a wind, blowing from the north-west crated a light chop on Lake Ontario. The "Ogopogo" with the defendant at the helm was proceeding at a speed of 10 to 12 knots; at that time Matthews, who had looked after the bowline on leaving Port Credit, was still sitting on the port side of the foredeck: another passenger, the defendant Richard J. Jones, was in the pilot's cockpit and the other four passengers, i.e., Horsley, one Donald Marck, and the two ladies -- Mrs. MacLaren and Mrs. Jones -- were in the cabin below. Jones observed Matthews get up and proceed towards the stern along the narrow catwalk on the port side of the boat, holding on to the rail, with his back to the water, and topple over backwards at the level of the windscreen. Jones immediately hollered "Roly's overboard" and the rescue operation began.

The defendant threw the boat controls in the neutral position and on leaning back could see Matthews, floating, with head and shoulders out of the water, some 40 to 50 ft. astern to starboard: he reversed the motors and backed towards Matthews, having pinned the control wheel with his stomach and looking over his shoulder using the throttle to manoeuvre and, according to Jones, swerving a bit, until the man in the water disappeared from his view behind the transom. The defendant then shut the engines down completely to drift towards Matthews: meanwhile, Jones had gone to the stern and thrown a life ring which landed some 10 ft. in front of Matthews, and as the boat got closer Donald Marck, also at the stern, was attempting to hook Matthews with a six-foot pikepole. Matthews was still floating -- arms outwards with his eyes open and staring, apparently unconscious. The motors had been shut down when the stern of the boat got to within four or five feet from Matthews, who could not be hooked when the boat was blown or drifted away a distance of 10 to 20 ft. The defendant MacLaren started the engines and reversed again towards Matthews.

A recounting of the facts begins here. Sometimes judges use headings for the various parts of their judgment. Lacourciere J used some headings, but not many.

Judges often start their reasons with a description of the action, and the appeal history, if there is one. Because this is a trial judgment, there is no appeal history.

Meanwhile, Jones had thrown a second lifejacket which had fallen on top of Matthews or under his nose.

By then some three or four minutes had elapsed since Matthews had fallen overboard and the situation was getting desperate. Horsley from the stern took off his shoes and trousers and yelling "my friend, my friend!" dived in while the boat was moving, and surfaced some 10 ft. away from Matthews. Mrs. Jones then noticed Matthews' body fall forward -- face and head in the water: she then courageously jumped in, one foot away, to hold his head up but Matthews had gone under the starboard quarter and could not be helped. Jones, seeing his wife in the water, ran up to the defendant and took over the controls without argument, swung the boat around and approached his wife "bow on", getting her on the starboard side. MacLaren and Marck grabbed her arms and pulled her out of the water. MacLaren reassumed the controls and shortly thereafter Horsley was picked up, but could not be resuscitated and was pronounced dead later at Port Credit.

The court is describing some of the evidence here. Be careful to distinguish between evidence and fact. What is important are the factual conclusions of the judge (or jury), not the evidence of a particular witness.

Although the outside temperature had been warm and pleasant in the afternoon, with a temperature of approximately 65°, the water was extremely cold: the only person who survived the immersion, Jean Jones, described how she felt paralysed, as if in a vat of ice cubes. The witness Burtershaw, chief operator of the Waterworks Department of the Oakville Public Utilities, gave evidence that the recorded water temperature at the intake pipe some 2,400 ft. from shore was a constant 39° on that day, with surface temperature probably **five degrees higher**.

The pathologist, Dr. D.F. Brunsdon, who examined Horsley's body, ascribed the cause of death to cardiac failure resulting from either sudden shock on immersion or from prolonged immersion in cold water. In the latter case, unconsciousness would precede death. It was his opinion after conducting the autopsy that death was probably due to sudden shock as a result of immersion, in which case death would be immediate or extremely quick; the deceased had been perfectly healthy before and there was no evidence of heart or any other disease. The body of Matthews was never recovered and the cause of his death remains undetermined.

Because of the allegation made in both actions (among other items of negligence) that the defendant was operating his motor boat while his ability to do so was impaired by alcohol, I will summarize the events leading up to the tragic occurrence.

The defendant, then a 51-year old steel salesman, had earlier in the morning one pint of beer with a sandwich at the Oakville Club, later a hamburger and one beer at the Oakville Powerboard Club with Mr. and Mrs. Jones; the outing was improvised, and a case of 24 pints of beer put on board: the defendant and each passenger had one pint of beer on the trip to Port Credit. The arrival of the "Ogopogo" at the Port Credit Club, and the docking process there was described in great detail by various witnesses because of the incident of damage to the stanchion, a vertical member of the stainless steel pulpit, on the stern of the "Stormalong" which was slightly damaged when hit by the bow of the "Ogopogo". **I am satisfied that this was a mere mishap caused by the temporary failure of one engine of the "Ogopogo", which can in no way reflect on the ability of the defendant who was at the helm.**

The defendant, as captain of the first boat -- so he claimed -- to dock at the Port Credit Yacht Club that season, arrived in jovial and exuberant mood and ordered champagne for all present. The steward of the yacht club relates that approximately forty people in the club shared four large (32 oz.) bottles of champagne. The MacLaren party was in the club between 3:30 and 6:30. The defendant admits having consumed two glasses of champagne during that period, intermingling freely with the Port Credit members, many of whom were friends. There is no evidence that the defendant had any of the other drinks being ordered and served that afternoon. After the accident, a glass of amber coloured liquid, presumably containing whisky, was found in a glass-holder near the controls of the cockpit. The defendant disclaims any knowledge of its contents and says that it must have been pressed upon him by friends upon leaving the dock of the Port Credit Yacht Club and forgotten and untouched by him.

This heading tells us that the analysis of issues dealing with liability begins here. Headings make judgments easier to read.

Liability:

1. Re Matthews' Claim

Notwithstanding the allegations pleaded that the defendant failed to ensure the safety of his passengers and particularly of the deceased Matthews by having **them wear life-preservers on board, I am satisfied that in the circumstances this** does not constitute actionable negligence. The only negligence argued here relates to the defendant's condition and to his conduct following Matthews' fall **into the water. The first question therefore is whether there existed a legal duty** on the part of the defendant to come to the rescue of a passenger who fell overboard by reason of his own misfortune or carelessness, and without any negligence on the part of the defendant or any person for whom the defendant would be vicariously responsible. This question, strictly a determination of law for the Court and not a question of fact for the jury, was repeatedly answered in the negative in the 19th century decisions (based on the distinction between "misfeasance" and "non-feasance") illustrated in Ontario by the 1913 decision of the Ontario Court of Appeal in *Vanvalkenburg* v. *Northern Navigation Co.* (1913), 30 O.L.R. 142, 19 D.L.R. 649. In that case, a seaman employed on a steamboat had fallen overboard by his own carelessness, and drowned: Mulock, C.J.Ex., speaking for the Appellate Division said at p. 146 O.L.R., p. 652 D.L.R.:

Lacourciere J begins his discussion of the first issue here. Look for pointer words and phrases, such as "The question is ..." to help isolate the issues in a case. Based on the detailed analysis that follows, it is clear that this is the most significant issue in the case.

> The question then arises whether the defendants were guilty of any actionable negligence in not using all reasonable means in order to rescue the drowning man. Undoubtedly such is one's moral duty, but what legal duty did the defendants owe to the deceased to rescue him if possible, from his position of danger, brought about, not by their, but his own, negligence?

And at p. 148 O.L.R., p. 653 D.L.R.:

> His voluntary act in thus putting himself in a position of danger, from the fatal consequences of which, unfortunately, there was no escape except through the defendants' intervention, could not create a legal obligation on the defendants' part to stop the ship or adopt other means to save the deceased.

This decision was followed by an amendment to the *Canada Shipping Act*, R.S.C. 1927, c. 186, enacting [1934, c. 44, s. 519] what is now s. 526 [R.S.C. 1952, c. 29]:

> 526(1) The master or person in charge of a vessel shall, so far as he can do so without serious danger to his own vessel, her crew and passengers, if any, render assistance to every person, even if that person be a subject of a foreign state at war with Her Majesty, who is found at sea and in danger of **being lost, and if he fails to do so he is liable to a fine not exceeding one** thousand dollars.

The section may not be applicable to or refer to the assistance to a passenger who falls overboard, but the shocking reluctance of the common law to recognize as a legal duty the moral obligation to assist a fellow human being in this predicament has been overcome in cases where a special relation exists, such as that of a carrier to a passenger in peril overboard, by thinly disguising the moral obligation as an "implied contract": See *Prosser on Torts,* 3rd ed., c.10, p. 336 under the heading "Duty to Aid One in Peril"; *Fleming on Torts*, 2nd ed., p. 166; *Salmond on Torts*, 14th ed., p. 57.

Two American decisions illustrate this trend: In *Harris* v. *Pennsylvania Railroad Co.* (1931), 50 F. 2d 866, where the evidence disclosed that a seaman on a flat had fallen overboard, it was held on appeal that the negligence of the crew in failing to assist the seaman should have been left to the jury on the evidence, the Court making the following comment at pp. 868-9:

> . . . it is implied in the contract that the ship shall use every reasonable means to save the life of a human being who has no other source of help. The universal custom of the sea demands as much wherever human life is in danger. The seaman's contract of employment requires it as a matter of right.

The decision, *The "Cappy", Hutchinson* v. *Dickie*, [1947] Am. Mar. Cas. 1467, 162 F. 2d 103, was quoted and relied upon by the defendant's counsel. The facts of the case are somewhat similar to those of the present case, in that during the daylight hours, after the consumption of intoxicating liquor, the owner of a 38-foot cabin cruiser who was at the wheel lost an invited guest who fell overboard in Lake Erie near Cleveland. The trial Judy found that the helmsman was incapable of co-ordination due to the excessive use of alcoholic stimulants coupled with physical impairment, and was negligent in failing to turn his cruiser about instead of back it astern. The Circuit Court of Appeal reversed the trial judgment and dismissed the case, on the basis that the decree had no substantial support in the evidence, and commenting at p. 1473:

> We think that if appellant erred at all in backing instead of turning the cruiser, the error was one of judgement and not of negligence. Further, we think an insurmountable objection to the judgement in appellee's favor is the entire lack of evidence that anything appellant did or left undone caused his efforts at rescue to fail. It does not appear that if appellant had turned the cruiser instead of backing it, Dickie would or should have been save.

The Court did not disagree, however, with the universally recognized duty of the owner to make a reasonable effort to rescue the man overboard.

In *Silva's Fishing Corporation (Pty.) Ltd.* v. *Maweza*, [1957] (2) So. Afr. L.R. 256 at p. 263, the following appears in a discussion whether there exists a legal or a moral duty to rescue:

> A duty to rescue is not special or subject to peculiarly restricted rules. It is simply a duty to act reasonably and such a duty may arise out of the circumstances of the case. It will be for the Court to decide in each case whether the circumstances are such as to give rise to a legal duty.

The learned author of *Fleming on Torts*, 3rd ed., discussed at p. 145 under the heading "Duty of Care", "Duties of Affirmative Action", the distinction above referred to, between misfeasance and nonfeasance, and compares it to the distinction, ". . . between active misconduct working positive injury to others **and passive inaction, failing merely to take positive steps to benefit others or** to protect them from some impending harm". It is still in the modern law of negligence that there is no general duty to come to the rescue of a person who **finds himself in peril from a source completely unrelated to the defendant, even** where little risk or effort would be involved in assisting: thus a person on a dock can with legal impunity ignore the call for help of a drowning person, even refusing to throw a life ring. The law leaves the remedy to a person's conscience.

There is, however, in the words of Fleming, *ibid*, at p. 148, ". . . strong **support for a duty of affirmative care, including aid and rescue, incidental to** certain special relations, like that of employer and employee, carrier and passenger, and occupier and his lawful visitors".

Extending the *quasi*-contractual duty of a carrier to his passenger in peril, it seems to me that the relation between the master of a pleasure boat and his invited guest should also require a legal duty to aid and rescue. Parliament **reflecting the conscience of the community has seen fit to impose on the master** a duty to render assistance to any stranger, including an enemy alien "found at sea and in danger of being lost" (s. 526, *Canada Shipping Act*); the common law

After a lengthy discussion of the law that included cases (precedents), a statute, and some texts (secondary authorities), the judge reaches his conclusion as to the applicable principle. He has extended the rule to include a new situation, and in so doing has created new law. This is one way that the common law develops, by incremental changes to existing rules.

can be no less solicitous for the safety of an invited guest and must impose upon the master the duty to attempt a rescue when this can be done without imperilling the safety of the vessel, her crew and passengers. The common law must keep pace with the demand and expectations of a civilized community, the sense of social obligation, and brand as tortuous negligence the failure to help a man overboard in accordance with the universal custom of the sea.

Lacourciere J applies another principle (apparently, this one is "established") to resolve the first issue.

In any event, if the defendant, as he did here, affirmatively undertakes the rescue operation, he is by law regarded as assuming a duty to act, and will thereafter be liable for his negligence: *Prosser on Torts* (1941), pp. 194-5, puts it this way:

> But further, if the defendant attempts to aid him, and takes control of the situation, he is regarded as entering voluntarily into a relation of responsibility, and hence as assuming a duty. Thereafter he will be liable for any failure to use reasonable care in dealing with him, until the emergency has ended, and particularly if he abandons him in a position of danger.

The analysis of the second issue starts here.

Having found a legal duty to rescue, or a voluntary assumption of duty, the next question is, is the standard of conduct applicable in the performance of such duty? Bearing in mind that the man in the street would not have any knowledge of a sea rescue operation, the test here is: what would the reasonable boat operator do in the circumstances, attributing to such person the reasonable skill and experience required of the master of a cabin cruiser who is responsible for the safety and rescue of his passengers?

Expert witnesses were called on behalf of the plaintiffs to assist the Court in setting out what such ordinary, prudent, reasonable boat operator would have done in the circumstances. The first was Captain Livingstone, Chairman of the Marine Department at George Brown Community College, Toronto, a qualified sea captain under a British certificate who recently acted as Education Vice-Commander of the Toronto Power Squadron, with considerable experience since 1925 on all ships including yachts of the "Ogopogo" type. The other expert was Captain John Kenneth Mumford, Communications Office of the Toronto Harbour Commission, British Master's Certificate 1957, and the author of a boating course covering all safety aspects of operating a power cruiser, and winner of every major navigation contest on Lake Ontario. These two highly qualified seamen agree that there are no statutory regulations or guidelines covering the rescue procedure in a "man overboard" situation, and that none is mentioned in the well-known Canadian booklet "Safety Afloat". This situation, according to them, is a common emergency calling for the common sense of every prudent seaman who should be prepared to react quickly and instinctively, so to speak automatically.

The following should be the procedure followed: having ascertained on which side the man fell, the master first turns his boat towards the same side to clear the propellers and leaves the engine in neutral unless the man overboard is astern and in no danger from them. A life ring is cast, and the master then turns around to approach the man against the wind, allowing him to come on the leeward side where passengers or crewmen can grasp him and haul him in at the lowest point of the boat. The maximum time involved would be one to two minutes or slightly more. Both experts emphasized many reasons why the procedure of reversing the engines and backing should never be adopted, unless in a confined area where the boat cannot be turned around: in addition to loss of control and manoeuvrability, there is the impossibility of keeping sight of the man astern when approaching, the danger of the propellers, and complete loss of control, at the mercy of wind and wave, on shutting down the engines. In the opinion of Captain Mumford, the bearing down stern first here adopted by the defendant was the sign of an incompetent operator: the average prudent owner of a 30-foot boat according to both experts should be competent in the rescue procedure described, and if not should not undertake to operate his boat. It is the procedure taught to students, and one in fact known by the defendant and practised by him on many previous occasions.

I can only conclude that the defendant's adoption of the wrong procedure in the circumstances was negligent, being a failure to exercise the reasonable care that the ordinary, prudent, reasonable operator would have shown in effecting the "man overboard" rescue. The defendant in his evidence admitted that he made what he described as an error of judgement and did not attempt to justify the rescue procedure adopted.

Detective Sergeant John Brooks of the Town of Port Credit Police, who had ample opportunity to observe the defendant at the yacht club, and at the Police Station after the accident, formed the opinion that MacLaren's ability to drive an automobile or operate a vessel was impaired by alcohol, and he would have recommended the laying of criminal charges to the Crown Attorney. The admitted consumption by the defendant and the necessary inferences from surrounding circumstances, plus the extraordinary conduct of the defendant during the rescue attempt, force me to the conclusion that the defendant was unable to exercise proper judgement in the emergency created because of his excessive consumption of alcohol.

The third issue. —— It is trite law that liability does not follow a finding of negligence, even where there exists a legally recognized duty, unless the defendant's conduct is the effective cause of the loss: *Cork* v. *Kirby MacLean, Ltd.,* [1952] 2 All E.R. 402 at p. 407, *per* Denning, L.J.:

> Subject to the question of remoteness, causation is, I think, a question of fact. If you can say that the damage would not have happened but for a particular fault, then that fault is in fact a cause of the damage; but if you can say that the damage would have happened just the same, fault or no fault, then the fault is not a cause of the damage.

In the present case the burden is on the plaintiff to prove by a preponderance of evidence that the defendant's negligence was the effective cause of Matthews' death. Obviously the defendant is not responsible for Matthews' fall overboard. There is no evidence in the present case that Matthews was ever alive after falling in the water: all witnesses agree that he was motionless and staring. Bearing in mind that Horsley, a young man than Matthews, in the opinion of the pathologist probably died of shock immediately or shortly after his immersion, it is reasonable to think that Matthews, 16 years older, did not survive longer, and after he hit the water there never was a sign of life or consciousness. It was impossible in the present case to discharge this burden by a pathologist's report; in the case of a missing body, witnesses' evidence of some struggle or sign of life on the part of the deceased during rescue operations would be required. I **The plaintiffs have** —— am reluctantly forced to the conclusion that, on the balance of probabilities, it has not been shown that Matthews' life could have been saved. The defendant's negligence therefore was not the cause of Matthews' death and there can be no liability.

The plaintiffs have failed to prove one of the essential elements in a negligence action: causation. While they succeeded on the first two points, their failure on this one means they lose the whole case.

* * *

CASE BRIEF

The following case brief summarizes the preceding decision using headings as described above.

Matthews v MacLaren

Facts

The defendant (Δ) was the owner/operator of a cabin cruiser. On the day in question, he invited some guests for an outing on his boat. One of his guests, Matthews, fell overboard. The Δ reversed the motors and backed toward Matthews. Approximately four minutes elapsed as various rescue attempts were made. Matthews was apparently unconscious in the water, and he eventually disappeared under the boat and his body was never found. The Δ was impaired because of excessive consumption of alcohol. The "standard" rescue procedure in a "man overboard" situation is to approach the person overboard "bow on."

The Greek letter delta (Δ) is often used as an abbreviation for the defendant, and the Greek letter pi (π) is used for the plaintiff.

In applying the guidelines to isolate the key facts, the parties, the cause of action, and the elements of the claim were noted. Only facts relating to these specifics were included.

Proceedings

The plaintiffs (π s), the widow and children of Matthews, commenced this action under fatal accidents legislation claiming negligence on the part of the Δ.

Issues

1 a) Whether there exists a duty on the part of the master of a pleasure boat to rescue a gratuitous passenger who falls overboard through no negligence on the part of the former?

   b) In any event, whether there existed a duty on the Δ to rescue Matthews having commenced the rescue operation?

2 a) Assuming the Δ owed a duty to rescue, what is the requisite standard of care?

   b) Assuming the Δ owed a duty to rescue, did the Δ breach the requisite standard of care by using the wrong procedure and by being impaired?

Note the two types of issues. 1a and 2a are *rule formulation issues*. The questions were about the nature of the applicable rule. The law was not clear and required some analysis (although for 2a, not much). 1b and 2b were *rule application issues*.

Holdings

1 a) Extending the quasi-contractual duty of a carrier to his passenger in peril, the relation between the master of a pleasure boat and his invited guest requires a duty to aid and rescue.

   b) Also, the Δ having commenced the rescue operation was by law regarded as having assumed a duty to act.

2 a) The test here is: what would the reasonable boat operator do in the circumstances, attributing to such person the reasonable skill and experience required of the master of a cabin cruiser who is responsible for the safety and rescue of his passengers?

b) The Δ failed to exercise the reasonable care of a reasonable boat operator in his rescue attempt by adopting the wrong procedure and by being impaired.

Reasoning

1 a) The court affirmed the rule that there is no general duty to rescue, but declined to follow the *Vanvalkenburg* case where the court held that the operators of a ship were not under a duty to rescue a seaman in their employ, who had fallen overboard through his own negligence. The court cited an amendment to the *Canada Shipping Act* enacted after the *Vanvalkenburg* case imposing a statutory duty on the master or person in charge of a vessel to rescue every person found at sea. The court also cited *Fleming on Torts* where it was stated that there was support for a duty to rescue incidental to certain special relations, like that of employer-employee, carrier-passenger, and occupier-visitor. In light of these authorities and the "expectations of a civilized community," the court extended the common law duty to rescue to include the relation of master of a pleasure boat and his invited guest.

b) The court simply applied the established rule that where a person attempts to rescue someone and takes control of the situation, he is regarded as entering voluntarily into a relation of responsibility, and hence assuming a duty.

2 a) The court adopted the standard of the reasonable boat operator stating that the man in the street would not have any knowledge of a sea rescue operation.

b) The court offered no arguments in support of its finding as a fact that the Δ had not exercised the care of an ordinary, prudent, reasonable boat operator.

Disposition/Judgment

The π s' action was dismissed. Although the court found the Δ in breach of his duty to Matthews, the court found that the Δ's conduct had not in fact caused Matthew's death.

Causation was not set out as a separate issue because there was no analysis of the legal principle involved. The judge made a purely factual determination: the Δ did not cause the loss.

FIGURE 6.4 Sample Case Report

The *Doern* case was seen as a case of interest to the legal community and was published in a number of report series. This excerpt is from the *British Columbia Law Reports*. At the beginning, the publisher has added a catchwords summary followed by a headnote.

Doern v. Phillips Estate   Kirkpatrick J. 349

[Indexed as: Doern v. Phillips Estate]

DOUGLAS ALLEN DOERN

v.

Estate of RONALD MICHAEL PHILLIPS, DECEASED,
his representative ad litem, PUBLIC TRUSTEE, said
PUBLIC TRUSTEE, VANCOUVER POLICE DEPARTMENT,
CITY OF VANCOUVER, FRED MANSVELD and R.. IN
RIGHT OF PROVINCE OF BRITISH COLUMBIA;

FRED MANSVELD, VANCOUVER CITY POLICE
DEPARTMENT, CITY OF VANCOUVER, R. IN RIGHT
OF PROVINCE OF BRITISH COLUMBIA, Estate of
RONALD MICHAEL PHILLIPS, DECEASED, his
representative ad litem, PUBLIC TRUSTEE and
said PUBLIC TRUSTEE (Third Parties)

Supreme Court
Kirkpatrick J.

Heard – September 14-16, 21, 26-30, October 3-7, 13-14
and 24-26, 1994
Judgment – December 13, 1994

Catchwords summary

Police — Duties and liability — Negligence — During police chase fleeing driver striking and severely injuring plaintiff driver — Injured driver suing police department and one officer — Court considering standard of care of police under s. 118 of Motor Vehicle Act and protection of officers from liability under s. 21 of Police Act — Police department 25 per cent liable for negligence involving pursuit guidelines — Officer not following guidelines but not liable as not grossly negligent — Fleeing driver 75 per cent liable.

Negligence — Remoteness of damage — Causation — During police chase fleeing driver striking and severely injuring plaintiff driver — Police negligence being one proximate cause of accident — Police 25 per cent liable to injured driver — Fleeing driver 75 per cent liable.

Administrative law — Judicial review of decisions — Characterization of function of tribunal — During police chase fleeing driver striking and severely injuring plaintiff driver — Police implementation of pursuit guidelines being operational matter and open to judicial review — Police negligent in implementation of guidelines.

Headnote

The Vancouver police manual prescribed the policy for police pursuits by car. The underlying principle was the capture of a fleeing suspect without unnecessarily endangering the police or other persons. Pursuits were normally limited to the primary unit which started the pursuit and one secondary unit. Other units were not to join the pursuit unless assigned. "Paralleling" a pursuit on a nearby street was forbidden. The duties of the chief dispatcher and field supervisor were to assume command, control police actions and ensure that police procedure was followed. The chief dispatcher was to obtain, assess and disseminate information. The pursuing units were to inform him of all relevant facts. If the police "lost" the fleeing car, the primary unit was immediately to inform the chief dispatcher and all police units were to resume their normal duties. Discontinuing a pursuit was to be considered when a

FIGURE 6.4 Sample Case Report   continued

Doern v. Phillips Estate   Kirkpatrick J. 351

command and the dispatcher failed to elicit vital information. The accumulation of occurrences of clear danger in the pursuit, which went unreported to those in command, would have mandated ending the pursuit. In failing to terminate in the face of clear danger, the police failed to meet the required standard of care.

Section 21(3) of the *Police Act* holds an officer liable for acts of gross negligence. "Gross negligence" is a very marked departure from the standards by which responsible people habitually govern themselves. The definition is not rigid, but reflects the degree to which the conduct falls below the appropriate standard of care. Police officers engaged in a pursuit have a reasonably high standard of care because of the inherent danger of such pursuits. Such higher standard of care raises the standard for gross negligence. The officer in the third unit had the hardest role in the pursuit because he had no partner to communicate with the dispatcher. In the circumstances, the line between negligence and gross negligence was very fine indeed. However, the officer's conduct was not grossly negligent.

The test for causation-in-fact is the "but-for" test. A defendant has caused a plaintiff's loss if the plaintiff would not have suffered the loss but for the defendant's act. Where a defendant creates or materially contributes to a significant risk of injury, and injury occurs that is squarely within the risk, the defendant is liable for the injury even though there are other later factors also causing or materially contributing to that injury. "But for" the pursuit the police initiated and negligently conducted, the injured driver's injuries would not have occurred. The police thus caused his loss. Further, the police materially increased his risk of injury by conducting the pursuit as they did, and by so doing materially contributed to the cause of his injury. The fact that the fleeing suspect actually collided with the injured driver's car was immaterial. Such an event was within the risk created by the police. As such, their negligence was also a proximate cause of the accident.

The implementation of government policy decisions is an operational matter and thus open to judicial review. The police implementation of their pursuit guidelines was negligent. That implementation was an operational matter. Thus whether the guidelines themselves were policy or operational decisions was immaterial. The police were not exempt from the duty which they would otherwise owe to users of the road.

Section 1 of the *Negligence Act* provides that where it is not possible to establish different degrees of fault, liability shall be apportioned equally. Here, it was not impossible to establish different degrees of fault. While the police were negligent and a proximate cause of the accident, one could not ignore the fleeing driver's negligence. Having regard to his reckless actions and his apparent response to the accelerations of the police, he should be found 75 per cent liable and the police 25 per cent liable.

Cases considered

Almeida v. Town of North Providence, 468 A. 2d 915 (R.I. Sup. Ct., 1983) — referred to.
Anns v. Merton London Borough Council, [1978] A.C. 728, (sub nom. *Anns v. London Borough Council of Merton*) [1977] 2 All E.R. 492 (H.L.) — considered.

At the end of the headnote, the *Cases considered* section lists all cases considered in the decision.

FIGURE 6.4 Sample Case Report   continued

Barratt v. North Vancouver (District), [1980] 2 S.C.R. 418, 27 B.C.L.R. 182, 8 M.V.R. 294, 13 M.P.L.R. 116, 14 C.C.L.T. 169, 114 D.L.R. (3d) 577, 33 N.R. 293 — considered.

Brown v. British Columbia (Minister of Transportation & Highways), [1994] 1 S.C.R. 420, [1994] 4 W.W.R. 194, 89 B.C.L.R. (2d) 1, 19 C.C.L.T. (2d) 268, 164 N.R. 161, 42 B.C.A.C. 1, 112 D.L.R. (4th) 1, 20 Admin. L.R. (2d) 1, 2 M.V.R. (3d) 43 — applied.

Jones v. Denomme (February 28, 1994), Doc. 5411/90 (Ont. Gen. Div.) — considered.

Just v. British Columbia (1989), [1989] 2 S.C.R. 1228, [1990] 1 W.W.R. 385, 41 B.C.L.R. (2d) 350, 1 C.C.L.T. (2d) 1, 18 M.V.R. (2d) 1, 103 N.R. 1, 64 D.L.R. (4th) 689, 41 Admin. L.R. 161 — applied.

McCulloch v. Murray, [1942] S.C.R. 141, [1942] 2 D.L.R. 179 — applied.

McGhee v. National Coal Board, [1973] 1 W.L.R. 1, [1972] 3 All E.R. 1008 (H.L.) — considered.

Moore v. Fanning (1987), 49 M.V.R. 161, 60 O.R. (2d) 225, 41 C.C.L.T. 67 (H.C.) — considered.

Ogilvie v. Donkin, [1949] 1 W.W.R. 439 (B.C. C.A.) — applied.

O'Reilly v. C., [1978] 3 W.W.R. 145, affirmed [1979] 3 W.W.R. 124, 8 C.C.L.T. 188, 99 D.L.R. (3d) 45 (Man. C.A.) — considered.

Pepper v. Hoover (1976), 71 D.L.R. (3d) 129 (Alta. T.D.) — considered.

Powell v. Guttman, [1978] 5 W.W.R. 228, 6 C.C.L.T. 183, 89 D.L.R. (2d) 180, 2 L. Med. Q. 279 at 291 (Man. C.A.) — applied.

Priestman v. Colangelo, [1959] S.C.R. 615, 30 C.R. 209, 124 C.C.C. 1, 19 D.L.R. (2d) 1 — applied.

R. v. Rahey, [1987] 1 S.C.R. 588, 75 N.R. 81, 78 N.S.R. (2d) 183, 193 A.P.R. 183, 57 C.R. (3d) 289, 33 C.C.C. (3d) 289, 39 D.L.R. (4th) 481, 33 C.R.R. 275 — applied.

Smith v. British Columbia (Attorney General) (1988), 30 B.C.L.R. (2d) 356 (C.A.) — considered.

Snell v. Farrell, [1990] 2 S.C.R. 311, 110 N.R. 200, 4 C.C.L.T. (2d) 229, 72 D.L.R. (4th) 289, 107 N.B.R. (2d) 94, 267 A.P.R. 94 — considered.

Thornton v. Shore, 666 P. 2d 655, 233 Kan. 737 (Sup. Ct., 1983) — referred to.

Vallery v. Po (1971), 23 D.L.R. (3d) 92 (B.C. S.C.) — applied.

Walker v. Coates, [1968] S.C.R. 599, 64 W.W.R. 449, 68 D.L.R. (2d) 436 — considered.

Watt v. Hertfordshire County Council, [1954] 1 W.L.R. 835, [1954] 2 All E.R. 368 (C.A.) — applied.

Whitehouse v. Jordan, [1981] 1 W.L.R. 246, [1981] 1 All E.R. 267 (H.L.) — applied.

Statutes considered

Good Samaritan Act, R.S.B.C. 1979, c. 155
    s. 1 — considered.

Motor Vehicle Act, R.S.B.C. 1979, c. 288
    s. 76 — considered.
    s. 79 — considered.
    s. 118 — considered.

Municipal Act, R.S.B.C. 1979, c. 290
    s. 755.1(3) — considered.

Most editors also include a *Statutes considered* section.

FIGURE 6.4 Sample Case Report   concluded

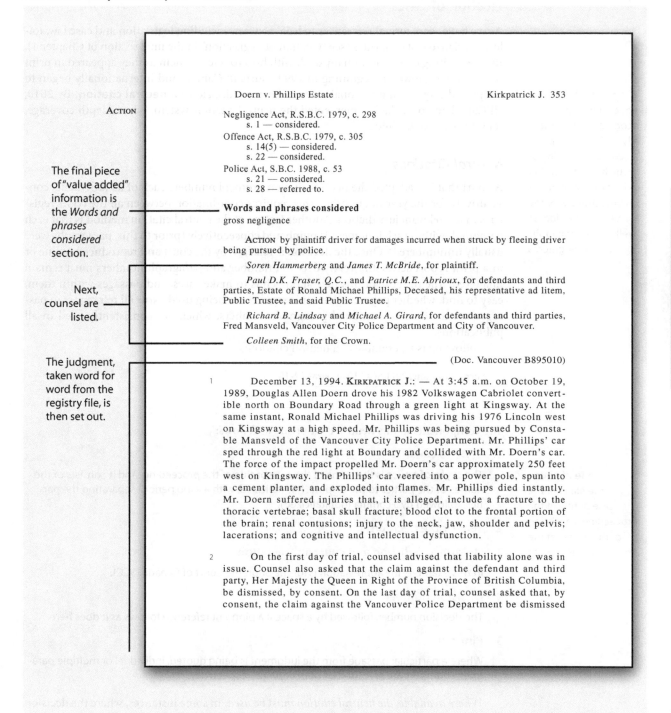

The final piece of "value added" information is the *Words and phrases considered* section.

Next, counsel are listed.

The judgment, taken word for word from the registry file, is then set out.

Doern v. Phillips Estate   Kirkpatrick J. 353

Negligence Act, R.S.B.C. 1979, c. 298
    s. 1 — considered.
Offence Act, R.S.B.C. 1979, c. 305
    s. 14(5) — considered.
    s. 22 — considered.
Police Act, S.B.C. 1988, c. 53
    s. 21 — considered.
    s. 28 — referred to.

Words and phrases considered
gross negligence

ACTION by plaintiff driver for damages incurred when struck by fleeing driver being pursued by police.

Soren Hammerberg and *James T. McBride*, for plaintiff.

Paul D.K. Fraser, Q.C., and *Patrice M.E. Abrioux*, for defendants and third parties, Estate of Ronald Michael Phillips, Deceased, his representative ad litem, Public Trustee, and said Public Trustee.

Richard B. Lindsay and *Michael A. Girard*, for defendants and third parties, Fred Mansveld, Vancouver City Police Department and City of Vancouver.

Colleen Smith, for the Crown.

(Doc. Vancouver B895010)

1   December 13, 1994. KIRKPATRICK J.: — At 3:45 a.m. on October 19, 1989, Douglas Allen Doern drove his 1982 Volkswagen Cabriolet convertible north on Boundary Road through a green light at Kingsway. At the same instant, Ronald Michael Phillips was driving his 1976 Lincoln west on Kingsway at a high speed. Mr. Phillips was being pursued by Constable Mansveld of the Vancouver City Police Department. Mr. Phillips' car sped through the red light at Boundary and collided with Mr. Doern's car. The force of the impact propelled Mr. Doern's car approximately 250 feet west on Kingsway. The Phillips' car veered into a power pole, spun into a cement planter, and exploded into flames. Mr. Phillips died instantly. Mr. Doern suffered injuries that, it is alleged, include a fracture to the thoracic vertebrae; basal skull fracture; blood clot to the frontal portion of the brain; renal contusions; injury to the neck, jaw, shoulder and pelvis; lacerations; and cognitive and intellectual dysfunction.

2   On the first day of trial, counsel advised that liability alone was in issue. Counsel also asked that the claim against the defendant and third party, Her Majesty the Queen in Right of the Province of British Columbia, be dismissed, by consent. On the last day of trial, counsel asked that, by consent, the claim against the Vancouver Police Department be dismissed

Citation of Cases

As we have seen, formal references to legal sources, including legislation and case law, follow specialized citation rules (see "Citation of Legislation" in the final section of Chapter 4). Rules for citing cases traditionally dealt with how to refer to them as they appeared in print report series. However, beginning in 1999 courts in Canada and internationally began to adopt and require an additional citation for their decisions: a **neutral citation**. By 2010, all Canadian courts had implemented the neutral citation system. For in-depth coverage, refer to the McGill Guide.[39]

neutral citation
unique citation protocol, recognized internationally and in all Canadian courts, according to which courts number each of their judgments consecutively for the year in question, as well as the paragraphs within judgments

Neutral Citations

A court that has adopted the neutral citation protocol numbers each of its judgments consecutively for the year in question. This requires coordination between all the court registries in the relevant jurisdiction. Another feature of the neutral citation method is that each paragraph within each judgment is numbered consecutively (prior to this, paragraphs were usually unnumbered). Once the decision is released by the court and reproduced online or in a print report series, the yearly decision number and paragraph numbers must remain unaltered. The purpose of this new approach is to make cases, and passages within them, easy to find, whether paper or electronic sources are being used. Now all references to passages are to the court-assigned paragraph numbers, which are consistently used in all publications.

Following is an example of a neutral citation:

Kerr v Baranow, 2011 SCC 10 at paras 12-15

1   2   3   4   5

The components in this neutral citation are as follows:

1   **Style of cause**

style of cause
the name of the case or title of the proceeding, consisting of the names of the parties to the dispute

The **style of cause** is the name of the case or title of the proceeding, and it consists of the names of the parties to the dispute. It is italicized, with a *v* (no period) separating the parties, followed by a comma (not italicized).

2   **Year of the decision**

3   **Unique jurisdiction and court abbreviation**

In this example, the abbreviation is for the Supreme Court of Canada (SCC).

4   **Decision number**

The decision number, followed by a space if a pinpoint reference follows as it does here.

5   **Pinpoint**

Where a particular passage from the judgment is being quoted, individual or multiple paragraph numbers are preceded by *para* or *paras*, respectively.

Where available, the neutral citation must be used. In some instances, where the decision has not been reported in a print report series, it will be the only citation available. Such cases will almost always be available online, because most courts now publish their decisions online soon after they are handed down.

---

39   McGill Law Journal, *Canadian Guide to Uniform Legal Citation*, 9th ed (Toronto: Carswell, 2018).

Print Report Citations

As mentioned, all Canadian court systems adopted the neutral citation protocol as of 2010. Since then, all reported citations will also have a neutral citation. For example:

Kerr v Baranow, 2011 SCC 10 at paras 12-15, 18, [2011] 1 SCR 269.

It was common practice to also include at least one print report citation if one was available, as a parallel (or extra) citation following the neutral citation. However, with the 9th edition of the McGill Guide, the recommended protocol is to no longer include parallel citations if there is a neutral citation.[40] This is a general rule, however, and a print citation should be included if it is otherwise necessary. For instance, it might be appropriate to include a parallel print citation if you know the reader will not have access to the decision online (an unlikely occurrence), but will have access to the print reporter. Assuming this is the situation, as you can see in the example just given, the neutral citation is set out first, together with any pinpoint reference (*paras 12-15, 18*). Where the report series reports by year (rather than by volume), the year is set out in square brackets. In this particular instance, the year of the decision and the year of publication are the same. (Sometimes, the year of publication is later than the year of the decision.) Set out the volume number after the year of the publication. Next is the law report abbreviation (*SCR*). Note that no periods separate the letters, in keeping with the McGill style. The last element in the citation is the page number—the first page of the case in the report series volume.

The following is an example of a print report citation *without* a neutral citation:[41]

Doern v Phillips Estate (1994), 2 BCLR (3d) 349 at 359 (SC).
 1   2 3 4 5 6 7 8

The components shown in this example are as follows:

1   **Style of cause**

The style of cause, set in italic, appears first in a case citation. As with neutral citations, the plaintiff's name precedes the defendant's, and the names are separated with a *v* (no period). Usually, last names are used, not titles or first names. When referring to business entities (corporations and partnerships), always include *Co, Corp, Inc, Ltd, Limited,* or *LLP* (or other words or abbreviations identifying the business).

In criminal cases, the Crown is usually *R*; however, if the Crown is the defendant/respondent, terms such as *The Queen* or *Regina* are used. In civil cases, the Crown is *Canada* or *Manitoba*, for example (depending on whether it is the federal Crown or a provincial Crown that is the party to the lawsuit). Specific bodies representing the Crown are designated in parentheses: for example, "New Brunswick (Workplace Health, Safety and Compensation Commission)." Where there are multiple parties, only the names of the first plaintiff and the first defendant are shown.

2   **Year of decision**

After the style of cause, the decision year is included in round brackets. This is done in cases where, as here, the report series reports by volume number and not by year. If the report series reports by year, include the year in the report series portion of the citation, in square brackets. Sometimes a case is published in the year after the case is decided, in which case you may need to include both a year in round brackets (indicating the year of decision)

---

40   Note that it is still recommended to include at least one parallel citation for older cases that do not have a neutral citation.

41   The purpose of this example is to highlight the elements of a print citation and does not include parallel citations.

and a year in square brackets. (Note, however, that if there is a neutral citation preceding a report series citation, it will never be necessary to include the year in round brackets; the neutral citation makes it clear what the year of the decision is.)

3 **Volume of law report**

Set out the volume number, followed by a space. Law reports consist of numerous volumes that cover many years. If the report series being cited reports by volume number and not by year, the volume numbers can get quite high, sometimes in the hundreds. If the report series reports by year, there still may be a volume number following the year in square brackets, but the numbers run only for the year in question and will never be that high.

4 **Law report abbreviation**

Next is the law report abbreviation. Cases are always cited according to the abbreviated form of the law report in which they are found. Many law reports state in the front of each volume how they are to be cited—what abbreviations should be used.

5 **Law report series**

The law report series appears, where applicable, after the law report abbreviation. Periodically, a law report may change its format and binding, or make other editorial changes. When this occurs, the law report may begin a new series. This means that the numbering system begins over again. If a law report has multiple series, the series number, starting with the second one, is indicated in round brackets—(2d)—followed by a space. The abbreviations are 2d, 3d, 4th, 5th, and so on. Superscript is not used, and there is no *n* in 2d or *r* in 3d.

6 **Page**

After the law report abbreviation or (if there is one) series indication, the page number on which the case begins in the law report is set out. The reference is to the first page only and does not include *p* for *page*.

7 **Pinpoint**

Indicate the relevant page number in the form "at *n*." There is no *p* or *pg* prior to the number.

8 **Jurisdiction and court**

The jurisdiction of the case—that is, the province or territory in which the case originated—and the court that rendered the decision are often placed in round brackets after the page reference. Some or all of this information may be omitted where it is redundant. In the above example, only *SC* is included to indicate the British Columbia Supreme Court, since the jurisdiction is clear from the name of the law report (*BCLR*). To take another example, the *Supreme Court Reports* contain only decisions of the SCC, so it is not necessary to include *(SCC)* at the end of the citation. Only include necessary information. (Note that where there is a neutral citation, it will never be necessary to include this information; it will already be part of the neutral citation.)

LEGAL ABBREVIATIONS

Most legal citations, whether of statutes, cases, or secondary material, use abbreviations. The publication in which you have located the relevant legal source will often indicate how it is to be abbreviated when cited. However, sometimes it is not clear how to abbreviate a particular source, either because the original source omits this information or because you are not looking at the original source. When this occurs, it is necessary to consult a secondary source that lists abbreviations. Two excellent resources are the following:

- The appendices to the McGill Guide, which include comprehensive listings of abbreviations required to correctly cite legal materials.
- The online Cardiff Index to Legal Abbreviations: http://www.legalabbrevs.cardiff .ac.uk>.

CHAPTER SUMMARY

The third branch of government, the judiciary, plays an important role in resolving all manner of disputes. Some of these disputes involve private law claims, some involve public law issues, and some involve common law principles. Other disputes deal with statutory interpretation, and still others require answers to important questions concerning the constitutional validity of our laws.

Two overarching principles inform the Canadian judicial system: (1) the open court principle, which requires proceedings to take place in public unless there is a justifiable exception, and (2) the principle of judicial independence. These two principles, when adhered to, help safeguard the rule of law and promote public confidence in our justice system.

Understanding how cases get before the courts requires a basic knowledge of the constitutional basis and structure of our courts. There are three broad categories of courts: (1) inferior courts, (2) superior courts, and (3) the SCC. The jurisdiction to create courts is split between the federal and provincial legislative branches. The power to appoint judges is also a split jurisdiction, between the federal and provincial executive branches. The involvement of both levels of government creates a balance of power in the judicial branch.

The provincial and territorial inferior courts handle most of the cases in the system overall, dealing as they do with the less serious criminal and civil cases. The provincial

superior courts have inherent jurisdiction to hear most disputes but are used primarily to resolve more serious claims. The federal courts have a more limited jurisdiction; they hear matters concerned with federal laws, such as intellectual property and taxation disputes. The SCC is the final court of appeal for Canada and generally hears only matters of national importance, whether criminal, civil, or constitutional in nature. Precedent flows downward, from the SCC to the various jurisdictionally separated court systems.

Understanding the structure and jurisdiction of the courts is only part of the puzzle, however. Knowing how to read and analyze court judgments, and how to cite them, is also important. Reading and briefing cases is one of the most effective ways to learn how to analyze legal problems. Most judgments have similar components, such as a factual base, defined legal issues, holdings (or decisions), and reasons for those holdings. The governing rule is often referred to as the *ratio* of the case and is one of the most important components to isolate when you are trying to understand a case. Finally, knowing about the basic rules of legal citation can help legal researchers locate relevant judgments and reference them accurately. Case law that has been properly cited provides important information about the decision, such as the name of the case, the year of the judgment, publication details (if reported), and the level of the court and its jurisdiction.

KEY TERMS

appellant, 181

binding, 173

case, 180

case brief, 184

court, 156

decision, 180

defendant, 181

dissent, 166

facta (sing. *factum*), 165

federal superior courts
 (or federal courts), 160

headnote , 182

inferior courts, 158

judgment, 180

judicial independence, 178

majority, 166

neutral citation, 198

obiter dicta or *obiter*
 (sing. *obiter dictum*), 182

open court principle, 177

persuasive, 173

plaintiff, 181

precedent, 172

provincial superior courts, 159

puisne, 162

reference, 164

reserve, 166

respondent, 181

section 96 courts, 159

style of cause, 198

Supreme Court of Canada, 160

territorial superior courts, 160

unified family courts, 168

FURTHER READING

BOOKS

Bushnell, Ian. *The Captive Court: A Study of the Supreme Court of Canada* (Montreal: McGill-Queen's University Press, 1992).

Hausegger, Lori, Matthew Hennigar & Troy Riddell. *Canadian Courts: Law, Politics, and Process*, 2nd ed (Toronto: Oxford University Press, 2015).

Hogg, Peter W. "Courts" in *Constitutional Law of Canada*, 2018 student ed (Toronto: Carswell, 2018) ch 7.

Hogg, Peter W. "Supreme Court of Canada" in *Constitutional Law of Canada*, 2018 student ed (Toronto: Carswell, 2018) ch 8.

McGill Law Journal. *Canadian Guide to Uniform Legal Citation*, 9th ed (Toronto: Carswell, 2018).

Russell, Peter H. *The Judiciary in Canada: The Third Branch of Government* (Toronto: McGraw-Hill Ryerson, 1987).

WEBSITES

Gateway Site for Canadian Legal Databases

Canadian Legal Information Institute (CanLII): <http://www.canlii.org>.

Federal Courts

Supreme Court of Canada: <http://www.scc-csc.gc.ca>.

Federal Court of Appeal: <http://www.fca-caf.gc.ca>.

Federal Court: <http://cas-cdc-www02.cas-satj.gc.ca/fct-cf>.

Tax Court of Canada: <http://www.tcc-cci.gc.ca/>

Court Martial Appeal Court of Canada: <http://www.cmac-cacm.ca>.

Courts of the Provinces and Territories

Alberta Courts: <http://www.albertacourts.ca>.

British Columbia Courts: <http://www.courts.gov.bc.ca>.

Manitoba Courts: <http://www.manitobacourts.mb.ca>.

New Brunswick Courts: <http://www.gnb.ca/cour>.

Newfoundland and Labrador Courts: <http://www.court.nl.ca>.

Northwest Territories Courts: <http://www.nwtcourts.ca>.

Nova Scotia Courts: <http://www.courts.ns.ca>.

Nunavut Courts: <http://www.nunavutcourts.ca>.

Ontario Courts: <http://www.ontariocourts.on.ca>.

Prince Edward Island Courts: <http://www.gov.pe.ca/courts>.

Quebec Courts: <http://www.tribunaux.qc.ca/mjq_en/index.html>.

Saskatchewan Courts: <http://www.sasklawcourts.ca>.

Yukon Courts: <http://www.yukoncourts.ca>.

Legal Abbreviations

Cardiff Index to Legal Abbreviations: <http://www.legalabbrevs.cardiff.ac.uk>.

REVIEW QUESTIONS

1. Explain how the role of the judiciary is still significant despite the prevalence today of legislated rules as a means of regulating society.

2. Explain why the provincial superior courts, which are constituted under section 92 of the *Constitution Act, 1867*, are sometimes referred to as *section 96 courts*.

3. What are the main criteria the SCC considers when deciding whether to grant leave to a party to appeal to the court?

4. How does the source of the jurisdiction of provincial and territorial *inferior* courts to hear cases differ from that of their superior court relatives?

5. Name three types of cases over which the Federal Court of Appeal has jurisdiction.

6. Describe the flow of precedent in the Canadian court system.

7. Describe the role of the Office of the Commissioner for Federal Judicial Affairs Canada (FJA) in the appointment process of superior court judges.

8. How does the National Judicial Institute (NJI) help prepare new judges for the transition from lawyer to adjudicator?

9. Explain the purpose of the open court principle and name two exceptions to it.

10. What are the three main facets of judicial independence?

11. What is the *ratio decidendi* (or *ratio*) of a case?

EXERCISES

1. Using Figure 6.1 as a reference point, research the website for the courts in your province or territory and chart the four levels of the court system using the correct names for the courts at all levels.

2. Using the website for the courts in your province or territory, determine who are the three most recent appointees to the trial level of the superior court. Read their biographical information and prepare a short opinion concerning each, focused on the following question: Do you think political patronage or professional competence was the primary factor in his or her appointment?

3. Search the SCC's judgments database (<http://scc-csc.lexum.com>) and locate a decision that involves the open court principle.

4. The following case citations all contain mistakes. Circle the mistakes and redo the citations in the correct format, following the style prescribed by the McGill Guide:

a. Westendorp v The Queen, [1983] 1 S.C.R. 43 (SCC

b. *Downing v Graydon* [1978], 92 DLR (3rd) 355 at pp. 370-71 (Ont CA)

c. *Fullowka v. Pinkerton's of Canada Ltd*, 2010 S.C.C. 5, (2010) 1 SCR 132

d. *Blair v Western Mutual Benefit Association*, 1972 4 W.W.R. 284 (BC CA)

5. Read the discussion about briefing cases in the final section of this chapter, and then prepare a case brief of the following SCC case, which is available online (there are two judgments):

Skoke-Graham v The Queen, [1985] 1 SCR 106, 1985 CanLII 60

6. Locate the statute for your province or territory that constitutes the provincial/territorial court. Review the provisions in the statute dealing with judicial independence and then prepare a reasoned argument as to why, in your opinion, these provisions adequately or inadequately support judicial independence.

7 Civil Liberties

After reading this chapter, you will understand:

- The historical evolution of civil liberties and human rights in Canada.
- How human rights are protected in the private sector by provincial and federal human rights legislation.

- How rights and freedoms are protected by the *Canadian Charter of Rights and Freedoms* in matters involving governments.
- The future of civil liberties in Canada.

Civil liberties encompass a broad range of values that support the freedom and dignity of the individual, and that are given recognition in various ways by Canadian law. The political civil liberties include the freedoms of speech, religion, assembly and association; the right to vote and be a candidate for elected office; and the freedom to enter and leave Canada and to move from one province to another. Legal civil liberties include the freedom from search, seizure, arrest, imprisonment, cruel and unusual punishment and unfair trial procedures. Egalitarian civil liberties include equality of access to accommodation, employment, education and other benefits, implying, at least, an absence of racial, sexual or other illegitimate criteria of discrimination. Particular to Canada are language rights, covering the right to use the English or the French language; and educational rights, covering the rights of denominational (or separate) schools.

Peter W Hogg, *Constitutional Law of Canada*, 2018 student ed
(Toronto: Carswell, 2018) at 34-1

Introduction

In Canada, there is a distinction between the terms *civil rights* and *civil liberties*. Section 92(13) of the *Constitution Act, 1867*[1] gave provinces jurisdiction over "Property and Civil Rights in the Province." When the Act was drafted, it was understood that the term *civil rights* referred to *private law rights* between individuals in areas such as torts, contracts, and property.[2]

civil liberties
rights and freedoms protected by the Charter

The term **civil liberties** has a different meaning. As our chapter's opening quotation from Peter Hogg suggests, civil liberties reflect values related to the freedom and dignity of

---

1   (UK), 30 & 31 Vict, c 3.

2   Peter W Hogg, *Constitutional Law of Canada*, 2018 student ed (Toronto: Carswell, 2018) at 21-3, 21-4. Note, however, that despite this formal distinction in Canada, *civil rights* is sometimes also used here to mean *civil liberties*. Context should make the intended meaning clear.

all individuals in their dealings with government, such as in politics and when interacting with the justice system, as well as in areas associated with the private sector, such as accommodation and employment. Human rights legislation in Canada—at the provincial, territorial, and federal levels—supports these values, perhaps most importantly through the prevention of discrimination.

This chapter begins by tracing the historical evolution of civil liberties in Canada, from their origins in England to their eventual inclusion in our regional and federal human rights acts and in our Charter. Next, we explain how these human rights acts protect rights and freedoms in the private sector. Following this is an overview of the Charter, which provides a similar kind of protection when governments are involved. We conclude with a look at possible future directions for civil liberties in Canada.

The Evolution of Civil Liberties in Canada

Civil liberties in Canada eventually gained legislative protection because of four main factors:

1. growing dissatisfaction in Canada, after the Second World War, with having only an "implied" bill of rights;
2. the influence of the civil rights movement in the United States;
3. dissatisfaction with the *Canadian Bill of Rights*[3] (1960); and
4. the advent of the *Canadian Charter of Rights and Freedoms*[4] in 1982.

These factors are described next.

Canada's "Implied" Bill of Rights

Canada's "implied" bill of rights is based on the *Constitution Act, 1867*, which states in its preamble that Canada is to have "a Constitution similar in Principle to that of the United Kingdom." These words reflect the drafters' intention that, among other features of England's Constitution, its historical legacy of civil liberties—and the rules that were developed to safeguard them—was also included in our Constitution.

Some examples of the civil liberties and safeguards that Canada has derived from England include a respect for the rule of law and due process, or fairness, in criminal matters, which includes legal rights upon arrest, the presumption of innocence, and the right to an open and fair trial. Many of these "liberties" can be traced to the *Magna Carta* (1215). (See also Chapter 1.) In addition to these legal rights, certain political civil rights developed that stemmed from England's system of government. Among these were the rights to freedom of speech, freedom of religion, freedom of the press, and peaceful assembly.

What is significant about the British system, from a Canadian perspective, is the absence of a single entrenched constitutional bill of rights. Civil liberties were and are protected in Britain, instead, by a combination of sources, including the common law, legislation, its political system, a free press, and the country's popular support for democracy. According to some Canadian court decisions, including by the Supreme Court of Canada (SCC),

---

3 SC 1960, c 44.

4 Part I of the *Constitution Act, 1982*, being Schedule B to the *Canada Act 1982* (UK), 1982, c 11.

FIGURE 7.1 When Martin Luther King (1929-1968) became the youngest man to receive the Nobel Peace Prize, in 1964, he contributed all of the prize money to the civil rights movement.

having "a Constitution similar in Principle to that of the United Kingdom" means Canada is similarly protected—this clause in our Constitution gives Canada an "implied bill of rights" that pre-dates the Charter and protects Canadians against misuse of government power.[5]

What concerned civil libertarian activists in Canada, particularly in the period after the Second World War, was a sense that such an implied bill of rights was not effective enough to protect the civil liberties of Canadians. This post-war period saw an international trend toward the global protection of human rights. The genocide and atrocities of the Second World War, once they came fully to light at the end of the war, led to the founding of the United Nations and to the proclamation, in 1948, of the UN's Universal Declaration of Human Rights. A growing number of Canadians, some important lawyers among them, believed that civil liberties in this country likewise needed to be codified and protected by constitutional legislation to achieve legitimacy.[6]

Influence of the Civil Rights Movement in the United States

The 1950s and 1960s were important decades for the civil rights movement in the United States. In the landmark 1954 US Supreme Court case of *Brown v Board of Education*,[7] the court outlawed racial segregation of Blacks and whites in public schools. The 1950s also saw the mobilization of activist organizations such as the National Association for the Advancement of Colored People (NAACP). Inspired by Dr Martin Luther King Jr, Black Americans began to engage in protest marches, boycotts, and sit-ins, particularly in the American South, with the aim of ending segregation in public places such as transit systems, lunch counters, and voting districts.

Such actions in America, as well as civil rights movements abroad—for example, the movement to end apartheid in South Africa—further influenced civil rights activists in Canada to seek anti-discrimination legislation here. Canada's "implied" bill of rights does not clearly address all civil liberties matters—in particular, discrimination.

Dissatisfaction with Canada's 1960 Bill of Rights

Among Canadians strongly influenced by these civil rights movements in the US and elsewhere was Prime Minister John Diefenbaker. In 1960, his government enacted the *Canadian Bill of Rights*. One of its notable provisions was section 1, which states:

5 See *Reference Re Alberta Statutes*, [1938] 2 SCR 100, 1938 CanLII 1; *Saumer v Quebec and Canada (AG)*, [1953] 2 SCR 299; *Roncarelli v Duplessis*, [1959] SCR 121, 1959 CanLII 50, and Hogg, *supra* note 2 at 34-11.

6 See EM Adams, "'Guardians of Liberty': RMW Chitty and the Wartime Idea of Constitutional Rights" in Constance Backhouse & W Wesley Pue, eds, *The Promise and Perils of Law: Lawyers in Canadian History* (Toronto: Irwin Law, 2009) 173, and FR Scott, *Civil Liberties and Canadian Federalism* (Toronto: University of Toronto Press, 1959).

7 347 US 438 (Kansas 1954).

> It is hereby recognized and declared that in Canada there have existed and shall continue to exist without discrimination by reason of race, national origin, colour, religion or sex, the following human rights and fundamental freedoms, namely,
>
> (a)   the right of the individual to life, liberty, security of the person and enjoyment of property, and the right not to be deprived thereof except by due process of law;
>
> (b)   the right of the individual to equality before the law and the protection of the law;
>
> (c)   freedom of religion;
>
> (d)   freedom of speech;
>
> (e)   freedom of assembly and association; and
>
> (f)   freedom of the press.[8]

Diefenbaker's initiative started a new approach to protecting civil liberties in this country—a movement away from the older, convention-based Anglo-Canadian implied-bill-of-rights idea toward the American approach of having rights codified in one central document. Many Canadians welcomed this initiative.

However, Diefenbaker's 1960 Bill of Rights proved disappointing. Where the US Bill of Rights was entrenched in that country's Constitution, Diefenbaker's Bill of Rights was not. It was also an ordinary act of the federal Parliament and applied only to federal laws, not provincial ones. Furthermore, in several cases pertaining to equality before the law using the Bill of Rights, the SCC was reluctant to use section 1 in any forceful way to invalidate federal legislation that concerned equality under the law between men and women (see Chapter 3).

The SCC's cautious interpretation of the Bill of Rights and deference to legislative supremacy concerned many civil rights activists and, especially, many women.[9] They were highly motivated to support then Prime Minister Pierre Elliot Trudeau's efforts in the 1970s and 1980s to patriate Canada's Constitution from England and supplement it with a charter of rights and freedoms that *would* be entrenched. In particular, they wanted stronger wording to overcome perceived limitations in section 1 and a document that was more effective than Diefenbaker's Bill of Rights.[10] By the 1980s, conditions at last were ripe for such a development. Former Chief Justice Dickson succinctly summarized the legal and socio-historical context in which Canada acquired the Charter:

> By the 1980s, many of the elements necessary for a *Charter of Rights* were present: a commitment to a unified set of norms governing the individual's relation with the state in a criminal law setting; experience with constitutionally mandated judicial review of legislative action in the realm of the division of powers; tentative steps by the judiciary to uphold rights in the implied *Bill of Rights* cases; a growing recognition at an international level that human rights should be constitutionally protected; and further steps on the part of the legislature and the courts to marry

---

8   SC 1960, c 44, reprinted in RSC 1985, App III.

9   See Anne F Bayefsky, "Defining Equality Rights" in Anne F Bayefsky & Mary Eberts, eds, *Equality Rights and the Canadian Charter of Rights and Freedoms* (Toronto: Carswell, 1985) at 1; and Lise Gotell, *The Canadian Women's Movement, Equality Rights and the Charter* (Ottawa: Canadian Research Institute for the Advancement of Women, 1990).

10   Sandra Burt, "What's Fair? Changing Feminist Perceptions of Justice in English Canada" (1992) 12 Windsor YB Access Just 337; P Leclerc, "Women's Issues" in P James & M Kasoff, eds, *Canadian Studies in the New Millennium* (Toronto: University of Toronto Press, 2008) 185.

this international movement with the dictates of a parliamentary democracy through the adoption of a *Bill of Rights*. In this rich environment, one critical ingredient was lacking: constitutional legitimization of these fundamental rights.[11]

The Advent of Canada's New Charter of Rights and Freedoms

The "critical ingredient" referred to by Chief Justice Dickson eventually arrived. After a number of years, Prime Minister Pierre Trudeau's efforts to patriate Canada's Constitution and add a charter of rights came to fruition (see Chapter 3). Fundamental rights became legitimized in Canada. On April 17, 1982, Queen Elizabeth proclaimed the *Constitution Act, 1982*[12] in force, and the *Canadian Charter of Rights and Freedoms*[13] was officially entrenched in Canada's Constitution.

Spheres of Protection

Again referring to the chapter's opening quote, we see that civil liberties issues sometimes arise in political or legal contexts when governments are involved, and they sometimes arise in areas associated with private sector activities (which may be federally regulated or under provincial or territorial jurisdiction).

Figure 7.2 summarizes they key areas of protection and the legislation that applies. The next two sections describe the relevant legislation in the private sector context and when governments are involved.

Human Rights Protection in the Private Sector

While the Charter is an important instrument for the protection of civil liberties, it applies only to governments, which are generally involved in public sector activities such as making, implementing, and enforcing laws. For protection in the private sector, other legislation is needed.

Provincial and Territorial Legislation

human rights
rights that respect the dignity and worth of an individual

discrimination
prejudicial treatment of people on the ground of race, age, sex, disability, or other recognized ground; prohibited by human rights legislation

Canada's provinces introduced **human rights** legislation in this country before the federal government did. By the middle of the 20th century, Canada was starting to undergo demographic changes because of a growing influx of visible-minority immigrants from non-European countries. Many of these new Canadians encountered **discrimination**, especially in finding housing, getting service in restaurants and hotels and in other public areas, and finding employment.[14] This discrimination occurred mainly in the private sector—that is,

---

11 B Dickson, "The Canadian Charter of Rights and Freedoms: Context and Evolution" in Errol Mendes & Stéphane Beaulac, eds, *Canadian Charter of Rights and Freedoms*, 5th ed (Toronto: LexisNexis, 2013) at 10.

12 Being Schedule B to the *Canada Act 1982* (UK), 1982, c 11.

13 Part I of the *Constitution Act, 1982*, being Schedule B to the *Canada Act 1982* (UK), 1982, c 11.

14 See, for example, George Tanaka, "Wartime Toronto and Japanese Canadians" (1984) 6 Polyphony 240, and Constance Backhouse, *Colour-Coded: A Legal History of Racism in Canada, 1900-1950* (Toronto: University of Toronto Press, 1999).

by landlords, employers, service providers, and companies. To help prevent it, provinces and territories began to enact human rights codes that prohibited discrimination in the private sector on certain defined grounds. The codes also applied to provincial and territorial governments when they engaged in private sector activities (for example, when acting as landlords or employers). Ontario passed the *Racial Discrimination Act*[15] in 1944, and, due in large part to the efforts of Tommy Douglas, Saskatchewan enacted a Bill of Rights in 1947—the first legislation of this kind in Canada.

FIGURE 7.2 Protection of Human Rights in Canada

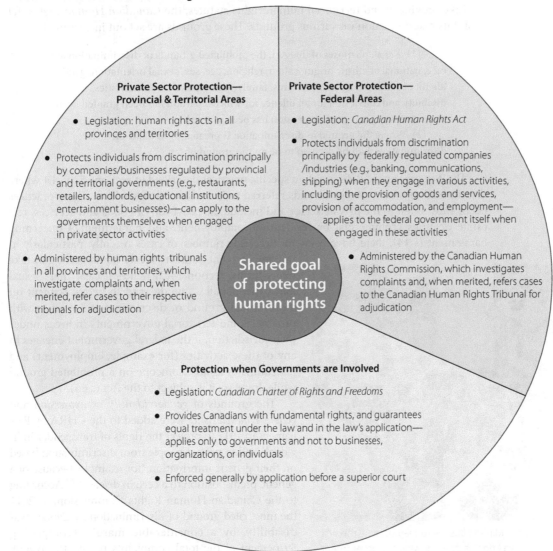

Private Sector Protection— Provincial & Territorial Areas

- Legislation: human rights acts in all provinces and territories

- Protects individuals from discrimination principally by companies/businesses regulated by provincial and territorial governments (e.g., restaurants, retailers, landlords, educational institutions, entertainment businesses)—can apply to the governments themselves when engaged in private sector activities

- Administered by human rights tribunals in all provinces and territories, which investigate complaints and, when merited, refer cases to their respective tribunals for adjudication

Private Sector Protection— Federal Areas

- Legislation: *Canadian Human Rights Act*

- Protects individuals from discrimination principally by federally regulated companies /industries (e.g., banking, communications, shipping) when they engage in various activities, including the provision of goods and services, provision of accommodation, and employment— applies to the federal government itself when engaged in these activities

- Administered by the Canadian Human Rights Commission, which investigates complaints and, when merited, refers cases to the Canadian Human Rights Tribunal for adjudication

Shared goal of protecting human rights

Protection when Governments are Involved

- Legislation: *Canadian Charter of Rights and Freedoms*

- Provides Canadians with fundamental rights, and guarantees equal treatment under the law and in the law's application— applies only to governments and not to businesses, organizations, or individuals

- Enforced generally by application before a superior court

Today, all provinces and territories have similar legislation. Human rights tribunals hear complaints involving discrimination, investigate and remedy them, and take measures to help prevent discrimination from occurring (see Further Reading at the end of this chapter).

---

15 SO 1944, c 51.

Federal Legislation: The Canadian Human Rights Act

The federal government passed its own *Canadian Human Rights Act*[16] (CHRA) in 1977 and established the Canadian Human Rights Commission one year later to administer it. The Act applies to private sector matters that, under section 91 of the *Constitution Act, 1867*, come under federal jurisdiction (see Chapter 4). For example, section 91(15) of the *Constitution Act, 1867* gives jurisdiction over banking to the federal government. Accordingly, if a human rights complaint were made against a bank manager, the federal *Canadian Human Rights Act*, not one of the provincial human rights acts, would apply to the complaint.

Like provincial and territorial human rights statutes, the *Canadian Human Rights Act* prohibits discrimination on various grounds. These grounds are set out in section 3:

> 3(1) For all purposes of this Act, the prohibited grounds of discrimination are race, national or ethnic origin, colour, religion, age, sex, sexual orientation, gender identity or expression, marital status, family status, genetic characteristics, disability and conviction for an offence for which a pardon has been granted or in respect of which a record suspension has been ordered.
>
> (2) Where the ground of discrimination is pregnancy or child-birth, the discrimination shall be deemed to be on the ground of sex.

The Act goes on the define certain specific practices described in sections 5 to 14.1 where discrimination on any of the grounds referred to in section 3 is forbidden. These practices occur most often in the private sector and include the provision of goods and services, real estate dealings (commercial or residential), employment, and harassment. Concerning harassment (s 14), there have been an increasing number of cases recently, particularly in the employment context. While harassment can take many forms, section 14(2) makes it clear that "sexual harassment shall ... be deemed to be harassment on a prohibited ground of discrimination." And as with provincial and territorial governments in areas under their jurisdiction, if the federal government engages in any of these activities (for example, employment) and discriminates against someone on a prohibited ground while doing so, it is subject to the Act (s 66).

The grounds of *gender identity or expression* and *genetic characteristics* were added to the CHRA by Parliament in 2017 to protect the rights of transgender individuals and to protect people from discrimination based on their genetic information (for example, because of a genetic predisposition to a certain disease).[17] According to the Canadian Human Rights Commission, in 2017 the most cited ground of discrimination in Canada was disability, by a considerable margin (comprising 59 percent of the total complaints received). Overall, 18 percent of complaints were related to mental health.[18]

FIGURE 7.3 In 2016, Prime Minister Justin Trudeau became the first prime minister to march in a Pride parade, showing the government's support of the LGBTQ2+ community.

---

16 RSC 1985, c H-6.

17 Canadian Human Rights Commission, "People First—The Canadian Human Rights Commission's 2017 Annual Report to Parliament" (Ottawa: CHRC, 2017), online: <http://chrcreport.ca/assets/pdf/CHRC_rapport_annuel_2017_ang.pdf>.

18 *Ibid.*

Indigenous People and the Canadian Human Rights Act

The original version of the *Canadian Human Rights Act* included section 67, which stated: "Nothing in this Act affects any provision of the *Indian Act* or any provision made under or pursuant to that Act." Effectively, this prevented anyone from filing a complaint with the Canadian Human Rights Commission (CHRC) about a decision that was made or an action that was taken by the federal government, a band council, or a related agency, such as a school board, pursuant to or under the *Indian Act*.[19] While the *Human Rights Act* protected Canadians and First Nations persons living or working *off* reserves from discrimination by an employer or a service provider, First Nations persons living or working *on* a reserve were unable to file complaints with the CHRC. In other words, they did not have full access to human rights protection.

In 2008, section 67 was repealed, and since then Indigenous people have been able to file complaints against the federal government; as of 2011, they have also been able to file complaints against First Nations governments and federally regulated Indigenous organizations. The majority of the complaints against the federal government following the repeal cite national or ethnic origin, family status, or race as the grounds for discrimination and relate to issues including Indian registration pursuant to the *Indian Act*; funding for child and family services, special education, and programs for individuals with disabilities and their families; and other issues, including consultation issues.[20] Complaints against First Nations governments primarily cite family status and national or ethnic origin as grounds for discrimination and relate to the provision of services, retaliatory action, and employment.[21]

Exceptions

A number of exceptions are built into human rights acts. Under the *Canadian Human Rights Act*, there are certain defined exceptions in which a *discriminatory practice* cannot be applied to an employer's actions. A key one is where a **bona fide occupational requirement** for a job is involved. This means that a job requirement exists for a legitimate reason and that it cannot be removed without undue hardship for the employer. Section 15(1)(a) states:

> 15(1) It is not a discriminatory practice if
>
> (a) any refusal, exclusion, expulsion, suspension, limitation, specification or preference in relation to any employment is established by an employer to be based on a *bona fide* occupational requirement.

One example of this could be where an employer specified that all its employees must wear a hard hat on the company's construction site. If an employee's religion prevents him from wearing head apparel, would the company be discriminating against him on religious grounds by requiring him to wear a hard hat—or is the requirement a bona fide occupational requirement to ensure worker safety?

Other exceptions in which discrimination of a kind is permitted by the *Canadian Human Rights Act* are **affirmative action** programs, under section 16(1). These are special government or business initiatives to help certain identifiable groups who have experienced

bona fide occupational requirement
in the context of employment, a bona fide (Latin for "in good faith") requirement is one that exists for a legitimate reason—for example, safety—and that cannot be removed without undue hardship on the employer

affirmative action
policy, particularly in relation to education or employment, intended to assist groups who have suffered past discrimination

---

19   RSC 1985, c I-5.

20   Aboriginal Affairs and Northern Development Canada, "Report to Parliament on the Five-Year Review of the Repeal of Section 67 of the Canadian Human Rights Act" (Gatineau, Quebec: September 2014), online: <http://publications.gc.ca/pub?id=9.699842&sl=0>.

21   *Ibid.*

discrimination in the past—for example, women, Indigenous persons, visible minorities, and persons with disabilities—achieve equality with others. Section 16(1) states:

> 16(1) It is not a discriminatory practice for a person to adopt or carry out a special program, plan or arrangement designed to prevent disadvantages that are likely to be suffered by, or to eliminate or reduce disadvantages that are suffered by, any group of individuals when those disadvantages would be based on or related to the prohibited grounds of discrimination, by improving opportunities respecting goods, services, facilities, accommodation or employment in relation to that group.

In the context of employment, this means that an employer may pass over one applicant and choose another on the basis of an affirmative action program (that is, a program designed to improve opportunities for the group to which the successful applicant belongs), and the unsuccessful applicant will have no grounds for a complaint of discrimination.

Protection of Civil Liberties When Governments Are Involved: The Charter

As we have seen, the arrival of the Charter was a significant milestone in the history of civil liberties in this country. The Charter entrenches many of the rights, freedoms, and protections we inherited from England and adds new ones. It clearly sets them out in a formal document and allows for change in the future, if necessary, following a constitutional amendment procedure.

The Charter applies to governments and their relationship to others; which "others" depends on the particular right or freedom.[22] It does not apply directly to the private sector.

An Overview of the Charter

The following is a brief examination of Charter provisions. See Appendix B for the full text of these provisions.

Section 1: Guarantee of Rights and Freedoms

Section 1 of the Charter guarantees the rights and freedoms it sets out, but also states that they are not absolute. They are subject to "reasonable limits prescribed by law as can be demonstrably justified in a free and democratic society."

One of the most important early Charter cases for the SCC, *R v Oakes*,[23] concerned the test for determining whether a law that infringes the Charter can be justified under section 1. Normally, a law that is inconsistent with the Constitution runs the risk of being struck down pursuant to the supremacy clause, section 52 of the *Constitution Act, 1982*. However, if the law is a "reasonable" limit on a right, it can be "saved" under section 1. Today, the courts still apply the two-part test set out in the *Oakes* case when making this

---

22 The Charter uses different words—such as *citizen, individual, person,* or *everyone*—when describing the various rights and freedoms. Who exactly is protected by, or receives the benefit of, a particular Charter provision depends on the word used. *Citizen* means *Canadian citizen, individual* means a human being as opposed to a corporate entity (and not necessarily a citizen), and *person* generally includes both human beings and corporate entities. Words such as *everyone* and *anyone* are also generally inclusive.

23 [1986] 1 SCR 103, 1986 CanLII 46.

determination. Briefly stated, for a Charter infringement that is "prescribed by law" to be saved under section 1, the law must:

1. serve an important social objective (one that is "pressing and substantial"); and
2. use proportionate means to reach that objective (the measures must be clearly connected to the objective and must impair individual rights as little as possible, and the social benefits of the law must outweigh the negative effects on those whose rights are affected by the law).

For instance, we have laws that prohibit a person from threatening to kill someone; from making, distributing, or possessing child pornography; and from inciting hatred against an identifiable group. Could a person charged with one of these offences argue that the law infringed her "freedom of thought, belief, opinion and expression" under section 2 of the Charter? The answer is "yes" (it is up to the accused to prove the infringement), but the government could successfully argue that the infringement is justified under section 1 (it is up to the government to prove the infringement is a "reasonable limit").

For further discussion of the *Oakes* case and an illustration of the section 1 analysis, see Box 7.1.

BOX 7.1

Section 1: The "Reasonable Limits" Clause and the Oakes Test

In 1982, David Oakes was found with a small quantity of narcotics and charged with unlawful possession of a narcotic for the purpose of trafficking, an offence under section 4(2) of the *Narcotic Control Act*.* At the time, section 8 of the Act stated: "[I]f the court finds that the accused was in possession of the narcotic he shall be given an opportunity of establishing that he was not in possession for the purpose of trafficking." The constitutionality of this provision, which placed a reverse onus on the defendant by requiring him to prove he did *not* intend to traffic, was challenged by Oakes on the grounds that it infringed his right under section 11(d) of the Charter to be presumed innocent until proven guilty.

The case eventually made its way up to the SCC.† The SCC noted that Canadian Charter jurisprudence accords a high degree of protection to the presumption of innocence and that section 11(d) had been infringed. The court then had to determine whether, in light of this, the infringement was justified by section 1 of the Charter. In other words, was section 8 of the *Narcotic Control Act* and its reverse onus a "reasonable limit" on Mr Oakes's right to be presumed innocent under section 11(d) of the Charter? Under section 1, it had to first be established that the limit was "prescribed by law." This was easy to show—the reverse-onus requirement was set out in section 8 of the *Narcotic Control Act*. Next, it had to be shown that the infringement was a "reasonable limit … demonstrably justified in a free and democratic society." The court developed a general two-part test, now known as the *Oakes* test,

to determine whether a law that infringes the Charter is a "reasonable limit" on one's Charter rights. The onus is on the Crown to show on a balance of probabilities (or preponderance of probability) that the limit is a reasonable one by proving (1) that it relates to an important social objective and (2) that it is a proportionate response to the problem. Specifically, the Crown must prove the following:

1. *Important social objective ("pressing and substantial" concern)*

    The government's objective in creating the law must be shown to be "of sufficient importance" to warrant overriding a Charter right. The standard for this part of the test is high, but is often met by the government in Charter cases. In the words of the SCC, for an objective to qualify as sufficiently important, it must relate "to concerns which are *pressing and substantial* in a free and democratic society."

2. *Proportionality*

    If the objective is found to be sufficiently important, the government must then show that the means used are a reasonable and fair way to achieve its legislative objective. To make this determination, a court considers three components or criteria, all of which must be satisfied in the circumstances:

    i. *Rational connection*: The measures that impair the Charter right must be designed to achieve the government's objective—in other words, the measures must be "rationally connected" to the objective. They must not be "arbitrary, unfair, or based on irrational considerations."

ii. *Minimal impairment*: If a rational connection exists, the court will then examine the degree to which the measures impair the right or freedom. The right should be impaired "as little as possible," and if it is possible to impair a right to a lesser degree and still achieve the objective, the government must do so in drafting its legislation. Many arguments put forward by governments in defending legislation fail this part of the test.

iii. *Proportionate effect*: The effects of the measures that limit the right or freedom must be proportionate to the objective identified in the first part of the test. In other words, this third part of the test weighs the benefit to society as a result of the law's being in place with the negative effects on those whose rights the law impairs. The greater the impairment of the right, the more important the objective must be.

Applying the test to section 8 of the *Narcotic Control Act*, the court held that the social objective involved was "pressing and substantial" and that the first part of the "reasonable limits" determination was satisfied. Controlling drug trafficking is a sufficiently important social objective to justify a violation of Charter rights. However, the provision failed to pass the proportionality test. Specifically, the first component of the test was not satisfied because the court found that there was no rational connection between the reverse-onus requirement and the objective of controlling trafficking. Chief Justice Dickson stated:

> [I]t would be irrational to infer that a person had an intent to traffic on the basis of his possession of a very small quantity of narcotics. The presumption required under s. 8 of the *Narcotic Control Act* is overinclusive and could lead to results in certain cases which would defy both rationality and fairness. In light of the seriousness of the offence in question, which carries with it the possibility of imprisonment for life, I am further convinced that the first component of the proportionality test has not been satisfied by the Crown.

As a result of its analysis, the SCC found that section 8 of the *Narcotic Control Act*, which infringed the Charter, could not be saved under section 1 and was therefore of no force or effect.

FIGURE 7.4   Section 1 Analysis: The Oakes Test

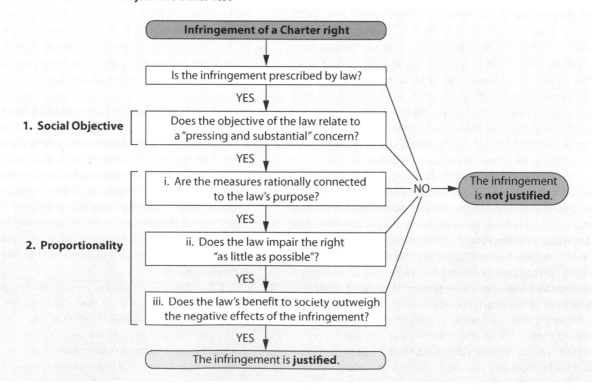

*   RSC 1970, c N-1.

†   R v Oakes, [1986] 1 SCR 103, 1986 CanLII 46.

Section 2: Fundamental Freedoms

Section 2 of the Charter lists four fundamental freedoms: freedom of *conscience and religion*; freedom of *thought, belief, opinion, and expression*; freedom of *peaceful assembly*; and freedom of *association*. These freedoms were established ones in English constitutional history and are essential to the functioning of our democracy in Canada. For example, our right to criticize government action or policy on television or in a newspaper, without fear of reprisal, or to peacefully protest against government actions, is fundamental to our parliamentary system of government and free and democratic society.

Sections 3-5: Democratic Rights

Sections 3-5 of the Charter further allow our democratic system of government to function by giving every citizen of Canada the right to vote and by limiting the duration of legislatures (no longer than five years, with the possibility of extensions in certain circumstances, such as war) and ensuring that there is an annual sitting of our legislative bodies.

Because the Charter gives every citizen the right to vote, Canadian women would have had the right to vote long ago if our country had had the Charter decades earlier. In 2002, section 3 of the Charter was used successfully to give prison inmates in Canada the right to vote.[24]

BOX 7.2

Freedom of Religion and Development Within Indigenous Territory

In *Ktunaxa Nation v British Columbia (Forests, Lands and Natural Resource Operations)*,* the SCC had to consider freedom of religion in the context of the development of a glacier sightseeing and ski resort in southeastern British Columbia, the Jumbo Glacier Resort. With respect to the Crown's duty to consult concerning development within disputed territory (where Aboriginal title had not been proven), a majority of the court held that the Crown had satisfied this obligation under section 35 of the *Constitution Act, 1982*. (See also Box 9.1 on Aboriginal title in Chapter 9.)

However, the Ktunaxa Nation also claimed that the proposed resort lay in an important sacred area called Qat'muk, which is the grizzly bear's spiritual home, and that the development would drive the Grizzly Bear Spirit from its home. This, they argued, would interfere with their freedom of religion under section 2(a) of the Charter. The court held that to establish this infringement, a claimant must demonstrate:

1. that he or she sincerely believes in a practice or belief that has a nexus with religion, and
2. that the state conduct interferes, in a manner that is non-trivial or not insubstantial, with his or her ability to act in accordance with that practice or belief.

Jumbo Glacier, Lake of the Hanging Glacier protected area, and Glacier Dome (British Columbia).

The majority found that the second part of the test was not met. They stated that the state's duty is to protect everyone's "freedom to hold [his or her] beliefs and to manifest them in worship and practice or by teaching and dissemination," but "not to protect the object of beliefs, such as Grizzly Bear Spirit." In short, they held that the Charter

---

24 *Sauvé v Canada (Chief Electoral Officer)*, 2002 SCC 68.

"protects the freedom to worship, but does not protect the spiritual focal point of worship." Indigenous spiritual beliefs would not forestall development in this case.

Some have argued that this decision diminishes the sphere of protection that this particular Charter freedom provides. It also raises questions about when the interference with a sacred

place affects the right to worship and how to prove that it does. If an "object of belief" is central to the belief itself, what kind of interference with the object will also be characterized as an interference with the freedom to worship?

* 2017 SCC 54 at paras 68 and 71.

Section 6: Mobility Rights

Section 6 of the Charter makes it clear that Canadians living in one part of the country can move to another province and obtain work there. For example, many people living in the maritime provinces work in the oil sands of Alberta. Generally speaking, a province cannot enact laws preventing citizens from other provinces (or from the territories) from setting up residence or working there. One exception to this, however, is where a province with a low rate of employment enacts laws to help its current residents who are socially or economically disadvantaged (and this prejudices out-of-province citizens).

Sections 7-14: Legal Rights

Sections 7-14 of the Charter set out important safeguards for everyone who enters the Canadian criminal justice system. They ensure that fairness is an essential part of our system.

Section 7 is a complex provision that provides significant protection for everyone encountering the Canadian criminal justice system.[25] It states that everyone has the "right to life, liberty and security of the person" and that an individual cannot be deprived of these things unless the "principles of fundamental justice" have been followed. In simple terms, this means that one's basic liberties, including both physical and psychological freedoms, cannot be taken away without both procedural *and* substantive fairness. For example, procedural unfairness could occur if a person were forced to speak or give evidence against himself (an accused person has the right to remain silent), while substantive unfairness could occur if a defendant were convicted of a crime for actions only, without the requirement of a guilty mind, or *mens rea* (see Chapter 12).

Section 8 protects against "unreasonable search or seizure." Section 9 covers the "right not to be arbitrarily detained or imprisoned." And section 10 concerns rights on arrest and detention (the right to be given reasons for the arrest or detention, the right to retain counsel, and the right to have the validity of the detention determined by way of *habeas corpus*).

Section 11 sets out the rights of individuals who are charged with an offence, while section 12 safeguards against cruel and unusual treatment or punishment. Section 13 protects witnesses against self-incrimination, providing that "[a] witness who testifies in any proceedings has the right not to have any incriminating evidence so given used to incriminate that

---

25 A detailed examination is beyond the scope of this text. For a full examination of s 7, see Peter W Hogg, "The Brilliant Career of Section 7 of the Charter" (2012) 58 SCLR (2d) 195.

witness in any other proceedings, except in a prosecution for perjury or for the giving of contradictory evidence." Finally, section 14 guarantees the right to an interpreter.

In a sense, sections 8-14 are specific examples of the broad protection afforded by section 7. Indeed, it is possible for one government law or action to infringe both section 7 *and* one of these other sections.

Section 15: Equality Rights

Section 15(1) of the Charter concerns equality rights. As noted in Chapter 3, in the lead-up to the Charter's enactment, concerns were expressed about the limited scope of Diefenbaker's 1960 *Canadian Bill of Rights*. One specific concern related to its phrasing of equality rights, referring as it does to "equality before the law and the protection of the law." The language in section 15(1) is stronger—it refers to the individual's equality "before *and under the law*" and grants every individual the "right to the equal protection *and equal benefit of the law*" (emphasis added). Clearly, this wording refers to equality not only when it comes to procedural protection (process issues), but also substantive protection (the content or substance of the laws themselves). Benefits, as well, must be equally distributed.

The Charter's equality rights apply with reference to prohibited grounds of discrimination.[26] Specifically, section 15(1) guarantees these rights without discrimination based on "race, national or ethnic origin, colour, religion, sex, age, or mental or physical disability." Further, the SCC has held that the listed grounds are not exhaustive and that discrimination must not occur on "analogous" grounds either (see Box 7.3).

Section 15(1) has limits, however. It does *not* protect against discrimination based on grounds that are not listed or grounds that are not analogous to listed grounds (examples of non-protected grounds include employment status and poverty). Further, there is always the possibility that a particular discriminatory law could be justified as a reasonable limit under section 1. Lastly, section 15(2) expressly permits affirmative action programs and allows discrimination against individuals in order to help certain disadvantaged groups by giving them special consideration.

BOX 7.3

Sexual Orientation: An Analogous Prohibited Ground

Delwin Vriend worked for a Christian college in Alberta. When the college found out that Vriend was homosexual, it terminated his employment. Vriend complained about this to the Alberta Human Rights Commission. The commission said that it could not intervene on Vriend's behalf because Alberta's *Individual's Rights Protection Act** (IRPA) did not have "sexual orientation" as a prohibited ground of discrimination.

The case was appealed to the SCC. The issue the court had to decide was whether Alberta's IRPA violated the Charter by not including sexual orientation as a prohibited ground of discrimination. Justice Cory stated that sexual orientation was a "personal characteristic which has been found to be analogous to the grounds enumerated in s. 15."† However, rather than strike down the Alberta Act, the court

---

26 Women have lobbied forcefully for gender equality, but other groups (for example, seniors and Canadians with mental and physical disabilities) have also applied concerted pressure on governments for recognition.

instead made it comply with the Charter. Sexual orientation was "read into" Alberta's IRPA—in other words, added by analogy to the Act's prohibited grounds of protection. Justice Iacobucci stated the following: "I conclude that reading sexual orientation into the impugned provisions of the IRPA is the most appropriate way of remedying this under inclusive legislation."‡

This case also illustrates how the Charter can *indirectly* affect private sector rights. Vriend did not have a claim directly against his employer for discrimination based on the Charter, but he had a claim against the Alberta government because its human rights legislation was discriminatory and violated the Charter. Once the IRPA was brought into compliance with the Charter, Vriend would have a private sector claim based on the IRPA.

*   RSA 2000, c A-25.5.

†   *Vriend v Alberta*, [1998] 1 SCR 493, 1998 CanLII 816 at para 107.

‡   *Ibid* at para 179.

Delwin Vriend (right) and his partner, Andrew Gagnon, at the Supreme Court in 1997.

Sections 16-23: Official Languages of Canada and Minority-Language Educational Rights

These sections of the Charter include a number of language provisions that are important for our country. Section 16(1) provides, for example, that "English and French are the official languages of Canada and have equality of status and equal rights and privileges as to their use in all institutions of the Parliament and government of Canada." They also provide that Canadians have the right to communicate and receive bilingual services in either English or French when dealing with any institution of the federal government. Section 23 also covers minority-language educational rights for citizens of Canada.

Section 24: Enforcement

We have seen that the supremacy clause (s 52(1) of the *Constitution Act, 1982*) provides for various forms of remedial relief in the event that a law is found to be unconstitutional, including because it violates the Charter. The two subsections of section 24 provide some additional forms of relief specifically in connection with Charter violations.

Section 24(1) provides for a wide range of remedies based on what the court considers "appropriate and just in the circumstances." For example, using this provision, courts can grant defensive remedies to prevent a legal wrong from continuing, as well affirmative remedies that are more compensatory in nature.

Section 24(2) is narrower in scope and provides for the exclusion of illegally obtained evidence if its admission in the proceedings would "bring the administration of justice into disrepute." To make this determination, the courts apply a three-part test, considering the seriousness of the Charter infringement, its impact on the accused, and society's interest in having reliable evidence admitted in criminal cases.

For more analysis of section 24, see Box 7.4.

Section 24: The "Remedies" Section

In most cases, when a *law* is inconsistent with the Constitution, including when it infringes the Charter and cannot be saved under section 1 (see Box 7.1), the courts will use their power to provide some form of relief under section 52 of the *Constitution Act, 1982*. As described in Chapter 4, section 52, the supremacy clause, has been interpreted as allowing for a range of responses or remedies, including striking down the legislation or a part of it, or interpreting it narrowly to bring it in line with the Constitution.

Section 24 can be contrasted to courts' remedial powers under section 52 in several respects. Some of the more important distinctions are:

- section 24 is restricted to remedies for Charter infringements;
- the range of possible relief is broader and is limited only by what is "appropriate and just in the circumstances";
- only "courts of competent jurisdiction" can hear applications under this section (this often means a superior court, because they have the broadest power to grant remedies); and
- a section 24 remedy is possible not only when a law infringes the Charter, but also when an *administrative action* offends the Charter (such as when a police officer performs an illegal search and seizure).

Section 24 has two subsections, the first of which deals with general remedial relief, and the second with the exclusion of evidence.

Section 24(1): General Relief

A wide range of remedies is possible under section 24(1), and what is "appropriate and just" will vary with the specific circumstances of the case. "Defensive" remedies may be issued to prevent the continuation of an illegal state of affairs (for example, a court may dismiss a charge, quash a search warrant, or declare a law invalid, which is also a possible remedy under s 52). The courts may also provide "affirmative" remedies (for example, by ordering the return of property that has been seized or by awarding damages to a person whose Charter rights have been infringed). In one case, the SCC ordered a provincial government to use its best efforts to build French-language schools to enforce minority-language education rights under section 23.* Finally, the court may issue a declaration in which it declares a particular state of

affairs unconstitutional (for example, declaring that it is a contravention of the Charter for a province not to have a law providing for absentee voting). A declaration does not positively order the government to change its laws or act in a particular way, but in practice it may have this effect, because the government may need to make changes to avoid a continued breach of its Charter obligations.

Section 24(2): Exclusion of Evidence

When an application is made under section 24(1) and the court finds that evidence was obtained in contravention of the Charter, the court is required to exclude the evidence under section 24(2) if its admission "would bring the administration of justice into disrepute." At common law, the primary guide for the admissibility of evidence is its relevance; the admissibility of relevant evidence is not affected by the way in which it was obtained (that is, legally or illegally). Section 24(2) changes this rule to exclude illegally obtained evidence in some situations.

The leading case on section 24(2) is *R v Grant*.[†] In 2003, Donnohue Grant attracted the attention of several officers while walking in an area known for its high crime rate. The officers questioned him and while doing so required him to keep his hands in front of him and obstructed his movement so that he was prevented from leaving. In the course of the questioning, Mr Grant admitted to having "a small bag of weed" and a firearm. The officers arrested and searched Mr Grant, seizing the marijuana and a loaded revolver. They then advised him of his right to counsel and took him into custody. He was later charged with a number of firearms offences.

Mr Grant was convicted at trial, and his case ultimately went to the SCC. There were several issues before the court, including whether the evidence the police had obtained was admissible. The court found that Mr Grant had been psychologically detained when he was first questioned and that his legal rights under sections 9 and 10 of the Charter had been infringed. In assessing whether admitting the evidence thus obtained would "bring the administration of justice into disrepute," the court set out a three-part test that assesses and balances the following factors:

1. *The seriousness of the Charter-infringing state conduct.* The more serious the Charter violation, the more likely the administration of justice will be brought into disrepute. Deliberate or blatant breaches, for example, are more serious than breaches occurring where the police are acting in good faith.

2. *The impact on the Charter-protected interests of the accused.* The greater the intrusion on the Charter right, the more likely the evidence will be excluded. For example, serious intrusions into one's privacy or dignity, such as might occur from an illegal search, would have more impact than a "fleeting and technical" breach, such as where a slight delay occurs in informing a person of the reasons for her arrest.
3. *Society's interest in an adjudication on the merits.* This last factor focuses on whether the conduct calls into question the reliability of the evidence (for example, was the conduct of police likely to produce a false confession?), and the importance of the evidence to the Crown's case. The less reliable the evidence appears to be, the more likely its

admission will bring the administration of justice into disrepute.

On the facts of this case, the court concluded that the evidence could be admitted. First, the police conduct in breaching Mr Grant's Charter rights was not "deliberate or egregious" and could not be characterized as serious. Second, there was no physical coercion or abuse and, therefore, while the impact on Mr Grant's rights was more than minimal, it was not severe. Finally, the gun was important evidence, and the method by which the evidence was obtained in this case did not affect its reliability.

* See *Doucet-Boudreau v Nova Scotia (Minister of Education),* 2003 SCC 62.

† 2009 SCC 32.

Sections 25-31: General

As mentioned in Chapter 3, section 25 ensures that existing Aboriginal and treaty rights will not be affected by the Charter. Section 35, which is in part II of the *Constitution Act, 1982* and not part of the Charter, formally recognizes and affirms the existing rights of Aboriginal peoples referred to in section 25.

Section 26 states that the Charter guarantees of rights and freedoms do not preclude the existence of other rights, such as may exist as part of the "implied" bill of rights, for example. Section 27 provides that the Charter must be interpreted in a way that is consistent with our multicultural heritage. Section 28, again as noted in Chapter 3, further protects gender equality (beyond the protection afforded by s 15) by ensuring that the Charter rights and freedoms themselves are guaranteed equally to male and female persons.

Sections 29-31 cover some miscellaneous matters.

Sections 32 and 33: Application of the Charter

Section 32 states that the Charter applies to the federal, provincial, and territorial governments in respect of all matters within their respective jurisdictions or spheres of authority. These include the laws within their jurisdiction (legislation and common law) and their administrative actions (which can include, for example, the conduct of police operating on behalf of government).

As we have seen, the Charter does *not* apply directly to private sector disputes involving only individuals or corporations—for example, to disputes between you and your neighbour, your landlord, or your employer or to how you are treated in a restaurant or a department store. Such situations, however, may be covered by federal, provincial, or territorial human rights legislation. Note that in situations where the government is involved in private sector activities (for example, as a landlord or employer), the Charter will apply, *as well as* any relevant human rights legislation.

Section 33 is commonly referred to as the *notwithstanding* or *override* clause. It allows the federal Parliament or provincial legislatures to pass legislation that may operate even though it may infringe certain sections of the Charter—specifically, section 2 or sections 7-15. To do so, however, the government must expressly declare in the Act that it is to operate "notwithstanding" those sections. The declaration lasts only for five years, but it can be renewed. Section 33 cannot be used to override voting rights under section 3 or Aboriginal rights under section 25.

Governments rarely exercise their power under section 33 because of the political consequences of openly stating that the Charter is being ignored when enacting a particular law. So far, the most noteworthy example of a government using this power was when the Quebec government used it in the late 1980s to protect its language law—the *Charter of the French Language* (also referred to as Bill 101)—from Charter challenges. In the previous year, the SCC had found that some of the provisions in this legislation contravened the Charter.[27] Following this case, the language law was re-enacted and section 33 was invoked to shield it from further Charter challenges for five years. In 1993, the language law was amended so that it no longer contravened the Charter—the use of the notwithstanding clause was no longer necessary.

The Future of Civil Liberties in Canada

Civil liberties around the world have evolved differently and at different paces. However, across all cultures, they evolve over time and with changing social values. In Canada, we have seen a dramatic growth in the recognition of civil liberties from the time of Tommy Douglas's Bill of Rights (1947) to the Charter (1982), and to the changes occurring today.

Canada's legislatures will continue to play a key role in this area. As new rights are identified, there will be calls for new legislation. For instance, in connection with transgender rights, governments have responded with changes to human rights legislation to expressly list gender identity as a prohibited ground of discrimination.[28]

Similarly, our courts—particularly the SCC—will continue their work in the development of civil liberties. For example, the "implied" bill of rights may be expanded. More significantly, however, the Charter will be used as an instrument of growth. Confronted with new situations, the courts will develop new interpretations and new tests (or modify old ones) for the broad phrases in the Charter—phrases such as *reasonable limits*, *freedom of conscience*, *fundamental justice*, *unreasonable delay*, and *appropriate and just*, among others. New grounds of discrimination will be recognized, and new remedies will be fashioned to respond to novel forms of infringement. Further, parallel work will occur as the courts interpret similar language in federal, provincial, and territorial human rights legislation.

We live in an era of rapid social change. With respect to civil liberties, Canada seems well equipped legally, and culturally, to respond positively.

---

27 See *Ford v Quebec (AG)*, [1988] 2 SCR 712, 1988 CanLII 19.

28 As of 2017, the federal government (see discussion of the *Canadian Human Rights Act* above) and all provinces and territories had amended their human rights legislation to include this ground. One of the consequences of gender identity protection is that provinces and territories are increasingly allowing for the issuance (or reissuance) of birth certificates, health cards, and other government documents that are gender neutral—that is, without a female or male designation. This may be important to individuals who are intersex or who do not self-identify as male or female. In 2017, British Columbia issued its first gender-neutral health card, with a *U* marker, and in 2018, Ontario issued its first non-binary birth certificate, with an *X* marker. As of 2017, Canadian passports can be issued, when requested, without a male or female gender designation (with an *X* marker). Before the issuance of gender-neutral documents, it was (and still is) possible to change one's designation from male to female, or female to male—initially, proof of gender reassignment surgery was required, but this requirement has been removed in most Canadian jurisdictions.

CHAPTER SUMMARY

Civil liberties in Canada evolved over many years and gained legislative protection as a result of various factors, such as dissatisfaction with our "implied" bills of rights, the US civil rights movement, weaknesses in the *Canadian Bill of Rights* (1960), and the patriation of the Constitution, which included the Charter.

In Canada, we distinguish between civil liberties in the private sector and civil liberties where governments are involved (based on their actions or laws under their jurisdiction). The former concerns the private sphere—in other words, relations between (for example) landlords and tenants, employers and employees, or customers and service providers. Various provincial and territorial human rights statutes and codes—and, at the federal level, the 1977 *Canadian Human Rights Act*—provide protection against such discrimination, subject to certain limits, in the private sector. Sections 91 and 92 of the *Constitution Act, 1867* set out the different jurisdictional areas and are used to determine whether a particular private

sector civil liberties matter falls under federal or provincial jurisdiction.

Civil liberties where governments are involved are primarily regulated by the Charter, which constitutionally entrenches and guarantees a number of rights and freedoms, such as the fundamental freedoms of conscience, expression, and association; various democratic rights, including the right to vote; mobility rights; legal rights, including the right to "life, liberty and the security of the person"; equality rights; and language rights. As in the case of private sector protection, Charter rights are also not absolute—most notably, they are subject to "reasonable limits" under section 1.

Civil liberties in Canada continue to evolve in response to social change, through new legislation and the work of courts in interpreting and developing the rights and freedoms Canadians currently enjoy.

KEY TERMS

affirmative action, 213

bona fide occupational
   requirement, 213

civil liberties, 206

discrimination, 210

human rights, 210

FURTHER READING

BOOKS

Corbett, SM. *Canadian Human Rights Law and Commentary* (Toronto: LexisNexis, 2007).

Greenspan, Edward L, John B Laskin & Melanie Dunn, eds. *Canadian Charter of Rights Annotated* (Toronto: Canada Law Book, 2009) (loose-leaf).

Mendes, Errol & Stéphane Beaulac, eds. *Canadian Charter of Rights and Freedoms*, 5th ed (Toronto: LexisNexis, 2013).

Sharpe, Robert J & Kent Roach. *The Charter of Rights and Freedoms*, 6th ed (Toronto: Irwin Law, 2017).

LEGISLATION

Canada

Canadian Bill of Rights, SC 1960, c 44, reprinted in RSC 1985, App III: <http://laws.justice.gc.ca/eng/acts/C-12.3/index.html>.

Canadian Human Rights Act, RSC 1985, c H-6: <http://laws.justice.gc.ca/eng/acts/H-6/index.html>.

Alberta

Alberta Human Rights Act, RSA 2000, c A-25.5: <http://www.qp.alberta.ca/documents/Acts/A25P5.pdf>.

British Columbia

Human Rights Code, RSBC 1996, c 210: <http://www.bclaws.ca/Recon/document/ID/freeside/00_96210_01>.

Manitoba

The Human Rights Code, CCSM c H175: <http://web2.gov.mb.ca/laws/statutes/ccsm/h175e.php>.

New Brunswick

Human Rights Act, RSNB 2011, c 171: <http://laws.gnb.ca/en/showdoc/cs/2011-c.171>.

Newfoundland and Labrador

Human Rights Act, 2010, SNL 2010, c H-13.1: <http://assembly.nl.ca/Legislation/sr/statutes/h13-1.htm>.

Northwest Territories

Human Rights Act, SNWT 2002, c 18: <https://www.justice.gov.nt.ca/en/files/legislation/human-rights/human-rights.a.pdf>.

Nova Scotia

Human Rights Act, RSNS 1989, c 214: <https://humanrights.novascotia.ca/content/legislation>.

Nunavut

Human Rights Act, SNu 2003, c 12: <http://www.nunavutlegislation.ca/en/download/file/fid/11459>.

Ontario

Human Rights Code, RSO 1990, c H.19: <http://www.ohrc.on.ca/en/ontario-human-rights-code>.

Prince Edward Island

Human Rights Act, RSPEI 1988, c H-12: <http://www.gov.pe.ca/law/statutes/pdf/h-12.pdf>.

Quebec

Charter of Human Rights and Freedoms, CQLR, c C-12: <http://legisquebec.gouv.qc.ca/en/showdoc/cs/c-12>.

Saskatchewan

The Saskatchewan Human Rights Code, SS 1979, c S-24.1: <http://www.qp.gov.sk.ca/documents/English/Statutes/Statutes/S24-1.pdf>.

Yukon

Human Rights Act, RSY 2002, c 116: <http://www.gov.yk.ca/legislation/acts/huri.pdf.>

REVIEW QUESTIONS

1. What is the distinction between civil rights and civil liberties in the Canadian context?

2. In Canada, what were four main factors in the development of legislative protection for civil rights?

3. What is the basis of Canada's "implied" bill of rights?

4. Why did Diefenbaker's 1960 Bill of Rights prove disappointing?

5. Why was the US civil rights movement important for the development of Canadian human rights legislation?

6. What is a bona fide occupational requirement? What do you think would be a bona fide occupational requirement for a firefighter?

7. If an employee were fired from her job at Canadian Tire, would the Charter or a provincial human rights act apply? Explain.

8. If there were a human rights complaint brought against a bank manager, what human rights act would apply—federal or provincial? Give reasons.

EXERCISES

1. Weigh the pros and cons of affirmative action programs. Do you approve or disapprove of them? Explain.

2. Assume you are an employer concerned with prohibiting harassment in your workplace. You are determined to be proactive in preventing occurrences of it. List three steps you might implement in this regard.

3. Locate the human rights code for your province or territory online. Compare and contrast your provincial or territorial code's prohibited grounds of discrimination with those in section 15 of the Charter.

4. Research Bill 62 (*An Act to foster adherence to State religious neutrality and, in particular, to provide a framework for requests for accommodations on religious grounds in certain bodies*, SQ 2017, c 19), a controversial bill that was passed into law by the Quebec government in 2017. Do you think the law and its proposed application contravene the freedoms of religion and expression guaranteed by section 2 of the Charter? If yes, is the law justified as a reasonable limit on these freedoms under section 1 of the Charter?

5. Discuss what you think might in time become a new prohibited ground of discrimination under section 15 of the Charter.

PART III
Key Subject Areas in Law

8 Private Law I: Tort Law and Contract Law

After reading this chapter, you will understand:

- The nature of private law and its relationship to other areas of the law.
- The constitutional basis of private law.
- The burden and standard of proof in private law claims.
- The scope of tort law, its main categories and subcategories, defences to tort liability, and the remedies available to victims of torts.
- The importance of contractual arrangements, how contracts are formed, important types of contracts and contract terms, excuses for non-performance, and remedies for breach of contract.

Private law is a pervasive phenomenon of our social life, a silent but ubiquitous participant in our most common transactions. It regulates the property we own and use, the injuries we inflict or avoid inflicting, the contracts we make or break. It is the public repository of our most deeply embedded intuitions about justice and personal responsibility.

Ernest J Weinrib, *The Idea of Private Law*, revised ed
(Oxford: Oxford University Press, 2012) at 1

Introduction

In Chapter 1, we described the divisions of law in broad terms. In Part III of this text, we examine some key domestic law subjects, explore the bounds of public international law, and conclude with a survey of some remaining areas. Private law, which governs the relationships between persons, is a large subcategory of domestic law and is the focus of this chapter and the next. Public law, another significant subcategory of domestic law, governs the relationship between persons and the state and between the various organs of the state; public law topics are the focus of Chapters 11 and 12. (Note that constitutional law, which we covered in Part II, is also part of public law.) Business and consumer law, the subject of Chapter 10, includes both private law and public law aspects.[1]

---

1 There are a number of subject areas that we are not able to cover in detail in this book: for example, certain public law areas (such as municipal, immigration, and tax law), various private law topics (including insurance, succession, creditors' remedies, and the civil law approach to private law in Quebec), and military law. See Figure 1.1 for a comprehensive listing of the divisions and areas of the law, and Chapter 14 for an overview of some of the areas that have not been more thoroughly discussed elsewhere. Also, keep in mind, as we alluded to in Chapter 1, that dividing the law into separate subject areas is somewhat artificial, though it is a useful learning tool. We speak of specific areas of law, but the reality is that many legal problems overlap subject areas, and some areas themselves overlap each other.

This chapter begins with a look at the constitutional basis of private law and matters of proof, and then surveys (from a Canadian common law perspective) two important areas of private law: torts and contracts. Chapter 9 examines property law and family law.

Constitutional Basis of Private Law

Most private law falls under the jurisdiction of the provincial and territorial legislatures. This is because the provinces have jurisdiction over "Property and Civil Rights" under section 92(13) of the *Constitution Act, 1867*.[2] The territories have a similar jurisdiction delegated to them by special federal legislation. As we noted in Chapter 7, the expression *civil rights* in this context means *private law rights* in areas such as torts, contracts, and property. However, there are areas of private law where Parliament's role is more significant. For example, under sections 91(22) and 91(23) of the *Constitution Act, 1867*, intellectual property is regulated federally.

In some areas, jurisdiction is more complex because it is split between the provinces and the federal government. For example, in the area of family law, section 91(26) of the *Constitution Act, 1867* gives Parliament jurisdiction over "Marriage and Divorce" (that is, the substantive requirements of a valid marriage and grounds for divorce), and section 92(12) assigns power to the provinces over "Solemnization of Marriage" (that is, the procedure or manner in which marriages must take place). The provinces also have jurisdiction over division of family assets when relationships break down, and over the adoption of children and child protection (based on their power over "Property and Civil Rights" noted above, and also over "Matters of a merely local or private Nature" assigned by s 92(16)). Support obligations and child custody matters are areas of shared jurisdiction. Family law is not the only area where jurisdiction is split—labour and employment law, business and consumer law, creditors' remedies, and entertainment law are other examples.

Burden of Proof and Standard of Proof in Private Law Claims

Private (or civil) law disputes are like most other disputes in that the party making a claim has the burden of proving it. Therefore, the plaintiff (or defendant on a counterclaim) generally has the burden of proving the allegations supporting the cause of action. In a few situations, however, a presumption in favour of the claimant reverses the burden and requires the person defending to prove that something did *not* happen (see below in connection with the trespass torts for an example).

Private (or civil) law disputes can involve significant amounts of money and may have life-changing consequences for the litigants. However, being involved in a private law dispute is generally considered less of a social concern than being involved in a public law dispute (particularly, a criminal matter). A criminal conviction, as we will see, has a moral stigma attached to it and can result in a loss of freedom (if the person found guilty is sentenced to a period of incarceration). This difference between private law and criminal law cases is reflected in the different standards of proof in these two types of cases. In civil claims, parties need only prove their allegations on a *balance of probabilities* (that is, prove that they

---

2   (UK), 30 & 31 Vict, c 3.

are more likely to be true than not). In criminal cases, on the other hand, the prosecution must adduce evidence proving that the person charged has committed the crime *beyond a reasonable doubt* (which requires a high degree of certainty). (See Chapter 12 for more on the burden of proof and standard of proof in criminal cases.)

Tort Law

Tort law is an area of private law that deals with certain types of wrongful conduct and the remedies available to those affected by that conduct. It covers a wide range of behaviours and is primarily concerned with providing a means of compensation (see Chapter 1 under the heading "Corrective Justice"). However, depending on the conduct in question, it can serve other purposes, such as deterrence and punishment. A **tort**, therefore, is a type of civil wrong for which the person wronged can obtain damages or some other remedy (the English word *tort* derives from the Latin *tortum*, meaning "something twisted" or "something crooked"). A **civil wrong** is a wrong defined by private law, which covers the relationships between persons.

Tort law is often seen as a "residuary" category within private law—in other words, a catch-all or miscellaneous category that includes all those civil wrongs that are not covered by other areas of private law, such as contract law, property law, family law, or equity.

Modern tort law can be divided into four categories, based on the type of fault involved:

1. intentional torts,
2. negligence,
3. strict liability torts, and
4. a miscellaneous group of torts, with unique principles of liability.

These four categories, along with some of the more commonly litigated torts in each, are described below (space restrictions prevent a discussion of all torts).

Intentional Torts

The defendant's intentional behaviour characterizes intentional torts. The defendant's behaviour is intentional where he intended to bring about the consequences of his actions, or at least knew that they were likely to result. It is the intentional nature of the conduct that makes these torts the most serious ones. In fact, many of the torts in this category are also crimes for which the defendant could be found criminally responsible.[3]

tort
a type of civil wrong for which damages can be obtained by the person wronged

civil wrong
a wrong that occurs in the context of relationships between persons and is addressed by one of the areas of private law

---

3 There have been many famous cases in Canada with both a criminal and a civil component: for example, cases involving on-ice violence in hockey, such as the Todd Bertuzzi and Steve Moore case (criminal assault and a related civil action, which ended up settling out of court), and the Colonel Russell Williams case (murders, sexual assaults, and related civil actions). Usually, the criminal proceedings are completed first, before any civil actions move forward. This can be an advantage to the victim: if there is a conviction in the criminal case, the underlying facts can be taken as proven in the civil case. Even if there is an acquittal in the criminal case, most civil cases still proceed because the standard of proof the plaintiff must meet in such cases (balance of probabilities) is more easily met than the standard of proof that must be met in criminal ones (beyond a reasonable doubt).

The intentional torts can be roughly divided into two categories:

1. intentional interferences with persons or property, and
2. intentional interferences with other interests.

Intentional Interferences with Persons or Property

The main intentional torts in this category are:

- trespass to person,
- trespass to land, and
- trespass to goods (also referred to as *trespass to chattels*).

These trespass torts all involve forms of direct interference, such as hitting, walking on, or moving. Actual damage is not a required element of these torts, although without actual damage any monetary award is likely to be small.

In Canada, once the plaintiff proves the direct interference in question, fault on the part of the defendant is *presumed*, and it is up to the defendant to prove that he didn't intend the consequences (and that he wasn't otherwise at fault—for example, by being careless). Other common law jurisdictions, such as the United Kingdom and the United States, require the plaintiff to prove intent as an element of the tort. It is customary in all common law jurisdictions to refer to these torts as *intentional*, regardless of whether intent must be proved or whether fault is presumed.

TRESPASS TO PERSON

Trespass-to-person actions are usually referred to by their more specific *sub*-tort names: *assault*, *battery*, and *false imprisonment*. **Assault** is a kind of psychological tort; it does not require actual physical contact. If the plaintiff is threatened and believes that harmful physical contact from the defendant may occur (that is, *apprehends* harmful contact), and if the defendant has the means to carry out the threat in the near future, an assault has occurred. For example, threatening to hit, shoot, stab, or sexually interfere with someone is an assault if the victim believes the threat will soon materialize, even if the assailant stops short of actual physical contact.

Battery requires that harmful or offensive physical contact *actually* occur. Many trespass-to-person claims have both an assault and a battery component. For instance, if a threat creates an apprehension of harm and then the threatened physical contact occurs, there has been an assault prior to contact and a battery once it occurs. Note also that, in criminal law, there is no distinction between assault and battery; both actions are covered by the crime of assault.[4]

False imprisonment occurs when one person totally restrains the movement of another person. The defining element here is the presence of an enclosed boundary around the

trespass to person
an intentional tort encompassing three subcategories of tort: assault, battery, and false imprisonment

assault
psychological tort involving one person's apprehension of harmful physical contact from another person

battery
tort requiring actual occurrence of harmful or offensive physical contact

false imprisonment
tort whereby one person totally restrains the movement of another person

---

4   Concerning wrongful sexual conduct, it is criminal conduct and may be prosecuted as a sexual assault under the *Criminal Code*, RSC 1985, c C-46 (in other words, in the sphere of public law), but there are also a number of potential tort claims based on sexual wrongdoing. Such actions, however, are not based on a stand-alone tort; there is no tort known as *sexual wrongdoing*. Rather, these actions are founded on established torts, such as assault, battery (often referred to in this context as *sexual battery*), or intentional infliction of nervous shock.

person being restrained, so that there is no reasonable means of escape. The boundary can be physical (for example, a locked jail cell) or psychological (for example, someone with a gun telling another person not to move). This tort is sometimes referred to as *false arrest* in cases where a police officer or security guard is the person being sued. But *false imprisonment* and *false arrest* are, legally speaking, the same action. In both cases, the word *false* is a bit misleading. The plaintiff is not required to prove that his imprisonment was false (that is, unjustified), only that he was imprisoned. Once that is established, the onus is on the defendant to establish that the imprisonment was authorized. If the defendant is a police officer, this authority usually comes from a statutory power of arrest.

TRESPASS TO LAND

trespass to land
tort involving the physical intrusion by one person onto land occupied by another

Trespass to land involves the physical intrusion by one person onto land occupied by another. This may take the form of a person entering another's land, or it may involve a person propelling an object onto another person's land. There are also criteria related to height and depth when determining whether trespass has occurred. Intruding on another person's airspace—that is, the space above that person's piece of land—up to a reasonably usable height (for example, by an overhanging sign) may qualify as a trespass. So may the intrusion on another person's subsoil down to a reasonably usable depth—for example, in a case where one person, to secure a structure on her own land, has inserted anchor rods into the plaintiff's land.

TRESPASS TO GOODS

trespass to goods (or trespass to chattels)
a tort whereby one person intentionally interferes with another's rightful possession of movable property

Trespass to goods (or **trespass to chattels**) is a tort whereby one person intentionally interferes with another's possession of movable property, such as a motor vehicle (for example, by moving it).

There are other torts besides trespass to goods that concern movable property. *Conversion* is the civil law equivalent of theft in criminal law. It involves one person substantially interfering with—including stealing or destroying—another person's goods. Another tort in this category is *detinue*, which involves the wrongful withholding of the owner's goods (even if the defendant initially came into possession of the goods lawfully, as in a case where the goods were loaned to the defendant by the owner).

OTHER INTENTIONAL INTERFERENCES WITH PERSONS OR PROPERTY

The torts of trespass are the most established of the torts involving intentional interferences with persons or property. But there are many others, including the following:

- invasion of privacy (covering all manner of intrusions, such as surveillance, eavesdropping, publishing private communications, and posting sexually explicit material of a person online without the person's permission);
- expropriation of personality (a special form of invasion of privacy whereby the defendant uses the plaintiff's name or likeness to promote the defendant's business without the plaintiff's consent); and
- harassment (which could involve sexual or non-sexual behaviour that is persistent and offensive).

These torts are relatively new and have not been fully considered and clearly defined by the Supreme Court of Canada (SCC). So we might say they are "under development" in the courts of the territories and common law provinces.[5] In the case of the first of them, however—that is, invasion of privacy—the provinces of British Columbia, Manitoba, Newfoundland and Labrador, and Saskatchewan have bypassed the development of the common law and have enacted legislation clearly making the invasion of privacy a tort.[6]

Intentional infliction of nervous shock is another example of a tort that is not considered a trespass tort but that does involve intentional interference with a person. This tort involves one person's intentionally inflicting mental suffering on another person. It is, like assault, a psychological tort, and a long-established one. But it is extremely difficult to prove. Its defining elements are extreme, flagrant, or outrageous conduct by the defendant, and consequent injury to the plaintiff in the form of a psychological disorder—typically, a disorder recognized in the *Diagnostic and Statistical Manual of Mental Disorders* (DSM-5).[7]

Intentional Interferences with Other Interests

The torts in this category all involve indirect forms of injury, and they generally have more to do with purely financial losses than with physical or psychological losses.

Misuse of court proceedings by a defendant can be tortious. The two most important torts in this area are *malicious prosecution* and *abuse of process*. Malicious prosecution is based on an earlier misuse of *criminal* (as opposed to civil) proceedings. In this case, the defendant is sued for having had groundless charges laid against the plaintiff—charges of which the plaintiff was later acquitted—while knowing they were groundless. Abuse of process is based on an earlier misuse of *civil* proceedings. In this case, the defendant commenced proceedings against the plaintiff for purposes unrelated to the claim itself—for example, in order to embarrass the plaintiff or put him out of business. These two torts are difficult to establish because they require proof of bad faith on the part of the defendant. Such proof is often lacking.

Other torts in this category—that is, torts involving intentional interferences with other interests—are certain business torts. Most of these involve some form of intentional behaviour that has led to purely financial or economic loss by the plaintiff. Some commonly litigated examples are:

- deceit (or fraud),
- passing off (that is, where one person misrepresents his goods or services as those of another person),
- inducing breach of contract,
- intimidation, and
- abuse of power.

---

5 For example, in 2012, the Ontario Court of Appeal recognized a tort of *intrusion upon seclusion*, finding the defendant liable when she used her position at a bank to repeatedly look at the banking records of her spouse's ex-wife (*Jones v Tsige*, 2012 ONCA 32). This decision was followed in 2016 by the Ontario Superior Court of Justice when it found a defendant liable who had posted a sexually explicit video of his ex-girlfriend on a pornography website without her consent (*Jane Doe 464533 v ND*, 2016 ONSC 541).

6 See *Privacy Act*, RSBC 1996, c 373; *The Privacy Act*, RSM 1987, c P125; *Privacy Act*, RSN 1990, c P-22; and *The Privacy Act*, RSS 1978, c P-24.

7 American Psychiatric Association, *Diagnostic and Statistical Manual of Mental Disorders*, 5th ed (Arlington, Va: American Psychiatric Association, 2013). The DSM has been a standard reference in non-legal and legal matters involving mental disorders since it was first published in 1952.

DECEIT

The tort of *deceit* occurs when the defendant intentionally misleads the plaintiff into taking a course of action that results in damage to the plaintiff. In a common example of this tort, the plaintiff invests in a doomed venture based on false information provided by the defendant, who knows the information is false. Deceit claims can also be based on physical or personal injury losses. For example, deliberately misleading someone about how to use dangerous equipment could support a deceit claim if personal injury resulted.

PASSING OFF

Passing off is related to expropriation of personality, except that it is not the plaintiff's name or likeness that the defendant is trading on, but the plaintiff's superior goods or services. This tort covers "knock-offs"—inferior products that the defendant passes off as having been produced by the plaintiff. The damage here consists in the fact that the plaintiff's brand can lose market share and consumer goodwill through being associated with an inferior product.

INDUCING BREACH OF CONTRACT

It is a tort to intentionally and unlawfully interfere with the contracts of others. The tort of *inducing breach of contract* (also known as *interference with contractual relations*) occurs as follows: one party, in pursuit of its own interests, deliberately pressures a second party to break its contractual obligations to a third party. The third party, if damaged by the broken contract, can sue the meddling first party.

INTIMIDATION

Intimidation, as the name suggests, is a tort involving threats. The plaintiff in an intimidation case must show that the defendant unlawfully threatened the plaintiff or a third party and that the plaintiff has suffered a loss as a result of the threat. In a labour dispute, for example, if a group of striking workers threatened to harm a worker who was planning to go to work, the latter could make an intimidation claim if she stayed away from work on the basis of the threat and lost wages as a result.

ABUSE OF POWER

Related to the tort of intimidation is a tort involving misuse of public office by a public official—in particular, the *abuse of power* involving the misuse of discretion. For example, if a public official gives a political appointment to a family member rather than to the person best qualified for the job, he is misusing discretion in this way. In another example, a public official might use her power to create economic hardship for a political opponent. *Roncarelli v Duplessis*[8] is the most famous example of this tort. (See Box 1.8 in Chapter 1 for a discussion of this case.)

Defences to Intentional Torts

There are many defences to the intentional torts. The defences argued most frequently—consent, self-defence, and legal authority—typically arise in the context of intentional

---

8   [1959] SCR 121, 1959 CanLII 50.

interferences with persons or property. *Consent* occurs where a claimant agrees to the interference in question. For example, inviting someone onto your land would negate your trespass-to-land claim. Consent can be given *expressly* (for example, in a written release) or *implicitly* (for example, by voluntarily participating in the activity). Consent issues often arise in cases involving medical procedures, sporting injuries, and sexual misconduct.

Self-defence applies if the defendant can show that she committed the tort, such as assault or battery, to protect herself. Two important requirements in this case are that the defendant:

1. honestly and reasonably believed that she was going to be attacked, and
2. responded in a way that was reasonable in the circumstances.

With respect to the first requirement, the defendant's belief need not have been correct; it must simply have been a belief, reasonable under the circumstances, that force was necessary to prevent immediate harm to herself. With respect to the second requirement for this defence, what is reasonable will depend on the facts of each case. If the force used is beyond what is reasonable, then it is excessive and the defence will not apply. Deadly force may be seen as having been reasonable if the person was required to protect herself from death or serious physical injury. Similar rules apply in cases where the defendant was defending third parties and property.

Legal authority, as a justification for committing a tort, is not one cohesive defence but a collection of defences based on various statutory (and sometimes common law) rules, each of which allows for intentional interferences with persons or property in specified circumstances (for example, a police officer searching a person for drugs). For these defences to apply, generally:

1. there must be reasonable grounds for the interference (for example, because a crime was being or was about to be committed), and
2. any force used must be reasonable (for example, a punch to temporarily disable a drunken aggressor as opposed to lethal force).

See Box 8.1 for a discussion of capacity to commit torts. *Lack of capacity*, when raised by a defendant, can operate like a defence.

Negligence

The largest area of tort law is the law of negligence. It covers almost every type of human activity. Personal injury cases, especially those resulting from motor vehicle accidents, are the most commonly litigated negligence cases. Unlike intentional tortious behaviour, which is made up of numerous individual torts with their own names and special rules, the tort of negligence has one set of rules, developed by the courts, that cover most instances of *carelessly* inflicted injury.

The word **negligence**, it should be noted, can have at least two legal meanings. In its broadest sense, negligence refers to the tort itself, meaning the entire cause of action or claim in negligence, including all its constituent elements. In its narrowest sense, it refers to just one element in the claim, the standard of care, or more specifically *breach* of the standard of care (a defendant who falls below the required standard of care for the activity in question is said to be *negligent*, or careless in a legal sense). The elements of a basic negligence claim are described next.

negligence
area of tort law that addresses harm caused by carelessness, not intentional harm

BOX 8.1

Capacity to Commit a Tort

Lack of capacity is sometimes raised as a defence in the case of intentional torts, usually on behalf of infants (that is, people under the age of majority) or mentally incompetent adults. Technically, capacity is a required *element* in all of the intentional torts. However, it is presumed that the defendant had the capacity to commit the tort in question unless the defendant challenges this presumption. There is no fixed age when children begin to be held responsible for intentionally inflicted injury; it depends on the intelligence and cognitive ability of the child in question. For both children and mentally incompetent adults, the key question is whether they have the mental ability to understand and appreciate the nature and consequences of their actions. If they do, then they have the capacity to be sued. A four-year-old child could potentially be held tortiously responsible for his actions. A similar approach to capacity applies to all areas of tort law, not just the intentional torts. See also the heading "Vicarious Liability," below, concerning the responsibility of parents for their children's tortious behavior.

"THE MAN WAS REAL NICE ABOUT IT. HE GAVE ME MY BALL BACK AND EVEN SAID YOU CAN EXPECT A NICE CALL FROM HIS LAWYER."

Elements of a Negligence Claim

The elements of a basic negligence claim have been variously named, described, and numbered. There is still no consensus on terminology, although the courts in Canada today generally refer to five elements:

1. duty,
2. standard of care and breach,
3. factual causation,
4. legal causation, and
5. damages.

While the plaintiff has the burden of proof with respect to all of these elements, in most cases the defendant will concede some of them and the litigation will focus on just one or two (most often, breach of the standard of care, and damages).

DUTY

In order for the law of negligence to apply, the law must recognize that the defendant had an obligation or duty to take care to avoid injuring the plaintiff, given the relationship between the parties and the activity in question. If the law has recognized a similar duty in the past, this element will be easy to establish.

If the situation is new and unprecedented, however, the court will engage in a detailed analysis to determine whether to recognize a new duty; it will consider, among other things:

1. whether the defendant could have reasonably foreseen the injury while engaged in the activity,

2. the nature of the relationship between the defendant and the plaintiff, and

3. policy considerations for or against the recognition of such a new duty (for example, the new duty might have a deterrent effect on others and reduce accidents, or it might lead to indeterminate liability costs for defendants).

See Box 8.2 for an example involving the alleged duty of a mother to her child for injuries caused to the child while the mother was pregnant.

BOX 8.2

Does a Mother Owe a Duty to Her Unborn Child?

In *Dobson (Litigation Guardian of) v Dobson*,* the SCC dealt with a case involving a pregnant woman who was driving her vehicle carelessly when it collided with another vehicle. Her child was born with permanent mental and physical disabilities as a result of the prenatal injuries sustained in the accident.

There was no precedent for this, and the court had to decide for the first time whether a mother owes a duty to her child with respect to her behaviour while pregnant. The court had to consider the law's role in regulating the lifestyle choices of pregnant women. It was clear that injury is foreseeable if a pregnant woman drives without care and attention and that the relationship between mother and child is a close one.

However, after weighing various policy considerations—in particular, the concern over imposing additional burdens on pregnant women, and the possible psychological consequences of liability for a new mother and the family—the court concluded that imposing a duty on women in these circumstances was not appropriate.

Note that the child was suing his mother (through a representative) because she was covered by insurance. The insurance money would have been used to offset the extra expenses his disability brought to his upbringing. Courts do not generally consider the existence of insurance in making their decisions about liability.

* [1999] 2 SCR 753, 1999 CanLII 698.

STANDARD OF CARE AND BREACH

Assuming that there is a duty, the question then arises whether the defendant has acted in accordance with that duty. This is the most frequently disputed element in negligence cases.

Standard of Care

Ordinarily, the test for standard of care is based on the following question: How would a reasonable person have acted in the circumstances? However, the test is modified for certain defendants (for example, professionals—whether doctors, lawyers, or engineers—are held to the same standard as reasonable professionals in the same field with the same specialization, and children are required to act as would other children of like age, intelligence, and experience).

Breach

To determine whether a defendant, measured by the applicable standard, has fallen below or breached the relevant standard, the court will consider all the circumstances of the case, including factors such as:

- the risk of injury inherent in the activity,
- the existence of any social benefits flowing from the activity,

- the extent to which others have acted similarly (that is, was the behaviour customary for someone in the defendant's position?), and

- the existence of legislative rules governing the activity and whether they have been followed or ignored.

For example, in one famous case, the court had to consider whether a municipality was liable for injuries caused to one of its firefighters when a jack in the back of a fire truck rolled on to the firefighter while the truck was responding to a fire. The jack was needed for the fire but couldn't be properly secured on this particular truck, which was the only one available at the time. In weighing the risk of injury by deploying the truck with an improperly secured jack against the benefit of saving "life and limb" in responding to the fire, the court concluded that in all the circumstances, the standard of care had not been breached.[9]

FACTUAL CAUSATION

Often simply referred to as *causation*, this element concerns whether the defendant's negligent conduct has actually caused the loss. Two tests are commonly used here:

1. the but for test, which asks whether there would have been no loss *but for*—that is, *in the absence of*—the defendant's conduct (or, framed another way, whether the defendant's conduct was necessary for the loss to occur), and

2. the material contribution test, which asks whether the defendant's conduct materially contributed to the loss (this test is the preferred test where there are multiple tortfeasors[10] contributing to the loss).

Recall the sample case in Chapter 6, *Matthews v MacLaren*.[11] This case illustrates the duty and standard of care elements above, but was in fact decided against Matthews's estate on the basis of this third element, factual causation. The court applied the but for test and found that Matthews would likely not have survived even if the defendant, MacLaren, had exercised proper care in rescuing him. Lake Ontario was very cold at the time, and the evidence was that Matthews probably died shortly after hitting the water.

LEGAL CAUSATION

Because negligence liability concerns *carelessness* rather than *intentional wrongdoing*, the law places a limit on the extent of the defendant's liability. For defendants to be liable, there must be a sufficiently close connection between their conduct and the loss. The question here is whether the defendant's conduct was a "proximate cause" of the loss; it concerns the conduct's "remoteness"—or, more precisely, *lack* of remoteness—as a causal factor in the loss.

The test used to limit liability is the reasonable foreseeability test; a defendant is responsible only for losses that are a reasonably foreseeable consequence of his behaviour.

In 2008, the SCC had to decide whether a supplier of bottled water was responsible for a serious psychological illness suffered by a consumer who witnessed a dead fly in an

---

9   See *Watt v Hertfordshire County Council*, [1945] 2 All ER 368 (CA).

10   A *tortfeasor* is a person who commits a tortious wrong.

11   1969 CanLII 227, 4 DLR (3d) 557 (Ont H Ct J).

unopened bottle. The SCC held that all of the elements of the negligence cause of action were met on these facts, except legal causation. The injury in this case was too remote to be compensable; it was not reasonably foreseeable that a person of ordinary fortitude would suffer serious injury from seeing a dead fly in a bottle of water.[12]

DAMAGES

The plaintiff has to show that she has suffered, or will suffer, a loss or injury that the court recognizes as worthy of compensation, such as personal injury, serious psychological injury, property damage, or financial loss (for example, loss of earnings, cost of care, or investment loss). "Ordinary" inconvenience, stress, or aggravation resulting from a careless defendant's behaviour is not compensable.

Misfeasance and Nonfeasance

Negligence liability usually applies to conduct that involves positive "doing." Such conduct might involve, for example,

- driving too fast or driving while impaired,
- operating on a patient and taking out the wrong kidney, or
- designing a bridge and miscalculating the stress points.

Doing something carelessly in this way is referred to as **misfeasance**. However, in special cases, the law imposes liability for injuries resulting from a failure to act—in other words, from "not doing." Examples of this would include situations where, for example,

- the driver of a motor vehicle fails to properly secure a child passenger,
- a bar owner fails to ensure that a drunken patron has a safe ride home, or
- a manufacturer omits to warn consumers about the risks associated with its product.

Not doing something you have an obligation to do is referred to as **nonfeasance**. See again the sample case, *Matthews v MacLaren*, in Chapter 6, which concerned a duty to rescue in the context of a boating mishap.

Common Types of Negligence and Forms of Loss

The following activities and contexts produce most negligence claims:

- *Motor vehicle accidents.* The largest number of negligence cases are a consequence of speeding, impairment by drugs or alcohol, or some other failure to exercise reasonable care when driving a motor vehicle.
- *Sports.* Participants in athletic activities can expect varying degrees of physicality depending on the sport and on whether they play professionally, at the amateur level, or in pick-up games with friends. Sometimes, the degree of violence exceeds what is expected in the given context. Aggressive behaviour can lead to intentional

misfeasance
negligent tort that involves doing something carelessly (as opposed to omitting to do something)

nonfeasance
negligent tort that involves omitting to do something the law requires you to do

---

12 See *Mustapha v Culligan of Canada Ltd*, 2008 SCC 27.

tort claims such as battery. Excessively careless behaviour can similarly lead to negligence claims.

- *Manufacture of defective products.* Product liability cases arise where manufacturers negligently design or produce goods.
- *Substandard construction.* Architects, engineers, and builders can be liable for negligently designing or constructing buildings.
- *Professional malpractice.* Professionals such as doctors, lawyers, architects, engineers, and accountants are liable if they are negligent in the services they provide to their clients.
- *Careless words* (or *negligent misrepresentation*). In situations where a special relationship exists between the defendant and the plaintiff (for example, where it is reasonable for the plaintiff to rely on the defendant because of the latter's expertise and position of trust), the court will impose an obligation on the defendant to exercise care in providing information to the plaintiff.
- *Careless inspections.* Government agencies, particularly municipalities, perform many kinds of inspections—for example, approving new construction and checking roads and highways for hazards. Negligently performed inspections resulting in loss can be actionable.

Different activities can lead to different types of harm. The following forms of loss or injury can be the basis of a negligence tort claim:

- *Personal injury.* Bodily injuries, ranging from broken bones to soft tissue injuries, including brain damage, occur as a result of many activities. In assessing the awards for such losses, courts refer to awards in similar cases. The SCC has set an upper limit for non-pecuniary losses (that is, losses such as pain and suffering that are not financial in nature): $100,000, in 1978 dollars. With inflation factored in, the maximum award is now over $300,000. Psychological injuries often accompany these bodily injuries and make up another element of the plaintiff's claim. So do financial losses—for example, loss of earnings and care costs. Financial losses are not subject to the SCC's upper limit and, in serious cases, such as those involving paralysis, can be in the millions of dollars.
- *Psychological injury.* When psychological injury alone is claimed (that is, where there is no accompanying physical injury), the injured party must prove that the injury is a recognized mental disorder—for example, the clinical depression or post-traumatic stress disorder that a person might suffer after witnessing a horrific accident. Financial losses may accompany such claims.
- *Property damage.* Negligent conduct resulting in damage to property—for example, when motor vehicles are damaged in accidents or buildings are flooded—can lead to liability. Again, any accompanying financial losses (such as the cost of replacement transportation while a damaged vehicle is repaired) may be part of the claim.
- *Pure economic loss.* A pure economic loss is one that is not connected to any of the previous three types of loss. In limited circumstances, such losses can be recovered. Common examples are investment losses—a case where a financial advisor negligently advises a client about an investment—or a loss resulting from an accountant or lawyer's carelessly structuring a business transaction.

Defences to Negligence

There are a number of defences available to a person sued in negligence. The onus is on the defendant to raise and prove these defences. There are three main ones:

1. contributory negligence,
2. consent, and
3. illegality.

Contributory negligence applies in a case where the plaintiff has negligently contributed to her own losses. It is not a complete defence, however; where the court finds contributory negligence, it will apportion liability between the plaintiff and the defendant. Where it is not clear that one party is more at fault than the other (or others, if there are multiple defendants), the court will apportion liability equally.[13]

Consent and illegality are complete defences. This means that, if the court finds that these defences applicable to the case, the plaintiff recovers nothing. **Consent** (also referred to as *voluntary assumption of risk*, or by its Latin name, *volenti non fit injuria*, or *volenti* for short) applies if, prior to engaging in the activity that led to injury, the plaintiff consented to the physical risks associated with it (for example, a sporting event) *and* expressly or implicitly agreed to give up the right to sue the defendant in the event of injury. Releases and exclusion clauses on the backs of tickets can be used as evidence of such an agreement.

The defence of **illegality** (sometimes referred to by its Latin name, *ex turpi causa non oritur action*, or *ex turpi* for short) historically applied only if the plaintiff and defendant had been involved in criminal or immoral activity at the time of the injury. More recently, this defence has been severely restricted by the SCC. It may now be used only in very limited situations—for example, in a case where the plaintiff is trying to use the negligence action to avoid a criminal penalty (this might occur if the plaintiff was sentenced to pay a fine and sued the defendant, an accomplice in the crime, to help pay for the fine).

Lack of capacity is sometimes used as a defence in negligence cases, as it is in intentional tort cases (see Box 8.1). As with the latter, however, the defendant's capacity is technically an element of the tort and is taken for granted unless the defendant challenges this presumption. There is no fixed age when children begin to be held responsible for negligence. For both children and mentally incompetent adults, the issue is whether the defendant has the mental ability to appreciate the nature of the duty imposed on him and to fulfill the duty by adhering to the requisite standard of care.

Strict Liability Torts

As we have seen, much of tort law is focused on the fault of the defendant. For the intentional torts, the defendant must have intended to bring about the consequences of her actions. With the tort of negligence, it is necessary to prove that the defendant's conduct fell below a reasonable standard of care. However, some forms of tort liability are not based on either intention or negligence. Under certain conditions, a defendant can be held responsible even if the consequences of her tortious actions were *not intended* and even if she was *not negligent*. Such actions are known as **strict liability torts**.

contributory negligence (defence of)
a defence against negligent tort claims that is based on the idea that the plaintiff negligently contributed to her losses

consent (defence of)
a defence against a variety of tort claims that is based on the idea that the plaintiff was aware of the risks associated with the activity that led to damages and agreed to participate in the activity anyway

illegality (defence of)
a defence to negligence claims that used to be applied when the plaintiff and defendant were involved in criminal or immoral activity at the time of the injury, but is now applied mainly when the plaintiff is trying to use the negligence action to avoid a criminal penalty

strict liability tort
a tort for which the defendant is held responsible even if the damaging action was neither intentional nor a result of negligence

---

13 All provinces and the Yukon have enacted legislation setting rules regarding apportionment of liability under this defence. See, for example, *The Tortfeasors and Contributory Negligence Act*, RSM 1987, c T90; *Negligence Act*, RSO 1990, c N.1; and *The Contributory Negligence Act*, RSS 1978, c C-31.

occupiers' liability
the liability of occupiers of land for injuries that visitors sustain while on the occupiers' property

Strict liability torts in Canada most often involve the following three activities:

1. the use of dangerous substances,
2. the ownership of animals, and
3. the use of agents (vicarious liability).

BOX 8.3

Occupiers' Liability: A Tort Related to Negligence

An area of liability closely related to negligence but with its own set of rules is **occupiers' liability**. It concerns the liability of occupiers of land for injuries that visitors (that is, entrants) sustain while on the property. At common law, the occupier's duty or obligation varies according to the type of entrant. The four main categories of entrant are

1. trespasser,
2. licensee (a person on the property with permission),
3. invitee (a person on the property for a business purpose—for example, a customer in a store), and
4. contractual entrant (someone who has a contract with the occupier allowing him to be there, such as a patron at a hotel, a movie theatre, or a fitness club).

The required level of care increases incrementally with each category. In the case of a trespasser, an occupier of land has only a duty to act with "common humanity"—for example, an occupier would not be required generally to make her property safe for trespassers, but still she would not be permitted to set traps to seriously harm someone cutting across her front yard. On the other hand, if someone has come onto your property with permission, or is there for a business purpose, the duty increases considerably. And in the case of a contractual entrant, there is a duty to ensure that the property is "reasonably safe" to use.

 In most provinces, legislation has modified the common law concerning occupiers' liability, simplifying the rules. This legislation has abolished the formal categories of entrants and imposed one general statutory duty that can be adjusted

to cover different circumstances. Typically, the new statutory duty requires occupiers to ensure that entrants and their property are reasonably safe "in all the circumstances of the case." Given that the duty is to take reasonable care *in the circumstances*, the level of care will vary depending on whether the visitor is a violent intruder, a friend over for dinner, or a customer at a store. (Saskatchewan, Newfoundland and Labrador, and the territories still apply the common law in this area, and New Brunswick has no specialized occupiers' liability rules and relies, for the most part, on basic negligence liability to regulate occupiers' liability disputes.)

 The same defences apply to occupiers' liability (at common law and under legislation) as to negligence generally.

rule in *Rylands v Fletcher*
the strict liability rule that the person who brings a dangerous substance onto his property is answerable for the damage it causes if it should escape

Dangerous Substances

Strict liability involving dangerous substances is based on the so-called **rule in *Rylands v Fletcher***.[14] The rule here is that a person who brings a dangerous substance (or uses in a dangerous way a substance that is not ordinarily dangerous) onto his property is answerable for the damage it causes if it should escape.

---

14   (1868), LR 3 HL 330.

The property owner's strict liability under *Rylands v Fletcher* is subject to two conditions. These conditions are that

1. the substance brought onto the defendant's land must *escape* to a neighbouring property and cause property damage or personal injury there, and
2. the use of the substance must be a *non-natural use*, meaning that it is unusual, extraordinary, or unsuitable and that it increases the risk of danger to others.

The main defences to *Rylands v Fletcher* claims are the following:

*   the plaintiff consented to the use of the escaping substance;
*   the escape was caused by an "act of God" (an unforeseeable natural disaster, such as a violent storm);
*   the substance escaped through the deliberate act of a third party (for whom the defendant is not responsible); and
*   legislative authority (where legislation shields the defendant from this form of liability).

Animals

Strict liability principles can also apply to owners of animals. Unlike dangerous substances, strict liability for damage caused by animals, whether they are wild or domestic, is generally not predicated on their escape from the defendant's property. Wild animals (for example, bears, lions, chimpanzees, and alligators) are always presumed to be dangerous, and their owners are strictly liable for the damage they cause.

For domestic animals that cause injury or damage, liability is strict only if the following conditions are met:

1. the animal had previously manifested a vicious or mischievous propensity to cause the type of harm in question, and
2. the owner knew of this propensity.

The second condition—the owner's knowledge of the animal's dangerous nature—is the most contentious point in actions involving domestic animals (usually dogs). The legal word for this knowledge is *scienter* (from the Latin for "knowingly"), and a plaintiff's action for damage caused by a domestic animal is often called a **scienter action**.

Another type of animal liability is **cattle trespass**. Strict liability for damage caused by straying cattle or other farm animals, unlike liability for domestic (or wild) animals generally, does require escape onto a neighbour's property. (Damage caused by animals that stray onto highways is governed by ordinary rules of negligence.) In that respect, cattle trespass is related to liability for dangerous substances.

The defence of consent is one of the very few defences available in actions based on strict liability for animals. For example, this defence would be available if the plaintiff had entered the defendant's property despite a "Beware of Dog" sign and then was mauled by the defendant's pit bull.

Vicarious Liability

The final type of strict liability tort is the kind involving **vicarious liability**. It is an important one. Vicarious liability involves the liability of one party for the fault of another, due to the special relationship between them. A special relationship of this kind exists, for example,

scienter action
a strict liability tort claim concerning damage caused by a domestic animal; based on the idea that the defendant (the owner) had knowledge the animal was dangerous

cattle trespass
a strict liability tort involving damage caused by straying cattle or other farm animals

vicarious liability
the strict liability of one party for the fault of another due to the special relationship between them (typically, an employer–employee relationship)

between a car owner and the people who drive the owner's car with her permission. When such people commit a tort in the course of driving the owner's car, the owner is generally held vicariously responsible, under provincial and territorial motor vehicle legislation.

The relationship to which vicarious liability most often applies is the principal–agent relationship. And the most commonly litigated principal–agent relationship is that of employer–employee. The general rationale for vicarious liability is as follows: even though the employee rather than the employer has caused the damage, the employer should bear the responsibility for the damage because the employer's enterprise has put the risk into the community. The plaintiff can still sue the employee as the primary tortfeasor, but vicarious liability gives the injured party an additional and typically "deeper pocket" to claim from.

Two conditions must be met before an employer will be found vicariously liable for the actions of an employee:

1. An employer–employee relationship, as opposed to a business–contractor relationship, must be established. The more control exercised over a person's work, the more likely the person will be classed as an employee.
2. The tort must have been committed in the course of employment. Employers are not responsible for torts committed by their employees on the latter's own time.

There are no specific defences to vicarious liability, although the employer can argue any of the defences that the employee can. If found liable, the employer can always choose to seek indemnity (that is, compensation) from the employee. Generally speaking, however, employers don't pursue this avenue.

Note that parents are generally *not* vicariously liable for torts committed by their children. Parents can be found primarily responsible in negligence, though, if a person is injured as a result of the parents' failure to properly supervise their children. A few provinces (for example, British Columbia, Manitoba, and Ontario) have enacted legislation making it easier to hold parents responsible for their children's actions in certain situations.

Miscellaneous Torts

Two important torts that do not fit neatly into the three categories discussed above (intentional torts, negligence torts, and strict liability torts) are *nuisance* and *defamation*. These torts have their own special rules. Arguably, they could both be considered forms of strict liability torts because the focus in assessing them, as with strict liability torts, is on the *effect* of the defendant's actions on others, not on whether the defendant intentionally or negligently brought about the damaging consequences.

Nuisance

In law, **nuisance** can be one of two kinds: public nuisance or private nuisance (see Table 8.1). A **public nuisance** occurs when a public interest is interfered with, such as when a highway is obstructed or a river is polluted through the defendant's actions. Generally, it is up to the government to seek redress for public nuisances—private citizens can sue for public nuisances only if they have suffered "special" damage that distinguishes them from the public at large.

A **private nuisance** occurs when the defendant has interfered with a person's reasonable use and enjoyment of his land. Trespass and/or physical damage may be involved—for example, where the defendant neighbour's felled tree lands on the plaintiff's house. But neither trespass nor physical injury is required. Interferences may involve foul odours or loud noises.

nuisance
in law, either public or private nuisance

public nuisance
occurs when a public interest is interfered with—for example, when a highway is obstructed or a river is polluted through the defendant's actions

private nuisance
a tort that involves one person's using her property in such a way as to substantially interfere with another person's enjoyment or use of his property, but without any actual trespass occurring

TABLE 8.1   Public Nuisance and Private Nuisance

PUBLIC NUISANCE	PRIVATE NUISANCE
• Unreasonable interference with public interests, such as obstructions of highways and pollution of waterways • If a crime has been committed, charges may be laid • Generally, the attorney gerneral has to bring any civil actions for damages or an injunction • A private citizen can bring an action for a public nuisance only if she has suffered special damage, such as personal injury, interference with private property interests, or economic losses that are substantially different from others also affected by the nuisance	• Unreasonable interference with plaintiff's use and enjoyment of his land • If the plaintiff has suffered material damage, an unreasonable interference is presumed • Where the damage is intangible, such as personal inconvenience or injury to the "senses or nerves" caused by noise or smell, whether the interference is unreasonable will depend on the court's assessment of the following factors: (1) nature, severity, and duration of interference; (2) character of the neighbourhood; (3) utility of the defendant's conduct; and (4) whether the plaintiff displayed abnormal sensitivity

The main defences to nuisance claims are the same as for claims based on *Rylands v Fletcher*—namely:

- the plaintiff consented to the activity causing the nuisance;
- the nuisance has come about by an act of God (that is, an unforeseeable natural disaster);
- the nuisance has come about through the deliberate act of a third party (for whom the defendant is not responsible); and
- legislative authority (where legislation shields the defendant from liability for nuisance).[15]

Defamation

Defamation is concerned with published allegations of impropriety that injure a person's reputation. The word *published*, in this context, simply means "communicated to others"; it doesn't necessarily mean these allegations have appeared in print. The rules relating to defamation attempt to balance individual rights with broader rights relating to free speech and access to information. The two main types of defamation are **libel** and **slander**. Libel deals with defamatory language that is written—for example, in a newspaper article or a book, whether in print or online. Slander deals with oral communications as well as other transitory kinds of communications (for example, looks or gestures). The common law considers libel a more serious form of defamation than slander; it doesn't require proof of damage for libel, but it does, in most cases, for slander.

The distinction between libel and slander has been abolished in a number of provinces—Alberta, Manitoba, New Brunswick, Newfoundland and Labrador, Nova Scotia, and Prince Edward Island—and in the territories. In these jurisdictions, libel and slander are treated equally and damage is presumed or not required to support an action for either.

defamation
a tort involving allegations of impropriety that injure a person's reputation

libel
a kind of defamation that involves defamatory language in writing, such as in a newspaper article or book, whether in print or online

slander
a kind of defamation transmitted via oral or other transitory forms of communication

---

15 Municipalities, for instance, are protected by legislation in most provinces and territories from being sued in nuisance by citizens for damages caused by blocked storm drains and sewers. The same legislation also usually protects municipalities from strict liability under *Rylands v Fletcher*.

BOX 8.4

Hyperlinking and Defamation

In *Crookes v Newton*,* new information practices ran up against old law. The SCC had to determine whether placing a link to a defamatory article on a website was the same as reproducing the article on the website. In other words, was the website owner liable for defamation? Newspapers and other publishers are responsible for checking the accuracy of the information they publish and print. Are website owners similarly responsible if they provide a hyperlink to defamatory material?

The plaintiff, Crookes, owned a business and commenced a number of lawsuits against various persons, including Newton, who he felt had defamed him. Crookes claimed to be the victim of a smear campaign. Newton owned a website that contained commentary on political matters, including free speech, and that included a hyperlink to another site that allegedly contained information that was defamatory of Crookes.

The narrow issue in this case was whether hyperlinking is publishing. A majority of the SCC concluded that it is not. They concluded that placing the burden of defamation lawsuits on website owners who had done no more than link to other sites that were defamatory would unduly restrict the free flow of information on the Internet. There was nothing on Newton's site itself that was defamatory. A site's providing a link to a second site is not the same thing as the first site's publishing that information itself, and the victim of defamation can always go after the owner of the site that actually contains the defamatory words.

*   2011 SCC 47.

DEFENCES TO DEFAMATION

It is frequently said that, where defamation actions are concerned, "truth is a defence." This defence is also referred to as *justification*. The defendant's own belief in the truth of the information is not a sufficient defence. Likewise, accurately repeating what someone else has said to you is still defamatory if what was said is untrue. That is why, especially for publishers, it is important that sources be checked.

Other important defences against a claim of defamation are the following: (1) *privilege*, which can be absolute or qualified; (2) *responsible communication on matters of public interest*; and (3) *fair comment*. These defences apply even if the statements are untrue.

Examples of statements protected by absolute privilege are statements by high-ranking government officials made in the course of official duties, and statements made during parliamentary proceedings. Such statements cannot be sued as defamatory even if they are made maliciously. The rationale for this defence is simply that public officials need absolute protection for their on-the-job defamatory words so that they can aggressively pursue the public good without fear of private actions against them.

The defence of qualified privilege applies to a variety of situations. It could apply to information published by a journalist if that information is in the public interest—for example, information related to public meetings or to public bodies such as the police or fire department. Also, this defence is available to a defendant who made the defamatory statements in the course of trying to protect her own interests or those of third parties. Such privilege is qualified in the sense that, unlike absolute privilege, it no longer applies if the plaintiff can show that the defendant was motivated by malice in making the statements. For example, a newspaper reporter who maliciously publishes false information about a public figure against whom she bears a personal grudge would not be able to claim privilege.

Until recently, the Canadian courts had never clearly defined, in the context of media reporting, the exact extent of the qualified privilege defence with respect to matters of public interest. In 2009, the SCC recognized a new defence to clear up the confusion.[16] *Responsible communication on matters of public interest* (commonly known by its shorter, less accurate name: *responsible journalism*) is available as a defence to any person who reports responsibly on matters of public interest, even if the some of the facts turn out to be untrue. Under this defence, matters of public interest can include anything that invites public attention, affects public welfare, or concerns matters of notoriety or controversy. The reporter must be responsible, however, in the sense of having been diligent in trying to verify the accuracy of the allegations.

Fair comment is a defence to defamation if the false statements are made in the context of commentary on matters of public interest, provided certain conditions are met—for example, provided that the statement is clearly recognizable as commentary or opinion (rather than put forward as a statement of fact) and provided that it amounts to an opinion someone could honestly and reasonably hold. Strictly speaking, such commentary cannot be false because it is an opinion and does not claim to be factual in nature.

Tort Remedies

Among the remedies available to victims of torts are (1) damages, (2) injunctions, and (3) extrajudicial remedies.

Damages

The main remedy available to the victim of a tort is damages. There are many different ways to classify damage awards. One way is to classify them according to the purpose the award serves. By this classification scheme, there are three main types of damages:

1. compensatory,
2. nominal, and
3. punitive.

Compensatory damages compensate the plaintiff for proven and recognized types of losses. These are what most plaintiffs are seeking in most tort actions. Sometimes the losses are easy to quantify—for example, where there have been out-of-pocket expenses necessitated by the tort, and receipts can be entered into evidence. These are often referred to as *special damages*. In other cases, the calculation is less exact—for example, where the court is attempting to compensate the plaintiff for pain and suffering or for future lost earnings. These are called *general damages*.

Nominal damages refer to damages that reflect the breach of a right where no actual loss has been sustained. While many torts—negligence, most notably—require the plaintiff to prove an actual *compensable* loss in order to bring an action in the first place, some torts allow an action to be brought without proof of loss (such torts are said to be *actionable per se*). Torts in this latter category include trespass to land, trespass to person, invasion of privacy, and libel. Where no actual loss has been sustained as a result of one of these torts, an award of nominal damages is possible. The word *nominal* in this context does not mean small, and such awards are not required to be small; however, unless the tortious behaviour in question is particularly extreme, nominal damage awards do tend to be relatively small.

compensatory damages
damages in a tort claim that compensate the plaintiff for proven and recognized types of losses

nominal damages
damages in a tort claim that reflect the breach of a plaintiff's right where no actual loss has been sustained

---

16   *Grant v Torstar Corp*, 2009 SCC 61.

punitive damages
damages in a tort claim that are granted in situations where the court wishes to punish the defendant for socially objectionable behaviour

Punitive damages are granted in situations where the court wishes to punish the defendant for socially objectionable behaviour. Such damage awards are in a sense a windfall to the plaintiff because they are over and above any amount needed for compensation or for acknowledging the infringement of rights. The intentional torts more than other torts result in this kind of award. In extreme cases of negligence and defamation, however, punitive damages have been awarded.

Injunctions

After damages, the next most important remedy for the victim of a tort is the *injunction*. Injunctive relief is most commonly prohibitory (that is, it takes the form of an order to stop doing something—for example, to stop using the plaintiff's backyard as a shortcut). But injunctive relief can in some cases be mandatory (that is, it may take the form of an order to do something, such as removing an obstruction blocking the plaintiff's access to his property). Claims concerning the tort of nuisance, more frequently than any other tort, include requests for injunctions.

Extrajudicial Remedies

Extrajudicial remedies are available in limited circumstances and are rarely used. Two examples in this category are *abatement of nuisance* and *recapture of goods*. The remedy allows the claimant to bring an end to the nuisance himself, without waiting to go to court. For instance, this remedy could allow a claimant to cut down a branch from a neighbour's tree if the branch were overhanging the claimant's property. The remedy of recapture allows an aggrieved person to recover goods that have been wrongfully removed or withheld, provided that the person acts reasonably in doing so (and without violence or breaking and entering).

The exact limits of these remedies are not clear, and they should be exercised only with caution—if possible, after seeking legal advice. There is a risk that the court may find the claimant's response excessive, leaving him open to counterclaims.

Contract Law

Contract law is a special area of the law. It empowers us to enter into agreements with others and to create legal relationships based on our own set of rules. For the most part, we are free to choose these rules. This makes contract law different from many other areas of the law—for example, torts and criminal law—where the rules are *imposed* upon us by the common law or by legislation.

Freedom of contract has its limits, though. These limits have to do with accepted community standards. For instance, many types of contracts or contractual terms are subject to judge-made or statutory rules dealing with illegality, human rights, employment standards, business practices, and consumer protection. These contracts or terms may be unenforceable if they do not follow those rules.

Pervasiveness of Contracts

Contracts are everywhere. Most of us enter into multiple contractual arrangements every day, without realizing it. We enter into contracts when we purchase gasoline for our vehicles (contract with a gasoline retailer), take public transit or hire a taxi (common-carrier contracts), or purchase food for immediate consumption (contract with a fast-food business). Then there are our contracts for non-food items (for example, clothing); for personal services (for example, haircuts) and home services (for example, cable and Internet access); and for entertainment (for example, movie rentals or tickets to sporting events). The list is long.

And even when we're not making new contracts, we're living by the terms of old ones—meeting our continuing service obligations (for example, making monthly payments on a gym membership) and requiring that the goods we purchase meet the contractual terms concerning their fitness for their stated purpose. If your new condominium begins to leak soon after you purchase it, you may have a claim in contract against the developer who sold it to you. If your smoke alarm fails to sound during a fire, you may have a contract claim against the home supply store that sold it to you. These are just a few examples.

Elements of a Valid Contract

As with the tort of negligence, there is no firmly established list of or nomenclature for the elements of a valid contract, at least beyond the first three. There is, however, *some* degree of consensus that up to six elements may be required: (1) offer, (2) acceptance, (3) consideration, (4) certainty of terms, (5) intention to contract, and (in some cases) (6) formal requirements. (Figure 8.1, below, summarizes the components of an enforceable contract.) We saw in our discussion of tort law that capacity to commit a tort was a required element. Similarly, in contract law, capacity to contract is a required element—one that is presumed unless the defendant raises the issue (see "Excuses That Protect Weaker Parties," later in this section).

Offer

An offer is a statement by one person (offeror) to another (offeree) indicating a willingness to commit to a binding arrangement. If a reasonable person would think—considering what was said and done, and the surrounding circumstances—that the offeror intended to be bound by the terms of the proposal should it be accepted, then a court will conclude that an offer has been made. The courts are resorting to an *objective intention* test here, as they often do in contract law, to determine the will of a party. This means the courts are not concerned with what the party actually believed in her own mind (that is, her *subjective intention*), but what a "reasonable person" would think the party intended based on her actions and the surrounding circumstances.

The following points are also important to note concerning offers:

- Precise words or formalized language are not necessary in the offer.
- Statements that do not qualify as offers are considered negotiating statements, often referred to as *invitations to treat* or *invitations to deal*. Negotiating statements generally do not have much legal significance unless they are false and induced the other party to enter into the contract.
- For most contracts, offers can be made either orally, in writing (for example, by letter or brochure, by posting a reward notice, or by means of a newspaper advertisement), electronically (for example, by email, fax, or on a website), by conduct (for example, by gesture or by providing a service), or through a combination of these methods.
- Offers must be deliberately communicated to the offeree or offerees before they can be accepted.
- Offers can be revoked (or taken back) at any time prior to acceptance.

Acceptance

Acceptance is the signification by the offeree of her willingness to enter into an agreement with the offeror. The test for whether an acceptance has been made is whether the offeree has absolutely and unequivocally agreed with the terms of the offer.

Note as well the following features concerning acceptances:

- Precise words or formalized language are not required.
- Responses to offers that do not qualify as an acceptance can fall into a number of categories:
  - *A mere inquiry or simple request to modify terms.* Here, the offeree indicates a willingness to accept on the offeror's terms but wishes to know if there is room for "movement" by the offeror in modifying the proposed terms. Such an inquiry or request does not "kill" the original offer; it remains open for acceptance.
  - *A counteroffer.* Here, the response includes a material change to the offer, such as modifying the price. A counteroffer kills the offer and requires an acceptance of its terms before a contract will be formed.
  - *An outright rejection of the offer.* This brings the negotiation to an end unless a new offer is made by one of the parties.
- Like offers, acceptances can generally be made either orally, in writing, electronically, by conduct, or by a combination of these.
- If the offeror requires a particular method of acceptance (for example, a special form or a precise time or place of acceptance), then this requirement must be met before the acceptance will be effective and the offeror bound to the contract.
- As a general rule, acceptances must be communicated to the offeror to be effective. The principal exceptions to this rule are
  - when the "postal acceptance rule" applies (if it is reasonable in the circumstances to use the post, it is presumed that a mailed acceptance is effective as soon as it is posted, even if the acceptance is lost in the mail and is never received by the offeror), and
  - when the offeror has dispensed with the need for communication (see discussion of unilateral contracts below).
- After acceptance, a contract is formed (assuming all other elements are present) and the parties are bound. At this point, it is too late for the parties to withdraw.

Consideration

At common law, contracts require an *exchange*, or a *bargain*. Consideration is something of value given by one party (for example, a purchaser who agrees to pay for land) in return for the promise or obligation of the other party (for example, a seller who has promised to sell the land). Consideration is crucial to making the contract binding.

A contractual promise must be supported by a *requested* consideration *coming from the other party* (promisee), which is a *benefit to the promisor* (for instance, a promise to sell something could be supported by payment or a reciprocal promise to pay) and/or a *loss to the promisee* (using the same example, the loss of the purchase moneys by the purchaser/promisee to obtain what is being sold). However, if one party promises to "sell" something for nothing (or close to nothing, such as selling a $1,000,000 house for $10), the promise would not be contractually enforceable. The promisor would not be receiving any real benefit from the promisee in exchange for the promise, and neither would the promisee be suffering any real loss. In this situation the promise to sell is not supported by consideration.

An exception to the consideration requirement relates to promises made under seal. A seal is a mark, placed on a document, that indicates a degree of formality and is acknowledged by the promisor as his own. Types of seal include impression seals, wax seals, or common stationers' red wafer seals. Such promises are binding without consideration. For example, when a person guarantees a bank loan to another person, the bank will often require the guarantor to sign *and seal* the guarantee. In most cases, the bank will not have provided any consideration to the guarantor for his promise, but the guarantee will still be binding because of the seal.

Certainty of Terms

If important terms—for example, those relating to the price or the nature of the property or service in question—are so vaguely expressed or uncertain in the contract that the court cannot ascribe any reasonable meaning to them, then the contract will be struck down as void on the grounds of uncertainty. The same applies if important terms are omitted altogether or if they are left open to be negotiated at a later date.

However, if the uncertainty relates to less important terms—such as times and places of delivery—the court will usually imply terms based on what is reasonable in the circumstances, and the contract will still be binding.

Intention to Contract

For a contract to be valid, the parties must intend to be *legally* bound by the terms of their arrangement.

In commercial settings, it is presumed that the parties did intend a legally binding relationship. This presumption can be rebutted by clear language to the contrary, if the parties want the arrangement to be in "honour" only and not binding.

In family and social settings, it is presumed that the parties did *not* intend a legally binding relationship. (This presumption, too, can be rebutted by clear language to the contrary.) However, this presumption does not apply in the case of marriage contracts and separation agreements, where the intention is always to bind.

Formal Requirements

All provinces and territories have legislation requiring certain kinds of contracts, such as land contracts or specific types of consumer contracts (for example, direct sales contracts—contracts entered into away from a seller's regular place of business), to be in writing and to contain certain information. The legislation in this area can be complicated and must be read carefully to determine the precise requirements and consequences of failing to meet them.

FIGURE 8.1 Summary of Contract Elements

1 + 2	+	3	+	4	+	5	+	6
A mutual agreement—offer and acceptance		Consideration— the exchange of something of value		Certainty— important terms expressed with sufficient clarity		Intention to contract—parties intend to create legal relationship		Compliance with formalities— required for certain kinds of contracts

Duties of Good Faith and Honesty

Our capitalist economic system favours open competition and freedom of contract. Adhering to these principles, it is argued, promotes a healthy economy. Traditionally, a consequence of this approach was that parties to contracts, *as a general rule*, were not subject to duties of good faith and honesty in their dealings with each other, either during negotiations or during contract performance.

There have always been exceptions, though. For example, if one party's conduct falls within the bounds of an established cause of action, such as fraud or theft, the other party can pursue his legal remedies accordingly. And if the parties are in a fiduciary relationship[17] or their contract incorporates fiduciary obligations (as is the case with most financial services contracts, such as banking and insurance contracts), they will be subject to duties of good faith and honesty. Lastly, there are special fairness rules, both legislated and at common law, requiring honest behaviour when dealing with consumers and vulnerable parties (for example, elderly or sick persons who might otherwise be taken advantage of). However, in many cases the dishonest behaviour in question does not fall within any of these exceptions, or the aggrieved party cannot prove that it does. In these situations, the behaviour has been implicitly sanctioned, *legally*.

In 2014, the SCC decided in *Bhasin v Hrynew*[18] that this was no longer acceptable. They held that in *all* contracts—in commerce generally—there is a basic obligation to ensure that contracts are performed in good faith. The plaintiff in the case was an investment dealer who had a contract with a financial corporation, Can-Am, to sell its educational savings plans (ESPs). The contract was coming up for renewal, and a competing dealer, Hrynew, was interested in merging his business with Bhasin's. Can-Am misled Bhasin about its relationship with Hrynew and its support for Bhasin's agency's business plans. In the end, Bhasin's contract was not renewed, and he lost his business selling Can-Am's ESPs. He was forced to take on less profitable work elsewhere. Hrynew benefited from Bhasin's loss.

The SCC held that the time had come for the principle of good faith to be recognized as a general organizing principle in contract law and that this includes an obligation on parties to be honest with one other. The obligation was not extended to pre-contract negotiations, and the court was clear that this new approach does not mean parties have to sacrifice their own interests. Nor does it imply duties of loyalty or disclosure. What exactly will be required under this new organizing principle will depend on context and what, in each case, is reasonable considering the legitimate interests of the parties.

On the facts of this case, none of the traditional exceptions applied. However, the court found that Can-Am had misled Bhasin and acted dishonestly, and that the newly recognized duty of honest performance had been breached. Bhasin was awarded damages.

It has been suggested that this decision will have a significant impact on business practices. Time will tell if this is true and how exactly a broadly enforceable requirement

---

17 A fiduciary relationship is one that is based on trust and confidence. When the law recognizes that such a relationship exists between the parties, it requires the fiduciary—that is, the party with whom trust has been placed—to act in the best interests of the party placing that trust. General obligations of honesty and good faith between the parties are also imposed. Examples of fiduciary relationships include trustees and beneficiaries, principals and agents, lawyers and clients, and guardians and wards.

18 2014 SCC 71.

of honesty will change behaviour. At a minimum, parties will not be able to deliberately mislead each other. Canada is not the first country to adopt such a principle in business dealings (although it is the first whose top court has led the way). The US, Australia, and New Zealand also recognize a similar approach.

Basic Contract Structures

Contracts can be structured in many different ways. Important types or forms of contract include *unilateral* and *bilateral contracts*, *standard form contracts*, *future performance contracts*, *contingent agreements*, *options*, *deeds*, and *electronic contracts*. These types of contracts are not mutually exclusive. For instance, it is possible to have a bilateral, standard form contact that is to be performed in the future and has been entered into electronically.

Unilateral and Bilateral Contracts

Unilateral contracts are contracts in the form of a "promise for an action," and they are sometimes referred to as *if* contracts because the offeror promises something (usually payment) *if* the offeree accepts by performing a requested action. Service contracts and renovation contracts are frequently in this form. Such a contract might say, for example, "If you paint my house, I will pay you $5,000."

Bilateral contracts are in the form of a "promise for a promise." Here, the offeror promises something in exchange for a reciprocal promise. She might say explicitly, for example, "I promise to sell you my car in exchange for your promise to pay me $5,000." Or she might simply say, "I offer to sell you my car for $5,000." Such an offer will usually be interpreted as a promise that impliedly calls for a reciprocal promise; simply by accepting the offer, the offeree will be seen to have "promised" to pay in return.

The important difference between unilateral and bilateral contracts is that bilateral contracts become binding as soon as the offeree accepts the offer, even though the promised actions (for example, transfer of ownership and payment) may not have occurred yet. With unilateral contracts, the parties are not bound to each other until the act of acceptance commences (for example, the offeree starts to paint the house). Up to that point, either party can change his mind and walk away from the deal (by revoking or rejecting the offer).

In many cases, it is not clear how the parties intended to structure their contract. When faced with this kind of ambiguity, courts tend to interpret the contract as bilateral. The courts presume the parties must have intended a bilateral contract because of the certainty and security that come from having a binding arrangement at the outset.

Standard Form Contracts

Contracts may be based on a standard form or be individually negotiated. Individually negotiated contracts are tailored to the specific circumstances of a situation. They are time-consuming to draft and tend to be used when the transaction is specialized or unique (for example, a contract for the development of a new sports arena or for the creation of a work of art).

Standard form contracts, on the other hand, tend to be used for predictable, uniform, common transactions—situations where individual negotiation would be impractical. Examples of standard form contracts include the ticket you receive when using public transit or going to a movie. More complex transactions—such as banking, insurance, real estate purchases, and car rental agreements—can also involve standard form contracts. Most written contracts are standard form contracts.

unilateral contract
contracts that are in the form of a "promise for an action," the offeror promising something (usually payment) if the offeree accepts by performing a requested action

bilateral contract
contracts in the form of a "promise for a promise" whereby the offeror promises something in exchange for a reciprocal promise

Standard form contracts are sometimes referred to as *contracts of adhesion* or *take-it-or-leave-it contracts*. They can serve an important purpose by improving efficiencies, but there is the potential for abuse when consumers or unsophisticated parties are involved. For example, an unscrupulous seller could draft a standard form contract it was using in such a way that its customers' rights under the contract are severely limited—for instance, by specifying in the contract that only written representations are binding, knowing that it would be difficult for consumers to enforce oral promises made by the seller's representatives. Consumer protection is discussed more generally in Chapter 10.

Executed and Future Performance Contracts

Another way to characterize the structure of contracts is based on the timing of their performance. Contracts that are fully performed are said to be *executed contracts*. If they are fully performed at the time (or shortly after) they are entered into, they are also *immediately performed*. Such contacts can be termed *immediate performance contracts*, although there is no generally accepted name for such contracts. An example of an immediate performance contract would be one where you pay for and receive goods or a service contemporaneously, such as when you buy your coffee at a coffee shop or go for a haircut.

Other contracts, however, delay performance for, or are continuously performed over, a period of time (sometimes for days, months, or even years). These contracts are referred to as *future performance contracts* (they are sometimes also called *executory contracts*). Future performance contracts, which are binding at the outset, are used whenever the promised actions take place in the future and sometimes over a period of time. They cover the full spectrum of planned arrangements from gym memberships to home purchases to ongoing business relations.

Contingent Agreements

Related to future performance arrangements are *contingent agreements*, sometimes called *delayed performance* or *defeasible contracts*. Contingent agreements include special terms called *conditions precedent* and/or *conditions subsequent*. A condition precedent delays the start of performance of the contract (or, in some cases, the formation of the contract in the first place) until a defined event occurs. A "subject to financing" clause in a home purchase contract is an example of a condition precedent; until financing is obtained by the purchaser, the contract does not take effect. In other words, if no financing is obtained, the contract simply fizzles out before it begins. A condition subsequent makes a contract "defeasible," meaning that at some point *after* performance has started the contract can be brought to a premature end if a defined event occurs. For example, an ongoing supply contract could include a condition subsequent that protects the supplier and terminates the contract should something happen that makes the product no longer profitable to supply.

Options

An option contract is an offer in the form of a contract, whereby an offeror makes a binding promise to keep an offer open for a fixed period of time during which, at any point, the option holder can accept the offer. In order to be bound, the person granting the option must have received consideration from the option holder or have made the promise under seal. Stock options and options to purchase real property are common examples of this form of contract.

Deeds

A deed is technically not a contract but a promise that has been "signed, sealed, and delivered." It is the traditional instrument for conveying ownership of real property (although it can be used for most other transactions as well), and it operates much like a contract, except that consideration is not required in order for the promise to be binding. The seal acts as a substitute for consideration (see the discussion, above, under "Consideration").

Electronic Contracts

Contracts can be formed by electronic means. As mentioned, offers and acceptances can be made electronically through, for example, faxes, emails, text messages, website forms, or combinations of these methods. Virtually any contract, regardless of its subject matter, can be electronic, although there are a few legislated exceptions. For instance, real estate contracts that are fully electronic are not valid in all jurisdictions.

In the area of consumer contracts, some observers have expressed concern that not all consumers are aware of the legal consequences of the point-and-click contracts into which they enter. In 2017, in a split decision, the SCC refused to enforce a provision in an online contract between Facebook and one of its users.[19] All users are required to enter into a contract with Facebook as part of the registration process. In this case, the user wanted to sue Facebook in British Columbia, where she lived, because Facebook had used her name and likeness without her knowledge in an advertising campaign. In the contract, which one judge described as an "online consumer contract of adhesion," the user had agreed to sue Facebook *in California* if she had a dispute (a clause in a contract that requires court claims to proceed in a particular jurisdiction is called a *forum selection clause*). The majority followed an established approach to the interpretation of forum selection clauses (which generally favours their enforcement), but cited public policy concerns, including unfairness resulting from inequality of bargaining power. Ultimately, the majority refused to enforce the clause, perhaps signalling a shift in the common law toward greater protection for consumers in this area. The result was that the user was entitled to proceed with her action in British Columbia.

Despite the risks of entering into electronic contracts, their convenience has led to recent increases in e-commerce. For more information on these types of contracts, see Box 8.5.

Contract Terms and Terminology

There are many different types or categories of contract terms. Some of the more significant ones are: (1) representations and promises, (2) express and implied terms, (3) conditions and warranties, (4) conditions precedent and conditions subsequent, and (5) exclusion clauses. The specific content of these various types of terms will vary from contract to contract.

Representations and Promises

Terms in contracts can be simple *representations* of fact (for example, "This car I'm selling you has 100,000 kilometres on it"), or they can be in the form of *promises* (for example, "I promise to paint your house next week"). With respect to liability, there is no difference

---

19   *Douez v Facebook Inc*, 2017 SCC 33.

between the two. If a representation is untrue, the party who made it can be sued for breach of contract. Similarly, if a promised event does not come to pass, the promisor will be liable (unless he has a recognized excuse for non-performance).

Electronic Contracts and E-Commerce

All Canadian jurisdictions have legislation providing that contracts may be made by electronic means and that clicking on computer icons, touching computer screens, or even speaking to computers are effective means of communicating contractual intentions.* This legislation is modelled on a law for electronic transactions adopted in 1996 by the United Nations Commission on International Trade Law (UNCITRAL), supplemented by further work on the law by the Uniform Law Conference of Canada, a body dedicated to the harmonization of provincial and territorial laws (and federal laws, where appropriate).

Various terms are gaining acceptance to describe the precise method by which e-contracts are entered into, such as *shrink-wrap*, *click-wrap*, and *browse-wrap agreements*:

- A *shrink-wrap agreement* usually relates to software and gets its name from the fact that some software is sold in a box enclosed in shrink wrap, but when the software is loaded, often from a CD or DVD, a further agreement presents itself on the computer, this time between the software creator and the user as opposed to retailer and user. Such agreements are usually licences restricting the user's ability to copy the software.

- A *click-wrap agreement* refers to a purchase contract made over the Internet, including but not restricted to software purchases; it gets its name from the fact that the user of the website is required to read an online contract and click an "I agree" icon or something similar.
- A *browse-wrap agreement*, like a click-wrap agreement, refers to Internet purchases. It is distinguished by the fact that the user indicates assent or agreement simply by using the product after having been made aware of the product's terms of use.†

E-commerce is responsible for a larger percentage of overall consumer sales each year, and by some estimates now accounts for 50 percent of such sales. And decisions about 80 percent of all purchases, whether or not they are actually made online, are influenced by online research. M-commerce, which refers to purchases using mobile communication devices such as cellphones, although still a relatively small segment of total e-commerce, has been identified as a rapidly growing area.

* For example, see Ontario's *Electronic Commerce Act, 2000*, SO 2000, c 17, and BC's *Electronic Transactions Act*, SBC 2001, c 10.

† For a discussion of these kinds of agreements, see *Century 21 Canada v Rogers Communications Inc*, 2011 BCSC 1196.

Express Terms and Implied Terms

express terms
contract terms that the parties have considered and deliberately included in the contract

implied terms
contract terms that the parties have not explicitly included in the contract but that are nonetheless part of the agreement

An **express term** is one that the parties have put their minds to and deliberately included in the contract. In an oral contract, for instance, an express term is something that the parties have specifically discussed. In a written contract, an express term will be spelled out in the text of the document.

Implied terms are terms that the parties have not expressed in their contract but are nonetheless part of the deal. The SCC has held that there are three kinds of implied terms that *may* be included in a contract, depending on the circumstances. The three kinds are as follows:

1. *Terms implied in fact*. These are terms that, in the court's view, the parties would have agreed to if they had put their minds to it. The test of whether a term is implied in fact is whether it is needed to give business efficacy to the contract. In other words, is this term necessary for the efficient performance of the contract?

2. *Terms implied in law.* These terms are automatically part of the contract owing to the nature of the contract and the laws regulating the area in question. Terms implied in law are based on what the court feels is necessary for the fair functioning of the agreement. Also included in this category are terms that legislation makes part of the contract. For example, sale of goods acts in all provinces and territories make it an implied term of any sale of goods contract that the goods sold will be "reasonably fit for the purpose" for which they were intended.

3. *Terms implied by custom or usage.* These terms are based on industry standards for similar types of contracts. It is assumed that the parties intended similar terms to be part of their own deal. Generally, the parties can exclude any of these implied terms, if they choose to, by doing so expressly in their agreement. In some cases, legislation may prevent them from such exclusion.

Conditions and Warranties

Terms in a contract can also be differentiated according to their level of importance to the parties, and the available remedies can vary depending how they are characterized (see also below under the heading "Contract Remedies"). A *condition*, in this context, means an important contract term—for example, payment of the purchase price or delivery of the promised goods. In the event that a condition is not met, the innocent party can not only sue for damages but can also terminate the contract if she so chooses.

A *warranty* is a less significant term, such as one relating to the inclusion of some inexpensive furnishings in the sale of a building. All that an innocent party can recover for a breach of warranty is damages. The contract cannot be terminated for breach.

The parties' particular intentions determine which provisions in the contract are conditions and which are warranties. For example, a definition clause could make it clear how the parties wanted the various terms to be characterized. However, if the contract does not make the parties' intentions clear, the court will make the determination for them based on its assessment of the relative importance of the various terms.

Note that the words *warranty* and *condition* can mean different things in different contexts. For instance, both words can simply refer to a term of the contract generally. *Warranty* can also refer to a guarantee of quality or performance, usually for a limited period of time (for example, a manufacturer's warranty). And the word *condition* can be a shorthand way to refer to a condition precedent or condition subsequent. Context will usually make the intended meaning clear.

Conditions Precedent and Conditions Subsequent

A condition precedent is a special kind of term that delays the performance or formation of a contract until a defined event occurs. A condition subsequent terminates a contract that is being performed when a stated event occurs. See above under "Contingent Agreements."

Exclusion Clauses

Exclusion clauses can be found in all kinds of contracts but are often associated with standard form contracts. They typically limit the liability of one of the parties either to a fixed dollar amount or—for certain types of breaches—altogether. For example, a ski-hill ticket may limit the liability of the resort operator for any injuries the patron sustains while on the ski hill, even if these injuries are caused by the operator's negligence in grooming or marking the runs.

There are many different ways of referring to exclusion clauses. In addition to *exclusion*, the following adjectives are used: *exclusionary*, *exculpatory*, *exemption*, *exempting*, *limitation*, *limiting*, and *disclaimer*. Exclusion clauses are important, particularly for businesses, because they allow the parties to the contract to manage their risks and insure accordingly.

Forum selection clauses, choice of law clauses, and arbitration clauses are related to exclusion clauses. These clauses limit the *manner* in which one party may pursue a claim against the other party and are often used by large corporations providing a product or a service. A *forum selection clause* determines where disputes will be heard (see the discussion of the Facebook case above under "Electronic Contracts"). A *choice of law clause* requires the law from a particular jurisdiction be used to resolve claims under the contract. Very often, forum selection and choice of law clauses are combined, favouring a seller or service provider with customers from other jurisdictions who must come to its jurisdiction to pursue their claims.

Arbitration clauses provide that disputes between the parties must be pursued using an arbitrator (an impartial third party). Resolution through arbitration is generally faster and less expensive than the regular court process. Arbitration and other forms of alternate dispute resolution are described in Chapter 17.

While there is nothing inherently wrong with the use of limiting provisions in contracts, as noted above in connection with standard form contracts, there is the potential for abuse if unsophisticated parties agree to limitations without understanding the consequences.

BOX 8.6

Words for Terms

Many different words are used to describe contract terms in a general sense, words such as *term*, *clause*, *representation*, *condition*, *warranty*, *provision*, *stipulation*, and *rider*. Sometimes these words can have specific and even multiple meanings. For instance, the words *warranty* and *condition* can refer to contract terms generically, but they can also have a more technical meaning, referring to the level of importance of a term. For example, the word *condition* can refer to any general stipulation in a contract, but it may also refer more specifically to a condition precedent or a condition subsequent, or to an important term that, if not followed, triggers a right of termination.

Very often, context will determine the intended meaning. Also, the contract may include a definition clause setting out the meanings of various words used in the contract.

Excuses for Non-Performance of Contracts

After a contract has been entered into, problems may occur, information may come to light, or new circumstances may arise that make the agreement unfair or even impossible to fulfill as originally made. With contracts, we talk not of defences but of excuses for not having to perform one's contractual obligations. In a sense, the right of an innocent party to walk away from a contract without liability is a type of remedy (remedies *against* a guilty party are examined below). The more common excuses are described next.

Serious Breach of Contract

As noted, terms can be classified according to their relative importance to the parties. Obligations concerning payment and delivery of the subject matter of the contract, for example, are usually interpreted to be conditions of further performance. If a condition is breached, the innocent party will have the option of lawfully repudiating (or terminating) the contract and of being relieved of the obligation of further performance on her part.

Misrepresentation

During the course of negotiations, one party may falsely represent a fact relating to the contract—for instance, stating that a house for sale has just had a new roof put on it when in fact it hasn't. Even if the representation has not been made a term of the contract, it can still be legally significant. A false statement of this nature is called a **misrepresentation**. Misrepresentations may be:

misrepresentation
a false representation made during contract negotiations

- *innocent* (made without knowing the information was untrue),
- *negligent* (made without knowing the information was untrue, but made under circumstances where the party ought to have known the information was untrue), or
- *fraudulent* (made while knowing the information was untrue or at least while knowing there was a serious risk it was untrue).

All three types of misrepresentation may provide an excuse for terminating the contract if the misrepresentation was material—in other words, if it was significant enough to induce a reasonable person to enter into a contract she would not have entered otherwise. What usually happens is that, once the innocent party discovers the misrepresentation, she refuses to complete the contract—for example, by not paying the balance owing on the contract. The other party then sues, and the innocent party offers up the misrepresentation as an excuse for not paying. She may even get back any money already paid by claiming rescission. (For an explanation of rescission, see the discussion of remedies, below).

Mistake and Frustration

Mistake and frustration are also excuses for not performing. The law of *mistake* in contractual settings is complex and not always consistently applied by the courts. Two relatively clear instances of mistake occur:

1. where the parties are confused about the terms they have agreed to (for instance, where the terminology used in the contract is ambiguous and capable of multiple meanings), and
2. where both parties have made a mistaken assumption about some fundamental or essential matter underlying the contract (for example, in a construction contract where the parties assumed the land was zoned for the project in question when it wasn't).

In both situations, once the mistake is discovered, it may provide an excuse for discontinuing further performance.

Frustration, as an excuse for non-performance of a contract, is similar to the mistaken assumption excuse, but the timing involved is different. In the case of mistake, the problem exists at the time of the contract. With frustration, the problem develops *after* the contract has been entered into and during performance, and it comes about because of a change of circumstances. The changed circumstances must be significant enough to make continued performance impossible or at least to change the fundamental nature of the agreement. Consider the zoning example again. If a construction contract is based on existing zoning, and the municipality, during performance, changes the zoning rules so as to make it impossible to complete the contract, the contract may become frustrated, thereby excusing the parties. The question of who is responsible for any losses incurred up to the point where the contract becomes frustrated is not always clear under the law and varies somewhat across jurisdictions in Canada.

Excuses That Protect Weaker Parties

Some excuses for non-performance of a contract are intended to protect weaker parties. The main excuses of this type are duress, undue influence, unconscionability, and lack of capacity.

DURESS

Duress applies when one of the parties entered into the agreement against his will. It is a common law doctrine and does not apply unless the will of the victim is taken away. If someone holds a gun to your head to make you sign a contract, the agreement can be set aside. Traditionally, there had to be a threat of physical violence for duress to apply. More recently, the courts have started to recognize economic duress as an excuse, too. For economic duress to qualify as an excuse, however, the financial pressure has to be so extreme that it deprives the party experiencing it of his freedom to exercise his will. Simple commercial pressure is not enough.

UNDUE INFLUENCE

Undue influence can be thought of as *duress light*. Undue influence is an equitable doctrine; that is, it was developed by the courts of equity (see Chapter 2). It qualifies as an excuse for non-performance of a contract when one party has exerted unconscionable use of power over another and has thereby influenced the weaker party to enter the contract. This influence may fall short of depriving the weaker party of his will. Undue influence may be established in one of two ways:

1. proving *actual* undue influence (for example, where one party threatens to sue or prosecute a relative of the other party unless the other enters into a contract), and
2. proving that a recognized special relationship exists between the parties (for example, a doctor–patient or lawyer–client relationship), in which case the court may *presume* undue influence unless the stronger party proves otherwise.

UNCONSCIONABILITY

Unconscionability, like undue influence, is an equitable doctrine; it applies where there is a power imbalance between the two parties. The difference is that unconscionability doesn't necessarily involve the application of actual or presumed pressure. As an excuse for non-performance of a contract, it applies when one party takes advantage of another. To establish it, two elements are required:

1. inequality of bargaining power (such as might exist between a young, fit person and a seriously ill or mentally incompetent relative), and
2. an unfair bargain (meaning the stronger party obtains property or some other benefit for less than its fair market value by taking advantage of the weaker party).

INCAPACITY

Incapacity may also be raised as an excuse by weaker parties. Technically, capacity to contract is a required element of a valid contract. In contract law as in tort law, capacity is presumed; the onus is on the party seeking to escape responsibility to prove *lack* of capacity (see Box 8.1). Almost everyone has the capacity to enter into contractual arrangements. The two main exceptions today are:

1. infants, and
2. individuals who are deemed to be mentally incompetent.

An infant is someone under the age of majority, which has been fixed by legislation in all provinces and territories at either 18 or 19. Despite the legal view that infants lack the capacity to contract, common law and legislated rules grant them limited capacity to enter certain kinds of contracts—for example, contracts for necessities such as food and clothing, contracts for student loans, and contracts for property settlements in the event they are getting married. (In the latter case, a public trustee of the court would usually oversee the contract.)

Incapacity based on mental incompetence applies where one party's mental incapacity prevents her from appreciating the nature of the contact entered into. The incompetence may be a matter of permanent mental disability or a matter of temporary impairment by drugs or alcohol. Apparently, although the case law is uncertain in this respect, mental incompetence qualifies as an excuse for non-performance of a contract only where the person trying to enforce the contract was aware of the other party's incompetence at the time the contract was made.

Illegality

Finally, contracts that are contrary to public policy at common law or are illegal under legislation may be unenforceable. In such cases, the parties have an excuse for not adhering to the agreed-to terms. For example, contracts to commit criminal or tortious acts are contrary to public policy and are not enforceable; parties may in fact face criminal charges for such agreements.

Contracts with restraint-of-trade provisions generate the most litigation on the grounds of illegality. Non-competition arrangements in contracts of employment often include these kinds of provisions, whose purpose is to prevent employees from competing against their former employers. Restraint-of-trade provisions are also included in contracts for the sale of businesses; they are intended to prevent former business owners (the sellers) from competing with the purchasers. The courts will strike down such provisions and sometimes the whole contract if the restraint-of-trade provision is unreasonably restrictive, especially with respect to its duration and the geographical area it is supposed to cover.

Other kinds of contracts that may prove unenforceable owing to illegality include:

- contracts for unregulated medical services,
- surrogacy contracts,

- contracts with a sexual services component, and
- gaming and wagering contracts.

Gaming and wagering contracts are illegal under most provincial and territorial insurance statutes, although specific exceptions apply to government-sanctioned gambling.

Contract Remedies

Remedies are available for breach of contract, misrepresentations, and other problems connected with contractual formation or performance. Rights of non-performance for an innocent party were discussed above. The main remedies that may be pursued *against* a defendant[20] are:

- damages,
- specific performance,
- injunctive relief,
- rescission, or
- rectification.

Damages

TYPES OF DAMAGES

As in tort law, the most important remedy in contract law is damages. Contract damages are classified differently, though. The three main categories in contract law are

1. expectation damages,
2. reliance damages, and
3. restitution damages.

expectation damages
a remedy for contract disputes that attempts to place the innocent party in the position she would have been in if the contract had been performed as promised and all the contractual representations had been true

Expectation damages attempt to place the innocent party in the position she would have been in if the contract had been performed as promised and all the contractual representations were true. This method of assessing damages is the standard method used to calculate damages in contract disputes. Expectation damages typically claimed include out-of-pocket expenses to correct defective performance (for example, where construction work is shoddy and has to be fixed) and loss of profits (for example, where a commodity was not delivered and the purchaser was unable to resell for a profit as planned).

Expectation damages sometimes have alternate names depending on what they represent or how they are calculated. For instance, out-of-pocket expenses, just referred to, can also be called *special damages* because they have already been incurred and are certain. The term *general damages* can be used to describe the value of a lost expectation that is not specifically quantifiable, such as the enjoyment the plaintiff hoped to experience on a vacation (where a vacation planner failed to deliver as promised). *Liquidated damages*, which are another type

---

20 Generally, only parties to a contract acquire rights or incur obligations under it. This is known as the *privity rule*. Privity of contract—that is, being a party to it—is generally required in order to maintain an action for damages or other remedy. Some exceptions apply, however, in the case of *third-party beneficiaries*. A third-party beneficiary is someone mentioned in the contract who benefits in some way from it.

of expectation claim, refer to damages that the parties have calculated in advance. However, they can be claimed only where the parties have put a clause in the contract setting out what the damages are to be, and where the amount represents a genuine pre-estimate of the loss expected to be suffered in the event of breach. Liquidated damages clauses can save the parties the trouble of arguing about what the damages are if the contract is broken.

Reliance and restitution damages can be claimed as alternatives to expectation damages in cases where there is no expectation loss or it can't be proved. **Reliance damages** are intended to cover expenses incurred *preparing for* contractual obligations (for example, the cost of special materials purchased by a building contractor that become wasted when the other party cancels the contract). **Restitution damages** generally cover moneys—deposits and part payments, for example—that the innocent party paid over to the other party. By recovering such expenses and moneys paid, the innocent party at least breaks even and doesn't suffer a loss as a result of the other party's breach.

A party may be able to claim *punitive damages* in addition to either expectation, reliance, or restitution damages. As in tort claims, punitive damages are designed to punish the defendant for socially objectionable behaviour (however, this is difficult to show in most breach of contract situations). Again, they represent a windfall to the plaintiff because they are over and above what is needed for compensation.

MITIGATION OF DAMAGES

A party to a contract that has been breached by the other party has an obligation to take reasonable steps to minimize her losses. In determining what is reasonable, the courts consider all the circumstances of the case.

For example, if a seller fails to deliver property in breach of contract, the purchaser may be required to purchase replacement property. The court would consider the volatility of the market, the availability of replacement property, and whether or not the breach has left the innocent party with funds with which to mitigate (because the purchase has not been completed). In a rising market, a purchaser who failed to mitigate by purchasing a replacement property within a reasonable time would not be able to recover for the increased loss resulting from the delay.

A similar obligation exists in relation to tort damages, but the issue tends to be more contentious in the area of contract damages. Expectation damages are commonly claimed in contract disputes (not in tort claims), and a plaintiff will generally have more opportunity to manage the extent of these kinds of losses.

CAUSATION AND REMOTENESS OF DAMAGES

As in tort claims (particularly negligence claims), a party claiming damages must prove that the breach of contract caused the loss and that the loss is not too remote. The basic causation test in contracts is the *but for* test: Would there have been no loss *but for*—that is, *in the absence of*—the defendant's conduct? Or, stated another way, was the defendant's conduct necessary for the loss to occur? For example, a coffee shop owner who claimed loss of profits because the defendant sold him a defective espresso machine would receive nothing if the defendant could show that a municipal road diversion kept all customers away from the shop at the relevant time.

Even if causation can be established, if the type of damages is not a "reasonably foreseeable" consequence of the breach, the damages will be deemed too remote to be claimed. Using loss of profits as an example again, if a courier company delivered a machine part to a business one day late, the courier company would likely not be responsible for loss of profits because the

reliance damages
a remedy for contract disputes that compensates the innocent party for expenses he incurred preparing for the performance of contractual obligations

restitution damages
a remedy for contract disputes that compensates the innocent party for moneys usually paid over to the other party (deposits and part payments, for example)

entire business was at a standstill waiting for the part to arrive. Unless the courier company had been given notice that the part was that critical to the business's operation, or otherwise ought reasonably to have known that it was, such a loss would be considered too remote.

See also the "Factual Causation" and "Legal Causation" subheadings under "Elements of a Negligence Claim," above.

Other Remedies

Besides damages and lawful repudiation (see above under "Serious Breach of Contract"), a number of other remedies are sometimes available in contract disputes, including (1) specific performance, (2) injunctive relief, (3) rescission, and (4) rectification. These four remedies are all equitable remedies and are generally available only if damages would not adequately compensate the plaintiff in the circumstances. Also, because they are equitable remedies, the court will not grant them unless the plaintiff has come to court "with clean hands" (in other words, has been fair and reasonable in bringing the proceedings). Other equitable bars can apply to these remedies as well (such as where the plaintiff has misrepresented some fact in connection with the transaction). Also, the court will not order this remedy if it would negatively affect an innocent third party (see the example in connection with specific performance referred to next).

specific performance
a remedy for contract disputes whereby the court orders the party in breach to perform his obligations as promised

Specific performance is a remedy whereby the court orders the party in breach to perform his obligations as promised by transferring the property or—more rarely—by performing the service agreed to. Besides the other equitable defences, the rights of third parties can be significant in this context. For example, the court would not order a party to transfer a residence if that party's ex-spouse were still living on the property.

When courts grant *injunctions* in contract claims, it is usually to prevent a party from ignoring a contractual provision intended to prevent that party from engaging in certain behaviour, such as selling competing products or stealing customers.

rescission
a remedy for contract disputes whereby the contract is cancelled and the parties are returned to the positions they were in just before the contract was entered into

Rescission is a special remedy whereby the contract is cancelled and the parties are returned to the positions they were in just before the contract was entered into. Usually this involves returning anything received under the contract, such as money or property, up to the point of cancellation. Rescission is not available as a remedy for breach of contract; it is meant for problems that arose prior to contract formation. It is most often claimed for material misrepresentations that were made before the contract was entered into. If the misrepresentations were also negligent or fraudulent, they may support a separate claim for damages *in tort*.

As a remedy, rescission is subject to a number of limitations. One of these is the practical impossibility of returning any property in precisely the same form in which it was received; for instance, a car may be in an accident, and a building may be substantially renovated or torn down altogether.

rectification
for contract disputes based on errors in the written contract, a remedy whereby the court orders that the contract be rewritten to correct the mistake

Rectification is an unusual and limited remedy that applies where the parties have made a mistake in recording the terms of their contract in a written document. This remedy involves an order that the contract be rewritten so as to correct the mistake. What usually happens in rectification cases is the following: a mistake comes to light, and the party benefiting from the mistake tries to enforce the contact as written. The other party, in order to obtain the remedy, must prove, among other things,

- what terms were actually and clearly agreed to orally,
- that a mistake was made in recording the agreement, and
- that the mistake can be corrected easily by the substitution of a few words.

BOX 8.7

Damages for Wrongful Dismissal: A Special Case

Generally speaking, the measurement of expectation losses in breach of contract cases is "open." In other words, there is no fixed formula for calculating the damages. However, in wrongful dismissal cases, the courts have developed a unique approach.

This special approach applies specifically to open-ended employment contracts, which cover most employment arrangements. An open-ended employment contract is one that is *not* for a fixed term or based on a collective agreement negotiated on behalf of the employee by a union (labour legislation tightly regulates collective agreements). Employees covered by open-ended employment contracts can be let go *immediately* for cause (for stealing or serious insubordination, for example). This is not surprising. More surprising is that employees covered by these kinds of contracts can also be dismissed at any time *without cause* and for almost any reason or even for no reason.* The only difference is that, if an employee is dismissed without cause, *the employer must give the employee reasonable notice or salary in lieu*. Open-ended employment contracts include an implied term at common law that employers must provide reasonable notice or equivalent pay in the case of without-cause dismissals. The common law "formula" for calculating reasonable notice[†] factors in such things as length of service, type of employment, the employee's age, and availability of similar employment.

Employment standards legislation, federally and in the provinces and territories, also applies in this area and sets minimum notice periods for employees dismissed without cause; they work out to roughly one week of notice for every year of service. However, the common law assessment is almost always more generous—the more responsibility and seniority an employee has, the longer the required notice will be—and can be as much as one month (or more) of notice per year of service, far in excess of the statutory minimums.

The legislation doesn't prevent the employee from pursuing a claim at common law, and, in the event of a dispute, a dismissed employee will most often choose the common law remedy over (or in addition to) the legislation. For example, in a recent Ontario Court of Appeal decision, *Love v Acuity Investment Management Inc*,[‡] a 50-year-old senior vice-president with only two and a half years' service, who had been dismissed without cause or notice, was awarded nine months' salary. The statutory minimum was just two weeks.

There is one important qualification to an employee's right to pursue this common law remedy, however. It applies when an employee expressly agrees, when hired, to limit notice entitlement upon dismissal—generally, in this situation the employee is restricted to the termination rights, if any, as agreed. The employee would still be able to pursue a statutory notice claim, however, as this right cannot be taken away by such an express term in an employment contract.

---

* There are a few exceptions, though. Dismissing an employee for discriminatory reasons, for instance, is prohibited by human rights legislation, federally and in all provinces and territories.

† See, for example, *Bardal v Globe & Mail Ltd*, 1960 CanLII 294, 24 DLR (2d) 140 at 145 (Ont H Ct J), and *Honda Canada Inc v Keays*, 2008 SCC 39.

‡ 2011 ONCA 130.

CHAPTER SUMMARY

Private law regulates the relationships between persons in many areas. Canada's Constitution assigns jurisdiction over private law, for the most part, to the provinces. However, some areas rest with Parliament (for example, intellectual property), and for a few (such as family law), jurisdiction is split between the provinces and the federal government. Private law disputes are resolved, like most other disputes, by assigning the burden of proof to the plaintiff or person asserting the claim. The standard of proof is *balance of probabilities*, which is less than the criminal standard, *beyond a reasonable doubt*.

Two key areas of private law are torts and contracts. Tort law covers a wide and diverse range of civil wrongs not covered by other areas of private law. Tort claims can be classified according to whether they involve intentional or negligent wrongdoing, or whether they are based on strict liability principles. Classic examples of intentional torts are assault and battery. Torts involving negligence include many situations, from car accidents to professional malpractice. Strict liability torts deal with relatively few situations, such as using dangerous substances, owning dangerous animals,

and vicarious liability. A few miscellaneous torts, such as nuisance and defamation, are more difficult to classify, but are similar to strict liability torts insofar as they are focused on the effects of behaviour rather than fault associated with it.

Contract law is one of the few areas of law where parties can create their own rules and define the terms of their own relationship. Contracts apply to many aspects of our daily routines. The main elements of contract formation are offer, acceptance, and consideration (the parties' reciprocal exchange of something of value). Contract disputes often centre on the interpretation of terms and on whether excuses are available for non-performance of the contract. Excuses for one party's non-performance might be, for example, misrepresentations by the other party during negotiations, or mistakes made about the nature of the contract agreed to. Breach of contract occurs where one party fails to live up to the terms of the agreement. The most common remedies in contract disputes are damages to compensate the innocent party for her lost expectation, or a court order forcing the party in breach to specifically perform his obligations.

KEY TERMS

assault, 233

battery, 233

bilateral contract, 255

cattle trespass, 245

civil wrong, 232

compensatory damages, 249

consent (defence of), 243

contributory negligence (defence of), 243

defamation, 247

expectation damages, 264

express terms, 258

false imprisonment, 233

illegality (defence of), 243

implied terms, 258

libel, 247

misfeasance, 241

misrepresentation, 261

negligence, 237

nominal damages, 249

nonfeasance, 241

nuisance, 246

occupiers' liability, 244

private nuisance, 246

public nuisance, 246

punitive damages, 250

rectification, 266

reliance damages, 265

rescission, 266

restitution damages, 265

rule in *Rylands v Fletcher*, 244

scienter action, 245

slander, 247

specific performance, 266

strict liability tort, 243

tort, 232

trespass to goods (or trespass to chattels), 234

trespass to land, 234

trespass to person, 233

unilateral contract, 255

vicarious liability, 245

FURTHER READING

BOOKS

Duxbury, Robert. *Nutshells: Contract Law*, 10th ed (London, UK: Sweet & Maxwell, 2015).

Fridman, Gerald HL. *An Introduction to the Canadian Law of Torts*, 3rd ed (Toronto: LexisNexis, 2012).

Fridman, Gerald HL. *The Law of Torts in Canada*, 3rd ed (Toronto: Carswell, 2010).

Kerr, Margaret, JoAnn Kurtz & Lawrence M Olivo. *Canadian Tort Law in a Nutshell*, 4th ed (Toronto: Carswell, 2014).

Klar, Lewis N & Cameron Jefferies. *Tort Law*, 6th ed (Toronto: Carswell, 2017).

Linden, Allen M & Bruce Feldthusen. *Canadian Tort Law*, 10th ed (Toronto: LexisNexis, 2015).

McCamus, John D. *The Law of Contracts*, 2nd ed (Toronto: Irwin Law, 2012).

Osborne, Philip H. *The Law of Torts*, 5th ed (Toronto: Irwin Law, 2015).

Rock, Nora, Laurence M Olivo & Jean Fitzgerald. *Contract and Tort Law for Paralegals*, 2nd ed (Toronto: Emond, 2018).

Waddams, Stephen M. *The Law of Contracts*, 7th ed (Toronto: Canada Law Book, 2017).

REVIEW QUESTIONS

1. List three intentional torts.

2. Identify the most common defences to intentional torts and explain these defences.

3. List the elements of a negligence claim.

4. Of the three main defences to negligence liability, which one allows for the apportionment of liability between the parties?

5. How have the provinces modified the common law concerning occupiers' liability and simplified the rules concerning this tort?

6. Explain the law relating to defamation and describe the varieties of this tort.

7. List the elements of a valid contract.

8. Describe the difference between unilateral and bilateral contracts.

9. Describe what implied terms are and the three kinds of implied terms that may be part of a contract.

10. What are standard form contracts, and what kinds of transactions are they appropriate for? Provide an example.

11. When an employee is employed under an open-ended contract and is dismissed without cause, what factors do the courts consider in assessing how much notice the employer must give an employee at common law?

EXERCISES

1. Consent is a common defence to the intentional torts. In the case of *Norberg v Wynrib*, [1992] 2 SCR 226, 1992 CanLII 65, a young woman had sex with an elderly doctor in order to get prescription painkillers. Locate and read La Forest J's judgment in the *Norberg* case and answer the following questions:

   a. Why was the defence of consent not applicable on these facts?

   b. On the basis of what tort was the doctor found liable?

   c. Why do you agree or disagree with this decision?

2. First, refer to the summary of the duty principles for negligence. Then:

   a. Locate and read the SCC case of *Childs v Desormeaux*, 2006 SCC 18, in which the SCC had to decide whether a social host owed a duty of care to third parties injured by an intoxicated guest. Describe the reasoning of the court in reaching its decision that, generally, no such duty exists.

b. Consider the following problem. A psychiatrist has a patient who says he's going to kill his wife. The psychiatrist tells no one, and the patient does attempt to murder his wife. Although his attempt fails, the attack causes her serious injury. She now wants to sue the psychiatrist for not warning her. Assume that no duty to warn a potential victim of a patient has ever been imposed on a doctor. Prepare an argument explaining why you think such a duty should, or should not, be recognized.

3. Imagine that you have started a new job and have only two weeks' vacation time in your first year. As the end of this year approaches, you start to look forward to your first chance to relax and unwind since you started the job. You have just ended a relationship, and you book a holiday to a Caribbean island through a local tour operator, who promises luxurious five-star accommodations at a small boutique hotel that caters to "singles." The owner is described as a charming person who speaks fluent English, and you are told there will be beach parties, snorkelling and scuba diving in crystal-clear waters, local entertainment, and lots of other singles to meet. When you arrive, you find a decrepit, run-down hotel. The owner is bad-tempered and speaks almost no English (the only language you speak). There are two couples and an older single person already there, but they all leave after a few days. You are all by yourself and no one else comes. There is no equipment for snorkelling or scuba diving on the premises, although there is an inflatable inner tube to use. There is no entertainment (except when the owner's cousin drops by to play "Auld Lang Syne" on the steel drums for five minutes), the food is bad, and there are bugs in your room. Finally, you decide to book an early flight home, thoroughly disappointed and extremely depressed by the experience. You now have to wait another year for a holiday. Assume that you paid $2,500 for this vacation. Based on the types of damages available for breach of contract, how do you think your damages should be assessed? See *Jarvis v Swan Tours*, [1973] 1 QB 233 (Eng CA).

4. A general principle that underlies Canadian contract law is freedom of contract, meaning that parties *generally* have the freedom to enter into binding agreements according to the terms they choose. Based on the overview of contract law in this chapter, detail three scenarios where the law would impose limits on that freedom and explain which specific rule imposes the limit in each case.

9 Private Law II: Property Law and Family Law

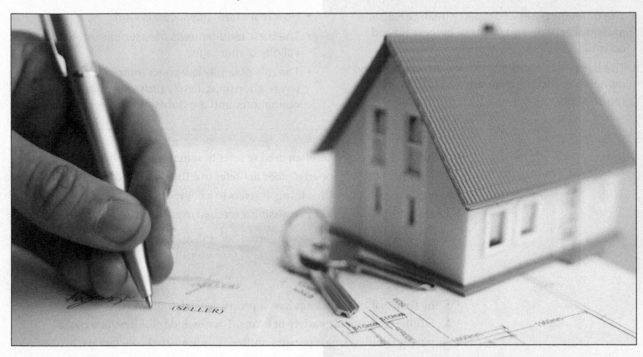

After reading this chapter, you will understand:

- The different types of property (real, personal, and intellectual), and forms of ownership and control.
- The basic rights and obligations attached to land ownership, and the different systems of land registration.

- How real estate transactions work.
- The basic requirements of essential and formal validity of marriage.
- The role of family law concerning divorce, common law relationships, family property, support obligations, and the rights of children and parents.

The word "property" is often used to refer to something that belongs to another. But ... "property" does not refer to a thing; it is a description of a legal relationship with a thing. It refers to a degree of power that is recognized in law as power permissibly exercised over the thing.

Bruce Ziff et al, A *Property Law Reader*, 4th ed
(Toronto: Thomson Reuters, 2016) at 13

The term "family" does not have a precise legal definition ... Canadian families take a wide variety of forms. They include childless marriages, two-parent families, single parent families ... , unmarried cohabitants with or without children, and blended or reconstituted families ... . Family structures may also vary according to ethnic and cultural factors.

Berend Hovius, Mary-Jo Maur & Nicholas Bala, *Family Law: Text, Cases, Materials and Notes*, 9th ed (Toronto: Thomson Reuters, 2017) at 1-2

Introduction

In Chapter 8, we considered torts and contracts. We now turn to two other key areas of private law—property law and family law.

The way that a society controls property—that is, how it is owned, used, and shared—and the nature of the society's family relationships are fundamental markers of its cultural values. The laws that govern property and families are a reflection of these values.

Property Law

Property law regulates the ownership and use of property. Three types of property are examined here: (1) real property, (2) personal property, and (3) intellectual property.

**real property
(or real estate)**
land and anything
attached to the land,
such as buildings
and resources

Real Property

Real property (or **real estate**) refers to land, and anything attached to land, such as buildings. A house, for example, is not owned separately from the land on which it is located; the owner of the land owns the house, too. She also owns the natural resources beneath the land unless they belong to the Crown by virtue of the original grant or according to legislation (the Crown owns the natural resources in most areas of Canada). Further, the owner of land owns and controls the airspace above the land to a reasonable height, unless that ownership and control has been taken away by legislation.

In most of Canada, the law relating to real property is based on concepts of ownership that evolved in Norman England 1,000 years ago. After the Norman conquest in 1066, William I (William the Conqueror) became the owner of all land in England, and he gradually imposed a feudal system on the country. He did this by dividing England into parcels of land over which—except for the portions that he kept for himself—his barons were given rights. However, the barons' control over their lands was conditional on their giving the king continued support (fealty) and military service. In other words, these feudal lords were not absolute owners but tenants of a kind. And they, in turn, assigned subtenancy rights to subordinates of their own in exchange for loyalty and service.

In countries such as Canada, where the British Crown remains the formal head of state, the feudal era has left a legacy—namely, the notion that the Crown owns all the land and that landowners below this station are, in a sense, tenants who hold a lesser interest or estate in the land (see below). This applies in Quebec, too, although there are slight legal and terminological differences owing to the influence of the French civil law tradition (mortgages, for example, are called *hypothecs* in Quebec).

Interests in Land and Types of Ownership

When we use the term **interest** in the context of real property, we mean any right, claim, or privilege that an individual has in relation to the property. In theory, the queen is the ultimate owner of all land in Canada. In reality, the executive authority here in Canada—that is, the federal and provincial governments, which we refer to as *the Crown*—holds the underlying title to all the land. Practically speaking, that underlying ownership manifests itself only if a person dies *intestate*—that is, without having made a will—and has no relatives who can inherit the land on an intestacy. The land, in that case, will revert back to the Crown and become "government" property. The technical phrase in this situation is that the Crown will take the land by *escheat*.

The Crown's underlying title to the land makes all other forms of ownership in Canada conditional and subordinate. These subordinate interests in the land come in many types. The most common types are:

- fee simple ownership,
- life estates,
- leasehold interests, and
- mortgages and other charges against land.[1]

Interests in land can be owned by one person or co-owned with others. Also, the ownership can be legal or equitable. These interests and types of ownership are described next.

interest
any right, claim, or privilege that an individual has with respect to real or personal property

---

1   Other interests in property confer a right to use property without transferring an interest *in* the property. For example, a licence creates a right to use property for a defined purpose; a person who has a hot dog concession in a shopping mall will in most cases have a licence from the mall owner to use the space. Another common example of a non-possessory interest is an easement, which typically provides a nearby owner with a right of way across the property or allows for water, sewer, or electrical lines to cross the property.

FEE SIMPLE OWNERSHIP

fee simple ownership
the most absolute form
of private ownership,
entitling the owner to
possess the property,
to build on it, and to
transfer it to others
during her lifetime or
in a will at her death

Owning land in **fee simple** is the closest a person can come to absolute ownership in Canada. The bundle of rights attached to the estate in fee simple gives the owner more power and flexibility to deal with the land than any other form of ownership. The fee simple owner has the right to possess the land and to build on it. She also has full power to transfer the estate to others while she is alive (a process known as *inter vivos transfer*) and to transfer the property in a will once she dies (a process known as *testamentary transfer*). Should the owner die intestate, the property will pass to her relatives according to statutory intestacy rules.

The fee simple owner also has the right to carve less permanent estates, such as life estates or leases (described below), out of the fee simple whole. When these lesser estates expire, they revert back to the fee simple owner, making her estate whole again. The fee simple owner's interest, when it is subject to one of these lesser estates, is referred to as a *reversionary interest*, and the fee simple owner is technically referred to as a *remainderman*.

BOX 9.1

Aboriginal Title

For a complete picture of land ownership in Canada, we must take into account Aboriginal title. Aboriginal rights, including Aboriginal title, are constitutionally recognized and protected under section 35 of the *Constitution Act, 1982** (see Chapter 3). As defined by court decisions, some Aboriginal rights, such as the right to hunt and fish, are not based upon exclusive occupancy of the land. In contrast, Aboriginal title (while associated with traditional uses) *is* based on exclusive occupancy. Claims to land and resources by Aboriginal peoples began to occur with increasing frequency in the 20th century (see Box 3.5).

When Europeans first settled and occupied Canada, their encounters with First Nations peoples were not governed by a legal protocol. After the Seven Years' War, King George III issued the *Royal Proclamation of 1763*,† claiming territory in North America for Great Britain. Part of the Royal Proclamation dealt with relations with First Nations and included a general proscription against purchasing or otherwise acquiring land from them—only the Crown could do this. The Proclamation is a key instrument in the history of Aboriginal title. Today, it is generally accepted that Aboriginal title can be extinguished only through surrender of lands to the Crown by treaty or, since 1982 and the constitutional protection of Aboriginal rights, by constitutional amendment (from the time of Confederation until 1982, title could be extinguished by ordinary federal legislation).

Historically, many treaties were entered into and land was surrendered to the Crown. Not all of these treaties were clear or fair, however, and in many instances the two sides have interpreted them differently. Disputes still arise concerning

their interpretation. Most of Canada is covered by these old treaties, but not all of it—for example, in parts of Quebec, Labrador, and the territories, and in almost all of British Columbia, no treaties were entered into and the land was never formally surrendered to the Crown. With respect to claims to land that has not been formally surrendered, the two main mechanisms by which claims are established are: (1) court challenge, or (2) participation in a land claims process leading to a treaty.

In several important cases—*Delgamuukw v British Columbia*,‡ *R v Marshall*; *R v Bernard*,§ and *Tsilhqot'in Nation v British Columbia* [*William*]#—the SCC has examined the concept of Aboriginal title more closely. In general terms, the court has recognized that Aboriginal title is *sui generis* (that is, in its own class, or unique) and is not based on "traditional real property rules." It is also, as noted, included within the broader conception of Aboriginal rights and is constitutionally protected. The following key principles have emerged concerning Aboriginal title:

1. Aboriginal title derives from the *exclusive occupation* of land, and that occupation must have existed at the time the Crown asserted sovereignty over the land. There can be breaks in the continuity of the occupation, provided that a substantial connection to the land has been maintained. Further, concerning the *sufficiency of the occupation*, title is not confined to specific settlement sites and includes areas over which effective control has been exercised when hunting and fishing, etc.

2. While the occupation of the land is determined by reference to particular uses (or activities) that create an attachment to the land, those *uses can change over time* provided they are not inconsistent with the uses that form the basis of the attachment.

3. It is a *communal title* that inheres in a particular group in relation to a particular area. Aboriginal title does not recognize rights of individual ownership in parcels of land the way the common law does, for example.

4. Aboriginal lands are *inalienable*, except to the Crown. In order for third parties to acquire Aboriginal lands, the lands must first be surrendered to the Crown and then transferred to the third parties.

5. Prior to the establishment of Aboriginal title in disputed lands, governments have a *duty to consult* in good faith about proposed uses and if appropriate make accommodations (this duty is based on the *honour of the Crown*, which is a type of fairness obligation arising because of the Crown's assertion of sovereignty over Aboriginal peoples and control of their lands). Once established, Aboriginal title includes the *right to manage and control* the land in question together with its economic benefits and resources. In exercising this stewardship, however, Aboriginal groups must not impair the rights of future generations over the land (for example, by clear cutting land and destroying traditional hunting habitats). Governments retain a limited jurisdiction over the land if justifiable (resource development and possibly pipeline construction could be justified if a "compelling and substantial government objective" is reconcilable with Aboriginal rights). (See, in particular, the *William* case.)

Not all Indigenous peoples agree that these principles are accurate markers of their title, and some believe they are still rooted in non-Aboriginal ideas of land ownership. Concerning the requirement of traditional occupancy, this has often been difficult to establish—the *William* case in 2014 is the first case where a specific claim of Aboriginal title has been proven and recognized by the Supreme Court of Canada. The recognition of Aboriginal title continues to inform the modern treaty process, however, and most modern claims to Aboriginal lands are being asserted through a formalized land claims negotiation process (for example, the BC treaty process or the comprehensive claims process). Prior to *William*, the greatest success in establishing rights to and control over land by Aboriginal peoples had come through such processes (for example, the Nisga'a Treaty entered into with the federal government in 2000).

*   Schedule B to the *Canada Act 1982* (UK), 1982, c 11.

†   RSC 1985, App II, No 1.

‡   [1997] 3 SCR 1010, 1997 CanLII 302.

§   2005 SCC 43.

\#   2014 SCC 44.

LIFE ESTATES

If the fee simple owner transfers title to land to someone (the transferee) for the life of the latter, a form of ownership called a **life estate** is created. The life estate holder is sometimes called a *life tenant*. A life estate cannot be inherited, but the life tenant can transfer it to another person *inter vivos*—that is, while the life estate holder is alive. But the life estate will end with the passing of the original life tenant and revert to the fee simple owner (or remainderman).

Uncommon today, the life estate is mostly used in a case where a deceased spouse leaves the surviving spouse (a second wife, say, who is stepmother to the deceased's children from a first marriage) a life estate, with the remainder going to the children or other relatives. This ensures that the surviving spouse has a place to live for life but that the children get the property eventually.

The life estate carries with it a right of exclusive possession. However, it is subject to the doctrine of waste. This means that the fee simple owner can hold the life tenant responsible for any damage the latter does to the property, though not for ordinary wear and tear or deterioration owing purely to the passage of time. The life tenant can also make improvements to the property. The rules associated with exclusive possession can be modified by express terms in the transfer documents or in a contract, if there is one.

life estate
type of ownership whereby the fee simple owner grants a person (the life tenant) exclusive possession of a property for that person's lifetime, with the condition that the estate reverts to the fee simple owner at the life tenant's death

defeasible
term used for life estates that can be terminated by the fee simple owner if certain conditions are not met or certain defined events occur

freehold interests
form of property ownership that does not imply an obligation to pay rent

leasehold interests
form of property ownership that implies an obligation to pay rent

Sometimes life estates are made **defeasible**. This means that they can be terminated if certain conditions are not met or if certain defined events occur. Such events could include changes in the use of the property. For example, if a life tenant held property subject to a condition that it be used for charitable purposes and began to use the property for commercial purposes, the fee simple owner could terminate the life estate.

LEASEHOLD INTERESTS

Leasehold interests are distinguishable from freehold interests. **Freehold interests** are a form of ownership that does not involve an obligation to pay rent. Fee simple ownership is a type of freehold estate. **Leasehold interests**, on the other hand, imply an obligation to pay rent.

When an owner leases her property to someone, she creates a landlord–tenant relationship. The owner is the landlord, or *lessor*, and the renter is the tenant, or *lessee*. A leasehold interest can be residential (renting a place to live) or commercial (renting a place to do business). It can also be in one of two main forms, fixed term or periodic. A fixed term tenancy is for a defined period of time (one year or two years, for example), after which it automatically comes to an end. There may or may not be a right of renewal. A periodic tenancy (for example, week-to-week or month-to-month) *automatically* renews itself at the end of each period, unless either party gives notice.

The lease, a type of contract, determines many of the rights and obligations of the parties under the tenancy. *Residential tenancies*, however, are regulated by provincial and territorial legislation, and residential lease agreements must comply with the legislation in matters relating to rents, repairs, notice obligations, compliance with health and safety regulations, etc. The main obligation of the tenant is to pay rent in exchange for the right to occupy and use the property. The legislation typically *requires* landlords to accept responsibility for ensuring the property meets health and safety regulations. As well, they must ensure that the rental property is in a good state of repair. Landlords are not permitted to contract out of these obligations. The same legislation also usually requires tenants to *maintain* the property according to reasonable standards of health and cleanliness and to repair any damage they cause.

Commercial tenancies are regulated too, but to a lesser degree, allowing the parties greater freedom to determine their respective rights and responsibilities under the lease. For example, the responsibility for repairs may be shifted to the tenant under the terms of the lease.

MORTGAGES AND OTHER CHARGES AGAINST LAND

charges and encumbrances
any claim on a parcel of real property—for example, mortgages, property taxes, or water rights

mortgage
a kind of charge against land that secures a debt owed by the landowner

Charges and encumbrances against real property secure debts or provide limited rights to the property. Interests in this category include rights of way, options to purchase, restrictive covenants, builders' liens, agreements for sale, and mortgages.

A **mortgage** is the most common type of charge or encumbrance; it secures a debt owed by the landowner. Traditionally, mortgages involved the landowner's title to the land being transferred to the lender. The lender would hold the title as security against the loan, with a promise to transfer title back to the owner once the latter had repaid the mortgage loan in full. If the owner/borrower (the mortgagor) missed a payment or otherwise went into default, the lender (the mortgagee, often a bank) was entitled to keep the land unconditionally. However, in equity, the mortgagor was given a period of time to come up with the balance—in other words, a redemption period (see the discussion of the Court of Chancery, in Chapter 2). The owner's right to redeem his property came to be known as the mortgagor's *equity of redemption*; it was valued at the worth of the property minus the amount of the mortgage debt still owing. Hence we now refer to a property owner's *equity* in the property, which refers to the net market value of his unencumbered interest in the property.

After a mortgagor went into default, the mortgagee would have to bring proceedings to foreclose the mortgagor's right to redeem the property. These proceedings were called **foreclosure proceedings**. If the redemption period expired without the mortgagor's coming up with the balance owing, the mortgagee could take absolute title to the property.

In many jurisdictions today, mortgages have been simplified by legislation and no longer involve the actual transfer of title to the creditor. In other respects, they operate the same way as before. Mortgagors are still given redemption periods, and mortgagees are still required to bring foreclosure proceedings if they wish to take over the property.

There are other charges against land that creditors use to secure property owners' debts. One of these is a *builders' (or construction) lien*, which builders use to secure amounts owed them for work done on landowners' property (see also under "Builders and Repairers: Security for Services Rendered" in Chapter 10). Another charge of this type is a *registered judgment*, which can be used to secure any judgment debt the landowner may owe. A judgment debt is an award granted in judicial proceedings. In the case of both the builders' lien and the registered judgment, the creditor can eventually force the sale of the property to recover the debt if the landowner doesn't repay it otherwise.

One charge that operates much like a mortgage is the **agreement for sale**. It is used only in real estate purchase situations. With an agreement for sale, a person who wants to sell her property agrees to finance the purchase herself, because the purchaser can't pay the full amount. The seller keeps title to the property but lets the purchaser take possession of it. The agreement for sale provides that once the balance of the purchase price is paid, the seller will transfer title to the purchaser. If the purchaser misses a payment or otherwise goes into default, the seller can begin a process called *cancellation proceedings*, which are similar to foreclosure proceedings. By this process, she can retake control of the property. An agreement for sale allows for vendor financing in much the same way as a *vendor take-back mortgage*; with the latter, the vendor sells the property outright to the purchaser at the time of purchase but immediately takes back a mortgage to secure the unpaid portion of the purchase price.

Other charges against property are concerned with securing not a debt but a right. These charges include the following:

- an *option to purchase*, which secures a right to purchase at the discretion of the option holder;
- a *right of first refusal*, which secures a right to purchase the property *if* it is offered for sale;
- a *caveat*, which prevents the owner from selling the property temporarily to allow the caveat holder to pursue its claim against the property; and
- a *right of way*, which, as mentioned above, allows limited access to the property (such as a right to cross over it).

CO-OWNERSHIP

It is possible for more than one person to own an interest in land, and the interest most commonly co-owned is the fee simple. All co-owners of possessory interests such as the fee simple have equal rights of possession and use of the property.

foreclosure proceedings proceedings that the mortgagee (the lender) brings against the defaulting mortgagor (borrower) in order to foreclose the mortgagor's right to redeem her property

agreement for sale agreement by which a person selling his property agrees to finance the purchase himself, keeping the title to the property while allowing the purchaser to take possession of it, and then transferring the title to the purchaser once the balance of the purchase price is paid

joint tenancy
a form of co-ownership that features the right of survivorship as well as the "four unities" of *possession* (each co-owner has an equal right to possess the entire property), *interest* (each co-owner has an identical interest in the property), *time* (the co-owners receive their interests at the same time), and *title* (the co-owners receive their interests under the same instrument, such as a will)

right of survivorship
a main condition of joint tenancy whereby the surviving co-owners automatically inherit a deceased owner's share

tenancy in common
a form of co-ownership that does not involve the four unities or the right of survivorship, meaning that a co-owner can transfer her interest to others during her lifetime or leave it to others in her will

trustee
someone who has legal title to the property but holds it for another and has the fiduciary responsibility to make decisions for the benefit of the other party

beneficial owner
also called an *equitable owner*, the person on whose behalf and for whose benefit the trustee holds and manages the property

The two principal forms of co-ownership are *joint tenancy* and *tenancy in common*. In order for a **joint tenancy** arrangement to exist, four *unities* must be present:

1. *Possession.* Each co-owner must have equal right to possess the entire property.
2. *Interest.* The interest of each co-owner must be identical in terms of nature, extent, and duration. The extent will depend on the number of joint tenants. For example, with two owners, each owns 50 percent. With three owners, each owns 33⅓ percent.
3. *Time.* The co-owners must each receive their interests at the same time.
4. *Title.* The co-owners must each receive their interests under the same instrument, such as a will or a transfer document.

The main feature of the joint tenancy is the **right of survivorship**, or *jus accrescendi*. This means that on the death of one co-owner the remaining co-owner(s) automatically inherit the deceased owner's share. The last remaining co-owner becomes the sole owner.

Joint tenants are not allowed to leave their share in a will because of the right of survivorship. They can, however, transfer their interest *inter vivos*—that is, during their lifetime—but this has the effect of severing the unities of time and title and thereby converts the co-ownership into a tenancy in common.

A **tenancy in common** is similar to a joint tenancy insofar as possession is equally shared. But the unities of interest, time, and title are not required for this kind of ownership. Tenants in common can own different percentage interests in the property, and they can become co-owners at different times and by different means. Also, there is no right of survivorship with this kind of ownership; tenants in common can leave their interests in their wills or transfer them to others *inter vivos* without destroying the tenancy in common.

Another special form of co-ownership exists when a *strata lot* (that is, a condominium or townhouse) is purchased. Ownership of a strata unit combines individual ownership with shared or common ownership. The individual ownership relates to the actual unit. The shared ownership relates to the common areas such as hallways, elevators, foyers, and exercise rooms. This form of co-ownership is relatively recent (first introduced in Australia in the 1960s) and is purely a creation of legislation; it requires a strata corporation to manage the property, and it requires the passage of by-laws to set the rules for this form of community living.

LEGAL AND EQUITABLE TITLE

A unique aspect of property ownership is the idea of *legal* and *equitable* ownership. This evolved out of the split jurisdiction between the royal courts and the Court of Chancery (again, see Chapter 2).

Title to estates in land can be split between a legal owner, called a **trustee**, and a **beneficial owner**, sometimes called an *equitable owner*. The legal owner's name will appear on any title documents, usually with an indication that the land is held "in trust" (or words to that effect), but this person (the trustee) will have to own and manage the property for the benefit of the equitable owner. The trustee may be required to ensure that the land and any buildings on it are cared for adequately and that any rents or profits are kept for or passed on to the beneficial owner. This split form of ownership is most common in connection with land, but it can apply to all forms of property, not just real property.

Split ownership of this kind is not recognized in Quebec, where ownership of property is *exclusive*; the civil law does not recognize a split between legal and equitable title.

Rights and Obligations Attached to Land Ownership

In addition to the basic rights and obligations described above, there are other important rights and obligations attached to land ownership, such as those relating to support, use of water resources, and land use generally.

A property owner is entitled to rely on the physical **support** that a neighbour's property provides to her own property. This obligation between neighbours is reciprocal, and it becomes a matter of legal significance when, for example, one party is having his property excavated as part of a construction project. Excavation on or close to the property line may cause the neighbour's soil to subside and thereby cause damage to her buildings. In this situation, the property owner who is doing such work must ensure that adequate steps are taken to shore up the neighbouring property. Otherwise, he may face a damage claim (see Box 9.2). Liability in this case is strict, and negligence or intent to cause damage does not have to be established.

Properties next to lakes or rivers may have something called **riparian rights** attached to them. Riparian rights include the right to make reasonable use of the water for activities such as swimming, fishing, and boating, and even the right to divert some of the water for drinking, washing, and irrigation. However, these rights are qualified by the obligation not to interfere unfairly with the riparian rights of others. A property owner would not be meeting this obligation, for example, if he diverted so much river water to irrigate his fields that the flow downstream was compromised, or if the discharge of effluent from his agricultural concern made the water unsafe for others to use.

Every jurisdiction has particular legislation relating to support and to the use of water. Property owners must carefully consider these rules when working close to their property lines or exercising their riparian rights.

Generally speaking, property ownership comes with many responsibilities and restrictions concerning use. The federal, provincial, and municipal (or local) governments all regulate it. Property owners must be aware of the relevant restrictions, which concern such matters as type of use (for example, single-family, multi-family, or commercial use), allowable construction, rentals, cutting down trees, and pollution.

support
property owner's obligation to consider how changes made to his property may affect his neighbour's property

riparian rights
rights that are attached to property fronting lakes or rivers and that include the right to make use of the water for certain activities and the obligation not to interfere with the riparian rights of others

---

BOX 9.2

Digging Holes and Collapsing Buildings: The Right to Lateral Support

In *Rytter v Schmitz,*[*] the plaintiffs and the defendant owned adjoining properties. There was a concrete-block building on the Rytters' property. Schmitz began to excavate his property with a view to constructing a building on his lot. His workmen excavated along the property line to a depth of 10 feet but didn't properly shore up the property. As a result, the subsoil on the Rytters' property fell away and caused the property to subside. Part of the Rytters' concrete-block building also collapsed and fell into the excavation.

The court held, among other things, that the plaintiff landowners were entitled to the lateral support of their land by their neighbour's property and that this right was a strict one—that is, it was not necessary to show that the defendant was negligent or intended to cause the damage. (See also "Strict Liability Torts" in Chapter 8.)

[*] 1974 CanLII 1169, 47 DLR (3d) 445.

Systems of Land Registration: Deed Registry and Land Titles

deeds
formal documents
showing ownership
of property

The common law procedure for transferring land, which evolved centuries ago, relied entirely on deeds. **Deeds** are formal documents showing evidence of ownership. They have always involved a certain amount of risk. After successive transfers and generations of owners, there was always the possibility that mistakes would be made, frauds committed, or deeds missed when tracing the line of ownership. There was always a risk that someone with a superior title to the property might pop up and, based on the *nemo dat* principle, challenge the current owner's rights over it.

Nemo dat—the full Latin expression is *nemo dat quod non habet*—means "one cannot give what one does not have." According to this principle, the purchase of a possession from someone who has no ownership right to it also denies the purchaser any ownership title. This usually applies even if the purchaser does not know that the seller is not a true owner.

To increase the certainty related to property ownership, registration systems were devised. Two main systems emerged, both used in Canada today: (1) the deed registration system and (2) the Torrens system. The deed registration system uses the traditional idea of transfer by deed. But it provides some certainty by requiring deeds to be registered, and it creates a deed repository to help with the tracing process. Mistakes can still be made, however, and *nemo dat* is still the guiding principle with this system.

**Torrens system (or
land titles system)**
system for registering
property ownership
that eliminates the
transfer of title by deeds
and replaces them
with statutory transfer
forms, meaning that
the title is guaranteed
(or *indefeasible*)

indefeasible
not able to be
annulled, made void,
or overturned

The **Torrens system** (or **land titles system**) is named after Robert Torrens, the Australian who first devised and implemented the system in 1858. The Torrens system and systems modelled on it eliminate the transfer of title by deeds, replacing them with statutory transfer forms. Title for all land within the jurisdiction must be registered, and anyone purchasing property can rely on the state of the register. Registered title is **indefeasible**. This means that the legislation essentially guarantees that "what you see is what you get" when you look at the registry entries for a particular piece of property. The true owner's name will appear on title, and any charges relating to the property—for example, mortgages or liens—must be registered against the title to be effective. An assurance fund, set up under the legislation, is there to protect any innocent parties in the event that a fraud is perpetrated and someone gets on the title improperly. In 1870, British Columbia became the first jurisdiction in North America to adopt the Torrens system.

In Canada, deed registration systems are used in the maritime provinces. Quebec uses a similar system. Deed registration systems had been used in Ontario since the 1700s, but recently Ontario has almost entirely converted to a land titles system. The four western provinces use the land titles system. The uncertainty over true title is less common than it used to be, but it still exists to some extent in jurisdictions using deed registration systems. There is a much greater demand for title insurance in these jurisdictions than there is in jurisdictions using the "newer" land titles system.

Real Estate Transactions

The law relating to the purchase and sale of real estate is often treated as its own subject because of the number of issues and the volume of litigation arising from such transactions. The following is a very brief outline of the area.

The transaction starts with property that is made available or listed for sale by a seller (sometimes referred to as the *vendor*). How exactly the sale proceeds depends on:

- whether the property is residential (and on whether it is a single lot with or without a house on it, or a strata unit);
- whether the property is commercial (and on what type of business is involved); or
- whether the property is for investment (and on what the particular tax implications are).

In most cases, the seller will hire a real estate agent to assist with the sale. The real estate agent will also frequently help prospective purchasers, although she has to be careful because of the potential for conflict of interest. Such a conflict would exist, for example, if the agent promoted certain bidders favoured by the agent and discouraged others at the expense of the seller, or if the agent took a secret commission from the successful purchaser. In a case where the seller has hired the agent, agency rules dictate that her primary responsibility and loyalty must be to the seller. In cases where purchasers have their own agents, this potential conflict is avoided.

The relationship between the real estate agents and other parties in the real estate transaction involves many contractual and fiduciary obligations, so the potential for litigation is great. For example, a real estate agent has to disclose to the parties any interest he may have in the property or any secret profits he may stand to gain as a result of the sale. Also, the agent can be responsible in tort for any negligent or fraudulent misrepresentations relating to the property (for example, telling a purchaser the property is zoned for a basement suite when it is not). It should be noted as well that real estate agents are regulated by real estate legislation in all provinces and territories and are subject to disciplinary action. They can lose their licences if they fail to follow required codes of conduct.

Disagreements concerning the terms in the contract of purchase and sale (sometimes called an interim agreement, because it precedes the actual transfer of title) can arise directly between the seller and the purchaser. This contract is frequently a standard form contract. Differences of interpretation may arise over particular terms in the contract—for example, terms dealing with the time for completing the contract and with conditions precedent (that is, terms defining events that must occur, such as financing or inspection, before the contract can move forward).

After the contract is entered into (sometimes months after negotiations begin), the actual transfer of title, or conveyance, occurs. **Conveyancing** is a very specialized process and is sometimes treated separately from the rest of the real estate transaction. The exact process varies according to the usual variables:

- whether a deed system or land titles system is involved;
- whether the transaction relates to single lot, strata lot, or a commercial or investment property; and
- the relevant legislative requirements concerning registration and other matters.

Financing matters are another prominent feature of real estate transactions. Financing can be managed in a variety of ways, including the following:

1. vendor financing (for instance, through the use of an agreement for sale or mortgage back to the vendor);
2. third-party financing (from a bank or other lender through the use of a mortgage); and
3. multiple investors, all participating in the purchase.

Which financing method is chosen will affect the whole process, including the legalities involved, from the start of the transaction through to the conveyance and completion.

Personal Property

Personal property includes not only tangible, movable objects such as computers and cars, but also intangible interests such as corporate securities. We have seen that there are many

conveyancing
the part of the real estate transaction that begins after the contract is entered into and that involves the actual transfer of title, or conveyance

personal property
tangible, movable objects as well as intangible interests such as shares in a company

kinds of estates or interests in real property. The case is different with personal property, ownership of which is usually absolute. However, liens and charges can be placed against personal property to secure debts, and tangible objects (goods) can be leased (for example, cars). Personal property can also be held in trust, meaning that ownership is divided between a trustee (the legal owner) and a beneficiary (the equitable owner).

The sale of personal property is regulated by legislation in most situations. Some of that legislation—legislation dealing with sales of goods, consumer protection, and business transactions, for example—is discussed in Chapter 10.

Tangible Personal Property

chattels
tangible, movable objects such as furniture, equipment, and cars

Tangible, movable objects—such as furniture, equipment, and cars—are sometimes referred to as **chattels**. Interests in them are referred to as *corporeal interests*.

Under certain circumstances, property that would ordinarily be considered personal property comes under the law relating to **fixtures**, or things that are attached to the land. The principle discussed at the beginning of this chapter—that is, the notion that anything that is attached to land becomes part of the land—influences these situations. For instance, a seller of equipment on credit may assume that the equipment sold can be retaken under the terms of the sale—for example, in the case of non-payment. But if, in the meantime, the equipment has become affixed to the buyer's land, recovering it may not be possible. Also, if there is a mortgagee (a lender) who has not been paid by the owner of the real property, priority issues could arise between the mortgagee and the seller who wants to recover his equipment. The mortgagee will likely want to recover his equipment to help satisfy the mortgage debt.

fixtures
things that are attached to the land

Determining whether goods have become affixed to the land requires looking at the *degree* of annexation and the *object* of annexation. The more easily the goods can be removed (for example, if they're attached merely by a few hooks, screws, or nails), the less likely they are to be classed as fixtures. On the other hand, if the object or purpose in attaching them was to improve the value or utility of the property, they are likely to be classed as fixtures (see Box 9.3). Each case is unique.

BOX 9.3

Is Wall-to-Wall Carpeting Personal Property?

In *La Salle Recreations Ltd v Canadian Camdex Investments Ltd*,* the British Columbia Court of Appeal had to decide whether wall-to-wall carpeting in a hotel was affixed to the building and therefore also to the land. The owner of the property had defaulted on his credit arrangement with the carpet seller as well as on his mortgage loan.

The carpet seller wanted to repossess the carpet. The mortgagee wanted it left in place because it would increase the value of the hotel. The legislation in place at the time dictated that if the carpet had become affixed to the land, priority over the carpet would be given to the mortgagee (whose charge covered the land).

The carpet had been attached to the floors by small nails or pins protruding upward around the perimeter of the unfinished plywood floors. The carpeting could be easily removed, causing little damage to the floors or the carpeting. On the other hand, the colour of the carpeting matched the colour scheme of the walls around it. The court applied the *degree* of annexation and the *object* of annexation tests and held that while the carpet was only lightly affixed (degree of annexation), the purpose of the carpeting was for the "better and more effectual use of the building as a hotel" (object of annexation), and therefore the carpet was a fixture. As a result, the mortgagee was successful and able to keep the carpeting.

* 1969 CanLII 740, 68 WWR 339 (BCCA).

There are a couple of well-known expressions concerning physical possession and ownership. One of these is *possession is nine-tenths of the law*; the other is *finders, keepers; losers, weepers*. The principle expressed here—the idea that physically possessing property is somehow proof of ownership—is not necessarily accurate, however. Possession may be *evidence* of ownership, but it is not *conclusive*. If it were, this would be very good news for thieves. All evidence of ownership needs to be considered, including any bills of sale or agreements of sale relating to the property.

Intangible Interests

Intangible interests are sometimes called *incorporeal interests*. The classic examples of these interests are corporate securities (for example, shares and bonds), as already noted. A **chose in action** is another example of an intangible personal property right. A chose (pronounced "shows") in action is the right to sue someone for an unpaid debt or other liability. For example, if a business owner had the right to sue a customer for property delivered but not paid for, the business owner could transfer that right, or chose in action, to a collection agency. In this situation, the collection agency often "purchases" the debt from the business owner at a discount.

> **chose in action**
> the right to sue some-one for an unpaid debt or liability; an intangible personal property right

Special legislative rules sometimes apply to the transfer of such interests, including notice requirements (for instance, effectively assigning or transferring a debt or chose in action may require notice to the debtor, depending on the type of debt).

Personal Property Security Legislation

Whenever a creditor (such as a seller or a lender) is owed money that is secured by personal property the debtor controls, there is a risk that the debtor will sell the personal property or further encumber it. This can lead to complex disputes over priority between the creditor and innocent third parties who dealt with the debtor in good faith, believing the property was not subject to any competing interests.

Personal property security legislation provides for the registration of a creditor's inter-est in personal property that the debtor controls or possesses. This enables others to check the state of the property in question before entering into dealings with the debtor. The common expression for this kind of background search is *checking for liens*.

> **personal property security**
> creditor's security based on the debtor's personal property

In the 1970s, Ontario adopted a new personal property security regime with the enact-ment of the *Personal Property Security Act*.[2] Since then, all common law provinces and the territories have adopted similar legislation by the same name. Quebec, too, has legislation based on civil law principles that protect creditors through a system of registration. These statutes are complicated. Among their key features are the following:

1. coverage of almost all forms of personal property, both tangible and intangible;
2. provisions that protect a creditor with respect to the debtor's personal property;
3. a special interest called a *purchase money security interest*, or PMSI, which can be granted to a lender who enables a debtor to acquire goods (for example, where a finance company lends money to a purchaser of a motor vehicle at the point of purchase);

---

2   RSO 1990, c P.10.

4. the protection of creditors through the registration of their security interests; and

5. the creation of a system of priorities and superpriorities, which starts from the principle that priority is given to creditors whose security interests in a debtor's property are registered earliest.

All provinces and territories have registries that can be checked electronically for security interests against personal property. If a check reveals no charge against the property, prospective creditors or lenders can be confident that when they register their security it will take priority over the securities of others who register later. For example, if a bank lends money to a client and registers the first security interest in the client's personal property, the bank knows that when the property is sold it will have first priority over the sale proceeds, which it can apply to the loan if it is not repaid by the client. If a second lender is approached by the client for another loan, the second lender will be able to see the bank's prior registered security interest. This will help the second lender decide whether loaning the client more money is too risky. The value of the property and the total value of the two loans will be important considerations.

Intellectual Property

intellectual property
property derived from the intellect, or mind—works of art, inventions, and designs

Intellectual property (IP) has gained prominence in recent years; it refers to property derived from the intellect, or mind—for example, works of art, musical creations, books, inventions, and designs. It is an intangible form of property, but it is usually classed separately from other forms of intangible personal property, such as securities.

As noted at the beginning of the previous chapter, IP is federally regulated. National standards make sense for this form of property, the precise location of which can be difficult to determine. Also, the federal government is best equipped to negotiate international agreements in this area. IP is increasingly traded—some would say *stolen*—across national boundaries, becoming part of the intellectual "human" commons. Federal regulators are better able to respond effectively to international changes and pressures than local regulators would be.

The Canadian Intellectual Property Office (CIPO) is the central registry for Canadian intellectual property. International cooperation and agreements have led to the creation of the World Intellectual Property Organization (WIPO), which is an agency of the United Nations. Its headquarters are in Geneva, Switzerland. Registration with WIPO can assist with the protection of IP rights on the international stage.

Table 9.1 summarizes four key areas of IP and their associated federal statutes.

Family Law

Family law is concerned with marriage, marriage breakdown and divorce, common law relationships, and the rights and obligations of family members (including those relating to children). It also covers matters such as adoption, child welfare, and support of parents.

This area is a fundamental part of the private law of any country and is influenced by religion more than any other area. In Chapter 2 in our discussion of religious law, we saw how some countries insist on the separation of church and state, while others accept a strong connection between the two. When the connection between the state and its religion is close, it tends to be expressed in the regulation of families. In countries that recognize Islamic law (that is, sharia), family relations are strictly governed by religious rules. In Israel, while civil or state law applies for the most part, religious law (that is, Halacha) applies to Jews exclusively in matters of marriage and divorce. And in India, Hindu law regulates family matters for the Hindu members of the population.

TABLE 9.1 Types of Intellectual Property

CATEGORY	DESCRIPTION	SOURCE
Copyright	Copyright refers to the right to copy, which only belongs to the copyright owner, who is usually the creator of the work or a person assigned ownership by the creator. Copyright exists as soon as the work is created and does not need to be registered to be enforceable. However, registration with CIPO provides evidence of ownership that can be used in court. Copyright protection lasts for the life of the creator plus 50 years, and applies in respect of • original dramatic, musical, artistic, and literary works (including computer programs); and • performances, communication signals, and sound recordings.	*Copyright Act*, RSC 1985, c C-42
Industrial Design	An industrial design is a design used in making an object by hand, tool, or machine. Industrial designs can be protected for up to ten years if registered with CIPO. Without registration, a person cannot claim ownership of the design and thereby prevent others from using it to make articles. To qualify for registration, the design must be an original design with unique visual features that is used to make objects (e.g., a unique design for an ordinary object, such as a chair).	*Industrial Design Act*, RSC 1985, c I-9
Patents	A patent is a right that the government grants to an inventor to prevent others from using his or her invention. Patent holders are protected for up to 20 years after the patent application is filed with the Patent Office, which is part of CIPO. If the patent has not been filed, the inventor has no protection. Patents cover only the following: • new inventions (which can be processes, machines, or compositions of matter), and new improvements in an existing invention; and • inventions that satisfy the three basic criteria of novelty, utility, and ingenuity.	*Patent Act*, RSC 1985, c P-4
Trademarks	A trademark distinguishes the goods or services of a person, business, or organization from those of others in the marketplace. Trademark registration provides evidence of ownership but, as with copyrights, it is not conclusive. A registered trademark gives its holder an exclusive right to use the trademark throughout Canada for 15 years, and it is renewable after that. A trademark, to be registrable, must be a word, symbol, or design (alone or in combination) used to distinguish goods or services.	*Trade-marks Act*, RSC 1985, c T-13

In Canada, however, the separation of religion and state means that it is our laws, rather than religious rules, that guide us *legally* in family matters. For instance, religious marriage ceremonies are not by themselves "official"—a legal marriage requires that a civil procedure (such as obtaining a licence) occur as well.

Under our Constitution, jurisdiction over family matters is split between the federal provincial governments (see "Constitutional Basis of Private Law" at the beginning of Chapter 8).

Marriage

Canadian law recognizes a difference between the *essential* validity and the *formal* validity of a marriage. **Essential validity** concerns a person's capacity to marry and the substantive

essential validity
concerns a person's capacity to marry and the substantive requirements of a valid marriage

requirements of a valid marriage. Questions of this kind are under federal jurisdiction. **Formal validity** refers to the formalities or ceremonial requirements of a marriage, and these matters come under provincial jurisdiction.

Essential Validity

Despite the federal government's power to regulate essential validity, there is no comprehensive legislation setting out the rules. There are just two statutes dealing with specific aspects of a person's capacity to marry (the *Civil Marriage Act*[3] and the *Marriage (Prohibited Degrees) Act*,[4] discussed below). In this area, courts have relied heavily on common law rules, which are strongly influenced by English canon (or church) law, which in turn relies on the Christian Bible and on other sources such as the Anglican *Book of Common Prayer*. It is an area where religious rules have clearly shaped the law, as mentioned above.

A marriage that has essential validity must meet the following six requirements:

1. two persons must be involved;
2. both parties must have the ability to consummate the marriage;
3. there must not be too close a degree of consanguinity or affinity between the two parties (for example, the marriage of a brother and sister is not valid);
4. the parties involved must be unmarried;
5. both parties must have given consent; and
6. both must be old enough to marry.

If it becomes apparent, after a marriage ceremony, that one or more of these requirements has not been met, the union can be set aside or annulled. Depending on which requirement is not satisfied and on the exact nature of the problem, the marriage will be either void from the beginning (regardless of whether it is challenged), referred to as being void *ab initio*, or voidable (that is, it will be set aside only if challenged; otherwise it will stand). The rules about the void/voidable distinction and about which party can challenge the validity of the marriage are complicated and not always clearly or consistently applied.

TWO PERSONS

This requirement used to be the common law opposite-sex rule. But in 2005, after a number of constitutional court challenges to this requirement, Parliament passed the *Civil Marriage Act*. Section 2 of this Act provides that "marriage, for civil purposes, is the lawful union of two persons to the exclusion of all others," and section 4 provides that "a marriage is not void or voidable by reason only that the spouses are of the same sex."

In Canada, then, same-sex marriages are now recognized. What used to be the "opposite-sex" element of essential validity can be restated as the *two individuals* (or *two persons*) requirement. The requirement that a marriage be a union of two people clearly also concerns the *number* of individuals involved. It means that polygamous marriages, for example—marriages involving more than two persons—are not legally recognized. In fact, polygamy is an offence under the *Criminal Code*.[5] Some religious and other groups have challenged the constitutional validity of limiting marriage to just two people and of specifically criminalizing polygamy (see Box 9.4).

---

3 SC 2005, c 33.

4 SC 1990, c 46.

5 RSC 1985, c C-46, s 293.

BOX 9.4

Polygamy and Canadian Law

The town of Bountiful, in southeastern British Columbia, is the home of a fundamentalist Mormon community that believes in polygamy. Its population is around 1,000. The first member of this Mormon group bought property there in 1946, and most of the town's residents today have descended from just six men.

In the wake of media attention and a police investigation into allegations of abuse involving Bountiful's young women and underaged girls, a special prosecutor was appointed to decide whether criminal charges should be laid. He concluded that there was little evidence of sexual abuse and exploitation in the community and recommended instead that a reference question be placed before the court concerning the constitutionality of the rarely used section of the *Criminal Code* dealing with polygamy, section 293.*

In a 335-page decision handed down by the chief justice of the BC Supreme Court in November 2011, the court concluded that while section 293 of the *Criminal Code* infringed the constitutional right to religious freedom (under s 2 of the Charter)† and to fundamental justice (under s 7 of the Charter), a criminal prohibition against polygamy was a "reasonable limit" on that freedom under section 1 of the Charter, which states that the rights and freedoms are subject "to such reasonable limits prescribed by law as can be demonstrably justified in a free and democratic society." The court found section 293's prohibition against polygamy justified because of the demonstrable "harm to women, to children, to society and to the institution of monogamous marriage" caused by the practice. In other words, the harms associated with polygamy outweigh any claims to religious freedom.

The decision was not appealed, and it set the stage for prosecution under section 293. In 2014, charges of polygamy

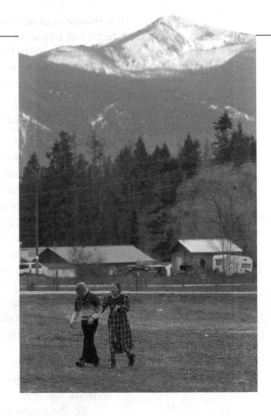

were laid against two men from Bountiful, Winston Blackmore and James Oler. In 2017, they were both convicted, and in 2018 they were sentenced to house arrest (six months and three months, respectively) along with community service work. These are the first polygamy convictions in Canada in over a century (there have only been two others, one in 1899 and one in 1906).

* *Reference re: Section 293 of the Criminal Code of Canada*, 2011 BCSC 1588.

† Part I of the *Constitution Act*, 1982, being Schedule B to the *Canada Act 1982* (UK), 1982, c 11]

ABILITY TO CONSUMMATE

For a marriage to be valid, both parties must have the ability to consummate it. The common law test for the consummation of an opposite-sex marriage is whether both parties are capable of having sexual intercourse at the outset of the marriage.[6] If one or both parties are impotent (that is, incapable of consummation) due to some incurable physical or mental disability, then the marriage may be annulled. Curable defects must be remedied and will not support an **annulment**. Note also that sterility—the inability to have children—is not the same thing as impotence and will also not support an annulment.

annulment
the legal cancellation or invalidation of a marriage

---

6   So far, the courts have not defined the consummation requirements for same-sex couples.

If a spouse is capable of consummating the marriage but simply refuses, or has a curable defect but refuses to fix it, the other party will not be able to obtain an annulment.

A marriage needs to be consummated only once for the consummation requirement to be satisfied. Once consummated, the marriage is always consummated. Lack of capacity or impotence that develops later is not grounds for annulment.

DEGREE OF CONSANGUINITY OR AFFINITY

consanguinity
a blood relationship between relatives

affinity
the relationship that a person has to the blood relatives of his or her spouse

Consanguinity refers to a blood relationship between relatives (that is, the relationship of people who descend from the same ancestor), and **affinity** refers to the relationship that a person has to the blood relatives of his or her spouse. Early in its development, the common law, adopting canon law rules, prohibited a wide range of relatives from marrying. The prohibited degrees of consanguinity and affinity extended up to and included the third degree of relationship. This means that third cousins and those lineally above and below them were prohibited from marrying. Later, these rules were relaxed—a gradual relaxation at common law over time.

In 1990, federal legislation was passed that clarified and simplified the rules. The *Marriage (Prohibited Degrees) Act*[7] states that marriage between relatives is generally permissible unless they are lineal relatives (parents, grandparents, children, grandchildren) directly up or down, or brothers or sisters (or half-brothers and half-sisters), including by adoption. Section 2 provides as follows:

> 2(1) Subject to subsection (2), persons related by consanguinity, affinity or adoption are not prohibited from marrying each other by reason only of their relationship.
>
> (2) No person shall marry another person if they are related lineally, or as brother or sister or half-brother or half-sister, including by adoption.

First cousins are permissible marriage partners in Canada, and nephews and nieces may marry their aunts and uncles.

UNMARRIED

Being married to one person, even if separated and apart from that person, is a bar to marrying a second person. Marrying one person while still married to another is bigamy, and it is an offence under the *Criminal Code*.

If one of the parties to a proposed marriage was previously married, the officiant or minister at the new marriage will need documentary evidence to prove that the prior marriage ended, either by annulment, divorce, or the death of the other spouse.

CONSENT

Both parties must consent to marry, freely and voluntarily. If one party consents to a marriage but lacks the capacity to understand the nature of its duties and responsibilities, the consent is invalid. This lack of capacity may be temporary—a matter of impairment due to drugs or alcohol—or it may be the effect of a permanent mental disability.

When one party enters a marriage under duress, compelled by fear of harm to herself or to a third person, the marriage will not be considered consensual and will not be valid. The expression *shotgun wedding* is based on this idea.

---

7   SC 1990, c 46.

Fraud or mistake can invalidate apparent consent. However, the misunderstanding must concern the nature of the ceremony or the actual identity of one of the parties. One party's misrepresentation of his wealth or status, for example, will not invalidate the other party's consent—though it might support a tort claim for deceit.

Finally, sham marriages that people enter into for immigration or other purposes, with no intention of living as a married couple, are considered not to involve real consent and are therefore invalid.

AGE

The common law age requirements for marriage are 12 for girls and 14 for boys. No federal legislation has changed these minimums. They are somewhat incongruous, for the following reason: depending on the exact ages and age differences between two young people getting married, the act of consummation necessary to validate the marriage could amount to a sexual offence under the *Criminal Code*.[8]

However, the issue of sexual offences in the context of marriages between infants (that is, people under the age of majority) has not been a problem in Canada. This is because the *Criminal Code* recognizes close-in-age and marriage defences starting at ages 12 and 14, respectively. Also, not many infants are able to obtain the necessary consents or approvals to get married in the first place. That is because provincial and territorial legislation requires parental (or guardian) consent to the solemnization of a marriage between young people under the age of majority. And infants under the age of 16 generally cannot be married even with the consent of parents or guardians. In very limited situations, however, courts are authorized under the legislation to order the solemnization of a marriage involving a person under 16. The usual test is that the marriage must be "in the interests of the parties." In making its decision, a court could consider such factors as cultural expectations or the pregnancy of one of the parties. Such marriages are rarely authorized, however.[9]

Formal Validity

The provinces and territories have jurisdiction over solemnization procedures or formalities that must occur for a marriage to be valid. The provincial and territorial marriage acts set the requirements, which typically include the following:

1. a marriage licence (some jurisdictions, such as Ontario, allow the **banns of marriage**—the public announcement in church of an impending marriage—to be used in place of licences);

2. a public marriage ceremony (religious or civil) before at least two witnesses;

3. a presiding official (religious or civil) who is authorized under the legislation to perform marriage ceremonies; and

4. registration of the marriage with the vital statistics office for the province or territory in question.

banns of marriage
the public announcement in church of an impending marriage

---

8   Sections 150-53.

9   Given that age is a matter of essential validity, there is at least an argument that these provincial and territorial age minimums are unconstitutional because they are higher than the ages set by the common law (in an area of federal jurisdiction). However, Canadian social norms today support barriers to marriage between youths, so it is unlikely any challenges will occur.

Basic Rights and Responsibilities in Marriage

During the marriage, the parties to the marriage have basic rights and obligations to each other and to their children.

At common law, and now as set out in provincial and territorial family law legislation, spouses are expected to financially support each other. The level of support is usually based on a test of what is reasonable in the circumstances, with regard to such things as the role of each spouse in the family, express or implied agreements on the matter, caregiving obligations for any children, and economic status.

Similarly, spouses within a marriage have an obligation to do what is reasonable and necessary to maintain and support their children, including providing for their education.

Matrimonial Property

Historically, the common law viewed marriage as creating a "unity of personality." This idea can be traced to the Christian belief that, upon marriage, the couple became one. What this meant in a patriarchal society, practically speaking, was that, upon marrying, the wife came under the husband's control. The husband assumed control over everything related to the family, including family property (even property that the wife brought into the marriage).

Manitoba was the first province, in 1871, to pass legislation enabling a woman to hold property in her own name and to control it free of her husband's influence and debts. Separate legislation was later passed in Manitoba to ensure that women's earnings during marriage were their own. By the early 1900s, most other provinces had followed suit, with similar legislation.[10] Legislation has since given women in Canada the same power as men to own and control property in their own right during marriage. In other words, the *unity*-of-personality concept has been replaced by a *separation*-of-personality concept.

Marriage Breakdown and Divorce

Marriage breakdown is usually a gradual process that begins while the parties are still together and moves next to separation and then divorce, although some parties may choose to stay separated without divorce. On marriage breakdown, support and other obligations are triggered under provincial legislation, whether or not there is a divorce.

Individuals in the midst of family breakdown are facing significant life decisions and are usually more emotionally fragile than are people involved in other kinds of legal conflicts. Dealing with individuals in such situations requires sensitivity from family law professionals. The special nature of disputes in this area is the reason that lawmakers in almost every Canadian jurisdiction have introduced unique measures for their resolution. These measures typically include:

- encouraging or requiring the parties to use alternative dispute resolution mechanisms (for example, collaborative law or negotiation-based approaches) before resorting to the courts; and
- creating unified family courts to simplify the process, should the courts be needed (see Chapter 6).

---

10 For examples of current legislation, see the following: *The Married Women's Property Act*, CCSM c M70; *Married Women's Property Act*, RSNWT 1988, c M-5; and *Family Law Act*, RSO 1990, c F.3, s 64.

Grounds for Divorce

Divorce in Canada is federally regulated, and the governing statute is the *Divorce Act*.[11] When it was first passed in 1968, the *Divorce Act* simplified the rules of divorce and introduced the idea of no-fault divorce.

For couples who want to formally end their relationship, there is just one ground of divorce under the *Divorce Act*—namely, marriage breakdown. Marriage breakdown can be established in one of three ways:

1. living separate and apart for one year (the no-fault basis),
2. adultery by the other party, or
3. physical or mental cruelty by the other spouse "of such a kind as to render intolerable the continued cohabitation of the spouses."[12]

The vast majority of divorces in Canada proceed under the first ground, with the couple first living separate and apart for one year. It is not necessary to actually go to court to get a divorce decree if the parties consent to the order. It can simply be filed in the appropriate court registry.

Spousal and Child Support

As mentioned, support obligations exist prior to marriage breakdown under provincial and territorial legislation. However, it is on marriage breakdown that they are most often disputed. Sometimes, different terms are used to describe the obligations. *Maintenance* and *alimony* are synonyms for payments one spouse makes to another once marriage breakdown has occurred, whether or not there has been divorce. The word *support* is more general and can refer to pre- and post-breakdown obligations, and can apply to both spousal and child payment obligations.

The parties can agree between themselves, by way of a separation agreement, who will support whom and for how long and what the payments will be, or they can go to court and have a judge make the determination for them. If they settle out of court, they may still file a consent order along with the agreement in court, which will make the settlement easier to enforce and can be adjusted if circumstances change.

Support orders, consent or otherwise, are made under provincial and territorial family law legislation until the parties proceed to divorce. If the parties proceed to divorce, support orders are made under the federal *Divorce Act*.

There are federal guidelines for spousal and child support obligations. In practice, these federal guidelines are followed in negotiated settlements involving legal professionals, as well as in court-ordered resolutions, and they are followed regardless of whether the support orders are made under provincial/territorial legislation or under the federal *Divorce Act*. Support orders can be changed at a later date if there is a significant change in circumstances.

Children: Custody and Access

When spouses who are separating have children, the main issue concerning the children is whether there will be joint custody, or whether there will be sole custody for one parent with (or without) access rights for the non-custodial parent.

---

11   RSC 1985, c 3 (2d Supp).

12   *Divorce Act*, s 8.

As with support, if there is no divorce, any non-negotiated resolution will have to be made under provincial or territorial family law legislation. And if there is a divorce, any custody and access orders will be under the *Divorce Act*. Regardless of which route is taken, the test for determining custody and access rights is essentially the same under all legislation, and that is to determine what is in the "best interests of the child" in light of all the circumstances.

Division of Family Assets

The provinces and territories have exclusive jurisdiction over the division of matrimonial property upon the breakdown of marriage. When a marriage collapses, family law legislation in all jurisdictions triggers rights to share in the marital possessions.

The legislation defines what constitutes family property, and the definitions vary depending on the province or territory. Typically, houses, pensions, retirement savings plans (RSPs), and bank accounts are included, while business assets are excluded. Inheritances are sometimes included and sometimes excluded, depending on the circumstances.

In general, this legislation creates a presumption that family assets should be split 50/50 between the parties. However, the court has the power to reapportion the division—that is, to split the assets otherwise than 50/50—in cases where an even split would be unfair or unconscionable. In choosing to reapportion, the court will consider various factors—for example, the length of the marriage, how much property each spouse brought into the marriage, the extent of each party's personal debts, and the economic self-sufficiency of each spouse. Marriage agreements and separation agreements that provide for a split other than 50/50 will also be considered by the courts, but they are not conclusive. The courts may choose to disregard such agreements.

Common Law Marriages

When two people live together in an intimate, marriage-like relationship but without going through a formal marriage ceremony, they take on some of the rights and some of the obligations of a married couple. There are various names for such relationships: common law marriages (or common law relationships), domestic partnerships, and civil unions.

Each province and territory defines what constitutes a common law marriage in its family law legislation and its financial legislation (for example, statutes dealing with taxes, pensions, and income supplements). The federal government does this, too, in its financial legislation.

In general, couples, including same-sex couples, living together in a marriage-like relationship for two years will take on some of the same rights and obligations as legally married couples. However, the applicable legislation must be read carefully. For example, under federal tax legislation, two people qualify as a common law couple if they cohabit in a conjugal relationship for just one year or if they have a child together. In Ontario, on the other hand, support obligations apply only to couples who have been together for three years or who have a child in common.

Assuming a couple satisfies the relevant legislative definition for common law marriage, the rights and obligations concerning spousal support and government financial matters will generally be the same as if they were married. Quebec is an exception and does not recognize support obligations between partners in common law relationships. Support obligations apply only to Quebec couples who are legally married or who are in a special type of civil union, not found elsewhere in Canada, that involves certain ceremonial formalities and a registration process similar to the process used for marriages.

Child support obligations are the same for common law couples as for married couples because they are based on parenthood, not marriage.

One area where a significant difference exists between common law marriages and conventional marriages has to do with the division of family property in the event of breakup. Most provinces and territories require couples to be legally married before the presumption of a 50/50 split will apply.[13] This means that a person living in a common law relationship whose partner owns most or all of the family property will be at risk of receiving little or no property if the couple breaks up.

Where no division-of-property rights exist, ownership is proved as it ordinarily is (through purchase, inheritance, etc.). The main way common law partners can protect themselves in the event of breakup is through a cohabitation agreement—in other words, an agreement between unmarried couples that deals with property rights. They may also insist on co-ownership of family property—for example, owning the matrimonial home as joint tenants or tenants in common. It is possible that if a common law spouse who is not on title has contributed in some way to the acquisition of property owned by the other spouse, a trust argument could be made that the contributing spouse is entitled to a share of the property. Such arguments are complicated and can be expensive to litigate. Generally, they are a last resort.

Protection of Children

The protection of children—that is, child welfare—is entrusted in all provinces and territories to government officials who have the power to intervene in situations where children are in need of protection.

Statutes in every jurisdiction impose duties on everyone—not just on family members, but also on friends, teachers, or social workers—to inform authorities about children who need protection from abuse or neglect.[14] Even in situations where the information is second-hand and is received in confidence, or in situations where privilege normally applies, as with communications between spouses (lawyer–client privilege is an exception to this), the legislation requires the person to report the matter and makes it an offence not to do so. It is also an offence to file a false report.

A child is in need of protection where there has been physical, sexual, or emotional abuse. Intervention is also required in cases where parents or guardians have neglected to care for or supervise the child, and harm to the child has occurred or is likely to occur because of this neglect.

After reports are received and assessed, childcare officials will respond according to the circumstances. They can offer support services to the family and meet with them; they can investigate the matter further and involve the police or courts; and, in extreme cases, they can remove the child from the home and make arrangements for alternative care, either temporarily or permanently. As a safeguard, child protection statutes allow the actions of the authorities to be challenged and reviewed in court at the request of the child or other affected family members.

The primary goals of the legislation are as follows:

- to protect children from harm;
- to keep immediate families together if possible;
- to maintain kinship ties (where care by the extended family is possible);

---

13   So far, only British Columbia has extended division-of-property rights to common law couples: see *Family Law Act*, SBC 2011, c 25.

14   See, for example, the *Child, Youth and Family Enhancement Act*, RSA 2000, c C-12, s 4; *Family Services Act*, SNB 1980, c F-2.2, s 30; and *Child and Family Services Act*, RSO 1990, c C.1, s 72.

- in cases involving Indigenous children, to preserve their cultural identity; and
- to do what is generally in the best interests of the child in all the circumstances.

BOX 9.5

Regulating the Adoption of Children

Each province and territory has legislation regulating the adoption of children.

Generally, there are two processes for adopting children: public adoption and private adoption. Public adoption involves applying to adopt a child through a government agency. While it also involves a screening process, the waitlists are generally much longer. Private adoption is done through a private agency. While it does involve a screening process, the waitlists are much shorter. Private adoptions also offer more opportunities for the adoptive parents to deal directly with the birth mother while she is pregnant or shortly after birth. Public adoptions are generally free, whereas private

adoptions can cost $10,000 or more. Despite this, most adoptions are done through private agencies. To be approved by the court, as is required in most jurisdictions, the adoption must pass the "best interests of the child" test.

International adoptions—that is, adoptions involving a child from another country—are more complicated than domestic adoptions. They must follow the rules in place for adoption and emigration in the country of birth, and they must also follow Canada's immigration rules. They are also more expensive.

An adopted child is legally the same as if she were the couple's biological child.

Support of Parents

Do adult children have an obligation to support their parents once the latter become elderly and unable to care for themselves? The answers to this question vary depending on the upbringing of the children and factors such as culture and religious beliefs.

With respect to the law in Canada, the *Criminal Code* imposes an obligation on adult children to care for their elderly parents if the parents are under their charge. The parents are most clearly under their charge if the children are living with them.[15] However, allegations and convictions for failing to live up to this obligation are rare.[16]

In some provinces and territories, family law legislation imposes civil obligations on adult children to support their parents. As with criminal charges, however, claims based on these obligations are rare. These civil obligations, where they exist, do not necessarily depend on whether the parent is under the charge of the child but on a number of factors, including the following:

- whether the parent had cared for and supported the adult child as a youth,
- the parent's current needs, and
- the adult child's current ability to support the parent.[17]

15 See s 215(1)(c) of the *Criminal Code*.

16 One such case is *R v Peterson*, 2005 CanLII 37972, 201 CCC (3d) 220 (Ont CA), which involved an adult son who was living in the family home with his 84-year-old father, who was suffering from Alzheimer's. The son, who failed to care for his father, was convicted and sentenced to six months in jail.

17 For example, see Ontario's *Family Law Act*, s 32. Some jurisdictions have moved away from such obligations, however. Alberta repealed its child–parent support requirements in 2003, and British Columbia did so in 2011.

CHAPTER SUMMARY

The regulation of private law was introduced in the previous chapter, and two key areas were examined: torts and contracts. In this chapter we looked at two more important areas, property law and family law.

Property has been a source of power in Western society since ancient times. The laws concerning the ownership and use of *real property*, or land, are among our oldest. In Canada, absolute ownership of land can rest only with the Crown, and the closest a person (who is not queen or king) can come to absolute ownership is with the fee simple estate. Fee simple ownership allows an owner full power to dispose of her land as she wishes during her life and upon her death. Various lesser estates and charges against property come with specific rights and obligations and with more limited powers of control. Co-ownership of property is possible, as is the separation of legal (right to control) and equitable (right to benefits) ownership. Interests in land can be registered, either in a deed registry or a land titles system, depending on the province or territory in which the land is located—registration provides a measure of security of ownership.

Besides real property, property law deals with the ownership and use of *personal property*, which includes tangible goods as well as some intangible interests, such as corporate securities. Ownership rules for personal property are generally simpler than for land. Personal property security legislation, in force in all provinces and territories, governs the process by which one party uses another's personal property as security, usually for a debt owing.

Finally, the law also regulates *intellectual property* (that is, property that is created through intellectual effort). IP has become a more important form of property in recent years

and is regulated exclusively at the federal level. The principal forms of IP protection relate to copyright, industrial designs, patents, and trademarks.

Family law governs marriage, marriage breakdown and divorce, common law relationships, and related matters (including those involving children and family assets). Certain aspects of family law—for example, the substantive requirements of a valid marriage and divorce—are federally regulated. Other aspects, such as the formal and ceremonial requirements of a marriage and the division of family assets on marriage breakdown, are under provincial jurisdiction. New laws concerning same-sex marriage, and permissible degrees of consanguinity (blood relation) and affinity, have expanded the range of marriageable couples.

When marriages end, most couples get divorced, and most divorces in Canada are based on the no-fault, one-year separation rule set out in the federal *Divorce Act*. Issues relating to support and care of children arise upon marriage breakdown. Spousal support focuses on what is reasonable for both parties in the circumstances. Child support and custody and access determinations are based on what is in the best interests of the child. Division-of-property rules, which are regulated by the provinces and territories, favour a 50/50 split of family property unless good reasons exist to adjust this division—a process known as *reapportionment*. The law treats common law relationships similarly to traditional marriages, except (in most jurisdictions) when it comes to division of property upon the breakup of the relationship; in such cases, ownership of property must be proved in the usual way.

Family law also covers other matters such as adoption, child welfare, and support of parents.

KEY TERMS

affinity, 288

agreement for sale, 277

annulment, 287

banns of marriage, 289

beneficial owner, 278

charges and encumbrances, 276

chattels, 282

chose in action, 283

consanguinity, 288

conveyancing, 281

deeds, 280

defeasible, 276

essential validity, 285

fee simple ownership, 274

fixtures, 282

foreclosure proceedings, 277

formal validity, 286

freehold interests, 276

indefeasible, 280

intellectual property, 284

interest, 273

joint tenancy, 278

leasehold interests, 276

life estate, 275

mortgage, 276

personal property, 281

personal property security, 283

FURTHER READING

BOOKS

Hovius, Berend, Mary-Jo Maur & Nicholas Bala. *Family Law: Text, Cases, Materials and Notes*, 9th ed (Toronto: Thomson Reuters, 2017).

Kurtz, JoAnn. *Family Law: Practice and Procedure*, 5th ed (Toronto: Emond, 2018).

Sinclair, Alan M & Margaret E McCallum. *An Introduction to Real Property Law*, 7th ed (Toronto: LexisNexis, 2017).

Ziff, Bruce. *Principles of Property Law*, 6th ed (Toronto: Carswell, 2014).

Ziff, Bruce et al. *A Property Law Reader*, 4th ed (Toronto: Thomson Reuters, 2016).

WEBSITES

Canadian Intellectual Property Office (CIPO): <http://www.ic.gc.ca/eic/site/cipointernet-internetopic.nsf/eng/Home>.

World Intellectual Property Organization: <http://www.wipo.int/portal/en/index.html>.

REVIEW QUESTIONS

1. What are the distinguishing features of the fee simple estate?

2. Define life estate ownership and outline its rights and obligations.

3. Explain how mortgages work and describe how the modern concept of a mortgage differs from the traditional concept.

4. What is the difference between joint tenancy and tenancy in common?

5. What does the term *support* mean in the context of property ownership?

6. What is the purpose of registration systems for property ownership, and what are the registry systems currently used in Canada?

7. What is the test for determining whether formerly movable property has become affixed to land and therefore part of the realty?

8. What are the six basic requirements of essential validity for marriage?

9. What is the difference between the annulment of a marriage and a divorce?

10. In terms of ownership and control of matrimonial property, what is the *unity of personality* principle, and does it apply today?

11. Upon marriage breakdown, what is the main test for determining custody and access rights concerning children?

EXERCISES

1. Locate the statute that regulates residential tenancies in your province or territory and review the provisions dealing with termination. For a month-to-month tenancy, name three no-fault reasons that will support a decision by a landlord to end the lease, and describe the specific notice requirements.

2. You have just written a script for an animated film that you believe has the potential to be Disney's next big hit. You want to send it around for others to read and critique but are concerned about its being plagiarized. Go to the CIPO website listed above and review the information about copyrights. What steps must be taken to register your original script? Once registered, does CIPO guarantee protection for your work? Explain.

3. In your opinion, should couples who choose not to get married but who live in a committed marriage-like relationship be treated the same way as married couples when it comes to division of family assets? Provide reasons for your answer.

10 Business and Consumer Law

After reading this chapter, you will understand:

- The most common business structures in Canada—sole proprietorships, partnerships, and corporations—and the advantages and disadvantages of each.
- The basic nature of business transactions, payment methods, and collection options.
- Circumstances that give rise to builders' and repairers' liens.
- The importance of sale of goods acts in Canada.

- How consumers are protected under the federal *Competition Act*.
- The role of the federal *Food and Drugs Act* and the *Canada Consumer Product Safety Act* in protecting the health and safety of Canadian consumers.
- Selected areas covered by provincial consumer protection legislation.
- How the Canadian advertising industry attempts to protect consumers.

M odern technology has placed at the disposal of the Canadian consumer a bewildering variety of highly complex products, consumable and non-consumable, many of which were unknown before the war. The notion of the consumer bargaining from a position of equal strength has become a fiction in any but the most attenuated sense.

JS Ziegel, "The Future of Canadian Consumerism" in MH Ogilvie, ed,
Consumer Law: Cases and Materials, 3rd ed (Toronto: Captus Press, 2007) at 2

Introduction

Choosing a business structure is one of the first decisions entrepreneurs make when planning a new business venture or developing an existing one. The most common ways of structuring a business—working alone and unincorporated, or with others in partnership, or behind the veil of a corporation—all have advantages and disadvantages. The nature of the business, the need for capital to grow it, and the risks involved in running the business are factors that will influence the choice of structure.

Regardless of the business structure chosen, all businesses must enter into business transactions; in almost all cases, these are based on contracts with customers that will determine the rights and obligations of the parties. Decisions about payment options, whether or not to offer credit or to take security for payment, and collection methods in the event of non-payment will be an important part of these transactions. And particular businesses, such as those involved in the building or repairing trades, need to consider whether any special rights apply to them.

Further, all businesses need to be aware of legislation, both federal and provincial, regulating the sale of products or services. Both levels of government have enacted legislation that sets standards and defines rights and responsibilities with regard to these products and services.

This chapter will consider all of these issues and will examine some basic rules under provincial sale of goods acts; the significance of certain federal consumer protection legislation (specifically, the *Competition Act*,[1] the *Food and Drugs Act*,[2] and the *Canada Consumer Product Safety Act*[3]); and how changes in the marketplace have led to increased protection of consumers at the provincial level. Lastly, it will consider a code of standards administered by Advertising Standards Canada designed to protect consumers.

Business Structures

In Canada, the three most common business structures are sole proprietorships, partnerships, and corporations.

Sole Proprietorships

The simplest form of business structure in Canada is the **sole proprietorship**. The business, in this case, is owned and operated by one person—the sole proprietor. For example, a sole proprietorship might be a neighbourhood dog-grooming business, a street vendor, or a business selling products on the Internet. With sole proprietorships, besides the owner there are generally few (if any) employees, and it is not unusual for the business to be based in the sole proprietor's home; however, depending on the size and type of business (and this applies regardless of how the business is structured), it could be in a retail store, warehouse, or office building, or even be a mobile business. Legal requirements for starting up a sole proprietorship are minimal, but still must be followed.

> **sole proprietorship**
> business that is owned and operated by an individual and that is not a legal entity separate from the owner

Depending on particular laws in each province, a sole proprietor may conduct her business under her own personal name. If the sole proprietor chooses to do otherwise—if she wishes to give her business a name different from her own name—she may (depending again on the province) be required to register that different name with the provincial government. There may be further restrictions in this regard. In Saskatchewan, for example, section 8(1) of *The Business Names Registration Act*[4] states that no business name shall be registered if, in the opinion of the registrar, it is the same as or similar to an existing corporation's name and would likely cause confusion, or if the name suggests or implies a connection with the Crown, the government, a political party, a professional association, or a university.[5]

With a sole proprietorship, there are federal and provincial laws and taxes that may also apply to its operation. There is the federal goods and services tax (GST), provincial sales tax (PST), and, in some provinces, including Ontario and the Atlantic provinces, a combined harmonized sales tax (HST) that is collected by the Canada Revenue Agency, which then remits a portion back to the participating provinces. Municipal by-laws may also apply to facets of the business, such as land use, zoning, parking, noise, and the location of advertising signs. Business permits and other licences may also be needed—for example, for electricians—depending on the type of business. Indeed, all of the business structures reviewed in this part are subject to taxes and other obligations under federal, provincial, and municipal laws.

---

1   RSC 1985, c C-34.

2   RSC 1985, c F-27.

3   SC 2010, c 21.

4   Being c B-11 of *The Revised Statutes of Saskatchewan, 1978* (effective February 26, 1979) as amended by the *Statutes of Saskatchewan*, 1980-81, c 3 and 21; 1986-87-88, c 40; 2006, c 14; and 2010, c B-12.

5   RSS 1978, c B-11.

Advantages and Disadvantages

A sole proprietorship is relatively easy to start up and operate. Income from the business is considered taxable income for the sole proprietor, but an income tax deduction based on a percentage of the costs of operating the business at home may be available.

The main disadvantage of a sole proprietorship is that it is not a separate legal business structure apart from its owner. Sole proprietors are legally liable for all of the business's debts and obligations. Such business debts may also put the sole proprietor's personal assets at risk.

Partnerships

Business owners may choose to change their business structure as their circumstances change. For example, a sole proprietor might wish to expand her home-based dog-grooming business. In order to raise capital to rent a storefront office and buy more equipment, she might convert her business into a partnership with a co-owner. This partnership structure could reduce business costs per person and increase business opportunities; the partners could share costs and work together to attract new customers.

A partnership exists whenever two or more persons carry on business together with a view to profit; collectively, they are referred to as a *firm*. Most partnerships are based in part on a *partnership agreement*, which defines their rights and obligations. However, partnership agreements are subject to any rules mandated by legislation, such as those relating to limiting liability in connection with the conduct of the business. Also, partners who are involved in the management of the business owe each other a **fiduciary duty**, which requires them to act in good faith (that is, to act honestly and for the common benefit of the partners) and to share profits and opportunities. They are also required to act carefully and reasonably in their partnership dealings.

The three types of partnerships available in Canada are:

1. general partnerships,
2. limited partnerships, and
3. limited liability partnerships.

A **general partnership** is the most common form of partnership. It exists when all of the partners manage the business together and share profits, as well as debts and obligations. All provinces and territories have partnership legislation, which sets out certain rules characterizing general partnerships.[6] Most importantly, partners are each other's *agents* (meaning that each is authorized to act on behalf of the others), and each partner is *jointly and severally liable* for the conduct of the business while she is a partner in it. This means that every partner is fully liable for all debts and liabilities of the firm (although an individual partner who is found liable for a partnership debt or other liability has a right to seek contribution from the other partners).

The main difference between a **limited partnership** and a general partnership is that, in a limited partnership, not all partners participate in the management of the business: a limited partnership consists of one or more *general* partners and one or more *limited* partners. The general partners are the ones who operate the partnership and are liable for any partnership liabilities. A limited partner, on the other hand, contributes money or property to the partnership, but does not operate the partnership or take part in managing its business.

---

fiduciary duty
in the context of a partnership, the responsibility to act carefully and reasonably in the best interest of the firm

general partnership
business structure in which two or more persons carry on business in common with a view to profit

limited partnership
partnership structure involving at least one general partner, who operates the partnership and is liable for any partnership debts, and at least one limited partner, who invests in the partnership but does not operate it or take part in managing its business and is not personally liable for its debts and obligations

---

6   See, for example, the *Partnerships Act*, RSO 1990, c P.5; *Partnership Act*, RSA 2000, c P-3; and *Partnership Act*, RSBC 1996, c 348.

The limited partner has the right to a share in the partnership profits but, unlike the general partners, is not liable for any partnership obligations. The liability of limited partners is restricted to only the value of money and other property they have contributed to the partnership. Specific rules dealing with the creation of limited partnerships and the liability of limited partners are regionally legislated.[7]

The **limited liability partnership** is a special form of partnership that, for the most part, is restricted to certain professionals, such as lawyers and accountants. It allows such professionals to limit their liability for the consequences of professional malpractice to their own conduct. In other words, they may not be held responsible for the malpractice of their partners. Limited liability partnerships (LLPs) are available across Canada—for lawyers and accountants in all provinces except PEI and in the Northwest Territories.[8]

See Table 10.1 for a comparison of the three types of partnerships.

limited liability partnership
partnership structure used by certain professions in Canada (accountants and lawyers, for the most part) whereby partners are not liable for the professional negligence of other partners

TABLE 10.1   Comparison of the Three Types of Partnership

	GENERAL PARTNERSHIP	LIMITED PARTNERSHIP	LIMITED LIABILITY PARTNERSHIP
Typical example	Two friends go into business together; they share capital costs, debts, work, profit, and liability.	A sole proprietor needs capital and finds investors who become limited partners; they provide capital, share debts, and are entitled to profit, but they do not work in the business and have limited liability. The sole proprietor becomes a general partner.	A group of accountants form a partnership; they share capital costs, debts, work, and profit; and they are not liable for each other's professional negligence.
Liability	All partners are jointly and severally liable for each other's debts and negligence, including professional negligence. Liability is unlimited.	At least one general partner must be fully liable for the debts of the firm and any negligence of the other partners. Liability of general partners is limitless. Limited liability partners are liable for the debts of the firm and any negligence of the other partners only to the extent provided in the partnership agreement (usually to the extent of their capital investment).	Some or all partners may be limited liability partners, who are liable only for the general debts of the firm and not for the professional negligence of the other partners.
Decision-making and profit taking	Partners often make decisions and share profit equally. A partnership agreement may provide that some partners have more decision-making power and are entitled to more profit (usually because of a larger initial investment) than others.	Limited partners have no decision-making powers. If they become involved in business decisions, they risk losing their limited liability status. Limited partners are entitled to profit according to the terms of the partnership agreement.	Limited liability partners may have decision-making powers and are entitled to profit according to the terms of the partnership agreement.

Source: Tamra Alexander & Pat Papadeas, *Canadian Business Law*, 3rd ed (Toronto: Emond, 2018) at 225-26.

---

7   These rules appear either in general partnerships legislation or in special limited partnerships acts, such as Ontario's *Limited Partnerships Act*, RSO 1990, c L.16. Under Ontario's legislation, a limited partnership is formed when a declaration is filed with the provincial government.

8   The governing legislation in each jurisdiction where LLPs are permitted sets out the rules for their creation and the attendant rights and responsibilities attaching to this business structure. In Ontario,

Advantages and Disadvantages

Concerning *general partnerships*, the main advantage is that, like sole proprietorships, they can be established with minimal expense. A general partnership can reduce business costs on an individual basis and increase business opportunities through the pooling of resources. A major disadvantage of this business structure is that, as mentioned, the individual partners are jointly and severally liable for the actions of the business (in other words, every partner is liable with the other partners for any debts or liabilities incurred by the firm). This liability places the partners' personal assets at risk of a creditor suing to collect money owing to it by the partnership.

An advantage of the *limited partnership* is that it enables the partners to raise the funds required by attracting new investors. These investors can share in the partnership profits while limiting the risks involved in their investment to only the money or property they have contributed. Not all investors in a partnership want to assume all its risks. One difficulty involved in a limited partnership is that the distinction between general and limited partners can become blurred. A limited partner who takes part in managing and controlling the partnership risks losing his limited partner status under the governing legislation and being held liable as a general partner for any debts or liabilities of the business.

The main advantage of the *limited liability partnership* is that one partner is not liable for the professional malpractice of the other partner(s), although the partner himself will be responsible for his own malpractice (he cannot hide behind limited liability protection with respect to his own conduct). One limitation on this business structure is that, even where it is recognized, it is generally not available to all professions or businesses.

Corporations

Two main concerns for those operating a sole proprietorship or a partnership are (1) raising new money for the business and (2), as noted, being personally liable for the business's debts and obligations.

corporation
company or group of people authorized by statute to act as a single entity (legally a person) and recognized as such in law

A **corporation** is a legal entity separate from those who create it. Because it is independent from its owners (the shareholders) and those who manage it (the directors and officers or their appointees), these individuals are in most cases not personally and legally liable for the company's debts and obligations. When first incorporating a company, one must consider who will provide the initial investment and be its shareholders, and who will be its directors and officers. Often in the initial stages of a corporation's existence, the owners, or shareholders, will also be the directors and officers—its first managers.

It is also necessary to consider where the head office will be located and whether to incorporate federally or provincially. Incorporating under the federal *Canada Business Corporations Act*[9] ensures a right to carry on business anywhere in Canada and provides increased name protection. If a company plans to carry on business locally, however, incorporation under the relevant provincial or territorial statute is common. These companies

---

for example, the legislation regulating lawyers allows them to carry on their business using the LLP business structure, and the province's *Partnerships Act* (RSO 1990, c P.5) provides that an LLP is formed when two or more persons sign a written agreement that designates their partnership as an LLP and states that the *Partnerships Act* governs the agreement. Under this Act (ss 44.1-44.3), the firm name of the LLP must be registered under Ontario's *Business Names Act*, and the firm name must also contain the words *limited liability partnership* or the abbreviation *LLP* as the last words or letters of the firm name. At the time of writing, British Columbia is the only province that allows LLPs for professions other than law and accounting, and for businesses generally.

9   RSC 1985, c C-44.

can still carry on business in other provinces and territories if they wish, provided that they register as required in those jurisdictions. (Federal companies have to register in jurisdictions in which they do business, too, but the process is simpler.)

A corporation is created when its incorporators file with the appropriate government office a document known either as (depending on the province) letters patent, memorandum of association, or—in the case of federal incorporation—articles of incorporation. These are standard form documents containing certain information the government requires, such as the company name, the location of its head office, the names and addresses of its first directors, and the number and types of company shares.

In addition, the application for incorporation must also include a NUANS (Newly Updated Automated Name Search) report. This is a report confirming that the government names database has been searched and that there are no existing corporations already using the proposed name. If the name is similar to that of an existing corporation, and the similarity is likely to cause confusion, the proposed new name may not be accepted. If the name proves problematic in this way and the incorporators want to get their new company up and running quickly, a company can be created using a number instead of a name. Once all the required paperwork is submitted and the submission fee is paid, the company comes into existence.

Corporations have the ability to raise capital by issuing and selling shares to the public, something not possible for a sole proprietor or partnership. Deciding whether to offer shares to the public, thereby creating a *public company*, or limiting the number of shareholders and operating as a *private company*, is one of many important matters to review with legal advisers when structuring or expanding a company. Public companies, whose shares can be sold on stock exchanges, are much more heavily regulated than private companies. *Securities regulation* is a very complex and detailed area of the law.

Advantages and Disadvantages

One legal advantage of corporations as a business structure is that the owners and directors of a company are not personally liable for its debts and obligations. Another advantage, for public companies, is that the corporation can sell shares to raise new capital.

BOX 10.1

Application of Charter Protections and Criminal Law to Corporations

What other implications flow from the special legal status of corporations? What treatment do corporations receive under statutes—such as the *Canadian Charter of Rights and Freedoms** or the *Criminal Code*†—that were primarily designed to apply to people? Generally, whether the special legal status of corporations entitles them to the protections of the Charter depends on the type of right or freedom under consideration. For example, freedom of expression has been interpreted as extending to corporations in the case of *Irwin Toy Ltd v Quebec (AG)*,‡ but the right to equality and the freedom of religion have been restricted to human beings.

Does criminal law apply to corporations? A corporation cannot be sent to jail for criminal acts, but governments are more and more willing to create criminal offences (such as environmental offences) for which corporations can be found guilty and punished through substantial fines. In some cases, the directors of a corporation may be jailed for serious criminal offences perpetrated by the corporation.

* Part I of the *Constitution Act, 1982*, being Schedule B to the *Canada Act 1982* (UK), 1982, c 11.

† RSC 1985, c C-46.

‡ [1989] 1 SCR 927, 1989 CanLII 87.

Source: Tamra Alexander & Pat Papadeas, *Canadian Business Law*, 3rd ed (Toronto: Emond, 2018) at 235-36.

Disadvantages for public companies include the cost and complexity of running them because of the detailed securities regulations that apply and because of the increased costs that are associated with those regulations.

Business Transactions

negotiable instrument

a document that promises the payment of a specific amount of money to the payee, on demand or at a set time, and that can be transferred to a third party

No matter what form of business structure one chooses, the successful operation of the business itself will depend on selling something—property, the use of property, services, or some combination of these things—to somebody (the customer or client) at a profit. Sales can be business-to-business or business-to-consumer, and the main vehicle used for accomplishing such sales is the contract. Contracts are used to define the rights and obligations of the parties in business transactions and, frequently, to place limits on the potential liability of the selling party (see Chapter 8 for a discussion of contract law generally).

There are numerous types of business transactions, and many have generated their own specialized standard form contracts (and some their own areas of law, such as real estate transactions and insurance). Further, the transactions can be local or can cross regional or national boundaries. Cross-boundary transactions introduce new levels of complexity because of the possible application of laws from jurisdictions other than the seller's.

BOX 10.2

Negotiable Instruments

A **negotiable instrument** is a document that promises the payment of a specific amount of money to a person, on demand or at a set time, and that can be transferred to a third party. Negotiable instruments are portable and easier to use when large sums of money are involved (a single page can represent the entire amount and be simply carried from one place to another) and can minimize the risk of theft because only the named payee (or another person, if the instrument is endorsed) can cash them. They can be used as a method of payment for most types of business transactions. In Canada, they are regulated under the *Bills of Exchange Act*** and come in three forms: cheques, promissory notes, and bills of exchange.

A *cheque* involves three parties: the *payer* (the person making payment and who has an account at a financial institution), the *drawee* (the financial institution), and the *payee* (the person to whom the financial institution is directed to make payment). A cheque is payable on demand on or after the date on the cheque. However, a bank is required to honour the cheque only if there are sufficient funds in the payer's account. The payee can transfer the cheque by endorsing it—that is, by signing the back of the cheque. If the cheque is simply endorsed without

naming another person as payee (this is called *endorsement in blank*), the cheque can be passed on multiple times to other bearers, until it is eventually presented to the bank for payment. If the cheque is endorsed and stated to be payable to a specific person (called a *restrictive endorsement*), only that person named can cash it; it cannot be passed on again.

A *promissory note* involves only two parties and is simply a promise by one person (the *maker*) to pay another person (a creditor) a specified amount according to the terms set out in the note (for example, the time of payment, interest charges, etc.). The maker must sign the note before it is enforceable. The creditor can endorse the note if she chooses and give it to another person, who becomes the *holder* and who has the same rights to enforce the note as the original creditor.

Bills of exchange can operate either like cheques or like promissory notes, depending on how they are structured. They are used infrequently today because of the popularity of cheques and promissory notes and because they are more complex and require more formalities when making them.

*   RSC 1985, c B-4.

Payment options for sellers include cash, cheque (and other negotiable instruments—see Box 10.2), credit card (which can be linked to smartphones and companies such as PayPal that facilitate online payments), debit card (allowing payment directly from the customer's bank account), wire transfer (bank-to-bank), and letter of credit (which can be used when a purchaser of goods resides in another jurisdiction, and usually comes in the form of a guarantee from the purchaser's bank promising to release funds to the seller as soon as the bank receives proof of shipment of the goods). New methods of payment will continue to evolve as technology changes and adapts.

When sellers sell on credit, and when the consumer or business debt is connected to personal property, the sellers can protect themselves by registering various security interests against the property (see Chapter 9 for a discussion of personal property security legislation).

More generally, in the event of non-payment, creditors have a large arsenal of techniques to help them collect their debts, including pre-judgment garnishment of bank accounts, post-judgment garnishment of wages, seizures and sales of personal property, and the registration of judgments against real property. In all cases, however, collections rules tend to be interpreted strictly and the requirements of the relevant legislation must be followed carefully.

Builders and Repairers: Security for Services Performed

The business of builders and repairers comprises a large part of the service industry. It includes building construction and renovation work, and storage of and repairs to (and other work related to) personal property (including motor vehicles, boats, aircraft, and other tangible property). In this section, we briefly examine some of the remedies available to builders and repairers when they are not paid for their work.

With respect to *construction and renovation work* done on real property, an unpaid contractor can pursue the civil remedy of damages for breach of contract. This is time-consuming and costly, and comes with the uncertainty associated with litigation generally. One well-established method of securing payment in these circumstances is the **builders' (or construction) lien**. An unpaid contractor has a lien for the amount owed for work done on the landowner's property, and this lien can be registered against the property. All provinces and territories have legislation detailing matters such as timelines for filing claims of liens against property, procedures for removal of liens after payment, and court-ordered sales of the land in the event of non-payment.[10]

With respect to unpaid work in relation to personal property (*storage and repair work*, etc.), all provinces and territories have legislation setting out rules for establishing liens against the property in question. For instance, Ontario's *Repair and Storage Liens Act*[11] provides that "a repairer has a lien against an article that the repairer has repaired for an amount equal to [the amount agreed upon or if there was no agreed amount the fair value of the repair], and the repairer may retain possession of the article until the amount is paid."[12] A similar lien exists with regard to unpaid storage costs. Further, these liens exist whether or not the contractor remains in possession of the property. The legislation allows for the registration of the lien in the personal property security registry of the relevant jurisdiction (see Chapter 9).

builders' (or construction) lien
charge against land that builders use to secure amounts owed them for work done on landowners' property

---

10 See, for example, the *Construction Act*, RSO 1990, c C.30; *Builders' Lien Act*, RSNS 1989, c 277; and *Mechanics' Lien Act*, RSNL 1990, c M-3.

11 RSO 1990, c R.25 [RSLA].

12 RSLA, s 3.

Product Sales and Consumer Protection Legislation

A business that sells products and services to the public today must comply with legislation covering a variety of issues relating to contract terms and product or service standards and safety. In the past, there was a much more lenient approach to the marketplace generally. Two phrases that are indicative of this approach are *laissez-faire* and *caveat emptor*. *Laissez-faire* (French: literally, "let do or make") refers to the economic philosophy that the marketplace should be free from constraints by government and that businesses should be free to profit from their ventures subject only to the contracts they negotiate with others. *Caveat emptor* (Latin: "buyer beware") refers to the idea that purchasers must take the property they purchase "as is." It is up to them to protect themselves by inspecting and testing the property before purchasing it, or by negotiating terms with respect to quality and to cover the risks of future defects.

The marketplace has changed significantly in the last 150 years and has become more complex. Businesses used to be smaller and have a closer connection with the communities where they sold their products or services. Many commercial operations today have grown into national or international enterprises, with few local allegiances. And many products now are mass-produced and technologically advanced, and it is difficult to inspect them before they are purchased, either because they are sealed (or their packaging is sealed) or because they are purchased online or from catalogues. Also, sellers often require purchasers to agree to standard form contracts, limiting their ability to negotiate favourable terms.

As Jacob Ziegel observed (see the quotation at the beginning of this chapter), "[t]he notion of the consumer bargaining from a position of equal strength has become a fiction in any but the most attenuated sense." The response of legislators to a changing marketplace and changing values has been varied and complex. In this section, we briefly examine: (1) sale of goods legislation and its impact on product sales contracts, (2) federal legislation specifically enacted to protect consumers, and (3) provincial and territorial legislative responses to consumer protection.

Sale of Goods Acts

The English *Sale of Goods Act*[13] was enacted in 1893. It was the first attempt to codify laws about buying and selling goods and to add some basic safeguards respecting the rights of buyers and sellers. All common law provinces and territories in Canada have passed similar acts based on this English statute. These acts modernize sale of goods law for the benefit of purchasers. In doing so, they help counter the traditional harshness of *caveat emptor*. One instance of this modernization is the introduction of some conditions implied into every contract of sale. We will use British Columbia's *Sale of Goods Act*[14] as an example in discussing these implied conditions.

Five major implied conditions listed in BC's *Sale of Goods Act* are the following:

1. *Seller's title and right to sell.* There is an implied condition under section 16 of the Act that a seller has a right to sell or lease the goods.

---

13 (UK), 56 & 57 Vict, c 71.

14 RSBC 1996, c 410.

2. *Sale by description.* If goods are sold by description, there is an implied condition under section 17 that the goods correspond with that description.

3. *Fitness for purpose.* If a buyer expressly or by implication indicates to a seller his particular purpose requiring a product and is relying on the seller's skill or judgment, and the seller is in the business of selling that product, then there is, under section 18(a) of the Act, an implied condition that the goods sold are reasonably fit for the purpose for which the product was bought.

4. *Goods of merchantable quality.* If goods are bought by description from a seller who deals in goods of that description, there is an implied condition, under section 18(b) of the Act, that the goods are of merchantable quality—that is, fit to be used for the ordinary purposes for which products of its kind are manufactured and sold.

5. *Sale by sample.* If goods are sold by sample, there is an implied condition under section 19 of the Act that the goods in bulk correspond to that sample in type and quality.

While this legislation protects consumers to a degree, as these five implied conditions illustrate, it is important to note that sale of goods acts are primarily about contractual rights and responsibilities generally and not consumer protection per se. These codified rules apply to all sale of goods transactions, whether they are between businesses (for example, one commercial enterprise selling machinery to another), between private individuals (such as a sale of goods at a garage sale), or between businesses and consumers (for example, a retail business selling clothing to a customer).

Federal Consumer Protection Legislation

Although provincial sale of goods acts assist purchasers by imposing implied conditions—along with additional safeguards—on sale transactions, these statutes do not cover all areas affecting consumers who buy an item for their own personal use. Increasingly, both the federal and provincial/territorial governments have enacted numerous other pieces of legislation more comprehensive in scope than sale of goods acts to help protect consumers from changing marketplace concerns, such as:

- anti-competitive and dishonest business tactics,
- false and misleading advertising,
- deceptive marketing practices, and
- products that may jeopardize the safety of consumers.

Three examples of this additional federal legislation are discussed below.

The Competition Act

In Canada, the *Competition Act*[15] is the principal federal statute regulating trade and commerce with respect to conspiracies, trade practices, and mergers that affect competition. It is the oldest competition (or antitrust) statute in the Western world and was first enacted in 1889. Its purpose, as set out in section 1.1, is "to maintain and encourage competition in Canada in order to promote the efficiency and adaptability of the Canadian economy."

---

15   RSC 1985, c C-34.

The Act authorizes the federal government to take action against those who it alleges violate its provisions, either through criminal proceedings or by administrative review. The Commissioner of Competition is responsible for the administration and enforcement of this Act.

Criminal matters relating to competition include such things as *price-fixing* (agreements fixing prices among competitors), *bid-rigging* (agreements restricting open bidding processes), *interferences with professional sports* (for instance, by unreasonably limiting opportunities to participate in professional sports or to negotiate contracts with clubs in professional leagues), and operating *pyramid schemes* (multi-level marketing plans that depend for profits on the recruitment of others who pay to participate). These kinds of offences are prosecuted in the criminal courts and, if the offending party is convicted, can result in fines or imprisonment.

Certain less serious market behaviours are classed as *reviewable conduct* and are not considered criminal matters; they are subject to administrative review by the Competition Bureau, the Competition Tribunal, or the courts. Reviewable conduct includes such things as *deceptive market practices* (for instance, *misleading misrepresentations* about product performance, *bait-and-switch selling*, or *sale above the advertised price* practices) and *mergers that substantially lessen competition* in a trade or industry (see Box 10.3 for an example). Administrative penalties for engaging in reviewable conduct are not as serious as criminal penalties and include orders to stop the offending practice or to publish notices informing consumers about the conduct, and administrative monetary penalties (which, for corporations, can be as high as $15 million).

BOX 10.3

Media Monopoly

Because of their significance as vehicles for airing diverse points of view, the news media are businesses in which healthy competition is extremely important. Although the case described below is a case that merely concerned an advertising supplement, it has wider implications.

In *Canada (Director of Investigation and Research) v Southam Inc*,* the defendant corporation, a media giant, purchased two British Columbia newspapers, the *North Shore News* and the *Real Estate Weekly*. The *North Shore News*, a profitable and widely read newspaper, contained a weekly real estate supplement. Before the defendant corporation purchased the papers, this supplement and the *Real Estate Weekly* were the only two real estate advertising papers distributed on the North Shore.

The Competition Tribunal's director of investigation and research brought an application asking the tribunal to order that the corporation sell one or the other of the two papers, alleging that the defendant's ownership of both papers eliminated competition in the real estate market in the area. The

defendant proposed, as an alternative remedy, that the *North Shore News* begin to carry, as an insert, an independent real estate supplement referred to as "HOMES."

The tribunal found that the corporation's ownership of both the *Real Estate Weekly* and the *North Shore News* eliminated competition in the real estate advertising sales market in the region. It was unconvinced that an independent HOMES supplement would be as attractive to advertisers or as financially viable as the existing *North Shore News* supplement (which at the time of the merger was slightly outperforming the *Real Estate Weekly*). The tribunal also believed that it lacked the power to make the order the defendant requested.

The tribunal ordered the corporation to sell either the *North Shore News* or the *Real Estate Weekly* to restore competition in the marketplace.

*   1991 CanLII 1702 (Comp Trib).

Source: Margaret Buchan et al, *Canadian Business Law*, 2nd ed (Toronto: Emond Montgomery, 2012) at 182.

The Food and Drugs Act

Canada's *Food and Drugs Act* is another key piece of federal legislation protecting consumers. It aims to protect the health and safety of Canadians in connection with the sale of food, drugs, cosmetics, and medical devices manufactured and sold in Canada. The Act prohibits sellers from selling the following:

- *food* that is unfit for human consumption, is deceptively labelled or packaged, or was manufactured or stored in unsanitary conditions (manufacturers are similarly prohibited from engaging in such practices) (ss 4, 5, and 7);
- *drugs* that were manufactured or stored in unsanitary conditions (a similar prohibition applies to manufacturers), that are adulterated, or that are deceptively labelled or packaged (ss 8, 9, and 11);
- *cosmetics* that contain injurious substances or were manufactured or stored in unsanitary conditions (a similar prohibition applies to manufacturers) (ss 16 and 18); and
- *medical devices* that may cause injury when used as directed (and any person who is involved with labelling or packaging such products can be liable if the labelling or packaging is misleading) (ss 19 and 20).

The Canada Consumer Product Safety Act

In 2011, the *Canada Consumer Product Safety Act*[16] (CCPSA) came into force, bringing Canada's consumer protection laws in line with the new realities of international manufacturing and the marketplace, and responding to the desire of consumers for more information about the products they use. The Act is administered by Health Canada.

The purpose of the CCPSA, as set out in section 3, is to protect the public by addressing or preventing dangers to human health or safety that are posed by consumer products in Canada, including imported products. The Act applies to consumer products that individuals may use for non-commercial purposes—such as domestic, recreational, and sports purposes—as well as to their parts, accessories, and packaging. A wide range of products is thus covered, from children's toys to household products and sporting goods, to name a few. The Act does not apply to goods that are governed by other specific legislation, such as food, cosmetics, medical devices, natural health products, drugs, and vehicles.

Sections 7(a) and 8(a) of the CCPSA contain what is known as the general prohibition. Section 7(a) prohibits manufacturers and importers from manufacturing, importing, advertising, or selling consumer products that constitute a danger to human health or safety, and section 8(a) prohibits anyone from advertising or selling a consumer product they know is a danger to human health or safety. Under the Act, the minister of health has the authority to order a manufacturer, importer, or seller to recall any product that the minister believes is a danger to human health or safety. Industry is expected to undertake recalls voluntarily when necessary.

Other key provisions of the Act include the following:

- Industry must provide Health Canada and suppliers of products with information related to safety incidents or product defects that could result in death or harmful health effects.

---

16 SC 2010, c 21.

- Packaging, labelling, and advertising must not mislead or deceive consumers as to the safety of a product.
- Certain records must be kept by manufacturers, importers, advertisers, vendors, and testers of consumer products in order to make it possible to trace unsafe products back to their source.
- Manufacturers or importers may be required to provide or obtain information about their products (including studies) so that Health Canada can verify that a product is in compliance with the requirements of the CCPSA.

Provincial and Territorial Areas of Consumer Protection

The federal government is not alone in protecting consumers. The provinces and territories are also involved in this area and have enacted legislation specifically focused on the protection of consumers. Typically, this legislation defines a consumer as someone who has entered into a transaction "for personal, family or household purposes" and excludes from its application business or commercial transactions. This is different from sale of goods acts, which apply generally to all transactions. In other respects, though, consumer protection legislation is broader than sale of goods acts, because it applies to sales of goods *and services*, and in some jurisdictions, even to the sale of real property.

One example of this legislation is Ontario's *Consumer Protection Act, 2002*,[17] which applies to all Ontario consumer transactions. For example, it covers consumer rights and warranties, credit agreements, leasing, and procedures for consumer remedies. The Act lists a number of "unfair practices," such as making a "false, misleading or deceptive representation" (s 14(1)) or pressuring a consumer to renegotiate a transaction by keeping custody or control of their goods (s 16). As well, the Act contains additional rights and obligations for some specific consumer agreements, such as those involving time shares, personal development services, and Internet agreements.

As illustrated in Box 10.4, businesses that are aware of serious defects in their products but fail to take swift action to resolve them may have punitive damages awarded against them by the courts.

Another specific area the Act covers is motor vehicle repairs, a major concern for all consumers who drive. Part VI of the Act helps to protect drivers against inflated bills for car repairs. Among its provisions are the following:

- No repairer shall charge consumers for any work or repairs without first giving them an estimate (s 56(1)).
- A repairer cannot charge a fee for giving the estimate unless the consumer is told in advance that a fee will be charged (s 57(1)).
- Repairers cannot charge for any work or repairs unless the work and repairs have been authorized by the consumer (s 58(1)).
- A repairer shall be deemed to warrant all new and reconditioned parts and labour for a minimum of 90 days or 5,000 kilometres, whichever comes first (s 63(1)).

---

17   SO 2002, c 30, Schedule A.

Punitive Damages for Failure to Protect Consumers

In the Supreme Court of Canada (SCC) case *Prebushewski v Dodge City Auto (1984) Ltd,** the consumer bought a brand new Dodge Ram half-ton truck from a dealership. She and her husband drove the truck without incident for 16 months until, one day, the husband's employer noticed a fire outside the office. The husband ran outside to discover the truck in flames. It was completely destroyed.

Both the dealer and the manufacturer denied liability, referring the consumer and her husband to their insurer. After some investigation, it was determined that the fire was caused by a defect in the daytime running light system. A representative of the manufacturer eventually testified that the manufacturer had known of this defect for several years without issuing a recall.

The trial court found a breach of a statutory warranty under the Saskatchewan *Consumer Protection Act*. In addition to

ordering regular damages of about $40,000, the trial judge ordered exemplary (punitive) damages of $25,000 against the manufacturer and dealer. The manufacturer and dealer appealed to the Court of Appeal and were successful in having the exemplary damage award struck out. The consumer appealed to the SCC.

The SCC restored the order of exemplary damages, finding that the consumer protection legislation had increased the accessibility of exemplary damages (under the common law, it is very difficult to win damages of this kind). (The Ontario *Consumer Protection Act, 2002* also permits awards of exemplary damages under s 18(11).)

* 2005 SCC 28.

Source: Reproduced from Margaret Buchan et al, *Canadian Business Law*, 2nd ed (Toronto: Emond Montgomery, 2012) at 172.

Advertising Standards

To supplement federal and provincial consumer legislation, major stakeholders in the advertising and marketing industries have formed industry associations that also help protect consumers. These associations have established self-regulating and industry-approved codes of standards and policy guidelines. Advertising Standards Canada (ASC), created in 1957, is one such body; it administers the *Canadian Code of Advertising Standards*, first published in 1963. The Code is widely endorsed by Canadian advertisers and sets out standards for advertising that is truthful, fair, and accurate in the following 14 areas:

1. accuracy and clarity,
2. disguised advertising techniques,
3. price claims,
4. bait and switch,
5. guarantees,
6. comparative advertising,
7. testimonials,
8. professional or scientific claims,
9. imitation,
10. safety,
11. superstition and fears,
12. advertising to children,
13. advertising to minors, and
14. unacceptable depictions and portrayals.

ASC updates the Code regularly to ensure that it keeps pace with consumer and societal expectations. It also administers it: the clauses above form the basis for the review of consumer and special interest group complaints, and trade disputes. As part of its commitment to a transparent consumer complaint process, ASC compiles reports of the complaints it receives and the decisions of its council on each one. The reports are listed by year on ASC's website. The following are several examples:[18]

- In 2009, an advertisement in a Punjabi-language newspaper in Ontario assured readers that, through black magic, the advertiser could eliminate all of their personal worries, fulfill all of their desires, remove all of the obstacles in the way of their marrying a loved one, and eliminate their lottery problems and business worries. The ad stated that results were 100 percent guaranteed. Council found that the ad exploited superstitions and played upon fears to mislead consumers, contrary to clause 11.
- In 2010, a manufacturer in the food/supermarkets industry in Quebec released a commercial in which a man shown in a deserted area was suddenly surrounded by a group of people who hit him repeatedly until he fell to his knees on the ground. Council considered a complaint that the commercial encouraged violence and found that, despite its humorous elements, the scenario did seem to condone violence, contrary to clause 14(b).
- In 2013, a popular Canadian clothing retailer advertised that all fall merchandise was being offered at a discount of 20-50 percent off the regular price. The complainant alleged that the discount was less than 20 percent off on many items. Council found that the ad contained a misleading savings claim contrary to clauses 1(a) and 3(a), and the advertiser agreed that the ad should have stated that only *select* items were being offered at 20-50 percent off.

---

18 Advertising Standards Canada, "Ad Complaints Reports," online: <http://www.adstandards.com/en/Standards/report.aspx>.

CHAPTER SUMMARY

There are many ways to carry on a business in Canada. The three most common business structures are the sole proprietorship, the partnership, and the corporation. Each one has its advantages and disadvantages. Sole proprietorships are relatively easy and inexpensive to set up and operate, but they are not a separate legal structure from their owners, who are liable for all debts and obligations that their businesses may incur and whose personal assets are thus put at risk.

There are several kinds of partnership structure, each with advantages and disadvantages. The *general partnership* structure is the standard one. It offers the advantage of being relatively inexpensive to create, and it provides the business with a collegial environment, an extended pool of capital based on cost-sharing, and a group of members whose connections may help the business attract new clients. Its main disadvantage is that each partner is personally liable for all of the firm's debts and liabilities, which may put the partners' personal assets at risk. A *limited partnership* has one or more general partners and one or more limited partners. A limited partner contributes money and property and shares in partnership profits, but is not liable for the partnership's obligations unless she takes part in managing the partnership. A *limited liability partnership*, if it meets certain criteria, has one key advantage: one partner is not liable for the professional negligence of the other partner(s).

A corporation is a legal entity separate from those who create it. The owners and directors are not personally liable for the company's debts and obligations, but the incorporation process can be expensive, and running a corporation can be a complicated undertaking.

All businesses engage in business transactions of various types with a view to profit. Contracts, which are frequently specialized for particular businesses, are important tools for determining rights and obligations and allocating risks. Payment methods are varied, but negotiable instruments (in particular, cheques and promissory notes) are important because they are portable, transferable, and safe. Businesses that are owed money and have rights against property have an option to register liens and other security interests to enforce their debts. In the event of non-payment, all businesses have a number of collections options, including garnishment of bank accounts and wages.

If a business is selling goods to other businesses or to consumers, sale of goods acts apply. These acts codify laws about buying and selling goods and add some basic safeguards respecting the rights of buyers and sellers. Particularly significant are the implied conditions and warranties relating to the seller's title and right to sell the goods, the correspondence of the goods with their description, and the fitness of the goods for their intended purpose.

Legislation protecting consumers has greatly expanded in recent times. Both the federal and provincial governments have enacted consumer protection statutes that are wider in scope than sale of goods acts. The federal *Competition Act* and *Food and Drugs Act*, for example, ensure that consumers have competitive prices and product choices, as well as laws protecting their health and safety respecting food, drugs, cosmetics, and medical devices manufactured and sold in Canada. Provincial consumer protection legislation, such as Ontario's *Consumer Protection Act, 2002*, protects consumers in a variety of other areas, including motor vehicle repairs. Advertising standards also aim to protect consumers by ensuring that advertising is truthful, fair, and accurate.

KEY TERMS

builders' (or construction) lien, 307

corporation, 304

fiduciary duty, 302

general partnership, 302

limited liability partnership, 303

limited partnership, 302

negotiable instrument, 306

sole proprietorship, 301

FURTHER READING

BOOKS

Alexander, Tamra & Pat Papadeas. *Canadian Business Law*, 3rd ed (Toronto: Emond, 2018).

DuPlessis, Dorothy et al. *Canadian Business and the Law*, 6th ed (Toronto: Nelson, 2017).

Ogilvie, Margaret, ed. *Consumer Law: Cases and Materials*, 3rd ed (Toronto: Captus Press, 2007).

Pritchard, Brenda & Susan Vogt. *Advertising and Marketing Law in Canada*, 5th ed (Toronto: LexisNexis, 2015).

Waddams, SM. *Products Liability*, 5th ed (Toronto: Carswell, 2011).

Weir, D Jan & Fran Smyth. *Critical Concepts of Canadian Business Law*, 6th ed (Toronto: Pearson, 2014).

Yates, Richard A, Teresa Bereznicki-Korol & Trevor Clarke, *Business Law in Canada*, 11th ed (Toronto: Pearson, 2016).

WEBSITES

Advertising Standards Canada: <http://www.adstandards.com/en>.

Cosmetics Alliance Canada: <http://www.cosmeticsalliance.ca>.

Competition Bureau: <http://www.competitionbureau.gc.ca/eic/site/cb-bc.nsf/eng/home>.

Health Canada: <http://www.hc-sc.gc.ca>.

Innovation, Science and Economic Development Canada: <http://strategis.ic.gc.ca>.

REVIEW QUESTIONS

1. List two advantages of a sole proprietorship.

2. Explain the meaning of the term *fiduciary duty*.

3. What is the advantage of a limited partnership for an investor?

4. What must be included in the name of a limited liability partnership?

5. List two main advantages to be gained by incorporating a company.

6. How can a contractor who performs work on real property—for instance, a renovation—protect herself in the event of non-payment?

7. List five implied conditions of sale under provincial sale of goods acts.

8. What are two ways the marketplace today causes difficulties for consumers who want to know more about a product before they buy it?

9. List four areas covered by the federal *Food and Drugs Act*.

EXERCISES

1. Four architects decide to form a general partnership and to work out of one office suite. List three advantages these architects could gain from such an arrangement, and list some potential problems that could arise from their partnership.

2. Why is the law providing ever more legislative protections for consumers? Is it a trend that you expect to continue? Why or why not?

3. Section 3(1) of the *Food and Drugs Act* states that "no person shall advertise any food, drug, cosmetic or device to the general public as a treatment, preventative or cure for any of the diseases, disorders or abnormal physical states referred to in Schedule A." Look at Schedule A to this Act, and discuss conditions that you think ought or ought not to be included on the list.

11 Administrative Law

After reading this chapter, you will understand:

- The nature of administrative law.
- The role of administrative agencies in society, their constitutional basis, and limitations on their power.
- The structure and functions of administrative agencies.

- Rights of appeal and grounds for judicial review.
- The various remedial options available when challenging administrative decisions.

> A dministrative law deals with the legal limitations on the actions of governmental officials, and with the remedies which are available to anyone affected by a transgression of these limitations.
>
> David P Jones & Anne S de Villars, *Principles of Administrative Law*,
> 6th ed (Toronto: Carswell, 2014) at 3

Introduction

Administrative law is a subcategory of public domestic law, and its objective, as one writer has stated, "is to regulate the relationships between the government and governed—the population."[1] Although criminal law is often highlighted when considering a person's relationship to the state, for the average person, administrative law is more important because it concerns how we interact with and are regulated by governments in many areas of everyday life.

Such interaction and regulation influence our lives from beginning to end and help define our place in society. For example, medical boards regulate the practices by which we are brought into the world. School boards determine what we learn. New Canadians interact with the Immigration and Refugee Board of Canada when it applies immigration laws to them. When we build our homes, building codes and municipal inspectors control our choices. The decisions of energy boards and utility commissions affect the price we pay for energy and fuel to keep ourselves warm. If an issue arises involving our employment, labour relations boards, workers' compensation boards, and human rights tribunals may be called upon to resolve our disputes. The Canadian Radio-television and Telecommunications Commission determines what we can watch for entertainment and the rates we pay to communicate with one another. The food we eat and drugs we ingest, the investments we make, the privacy we enjoy (or don't)—in fact, almost all aspects of our lives—are regulated to varying degrees through the instrument of administrative law.[2]

---

1   Guy Régimbald, *Canadian Administrative Law*, 2nd ed (Toronto: LexisNexis, 2015) at 1.

2   See also Sara Blake, *Administrative Law in Canada*, 6th ed (Toronto: LexisNexis, 2017) at 3 and *Newfoundland Telephone Co v Newfoundland (Board of Commissioners of Public Utilities)*, [1992] 1 SCR 623 at 634-35, 89 DLR (4th) 28.

However, the influence of administrative law, though inescapable, has its limits. The mass of regulation permeating modern societies, while connected to administrative law, is also separate from it in a sense. Complaints we may have with the amount or quality of government regulation (most of it in the form of subordinate legislation, as described in Chapter 4) are more political than legal in nature. Administrative law is not so much about the *value* of our regulation as it is about the *manner* in which this regulation is imposed on us. Put another way, "[i]t is more concerned with *the process for making a decision* than with the result."[3]

In this chapter, we examine the role of regulatory bodies in society. We consider the constitutional framework in which they operate and important limitations on their power connected to the delegatory relationship they have with governments. The structure and functions of administrative agencies are also examined, along with a consideration of the principal methods and grounds for challenging their decisions, and the types of remedies that may be claimed when seeking relief.

To see how administrative law is situated overall as an area of law in Canada, review Figure 1.1, "Divisions of Law," in Chapter 1.

The Role of Administrative Agencies in Society

Governments and elected officials cannot participate directly in all aspects of the implementation of our laws. This is due both to the *quantity* of regulation applicable to most activities involving the public and to the *complexity* of this regulation. To fulfill their obligation to administer the law, governments delegate many of their responsibilities to administrative agencies. **Administrative agencies** are regulatory bodies created under various federal, provincial, and territorial statutes. Their purpose is to administer the legislative schemes set out in these enabling statutes and their regulations. The word *agency* in this context simply means any person, institution, body, board, or tribunal that has been assigned governance powers under legislation.[4]

Delegating tasks to administrative agencies offers a number of advantages for both governments and the public. First, it speeds things up. Having more decision-makers on the ground enables the government to respond more quickly and efficiently to the needs of the public. A second advantage is specialization; agency officials are usually appointed on the basis of their familiarity with the area of regulation. Such expertise produces better decisions, which can, in turn, enhance the credibility of government.

As indicated, the reach of administrative agencies is extensive. They include not only traditional government entities—such as licensing bodies, securities commissions, and labour boards—but also hospitals, universities, self-regulating professions, and certain trade associations that have been delegated regulatory authority under legislation.

administrative agency
government bodies created under various federal, provincial, and territorial statutes with the purpose of administering particular statutory regimes

---

3   Blake, *ibid* at 4 (emphasis added).

4   Administrative agencies are referred to in various ways. Generically speaking, they are known as *bodies*, *entities*, or *agencies*. Their actual names or titles commonly include, if not the word *agency*, one of the following terms: *board*, *commission*, *council*, *institution*, *office*, *organization*, *service*, or *tribunal*. Generally, an agency's name tells us little about its particular delegated function. There is one exception to this. An administrative body that is referred to as a *tribunal* usually performs quasi-judicial functions (discussed in more detail below).

To appreciate their influence, it is important to understand:

- how these delegated entities are structured;
- the ways in which they interact with "the governed";
- the extent of their jurisdiction—that is, the types of activities they can engage in and the types of decisions they can make; and
- the means by which their actions and decisions can be challenged.

The following sections explore these issues in more detail.

The Constitutional Basis of Administrative Agencies

How do we determine whether the constitutional authority to create an administrative agency comes from the federal government or from the provincial government? We look to the *Constitution Act, 1867*,[5] which tells us which level of government has jurisdiction over the subject matter of the agency's enabling statute. To take one example, section 91(23) of the *Constitution Act, 1867* gives the federal government jurisdiction over copyrights. Thus empowered, the federal government has enacted legislation creating the Copyright Board, a federal administrative tribunal that makes decisions about copyright.

The provinces have jurisdiction over other areas. Section 92(8) of the *Constitution Act, 1867*, for example, gives the provinces power over "Municipal Institutions." With this power, the provinces have enacted legislation under which cities, towns, and other municipal organizations are created. The territories have a parallel jurisdiction assigned to them.

There are several constitutional provisions that are specifically relevant to administrative law. For instance, the federal government's power to appoint and to pay delegated officials to sit on administrative agencies is specifically reinforced under section 91(8) of the *Constitution Act, 1867*. The provincial government's power in this regard is spelled out in section 92(4).

Constitutional Limitations on Administrative Tribunals

As explained below, administrative agencies may be assigned different functions. Sometimes they are given the power to resolve disputes and exercise court-like (or quasi-judicial) functions. For example, a labour board may hear a dispute between an employer and a union about the right to picket. When court-like functions are assigned to an agency in this way, it is acting like a tribunal. One significant constitutional limitation on a government's ability to delegate court-like powers to administrative agencies is that the agency thus created must not be too close in operation to a section 96 court—that is, a provincial superior court (see Chapter 6).

If the constitutionality of an administrative agency's powers is challenged in court on the basis of this limitation, the court has to make a determination, based on three questions:

1. whether the subject matter of the dispute is one that had been historically assigned (that is, by common law at the time of Confederation) to superior courts;

---

5   (UK), 30 & 31 Vict, c 3, reprinted in RSC 1985, Appendix II, No 5.

2. whether the tribunal is exercising a judicial function by applying recognized rules in an impartial manner to resolve disputes; and

3. whether the judicial function is part of a wider institutional framework or whether, as with a section 96 court, the adjudicative role is its sole or primary function.

If the tribunal is exercising a power similar to that of a traditional superior court and is resolving disputes as a court does (that is, applying recognized rules), it may still be acceptable as an administrative agency if the decision-making aspect of its jurisdiction is merely *part* of what it does.

If the tribunal resembles a provincial superior court in all three ways, then it will be deemed to be a section 96 court and will be required, like other superior courts, to have federally appointed judges. Without federally appointed judges, the agency will be declared unconstitutional. This is a problem for provincial boards (and provincial inferior courts) that have been delegated too much power and too many responsibilities.

The requirement that only federally appointed judges can hear matters at the superior court level can be problematic for federal administrative tribunals as well as for provincial ones. It is not uncommon for some panellists on administrative tribunals to be lay appointees without formal legal training. Their qualifications and the process by which they are appointed are not necessarily the same as those for superior court judges.

Delegated Power and Functions of Administrative Agencies

Administrative agencies can exercise only power that has been delegated to them by the federal government or by provincial (or territorial) governments. They are charged with administering the legislative regime set out in the legislation that created (or enabled) them.

The government functions that can be delegated to these agencies reflect the three branches of government itself:

1. *legislative* functions (for example, passing by-laws or rules of procedure for appearing before a tribunal),

2. *administrative* or executive functions (for example, issuing business licences), and

3. *quasi-judicial* functions (for example, rendering decisions in labour disputes, as noted above).

A single administrative body may exercise more than one function. When an administrative action or decision is challenged, the available remedies vary according to function. For example, there are fewer opportunities to challenge legislative actions than administrative ones. (Challenging administrative decisions is discussed later in this section.)

With most administrative agencies, a single level of government—federal or provincial (or territorial)—creates an agency and delegates to it all the power it needs (basic delegation). But it is sometimes the case, depending on the area of regulation for which the agency is responsible, that an agency will require powers from more than one level of government.

Under the Constitution, *cross-delegation*—that is, the process whereby one level of government delegates power directly to the other level—is not permitted.[6] However, the

---

6 *Nova Scotia (AG) v Canada (AG)*, [1951] SCR 31, [1950] SCJ No 32 (QL).

Supreme Court of Canada (SCC) has recognized that *inter-delegation*, whereby one level of government creates an agency and the agency subsequently receives some of its power from the other level of government, *is* permissible.[7] For instance, a provincial agency that normally licenses trade within the province (*intra*provincial trade) may wish to license a business to do some trade outside the province (*inter*provincial trade). Interprovincial trade, however, is under federal jurisdiction. In this case, the federal government could delegate some power to that provincial agency. A final type of delegation arrangement is *subdelegation* (or redelegation), whereby an agency attempts to further delegate some of the power it has already received. Subdelegation is generally not permitted unless the enabling legislation authorizes it. This is the *delegatus non potest delegare* principle described in Chapter 4 in connection with subordinate legislation. For example, municipalities—which themselves exercise delegated power—are not able to delegate the power to make by-laws to a subordinate body they create, such as a planning committee. Figure 11.1, below, illustrates these delegation principles.

Administrative agencies, regardless of the delegation arrangement they involve or the particular functions they have been delegated, operate as part of the executive branch of government and are controlled by it, with the legislative branch authorizing the executive branch's power in this regard.

Legislative Functions

Administrative agencies fulfill legislative functions in two main areas: (1) municipal institutions making by-laws and (2) quasi-judicial tribunals creating rules of procedure.

In the case of municipalities, the delegation of legislative authority to administrative agencies works in the following way. The provincial or territorial legislation that provides for the incorporation of local governments delegates to these governments the power to pass by-laws. These by-laws concern a wide range of municipal matters, including the following:

- raising taxes for schools and utilities,
- setting zoning requirements, and
- city planning and land use.

The provincial or territorial legislation sets out procedures for passing by-laws, and these procedures usually parallel those for enacting primary legislation (see Chapter 4). As with primary legislation, for example, the enacting of by-laws usually requires three readings and the opportunity for public input.

Administrative tribunals with quasi-judicial powers can also fulfill legislative functions insofar as they are frequently empowered to make their own rules governing how they hold hearings and how they resolve disputes.

Administrative Functions

Many executive or administrative functions are commonly delegated to administrative bodies. The issuing of licences and permits is one such function. In Canada, licences are mandatory for numerous activities. This country requires, for example, driver's licences, fishing and hunting licences, business licences, liquor licences, broadcasting licences, special event permits, building permits, and pollution permits. All of these licences and permits require applications to administrative agencies.

---

7   *Coughlin v The Ontario Highway Transport Board*, [1968] SCR 569, 1968 CanLII 2.

FIGURE 11.1 Basic Rules of Delegation

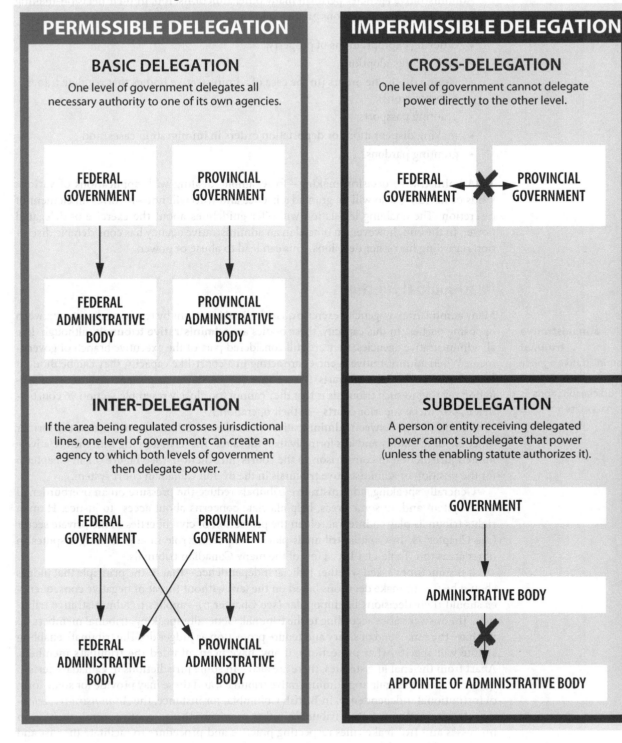

PERMISSIBLE DELEGATION

BASIC DELEGATION
One level of government delegates all necessary authority to one of its own agencies.

FEDERAL GOVERNMENT

PROVINCIAL GOVERNMENT

FEDERAL ADMINISTRATIVE BODY

PROVINCIAL ADMINISTRATIVE BODY

INTER-DELEGATION
If the area being regulated crosses jurisdictional lines, one level of government can create an agency to which both levels of government then delegate power.

FEDERAL GOVERNMENT

PROVINCIAL GOVERNMENT

FEDERAL ADMINISTRATIVE BODY

PROVINCIAL ADMINISTRATIVE BODY

IMPERMISSIBLE DELEGATION

CROSS-DELEGATION
One level of government cannot delegate power directly to the other level.

FEDERAL GOVERNMENT

PROVINCIAL GOVERNMENT

SUBDELEGATION
A person or entity receiving delegated power cannot subdelegate that power (unless the enabling statute authorizes it).

GOVERNMENT

ADMINISTRATIVE BODY

APPOINTEE OF ADMINISTRATIVE BODY

Administrative agencies perform many other functions, too, in their decision-making capacity. Among these functions are the following:

- ordering expropriations of property,
- authorizing adoptions,
- issuing discipline orders (in the case of administrative bodies that regulate trades or professions),
- granting passports,
- making dispensations or deportation orders in immigration cases, and
- granting pardons.

Administrative decision making—for example, dealing with applications of various kinds or deciding who will be granted a licence and who will not—involves an element of discretion. The enabling legislation will offer guidelines about the exercise of delegated power. In the end, however, an official in an administrative agency has considerable discretion regarding his or her decisions. This can lead to abuse of power.

Quasi-Judicial Functions

administrative tribunal

administrative agency that fulfills quasi-judicial functions as part of its mandate

Many administrative agencies exercise quasi-judicial functions by resolving disputes between opposing parties. In this capacity, these bodies are **administrative tribunals**, although, like all administrative agencies, they are still considered part of the executive branch of government. When administrative agencies are acting in a court-like capacity, they can be thought of as cousins to the inferior courts. (As we have discussed, one important constitutional limitation relating to such tribunals is that they cannot too closely resemble section 96 courts—that is, provincial superior courts—in their operation.)

The difference between administrative tribunals and inferior courts is that the former function more quickly and less formally than the latter. This is in keeping with their relatively limited jurisdiction in comparison to the courts' jurisdiction. (See Figure 6.1 in Chapter 6 for the position of administrative tribunals in the overall Canadian court system.)

Generally speaking, administrative tribunals reduce the pressure on an overburdened court system and, in some areas, help alleviate concerns about access to justice. Human rights tribunals play an integral role in the protection of civil liberties in the private sector (see Chapter 7). In Canada, tribunals play an important role in adjudicating disputes in other areas too. Table 11.1 lists a few of the many Canadian tribunals.

It is sometimes asked whether judicial independence—that is, the principle that judges should be free to make decisions based on the law, without threat of negative consequences should their decisions be unpopular (see Chapter 6)—applies to administrative tribunals. The answer varies according to the tribunal. Generally speaking, tribunal members do not have the same kind of salary and tenure protection as judges do. The tribunal's enabling statute will specify what protections, if any, have been afforded the tribunal's members. Apart from the enabling statutes, there are also—in some jurisdictions in Canada—certain "general" statutes regulating administrative tribunals, and these may provide for some form of institutional independence. In British Columbia, for instance, the *Administrative Tribunals Act* gives administrative tribunals in that province "the power to control [their] own processes and [to] make rules respecting practice and procedure to facilitate the just and timely resolution of the matters before [them]."[8] It is necessary to review these statutes to determine a tribunal's degree of judicial independence.

---

8 SBC 2004, c 45, s 11. See also Alberta's *Administrative Procedures and Jurisdiction Act*, RSA 2000, c A-3 and Ontario's *Statutory Powers Procedure Act*, RSO 1990, c S.22.

TABLE 11.1 Administrative Tribunals by Subject and Jurisdiction

SUBJECT	JURISDICTION	ADMINISTRATIVE TRIBUNALS
Access to Information	British Columbia	Information and Privacy Commissioner
	Ontario	Information and Privacy Commissioner
Aeronautics	Federal	Canada Civil Aviation Tribunal
Corporate, Commercial Law	Federal	Competition Tribunal
	British Columbia	BC Securities Commission, Commercial Appeals Commission, Liquor Appeal Board
	Ontario	Securities Commission
Energy	Federal	National Energy Board
	Alberta	Energy Resources Conservation Board
	British Columbia	BC Utilities Commission
	Ontario	Energy Board
Environmental Law	Alberta	Environmental Appeal Board
	Ontario	Environmental Review Tribunal
Forestry Law	British Columbia	Forest Practices Board
Human Rights	Federal	Canadian Human Rights Tribunal
	British Columbia	BC Human Rights Tribunal
	Nova Scotia	Human Rights Commission
	Ontario	Human Rights Tribunal of Ontario
Immigration	Federal	Immigration and Refugee Board of Canada
Intellectual Property	Federal	Copyright Board, Patent Appeal Board, Trade-marks Opposition Board
Labour and Employment Law	Federal	Canada Industrial Relations Board, Public Service Relations Board, Umpires under the *Employment Insurance Act**
	Alberta	Workers' Compensation Appeals Commission
	British Columbia	Labour Relations Board, Employment Standards Tribunal, Workers' Compensation Board
	Manitoba	Labour Board
	Ontario	Workplace Safety and Insurance Appeals Tribunal
Telecommunications	Federal	Canadian Radio-television and Telecommunications Commission
Trade	Federal	Canadian International Trade Tribunal
Transportation	Federal	Canadian Transportation Agency

* SC 1996, c 23.

The Public's Interaction with Administrative Bodies

Most interactions between the public and administrative agencies occur in connection with the latter's exercise of administrative or quasi-judicial functions. But tribunals' legislative functions can be particularly significant where the public is concerned. These legislative activities are the source, for example, of proposed municipal by-laws that may affect the public interest, and the process may allow for members of the public to consult with the tribunals about such by-laws.

Generally speaking, there are two sets of rules for the public to be aware of when dealing with administrative bodies: substantive rules and procedural rules.

Substantive Rules

Substantive rules are the public's fundamental rights and obligations with respect to an administrative regime. For the most part, these rules will be found in the relevant legislation. For example, if a person were applying for a broadcasting licence from the Canadian Radio-television and Telecommunications Commission (CRTC), the substantive rules of which the applicant needs to be aware—for example, Canadian-content restrictions and the various media delivery limitations—are located in the *Canadian Radio-television and Telecommunications Commission Act*,[9] the *Broadcasting Act*,[10] and a few other statutes, along with the regulations passed pursuant to them. The substantive rules will also include any CRTC and judicial interpretations of the legislation.

Occasionally, substantive rules may be found in the common law as well, such as in the area of civil liberties (for example, the right of free speech).

A review of all the relevant substantive rules is the first step in dealing successfully with administrative agencies.

Procedural Rules

Many administrative agencies have established their own rules of practice and procedure that members of the public must follow in order to move forward with applications and hearings. These rules concern such things as what documents need to be filed with the agency, who else needs to receive copies, what the timelines are, and whether legal representation is allowed. Generally, the procedural rules for administrative agencies are less formal or rigid than those for court proceedings.

When trying to determine what the procedural rules are, one begins by checking the enabling legislation, then proceed to the administrative agency itself. Checking agency websites and contacting agency personnel are generally the best ways to obtain information about procedural rules.

In addition to considering the legislated rules that are in place for a particular administrative agency, one must also consider common law rules. Common law rules concerning procedural

---

9 RSC 1985, c C-22.

10 SC 1991, c 11.

fairness and natural justice in relation to administrative bodies are well established (see below). They must be followed unless they have been abrogated by the legislation.

Challenging Administrative Decisions

A party negatively affected by an administrative decision (or action) may wish to challenge it. There are various means of doing so. The following discussion primarily concerns decisions involving administrative and quasi-judicial functions.

Internal Means of Challenge

As a first step, a party wishing to contest an administrative decision should exhaust all internal means of challenge. The agency structure may have mechanisms providing for this. Once these options have been exhausted, it may be necessary to consider intervention by the courts.

Challenging in the Courts

There are two ways in which an administrative decision can be challenged in the courts: on appeal or by judicial review. Note that the expression *judicial review* in this context refers to the review of the decisions of administrative bodies and is not the same as judicial review of provincial and federal legislation on constitutional grounds, as discussed in Chapters 3 and 4.

    The process of appealing an administrative decision is generally similar to the process of appealing a court decision. The difference has to do with the scope of the appeal available and the remedies available. When a court decision is appealed, the court engages in a full substantive reconsideration of the merits of the decision, corrects any errors that were made, and makes orders as it normally would. With an administrative decision, the scope of the appeal and the available remedies are always subject to the enabling legislation. Generally speaking, *any right to appeal exists only if the enabling legislation expressly provides for it.* There is no inherent common law right to appeal an administrative decision. Where the enabling legislation does provide for such a right, the person contesting the administrative decision must go this route before mounting a challenge by the other possible means—namely, judicial review.

    Judicial review, as a means of challenging an administrative decision, is a final option. Sara Blake has made this point as follows:

> Application to the court for review of a decision of an inferior tribunal should be made only as a last resort. Parties should take advantage of internal procedures available to a tribunal to correct its errors and of rights of appeal granted by statute. These other ways of correcting tribunal errors tend to be more satisfactory especially as an application for judicial review may be dismissed for failure to pursue other processes. Only when those routes are unavailable, or have been tried without success, should parties resort to judicial review.[11]

    Judicial review of an administrative decision tends to be more limited in scope than proceeding by way of an appeal (when such a right is granted by statute). Substantive

judicial review (of decisions by administrative bodies)
process by which a superior court can review the decision of an administrative body or inferior court on a number of grounds, including substantive review (review of the merits of the decision), review of discretionary decisions, and procedural review (review of the *process* followed in making the decision)

---

11 Blake, *supra* note 2 at 193.

reviews are possible, but they are not typical. When it comes to procedural reviews, for example, the courts are confined to reviewing the *process* by which decisions have been reached.

Jurisdiction of Superior Courts to Review

The provincial superior courts have an inherent common law power to oversee and review the decisions of both inferior courts and administrative boards and tribunals. This jurisdiction has been modified by legislation. The *Federal Courts Act*[12] assigns exclusive jurisdiction to review federal tribunals to the Federal Court and to the Federal Court of Appeal.

Sections 18 and 18.1 of the *Federal Courts Act* combine to give the Federal Court exclusive power to review federal agencies in general. The exceptions are set out in section 28 of the Act; it gives the Federal Court of Appeal exclusive jurisdiction to review the decisions of certain federal agencies, which are specifically identified. Section 28 provides in part that:

> 28(1) The Federal Court of Appeal has jurisdiction to hear and determine applications for judicial review made in respect of any of the following federal boards, commissions or other tribunals:
>
> (a) the Board of Arbitration established by the *Canada Agricultural Products Act*;
>
> (b) the Review Tribunal established by the *Canada Agricultural Products Act*;
>
> (b.1) the Conflict of Interest and Ethics Commissioner appointed under section 81 of the *Parliament of Canada Act*;
>
> (c) the Canadian Radio-television and Telecommunications Commission established by the *Canadian Radio-television and Telecommunications Commission Act*; ...
>
> (e) the Canadian International Trade Tribunal established by the *Canadian International Trade Tribunal Act*;
>
> (f) the National Energy Board established by the *National Energy Board Act*. ...

Section 28 goes on to list other tribunals over which the Federal Court of Appeal has the power of review. These include the following:

- the Canada Industrial Relations Board,
- the Public Service Labour Relations and Employment Board,
- the Copyright Board,
- the Canadian Transportation Agency,
- the Competition Tribunal,
- the Public Servants Disclosure Protection Tribunal, and
- the Specific Claims Tribunal.

To summarize, the *Federal Courts Act* gives the Federal Court of Appeal exclusive jurisdiction over certain federal agencies and the Federal Court exclusive jurisdiction over all the others. The provincial superior courts, based on what remains of their inherent common law jurisdiction, have exclusive jurisdiction over provincial agencies, but have no general

---

12 RSC 1985, c F-7.

power of review over federal ones. Review of territorial tribunal decisions is assigned by federal legislation to the territorial superior courts.

Privative Clauses

A privative clause is a statutory provision that restricts or prevents altogether the judicial review of an administrative agency's decision. Legislatures sometimes include such provisions because they want a particular administrative process to be final. There can be a variety of reasons for their wanting this finality—for example, the special expertise of the tribunal officials may make judicial review of their decision especially difficult.

The specific terms of the statutory provision will determine the limits of judicial review. Judicial review is always a possibility, however, whatever the legislation says. Even where a privative clause states that the administrative agency's decision is "final and conclusive" or states that the tribunal has "exclusive jurisdiction" in the matter or states—even more strongly—that judicial review is prohibited, the court has the jurisdiction to review. Any attempt by a legislature to enact a privative clause so strong as to exclude review in all cases— even in a case, for example, where a tribunal has exceeded its jurisdiction—would likely be declared unconstitutional.

This is not to say that the privative clause has no function. The strength of the privative clause is one of the factors the court will consider in determining how much deference it will pay to the administrative decision. The clearer and stronger the privative clause, the more the court will defer to the administrative agency's decision. In the end, however, the courts always have the right to review an administrative agency's decision. Let's say, for example—to take an extreme case—a labour board passed a decision ordering a union official to assassinate the head of a multinational corporation. In such a case, even a privative clause clearly prohibiting review by the court under any circumstances would not prevent the judicial review of the board's decision.

Grounds for Review

There are several possible bases for challenging administrative decisions by review. They are variously named in federal, provincial, and territorial legislation as well as in the academic literature on the subject. Recent case law emphasizes three broad grounds: (1) substantive review, (2) review of discretionary decisions, and (3) procedural review. These grounds are distinct, but, in a given case, more than one ground may be cited (see Box 11.1).

Substantive Review

Substantive review refers to a review that considers both the legal and factual bases of the tribunal's analysis. When conducting a review of this kind, the courts have to first decide what **standard of review** is applicable. The standard of review defines the level of deference the court pays to the tribunal. The SCC has recently simplified this decision-making area, stating that there are only two standards of review: (1) correctness and (2) reasonableness.[13]

When, in the course of a substantive review, the court is reviewing the legal basis of an administrative decision, it applies the correctness standard and pays no deference to the

substantive review
review of an administrative decision's merits that considers both the legal and factual bases of the tribunal's analysis

standard of review
defines the level of deference the court pays to the tribunal when conducting a judicial review

---

13 *Dunsmuir v New Brunswick*, 2008 SCC 9.

tribunal. It simply substitutes its decision for the tribunal's. The legality of a decision is in issue when the court is reviewing fundamental questions of law—for example, whether the tribunal had the jurisdiction to make the particular decision being reviewed. When a tribunal has made a decision it had no authority to make under the enabling legislation, it has exceeded its jurisdiction. Such a decision is said to be *ultra vires*, or without jurisdiction. (A decision by a tribunal that is within its jurisdiction is *intra vires*.) Jurisdictional questions usually turn on statutory interpretation and the intended scope of delegated power under the legislation. For example, a provincial human rights tribunal would clearly have no jurisdiction to issue a federal patent for a new type of cellphone. The courts would review such a decision according to the correctness standard.

When reviewing decisions with regard to less fundamental questions of law, or to fact, discretion, or policy, the court applies the reasonableness standard. Here, instead of simply substituting its own decision for the tribunal's, the court pays deference to the tribunal. It does so in the following way. First, it will determine if any previous cases have already defined the level of deference owed the tribunal. If such cases exist and a level of deference has been established, the court will generally follow the established level. If there are no precedents of this kind, the court will determine the level of deference by referring to a number of factors, including the following:

- whether the enabling legislation contains a privative clause, and
- whether the agency adjudicator possesses expertise in relation to the matter in question.

If the legislation contains a privative clause and the adjudicator who made the decision possesses expertise in the area, the decision under review will have to be clearly unreasonable before the court will overturn it.

It is the reference to different standards of review that distinguishes judicial review of an administrative decision from substantive review based on a statutory right of appeal. In the latter case, the standard is always correctness in the opinion of the court.

Review of Discretionary Decisions

Review of discretionary decisions is hard to categorize. Depending on how discretion is exercised, it can have aspects of either a substantive error or a procedural one (as described next).

fairness (also procedural fairness or natural justice) principle that fairness requires that certain "rights" be accorded to persons engaged with an administrative process, such as the right to notice, the right to be heard and to respond, the right to representation, and the right to an adjudicator who is free from bias or an appearance of bias

Administrative officials must exercise any discretion delegated to them under legislation with a view to furthering the legislative objectives. The granting of licences, for example, involves a discretionary element (that is, the agency *may* grant a licence to someone who applies for one). In exercising discretion, administrative officials must not act arbitrarily or capriciously or be influenced by factors that are unconnected with advancing the legislative purposes—for example, by considerations related to personal gain, religious beliefs, or political leanings. Conversely, they must not neglect to consider relevant factors under the legislation (see Box 11.1).

Procedural Review

Arguments concerning process or procedure generate the most litigation. Even if there are no substantive issues surrounding a decision and no problems with the exercise of discretion, there may still be procedural grounds for review.

At common law, administrative officials are required to adhere to standards of **fairness**, also referred to as **procedural fairness** or **natural justice**, when making decisions that affect a person's interests. Natural justice dictates that certain rights will be accorded to persons engaged with an administrative process, regardless of whether the process involved is administrative or quasi-judicial. Some of these rights include the following:

- the right to notice (in other words, the right to know what the opposing case is),
- the right to be heard and to respond,
- the right to representation,
- the right to cross-examine,
- the right to reasons, and
- the right to an adjudicator who is free from bias or an appearance of bias.

BOX 11.1

Discretion and Procedural Fairness in Administrative Decisions

In 1992, Mavis Baker was ordered to be deported to Jamaica. She came to Canada in 1981 as a visitor but never received permanent resident status. When her visitor's visa expired, she stayed in Canada and worked illegally as a live-in domestic worker. During her time in Canada, she had four children, all Canadian citizens. She also suffered from mental illness, for which she was receiving treatment.

The deportation order required her to apply for permanent residency status from outside Canada. She argued that she should be exempted from this requirement on humanitarian and compassionate grounds; the order would cause her to be separated from her children, and treatment for her mental condition might not be available in Jamaica.

The senior immigration officer handling her file gave her the opportunity to make written submissions but not to appear in person and make oral submissions. She argued that this infringed her right to procedural fairness. Her case eventually made it to the SCC.* The SCC held that procedural fairness was a flexible and variable concept. She had been given the opportunity to respond fully and completely in writing, and this was sufficient in the circumstances. The court deemed that there was no violation of the requirement of procedural fairness.

However, the court went on to hold that the immigration officer, in exercising his discretion, had failed to consider important factors relevant under the legislation, such as the impact of the decision on Ms Baker's children. The order was overturned on this basis.

* *Baker v Canada (Minister of Citizenship and Immigration)*, [1999] 2 SCR 817, 1999 CanLII 699.

The degree of fairness and the number of these rights that natural justice requires in a particular case will vary according to a number of factors, including the following:

1. the nature of the decision to be made by the administrative body,
2. the relationship existing between that body and the individual, and
3. the effect of that decision on the individual's rights.

Legislation may also dictate that certain procedural standards be adhered to in a given situation. Generally, the more significant the decision's impact, the more procedural safeguards that will be required.[14] For instance, a decision that resulted in a person losing her

14   See *Knight v Indian Head School Division No 19*, [1990] 1 SCR 653, 1990 CanLII 138, the leading case in Canada on procedural fairness.

job or means of livelihood would trigger more procedural protection than a decision denying a person the right to light fireworks in her backyard on her birthday.

Remedies on Review

prerogative writs
special common law remedies for administrative infractions

A number of special common law remedies are available to those who have suffered as a result of substantive or procedural errors made by administrative bodies. These remedies, called **prerogative writs**, are granted following an application to the superior courts. There are various kinds of prerogative writs (see Box 11.2). Historically, subjects would apply to the Crown, which could issue these writs as part of the monarch's royal prerogative power (see Chapter 5). Control over these writs has long since passed into the hands of the courts.

In addition to prerogative writs, the courts also have the power to grant injunctive relief (that is, ordering someone to do something) as well as declaratory relief (that is, simply declaring what the legal position is). Most provinces and territories have now enacted legislation simplifying the procedure for applying for prerogative writs and for these other remedies. At one time, a separate application was required for each prerogative writ. Ontario and British Columbia have the simplest application procedure. In these provinces, one statutory application for judicial review serves as an application for all available remedies (except damages).[15]

In addition to any rights of appeal or review, a person challenging an administrative decision may also have a private law claim, depending on the circumstances.[16]

BOX 11.2

Prerogative Writs

The main prerogative writs are the following:

- Writ of *certiorari*: In the context of Canadian judicial review proceedings, this kind of writ is used to "quash" or overturn an administrative body's decision in cases where there have been substantive errors, abuse of discretion, or procedural unfairness.
- Writ of prohibition: This writ is an order, issued by the superior court, requiring the administrative body not to proceed with a planned action.
- Writ of *mandamus*: This writ is the reverse of a writ of prohibition. It is an order by the superior court requiring the administrative body to proceed with an action it wouldn't have proceeded with otherwise (for example,

the court might order the administrative body to issue a permit).
- Writ of *quo warranto*: With this remedy, a public official is ordered to give up his office because he has not been validly appointed. Such an order would of course prevent the official from making any official decisions.
- Writ of *habeas corpus*: This most ancient of the prerogative writs is mentioned in the *Magna Carta* of 1215. It concerns the lawfulness of an individual's detention by government authorities. Today it is most significant in connection with the detention of immigrants (by immigration officials), of prisoners (by prison officials), of children (by child protection agencies), and of the mentally disabled (by mental health facilities).

---

15 See the *Judicial Review Procedure Act*, RSBC 1996, c 241, and *Judicial Review Procedure Act*, RSO 1990, c J.1.

16 Sometimes, it is possible to sue agencies in negligence if they have been careless in carrying out their duties under legislation. A number of cases involving negligent inspections have resulted in successful claims for damages. For example, see *Just v British Columbia*, [1989] 2 SCR 1228, 1989 CanLII 16. And if a government official abuses his discretionary power, damages in tort based on a claim of "abuse of power" may be recoverable.

CHAPTER SUMMARY

Administrative law is an important area of public domestic law that affects individuals and businesses in various contexts. Because of the degree and complexity of regulation in developed societies today, it is necessary for governments to delegate many governmental tasks to specialized agencies. Administrative law is concerned with the governance structures of these agencies and the limitations on their powers in their dealings with the objects of their power: the governed.

Some limits on the power of administrative agencies are based on the Constitution—specifically, rules relating to the delegation of power. For instance, if the federal government sets up an administrative agency under federal legislation, as a general rule only matters over which Parliament has jurisdiction under the Constitution can be delegated to the agency (inter-delegation is an exception to this, allowing the provinces to delegate some power to federal agencies). A similar approach applies to provincial boards. Another important limitation relates to the power of governments to set up tribunals exercising court-like functions. Administrative tribunals whose sole or primary function is to exercise powers that were traditionally assigned to section 96 courts must have federally appointed judges.

Regulatory agencies are created under specific statutes—federal, provincial, or territorial—that determine their structure and outline many of the rules governing their interactions with the public. Their functions range from making rules and regulations to administering the law and adjudicating disputes.

The public can challenge administrative decisions in various ways. The exact methods depend on the particular agency, its functions, and the legislation involved. A statutory right of appeal, if available, is the most effective method. When such a right of appeal exists, the scope of the appeal and the available remedies are determined by and subject to the enabling legislation.

If there is no statutory right of appeal, the decision can be challenged through judicial review. Judicial review of regulatory decisions is based on one of three broad grounds: (1) substantive review of the merits of the decision; (2) review of discretionary decisions; and (3) procedural review, which concerns the fairness of the process by which the decision was reached. Key remedies on review include the writs of *certiorari* (used to *quash* or overturn an administrative body's unlawful decision), *mandamus* (which orders an administrative body to proceed with an action it wouldn't have proceeded with otherwise, such as issuing a permit), and *habeas corpus* (which concerns the lawfulness of an individual's detention by government authorities, such as in immigration or child protection cases).

KEY TERMS

administrative agency, 319

administrative tribunal, 324

fairness (also procedural fairness or natural justice), 330

judicial review (of decisions by administrative bodies), 327

prerogative writs, 332

standard of review, 329

substantive review, 329

FURTHER READING

BOOKS

Blake, Sara. *Administrative Law in Canada*, 6th ed (Toronto: LexisNexis, 2017).

Jones, David P & Anne S de Villars. *Principles of Administrative Law*, 6th ed (Toronto: Carswell, 2014).

Mullan, David J. *Administrative Law* (Toronto: Irwin Law, 2001).

Régimbald, Guy. *Canadian Administrative Law*, 2nd ed (Toronto: LexisNexis, 2015).

Swaigen, John & Jasteena Dhillon. *Administrative Law: Principles and Advocacy*, 3rd ed (Toronto: Emond, 2016).

WEBSITE

Research Guide for Canadian Administrative Boards and
Tribunal Decisions: <http://guides.library.ubc.ca/
cases/can>.

REVIEW QUESTIONS

1. What three factors do the courts consider in
determining whether an administrative tribunal is too
close in operation to a section 96 court?

2. What does *inter-delegation* refer to in relation to an
administrative body's power?

3. Name and briefly describe the three general types of
functions or powers that are delegated to
administrative agencies.

4. Explain the difference between substantive and
procedural rules as they relate to dealings with
administrative agencies.

5. Which court has exclusive jurisdiction to review
Copyright Board decisions?

6. Describe the remedy sought with the prerogative writ
of *quo warranto*.

EXERCISES

1. Using the Canadian Administrative Boards and
Tribunal Decisions database link provided above,
select a board or tribunal (human rights, labour, or
employment standards, for example) and then choose
a decision listed in the database. Read the decision
and prepare a short summary of it.

2. In your own words, explain how the "standard of
review" concept limits the judicial review of
administrative decisions in comparison with a full
appeal of such a decision.

3. Locate and read the full text of the decision in *Baker v
Canada (Minister of Citizenship and Immigration)*,
[1999] 2 SCR 817, 1999 CanLII 699 (see Box 11.1).
Prepare a short commentary on this decision
explaining why you agree or disagree with the court's
reasons for overturning Baker's deportation order on
the basis that the immigration officer had failed to
take into account important factors in exercising his
discretion under the legislation.

12 Criminal Law

| LEARNING OUTCOMES |

After reading this chapter, you will understand:

- The division of responsibility between federal and provincial governments regarding criminal justice in Canada.

- The sources of Canadian criminal law.

- How criminal offences are classified and how offenders are prosecuted under Canada's *Criminal Code*.

- Police powers to investigate crime.

- Constitutional safeguards in the *Canadian Charter of Rights and Freedoms* applicable to criminal justice in Canada.

- Procedures for conducting a criminal trial, and the principles that apply to the sentencing of offenders.

- The application of the *Youth Criminal Justice Act* to young offenders and its key provisions.

- Indigenous perspectives on criminal justice.

For the ordinary person one of the most interesting and fascinating topics of discussion is that of law and order … To many people, the term "criminal law" simply refers to society's prohibitions against acts that threaten its very existence—acts such as murder, assault, and theft. In the same vein, "crime" simply means the breaking of these laws, and the "criminal" is the person who has broken them. Criminal law, then, may be seen as one form of social control—a term encompassing all kinds of pressure upon individuals to do what is customarily considered the right thing in a given society.

David Perrier, "An Introduction to Criminal Law" in Joel E Pink & David Perrier, eds, *From Crime to Punishment: An Introduction to the Criminal Law System*, 8th ed (Toronto: Carswell, 2014) at 1

Introduction

In addition to providing a continuous source of news headlines and heated political debates, the criminal justice system is a critical component of Canadian society. Unlike private law matters, in which private citizens take legal action against one another, criminal law concerns the state itself: criminal offences are seen as transgressions against society as a whole and are prosecuted by lawyers known as **Crown attorneys** or Crown prosecutors, so named because they represent the official head of government in Canada, the reigning British (and Canadian) monarch.[1]

Canada's criminal justice system works to determine whether or not persons charged with criminal offences are guilty according to the law and, if they are, what measures should be taken to punish, deter, and/or rehabilitate them and to protect the rest of society from

Crown attorney
a lawyer, also known as a Crown prosecutor, who is an agent of the attorney general and who represents the Crown in court, particularly in criminal matters

---

1   This is reflected in the style of cause of criminal cases, which generally begin with the letter *R*, standing for *regina* or *rex*, the Latin words for *queen* and *king*. See also the section on law reports at the end of Chapter 6 under the subheading "Names of Parties."

further harm. Our criminal justice system is jurisdictionally complex. Substantive criminal law and the procedures involved in the system—namely, police investigation of a crime, bringing the accused to court, trying the accused, and sentencing accused persons who are found guilty—are carried out within a constitutional framework that involves both the federal and provincial governments. Since the advent of the *Canadian Charter of Rights and Freedoms*,[2] constitutional safeguards protect an accused person's rights throughout the criminal process.

This chapter presents an overview of the criminal justice system in Canada. We will examine criminal law in relation to the division of federal and provincial powers under the Constitution, explain the classification of offences, and outline how a criminal offence is investigated by police, including a review of the Charter rights of persons who are detained or arrested and the limits on police powers of search and seizure. We will consider criminal pretrial matters and the conduct of a criminal trial, as well as sentencing. Lastly, we will briefly examine the correctional system in Canada, the *Youth Criminal Justice Act* (YCJA),[3] and the relationship between Indigenous peoples and the Canadian criminal justice system.

Figure 12.1 illustrates both the larger context of Canada's criminal justice system and the individual elements that comprise it.

When Canada became a nation in 1867, we adopted a Constitution that assigned jurisdiction over criminal law and criminal procedure to the federal Parliament. In the debates leading up to Confederation in 1867, John A Macdonald stated that "[i]t is one of the defects in the United States system, that each separate state has or may have a criminal code of its own—that what may be a capital offence in one state, may be a venial offence, punishable slightly, in another."[4]

Macdonald believed this potential for variance among state criminal codes produced confusion, and he argued that criminal law in Canada should be assigned to the general (that is, federal) government so that it would be the same throughout the country. Under our Constitution, said Macdonald:

> [W]e shall have one body of criminal law, based on the criminal law of England,
> and operating equally throughout British America, so that a British American,
> belonging to what province he may, or going to any other part of the
> Confederation, knows what his rights are in that respect, and what his punishment
> will be if an offender against the criminal laws of the land.[5]

Macdonald's view carried, and section 91(27) of the *Constitution Act, 1867*[6] gave the Parliament of Canada exclusive jurisdiction over criminal law and procedure in criminal matters. This means that criminal law and criminal procedure are *national* in scope. They apply throughout Canada.

Two major sources of criminal law in Canada today are statute law and common law. Originally, criminal law in Canada was largely judge-made law, as it was in England—there was no central criminal law statute. Our *Criminal Code*[7] was enacted in 1892, and today it is the main source of Canadian criminal law. Since its inception, it has been extensively amended.

---

2 Part 1 of the *Constitution Act, 1982*, being Schedule B to the *Canada Act 1982* (UK), 1982, c 11.

3 SC 2002, c 1.

4 Quoted in PB Waite, ed, *The Confederation Debates in the Province of Canada, 1865* (Toronto: McClelland & Stewart, 1963) at 46.

5 *Ibid* at 46.

6 (UK), 30 & 31 Vict, c 3, reprinted in RSC 1985, Appendix II, No 5.

7 RSC 1985, c C-46.

FIGURE 12.1 Overview of Canada's Criminal Justice System

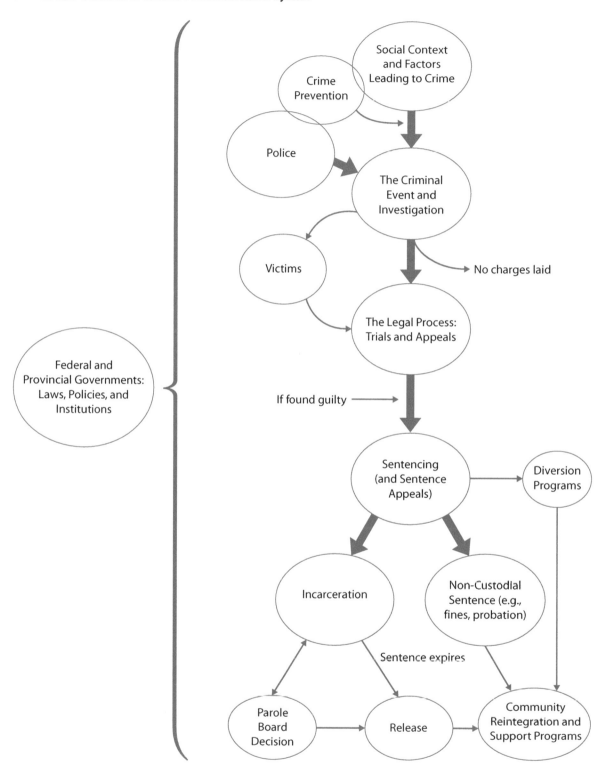

Source: Karla O'Regan & Susan Reid, *Thinking About Criminal Justice in Canada*, 2nd ed (Toronto: Emond, 2017) at xii.

The *Criminal Code* is a lengthy and complex statute that defines and classifies criminal offences, and describes the procedures for prosecuting them. It also provides directions for sentencing. The *Criminal Code* is composed of 28 parts, each concerned with a specific subject area.

Besides the *Criminal Code*, there are other important federal statutes that relate to the criminal law field, including:

- the *Canada Evidence Act*,[8]
- the *Controlled Drugs and Substances Act*,[9] and
- the *Youth Criminal Justice Act*.

The *Canada Evidence Act* covers witnesses and evidence law. Section 2 in part I, for example, provides that part I applies to "all criminal proceedings and to all civil proceedings and other matters whatever respecting which Parliament has jurisdiction."

The *Controlled Drugs and Substances Act* regulates certain kinds of dangerous drugs and narcotics in Canada, called "controlled substances." Search, seizure, and detention are covered in part II of the Act, which concerns enforcement, while part III covers the disposal of controlled substances.

The YCJA is a federal statute that deals with young persons who commit crimes in this country. It came into force on April 1, 2003, replacing the *Young Offenders Act*.[10] The YCJA applies to young persons who are between the ages of 12 and 17 when they commit a criminal offence. The Act outlines procedures for trying young persons separately from adult offenders, in youth justice courts. We will look at youth justice later in this chapter.

The common law, too, continues to be another important source of our criminal law, mainly in connection with defences (all *offences* are now legislated). There is also a considerable amount of case law interpreting the *Criminal Code* and other criminal law statutes. For this reason, many lawyers practising criminal law in Canada use annotated and easy-to-carry versions of the *Criminal Code* and related statutes. These all-in-one books are usually updated annually and include relevant case law together with the legislation. A well-known annotated version is *Martin's Annual Criminal Code*, and a useful small companion book is *Martin's Pocket Criminal Code*, both published by Carswell.[11]

True Crimes Versus Quasi-Criminal Offences

"True" crimes are offences over which the federal government has jurisdiction pursuant to its power under section 91(27) of the *Constitution Act, 1867*. These federal crimes are typically serious in nature and are often thought of as being inherently wrong. They generally have a *mens rea*, or guilty mind, element (see below under the heading "The Elements of a Criminal Offence"). In addition to penalties that can be severe, being convicted of a crime

---

8 RSC 1985, c C-5.

9 SC 1996, c 19.

10 RSC 1985, c Y-1.

11 *Martin's Annual Criminal Code*, 2019 ed (Toronto: Canada Law Book, 2018); *Martin's Pocket Criminal Code*, 2019 ed (Toronto: Canada Law Book, 2018).

carries with it a criminal record and a social stigma. Treason, terrorism, firearms offences, sexual assault, murder, robbery, and arson—all dealt with in the *Criminal Code*—are just a few examples of criminal offences.

Quasi-criminal offences, on the other hand, are less serious offences and do not fall under the federal criminal law power. They are sometimes referred to as *regulatory offences* and deal with the regulation of conduct in the public interest. They may have a *mens rea* component, but are more frequently *strict liability offences* (that is, offences without a mental element and where an accused can argue as a defence that she exercised due diligence in trying to avoid committing the offence—for example, pollution offences) or *absolute liability offences* (offences based solely on the commission of the proscribed act—such as driving over the speed limit—and without a mental element or possible defence of due diligence).

Quasi-criminal offences can be federal, provincial, territorial, or municipal, but most of these offences are creatures of provincial legislation (provincial quasi-criminal offences are often simply referred to as *provincial offences*). Section 92(15) of the *Constitution Act, 1867* states that the provinces have jurisdiction over "[t]he Imposition of Punishment by Fine, Penalty, or Imprisonment for enforcing any Law of the Province made in relation to any Matter coming within any of the Classes of Subjects enumerated in this Section." The territories have an analogous power to create quasi-criminal offences in relation to the areas over which they have legislative jurisdiction (as devolved to them by the federal Parliament). Municipalities (or local governments) have a similar power delegated to them by the provinces. And the federal government can always pass legislation creating quasi-criminal offences under a power other than its criminal law power. (See Chapter 4 for a discussion of the areas or subjects over which Parliament, the provinces, and territories have legislative jurisdiction.)

There are a vast number of quasi-criminal, or regulatory, offences in Canada, including such things as:

- motor vehicle offences, such as careless driving and parking offences (for example, under Ontario's *Highway Traffic Act*);[12]
- offences related to the selling or supplying of liquor (for example, under New Brunswick's *Liquor Control Act*);[13]
- offences related to workplace safety covering a range of violations, such as an employer's failure to provide a safe work environment or to immediately report accidents causing critical injury or death (for example, under BC's *Workers Compensation Act*);[14]
- pollution offences covering land, air, or water (for example, under the federal *Fisheries Act*);[15] and
- offences relating to the sale and distribution of securities (for example, under Yukon's *Securities Act*).[16]

---

quasi-criminal offences

less serious offences, such as pollution or traffic offences, that do not fall under the federal criminal law power—they may be passed by all levels of government but are frequently created under provincial legislation

12   RSO 1990, c H.8.

13   RSNB 1973, c L-10.

14   RSBC 1996, c 492.

15   RSC 1985, c F-14.

16   RY 2007, c 16.

Quasi-criminal offences are prosecuted according to the procedures set out in the relevant act—for example, provincial offences in Ontario are prosecuted under the *Provincial Offences Act*.[17] Punishment for these types of offences is usually a fine (though it can involve imprisonment) and may also include other penalties, such as demerit points on a convicted person's driver's licence or the loss of the licence itself. Because quasi-criminal offences are not true criminal offences, they do not result in a criminal record.

Basic Principles of Criminal Law

Because the consequences of being convicted of a criminal offence are so serious and can result in individuals being deprived of their liberty, the Crown attorney's burden in proving that an accused committed a crime is very high. In this section, we will look at *what* the Crown must prove and *how* it must prove it.

The Elements of a Criminal Offence

Criminal offences in Canada are set out in the *Criminal Code* and several other statutes. We saw in Chapter 10, for example, that price-fixing agreements in relation to competition is a crime under the *Competition Act*.[18] Generally speaking, criminal offences are composed of an objective physical element, known as the *actus reus*, or "guilty act," and a mental element, known as *mens rea*, or "guilty mind."

In committing the guilty act component of an offence, an individual must engage in a proscribed action, conduct, or behaviour. In addition, the *actus reus* may involve the accused being found in particular circumstances; failing to act when required to do so by a legal duty; or causing particular consequences. An important feature of the *actus reus* is that, for criminal consequences to apply, it must be carried out consciously and voluntarily. Some defences go to these elements—for example, duress (see the discussion of defences later in this chapter).

For persons to be found guilty of a criminal offence, not only must they commit a particular criminal act, they must do so with a blameworthy guilty mind or with a particular intention. For example, section 265(1)(a) of the *Criminal Code* states that a person commits an assault when "without the consent of another person, he applies force intentionally to that other person, directly or indirectly." Such force might be applied in a variety of ways—intentionally in a fight or during a robbery, or unintentionally in a crowded public area due to factors beyond the person's control. While some of these acts are blameworthy and could attract criminal consequences, others might not.

Burden of Proof and Standard of Proof

A key principle of our criminal justice system that has existed for centuries is the *presumption of innocence*. This common law safeguard is now a Charter legal right: section 11(d) states that any person charged with an offence has the right "to be presumed innocent until proven guilty according to law in a fair and public hearing by an independent and impartial tribunal." In addition, section 6(1)(a) of the *Criminal Code* prescribes that a person shall be deemed not to be guilty until he is convicted or discharged of the offence. In other words,

---

17 RSO 1990, c P.33.

18 RSC 1985, c C-34.

the state has the *burden* or the *onus of proof* to establish its case, and an accused is presumed innocent until proven guilty in court.

In contrast to civil matters, which require proof on a balance of probabilities, the criminal *standard of proof* is a much higher standard of proof "beyond a reasonable doubt." This means that the Crown must also prove *all* of the elements of the offence beyond a reasonable doubt for the accused to be found guilty. If the defence is able to raise a reasonable doubt in the minds of the judge or jury as to whether the accused committed the offence, the accused must be found not guilty.

Organization and Classification of Criminal Code Offences

In this section, we will look first at how criminal offences are organized in the *Criminal Code* and then review its three categories of offences. These are:

1. summary conviction offences,
2. indictable offences, and
3. hybrid offences.

How an offence is classified largely determines, for example, the scope of investigatory powers granted to the police, the terms of the accused's pretrial release, how the offence is prosecuted, which court hears the matter, which punishments can apply on a conviction, and the process for an appeal.[19]

Organization of Criminal Code Offences

The *Criminal Code* organizes specific offences into general subject matter categories, as follows:

- Part II covers offences against public order—for example, treason, sedition, unlawful assemblies and riots, duels, piracy, and offences against air or maritime safety.
- Part II.1 covers terrorism.
- Part III covers offences involving firearms and other weapons.
- Part IV covers offences against the administration of law and justice, including corruption and disobedience, and misleading justice.
- Part V covers sexual offences, public morals, and disorderly conduct.

---

19   Richard Barnhorst & Sherrie Barnhorst, *Criminal Law and the Canadian Criminal Code*, 6th ed (Toronto: McGraw-Hill Ryerson, 2013); Kent Roach, *Criminal Law*, 6th ed (Toronto: Irwin Law, 2015); Nora Rock & Valerie Hoag, *Foundations of Criminal and Civil Law in Canada*, 3rd ed (Toronto: Emond Montgomery, 2011); Mary Ann Kelly, "Criminal Procedure" in Laurence Olivo, ed, *Introduction to Law in Canada*, Ont ed (Toronto: Captus Press, 1995–2009) at 245; Joel E Pink & David C Perrier, eds, *From Crime to Punishment: An Introduction to the Criminal Law System*, 8th ed (Toronto: Carswell, 2014); Michael Gulycz & Mary Ann Kelly, *Criminal Law for Legal Professionals*, 2nd ed (Toronto: Emond, 2018).

- Part VI covers invasion of privacy.
- Part VII covers disorderly houses, gaming, and betting.
- Part VIII covers offences against the person and reputation—for example, criminal negligence, homicide, murder, suicide, assault, kidnapping, defamatory libel, and hate propaganda.
- Part IX covers property offences—for example, theft, robbery, breaking and entering, and forgery.
- Part X covers fraudulent transactions relating to contracts and trade.
- Part XI covers wilful and forbidden acts in respect of certain property, including mischief and arson.
- Part XII covers offences relating to currency, and part XII.2 covers proceeds of crime.
- Part XIII covers attempts, conspiracies, and accessories.

There has been and continues to be much discussion and debate regarding the kind of behaviour that society should criminalize. For example, after years of considering the advantages and disadvantages involved, in 2018, Canada became just the second country in the world (after Uruguay) to fully legalize the recreational use of cannabis.[20] The arguments in favour of or against change often have their basis in the rights guaranteed by the Charter (see Box 12.1).

BOX 12.1

Canada's Prostitution Laws: Unconstitutional

In 2010, three Ontario sex workers challenged the constitutionality of Canada's prostitution laws in the Ontario Superior Court, and their case eventually made its way to the Supreme Court of Canada (SCC).* The women argued that certain provisions in the *Criminal Code* needlessly endangered them, violating their right to security of the person under section 7 of the Charter. The provisions in question were:

1. section 210, which prevented sex workers from working in a "bawdy house" (fixed indoor location) and limited them instead to street prostitution or outcalls (that is, meeting clients in different locations);
2. section 212(1)(j), which criminalized "living on the avails" of prostitution and made it illegal for sex workers to hire drivers, security, and so on to protect themselves against some of the risks inherent in prostitution under the regime in force at the time; and

3. section 213(1)(c), which prohibited communicating in public for the purposes of prostitution, effectively making it illegal for sex workers to negotiate terms related to their activities with clients.

In December 2013, the SCC delivered its landmark ruling on the prostitution provisions in the *Criminal Code*. Setting out the issue before the court, Chief Justice McLachlin stated that the appeals and cross-appeal were not about whether prostitution should be legal or not, but "about whether the laws Parliament has enacted on how prostitution may be carried out pass constitutional muster."† In a unanimous 9-0 ruling, the court declared that the sections in question were inconsistent with the Charter and therefore void. In the words of Chief Justice McLachlin:

> The prohibitions at issue do not merely impose conditions on how prostitutes operate. They go a

---

20 The *Cannabis Act*, SC 2018, c 16, which brought about this change, required amendments to the *Controlled Drugs and Substances Act*, the *Criminal Code*, and other legislation.

critical step further, by imposing *dangerous* conditions on prostitution; they prevent people engaged in a risky—but legal—activity from taking steps to protect themselves from the risks.‡

The bawdy-house and communication offences§ had as their main purpose the control of nuisances, but the court held that the outright ban against keeping a bawdy house or communicating in public for the purpose of prostitution was a grossly disproportionate response in pursuing this objective (in many cases, these activities would not create a nuisance); further, the outright ban made prostitution more dangerous because it took away opportunities for sex workers to increase their safety. Concerning the offence of "living on the avails,"# while the control of exploitive relationships was its objective, the court held that, as worded, it was an overbroad response because it also punished those who were not in exploitive relationships, including those who could increase the safety of sex workers, such as drivers and bodyguards. All three provisions were therefore held to be contrary to section 7 of the Charter.

Although the court declared the challenged provisions invalid, it acknowledged Parliament's right to impose limits on how prostitution may be conducted and noted that its

regulation is a "complex and delicate matter." With regard to all the interests at stake, the court decided to suspend the declaration of invalidity for one year to give Parliament the opportunity to redraft Canada's prostitution laws.

In 2014, the Conservative government passed the *Protection of Communities and Exploited Persons Act,*** which included amendments to the *Criminal Code* and created new offences relating to prostitution. There are provisions dealing with communicating and advertising for sexual purposes, and profiting from another person's sex work. It is also now an offence to purchase sexual services, although the sale of sexual services by sex workers is not criminalized. Whether the new prostitution laws will withstand a Charter challenge—and whether they adequately address the concerns expressed by the SCC in connection with the old laws—remains to be seen.

* *Canada (AG) v Bedford*, 2013 SCC 72.

† *Ibid* at para 2.

‡ *Ibid* at para 60.

§ *Criminal Code*, ss 210 and 213(1)(c).

Ibid, s 212(1)(j).

** SC 2014, c 25.

Summary Conviction Offences

summary conviction offence
the least serious type of offence in the *Criminal Code* (for example, trespassing or disturbing the peace), tried only in provincial court and subject to the lightest sentences

Summary conviction offences are the least serious offences in the *Criminal Code* and are dealt with under part XXVII. Such offences include, for example, making an indecent telephone call and public nudity. Trials for summary conviction offences are held before a provincial court judge; no jury is permitted and there is no preliminary hearing. **Limitation periods** apply to summary offences—in general, summary offence charges must be laid within six months from the time the offence was committed.

If convicted of a summary conviction offence, a person is liable, under section 787(1) of the *Criminal Code*, to "a fine of not more than five thousand dollars or to a term of imprisonment not exceeding six months or to both." The maximum penalty for a number of offences, known as *super summary conviction offences*, exceeds the general penalty. For example, the offences of assault with a weapon and sexual assault both carry a maximum summary conviction sentence of 18 months.

limitation period
the period in which a legal action must be taken or the ability to do so is lost

Indictable Offences

indictable offence
the most serious type of offence in the *Criminal Code* (for example, murder), carrying the most serious sentences

Indictable offences are the most serious offences in the *Criminal Code*, and the procedure by which they are prosecuted is more involved than the process for summary conviction offences. Limitation periods do not apply to indictable offences, and a person can be charged at any time. Being convicted of them also brings more severe penalties, to a maximum of life imprisonment. The seriousness of an indictable offence determines what court has jurisdiction to hear it. One of the most serious indictable offences is murder, along with some others listed under section 469 of the *Criminal Code*, such as treason and piracy. These offences must be tried before a judge and jury in a province's **superior court of criminal jurisdiction**,[21] unless both the accused and the attorney general consent to a trial before a superior court judge alone under section 473 of the *Criminal Code*. The least serious types of indictable offences are those listed in section 553 of the *Criminal Code*—for example, theft (other than theft of cattle), obtaining money or property by false pretenses, and failure to comply with a probation order. These offences are under the absolute jurisdiction of a provincial court judge, without a jury.

If charged with an indictable offence *not* listed in either section 469 or section 553, an accused may choose or elect his mode of trial. The accused can choose to be tried before either a provincial court judge alone, a superior court of justice judge alone, or a superior court of justice judge with a jury. Section 536 of the *Criminal Code* outlines the election procedure.

superior court of criminal jurisdiction
the highest court in each province and territory to hear criminal matters, sometimes with a jury, its designation varying by province and territory

Hybrid Offences

A **hybrid offence** is also called a *dual procedure offence* or a *Crown election offence*. This means that the Crown attorney has the option of choosing whether to prosecute it as a summary conviction offence or as an indictable offence. The offence of assault causing bodily harm is an example of a hybrid offence; the procedure and potential penalties are different depending on whether the Crown decides to proceed by indictment or summarily. Factors that will affect the Crown's decision include the accused's prior criminal record, the specific circumstances involved, and the time since the offence (limitation period). A hybrid offence is deemed to be an indictable offence by default unless the Crown attorney chooses to prosecute it as a summary offence.

hybrid offence
a dual procedure offence, meaning that the Crown attorney has the option of choosing whether to prosecute it as a summary conviction offence or as an indictable offence

Police Investigation of Crime

When a crime is committed and this fact becomes known to authorities in the criminal justice system, the first step is an investigation by the police. The police gather evidence and attempt to determine who is responsible for the offence; they may then arrest and charge the person or persons they believe to be responsible.

There are three levels of police forces in Canada: federal, provincial, and municipal. The federal police force is the Royal Canadian Mounted Police (RCMP). Not all provinces and territories have their own provincial/territorial police forces, and in such cases the RCMP is responsible for policing in that province or territory. The majority of police officers in Canada are members of municipal police forces.

Police do not have unlimited powers to investigate crime. The *Criminal Code*, the common law, and the Charter all place limits on the investigatory powers of police and safeguard the rights of individuals with whom police interact. Failure on the part of police to abide by the law in this regard may result in evidence against an accused being excluded in a criminal trial. As described in Chapter 7, section 24(2) of the Charter requires courts to exclude evidence

---

21 Section 2 of the *Criminal Code* provides the names of the superior court of criminal jurisdiction in each province and territory. For example, in Nova Scotia, British Columbia, and Newfoundland and Labrador, the superior court of criminal jurisdiction is the Supreme Court or the Court of Appeal, while in Ontario, it is the Court of Appeal or the Superior Court of Justice, and in Nunavut, it is the Nunavut Court of Justice.

whose admission "would bring the administration of justice into disrepute" when an application is made under section 24(1) (see Box 7.4).

In the following sections, we will look more closely at the law related to the detention and arrest of persons suspected of committing crimes, and the law governing the search and seizure of evidence by police.

Detention and Arrest

arrest
detaining or holding a person by legal authority

The Charter sets out further legal requirements with which police must comply whenever they are dealing with persons whom they detain or **arrest**. For example, section 10 of the Charter states:

>   10. Everyone has the right on arrest or detention
>   (a) to be informed promptly of the reasons therefor;
>   (b) to retain and instruct counsel without delay and to be informed of that
>   right; and
>   (c) to have the validity of the detention determined by way of *habeas corpus* and to be released if the detention is not lawful.

With respect to reasons, section 29(2)(b) of the *Criminal Code* states that it is the duty of everyone who arrests a person to give notice to that person of the reason for the arrest; the common law requires this, too. Sections 7 and 11(c) of the Charter provide an accused person with the right to remain silent while being questioned by police and during her trial.

If an accused decides to waive his right to silence and give a statement, the court must determine whether it was given *voluntarily* before the statement can be admissible against the accused; this is usually established in a *voir dire*, or a trial within a trial. The common law confessions rule aims to prevent wrongful convictions by requiring the Crown to prove that any statement made by an accused person to a person in authority was given voluntarily for the statement to be admissible against the accused (see Box 12.2).

> ### BOX 12.2
>
> # Voluntariness and Oickle
>
> In *R v Oickle*,* the court noted that false confessions are "rarely the product of proper police techniques"† and stated that, if a confession is produced in certain situations or under certain circumstances, the voluntariness of the confession is difficult to determine. Judges must look carefully at *all* of the circumstances surrounding a confession and how it was obtained and consider the degree to which the following four factors were present:
>
> 1. threats or promises (for example, the promise of preferential treatment, or the threat of physical violence/torture),
> 2. an atmosphere of oppression (contributing actions include prolonged interrogations, fabricated evidence, and disregard for the dignity/well-being of the accused),
>
> 3. an operating mind (the accused must have the cognitive ability to understand what is being said to her, what she is saying, and the consequences of saying it to police; the presence of an operating mind may be affected by shock, intoxication, presence of a mental disorder, etc.), and
> 4. police trickery (unacceptable trickery is determined by the "community shock test"—for example, an officer pretending to be a chaplain and extracting a confession).
>
> The first three factors are connected with the voluntariness of a statement; depending on the context in which the statement was made, the presence of just one of these three factors to a sufficient degree, or a combination of all three, may

be enough to render the statement involuntary. The presence of the fourth factor to a sufficient degree may be enough to exclude a statement on the basis of the fact that the actions of the police reflect negatively on the justice system and have the potential to bring the administration of justice into disrepute.

* 2000 SCC 38.

† *Ibid* at para 45.

Source: Reproduced from Kerry Watkins, Gail Anderson & Vincenzo Rondinelli, *Evidence and Investigation: From the Crime Scene to the Courtroom* (Toronto: Emond Montgomery, 2012) at 300.

Search and Seizure

Police investigation can involve searching people and places, as well as seizing physical evidence that is related to the crime. Prior to a criminal trial, the Crown has a legal duty to provide the accused with all relevant information in its possession that relates to the investigation (in the absence of any legal restrictions) so that the accused can better understand and prepare a defence to the charge(s) against him or her—in other words, make "full answer and defence." This duty, known as the **duty of disclosure**, exists at common law and is guaranteed by section 7 of the Charter. In the SCC case of *R v Stinchcombe*,[22] the court framed the duty as follows:

> [T]here is a general duty on the part of the Crown to disclose all materials it proposes to use at trial and especially all evidence which may assist the accused even if the Crown does not propose to adduce it.[23]

The court also explained the proper use to which the information gathered by the Crown should be put:

> The fruits of the investigation which are in its possession are not the property of the Crown for use in securing a conviction but the property of the public to be used to ensure that justice is done.[24]

The Crown's duty of disclosure places a corollary duty on police to disclose the "fruits of the investigation" to the Crown, and to ensure that the evidence they collect is not contaminated, lost, or destroyed and that the chain of continuity is not broken (that is, it must be possible to account for the whereabouts of any piece of physical evidence from the time of its collection to the time it is entered as an exhibit in the trial record).

The Charter places further limits on the ability of police to search for and seize evidence. Section 8 states that everyone "has the right to be secure against unreasonable search or seizure," and court decisions have determined what constitutes a reasonable or an unreasonable search. For a search to be considered reasonable, it must meet the following test as stated by the SCC in *R v Collins*:[25]

1. it must be authorized by law;
2. the law itself must be reasonable (that is, the law that authorizes the search); and
3. the search must be conducted in a reasonable manner.

duty of disclosure
the Crown's mandatory disclosure to the accused, before the trial, of the evidence against him

---

22 [1991] 3 SCR 326, 1991 CanLII 45.

23 *Ibid* at 338, adopting as correct law this statement from McEachern CJBC in *R v C (MH)*, 1988 CanLII 3283, 46 CCC (3d) 142 (BCCA).

24 *Supra* note 22 at 333.

25 [1987] 1 SCR 265, 1987 CanLII 84. See also Gulycz & Kelly, *supra* note 19 at 142.

search warrant
a warrant, issued by a justice of the peace or a provincial court judge, authorizing police to conduct a search

Section 487(5) of the *Criminal Code* authorizes a justice to issue a police officer a **search warrant**, which provides police with the legal authority to conduct a search. Once authorized to conduct a search, the police must then, as noted in *Collins* and following section 8 of the Charter, conduct the search in a reasonable manner. This normally requires them to have the search warrant with them and show it if asked; use reasonable force when executing the warrant; request voluntary admittance before making a forcible entry; and search premises only during the daytime, unless the search warrant authorizes execution at night.[26]

There are a limited number of exceptions to the general rule requiring police to obtain a warrant before conducting a search and seizure. For example, section 487.11 of the *Criminal Code* permits a peace officer to conduct a search without a warrant "if the conditions for obtaining a warrant exist but by reason of exigent circumstances it would be impracticable to obtain a warrant."[27]

The Criminal Trial Process

In this section, we examine the criminal courts, pretrial procedures, the trial itself, defences, and sentencing.

Criminal Courts

Although our federal Parliament has sole jurisdiction over criminal law and criminal procedure, section 92(14) of the *Constitution Act, 1867* gives the provinces jurisdiction over "[t]he Administration of Justice in the Province, including the Constitution, Maintenance, and Organization of Provincial Courts, both of Civil and of Criminal Jurisdiction." This means that most criminal cases are heard in the provincial (or territorial) inferior courts, or criminal divisions of them, and in the provincial (or territorial) superior courts. The inferior courts hear the vast majority of these cases, but the superior courts have *exclusive* jurisdiction over certain serious crimes, such as murder, treason, and piracy. Some serious crimes (including attempted murder, manslaughter, and sexual assault) can be heard in either the inferior or superior courts.

The Federal Court, constituted under section 101 of the *Constitution Act, 1867*, has limited criminal jurisdiction. For example, it has non-exclusive jurisdiction (that is, shared jurisdiction with the provincial courts) over trade and commerce offences under the *Competition Act* (see discussion in Chapter 10), and jurisdiction to hear certain matters in connection with terrorism offences under the *Criminal Code* (for instance, dealing with the forfeiture of property).

Appeals from decisions of any of these courts of original jurisdiction can make their way through the court system to the SCC. See Figure 6.1 and the descriptions of these courts in Chapter 6.

In addition to the courts just mentioned, a number of specialized courts have been created outside of the regular court system. The aim of these courts is to achieve better long-term outcomes for offenders in certain circumstances and for society as a whole. They include:

---

26 Kelly, "Criminal Procedure," *supra* note 19 at 252-54.

27 For a detailed discussion of police investigatory powers, see Kerry Watkins, Gail Anderson & Vincenzo Rondinelli, *Evidence and Investigation: From the Crime Scene to the Courtroom* (Toronto: Emond Montgomery, 2012) ch 6; and Gulycz & Kelly, *supra* note 19 at 142-54.

- *Gladue courts.* The first *Gladue* court was established in Toronto in 2001. Named for the Supreme Court decision *R v Gladue*[28] (see the discussion below, under the heading "Sentencing"), *Gladue* courts hear criminal matters involving Indigenous persons. At the time of writing, *Gladue* courts are operating in several cities in Ontario and are being considered for a number of others. Like regular courts, *Gladue* courts include a judge, duty counsel, Crown, and defence lawyers, but most of the individuals involved are trained in the issues pertinent to the offenders who appear before them. Caseworkers prepare reports on offenders' life circumstances, which are used to determine an appropriate sentence. In some other provinces, such as British Columbia, partnerships exist between courts and non-governmental organizations to ensure that *Gladue*-type information is systematically incorporated into sentencing procedures for Indigenous offenders.

- *Domestic Violence Court.* Created in 1997, Ontario's Domestic Violence Court (DVC) Program deals with criminal cases that involve allegations of domestic abuse. The DVC Program aims to facilitate the prosecution of such cases, provide early intervention and better support to victims, and increase offender accountability. It is the most extensive of such programs in Canada and includes specialized teams made up of police, Crown attorneys, community agencies, victim/witness assistance program staff, and others who aim to make the safety and needs of victims of domestic violence and their children a priority.

- *Toronto Mental Health Court.* The Toronto Mental Health Court (MHC) opened in 1998 in response to the growing number of accused suffering from mental disorders who were appearing before the courts. The Toronto MHC, which was the first court of its kind in Canada, is a non-adversarial court available to individuals suffering from mental illness who are charged with non-violent criminal offences. Ideally, arrested persons who meet the criteria for diversion will be sent to the MHC, where they will be seen by psychiatrists, legal aid, and social workers; they will then have a fitness hearing and a bail hearing. The goals of the court, whose underlying philosophy is that the justice system should aim to heal as well as to protect, include "to expedite case processing, create effective interactions between the mental health and criminal justice system, increase access to mental health services, reduce recidivism, improve public safety and reduce the length of confinement in jails for mentally disordered offenders."[29]

- *Drug Treatment Courts.* At the time of writing, six Drug Treatment Courts (DTCs) are operating across Canada: in Toronto (since 1998); Vancouver (since 2001); Edmonton (since 2005); and Winnipeg, Ottawa, and Regina (since 2006).[30] Participation is open to non-violent offenders with addictions who have been charged with possession or trafficking of small quantities of drugs such as crack, cocaine, and heroin; minor property crimes; or prostitution. The aim of DTCs is to reduce the amount of crime committed due to substance abuse by a combination of court-monitored treatment and community support for offenders; the larger

28 [1999] 1 SCR 688, 1999 CanLII 679.

29 Edward F Ormston, "Mental Health Court in Ontario" (2005) 2:8 Visions: BC's Mental Health & Addictions Journal 31.

30 See the Government of Canada's Canadian Drugs and Substances Strategy, online at <http://nationalantidrugstrategy.gc.ca/dtc-ttt.html>.

aim is to reduce, for Canadian law enforcement and legal and corrections systems, the costs stemming from addiction. Participation in the courts is voluntary, but participants are required to appear in court regularly, attend counselling sessions, receive medical attention as needed (for example, methadone treatment), and undergo random drug tests.

Pretrial Procedures

A number of procedures occur prior to a criminal trial.[31] Once the police have finished investigating a crime and have gathered and assessed their evidence, they may lay a criminal charge against a suspect. They must also ensure that the accused person comes before a court. Part XVI of the *Criminal Code* sets out several ways police may do this.

First, if the offence is an indictable type mentioned in section 553 (the least serious indictable offences), a hybrid offence, or a summary conviction offence, the police officer may issue an **appearance notice** to the accused person. The appearance notice is a document given to a person, usually at the scene of the offence, requiring that person to come to court on a certain date and time to answer to a charge. The accused must sign the appearance notice and then may leave. Having issued an appearance notice, the police officer must then swear an information before a justice that the accused person has committed an offence. The officer must do this as soon as practicable, before the date and time prescribed in the appearance notice for the accused's future court appearance.

Second, sometimes the accused will be brought to court by a **summons**. To start this process, the police officer goes before a justice and swears an information that there are reasonable grounds to believe an accused has committed an offence. If the justice is satisfied that an arrest warrant is not necessary, a summons is issued, following the requirements set out in section 509 of the *Criminal Code*. The summons requires the accused to attend court on a certain date and time to answer to the charge. It is served personally on the accused.

The third way of bringing an accused before the court is for a justice to issue a warrant for the person's arrest, directing the police to take the accused into custody and bring her to court. As always, police actions in compelling the accused to appear in court are subject to the rights everyone has under the Charter.

Generally, a considerable amount of time elapses between the date an accused is charged with an offence and the date the actual trial takes place. Note that section 11(b) of the Charter states that any person charged with an offence has the right "to be tried within a reasonable time." Given that an accused's trial may be some time in the future, the *Criminal Code* outlines procedures by which a police officer, a justice of the peace, or a judge may release an accused prior to his trial. Here, again, the Charter applies. Section 11(e) states that any person charged with an offence has the right "not to be denied reasonable bail without just cause."

Pretrial release of the accused, often called *bail*, is formally known in the *Criminal Code* as **judicial interim release**. If the accused is still in custody, the pretrial release of that person is determined at a bail hearing. The bail hearing follows different procedures depending on the seriousness of the charge. For less serious offences—that is, for offences not listed in section 469—the accused must be taken before a justice for her bail hearing within 24 hours of arrest and detention.

At this regular bail hearing, the Crown attorney has the onus to show cause why the accused should *not* be released or should be released with certain conditions attached. If

appearance notice
a document given to a person, usually at the scene of the crime, requiring that person to come to court on a certain date and time to answer to a charge

summons
a document served personally on an accused person requiring her to be in court at a certain date and time

judicial interim release
formal name for bail; the release of an accused prior to her trial

---

31   For more information on pretrial procedures, see Gulycz & Kelly, *supra* note 19, ch 17.

the Crown does not show cause, the justice must release the accused on an **undertaking** without conditions or "with such conditions as the justice directs" (the conditions that may be applied are set out in s 515(2) of the *Criminal Code*). However, the onus is not always on the Crown. There are a number of situations, set out in section 515(6) of the *Criminal Code*, in which the onus is on the accused to show why he should *not* be detained in custody prior to the trial. Such a reverse onus could happen if, for example, the accused were charged with an indictable offence while already out on bail for another indictable offence.

For an accused charged with a more serious section 469 indictable offence (for example, murder or treason), more stringent considerations apply. The accused must apply for a bail hearing before a judge in a superior court of criminal jurisdiction, under section 522 of the *Criminal Code*. In this case, due to the seriousness of the offence, the accused has the onus to show cause why her detention is not justified. If the judge is not persuaded, the accused will be detained until her trial.

Before the trial begins, the accused and his lawyer have a number of important matters to consider, including the following:

- Obtaining disclosure of all the Crown's relevant evidence against the accused. Such disclosure is required by common law, as per *Stinchcombe*, as well as the Charter.
- Having a pretrial hearing conference, as set out in section 625.1 of the *Criminal Code*. Such conferences are mandatory for jury trials.
- Discussing how to **plead** to the offence. Under section 606 of the *Criminal Code*, permitted pleas are either guilty or not guilty, or one of the special pleas authorized under section 607 of the *Criminal Code*. These are:
  - *autrefois acquit* (available when the person charged has been previously acquitted with respect to the charge),
  - *autrefois convict* (available when the person charged has been previously convicted with respect to the charge), and
  - pardon (the offence and the penalty are forgiven, usually by a head of state or Parliament).
- Considering whether a **plea bargain** should be negotiated with the Crown. A plea bargain comes about when the Crown attorney and the defence counsel negotiate an agreement on matters such as how the accused will plead to the offence and what sentence the Crown will ask for in court if the accused pleads guilty. For example, the accused may plead guilty to a lesser offence and receive a reduced sentence.
- Electing the mode of trial. This consideration is relevant if the accused is charged with an indictable offence that is not listed in either section 469 or section 553 of the *Criminal Code*. The options are trial by a judge of the superior court of justice with a jury, trial by a judge of the superior court of justice without a jury, and trial by a provincial court judge without a jury.
- Considering (in a case where the accused chooses to have the trial in the superior court) whether to have a **preliminary inquiry**. The procedure for a preliminary inquiry is described in part XVIII of the *Criminal Code*. It is conducted before a provincial court judge, who determines whether there is sufficient evidence to require the accused to stand trial for the offence.
- Deciding whether the accused will testify at his own trial. (There is no requirement that the accused do so.) This right is also protected under section 11(c) of the Charter.

undertaking
clear statement of intention by one person, usually a lawyer, that is reasonably relied on by another, amounting to a solemn promise that must be kept or the person who has given the undertaking will be liable for misconduct

plead
to answer to a criminal charge in ways permitted by the *Criminal Code*

plea bargain
agreement between the Crown and the defence on how the accused will plead in court and on the sentence he will receive

preliminary inquiry
hearing before a provincial court judge to determine whether the Crown has sufficient evidence for the accused to stand trial for the offence

The Trial

In Canada, trials are open to the public. If the trial is in a provincial court, the charging document describing the offence(s) with which the accused is charged is called an **information**. If the trial is in superior court, the charging document describing the offence(s) is called an **indictment** (although some indictable offences, which require indictments, can proceed in provincial court). The nature of a criminal trial is complex, and various sections of the *Criminal Code* outline how the trial proceeds. The trial itself starts with the **arraignment**, whereby the charge is read to the accused in open court and the accused is asked how she wishes to plead. If the accused pleads guilty to the offence, the Crown will read a summary of the facts to the judge, and the defence will admit to them. If the trial judge agrees, he finds the accused guilty and enters a **conviction**. The accused will then be sentenced (see the discussion below).

If the accused pleads not guilty to the offence, the Crown attorney presents its case first. The Crown then attempts to prove its case with evidence against the accused. Evidence may take a number of forms, including oral evidence (spoken evidence given by a witness under affirmation or oath), physical evidence (actual objects, such as DNA, photographs, or a weapon), and documentary evidence (any documents produced mechanically or by hand, such as medical records or transcripts).

In general, all relevant evidence is admissible unless a statutory or common law rule excludes it. For example, evidence may be deemed unreliable under the common law hearsay rule and excluded as a result (hearsay is an out-of-court statement by a person not before the court that is being used to prove the truth of what is asserted in the statement and is being related to the court by someone else). Or evidence may have been acquired in contravention of the Charter (for instance, by way of an illegal seizure) and may be excluded under section 24(2) (see Box 7.4). There are many other evidentiary rules under which relevant evidence may be excluded because the evidence is unreliable or because admitting it would be unfair (including rules relating to character evidence, privileged communications, and the competence and compellability of witnesses).

As mentioned, the Crown must prove all the elements of the offence beyond a reasonable doubt. Following the Crown's own examination-in-chief of their witness, the defence counsel may conduct a cross-examination, which the Crown may then follow with a re-examination. The judge may also question the witness, and then the next witness may be called. After the Crown has finished calling all of its witnesses and presenting all of its evidence, the Crown closes its case. If the defence believes the Crown has not provided any evidence on an essential element of the offence, the defence may make a motion to the trial judge for a directed verdict of acquittal. If the motion is allowed, the accused will be acquitted; if it is dismissed, the trial will continue, with the defence then opening its case and calling its evidence. At this stage of the trial, the defence conducts the examination-in-chief of their own witnesses; the Crown then cross-examines the witnesses and the defence re-examines them. As stated, the accused is not obligated to testify at her own trial.

A number of defences are set out in the *Criminal Code*. (These are discussed briefly in the following section.) When the defence has finished presenting all of its evidence, it closes its case. The Crown and the defence then both make closing submissions to the judge. If the trial is before a judge alone, the judge decides if the accused is guilty or not guilty. If the trial is before a judge and jury, the judge reviews the evidence and each side's case for the jury and instructs or charges them on how to apply the law to the facts of the case in order to reach their decision. The jury then retires to a jury room to deliberate and determine a **verdict** of guilty or not guilty. Jurors do not need to give reasons for their verdict, but their verdict must be unanimous. If they find the accused guilty, the trial judge imposes the sentence (see the discussion below).

information
written document, used in provincial court, describing the offences with which the accused is charged

indictment
written document, used in superior court, describing the offences with which the accused is charged

arraignment
procedure by which the charge is read to the accused in open court and the accused is asked how she wishes to plead

conviction
a judge or jury's finding an accused person guilty of an offence

verdict
the finding of a jury on the matter before it—for example, whether the accused is guilty or not guilty

Defences

Prior to the enactment of the *Criminal Code*, defences to criminal offences were based on the common law. Today, they are found in the *Criminal Code* and, by section 8(3), at common law. The following are some examples of defences:[32]

- *Self-defence.* The defence of self-defence is set out in section 34 of the *Criminal Code*. It states that a person is not guilty of an offence if (a) he believes on reasonable grounds that force is being used against him or another person or that a threat of force is being made against him or another person; (b) the act that constitutes the offence is committed for the purpose of defending or protecting himself or the other person from that use or threat of force; and (c) the act committed is reasonable in the circumstances. In determining whether the act committed is "reasonable in the circumstances," the court will consider factors including but not limited to the nature of the force or threat; the extent to which the use of force was imminent and whether there were other means available to respond to the potential use of force; whether any party to the incident used or threatened to use a weapon; and the size, age, gender, and physical capabilities of the parties to the incident.

- *Consent.* To rely on the defence of consent, the accused must prove that the alleged victim freely consented to the acts carried out by the accused. Assault is an offence to which the defence of consent may apply—for example, in sporting matches involving physical contact. Certain offences exclude the defence of consent—for example, the infliction of death.

- *Provocation.* This defence is available only where the accused is charged with murder. It is a partial defence, which, if established, does not result in the acquittal of the accused but rather in the accused being convicted of the lesser offence of manslaughter. The provocation may take various forms (such as words or gestures), but the result must be that the accused suddenly lost self-control and did not have time to take into account the consequences of her actions.

- *Duress.* The defence of duress exists at common law and in section 17 of the *Criminal Code*. It is a complex defence when the accused was compelled to commit a criminal offence as a result of threats of immediate death or bodily harm from a person present when the offence was committed. Section 17 does not apply to some specific offences, such as murder, sexual assault, or robbery.

- *Mental disorder.* Section 16 states that no person is criminally responsible for a criminal act or omission made "while suffering from a mental disorder that rendered the person incapable of appreciating the nature and quality of the act or omission or of knowing that it was wrong." Furthermore, the presence of such a disorder must be proved on a balance of probabilities. The burden of proof that an accused was suffering from a mental disorder that exempts him from criminal responsibility is on the party who raises the issue.

Other defences include necessity, automatism, intoxication, mistake of fact, and mistake of law.

---

32 For more information on defences, see Gulycz & Kelly, *supra* note 19, ch 10.

Sentencing

sentence
the punishment the
judge imposes on a
person convicted of
a criminal offence

A **sentence** is the punishment imposed by a trial judge on someone found guilty of a criminal offence. The sentence aims to protect society, as well as to punish the offender and deter others from committing crimes. Sentencing is dealt with in part XXIII of the *Criminal Code*.[33] The purpose and objectives are set out in section 718 as follows:

> 718. The fundamental purpose of sentencing is to protect society and to
> contribute, along with crime prevention initiatives, to respect for the law and the
> maintenance of a just, peaceful and safe society by imposing just sanctions that
> have one or more of the following objectives:
>> (a) to denounce unlawful conduct and the harm done to victims or to the
> community that is caused by unlawful conduct;
>> (b) to deter the offender and other persons from committing offences;
>> (c) to separate offenders from society, where necessary;
>> (d) to assist in rehabilitating offenders;
>> (e) to provide reparations for harm done to victims or to the community; and
>> (f) to promote a sense of responsibility in offenders, and acknowledgment
> of the harm done to victims or to the community.

The fundamental principle of sentencing is expressed in section 718.1 of the *Criminal Code*, which states: "A sentence must be proportionate to the gravity of the offence and the degree of responsibility of the offender." In determining the appropriate sentence, section 718.2 provides other sentencing principles. For example, section 718.2(b) states that a sentence "should be similar to sentences imposed on similar offenders for similar offences committed in similar circumstances," while section 718.2(c) states that "where consecutive sentences are imposed, the combined sentence should not be unduly long or harsh."

Note that there is a particular sentencing principle in the *Criminal Code* that applies specifically to Indigenous offenders, whose overrepresentation has been called "one of the most documented trends in the Canadian criminal justice system."[34] Section 718.2(e) states that "all available sanctions, other than imprisonment, that are reasonable in the circumstances and consistent with the harm done to the victims or to the community should be considered for *all* offenders, *with particular attention to the circumstances of [A]boriginal offenders*" (emphasis added). This principle, which was added to the *Criminal Code* in 1996, represents among other things an attempt to redress Indigenous overrepresentation in the criminal justice system. In the seminal case *R v Gladue*,[35] the Supreme Court first articulated the rules and principles applicable to this section when imposing sentences on Indigenous offenders. Particular background factors that judges must consider are the following:

> (A) The unique systemic or background factors which may have played a part
> in bringing the particular [A]boriginal offender before the courts; and

---

33   A detailed description of sentencing is outside the scope of this text. Interested readers should consult Gulycz & Kelly, *supra* note 19, ch 20.

34   Brian R Pfefferle, "Gladue Sentencing: Uneasy Answers to the Hard Problem of Aboriginal Over-Incarceration" (2009) 32:2 Man LJ 113.

35   *Supra* note 28. The case involved an Indigenous woman from British Columbia, Jamie Tanis Gladue, who pleaded guilty to manslaughter for killing her common law husband. For more information on the case and *Gladue* rights, see Jay Istvanffy's *Gladue Primer* under Further Reading at the end of this chapter.

(B) The types of sentencing procedures and sanctions which may be appropriate in the circumstances for the offender because of his or her particular [A]boriginal heritage or connection.[36]

The court elaborated on these further, as follows:

> The background factors which figure prominently in the causation of crime by [A]boriginal offenders are by now well known. Years of dislocation and economic development have translated, for many [A]boriginal peoples, into low incomes, high unemployment, lack of opportunities and options, lack or irrelevance of education, substance abuse, loneliness, and community fragmentation. These and other factors contribute to a higher incidence of crime and incarceration.[37]

The court also noted some differences between traditional Indigenous sentencing ideals and those of Canada's criminal justice system, highlighting their importance to the analysis:

> A significant problem experienced by [A]boriginal people who come into contact with the criminal justice system is that the traditional sentencing ideals of deterrence, separation, and denunciation are often far removed from the understanding of sentencing held by these offenders and their community. ... [M]ost traditional [A]boriginal conceptions of sentencing place a *primary* emphasis upon the ideals of restorative justice. This tradition is extremely important to the analysis under s. 718.2(e).[38]

Unfortunately, more than a decade after the precedent-setting *Gladue* decision, the Supreme Court observed that—according to statistics, and due in part to "a fundamental misunderstanding and misapplication of both s. 718.2(e) and this Court's decision in *Gladue*"—section 718.2(e) has not had a "discernible impact" on Indigenous overrepresentation in the criminal justice system to date.[39]

Under section 718.2, a judge must also consider possible aggravating circumstances before imposing a sentence. An **aggravating circumstance** is any circumstance related to the offence or the offender that increases the seriousness of the offence and that may result in an increased sentence. Section 718.2(a) sets out a number of circumstances that may be considered aggravating—for example, evidence that the offence was motivated by bias, prejudice, or hate based on a prohibited ground of discrimination; that the offender abused someone under the age of 18; that the offender, in committing the offence, abused a position of trust or authority in relation to the victim; and that the offence was a terrorism offence. A **mitigating circumstance** is any circumstance associated with the offence or the offender that decreases the seriousness of the offence and that may result in a reduced sentence. Although section 718.2 does not provide examples, some could include whether the offender cooperated with police, the offender's age and absence of a criminal record, whether the offender showed remorse, or whether the offender committed the offence as a result of having been provoked.

To help them decide on an appropriate sentence, particularly in the case of a first-time offender, judges may also request a **pre-sentence report**, prepared by a probation officer,

aggravating circumstance
a factor in the case that causes the judge to impose a harsher sentence on the convicted person than she would otherwise

mitigating circumstance
a factor in the case that causes the judge to impose a milder sentence on the convicted person than he would otherwise

pre-sentence report
a report, prepared by a probation officer that provides information about the background and character of the offender, to assist a judge in sentencing

---

36 *R v Gladue*, *supra* note 28 at para 66.

37 *Ibid* at para 67.

38 *Ibid* at para 70 (emphasis in original).

39 *R v Ipeelee*, 2012 SCC 13 at para 63.

to learn more about the background and character of the offender. In addition to the pre-sentence report, the victim and relatives of the victim may prepare and file a victim impact statement, describing the impact the crime has had on their lives. At the sentencing hearing, both the Crown and defence counsel have an opportunity to make submissions; they may also make a joint submission. Possible sentences include an absolute or conditional discharge, a fine, a suspended sentence and probation, or imprisonment (see Box 12.3). If either the Crown or accused person decides to appeal, part XXI of the *Criminal Code* governs appeals for indictable offences, while part XXVII governs appeals for summary conviction offences.[40]

BOX 12.3

Sentencing and Canada's Correctional System

In Canada, correctional jurisdiction is divided between the provinces/territories and the federal government. Adults who receive a custodial sentence of less than two years serve their sentence in a provincial or territorial correctional facility operated by the province/territory under relevant provincial/territorial legislation—in Ontario, for example, corrections are administered under the *Ministry of Correctional Services Act*[41] by the Ontario Ministry of Community Safety and Correctional Services. Adults who receive a custodial sentence of two years or more serve their sentence in federal institutions, referred to as penitentiaries, which are operated by the Correctional Service of Canada (CSC) under the *Corrections and Conditional Release Act*.[42]

Depending on the assessment and classification of a particular offender by correctional officials, the offender may serve her sentence in a maximum, medium, or minimum security facility, or in a multi-level institution. Offenders may be released once their entire sentence has been served, or by parole granted prior to completion of the sentence by either the Parole Board of Canada or various provincial/territorial parole boards established by some provinces/territories for inmates serving time in provincial/territorial correctional facilities. In addition to the provincial/territorial and federal correctional systems, the third correctional system in Canada is the youth criminal justice system for young persons (see the discussion under the heading "Youth Criminal Justice Act").

Another way in which someone convicted of an offence can serve their sentence in the community and remain out of custody is through a suspended sentence and probation. Under section 731(1)(a) of the *Criminal Code*, provided that no minimum punishment is prescribed by law, a judge can, having regard to the offender's age and character, the nature of the offence, and the circumstances surrounding it, suspend the sentence and release the offender on probation. This order prescribes certain mandatory conditions and permits the court to prescribe "additional conditions" listed in section 732.1(3). If, however, the offender fails or refuses to comply with the order without a reasonable excuse, he may be charged with an additional offence of breach of probation under section 733.1 of the *Criminal Code*.

Youth Criminal Justice Act

In Canada today, young people who commit criminal offences set out in the *Criminal Code* are treated differently from adults. Young persons 12 years of age or older but less than 18 years of age do not have their offence dealt with in adult criminal court, but rather are tried

---

40   For more information on appeals, see Gulycz & Kelly, *supra* note 19, ch 21.

41   RSO 1990, c M.22.

42   SC 1992, c 20.

in a youth justice court established under the provisions of the YCJA, which came into force in 2003.

The YCJA has a declaration of principle in section 3 that contains the policy in Canada for dealing with young persons. The Act is structured to process young persons charged with *Criminal Code* offences from their first contact with police through to (if applicable) their trial and sentence with this policy in mind. Special procedures aim to ensure the fair treatment of young persons and the protection of their rights.

Among the Act's features is the use of extrajudicial measures, requiring a police officer to consider, for example, giving a warning to a young person or making a referral to a community program before starting judicial proceedings (s 6); giving young persons the right to retain and instruct counsel without delay at *any* stage of the proceedings (s 25); requiring parental notice of their child's arrest (s 26); and provisions relating to the sentencing, custody, and supervision of young persons in parts 4 and 5 of the Act. The sentencing principles in section 38(1) state that

> [t]he purpose of sentencing under section 42 (youth sentences) is to hold a young person accountable for an offence through the imposition of just sanctions that have meaningful consequences for the young person and that promote his or her rehabilitation and reintegration into society, thereby contributing to the long-term protection of the public.

Sentences may include a judicial reprimand, a fine, compensation or restitution, or a community service order. Custody and supervision orders are also possible.

Youth sentences are generally less severe than adult sentences, but in some cases the Crown can apply to the court to have the youth sentenced as an adult. An adult sentence may be appropriate where the youth is convicted of a serious violent crime (such as murder, manslaughter, or aggravated sexual assault) or where the offence is part of a pattern of violent offences. Youths receiving adult sentences serve their sentences in youth facilities; however, if they turn 20 in a youth facility, they may be transferred to an adult facility (ss 64-81).

Indigenous Peoples and the Criminal Justice System

In recent decades, the overrepresentation of Indigenous peoples in Canada's criminal justice system, especially corrections, has reached alarming proportions.[43] The Office of the Correctional Investigator now estimates that the incarceration rate for Indigenous adults is as much as ten times higher than for non-Indigenous adults. As of 2013, although Indigenous peoples made up only approximately 4 percent of Canada's population, they accounted for over 23 percent of the federal inmate population.[44]

A range of studies, task forces, royal commissions, conferences, and inquiries have highlighted the adverse impact of the enforcement and administration of criminal law on

---

43 For a detailed discussion, see Darion Boyington et al, "Indigenous People and the Criminal Justice System" in *Diversity and Indigenous Peoples in Canada*, 3rd ed (Toronto: Emond, 2017) ch 11.

44 Canada, Office of the Correctional Investigator, "Aboriginal Offenders—A Critical Situation" (Backgrounder) (Ottawa: 16 September 2013), online: <http://www.oci-bec.gc.ca/cnt/rpt/oth-aut/oth-aut20121022info-eng.aspx>.

Indigenous peoples and put forth suggestions for intervention. The Office of the Correctional Investigator noted recently that, compared with non-Indigenous inmates, Indigenous inmates are:

- classified as higher risk and higher need in areas such as community reintegration, family supports, and unemployment;
- released later in their sentences, with most leaving prison at the statutory release or warrant expiry date;
- overrepresented in segregation and maximum security populations;
- disproportionately involved in self-injury and use-of-force interventions while incarcerated; and
- more likely to return to prison on revocation of parole for administrative reasons rather than criminal violations.[45]

In addition to the background factors described by the Supreme Court in *Gladue*, the fundamental differences between Euro-Canadian and traditional Indigenous notions of justice have been suggested as another contributing factor to the higher incidence of Indigenous crime and incarceration (see Table 12.1). Manitoba Justice Murray Sinclair, who served as the chair of the Truth and Reconciliation Commission, explains:

> The starting point is a difficult one for people raised with the liberal ideals of "civil rights" and "equality"; it requires one to accept the possibility that being Aboriginal and being non-Aboriginal involve being different. It requires one to come to terms with the concept that the Aboriginal Peoples of North America, for the most part, hold world views and life philosophies fundamentally different from those of the dominant Euro-Canadian society, and that these ... are so fundamentally different as to be inherently in conflict. ...
>
> There are areas of thought and belief that are substantially shared by both Aboriginal and non-Aboriginal peoples. Nevertheless, the differences are broad enough and general enough to make many Euro-Canadian institutions incompatible with the moral and ethical value systems and approaches of Aboriginal Canadians.[46]

The modern instruments of criminal justice—jails, police officers, and courts—were unknown to Indigenous peoples prior to European contact. Mediation was used to resolve disputes and restore the offender to a harmonious relationship with the rest of the community, through the acceptance of responsibility and through making the necessary amends, both to the victim and the larger community. All community members, and Elders in particular, played an important role.[47]

---

45 *Ibid.*

46 Murray Sinclair, "Aboriginal Peoples, Justice and the Law" in Richard Gosse, James Youngblood Henderson & Roger Carter, eds, *Continuing Poundmaker and Riel's Quest: Presentations Made at a Conference on Aboriginal Peoples and Justice* (Saskatoon: Purich, 1994) 173 at 175-76.

47 Boyington et al, *supra* note 43 at 332-33. These were the broad principles of Indigenous justice. Different moral codes, religious beliefs, and life philosophies existed among different Indigenous peoples.

TABLE 12.1 Euro–Canadian Versus Traditional Indigenous Justice

EURO–CANADIAN JUSTICE	TRADITIONAL INDIGENOUS JUSTICE
Laws formulated by elected representatives	Laws formulated by the community through tradition and consensus
Laws tied to man-made economy	Laws tied to the natural environment, only a few universally condemned actions
Protestant ethic and Christianity the moral foundation of law	Traditional Indian religions the foundations of codes of behaviour
Personal offences seen as transgressions against the state as represented by the monarch	Personal offences seen as transgressions against the victim and his/her family; community threatened only when the public peace is threatened
Law administered by representatives of the state in the form of officially recognized or operated social institutions	Laws usually administered by the offended party, i.e. family, clan
Force and punishment used as methods of social control	Arbitration and ostracism usual peacekeeping methods
Individualistic basis for society and the use of the law to protect private property	Communal basis for society; no legal protection for private property; land held in trust by an individual and protected by the group

Source: James S Frideres & René R Gadacz, *Aboriginal Peoples in Canada*, 9th ed (Toronto: Pearson, 2012) at 119.

Given all that has occurred over the past few hundred years, however, as Mary Ellen Turpel suggests in the Royal Commission on Aboriginal Peoples report on justice issues, it would be fruitless to attempt simply to return to pre-colonial ways:

> Can the pre-colonial regime ever be reconstructed? My own view is no, not except as a relic of the past. It cannot be resurrected because we have all been touched by imperialism and colonialism, and there is no simplistic escape to some pre-colonial history except a rhetorical one. In my view, we [Aboriginal people] need to regain control over criminal justice, indeed all justice matters, but in a thoroughly post-colonial fashion. ... One cannot erase the history of colonialism, but we must, as an imperative, undo it in a contemporary context. ... We have to accept that there are profound social and economic problems in Aboriginal communities today that never existed pre-colonization and even in the first few hundred years of interaction. Problems of alcohol and solvent abuse, family violence and sexual abuse, and youth crime—these are indications of a fundamental breakdown in the social order in Aboriginal communities of a magnitude never known before. A reform dialogue or proposals in the criminal justice field have to come to grips with this contemporary reality and not just retreat into a pre-colonial situation.[48]

The Royal Commission on Aboriginal Peoples recommended that the federal, provincial, and territorial governments "recognize the right of Aboriginal nations to establish and administer their own systems of justice,"[49] and others, such as Manitoba's Aboriginal

---

48 Royal Commission on Aboriginal Peoples, *Bridging the Cultural Divide: A Report on Aboriginal People and Criminal Justice in Canada* (Ottawa: Supply and Services Canada, 1996) at 65-66.

49 *Ibid* at 312.

Justice Implementation Commission, have recommended an autonomous Indigenous justice system to address the failure of the current criminal justice system for Indigenous peoples. Other possibilities include "Indigenizing" the current criminal justice system through increased Indigenous representation among police officers, lawyers, judges, and correctional officers; creating autonomous Indigenous agencies to work within the existing system; and the continued implementation of the Correctional Service of Canada strategic plan for Indigenous corrections, which aims to provide culturally appropriate programming and services in custody facilities.[50]

Despite some positive developments—for example, the eight healing lodges currently operating across the country, and the Indigenous-specific In Search of Your Warrior Violent Offender Healing Program—success has been limited. Many bridges still need to be built to cross the cultural divide between mainstream and Indigenous concepts of law and justice, and to address the underlying causes of Indigenous overrepresentation in the criminal justice system.

---

50 Boyington, *supra* note 43 at 336-37.

CHAPTER SUMMARY

Canada's *Constitution Act, 1867* gives the Parliament of Canada exclusive jurisdiction over criminal law and procedure in criminal matters. Pursuant to this power, the federal government enacted a *Criminal Code* in 1892, which, since then, has been the primary source of Canadian criminal law. The *Criminal Code* contains key principles of our criminal law. It organizes specific offences into general subject matter categories and classifies offences into three categories: summary, indictable, and hybrid. It also contains law relating to the criminal trial process, defences, sentencing, and appeals.

In addition to the *Criminal Code*, other federal statutes and the Charter play an important role in this area. As well, decisions of the courts—especially SCC decisions interpreting criminal law statutes and the Charter—are an integral part of our criminal law.

The larger field of criminal justice also involves policing, corrections, and youth justice. Police investigation of crime may lead police to charge an individual with a criminal offence. If, after their trial, individuals are found guilty, then depending on their offence they may be sentenced to incarceration in either a provincial or a federal correctional institution. In Canada today, young persons who commit criminal offences are treated differently than adults and are tried separately in a youth justice court.

KEY TERMS

aggravating circumstance, 355

appearance notice, 350

arraignment, 352

arrest, 346

conviction, 352

Crown attorney, 336

duty of disclosure, 347

hybrid offence, 345

indictable offence, 344

indictment, 352

information, 352

judicial interim release, 350

limitation period, 344

mitigating circumstance, 355

plea bargain, 351

plead, 351

preliminary inquiry, 351

pre-sentence report, 355

quasi-criminal offences, 340

search warrant, 348

sentence, 354

summary conviction offence, 344

summons, 350

superior court of criminal jurisdiction, 345

undertaking, 351

verdict, 352

FURTHER READING

BOOKS

Atkinson, Paul. *The Canadian Justice System: An Overview*, 4th ed (Toronto: LexisNexis, 2017).

Barnhorst, Richard & Sherrie Barnhorst. *Criminal Law and the Canadian Criminal Code*, 6th ed (Toronto: McGraw-Hill Ryerson, 2013).

Bell, Sandra J. *Young Offenders and Youth Justice: A Century After the Fact*, 5th ed (Toronto: Nelson, 2014).

Gulycz, Michael & Mary Ann Kelly. *Criminal Law for Legal Professionals*, 2nd ed (Toronto: Emond, 2018).

Hamilton, AC. *A Feather Not a Gavel: Working Towards Aboriginal Justice* (Winnipeg: Great Plains, 2001).

Hennessy, P. *Canada's Big House: The Dark History of the Kingston Penitentiary* (Toronto: Dundurn, 1999).

Ismaili, Karim, Jane B Sprott & Kim Varma, eds. *Canadian Criminal Justice Policy: Contemporary Perspectives* (Toronto: Oxford University Press, 2012).

Istvanffy, Jay. *Gladue Primer* (Vancouver: Legal Services Society, 2011), online: <http://www.lss.bc.ca/resources/pdfs/pubs/Gladue-Primer-eng.pdf>.

O'Regan, Karla & Susan Reid. *Thinking About Criminal Justice in Canada*, 2nd ed (Toronto: Emond, 2017).

Pink, Joel E & David C Perrier, eds. *From Crime to Punishment: An Introduction to the Criminal Law System*, 8th ed (Toronto: Carswell, 2014).

Roach, Kent. *Criminal Law*, 6th ed (Toronto: Irwin Law, 2015).

Stuart, Don. *Canadian Criminal Law: A Treatise*, 7th ed (Toronto: Carswell, 2014).

Watkins, Kerry, Gail Anderson & Vincenzo Rondinelli. *Evidence and Investigation: From the Crime Scene to the Courtroom* (Toronto: Emond Montgomery, 2012).

REVIEW QUESTIONS

1. What did John A Macdonald dislike about the American system of criminal law, and how did he prevent it from happening in Canada?

2. List four federal statutes that are sources of Canadian criminal law.

3. List and describe the two elements of a criminal offence in the *Criminal Code*.

4. Explain the criminal standard of proof "beyond a reasonable doubt." To whom does this standard apply?

5. What are the three classifications of criminal offences under the *Criminal Code*?

6. Why is disclosure so important to an accused person?

7. What is an aggravating circumstance? Give three examples.

8. List five important matters for an accused to consider before the trial begins.

EXERCISES

1. Do you think a specialized court like Ontario's Domestic Violence Court is a good idea? Why or why not?

2. Locate and read the SCC decision in *Bedford* (see Box 12.1). Next, locate and review the provisions in the *Protection of Communities and Exploited Persons Act*, SC 2014, c 25 amending Canada's prostitution laws. Do you think the provisions alleviate the concerns expressed by the SCC in connection with the old laws—particularly those relating to the safety of sex workers? Give reasons for your answer.

3. Examine the first paragraph in the preamble to the *Youth Criminal Justice Act*. What do you think are the "developmental challenges and the needs of young persons"? What members of society are best placed to guide young persons into adulthood, and why?

4. In recent decades, changes to the way Canada's criminal justice system deals with Indigenous peoples accused and convicted of crimes have sought to improve treatment and outcomes for Indigenous offenders. What do you think of these solutions and their potential for reform? Depending on your answer, should Indigenous peoples have jurisdiction to operate their own criminal justice system? Defend your answer.

13 Public International Law

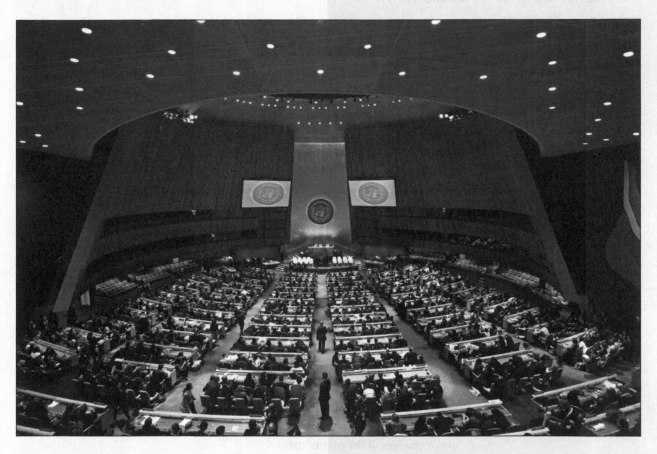

Inside the United Nations
General Assembly building in New York.

After reading this chapter, you will understand:

- The nature of international law and its historical development.
- The principal sources of international law.
- The relationship between international law and domestic law.
- The main branches of international law.
- How international law is enforced.

Public international law is not so much an area or topic of the law as it is an entire legal system that is conceptually distinct from the national legal systems that regulate daily life within states.

John H Currie, *Public International Law*, 2nd ed (Toronto: Irwin Law, 2008) at 1

Introduction

public international law (or international law)
law relating primarily to international treaties and customs and to inter-state relationships

In recent years, a number of global issues have highlighted the importance of **public international law (or international law)**, including:

- terrorism and state responses to it,
- continuing regional and ethnic conflicts around the world,
- the fragility of the global economy,
- a growing awareness of the economic interdependence of nations, and
- major changes to the environment.

This chapter presents an overview of the basic concepts and principles of international law, its sources, some of its key branches, and the ways in which it is enforced. For a brief history of international law, see Box 13.1.

What Is International Law?

In simple terms, international law is concerned with regulating the relationship between independent states, and to a lesser degree with the rights and obligations of non-state actors, including individuals. A fuller examination shows, however, that international law is a vast, complex, and developing field of regulation that concerns all of humankind. As stated in the opening quote, it more closely resembles a legal system than a discrete area of law.

The following question is frequently posed: Is international law about "law" at all, or is it about other types of norms? International law lacks a number of the elements that characterize most domestic legal systems. It lacks, for example, a centralized law-making structure, and it lacks executive and judicial branches that administer and apply the law. It also lacks an effective enforcement mechanism. Despite this, there is a general respect for the system of international law that is in place; its rules are followed more than they are broken.

There are over 190 independent countries in the world today, and even with the cultural, ethnic, religious, political, and economic differences that exist among these countries, most of them recognize the need for a stable framework of agreed-upon rules that can help them peacefully coexist.

It is important to keep in mind that not all legal relationships that involve an *international* component are the province of public international law. Private law relationships may have transnational aspects to them—for example, in cases where individuals or corporations residing in different countries do business together. These relationships are the province of *private* international law (or *conflict of laws*), as noted in the brief discussion of this area in Chapter 14.

BOX 13.1

History of International Law

Scholars recognize three distinct periods in the history of international law: (1) the so-called primitive period; (2) the classical, or traditional, period; and (3) the modern period.

Primitive Period: Before 1648

In the period leading up to the mid-1600s, relations between states in Europe were marked by a tension between two opposing ideas or premises:

1. States are free to do as they please in the international arena based on the "might is right" principle.
2. In both international and domestic affairs, states are subject to overarching natural law principles—that is, principles derived from a higher power or source that guides our behaviour and offers us an ideal standard.

Notions of what those natural law principles were precisely and the degree of control they ought to have over a state's actions varied according to the writer. A natural law thinker, Hugo Grotius, whose writings on international relations culminated in *On the Law of War and Peace* (1625), is generally regarded as the father of modern international law, and this work as the seminal international law treatise. He espoused a natural law system based on reason and asserted the notion of the interdependence of states.

Classical or Traditional Period: 1648-1919

The Peace of Westphalia was a series of treaties made in 1648 that marked the end of two long-standing wars: the Thirty Years' War between France and the Habsburg rulers of the Holy Roman Empire, and the Eighty Years' War between Spain and the Dutch. These treaties were significant because

they clearly gave the principle of state sovereignty priority over other considerations, such as religious and dynastic allegiances. State sovereignty focuses on the right of a state to control itself. Religious and dynastic allegiances recognize controls from outside.

The Peace of Westphalia marks the beginning of the classical or traditional period of international law. In the centuries that followed it, secularism in state affairs grew and religious influences declined. There was a rise in nationalism, and the independence of sovereign states in international dealings became entrenched. Grotius's idea of interdependence manifested itself primarily through treaty making.

In the 1800s, positivistic thinking, which was based on empiricism (or knowledge from experience), looked at state conduct as a possible basis of laws between states. In other words, the theory that custom—the established conduct of states in their international relations—could be a source of international law began to take hold. Most of this thinking arose in Europe, but eventually Middle Eastern and Oriental states also started to accept these general principles concerning state sovereignty, treaty making, and custom.

Modern Period: 1919-Present

Modern international law dates from the end of the First World War and the Paris Peace Conference of 1919, which led to the creation of the League of Nations in the same year. The league was an intergovernmental organization, consisting of 42 member states, whose main purpose was to maintain world peace. It sought to resolve international disputes through negotiation, and when these negotiations failed, it relied heavily on its strongest members to enforce its resolutions. Though US president Woodrow Wilson was a driving force behind the league's founding, the United States never joined it, and it was ineffective in stopping the Axis powers in the leadup to the Second World War. It was officially disbanded in 1946.

In 1945, the UN was formed as the successor organization to the League of Nations. Today, it has 193 member nations.

The UN and the UN Charter are at the centre of the modern system of international law. The guiding principles of international law have never been so clearly expressed and actively developed as they are today. Nor have they ever been so widely accepted as binding.

Subjects and Objects in International Law

subject of international law
usually a state that has as an "international legal personality" and is capable of possessing international rights and obligations

International law recognizes a loose distinction between *subjects* and *objects*. A **subject of international law** has an "international legal personality" and is capable of possessing international rights and obligations. An *object* is the focus of a subject's rights and obligations, and it can be a person, an entity, a geographical area, or a resource.

The main subjects are states. However, there are no clear limitations either on who or what can be a subject or on who or what can be an object. States can, by agreement or recognition, confer statehood on new members. Furthermore, a state can be a subject in one context and an object in another. So can an individual person. For example, a country as subject might owe an individual as object certain human rights obligations, and an individual as subject might owe a country as object an obligation not to perpetrate or orchestrate war crimes. The entities in the following list are *objects* in some contexts but have limited *subject* status in others:

- countries such as Taiwan, Palestine, and Tibet, which are not fully recognized as states internationally;
- peoples seeking self-determination (ethnic groups or Indigenous peoples within countries who don't fully accept state control), such as the Basques of Spain, the Chechens of Russia, the Kurdish people of the Middle East, or the Québécois separatists of Canada;
- international or intergovernmental organizations (IGOs), such as the North Atlantic Treaty Organization (NATO) or the European Union;
- non-governmental organizations (NGOs), such as Oxfam and Greenpeace;
- individuals; and
- corporations (multinational or otherwise).

State Sovereignty and State Jurisdiction

state sovereignty
principle that a state has exclusive power in certain areas, such as the power to make, administer, and adjudicate its own laws in relation to itself and its own citizens and residents

state jurisdiction
area of control within which a state's sovereignty can be exercised

Two key and related concepts in international law are *state sovereignty* and *state jurisdiction*. **State sovereignty** refers to the state's exclusive power in certain areas—for example, the power to make, administer, and adjudicate its own laws in relation to itself and its own citizens and residents. It is also clear that sovereign states can enter into relations with other states—for example, to make treaties. **State jurisdiction** is the area of control within which a state's sovereignty can be exercised. The area can be physical or territorial, or it can be conceptual—related, for example, to a subject matter such as civil or criminal liability. States have jurisdiction over almost all matters within their territorial limits.

States have restricted jurisdiction over matters outside their territorial limits. For nations bordering oceans and seas, their jurisdiction over the area off the coast is based on a complex system of customs and conventions; there are rules for 12-mile limits (exclusive control over virtually all matters), 200-mile limits (exclusive economic control), and other limits. With respect to its own nationals or citizens, a state may exercise jurisdiction over them outside its territorial limits if they "injure" the state there—for example, by threatening its security. (The term *nationals* usually refers to individual citizens, but it can also include corporations and ships that fly the state's flag.)

A state can also exercise jurisdiction over non-nationals—citizens of a different country—outside its territorial limits for conduct that affects or has affected the state and amounts to a crime against humanity.[1] (See the discussion of international criminal law in the next section.) Whether a state's extraterritorial jurisdiction can involve the use of force in another state to apprehend or punish a person (regardless of whether the conduct was committed territorially or extraterritorially) is another issue. Claiming jurisdiction over someone or something extraterritorially is one thing. Using force in another country is another. There are peaceful methods of exercising jurisdiction, such as diplomacy and international court processes. It is generally accepted that the use of such force requires the consent of the other state.

State Responsibility and State Immunity

Another important idea in international law is that of **state responsibility**. This refers to the state's accountability for breaches of international obligations. The equivalent of responsibility, in domestic law, is a person's being required to pay damages for breach of contract, or being sent to jail for committing a serious crime. Until recently, this area was unclear with respect to international law. In 2001, however, the International Law Commission adopted a draft set of articles that, while not yet officially adopted by the United Nations or by individual states at the time of writing, is gaining wide acceptance. The International Court of Justice (ICJ)—the main judicial arm of the United Nations—has already cited this set of articles with approval. It should pave the way for much greater certainty in the area of accountability.[2]

State immunity can be thought of as the flip side of state responsibility, although it is not precisely that. Based on customary international law, state immunity generally applies where one state, its representatives (mainly diplomats and consuls), or their property have been made subject to judicial proceedings in another state. This immunity, when claimed, prevents the judicial proceedings from progressing any further.

There are questions about how absolute this immunity is and what exceptions to it there might be. In 1982, Canada passed the *State Immunity Act*,[3] which clearly sets out a number of exceptions. Under this legislation, states and their representatives do not enjoy immunity in Canada either in relation to commercial activities—for example, buying and selling—or when they cause death, personal injury, or property damage in this country. There could be contractual, tortious, or criminal liability arising from such activities, depending on the circumstances.

The exceptions set out in Canada's *State Immunity Act* appear to be broader than the exceptions established by international custom. This disparity could prove problematic: for

state responsibility
principle that a state should be held accountable for breaches of international obligations

state immunity
immunity that a state or its officials have in the event they become the subject of judicial proceedings in another state

---

1 See *Israel (AG) v Eichmann*, judgment of the District Court of Jerusalem (1961), translated and reprinted in (1962) 56 Am J Int'l L 805.

2 International Law Commission, *Responsibility of States for Internationally Wrongful Acts*, UNILCOR, 53rd Sess (2001), online: <http://legal.un.org/ilc/texts/instruments/english/draft_articles/9_6_2001.pdf>.

3 RSC 1985, c S-18.

example, if Canadian courts were to permit judicial proceedings against a foreign official based on the exceptions set out in the Act, these proceedings could be contrary to international law. Finally, state immunity does not apply in international settings or venues—the ICJ, for example, which is not under the control of a single state. State immunity is territorially based. When it does apply, it is confined to protecting one state or its representatives from having to submit to judicial proceedings in another state.

The UN Charter: Core Principles of International Law

The United Nations (UN) is at the centre of the modern system of international law, and its principles are expressed in its constitution, the *Charter of the United Nations*[4] (UN Charter). These are core principles of international law and serve as guides for state behaviour, treaties, and policy making.

Article 1 of the UN Charter sets out the *purposes* of the UN. The following is a summary of them:

1. to maintain international peace and security and to resolve international disputes in conformity with the principles of justice and international law;
2. to develop friendly relations among nations based on a respect for equal rights and self-determination of peoples;
3. to solve economic, social, cultural, or humanitarian problems of an international character and to promote respect for human rights through cooperation; and
4. to be a centre for harmonizing the actions of nations in the attainment of these common ends.

Article 2 describes the *principles* that the UN and its members are to follow in pursuing the purposes identified in the UN Charter. The following is a summary of these principles:

1. recognizing sovereign equality of members,
2. fulfilling obligations in good faith,
3. settling international disputes peacefully,
4. not threatening or using force against other states,
5. assisting the UN as necessary,
6. respecting non-member states, and
7. not intervening in the domestic affairs of a state except to maintain or restore international peace, or in self-defence.

Sources of International Law

The principal sources of international law are set out in article 38 of the *Statute of the International Court of Justice* (ICJ Statute).[5] They are as follows:

> a. international conventions, whether general or particular, establishing rules expressly recognized by the contesting states [that is, *treaties*],

---

4 26 June 1945, Can TS 1945 No 7.

5 The ICJ Statute, which constitutes the ICJ, is annexed to the UN Charter and can only be changed by a two-thirds majority of the General Assembly of the UN.

b. international custom, as evidence of a general practice accepted as law [that is, *international custom*],

c. general principles of law recognized by civilized nations [that is, *general principles of law*], and

d. subject to the provisions of Article 59, judicial decisions and the teachings of the most highly qualified publicists of the various nations, as subsidiary means for the determination of rules of law [that is, *domestic judgments and commentary*].

According to article 38, then, the main sources of international law are (1) treaties, (2) international custom, (3) general principles of law, and (4) domestic judgments and commentary. Other sources of international law include resolutions by international organizations, such as the UN, and self-imposed obligations by states.

Treaties

Treaties are agreements between states concerning their legal rights and obligations in relation to specific matters. As noted above, they can be bilateral (between two states) or multilateral (between three or more states—for example, the UN Charter). There are hundreds of current treaties in the world today covering a multitude of topics, including state privileges and immunities, human rights, refugees and stateless persons, drugs, human trafficking, health, international trade, oceans, outer space, disarmament, and the environment.

Making treaties is governed by another treaty: the 1980 Vienna Convention on the Law of Treaties[6] (VCLT). The VCLT essentially codifies the customary rules concerning treaty making, rules that were already in place in 1980. As of 2010, the VCLT has been ratified by 111 nations, and even states that have not formally signed on to it recognize it as an authoritative guide. It applies only to treaties between states, not to agreements between states and non-state entities such as IGOs (public or governmental organizations created by treaty or agreement between states, such as the European Union or the Arab League) or NGOs (organizations established by individuals or associations of individuals, such as Greenpeace or Amnesty International). Nor does it apply to agreements between IGOs and NGOs.

The VCLT contains rules about a number of issues related to treaties, including their form, validity, interpretation, and dispute resolution. Regarding the latter, for example, the VCLT prescribes that any dispute involving *jus cogens*—that is, important international customs that have achieved a special status, as described below—must go before the ICJ.

International Custom

An international custom is a settled, general practice between states that has been accepted as law. Such customs develop over time. They begin as limited practices that states engage in with a view not to making law but to protecting their own interests, such as customs prohibiting genocide and torture. Some of the criteria defining a custom are the following:

1. *Duration of practice.* The longer the practice has existed, the more likely it is to have evolved into a custom. However, no particular amount of time is required to have elapsed before a practice qualifies as a custom, and the ICJ does not emphasize this element.

2. *Consistency of practice.* The practice must be one that has not varied substantially during its existence.

---

6   23 May 1969, 1155 UNTS 331 (entered into force 27 January 1980).

3. *Generality of practice.* For a practice to be considered a custom, there must be "substantial universality" in its use by world states. Absolute universality is not required.

4. *Accepted as law.* The Latin term for this, *opinio juris* ("opinion of law"), refers to the *belief* that an action is carried out because there is a legal obligation to do so; it is sometimes described as the "psychological" element of custom. States' official declarations of their motivations for some action could be evidence of *opinio juris*. In other words, a state may believe it has an obligation to do something and declare that it does have this obligation, leading to the conclusion that the action is based on a legal obligation. The more evidence of this kind exists, the more likely a practice will be held to be custom.[7]

The criterion of substantial universality means that not all states need to engage in or accept a practice that other states regard as a custom. If a state has persistently refrained from or rejected a practice that has developed into a custom for other states, that state is not considered subject to it.

As described below, some important customs reach the status of *jus cogens* and have a special status in international law. They take precedence over treaties that conflict with them. Apart from customs that have this *jus cogens* status, the interrelation between custom and treaties is a complex and somewhat unclear area.

General Principles of Law

Article 38 of the ICJ Statute lists "general principles of law" as another one of the sources of international law. This provision is not clear and has been the subject of much debate. It appears to refer to principles of general application commonly found in domestic legal systems—for example, the principle of *res judicata*, which prevents the relitigation of an already fully litigated matter; and equitable principles such as estoppel, which requires a party to act consistently with previous actions or declarations of intention.

Domestic Judgments and Commentary

Article 38 categorizes this last-listed source of international law as a "subsidiary means for the determination of rules of law." This phrasing suggests that domestic judgments and commentary are not true sources at all, but rather secondary sources to help evidence or buttress the other formal sources. Not all jurists agree, and some believe that these domestic sources should be considered binding.

Other Sources of International Law

UN Security Council resolutions are binding sources of international law. The Security Council is set up under the UN Charter and is charged with the primary responsibility of maintaining international peace and security. It is composed of 15 member states, some of which have permanent places on the Council; other states are elected for two-year periods. Its resolutions are made binding by virtue of article 25 of the UN Charter: "The Members

---

7   James Crawford, *Brownlie's Principles of Public International Law*, 8th ed (Oxford: Oxford University Press, 2012) at 24-27.

of the United Nations agree to accept and carry out the decisions of the Security Council in accordance with the present Charter."

Resolutions of the UN General Assembly—which is made up of all the members of the UN—are recommendations only and are not a source of international law. The contents of these resolutions, however, may evidence other sources of international law, such as customs.

Unilateral declarations by states about their obligations can also amount to sources of international law. However, they are binding only on the state making the declaration.

Hierarchy of Sources

Is there a hierarchy among the sources of international law listed above? If the sources disagree, which takes precedence? In the Canadian domestic system, when there is a conflict between legislation and common law, the doctrine of parliamentary sovereignty dictates that the legislation takes precedence. Is there a similar kind of doctrine in international law?

The short answer is a qualified "yes." Absolute certainty in this regard is not possible, however, because there is no formal, binding international constitution. The ordering in article 38 does not appear to be determinative, and it is the following hierarchy that has the support of most jurists:

1. *Jus cogens.* Latin for "compelling law," **jus cogens** are overriding or peremptory principles of international law, generally based on custom.[8] Once established, they cannot be changed by treaty, only replaced by new norms or principles that have acquired the status of *jus cogens*. Examples of such fundamental principles in international law include the prohibitions against the unlawful use of force, genocide, slave trading, and piracy.[9] Some customs, though compelling, are not considered overriding or peremptory and do not qualify as *jus cogens*. Where there are conflicts between treaties and these kinds of customs (that is, customs that are not *jus cogens*), the relationship is not clear.

2. *Law-making treaties.* Some treaties make law in the sense of creating or evidencing general norms of international behaviour. When one does, usually in the form of a multilateral treaty, it becomes a principal source of international law. Examples of these kinds of law-making treaties include treaties about international human rights and the Geneva Conventions, which deal with the humanitarian treatment of non-combatants during times of war. Not all treaties have this status, however; not all provide evidence of general norms of international behaviour. Some may simply be bilateral arrangements for limited purposes (for example, sharing a water source or a trade agreement). These types of treaties are sometimes referred to as *contract treaties* and are not a source of international law.

   The UN Charter provides that UN obligations take precedence over all other treaty obligations. Article 103 states: "In the event of a conflict between the

jus cogens
principles of international law, based on custom, that are overriding or peremptory and that cannot be changed by treaty

---

8   There is no reason in theory, however, why such peremptory principles could not be derived originally from treaty provisions: see John H Currie, *Public International Law*, 2nd ed (Toronto: Irwin Law, 2008) at 174-75. Further, such principles, when based on custom, may later be codified in treaties.

9   Malcolm N Shaw, *International Law*, 6th ed (Cambridge, UK: Cambridge University Press, 2008) at 126.

obligations of the Members of the United Nations under the present Charter and their obligations under any other international agreement, their obligations under the present Charter shall prevail." The UN Charter is itself a treaty and contains obligations. According to article 103, then, these obligations would clearly take priority over all other treaty obligations. Article 103 also suggests that UN Security Council resolutions that are passed under the UN Charter and that create obligations would take priority over other treaty obligations.

3. *Other sources.* There does not appear to be any consensus about the relative authority of other sources of international law except insofar as they are all subordinate to custom and treaties.

In terms of the hierarchical ordering of the sources of international law, it is clear the *jus cogens* customs are first and that law-making treaties are second. Beyond that, there is no consensus.

Relationship Between International Law and Domestic Law

It may appear that the UN Charter is the international equivalent of a nation's constitution and that the UN General Assembly is the equivalent of a legislature. The Secretariat—headed by the secretary-general, who is elected by the members—seems comparable to an executive branch of government. And the ICJ seems analogous to a nation's judiciary. The appearance, however, is not the reality.

This analogy breaks down on closer examination, for the simple reason that the UN is a voluntary organization. The General Assembly does not have the power to make binding laws, and the treaties that its members enter into are a matter of choice, not obligation. It is closer to a contract-facilitating organization than to a law-making power. The Secretariat has no laws to administer, and the ICJ's judgments have no precedential value the way decisions in common law jurisdictions do. Article 59 of the ICJ Statute expressly states the following: "The decision of the Court has no binding force except between the parties and in respect of that particular case." UN enforcement powers are also limited, as we discuss below. In short, the UN and its agencies do not have the same power on an international scale that parallel institutions have at the national level.

Reception of International Law into Canada

International law is not precisely analogous to domestic law. Nonetheless, it does exist, and there are increasingly well-defined sources for determining its content. In terms of how international laws are relevant at the state level, it is important to understand that there is a distinction between states' obligations to each other and the binding force of international law *within* a state.

The principle of state sovereignty means that international law, in order to be binding within a state, needs to be implemented or adopted using that state's law-making machinery. With respect to treaties, article 26 of the VCLT requires parties to perform their treaty obligations in good faith, and article 27 states that parties cannot use their own internal legal systems as an excuse for not performing their treaty obligations. Countries must *implement* treaties before they become binding within their territories. This means they must enact legislation making the treaties part of their domestic law.

In Canada, this process is slightly complicated by the fact that our country is a federal state. Some treaties deal with areas that, under section 92 of the *Constitution Act, 1867*, are provincial areas of jurisdiction. These treaties require the provincial legislatures to pass statutes implementing them.[10] If the treaty covers a purely federal matter, such as criminal law, Parliament can implement the treaty by itself, with federal legislation.

International customs, unlike treaties, are presumptively *adopted* by the common law in Canada. However, such customs can be changed by clearly worded legislation passed by the appropriate level of government (see Box 13.2).

BOX 13.2

Does International Custom Apply **Inside** Canada?

In 1943, there was an international custom according to which a state was prohibited from taxing property within its own territory if the property was owned by a foreign state or by officials of the foreign state. That year, the province of Ontario delegated to the city of Ottawa and to another municipality the power, under municipal legislation, to raise money for municipal purposes by taxing property based on ownership. The wording of the legislation was general and did not restrict the municipality's power to tax property or qualify that power according to who owned the property. Under the authority of this legislation, Ottawa and the other municipality taxed property owned by foreign officials. These officials objected to being taxed on the grounds that it was contrary to international law.

In a reference that year,* Duff CJC followed the English position regarding international custom. He held that *international custom is presumed to be part of the common law in Canada* unless it has been expressly changed by competent legislative authority. This is sometimes referred to as the *presumption of conformity* between domestic and international law. Duff CJC went on to hold that the Ontario legislation did not clearly abrogate the international custom in question—that is, the prohibition against taxing property owned by a foreign state or by its officials. Therefore, the legislation had to be interpreted as qualified and as not applying to foreign officials.

The other judges in the case were not as clear about whether the presumption rule applied. Nevertheless, Duff CJC's position is generally accepted as being correct, and the SCC has not had occasion to reconsider this issue.

* *Reference as to Powers to Levy Rates on Foreign Legations*, [1943] SCR 208, 1943 CanLII 39.

Branches of Public International Law

Earlier in this chapter, we approached the subject of international law from a conceptual perspective, discussing the key principles involved in this legal area. But international law is not only about concepts; it is also about specific areas of regulation. There are many

---

10 Section 132 of the *Constitution Act, 1867* appears to give the federal government the power to implement treaties by passing all necessary legislation, but it has been interpreted narrowly. The decision of the Privy Council in *Canada (AG) v Ontario (AG)*, 1937 CanLII 362, [1937] AC 326 (UKJCPC) established that treaties dealing with provincial subject matters require provincial legislation to implement them. For instance, when the federal government ratified the United Nations Convention on Contracts for the International Sale of Goods (1980), each province was required to pass legislation implementing it before it was binding within Canada. Sales of goods transactions generally fall within the "Property and Civil Rights" power belonging to the provinces (s 92(13)).

branches of international law. Each of these branches has its own subject-specific sources, which can include treaties, customs, general principles of law, and other sources. A few of the main branches are:

- law of war,
- international criminal law,
- international human rights law,
- international environmental law, and
- law of the sea (and related areas).

Law of War

International law came about largely to promote peace and security among nations. The *law of war* deals with justifications for war, acceptable conduct during war, and reparations following war. It has been the subject of legal philosophers, and the basis of international customs and treaties, for hundreds of years. The Geneva Conventions, which the nations of the world agreed to in the wake of the Second World War, still forms the basis of modern humanitarian rules for dealing with prisoners of war, for helping the sick and injured during war, and for protecting civilians. Other international conventions include the following:

- the Hague Convention for the Protection of Cultural Property[11] (1954), which, as its name suggests, covers the protection of cultural property;
- the UN Convention Against Torture and Other Cruel, Inhuman or Degrading Treatment or Punishment[12] (1987), which prohibits torture and has 150 signatory states; and
- the *Ottawa Treaty*[13] (1990), which bans land mines.

The complete catalogue of conventions concerned with the law of war is extensive.

International Criminal Law

International criminal law deals with atrocities often committed in the course of armed conflict—principally, genocide, crimes against humanity, war crimes, and acts of aggression. These are extremely serious offences that transcend national boundaries and are defined in treaties. As a branch of international law, international criminal law is somewhat unique because it focuses on individual responsibility as opposed to state responsibility. After the Second World War, for example, the Nuremberg trials—which brought international criminal law fully into public attention—prosecuted Nazi war criminals individually. There have been numerous tribunals and treaties in this area over the years. There remain in place multiple courts and conventions dedicated to this area of law.

---

11 Convention for the Protection of Cultural Property in the Event of Armed Conflict with Regulations for the Execution of the Convention 1954, 14 May 1954 (entered into force 7 August 1956).

12 10 December 1948, resolution 39/46 (entered into force 26 June 1987) [CAT].

13 Convention on the Prohibition of the Use, Stockpiling, Production and Transfer of Anti-Personnel Mines and on their Destruction, 18 September 1997, 2056 UNTS 211 (entered into force 1 March 1999).

The *Rome Statute* is the governing statute for the International Criminal Court (ICC) and gives the ICC jurisdiction over the crimes just mentioned.[14] The statute defines a number of terms, including the following:

- *Genocide*: acts "committed with intent to destroy, in whole or in part, a national, ethnical, racial or religious group";
- *Crimes against humanity*: acts such as murder, extermination, torture, or rape, when "committed as part of a widespread or systematic attack directed against any civilian population, with knowledge of the attack";
- *War crimes*: "serious violations" of the Geneva Conventions, other laws, and conventions applicable in armed conflicts, including those of a non-international character (war crimes can apply to attacks on combatants and civilians, and intentional attacks against "buildings dedicated to religion, education, art, science or charitable purposes, historic monuments, hospitals and places where the sick and wounded are collected"); and
- *Acts of aggression*: "the use of armed force by a State against the sovereignty, territorial integrity or political independence of another State, or in any other manner inconsistent with the Charter of the United Nations."[15]

As of 2018, 123 states are parties to the *Rome Statute*.[16] The ICC's first investigation began in 2004, and since then there have been over 30 indictments but just a handful of convictions.[17]

International Human Rights Law

The internationalization of human rights has led to the development of *international human rights law* as a separate branch of international law. It concerns the advancement of human rights at all levels—international, regional, and domestic. A key document in the field is the Universal Declaration of Human Rights[18] (1948), a UN General Assembly document that is not officially binding but that arguably enshrines customary law and that has formed the basis of subsequent conventions, including the following: CAT (generally considered a human rights instrument), the Convention Relating to the Status of Refugees[19] (1951), the Convention on the Rights of the Child[20] (1990), and the Convention on the Rights of Persons with Disabilities[21] (2008).

---

14 The *Rome Statute* (17 July 1998, online at: https://www.refworld.org/docid/3ae6b3a84.html) came into force in 2002. The ICC, unlike the ICJ, is independent of the UN. It is currently the most important international criminal court.

15 These serious crimes also amount to crimes in domestic legal systems, and perpetrators can face charges in national courts as well as in the ICC or other international courts.

16 Some notable states that are not signatories to the *Rome Statute* are the United States, Russia, China, India, Indonesia, and Israel.

17 For example, in 2016, arising out of the ongoing conflict in Mali, Ahmad Al Faqi Al Mahdi (also known as Abu Turab) was convicted of war crimes involving attacks in 2012 against ten buildings of a religious and historical character in Timbuktu, Mali. In sentencing him to nine years' imprisonment, the ICC considered Mahdi's admission of guilt, his remorse for his acts, and the damage he had caused his community. See also Box 13.4.

18 GA Res 217A (III), UNAGOR, 3rd Sess, Supp No 13, UN Doc A/810 (1948) 71.

19 28 July 1951, 189 UNTS 137 (entered into force 22 April 1954).

20 20 November 1989, 1577 UNTS 3 (entered into force 2 September 1990).

21 13 December 2006, 2515 UNTS 3 (entered into force 3 May 2008).

Other important international documents include those relating to the rights of women and Indigenous peoples. The Convention on the Elimination of All Forms of Discrimination Against Women[22] was adopted by the United Nations General Assembly in 1979 and has been ratified by 189 states, including Canada. It has been described as an international bill of rights for women. Indigenous issues have received increasing attention in recent decades, along with a growing recognition of the negative effects of colonization.[23] An international movement to redress the wrongs perpetrated against Indigenous peoples led to the UN Declaration on the Rights of Indigenous Peoples,[24] which was adopted by the General Assembly in 2007.[25] UNDRIP sets out an international framework for ensuring, for Indigenous peoples, dignity and respect, the enjoyment of all the human rights recognized under the UN Charter, the right of self-determination, the survival of their cultures and languages, the protection of their lands, and related objectives.

With respect to refugees, in recent times wars, famine, and religious and ethnic conflict have continued to highlight the problems associated with human displacement and migration. The plight of refugees was internationally acknowledged after the Second World War, which saw an unprecedented number of displaced persons, by the adoption of the 1951 Refugee Convention.[26] A core principle in this document is **non-refoulement**, which means that refugees will not be returned to countries where they would face serious threats to their life or freedom. Non-refoulement is also considered to be an international custom.[27] In practice, the degree to which individual countries accept responsibility for bringing in and helping to resettle refugees varies. Recent refugee crises, such as the Rohingya and Syrian crises, promise to keep the international community occupied for years to come.

The issues touched on in this section—the rights of refugees, children, women, persons with disabilities, Indigenous peoples, and other groups, at an international level—are complex. These areas can be classed as sub-areas under the broad heading of international human rights law or, in many cases, as separate branches of international law. In our discussion, we

non-refoulement
the internationally acknowledged principle that refugees will not be returned to countries where they would face serious threats to their life or freedom

---

22 18 December 1979, 1249 UNTS 13 (entered into force 3 September 1981).

23 The UN Charter's purpose of developing "respect for equal rights and self-determination of peoples" (article 1), specific chapters concerning the interests of dependent peoples (chapters XI-XIII), and the Declaration on the Granting of Independence to Colonial Countries and Peoples (1960) laid the groundwork for later developments specifically addressing the rights of Indigenous peoples.

24 UNHRCOR, 61st session, UN Doc A/RES/61/295 (2007) [UNDRIP].

25 UNDRIP was adopted by a majority of 144 states, with 4 votes against (Australia, Canada, New Zealand, and the United States) and a number of abstentions. Canada and the other three countries that voted against the declaration later reversed their position and now support it. Canada's initial objection was based on concerns about conflicts between UNDRIP and existing Canadian laws, but in 2016, it removed its objection and committed to implementing the declaration.

26 The 1951 Refugee Convention (as later amended) defines a refugee as a "person who owing to a well-founded fear of being persecuted for reasons of race, religion, nationality, membership of a particular social group or political opinion, is outside the country of his nationality and is unable or, owing to such fear, is unwilling to avail himself of the protection of that country; or who, not having a nationality and being outside the country of his former habitual residence as a result of such events, is unable or, owing to such fear, is unwilling to return to it." There is a general terminological distinction between *refugees* and *asylum seekers,* or *asylees*: the latter must meet the definition of a refugee; however, a refugee is a person applying from outside of the country in which she wishes to settle, whereas an asylum seeker is applying from inside or at the border of the country. The application processes for refugees and asylees are slightly different.

27 In Canada, the non-refoulement principle has been affirmed by legislation: see the *Immigration and Refugee Protection Act*, SC 2001, c 27, s 115.

have grouped them all together under the banner of international human rights law. The international documents, the secondary sources interpreting them, and the groups dedicated to rights and remedies in these areas have grown and become more focused, and it is possible today to specialize in just one of these areas.

International Environmental Law

International environmental law deals with many of the same issues as environmental law (see Chapter 14), but it addresses them in the international context. There are numerous treaties, protocols and conventions, customary laws, and judicial decisions from international tribunals in this area. Sample topics include climate change, pollution, biodiversity and wildlife conservation, sustainable development, trade and the environment, and nuclear testing and energy.

Law of the Sea and Related Areas

The *law of the sea*, like the law of war, has a long history. Part of the reason for its early development had to do with power imbalances on the seas; some states, such as England and Spain, had strong naval forces that allowed them to control the seas. The law of the sea attempts, in part, to provide a balance of power in this regard. Some of the main legal questions that this area of the law addresses concern the territorial boundaries of coastal nations, the ownership and development of mineral resources at sea, the protection of fisheries, and pollution (concerning this issue, there is overlap with international environmental law). This area of law is based on many conventions, customs, and judicial decisions, as well as copious commentary by jurists.

BOX 13.3

Maritime Boundary in the Gulf of Maine: Canada v US

In 1981, Canada and the United States asked the ICJ to resolve a territorial dispute regarding the delimitation of the maritime boundary dividing the continental shelf and fisheries zones in the Gulf of Maine area, including the Georges Bank, which at the time was one of the richest fishing areas in the world. Both countries pointed to historical ties as well as economic interests in their arguments.

In its judgment,* rendered in 1984, the court rejected arguments on both sides and instead referred to a number of rules and principles, including:

- treaty rules and rules of customary international law,
- the 1958 Convention on the Continental Shelf,[†] and
- the Convention on the Law of the Sea,[‡] adopted in 1982 by the Third United Nations Conference.

The court also noted the *absence* of detailed rules concerning the delimitation of the maritime projections of adjacent states. However, it stated that the fundamental rule of general international law governing maritime delimitations is to apply equitable criteria with a view to reaching an equitable result (at para 230); here, this meant applying geographical criteria and geometric methods to divide the disputed areas equally between the parties. After considering all the evidence and applying this approach, delimitation lines were drawn accordingly.

The judgment was accepted by the parties. Canada and the US continue to cooperate in the region (subject to a dispute concerning jurisdiction over an island in the northeastern part of the gulf) and have agreed to refrain from oil and gas exploration and development in the area in order to protect the marine habitat and sensitive ecosystem.

*   *Case Concerning Delimitation of the Maritime Boundary in the Gulf of Maine Area (Canada/United States of America)*, [1984] ICJ Rep 246.

†   29 April 1958, 499 UNTS 312 (entered into force 10 June 1964).

‡   10 December 1982, 1833 UNTS 3 (entered into force 16 November 1994).

FIGURE 13.1 Apollo 11 astronaut Buzz Aldrin stands next to the US flag on the moon (July 20, 1969). The United Nations Office for Outer Space Affairs (UNOOSA), which was created to promote the peaceful use and exploration of space through international cooperation, defines space law as "the body of law applicable to and governing space-related activities." Like international law generally, it is largely comprised of "international agreements, treaties, conventions, and United Nations General Assembly resolutions as well as rules and regulations of international organizations."

Other branches of international law also address stateless, "common" areas such as the polar regions, outer space, and cyberspace. Hence there are *polar regions law*,[28] *space law* (see Figure 13.1), and the *law of cyberspace*.

Enforcement of International Law

One of the major weaknesses of the UN and of international law generally is that there is no strong, consistently used machinery for enforcing breaches of international law.

---

28 In the Arctic, for example, while international law is clear that the North Pole itself and the waters surrounding it are not owned or controlled by any single country, the five coastal nations (Canada, the United States, Russia, Norway, and Denmark) have territorial claims in the region. The extent of their claims to the Arctic Ocean and seabed, the precise delineation of international waters around the North Pole (the "high seas"), and rights of passage are in dispute.

Non-Violent Infractions

In 2001, as we mentioned above, the International Law Commission adopted a draft set of articles concerning states' accountability for breaches of their international obligations. This set of articles, which has gained the approval of the ICJ, is gaining wide acceptance. However, it has not been officially adopted by the UN. At the time of writing, there is no enforceable requirement that states submit to the jurisdiction of the ICJ to resolve non-violent disputes, such as those arising from trade-agreement violations or boundary disagreements (see Box 13.3). Settling such disputes or accepting the ICJ's jurisdiction over them is essentially voluntary. The ICJ resolves disputes submitted to it by states (contentious jurisdiction) and also provides advisory opinions on legal questions submitted to it by the UN Assembly and international organizations (advisory jurisdiction). It is a basic principle of international law, though, that states must consent to the jurisdiction of an international court such as the ICJ before it can assume jurisdiction in a particular case. That consent may be with or without limitations.[29]

Breaches of International Peace and Security

There is no global police force or army. When breaches of international peace and security occur, the response usually comes from one of the following: ad hoc groups of nations directed by the UN Security Council; other organizations, such as NATO; or individual nations.

Collective Responses

The UN Security Council is charged with maintaining international peace and security. Under chapter VII and in particular article 42 of the UN Charter, this responsibility can involve armed responses without the consent of the state directly affected. Such armed responses depend on the Security Council's being able to negotiate an agreement or agreements with UN members for the supply of air, sea, and land forces, as described in article 43 of the Charter. So far, no such agreements have been negotiated, and collective responses have usually depended on ad hoc responses of states that—while acting in support of a Security Council resolution—are under national command.[30]

Article 52 of the UN Charter also provides for regional arrangements to be made for maintaining peace and security as long as these arrangements are "consistent with the Purposes and Principles of the United Nations." This has been the basis for NATO responses to aggressive behaviour, such as the 2011 NATO-led armed support of rebels in Libya that resulted in the fall of the Gadhafi regime. This response was sanctioned by UN Security Council Resolution 1973.

By way of contrast, there have been many examples where the UN has sanctioned peacekeeping missions involving military or police forces that have been based on the consent of the states where the forces (sometimes called *Blue Helmets* because of their light blue helmets or berets) are deployed.[31] Armed responses in these situations are permitted where necessary for self-defence or in defence of the mandate. The UN Charter does not

---

29 Thomas Buergenthal & Sean D Murphy, *Public International Law in a Nutshell*, 6th ed (St Paul, Minn: West Publishing, 2019) at 95.

30 *Ibid* at 402.

31 Examples include missions in the Democratic Republic of Congo, Darfur, South Sudan, Haiti, Kosovo, and Mali.

specifically provide for peacekeeping missions where force *may* be used in these circumstances. These missions fall somewhere between chapter VI of the Charter (dealing with peaceful settlement of disputes) and chapter VII (which includes articles 42-43 and deals with peace *enforcement* without the consent of the state affected); for this reason, they have been described as "Chapter VI 1/2" operations.[32] See Box 13.4.

BOX 13.4

Peacekeeping in Mali (MINUSMA)

The West African country of Mali has a long and rich history; however, famines and ethnic tensions have presented serious challenges for this region from early times. Mali came under French colonial rule in the late 1800s but gained independence in 1960. A military regime took power in 1968, and unrest and upheaval persisted until 1992, when Mali's first democratically elected government assumed control.

Relative peace and stability lasted for 20 years, but in 2012 a rebellion by the Tuareg people—ethnic Berbers seeking independence in the country's northeast—brought renewed tension to the region. A military coup d'état soon followed, and in 2013, the new government requested the intercession of the French armed forces and then of the UN.

The United Nations Multidimensional Integrated Stabilization Mission in Mali (known by its French acronym, MINUSMA) was established pursuant to UN Security Council resolution 2100. The first Blue Helmets were on the ground by July 2013. Their mission was to assist in the restoration of peace by Mali's government (supporting its defence and security forces), to protect civilians, and to promote and defend human rights. It has become one of the UN's most dangerous peacekeeping missions. By mid-2018, over 160 peacekeepers had lost their lives.

In 2018, Canada committed to sending helicopters and hundreds of troops to the region. Some commentators have questioned the effectiveness of the UN's peacekeeping model in complex and deep-rooted conflicts such as this one, citing experiences in Afghanistan and Iraq. With an annual budget of US$1 billion for MINUSMA, they ask whether the money would be better spent on political or educational initiatives.

Responses by Individual States

Generally, an individual state's right of enforcement in relation to a breach of international law is confined to breaches directly affecting the state itself. Article 2 of the UN Charter requires the peaceful settlement of disputes and prohibits the use of force against other states. However, article 51 provides that individual states have the inherent right to defend themselves in the event of an armed attack until the Security Council takes measures to maintain peace.

Whether pre-emptive self-defence is permissible under customary law has been a subject of debate for many years. Most of the evidence of custom in this area comes from the 1800s and is less than clear. To the extent that such a right exists, it must be based on a credible threat of attack. Until there is a ruling by an international tribunal, it is likely the debate will continue.

In the absence of a self-defense rationale, some analysts have argued that a new norm is developing that would justify an aggressive response by one state against another based on violations of *jus cogens* within the other state (for example, genocide) or where other serious humanitarian concerns exist there (such as the use of chemical weapons against civilians). However, there is no consensus at this time whether such a norm is developing, and many argue against such responses outside of the UN framework.

---

32   See Hugh M Kindred et al, *International Law: Chiefly as Interpreted and Applied in Canada*, 8th ed (Toronto: Emond Montgomery, 2014) at 866.

CHAPTER SUMMARY

Public international law is a system of law primarily regulating the relations between countries, but also covering, in certain circumstances, the rights and obligations of non-state actors, including peoples seeking self-determination, IGOs and NGOs, individuals, and corporations. Its basic concepts and principles have been evolving for hundreds of years; the modern system began with the peace process at the end of the First World War. Some of the fundamental principles guiding nations since then have been the sovereign equality of states, the peaceful settlement of disputes, and non-intervention in the domestic affairs of other nations.

The two main sources of international law are (1) treaties—that is, agreements between states; and (2) customs, which are established, settled practices between countries. Concerning the hierarchy of sources, there is some degree of certainty that *jus cogens*, which are peremptory principles of international law (including prohibitions against genocide, slavery, and piracy), rank first and cannot by changed by treaty. Treaties are ranked second and are followed by all other sources, amongst which there is no agreed ranking.

With respect to the application of international law principles within individual states, the rules must be brought into the domestic legal system either through the passage of legislation (in the case of treaty rules) or through adoption by the courts (in the case of custom).

There are many branches of public international law, including the law of war, international criminal law, international human rights law, international environmental law, and the law of the sea (among others). Newer areas are developing, such as the law of cyberspace.

The weakness of the current international law system is the lack of an effective enforcement mechanism. The institutional infrastructure at the international level is largely based on consent. Countries generally resolve their disputes by negotiation, but they can also voluntarily submit matters to the International Court of Justice for adjudication. In cases of serious disturbances of international peace, enforcement depends on the will and financial support of a few of the most powerful nations in the world. The international system continues to evolve, however, and generally there is a desire worldwide to see it become stronger and more effective.

KEY TERMS

jus cogens, 371

non-refoulement, 376

public international law
(or international law), 364

state immunity, 367

state jurisdiction, 366

state responsibility, 367

state sovereignty, 366

subject of international law, 366

FURTHER READING

BOOKS

Buergenthal, Thomas & Sean D Murphy. *Public International Law in a Nutshell*, 6th ed (St Paul, Minn: West Publishing, 2019).

Currie, John H. *Public International Law*, 2nd ed (Toronto: Irwin Law, 2008).

Currie, John H et al. *International Law: Doctrine, Practice, and Theory*, 2nd ed (Toronto: Irwin Law, 2014).

Kindred, Hugh M et al. *International Law: Chiefly as Interpreted and Applied in Canada*, 8th ed (Toronto: Emond Montgomery, 2014).

Madsen, Chris. *Military Law and Operations* (Toronto: Canada Law Book, 2008) (looseleaf).

Shaw, Malcolm N. *International Law*, 6th ed (Cambridge, UK: Cambridge University Press, 2008).

Walker, James. *Brownlie's Principles of Public International Law*, 8th ed (Oxford: Oxford University Press, 2012).

WEBSITES

Court Martial Appeal Court of Canada. *Overview of Canadian Military Law and Courts*: <http://www.cmac-cacm.ca/business/military_law-eng.shtml>.

International Court of Justice: <http://www.icj-cij.org>.

International Criminal Court: <http://www.icc-cpi.int/>.

Research Guide for Canadian Administrative Boards & Tribunal Decisions: <http://guides.library.ubc.ca/cases/can>.

United Nations: <http://www.un.org/en/index.html>.

United Nations Treaty Collection: <http://treaties.un.org>.

REVIEW QUESTIONS

1. Name three global issues that highlight the importance of international law.

2. What was significant about the Peace of Westphalia in the development of international law?

3. What are *objects*, as opposed to *subjects*, in international law?

4. Explain the idea of state responsibility in international law, and provide two examples of a state being responsible to another state.

5. What is *opinio juris*, and what is its significance in international law?

6. Briefly describe the ICJ and its jurisdiction.

7. How are treaties that the Canadian government enters into made part of our domestic law?

8. Name three specific branches of public international law.

9. What is international criminal law concerned with?

10. Why are UN peacekeeping missions where armed personnel are deployed with the consent of the state affected sometimes referred to as "Chapter VI 1/2" operations?

EXERCISES

1. Review the institutional framework of the UN and compare it with Canadian government branches. On the assumption that having a strong and effective UN is a desirable objective, do you think the UN could be improved by changing its infrastructure? If so, how? Explain what changes you would recommend and how those changes could be implemented. If you think no changes are needed, explain why.

2. Go to the ICJ website and choose a decision from the list of cases (all cases are listed from the first one in 1947 to present time, including three where Canada is one of the parties). First read the court's overview of the case and then the full text of the judgment. Prepare a case brief following the format described in Chapter 6, and then comment on what you believe are the strengths and/or weaknesses of the decision or the process by which it was reached.

3. Go to the ICC website and choose one of the cases from the list. If a judgment has been rendered concerning the charges, prepare a case brief following the format described in Chapter 6. If the investigation is ongoing or has been terminated in the preliminary stages, summarize the progress of the case to date. Next, comment on what you believe are the strengths and/or weaknesses of the ICC process, and the judgment if one has been reached.

4. Review the general principles of international law set out in article 2 of the UN Charter and then the basic principles relating to the enforcement of international rules. Prepare an argument based on these principles demonstrating why you think the US-led missile strikes against Syria in 2018—following alleged chemical attacks by the Syrian government against civilians in Syria—were either justified or not justified.

14 Other Areas of Law: An Overview

The Great Library in Osgoode Hall (Toronto). Its extensive collection of print and electronic legal resources serves the needs of lawyers, paralegals and other legal researchers, and it is open to the public.

After reading this chapter, you will understand:

- The range of subject areas covered by the field of law.
- The division of the law and its practice into the broad categories of substantive law, procedural law, and practice norms.
- How some legal subjects have elements of more than one classification type.
- The nature of subjects that deal with issues crossing jurisdictional lines.

Canada's laws are extensive, filling hundreds of volumes, and have specialized libraries devoted to them. With so many statutes, regulations and reported cases, some classification is necessary, not only to adequately organize and comprehend them, but also to work out their applicability to real situations and the resolution of disputes.

Patrick Fitzgerald, Barry Wright & Vincent Kazmierski, *Looking at Law: Canada's Legal System*, 6th ed (Toronto: LexisNexis, 2010) at 61

Introduction

In Chapter 1, we saw how the law can be divided into a number of subject areas (see "Divisions of Law" and Figure 1.1). In Part II, we examined constitutional law, a substantive area of public law. Earlier in Part III, we explored various key substantive domestic law areas and concluded with a discussion of public international law. In Part IV, we consider, among other things, legal ethics (Chapter 16), which deals with practice norms, and alternative dispute resolution (Chapter 17), which can be classed as an area of procedural law.

In this chapter, we attempt to fill in the legal landscape a little more. We outline a number of *other* areas under the broad headings of substantive law, procedural law, and practice norms, following the basic organizational structure provided in Figure 1.1. And while substantive law, procedural law, and practice norms feed into both domestic law and international law systems, our focus in this chapter is on domestic law topics (international law and its branches were discussed in Chapter 13). In the final section, we briefly consider some mixed areas—those that either involve significant hybrid aspects or are transnational in scope (that is, that have an impact beyond jurisdictional boundaries).[1]

---

1   To reiterate an earlier caveat, the law is a vast and complex field of study, and it is not possible to cover all areas in an introductory book. As well, the process of division and categorization, while helpful for the purposes of study, is not always exact (some areas defy easy classification, some belong to multiple categories, and some overlap with other subject areas). Further, resolving the legal problems with which we are confronted in practice often requires analyzing multiple areas of law.

Note that in this survey, subject areas that belong to multiple categories, or that are strongly associated with areas in other categories, are described just once, where it seems most appropriate. For example, *conflict of laws*, which is both a procedural and a transnational law area, is described just once under transnational law.

Substantive Law

Two broad categories of domestic substantive law are those relating to public law and those relating to private law. The following is a look at some of the subjects in these categories not covered in other chapters.

Other Public Law Areas

Major areas of public law (which deals with the relationship between persons and the state, and between the various organs of the state) are discussed elsewhere in this book: constitutional law in Part II, administrative law in Chapter 11, and criminal law in Chapter 12. We also consider certain legal issues concerning Indigenous peoples, such as the customary basis of Indigenous legal traditions and the constitutional protection of Aboriginal rights, including Aboriginal title (see, in particular, Chapters 3, 4, and 9).

Other areas of public law, briefly described next, include municipal law, immigration law, taxation law, and certain sub-areas of criminal law.

Municipal Law

Among the areas of public law we have not yet discussed is *municipal law*, which concerns the powers and activities of local governments. Municipal law is generally classed by itself as a separate sub-area of administrative law because of the special nature of the issues it addresses and because of the size, power, and complexity of municipalities. Often referred to as *local governments*, municipal governments are the third level of government after the federal and provincial and territorial governments. They are incorporated under provincial and territorial legislation, which delegates to them legislative, administrative, and quasi-judicial powers to govern at the local level. They have the power to raise taxes, and they often own and control assets of substantial value. Many of the issues that arise in this area of law are related to the following:

- the extent of the local government's delegated power,
- judicial review of the local government's actions,
- conflicts of interest,
- municipal regulation of business activities,
- land use and planning by local governments, and
- private law liability in tort and for breach of contract.

Immigration Law

Immigration law is another area of public domestic law. It is under federal jurisdiction and covers a wide range of matters that arise under the *Immigration and Refugee Protection Act*[2]

---

2 SC 2001, c 27.

and other legislation. These matters include the following: the procedure for immigrating to Canada; the various visas and other documents that are required; sponsorship rules for family members and others; provincial nominee programs; criteria for eligibility (or ineligibility, for reasons related to criminality or health), and removals and deportation orders (see Box 11.1).

Taxation Law

taxation law
complex, wide-ranging area of public law encompassing federal, provincial, and municipal taxation laws applicable to personal, property, and business income; capital gains; property ownership; and sales transactions

Taxation law is a complex, wide-ranging area of public domestic law. It encompasses federal, provincial, and municipal taxation laws applicable to personal, property, and business income; capital gains; property ownership; and sales transactions. Adding to the complexity of this area is that its rules are frequently changing, perhaps more quickly than in any other area of law. Income tax is the largest source of revenue for governments and an important area of taxation law. It concerns the taxation of various types of income, allowable deductions, and the calculation of gains and losses. Income tax law is focused largely on the statutory interpretation of the federal *Income Tax Act*[3] and of other tax statutes.

Sub-Areas of Criminal Law

Criminal law includes a number of sub-areas that could be classed as separate subjects or areas of public law. (See Chapter 12 for a discussion of criminal law generally.) For example, *competition law* (in the United States referred to as *antitrust law*) deals with unfair competition in the marketplace; *proceeds-of-crime law* covers dealings with assets illegally obtained through or used in the commission of crimes; and *public safety law* concerns laws that are in place to combat serious risks to public safety (including anti-terrorism measures).

Other Private Law Areas

We considered some key areas of private law in Chapters 8 and 9: tort law, contract law, property law, and family law. The following is an overview of a number of areas that are related to these subjects but that are frequently treated as discrete topics. In addition, we reference a few areas based in equity law.

Areas Related to Tort Law

Two areas with a torts connection that can be considered distinct subjects are sports law and professional malpractice. Sports law is briefly described below under "Hybrid Areas: Public Law and Private Law Aspects."

Professional malpractice concerns the liability of professionals to their clients for a wide range of misdealings, from incompetence to fraud. Tort law features prominently with claims in negligence and deceit, but contract claims (for example, breach of obligations to exercise reasonable care), claims in equity (for example, breach of fiduciary duties), and occasionally criminal charges play a role, too. To the extent that criminal law may apply—in extreme cases only—this area has a hybrid nature as well, consisting of both public law and private law aspects. Professional malpractice claims also invariably involve breaches of ethical norms, mentioned below and described in more detail in Chapter 16.

---

3 RSC 1985, c 1 (5th Supp).

Areas Related to Contract Law

Contract law is its own area, but it also informs many areas of law that we think of as distinct, including employment law, insurance law, and corporate and commercial law.

Employment law is largely focused on the contractual relationship between employer and employee in a non-unionized environment (see also Box 8.7 in Chapter 8). Employment law also has a legislative component, from employment standards and workers' compensation legislation to human rights legislation concerning (for example) discrimination in the workplace. *Labour law* deals primarily with unionized work environments and the collective bargaining process. Federal, provincial, and territorial labour legislation determines rights to strike, picket, and lock out workers, among other things. Administrative law and civil liberties issues are also part of this area. *Workers' compensation* is sometimes considered as a separate area of law. It covers a special government-run insurance scheme for injuries sustained at work. These areas are sometimes combined and referred to as the *law of work* or *workplace law*.

Insurance law is based on a contract between an insured person and an insurer (usually a large insurance company). It covers risk planning for businesses and individuals, handling of claims, interpretation of contract clauses, fiduciary obligations, and many other topics. Various legal issues can arise depending on the type of insurance involved. These types include property insurance, motor vehicle insurance, life insurance, fire insurance, and business-interruption insurance. They vary in their contractual provisions, and the legislation regulating the different types of insurance also varies. Insurance law can have a public law component in some jurisdictions, if certain forms of insurance are mandated by legislation (as in the case of motor vehicle insurance) and if regulatory penalties result from a failure to insure as required.

Corporate and commercial law has a number of subcategories that we can address individually; all have a significant contracts component. *Company law* (or corporate law) concerns the law of business associations with respect to the formation, structure, and management of corporations. This law covers shareholders' rights and remedies as well as the duties and obligations of corporate managers. Legislation (federal, provincial, and territorial) heavily regulates the area of business corporations. *Close corporations* (small companies that are not publicly traded), *corporate transactions* (for example, mergers and acquisitions), and *corporate finance* (raising funds for corporate purposes) generate particular issues and are often treated as discrete subject areas.

Securities law regulates the public trading of shares and other corporate instruments. It is a complex area with elaborate public disclosure requirements (which involve prospectuses and other documents) and liability rules, all designed to protect members of the public when they are investing in the market. The requirements of securities commissions, stock exchanges, and other organizations have to be satisfied, often in multiple jurisdictions if the shares are sold across provincial and/or international boundaries. Securities law could be classed as a mixed area, with public law aspects (in that there is the potential for criminal or regulatory penalties) and transnational elements.

Business and consumer law, described in Chapter 10 and referenced below under "Hybrid Areas: Public Law and Private Law Aspects," overlaps with some of these areas.

Areas Related to Property Law

As described in Chapter 9, *real estate transactions* and *conveyancing* are frequently considered to be subcategories of real property law. *Landlord and tenant law*, which concerns the relationship between lessors and lessees of real property, whether in the context of residential or commercial tenancies, is also often classed as its own subject.

insurance law
area of private law based on a contract between an insured person and an insurer (usually a large insurance company); covers many topics, including risk planning for businesses and individuals, handling of claims, interpretation of contract clauses, and fiduciary obligations

Other subcategories within property law in general are *commercial transactions* and *secured transactions*. The law concerned with commercial transactions covers all goods transactions, from the point of manufacture through supply and retail to final purchase by consumers or businesses. It is concerned with the transfer of property rights.

The area of secured transactions covers the use of personal property as security for obligations, usually consumer or business debt. The focus of this area of law is the relatively uniform personal property security legislation in force in all jurisdictions across Canada, briefly described in Chapter 9.

Animal law considers a wide range of issues relating to animals. Animals are still considered a form of property, despite attempts to change the law and recognize them as sentient beings. The issues involving animals go beyond just the property rights of animal owners, however. Owners can be held liable in tort for any damages their animals cause, and issues related to family law, contract law, criminal law, and environmental law issues can also arise. Animal rights and welfare are developing areas at both the domestic law and international law levels. Animal law could be classed as a hybrid subject.

Areas Related to Family Law

elder law
area of private law that covers the various legal issues facing the elderly

Elder law, as the name suggests, deals with the various legal issues facing the elderly. With an aging population, it has emerged in recent years as a separate area of study and practice. While elder law is obviously related to family law, it touches on other legal areas; in fact, it could be described as a collection of the legal areas most often related to elders' lives (and to the degree that it touches on public law issues, like criminal law, it is a hybrid area). Elder law comprises the following, for example:

- torts and criminal law (to address, for example, the various forms of physical, emotional, and financial abuse suffered by the elderly);
- contracts (for example, to address the validity of contracts that the elderly negotiate under duress or undue influence, and to consider the need for powers of attorney or representation agreements authorizing representatives to make financial and personal care decisions for the elderly);
- property and succession (to address the validity of wills executed under pressure); and
- family law (to address, for example, the obligations owed to parents by adult children).

Other topics addressed by elder law include assisted-living opportunities, the loss of driving privileges, powers of attorney, and issues to do with end-of-life and palliative care.

succession law
area of private law that covers issues concerning wills and estates and the transmission of property upon death

Succession law is also related to family law. However, it also has a strong connection to property law. The law of succession covers issues dealing with wills and estates and the transmission of property upon death. Most often, the property goes to family members. Legally speaking, however, there is nothing to prevent a person from leaving everything to a favourite charity instead. Specifically, succession law concerns the following:

- estate planning (sometimes viewed as a specialized field by itself);
- wills (drafting them, interpreting them, and challenging them based on, for example, a lack of testamentary capacity);
- succession legislation (including rules relating to the limited power of the court to vary wills and a testator's wishes on the basis of fairness; rules in connection with

the transmission of property in the event that someone dies intestate [that is, without a will]; and rules relating to the rights and responsibilities of personal representatives [for example, executors and administrators] who manage the estate pending the transfer of the deceased's property to beneficiaries and others); and

- other estate matters, such as applicable taxes and fees.

Equity

The Courts of Chancery were courts authorized to apply principles of equity (rather than common law) to cases brought before them (see Chapter 2). For the most part, equity served to modify, soften, or put a gloss on the common law—for example, in setting rules for the interpretation of contract clauses or provisions in property transfers. Many of the rules developed according to these principles are still with us today, and modern courts continue to refine and expand upon some of them. Generally speaking, the discussion of equity and its modifications comes up in the context of the areas of law to which these modifications apply—contracts or property transfers, for example. Occasionally, however, equity went further and created stand-alone actions or claims for remedies. These actions or remedies can be treated as separate areas of private law.

Three discrete equity subjects stand out:

1. trusts,
2. fiduciary duties, and
3. equitable remedies.

The **law of trusts** deals with how trusts are created, the relationship between the legal owner of property (the trustee) and the equitable owner (or beneficiary), the regulation of trust relationships by legislation, and the remedies for breach of trust.

The study of *fiduciary duties* examines the obligations that arise in certain kinds of relationships—for example, between lawyers and clients, between banks and customers, and between financial advisors and investors. This area of law concerns such aspects of fiduciary duty as obligations of good faith, openness, and accountability (for example, with respect to any secret profits).

The area of law concerned with *equitable remedies* looks in detail at the various remedies developed by the courts of equity. These remedies include injunctions, specific performance, rescission, rectification, equitable damages, and equitable compensation. Some of these were described in Chapter 8, in connection with contract remedies. From a classification standpoint, remedies arguably belong under the procedural law banner, but these particular ones are mentioned here because they are based in equity.

trusts (law of)
private law area dealing with how trusts are created, the relationship between the legal owner of property (the trustee) and the equitable owner (or beneficiary), the regulation of trust relationships by legislation, and the remedies for breach of trust

Procedural Law

Procedural law concerns the *process* by which legal matters are managed or resolved, whether they require adjudication or not, and whether they are grounded in private law or public law (including criminal cases). Procedural law is not concerned with the actual substantive rights and obligations involved. However, it is still an extremely important part of the legal system—overlooking or ignoring the required procedures may result in legal matters failing to be managed through completion or resolved on their merits because of a "technical" problem. Many legal practitioners spend most of their time working with procedures, where the relevant substantive rules operate in the background and are not in dispute. For example, a lawyer with a conveyancing practice might deal almost exclusively with the procedures involved in transferring interests in land, knowing what the governing substantive rules are but not challenging or litigating them.

The following is a synopsis of some key procedural law areas dealing with court and tribunal procedures, evidence, alternative dispute resolution, and collections. There are many other procedural areas besides these, including those mentioned elsewhere in this chapter (for example, conveyancing in connection with real property law; equitable remedies, mentioned above; and conflict of laws, which we discuss later in this chapter).[4]

Court and Tribunal Procedures

All courts and tribunals have procedures relating to their decision-making functions. Two key areas are procedures relating to civil (or private) law claims and those relating to criminal prosecutions.

Litigation Procedures

litigation procedures
procedural law area involving court and tribunal procedures in civil proceedings and including such matters as the steps involved in commencing actions, notice requirements, and time limitations

Litigation procedures (or *litigation process* or *civil litigation procedures/process*) refers generally to the procedures or processes involved in civil proceedings before courts and tribunals. As noted, different procedures apply depending on the subject matter of the hearing and the specific court or tribunal in question.

Among other things, these rules cover:

- the steps involved in starting an action,
- the notice requirements for opposing parties,
- time limitations,
- the security required for the costs involved in the action, and
- discovery processes.

Legal representatives must be knowledgeable about the relevant process for a given dispute if the matter is to proceed smoothly though the court system. The rules must be followed carefully; otherwise, there is a risk that claims or defences will be rejected because of procedural failings. Due to the complexity of the rules, unrepresented litigants frequently have difficulties navigating their way through the system.

---

4 Procedural law affects all parts of the legal system. Most substantive law areas have related procedural sub-areas: for example, real property law and conveyancing, intellectual property and related procedures (including registration of trademarks and patents), company law and *corporate procedures* (such as registry filings and maintaining corporate books), securities law and *securities procedures* (for instance, securities commissions and stock exchange filings), *family law procedures* (specialized court applications and other processes), *estate procedures* (probate applications and estate administration), and many others. With respect to court procedures, we summarize civil and criminal court procedures in general terms next, but almost all courts and tribunals—for example, human rights tribunals, labour boards, small claims courts, youth courts, provincial and territorial superior courts and courts of appeal, the Tax Court of Canada, the Federal Courts, and the Supreme Court of Canada—have their own specific procedures. An exhaustive list of procedural law areas and sub-areas would be lengthy.

Criminal Procedure

There are also specialized processes when public law matters are dealt with before the courts. An important and specialized area here is *criminal procedure*. As with civil procedure, the rules vary depending on the subject matter (in this context, the crime in question) and the various courts that may be involved (which, again, can be from the provincial or territorial court level all the way up to the Supreme Court of Canada [SCC]). For more on the criminal trial process, see Chapter 12.

Evidence

The **law of evidence** is relevant to any legal concern where proof is required. This includes non-litigious situations—such as applying for licences, corporate registrations, and vital statistics applications—but it features most notably in court and tribunal proceedings. Evidentiary rules vary according to the issue and are found in the common law and in legislation (federal, provincial, and territorial). In criminal matters, the Charter may also be relevant.[5]

During adjudications, the law of evidence governs a wide array of matters, including:

- the tests for relevancy and privilege;
- the use of oral testimony, including the competency of witnesses to testify;
- special issues relating to the admission of written or documentary evidence;
- the admissibility of hearsay evidence;
- the use of expert evidence (for example, evidence of medical professionals about the nature of injuries or in connection with competency or mental disorders); and
- the authentication of real evidence and demonstrative evidence (that is, physical objects, such as materials, weapons, recordings, photographs, and models).

While evidence is in essence a procedural law topic, it has aspects that are arguably substantive in nature: for example, concerning the right not to incriminate oneself when giving testimony, and the presumption of innocence in criminal matters. It also relates to both public law and private law matters.

evidence (law of) procedural law area detailing rules relevant in all matters of proof, including non-litigious situations (such as applying for licences) but more commonly in court and tribunal proceedings

Alternative Dispute Resolution

Approximately 90 percent of legal disputes are settled out of court, either before any court process commences or at some point during the process. Three important reasons for this, which are particularly relevant in the context of private law disputes, are:

1. *Expense.* A few days in court with the legal fees and all of the associated disbursements can easily eat away at any expected award.
2. *Time.* It can take years to proceed through all levels of court if decisions are appealed.
3. *Uncertainty.* If a dispute gets as far as court, there is likely some uncertainty about what the law is or how it should be applied.

---

5   For the use of evidence in criminal matters more generally, see Chapter 12 under the heading "The Trial."

These three reasons provide a significant incentive to settle disputes outside of court whenever possible. Negotiation, mediation, collaborative law (which has become more and more common in family law matters), and arbitration (often used for long-term business relationships) are examples of an increasingly important area known as *alternative dispute resolution* (ADR). Access-to-justice issues are driving this field, and many legal professionals are being trained specifically in ADR. See Chapter 17 concerning ADR in non-criminal matters generally, and Chapter 12 in connection with criminal prosecutions outside of the regular court system (under the heading "Criminal Courts").

Collections Procedures

During the pursuit of a civil claim and after its resolution—either by court judgment, administrative processes, or settlement—the successful party may have to concern herself with collecting what is owed. If the debtor pays willingly, then all is well.

If the debtor does not pay willingly, then there is more work to be done. Establishing a claim is very often just the first half of the process. Collecting the debt is the second half, and generally speaking it is up to the creditor to make this happen. The courts, for instance, will not pursue collections after judgment on the creditor's behalf.

The creditor—on her own, with legal representation, or by hiring a debt collections agency—may have a number of procedural options open to her. These options vary depending on whether the debtor is solvent (that is, able to pay) or insolvent (or unable to pay).

General Collections

Assuming a creditor is dealing with a debtor who is reluctant to pay but who is generally solvent, then the general area of **creditors' remedies** becomes important.

Creditors have a large arsenal of available techniques to collect their debts, including pre-judgment garnishment of bank accounts, post-judgment garnishment of wages, seizure and sales of motor vehicles, and the registration of judgments against real property. The exact number of techniques varies according to the nature of the claim or debt (for example, builders' liens are available only to building contractors), and additional options are available to secured creditors (that is, those with security against a particular asset, such as a mortgage over real property). In all cases, however, collections rules tend to be fairly strict and the requirements of the relevant legislation must be followed carefully.

Insolvency Collections

Insolvency law deals with specialized legal responses to unmanageable debt incurred by businesses and individuals. Some of the issues debtors and creditors face relate to debt restructuring, settlements with other creditors, collection of secured debts, the priority between different types of debts, and bankruptcy options (being excused from debts with or without conditions). While there are some common law insolvency rules, this area is mainly governed by federal legislation. Two of the key statutes are the *Bankruptcy and Insolvency Act*[6] and the *Companies' Creditors Arrangement Act*.[7]

creditors' remedies
procedural law area that governs techniques available to creditors to collect their debts, including pre-judgment garnishment of bank accounts, post-judgment garnishment of wages, seizure and sales of motor vehicles, and the registration of judgments against real property

---

6   RSC 1985, c B-3.

7   RSC 1985, c C-36.

From a classification standpoint, insolvency law is a difficult area. It is mainly concerned with collection procedures for creditors pursuing claims against debtors faced with financial obligations they cannot meet. However, it also has a substantive element to it to the extent that it regulates the priority of claims between creditors and the conditions under which debtors may be entitled to partial or complete forgiveness of their debts. It is therefore a rare hybrid of procedural and substantive law. Further, it has aspects of public law (at least to the extent that it deals with the collection and forgiveness of tax debts) and private law (when it involves personal or commercial debts to individuals or corporate entities). And last, it is a jurisdictional hybrid: while federal legislation generally governs, there is sometimes also an interplay with provincial (or territorial) rules.

Practice Norms

Practice norms concern the necessary ethical standards and skills that legal practitioners must follow and possess to deliver legal services effectively. The legal profession and the public expect high standards in the practice of law. In individual cases, the failure to adhere to these norms at an optimal level often means the difference between good representation and a positive outcome, and a poor result for the client. General adherence to these standards across the profession, however, goes beyond this and is vital for a just and stable legal system.

Despite the importance of high standards in practice, it is the marketplace that is the main regulator—less than ideal performance by legal representatives usually results in the loss of reputation and business for the practitioner. However, more serious cases can also result in disciplinary consequences enforced by the governing law society or other regulatory body. In extreme cases, clients may also have *legal* claims against their representatives (where the ethical or competency lapse is so serious that it also amounts to a breach of contract or a tortious wrong, for instance).

Legal Ethics

Legal ethics is one of the most important subjects in law. It deals with the ethical issues facing legal professionals in all facets of their practice and, in particular, in connection with their duties to their clients, the courts, and the public. Legal ethics issues are most often highlighted when legal professionals are sued or disciplined for professional malpractice. In Chapter 16, legal codes of ethics and the specific types of ethical issues arising in the practice of law are described in detail.

Legal Skills

Legal practitioners need to develop skills in a variety of areas: the more varied their practice, the more skills they will need. Commonly required legal skills include those relating to interviewing, drafting, researching, and advocacy.

Good *legal interviewing* skills help build a relationship of trust with the interviewee (a client, witness, or other person connected to the matter) and support the information-gathering process. Advance preparation and research, when possible, assist the interviewer in structuring the interview and using time efficiently. Knowing whether there are any special circumstances affecting the interviewee's perception of events can help determine the style of questioning that will be most effective. Knowing when and how to listen is also important.

Legal representatives are commonly required to draft correspondence, contracts, pleadings, affidavits, and other legal documents on behalf of their clients. Clear, precise, and correct use of language is critical. And despite the law's reputation for the use of obscure and arcane language, the current trend is toward plain language. Effective *legal drafting* can mean the difference between a successful outcome and a significant financial loss.

Legal research skills are required to keep abreast of changes to the law. The ability to find, read, and understand relevant legislation, case law, and secondary sources (for example, books and articles describing the primary sources) are necessary to properly advise clients. Some areas of practice change frequently (taxation law, for example, is constantly changing), but even more "stable" areas (for example, property law) undergo change at some point.

Legal advocacy is an area of expertise that concerns the effective presentation of evidence, including examination of witnesses and use of argumentation. Not all legal representatives have practices that require them to present before courts and tribunals, but those who do can spend years developing their skills as litigators.

Mixed Areas

A number of subject areas are considered "mixed." This can happen when areas have hybrid aspects, in the sense of crossing major classification lines. For example, a subject may have both substantive and procedural law aspects (see insolvency law, mentioned above) or substantive law and practice norms elements (ethical obligations can cross into the private law and even the criminal law domain). It can also happen where the application of laws across jurisdictional boundaries is concerned.

In this section, we discuss a few subjects with substantial hybrid natures, those crossing the public law–private law divide and the domestic law–international law divide. We also discuss transnational subject areas, which cross jurisdictional boundaries (some subjects, such as aviation law, are hybrids *and* transnational).

Hybrid Areas: Public Law and Private Law Aspects

Subjects with both public law and private elements are common. In Chapter 10, we covered such a subject, *business and consumer law*, which is arguably two subjects combined. When company law is examined in a broader context along with other forms of business organization and together with various types of business transactions, the area is commonly referred to as *business law*. *Consumer protection law*, also referred to simply as *consumer law*, has developed from the increasing attention paid by lawmakers to the protection of consumers, who are on the "demand" side of business and economics. *Business and consumer law* covers the two areas together.

Here, we consider some other subjects with public law and private law aspects: sports law, entertainment law, natural resources law, and environmental law. A few areas considered above—such as animal law, securities law, elder law, and insolvency law—could also be placed in this category.

Sports law deals with the law as it relates to professional and amateur sports. Many of the injuries that occur in sporting activities produce claims in negligence and even the intentional torts. Of course, sports law touches on other areas of law as well, including, for example, the following:

- contracts (agreements between professional athletes and their agents and teams, as well as waivers and releases),
- criminal law (in the case of recklessly or deliberately caused injuries),
- labour law (player associations),
- civil liberties (equal opportunity and drug testing), and
- other areas.

Entertainment law touches on many areas, including taxation, intellectual property, and broadcasting and telecommunications regulatory issues. It covers rules regarding marketing and advertising, the financing of films and other entertainment ventures, and the negotiation and performance of production contracts as well as contracts with actors, musicians, writers, and composers. The legal framework for the area spreads across all jurisdictions, and it bridges the divide between private and public law.

The matters dealt with by *natural resources law* include (1) transactions and royalties involved in the extraction of natural resources (for example, purchase and sale of oil and gas leases, under which the freehold natural resources owner—either the owner of the surface rights or the government if natural resources have been reserved—transfers rights to a resource company to remove the resource) and (2) the regulatory structure for the particular resource being developed. The nature of the transactions, royalties, and regulatory structure vary according to whether the resource is oil and gas, minerals, coal, water, forests, or wildlife and fisheries.

Environmental law has a large regulatory component. It involves governments defining such matters as the following: their obligations concerning land, air, and water pollution; the requirements for environmental impact studies; property reclamation; and environment-related issues concerning Indigenous peoples. Private law issues can arise in the context of land transfers when responsibility for pollution is unclear. Transnational law issues can arise when pollution crosses borders and thereby violates treaties or other international rules.

environmental law
hybrid area of law with public law and private law aspects involving land, air, and water pollution, and that has a large regulatory component

Transnational Law

Transnational law subjects focus on legal matters that cross jurisdictional boundaries, whether involving individuals, corporations, or governments. In federal states such as Canada, it might be more appropriate to refer to this area as *transjurisdictional law*, because crossing provincial lines can raise similar issues to crossing national boundaries. Laws can vary from province to province as well as from country to country.

Transnational law subjects can be based on domestic law, international law, or hybrids of the two. The following discussion is concerned with domestic law and hybrids. Legal matters that are covered by international law and its branches are examined in Chapter 13.

Domestic Law Areas

Two transnational law areas that are rooted in Canada's domestic law (private law) are conflict of laws and admiralty law.[8] They are considered next. See also Box 14.2.

---

8   Issues arising in these areas may have an international law component if they are covered by international treaties or customs that have been implemented or adopted by domestic law (for example, in admiralty law, federal legislation implementing international conventions concerning civil liability for oil pollution damage).

CONFLICT OF LAWS

conflict of laws
area of law—also
referred to as *private
international law*—that
covers private law
disputes that have an
interprovincial or inter-
national component

Conflict of laws, also referred to as *private international law* (to distinguish it from *public* international law), is an area of law that covers private law disputes that have an interprovincial or an international component. These disputes could include, for example,

- product liability disputes where the goods were manufactured abroad,
- contracts between parties residing in two different countries,
- marriages and divorces involving two people from outside the country or people with different citizenships, and
- succession cases involving foreign property.

Conflict of laws is always relevant to international trade or business transactions. Within this general context, some of the specific topics covered are jurisdiction or choice of forum (that is, which jurisdiction's courts should hear the dispute), applicable law (which jurisdiction's laws govern the dispute), and the enforcement of foreign judgments.

When determining jurisdiction (assuming there is no forum selection or choice of forum clause in a contract between the parties), Canadian courts use the following approach. First, they consider whether a "real and substantial connection" exists between the court and the subject matter of the dispute (this is called the *jurisdiction simpliciter test*). To assist in making this determination, the court looks for any presumptive factors that point in the direction of one forum or another. For example, if the defendant resides or carries on business in a particular jurisdiction, it may be appropriate for a court in that jurisdiction to hear the dispute. Similarly, the place where the tort was committed (in tort cases) or the contract was made (contract cases) will point to the forum with the strongest connection. Other factors may also be considered.

However, there is a second stage to the jurisdiction analysis (called *forum non conveniens*). Despite the existence of presumptive factors indicating a real and substantial connection with a particular court, the court may ultimately decide in favour of another court based on other considerations, such as fairness and efficiency. See Box 14.1.

BOX 14.1

SCC Rules Against Canadian Man in Transnational Online Defamation Suit

In 2018, the SCC considered the case of a Canadian businessman, the plaintiff, who owned a popular soccer team in Israel. He had a residence there and visited regularly. The defendant was an established Israeli newspaper, and it published an article criticizing the plaintiff's management of the team. The print edition of the newspaper was not generally available in Canada, but an online edition was. The plaintiff commenced an action in Ontario, arguing that he had been libelously defamed and his reputation damaged. The defendant resisted the claim on the procedural ground that Ontario courts lacked jurisdiction. The motion judge and the Ontario Court of Appeal held that the claim could proceed in Ontario. The defendant appealed to the SCC.*

The SCC followed the two-stage analysis for determining jurisdiction (described above). The court looked first at whether the jurisdiction *simpliciter* test was satisfied, and all judges concluded that it was. There was a real and substantial connection with Ontario, considering, among other things, that the tort was committed in Ontario.

Next, the court analyzed the *forum non conveniens* issue; it was divided in its reasons at this second stage. A majority (six of nine judges) concluded that despite the presumptive connection of the case to Ontario, it was more appropriate for the matter to be heard in Israel. The minority of three concluded that the presumption in favour of Ontario was not rebutted. There was further disagreement amongst the majority about the determinative factors rebutting the presumption—three of the six concluded that fairness and efficiency favoured Israel (considering, principally, the plaintiff's connection to Israel and the defendant's lack of assets or presence in Ontario), and the remaining three wrote their own judgments with slightly differing analyses.

This case raises issues about how legal principles are adapted to deal with changing technologies, and specifically with jurisdiction in Internet defamation cases. Because in such cases the tort will almost always be committed in the jurisdiction of the defendant (as well as in other jurisdictions), a presumption will always arise in favour of hearing the dispute in the defendant's jurisdiction. Is this a bad thing? Does this mean that a different approach to jurisdiction should be employed in these kinds of cases? Despite the differences of opinion of the judges on the application of *forum non conveniens*, the view of the court as a whole was that the current approach to determining jurisdiction was flexible enough to accommodate Internet defamation.

* *Haaretz.com v Goldhar*, 2018 SCC 28.

When determining jurisdiction in cases where the parties have agreed to a particular forum (that is, where they have a contract that includes a forum selection clause), the analysis is slightly different. Assuming that no legislation overrides the clause, there is another two-stage analysis. First, the court looks at whether the clause is generally clear and valid. If so, the clause will in most cases be enforced. Where another court has been chosen (which is the usual situation), this means that the proceedings will be stayed and will have to be re-commenced in the other jurisdiction. However, there is a second stage, which allows the party opposing the enforcement of the clause to show "strong cause" why it should not be enforced. At this second stage, the court can consider a range of factors, such as the convenience of the parties, fairness, justice, and public policy.[9] In rare cases, based on these factors, the court can refuse to follow the forum selection clause and assume jurisdiction over the dispute despite the clause (for an example, see the discussion of *Douez v Facebook* in Chapter 8).[10]

Once a court determines that it has jurisdiction, the question of the applicable law comes up: specifically, what *substantive* law should be applied—local law (the *lex fori*) or the law of another jurisdiction?[11] If no one questions the application of the *lex fori*, then that law will apply. However, if it is challenged and one party wants the law of another of another jurisdiction to apply, the analysis can be a complicated. Sometimes, however, the approach is relatively straightforward. For example, in basic torts cases the substantive law of the jurisdiction where the tort was committed applies. And in contracts cases where the parties have included a choice of law clause, the courts will generally follow the parties' wishes and apply the substantive law of the jurisdiction chosen, provided that the clause is otherwise valid and there are no policy reasons for overturning the clause.

ADMIRALTY LAW

Admiralty (or maritime) law concerns maritime trade and commerce and the rules for resolving maritime disputes. Some of the issues it addresses are wages and conditions for sailors, shipowners' obligations toward people injured on board, responsibility for

admiralty (or maritime) law
area of law that concerns maritime trade and commerce and that has a private international law component

---

9 See *ZI Pompey Industrie v ECU-Line NV*, 2003 SCC 27.

10 *Douez v Facebook*, 2017 SCC 33, applied the two-stage analysis from *Pompey*.

11 Note that once jurisdiction has been assumed, while the question of the applicable substantive law may be up in the air, the relevant procedural law (for instance, court procedures) is clear: procedural law is determined according to the *lex fori*.

damages and injuries caused at sea, rights of salvage (in other words, reward for recovering the property of others lost at sea), and rules relating to piracy. Admiralty law is not the same as the *law of the sea*. The latter is a branch of public international law described in Chapter 13, and it defines, among other things, the rights and responsibilities of nations in their use of the world's oceans.

BOX 14.2

Comparative Law

Comparative law is the study of legal responses to similar problems in different jurisdictions and sometimes within jurisdictions with more than one legal tradition (see also Table 2.1 in Chapter 2 comparing the civil law and common law systems). Comparative law is a developing area and, in recent cases, courts in Canada and elsewhere have demonstrated a greater willingness to consider legal approaches in other countries when developing new rules or extending existing ones in their own jurisdictions. For example, in the *Bhasin v Hrynew* case (described in Chapter 8) before the SCC recognized a new organizing principle in contract law requiring parties to act in good faith and be honest with one another, the court considered the law in the United States and Australia (along with the civil law position in Quebec), where similar approaches had been adopted.

Comparative law analyses can occur in any kind of case involving domestic law. While comparative law is not a transnational law subject in the usual sense of dealing with how litigants resolve cross-jurisdictional legal issues, its goal of improving local law by comparing legal approaches to similar problems in other jurisdictions makes it a companion area.

Hybrid Areas: Domestic Law and International Law Aspects

Important areas with domestic law and international law elements concern trade and business, and aviation.

International trade law and *international business transactions* are areas that are part international law and part domestic law. International trade law focuses on how trade between countries is regulated; it addresses treaties (for example, the North American Free Trade Agreement), customs rules, and organizations such as the World Trade Organization. International business transactions law in Canada focuses on specific types of transactions, such as international sales of goods, cross-border financing arrangements, and the regulatory frameworks in other countries, as well as some of the non-legal subtleties of cross-cultural business dealings.

Aviation law is another hybrid area. It concerns business rules and regulations both in the airline's home state and in destination states. Domestic laws and foreign laws are involved, potentially also giving rise to conflict of laws issues. It also involves public international law issues insofar as the airline must adhere to international conventions relating to air travel.

CHAPTER SUMMARY

The law regulates almost all forms of human conduct. As accepted behaviours continue to evolve, legal subjects are refined and developed. Classification and categorization is challenging at times, but a basic understanding of the differences between substantive law, procedural law, and practice norms—and how the law is further divided into specific subject areas—can help situate legal issues and the way in which legal problems are analyzed.

Substantive law topics define the core rights and obligations that regulate our interactions with one another and with the state, and that regulate the apparatus of the state itself. Public law and private law topics range from the most significant at the societal level (constitutional law) to the very specific at the private law level (such as corporate finance, and landlord and tenant law).

Procedural law and practice norms are important in the everyday practice of law. Procedural law concerns the processes that must be followed in order to achieve a legal result. Procedures affect almost every area of the law and include the adjudication of disputes before the courts, the use of evidence, the application of ADR techniques to resolve claims, and the collection of debts. Practice norms are similarly wide-ranging, featuring in all contexts where legal professionals are employed as representatives. The adherence to high ethical standards and proficiency in a range of legal skills on the part of legal representatives is critical to the maintenance of a fair and workable legal system.

Some areas have a mixed nature as subject hybrids or transnational subjects. Hybrid areas cross classification lines (for example, subjects with public law and private law elements or domestic law and international law elements). Transnational subjects, such as conflict of laws, cover legal issues that cross jurisdictional boundaries.

Our system of justice is far-reaching and varied and has adapted to cover most forms of human activity.

KEY TERMS

admiralty (or maritime) law, 397

conflict of laws, 396

creditors' remedies, 392

elder law, 388

environmental law, 395

evidence (law of), 391

insurance law, 387

litigation procedures, 390

succession law, 388

taxation law, 386

trusts (law of), 389

FURTHER READING

BOOKS

Boivin, Denis. *Insurance Law* (Toronto: Irwin Law, 2015).

Brown, Craig & Andrew Mercer. *Introduction to Canadian Insurance Law*, 3rd ed (Toronto: LexisNexis, 2013).

Chase, Oscard G & Janet Walker. *Common Law, Civil Law and the Future of Categories* (Toronto: LexisNexis, 2010).

Chircop, Aldo et al, eds. *Canadian Maritime Law*, 2nd ed (Toronto: Irwin Law, 2016).

Delisle, Ron & Lisa Dufraimont. *Canadian Evidence Law in a Nutshell*, 3rd ed (Toronto: Carswell, 2009).

Duff, David R et al. *Canadian Income Tax Law*, 6th ed (Toronto: LexisNexis, 2018).

Fitzgerald, Patrick, Barry Wright & Vincent Kazmierski. *Looking at Law: Canada's Legal System*, 6th ed (Toronto: LexisNexis, 2010).

Fuerst, Michelle, Sidney N Lederman & Alan W Bryant. *Sopinka, Lederman & Bryant—The Law of Evidence*, 5th ed (Toronto: LexisNexis, 2018).

Hull, Ian, James MacKenzie & Suzana Popovic-Montag. *Feeney's Canadian Law of Wills*, 4th ed (Toronto: LexisNexis, 2000) (loose-leaf).

Li, Jinyan, Joanne Magee & J Scott Wilkie. *Principles of Canadian Income Tax Law*, 9th ed (Toronto: Carswell, 2017).

Liew, Jamie Chai Yun & Donald Galloway. *Immigration Law* (Toronto: Irwin Law, 2015).

Lucas, Alastair R et al. *Canadian Environmental Law*, 3rd ed (Toronto: LexisNexis, 2017) (loose-leaf).

Olivo, Laurence M & DeeAnn Gonsalves. *Debtor-Creditor Law and Procedure*, 5th ed (Toronto: Emond, 2018).

Walker, Janet. *Castel & Walker: Canadian Conflict of Laws*, 6th ed (Toronto: LexisNexis, 2005) (loose-leaf).

REVIEW QUESTIONS

1. Name three subject areas in the category of domestic public law other than constitutional law and criminal law.

2. Define employment law.

3. Name three subject areas that are part of the law of equity.

4. Describe litigation procedures, including some of the processes covered.

5. Define practice norms.

6. What are transnational law subjects? Provide two examples.

EXERCISES

1. Choose a subject area listed under the heading "Substantive Law." Prepare a brief summary of the law on a particular issue covered by that area (for example, immigration law and sponsorship rules for family members, or elder law and the validity of contracts entered into by the elderly). Base your research on online resources (for instance, use CanLII to locate relevant case law) and/or a textbook on the subject (see "Further Reading" for some suggestions).

2. Students sometimes accumulate significant debt by the time their education is finished. Locate and summarize the relevant provisions of the *Bankruptcy and Insolvency Act* that set out the seven-year rule and the five-year hardship exception dealing with student loans. In your opinion, are these provisions adequate? Why or why not? If you believe they are not adequate, what changes could be made to the provisions to improve them? See the discussion under "Insolvency Collections" for a general description of this area.

3. Locate and read *Haaretz.com v Goldhar*, 2018 SCC 28, a split decision with five different judgments (see Box 14.1). Next, review the discussion of multiple judgments under "Multiple Judgments" in Chapter 6. Based on your analysis of this case and your review of the approach to multiple judgments, what in your opinion is the *ratio* (or *ratio decidendi*) of the case—or is there no *ratio*? Support your opinion by referencing specific passages in the case.

PART IV

Working with the Law

15 The Legal Profession

TORONTO. OSGOODE HALL.

Hand-tinted postcard showing Osgoode Hall,
home of the oldest law society in Canada, ca. 1912.

After reading this chapter, you will understand:

- The origins and development of the legal profession.
- The practice of law in Canada today and the various practitioner classes.

- Educational requirements for legal professionals.
- The range of law-related career opportunities.

As capital markets and businesses have become more global and law firm clients more sophisticated, there has been increasing pressure on law firms, law societies and provincial legislatures to modernize and harmonize the options for the practice of law across the country. In response, legislative and regulatory changes over the past two decades have allowed lawyers to practice through professional corporations, limited liability partnerships and multidisciplinary practices, as well as combinations of the traditional and newer practice structures.

Adam M Dodek, *Canadian Legal Practice: A Guide for the 21st Century*
(Toronto: LexisNexis, 2009) (looseleaf) at 7-1

Introduction

The legal profession is an essential part of the Canadian system of law. Lawyers are prominent in public life, and they play a significant role in our three branches of government. Judges in the judicial branch are appointed from the legal profession. Numerous members of our legislatures, including Parliament, have been and are lawyers. In the executive branch, many prime ministers, premiers, and Cabinet ministers also have been and are lawyers (see Box 15.1). Lawyers also play a key role in the civil service, formulating government policies, drafting new legislation, and serving on various administrative boards and tribunals.

This chapter begins by looking at the historical development of the legal profession. Next, it examines the main players in the practice of law in Canada today; in addition to lawyers and judges, these include paralegals, law clerks, legal assistants, notaries, immigration consultants, and others. The educational requirements of legal professionals are also considered, with a focus on common law lawyers and those with whom they work.

Origins and Development of the Legal Profession

In Early Times

The legal profession in Western society can be traced to ancient Greece, where the use of orators to argue legal points developed. These skilled speakers were not formally recognized as belonging to a legal *profession*. Athenian law, for example, forbade the charging of fees for such work. (*Public* advocates, appointed to prosecute important criminal cases, were, however, paid a small fee.[1])

The situation was similar for many years in ancient Rome, where orators or advocates would plead cases for others without remuneration. Over time, Rome saw the emergence of a class of legal specialists, called *jurisprudents*, who had a recognized expertise in the law, acquired through study.[2] Like the unpaid orators before them, however, they were amateurs and also worked for free. It was not until the reign of Emperor Claudius (41-54 CE) that the practice of law was "professionalized," and legal representatives in Roman society could charge fees for their services up to a maximum of 10,000 sesterces (approximately $5,000 in today's currency).[3]

With the fall of the Western Roman Empire and the onset of the Dark Ages, the legal profession essentially disappeared. The Church became the dominant force, and ecclesiastical, or canon, law provided the basis of social regulation. However, in the Middle Ages and with the rise of civil government, a separate legal profession re-emerged. Initially, these legal practitioners were thought of narrowly as *canonists*—that is, experts in ecclesiastical law. But by the 1200s, throughout Europe and in England, paid jurists again established themselves as part of the state's regulatory structure.

The early history of the English legal profession is complicated, due to the wide variety of practitioner classes. There were many kinds, or classes, of lawyers, each with its own set of responsibilities. This complexity diminished over time, until two main types of lawyers remained: barristers and solicitors. This distinction between barristers (that is, litigators) and solicitors (who generally do not litigate, but restrict their practice to giving advice and preparing legal documentation) is still observed in England today, though it is less pronounced than it once was.

In Canada

The distinction between barristers and solicitors has never been as significant in Canada as it has been in England; Canadian common law lawyers, once called to the bar, can practise as both barristers and solicitors. That said, most lawyers in Canada have practices centred on either arguing cases before courts and tribunals (barrister work) or on representing and serving clients in non-litigious matters (solicitor work).

Despite the apparent simplicity of general practice styles in this country, however, the history of the profession illustrates an evolution toward complexity and specialization. As legal historian Carol Wilton has written, "law firms are not islands unto themselves. On the contrary, their work, organization, and culture are intimately tied to the economies and societies of which they are a part."[4] Ged Baldwin, a lawyer who established his law practice in the Peace River district of Alberta in the early 1900s, wrote a book about his career that

---

1   Robert J Bonner, *Lawyers and Litigants in Ancient Athens: The Genesis of the Legal Profession* (New York: Benjamin Blom, 1927) at 201.

2   John A Crook, *Legal Advocacy in the Roman World* (London, UK: Duckworth, 1995) at 40.

3   *Ibid* at 129-30.

4   Carol Wilton, "Introduction" in Carol Wilton, ed, *Essays in the History of Canadian Law*, vol 7, *Inside the Law: Canadian Law Firms in Historical Perspective* (Toronto: University of Toronto Press, 1996) 3.

illustrates Wilton's point and gives us some idea of how much the legal profession has changed in the past century. The following passage, for example, describes Baldwin's early start in the town of Berwyn:

> For my legal services on behalf of the town and my hockey-playing skills on behalf of the town team, they would pay me a small salary. I accepted. I opened a little law office in Berwyn. One by one other clients began to trickle in. Some even managed to pay for my services in coin of the realm. More often, my recompense was stove wood, or lumber, or crop produce, even livestock sometimes. These were, after all, the Depression years.[5]

Prior to Confederation in 1867, Canada was largely a pre-industrial, rural country. Cities were small. A transportation infrastructure composed of canals, roads, bridges, and railways was just getting started. Natural resources such as furs, timber, minerals, and fish were key staples of the economy. Commercial life was expanding with the rise of banks, insurance companies, and corporations, but these institutions were not as developed as they are today. Legal practice was intimately tied to the economy and society of this era. Lawyers had a general practice doing land conveyancing and mortgages, drafting wills and contracts, and doing collections and litigation work. Most lawyers worked as sole practitioners or in small two-person partnerships.[6]

However, with social and economic change after Confederation, the practice of law evolved. For example, the era of railway building began and, as the railway business grew in importance, so did the responsibilities of the lawyers associated with it. Aemilius Irving of Ontario, for instance, became in-house corporate counsel for the Great Western Railway, making him one of the first lawyers in Canada to hold this new kind of in-house corporate position.[7] As the country's economy developed further, there were more and more positions for lawyers in business. Lawyers with corporate clients, or those who went on to manage businesses, often found the move to positions of power in government a natural progression. The legal career of John A Macdonald exemplifies this evolution (see Box 15.1).

Other economic developments in Canada after Confederation affected the nature and practice of law. Electricity began to power new factories, and people moved from farms to the cities in greater numbers. New industries arose during this period—iron and steel, for example, and, in Western Canada, wheat, pulp and paper, and oil and gas. Inventions such as the car, the airplane, and the telephone continued to further transform society.[8] Every change helped create new roles and opportunities for legal professionals and helped shape the legal landscape in Canada today.

---

5 Ged Baldwin, *Frontier Justice: The Reminiscences of Ged Baldwin* (Edmonton: University of Alberta Press, 1987) at 3.

6 Wilton, *supra* note 4. See also Philip Girard, *Lawyers and Legal Culture in British North America: Beamish Murdoch of Halifax* (Toronto: University of Toronto Press, 2011).

7 Jamie Benidickson, "Aemilius Irving: Solicitor to the Great Western Railway" in Wilton, *supra* note 4 at 100.

8 Wilton, *supra* note 4.

BOX 15.1

John A Macdonald: Corporate Lawyer

Much is known about the significance of Sir John A Macdonald's role in bringing about Confederation and his efforts as Canada's first prime minister in nation building. His recently acknowledged racist views and harmful policies concerning Indigenous peoples, however, have tarnished his legacy for many. His career, though, still illustrates how lawyers can transition, perhaps more easily than other professionals, into the political arena.

It is not as well known that Macdonald acted as a leading corporate lawyer for business and commercial clients in Kingston and elsewhere both before and during his career in federal politics. As a corporate lawyer, according to historian JK Johnson, Macdonald held the following positions:

- a director of the Commercial Bank of the Midland District, Kingston's main financial institution;
- member of the board of directors for two British firms—the Trust and Loan Company of Upper Canada and the Times and Beacon Assurance Company of London; and
- president of the St Lawrence Warehouse Dock and Wharfage Company of Quebec City from 1864 to 1889.

Macdonald was also involved with railways, steamships, road companies, and real estate speculation across southern Ontario.

Johnson argues that Macdonald's extensive business background helped facilitate economic activity in Canada. He cites as evidence of this Macdonald's later support of a "National Policy" for a high tariff to protect domestic Canadian manufacturers, a policy favoured by a majority of urban Canadian business leaders.

Sources: JK Johnson, "John A Macdonald, the Young Non-Politician" (1971) 6:1 Historical Papers 138; JK Johnson, "John A Macdonald and the Kingston Business Community" in Gerald JJ Tulchinsky, ed, *To Preserve and Defend: Essays on Kingston in the Nineteenth Century* (Montreal and London: McGill-Queen's University Press, 1976) 141.

Legal Practitioners in Canada Today

Lawyers and judges are the primary actors in the legal profession but, in the modern era, other professionals, such as paralegals and notaries, have joined lawyers in delivering legal services to the public. The main kinds of legal practitioners working in Canada today, as well as their educational requirements, are described next.

Judges and Other Adjudicators

Judges are usually senior lawyers who have been appointed to the bench after many years of successful and distinguished practice. They can also be lawyers who have made their careers in academia or politics. Legislative rules set minimums for required years of experience before a lawyer can become a judge, along with frameworks for the appointment process. There are some differences depending on the court involved and whether the appointments are federal or provincial.

See Chapter 6 for a detailed discussion of judicial qualifications and appointments. The specialized education that judges receive upon their appointment to the bench is described in Box 6.4, "The National Judicial Institute."

Justices of the peace (JPs) are judicial officers affiliated with the provincial courts. They perform a variety of functions related to the administration of justice, including the adjudication of minor criminal or quasi-criminal matters. JPs play an important role in rural communities far from the regular courts. Although not all jurisdictions require JPs to be lawyers, a record of community involvement and some post-secondary education is generally a condition of appointment.

Administrative tribunals resolve disputes in a multitude of areas. Adjudicators appointed to such tribunals are often lawyers, although in some instances they may not be. Appointment qualifications and processes depend on the board and jurisdiction involved (see Chapter 11).

Increasingly, disputes are being resolved outside of formal adjudicative processes.

Alternative dispute resolution (ADR), examined in Chapter 17, deals with the resolution of disputes primarily through negotiation, mediation, or arbitration. ADR is used in various contexts, including business disputes and family matters. Third parties participating in ADR processes often have legal training.

Lawyers

Lawyers can perform almost all forms of legal work. For example, they can advise clients on legal matters, draft legal documents, and prepare for and represent clients at hearings before courts and tribunals. Legislation in every province and territory has empowered law societies to regulate their members and to set standards of practice for the profession. All lawyers must be members of the **law society** for their jurisdiction in order to practise law. The names of these law societies vary. For example, the law society in Nova Scotia is known as the Barristers' Society; in Ontario, it is called the Law Society of Ontario (LSO). In Quebec, the law society has two divisions—the *Barreau du Québec* and the *Chambre des notaires du Québec*.

law society
the governing body of lawyers in a province or territory

Law societies are responsible for, among other things, establishing qualifications to be called to the bar (that is, to be a member of the law society), monitoring professional competence and providing continuing education, and handling public complaints about lawyers and disciplining lawyers in cases of malpractice. Law societies are composed of a small executive group of elected lawyers known in most jurisdictions as **benchers** and may also have some government-appointed non-lawyers known as *lay benchers*. One of the benchers, called the president or treasurer, acts as the head. All of the benchers meet in convocation and form committees—the discipline committee, for example. The profession is, therefore, essentially self-regulated.[9]

benchers
lawyers (and some non-lawyers) who are responsible for administering and governing a provincial or territorial law society

The business structures and settings in which lawyers work are varied (see Box 15.2). Lawyers can practise law independently as sole practitioners with general or specialized practices (such as personal injury or criminal law), in firms of all sizes (see the discussion of partnerships in Chapter 10), in corporate legal departments, or with government departments and agencies. They can also work with regulatory bodies, for unions, for non-profit societies (for instance, civil liberties associations and legal aid societies [described in Chapter 17]), and for other organizations, including international bodies such as the United Nations.

---

9   Some commentators question whether the legal profession in Canada should continue to be self-regulated. There is a global trend away from self-regulation toward co-regulation, in which a separate body comprising both lawyers and non-lawyers provides regulatory oversight, such as in the United Kingdom and Australia; see Laurel S Terry, "Trends in Global and Canadian Lawyer Regulation" (2013) 76 Sask L Rev 145 at 152.

BOX 15.2

Hamilton's "United Nations" Law Firm

The small firm of Millar, Alexander, Tokiwa, and Isaacs, which existed from 1962 to 1993, nicknamed Hamilton's "United Nations law firm," was a leader and an inspiration in addressing the issue of race and the practice of law. The firm's four partners were Irish, Black, Japanese, and Indigenous lawyers, respectively, at a time when multiracial law firms were rare in Canada.

Over time, it became one of the most prominent and successful law firms in Hamilton. Its underlying success was partly owing to political, social, and economic forces that were reshaping Canadian society in the era following the Second World War. These forces began to change how—and by whom—law was practised in this country. The post-war era in Hamilton saw a broad transition away from a predominantly white male and Anglo-Celtic bar to one that included more visible minorities and women. Under these changing circumstances, the firm of Millar, Alexander, Tokiwa, and Isaacs was able to transform what would have been a disadvantage in an earlier era—its multiracial character—into an advantage.

The firm's multiracial character kept it in touch with the changing times. Many immigrants who settled in Hamilton after the war were anxious to buy their first home and sought out this multiracial firm to meet their legal needs in this regard. Paul Tokiwa, for example, could speak to the firm's new Japanese-Canadian clients in their own language.

There were other reasons for the firm's success. Lincoln Alexander's rise to political prominence as the first Black member of Parliament in 1968 brought the firm national goodwill and further recognition. Moreover, all of the firm's members were excellent lawyers, whose reputations for doing good legal work brought in many new clients. As a small law firm, it also had the advantage of being able to service these new clients on a one-to-one basis.

The success of Millar, Alexander, Tokiwa, and Isaacs showed that in a modern Canadian multicultural society, diversity within a law firm could be a benefit. Indeed, this benefit is becoming more apparent as Canada grows ever more multicultural and multiracial, and business becomes more global.

Source: Philip Sworden, "'A Small United Nations': The Hamilton Firm of Millar, Alexander, Tokiwa, and Isaacs, 1962-1993" in Carol Wilton, ed, *Essays in the History of Canadian Law*, vol 7, *Inside the Law: Canadian Law Firms in Historical Perspective* (Toronto: University of Toronto Press, 1996) 469.

In the last century, with the growth and increased sophistication of our economy and regulatory frameworks, some law firms saw a corresponding growth both in terms of size and in terms of breadth of expertise. Larger firms today might have departments specializing in corporate law and securities, taxation, insurance, labour and employment, administrative and regulatory law, real property, personal injury law, family, succession, and other areas, allowing them to service all or most of their clients' legal needs.[10] Some firms have become so large through mergers and alliances that they have national, North American, and even international reach—these *megafirms* hope to improve efficiencies and better serve large commercial and international clients. Other firms have expanded their practices through collaborations with non-legal professionals such as accountants, financial services professionals, health care professionals, engineers, and architects (such collaborations are commonly referred to as *multidisciplinary practices*, or *MDPs*).

---

10   See Ronald J Daniels, "Growing Pains: The Why and How of Law Firm Expansion" (1993) 43:2 UTLJ 147; Christopher Moore, *McCarthy Tetrault: Building Canada's Premier Law Firm, 1855-2005* (Vancouver/Toronto: Douglas & McIntyre, 2005); Christopher Moore, "Megafirm: A Chronology for the Large Law Firm in Canada" in Constance Backhouse & W Wesley Pue, eds, *The Promise and Perils of Law: Lawyers in Canadian History* (Toronto: Irwin Law, 2009) 103.

Educational Requirements

Historically, in Canada, there was debate over rival methods for teaching law. Some members of the legal community believed that traditional English vocational methods for training lawyers should be followed. These methods were based on an apprenticeship model whereby law students served "under **articles**" and obtained practical experience and direct knowledge of the law by working with and under the supervision of a practising lawyer. This training could also be supplemented with law society lectures. Ontario, for example, followed this apprenticeship, or articling, model for a long time.

On the other side of the legal education debate were those who favoured the idea of formal university training at a recognized law school, where professors (rather than practising lawyers) taught the law. Those in Canada who supported this rival academic approach had American law schools (most notably Harvard University) and university law schools in Canada (such as McGill, in Quebec, and Dalhousie, in Nova Scotia) as examples to follow.[11]

The first Canadian common law province to teach future lawyers at a university law school was Nova Scotia, in 1883, at Dalhousie University law school in Halifax.[12] There, law students studied full-time and then articled for a period of time, as prescribed by that province's law society (the Barristers' Society of Nova Scotia), before becoming lawyers.

The debate over how best to train lawyers continued in other common law provinces as they were formed, especially in Western Canada.[13] The model currently in place in the common law provinces, which combines academic coursework with articling requirements, is now the generally accepted one.[14]

Prospective lawyers in common law provinces must now generally meet the following educational requirements:

- an undergraduate bachelor's degree with a high grade-point average (though many applicants have more advanced degrees, such as master's degrees, and some law schools may take incoming students with a minimum of two years at a university);
- a high score on the Law School Admission Test (LSAT);
- three years of full-time study at law school completing an LLB or JD degree;
- a period of articling as determined by their province's law society; and
- completion of a bar admission course, consisting of a series of lectures and examinations established by a province's law society.

articles
an apprenticeship under a practising lawyer

---

11 See Ian C Pilarczyk, *A Noble Roster: One Hundred and Fifty Years of Law at McGill* (Montreal: McGill University Faculty of Law, 1999); Léon Lortie, "The Early Teaching of Law in French Canada" (1976) 2 Dal LJ 521; C Ian Kyer & Jerome Bickenbach, *The Fiercest Debate: Cecil A Wright, the Benchers and Legal Education in Ontario, 1923-1957* (Toronto: University of Toronto Press, 1987); JPS McLaren, "The History of Legal Education in Common Law Canada" in RJ Matas & DJ McCawley, eds, *Legal Education in Canada* (Montreal: Federation of Law Societies of Canada, 1987) 111.

12 John Willis, *A History of Dalhousie Law School* (Toronto: University of Toronto Press, 1979).

13 JR London, "The Admissions and Education Committee: A Perspective on Legal Education and Admission to Practice in the Province of Manitoba, Past, Present and Future" in C Harvey, ed, *The Law Society of Manitoba, 1877-1977* (Winnipeg: Peguis, 1977) 74 at 75; W Wesley Pue, *Law School: The Story of Legal Education in British Columbia* (Vancouver: University of British Columbia Faculty of Law, 1995).

14 William H Hurlburt, *The Self-Regulation of the Legal Profession in Canada and in England and Wales* (Calgary and Edmonton: Law Society of Alberta/Alberta Law Reform Institute, 2000) 69.

Once all these educational and placement requirements are met, law students are then **called to the bar**, a formal ceremony whereby they are admitted to the law society of their province and may begin to practise law. In Canada, they are usually called lawyers and formally called barristers and solicitors.

called to the bar
formal ceremony
whereby a law student
becomes entitled
to practise law

Paralegals

In most jurisdictions in North America, other than Ontario, the term *paralegal* refers to a person who is qualified by education and experience to perform specifically delegated substantive and procedural legal work while working *under the supervision of a lawyer*. Paralegals can work in all of the same legal settings that lawyers can. They are not formally regulated or certified under legislative authority, and the stature they enjoy comes from the specific education they have received and the experience they have gained through their employment in the legal field. In Ontario, a person referred to as a paralegal in other Canadian jurisdictions and in the United States would be referred to as a *law clerk* (see below).

In most jurisdictions, then, paralegals can provide the same legal services as lawyers can (and at a reduced cost to the client or employer), subject to the limitations set out in the legislation regulating the legal profession generally and law society rules. Their work typically includes the following:

- file management;
- interviewing clients and witnesses;
- drafting pleadings, contracts, wills, and conveyancing and corporate records documents;
- legal research; and
- assisting with trials.

Paralegals are typically restricted from doing the following:

- giving legal advice directly to clients,
- providing undertakings to third parties, and
- appearing in courts and tribunals by themselves as advocates.

These restrictions are not rigid, however, and may not apply if the relevant rules of practice and rules of procedure before particular courts and tribunals permit the activities described.

Paralegals in Ontario

In Ontario, the term *paralegal* refers to a person with a unique classification. In that province alone, paralegals are permitted to practise independently of lawyers. In most common law jurisdictions in Canada, lawyers have long had a virtual monopoly over the practice of law. Historically, Ontario was the one jurisdiction where lawyers did not have this kind of monopoly. The Ontario legislation used to define specific areas of practice that were reserved for lawyers, and it left all other areas unregulated. One consequence of this was the emergence of an unregulated "paralegal" profession. In 2007, however, the legislative framework in Ontario changed. Lawyers in Ontario, as in other jurisdictions, are now given a virtual monopoly over the practice of law except in certain broad areas where paralegals, who are now regulated, are allowed to practise.

Paralegals in Ontario, then, licensed by the Law Society of Ontario (LSO), are authorized to provide certain legal services *independently* of lawyers—that is, the work need not be delegated—within the limits set out in the relevant legislation and the LSO rules (by-laws). Work that licensed paralegals in Ontario can perform independently of lawyers includes the following:

- representing clients in Small Claims Court, in the Ontario Court of Justice in respect of provincial offences, on summary conviction offences where the maximum penalty does not exceed six months' imprisonment, and before administrative tribunals;
- giving legal advice concerning rights and responsibilities in connection with the subject matter of a proceeding;
- drafting court documents for use in a proceeding; and
- negotiating on behalf of a client who is a party to a proceeding.[15]

Educational Requirements

As described, paralegals outside of Ontario cannot practise independently and are not formally regulated or obliged to fulfill specific educational requirements in order to practise. Increasingly, however, employers are making formal training a condition of employment for the paralegals they employ. In addition, voluntary industry associations may set educational or experiential standards as conditions of membership.[16]

Most paralegals today are graduates of specialized certificate or diploma programs offered by colleges or universities. These programs may be offered part-time or full-time, and onsite or online; admission requirements vary as well, with some programs requiring work or post-secondary educational experience and others allowing admission directly from high school. Some academic institutions also now offer four-year degree programs in paralegal education.[17]

In Ontario, as noted, paralegals may practise independently, representing clients in connection with certain kinds of offences and regulatory matters. They are licensed by the LSO and, as a condition of licensure, must graduate from an accredited paralegal program and pass a licensing exam. Other law societies are considering adopting a similar approach for paralegals in their jurisdictions.

Law Clerks

In most jurisdictions, the term *law clerk* refers to a person who assists judges or tribunal adjudicators. Frequently, law clerks are recent graduates of law school who are working and who, depending on the jurisdiction, may be able to use this experience in partial or full completion of their articling training. A law clerk's work can involve legal research, preparing draft judgments, and other work assisting the court or tribunal. Law clerks are sometimes also referred to as *judicial clerks*.

As law firms with strong connections to Ontario establish practices in other regions of Canada, the term *law clerk* may be used at those firms in the sense in which it is used in Ontario, as described next.

---

15 For a history of the legal profession in Ontario and the process, beginning in 2007, that led to the regulation of paralegals in that province, see S Patricia Knight, "Paralegal Governance in Ontario" in *Ethics and Professional Practice for Paralegals*, 4th ed (Toronto: Emond, 2018) ch 1. See also the Law Society of Ontario, online: <http://lso.ca/>.

16 See, for example, the Canadian Association of Paralegals (CAP), the Alberta Association of Professional Paralegals (AAPP), and the BC Paralegal Association (BCPA).

17 For example, Humber College in Ontario and Capilano University in British Columbia.

Law Clerks in Ontario

In Ontario, the term *law clerk* refers to an employee who works under the supervision of a lawyer, primarily providing assistance with basic administrative and legal matters. Legal tasks tend to focus more on practice and procedural matters than substantive legal work (such as legal research and preparing legal arguments), but they can involve the latter depending on the level of delegation by the lawyer.

Outside Ontario, a law clerk would generally be referred to as a paralegal, or a person working in a hybrid role as a legal assistant (see the next section).

EDUCATIONAL REQUIREMENTS

Like paralegals outside of Ontario, law clerks in Ontario cannot practise independently and are not formally regulated. The Institute of Law Clerks of Ontario (ILCO) is a voluntary organization that sets standards for membership, including educational requirements. Student members must be enrolled in an ILCO-approved Ontario law clerk program. Other membership categories are based on employment in the field and having passed an ILCO examination.

Legal Administrative Assistants and Legal Assistants

Legal administrative assistants are administrative assistants trained to work in the field of law. Typically, they work as assistants to lawyers, but can also work with paralegals, notaries, and other legal professionals. Their duties often include answering calls, responding to emails, scheduling appointments, and taking notes at meetings. They can assist with the preparation of all types of legal documents, including letters, litigation-related materials, contracts, wills, conveyancing documents, and corporate and securities documentation. They also work with paper and electronic filing systems, both internally (that is, belonging to their employers) and externally (such as with court and other government registries).

Job titles can be confusing in this area. Legal administrative assistants used to be called *legal secretaries*. Paralegals used to be called *legal assistants* in many jurisdictions, though not in Ontario; the term *legal assistant* can also refer to a hybrid position, somewhere in between a paralegal (outside of Ontario) and a legal administrative assistant. Increasingly, however, legal administrative assistants are being called legal assistants.

Educational Requirements

Like law clerks in Ontario, legal assistants and legal administrative assistants are similarly unregulated. However, as a condition of employment most employers require them to have a certificate or diploma designed for legal support staff from a public or private post-secondary institution.

Notaries

Notaries (or notaries public) provide certain types of legal services that could be classed as "solicitor" work. Examples of typical notarial work include the following:

- witnessing affidavits (used as evidence in court proceedings) and statutory declarations (generally used for purposes other than court proceedings, such as for name changes and lost passport declarations);
- preparing contracts;

- preparing real estate documentation (for example, transfers, mortgages, easements, and re-zoning applications);
- estate planning;
- assisting with passport documentation; and
- preparing powers of attorney and representation agreements.

In most jurisdictions, lawyers are *automatically* (or on application can become) notaries. Non-lawyers can also apply to be notaries and, after meeting defined criteria (which vary from region to region), they can be appointed by the government (generally by the attorney general or the minister of justice of the province or territory in which they reside, or by the Crown on their advice). Some jurisdictions, including Alberta and Ontario, require non-lawyer notaries to be affiliated with a specific organization that regularly requires notarized documents. Other jurisdictions, such as British Columbia, allow notaries to practise independently.

Notaries in Quebec are not the same as in other parts of Canada. Civil law notaries in Quebec are in fact lawyers and are required to have a civil law degree—their practice is roughly equivalent to a solicitor's practice in common law jurisdictions.

Educational Requirements

As mentioned, when lawyers are called to the bar, they qualify automatically as, or on application can become, notaries. In most jurisdictions, non-lawyers can become notaries after following an application process, which may or may not involve specific educational requirements. British Columbia, which allows notaries to practise independently, has the strictest educational requirements in Canada—prospective notaries must first complete a designated master's degree in legal studies.

Other Law-Related Positions

A legal education opens many doors, and legal professionals can and do change careers or take on additional roles. There are also many career possibilities and positions with a legal connection that are open to individuals from outside the legal profession who qualify and undertake the necessary training. For instance, a prospective patent agent could have a background in engineering or science and could train for the position without any prior legal experience. A lawyer, however, could also qualify as a patent agent and add that role to his intellectual property (IP) practice. In some instances—for example, commissioners for taking affidavits— lawyers, notaries, and certain government officials automatically qualify for the role.

The following are some positions and careers with a legal connection (some may be pursued as full-time occupations in their own right, while others may be taken on part-time, supplementing other legal or non-legal positions):

- *Commissioners for taking affidavits.* Sometimes referred to as *commissioners of oaths,* these professionals, whose scope of practice is limited, can administer oaths and witness affidavits and statutory declarations, usually in the context of other work, such as corporate business or government regulation.
- *Court administrators* (such as court clerks, reporters, or trial coordinators).
- *Court agents.* In some provinces, courts permit lay practitioners, known as *court agents,* to appear before them as advocates for individuals who would otherwise go unrepresented due to the unavailability of trained professionals.
- *Corporate compliance officers* (corporate officers charged with ensuring compliance with regulatory requirements and internal policies and procedures).

- *Human resources and office management* (involving employee services and control of office systems at a law firm or other organization).
- *Immigration consultants.* These federally regulated professionals, who are permitted to practise independently, provide advice on immigration matters, such as permanent residence applications, temporary residence and visa applications, and refugee claims.
- *Insurance* (including work as a claims adjuster, broker, or insurance agent).
- *Law librarians* (for instance, with courthouse, law school, law firm, or government libraries).
- *Legal education* (for example, teaching in a legal studies program).
- *Legal publishing* (for example, legal editors, legal software developers, or technical writers).
- *Legal recruiters* (employment specialists who recruit for law firms and other organizations).
- *Marriage commissioners* or other government appointees authorized to perform civil marriage ceremonies (titles and qualifications vary according to region).
- *Patent and trademark agents.* These are federally regulated IP professionals who are permitted to practise independently and who can assist with the registration of patents and trademarks and other related matters.
- *Private investigation* (involving investigative work collecting evidence, often for lawyers in business, insurance, family, or criminal matters).
- *Policing and corrections* (including work as RCMP officers, provincial and municipal police officers, and probation and parole officers).

Educational Requirements

The educational requirements for other legal professionals vary. They depend on whether the profession is regulated and on the employment market. For instance, immigration consultants are federally licensed through Immigration, Refugees and Citizenship Canada, and must take an accredited practitioner program and pass examinations (the Immigration Consultants of Canada Regulatory Council is the designated regulator for immigration consultants). Patent and trademark agents, who are federally licensed through the Canadian Intellectual Property Office, are similarly required to pass licensure examinations before they can practise.

Some professionals must meet certain educational standards, not because they are mandated by legislation, but because of industry expectations or requirements. For example, law librarians generally must have a library sciences degree, police officers and corrections workers are usually required to have post-secondary education and to complete agency-specific training, and law teachers usually must have a legal education (such as a law degree or paralegal credential).

CHAPTER SUMMARY

The practice of law has changed dramatically in the last 100 years, from a profession made up largely of sole practitioners and small partnerships to one that includes a greater number of large law firms, some megafirms, and MDPs. The legal landscape has also changed, through the introduction of new practitioner classes such as paralegals, law clerks, and notaries, among others.

Legal education in Canada has evolved, too. Lawyers are no longer trained according to the old English apprenticeship model, in which law students were taught by a practising lawyer while serving under articles. Instead, in the common law provinces today, they are educated through a combination of academic coursework with articling requirements. Education requirements for paralegals have changed significantly as well. Whereas, previously, no formal education was required, most paralegals today are graduates of a college diploma program or a degree program in paralegal studies. In Ontario, paralegals must satisfy defined educational standards as a condition of licensure with the LSO. Other legal professionals are similarly required to meet certain educational standards, because of either market demand or regulatory requirements.

In every province and territory, law societies composed of elected lawyers regulate and supervise the practice of law. Their functions include administering a code of conduct for lawyers, handling public complaints, providing continuing legal education, and disciplining lawyers. Other legal professionals may also have regulatory bodies governing their particular area of practice. In Chapter 16, the disciplinary consequences of professional malpractice are considered in more detail.

A range of opportunities exists for lawyers outside of the traditional law firm, including work at all levels of government, in community legal aid clinics, as in-house counsel for companies, and with administrative agencies and tribunals, public interest advocacy organizations, and legal publishers. Paralegals and other legal professionals also enjoy flexibility in career options because of their training; possibilities include work in court administration, private investigation, legal research, legal publishing, policing, insurance, and human resources.

KEY TERMS

articles, 410

benchers, 408

called to the bar, 411

law society, 408

FURTHER READING

BOOKS

Alexander, Lincoln M. *"Go to School, You're a Little Black Boy": The Honourable Lincoln M Alexander—A Memoir* (Toronto: Dundurn Press, 2006).

Backhouse, Constance & W Wesley Pue, eds. *The Promise and Perils of Law: Lawyers in Canadian History* (Toronto: Irwin Law, 2009).

Brockman, Joan. *Gender in the Legal Profession: Fitting or Breaking the Mould* (Vancouver: University of British Columbia Press, 2001).

Collis, Diana & Cynthia Forget. *Working in a Legal Environment*, 2nd ed (Toronto: Emond Montgomery, 2011).

Sheehy, Elizabeth & Sheila McIntyre, eds. *Calling for Change: Women, Law, and the Legal Profession* (Ottawa: University of Ottawa Press, 2006).

Williams, David Ricardo. *Just Lawyers: Seven Portraits* (Toronto: University of Toronto Press, 1995).

WEBSITES

Provincial and Territorial Law Society Websites

Alberta: <http://www.lawsocietyalberta.com>.

British Columbia: <http://www.lawsociety.bc.ca>.

Manitoba: <http://www.lawsociety.mb.ca>.

New Brunswick: <http://www.lawsociety-barreau.nb.ca>.

Newfoundland and Labrador:
   <http://www.lawsociety.nf.ca>.

Northwest Territories: <http://www.lawsociety.nt.ca>.

Nova Scotia: <http://www.nsbs.org>.

Nunavut: <http://www.lawsociety.nu.ca>.

Ontario: <http://lso.ca/>.

Prince Edward Island: <http://www.lawsocietypei.ca>.

Quebec: <http://www.barreau.qc.ca>.

Saskatchewan: <http://www.lawsociety.sk.ca>.

Yukon: <http://www.lawsocietyyukon.com>.

REVIEW QUESTIONS

1. In what ways do lawyers play a key role in the executive branch of government?

2. In Canada, is there a clear divide between lawyers who are barristers (litigators) and lawyers who are solicitors? Explain.

3. List three responsibilities of provincial and territorial law societies.

4. Describe the main practice settings for lawyers.

5. Describe some effects of economic and regulatory changes in Canada in the last century on the practice of law.

6. What were the two sides in the debate in Canada's common law provinces over how best to train lawyers? Explain.

7. In Canada's common law provinces today, what educational requirements must a prospective lawyer meet?

8. Explain the role of paralegals in your province.

9. Besides judges, lawyers, and paralegals, name four other types of legal professionals or law-related careers in Canada.

EXERCISES

1. Visit the website for your province's law society. Comment on how effectively the website provides information concerning how to find a lawyer practising in an area of the law of interest to you.

2. Assume you are studying at a college or university and are thinking of becoming a lawyer. List the academic requirements you will need to complete in order to become a lawyer in your province.

3. Do you think that Canada's increasing aging population will have an impact on the future practice of law? Discuss.

4. Why do you think an institutional client like a bank or large corporation is so valuable to a law firm?

5. Do you believe that lawyers should be self-regulated by their own professional body or be regulated by their provincial government? Discuss.

16 Legal Ethics

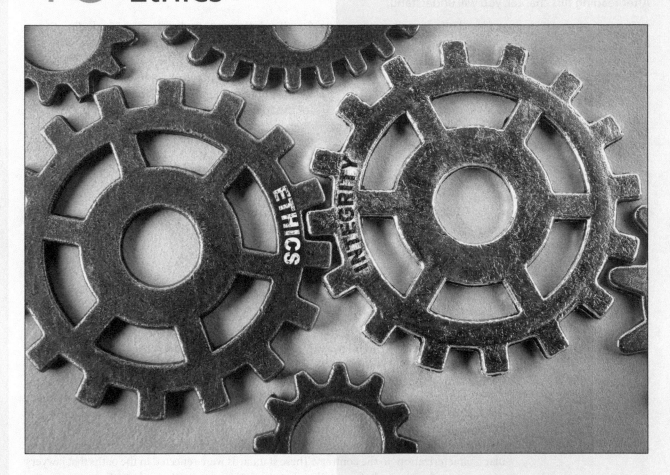

After reading this chapter, you will understand:

- The nature and purpose of legal ethics.
- Codes of conduct and the ethical obligations imposed on judges, lawyers, paralegals, notaries, and other legal practitioners.
- Professionalism and integrity in the legal profession.

- Specific duties imposed on lawyers, including those owed to the state, the court, the profession, the public, and the client.
- The regulatory framework for monitoring ethical behaviour in the legal profession and the process for disciplining ethical breaches.

> Integrity without knowledge is weak and useless, and knowledge without integrity is dangerous and dreadful.
>
> Samuel Johnson (1709-1784) from *Rasselas*, ch 41

Introduction

In Chapter 1, we compared law with other rules, or norms, including moral and ethical obligations. We noted that, while there is no generally accepted distinction between morality and ethics, the two terms can have slightly different connotations. For instance, ethical norms can be associated with specific social contexts, such as acceptable standards of behaviour within certain professions. The purpose of this section is to provide an overview of the ethics of the legal profession.

Ethical standards and the practice of law have long been closely connected, despite popular characterizations to the contrary. These standards were reflected in the oaths that lawyers were required to swear before civil and ecclesiastical courts throughout Europe after the legal profession's re-emergence in the Middle Ages. They were incorporated into England's first *Statute of Westminster*, enacted in 1275, which made it an offence to perpetrate a fraud before the court. And they are defined in the codes and rules that govern the profession today.

legal ethics
legal ethics involve the rules of conduct that govern the legal profession, and their primary purpose is the protection of the public

Legal ethics go beyond the rules proscribing civil wrongs or criminal behaviour generally; these rules apply to everyone. This area of the law involves the rules of conduct that govern the legal profession and covers a wide range of behaviours, including interactions with the court, with clients, and with others. Holding legal professionals to high ethical standards is necessary in order to protect the public. Legal professionals exercise considerable power. They have expertise in the workings of the state and often have access to personal and financial information that could be damaging to their clients and others if misused or disclosed.

The ethical rules that apply to judges, lawyers, paralegals, notaries, and other legal professionals are described next. However, our focus is on lawyers, whose codes of conduct, obligations of professionalism and integrity, and specific duties (including duties to the state, the court, the profession, the public, and the client) are well established and have been refined over many decades.

Judges

The judiciary is the third branch of government in Canada, and the independence of judges is constitutionally protected (see also Chapter 6 under "Judicial Independence"). Judicial tenure, which allows judges to render decisions without fear of losing their jobs if their decisions are not well received, is based on the judges maintaining a standard of "good behaviour"—a standard that is rarely breached.

Complementing the idea of tenure based on good behaviour is the expectation that judges maintain high ethical standards. The Canadian Judicial Council, a federal body created under the *Judges Act*[1] in 1971, has a mandate to (among other things) improve quality and promote accountability in courts with federally appointed judges, which include all superior courts. To that end, the council has published a document entitled "Ethical Principles for Judges." Its stated purpose is to provide "ethical guidance" for judges, but the council is careful to note that the principles are advisory in nature and do not constitute a list of prohibited behaviours or set standards for judicial misconduct. Otherwise, these guidelines could be interpreted as a form of interference with the principle of judicial independence.

Under these guidelines, federally appointed judges are encouraged to conduct themselves with integrity, be diligent in the performance of their judicial duties, assure equality before the law, and be impartial. Similar ethical obligations and guidelines apply to provincial and territorial inferior court judges and to other adjudicators.

Complaints about the conduct of federally appointed judges are handled by the Canadian Judicial Council, which will investigate in appropriate cases and make recommendations.[2] However, under the Constitution, only Parliament can formally remove superior court judges, and to date this has never happened. Comparable disciplinary processes, but with greater remedial flexibility (including possible removal), apply to provincial and territorial inferior court judges and other adjudicators; judges and adjudicators generally retire or resign before the process reaches the point of removal.[3]

---

1 RSC 1985, c J-1.

2 Until recently, there had been only four attempts (since Confederation) to remove superior court judges, but in 2017, the Canadian Judicial Council recommended the removal of two judges in separate investigations. In the case of Michel Girouard, a Quebec superior court judge, the council found that Girouard has misled its inquiry into his purchase and use of cocaine in 2010, just before he was appointed to the bench. His conduct, the council concluded, demonstrated a lack of integrity that prevented him from discharging his duties as a judge. Girouard is challenging the findings of the council on a number of grounds and, at the time of writing, has not resigned—he continues to collect his salary of over $320,000 per year and have the legal expenses connected to his challenges paid for by the government. In the second case, Robin Camp made inappropriate comments to an alleged rape victim, including asking her why she didn't keep her "knees together." His comments were made in 2014 during a sexual assault trial when he was an Alberta provincial court judge. The review of his conduct, however, didn't begin until over a year later, by which time he had been elevated to the federal court. Camp resigned shortly after the council recommended his removal.

3 As noted in Chapter 6, only a handful of lower court judges have ever been removed. And, as with superior court judges, findings of misconduct are uncommon. For example, in Ontario, since 2000, there have been just three findings of misconduct by the Ontario Judicial Council. In 2004, a provincial court judge was reprimanded for indiscreet comments she had made about an accused and her family. In the same year, the council found a judge guilty of misconduct for inappropriately touching a female staff member—the judge resigned before a penalty was imposed. And in 2007, the council officially warned a judge after he altered court transcripts to remove objectionable comments he had made. See Michael McKiernan, "Judging the Judges" (2012) 26:2 Can Lawyer 32 at 36.

Lawyers

The most developed and specifically defined rules and guidelines for ethical behaviour in the legal profession—and possibly across all professions—are those that apply to lawyers.

Written codes of conduct for lawyers are a relatively recent development in common law jurisdictions. In the past, there was some statute law and case law defining inappropriate conduct in the practice of law. But the profession initially resisted adopting anything more comprehensive than that. The common assumption seems to have been that the legal profession was, after all, an ancient, noble, and learned profession; it went without saying that honour and integrity governed its practice. This notion persisted until the 19th century.

Codes of Conduct

codes of conduct
written sets of rules regulating the ethical behaviour of professionals

In the late 1800s, the governing bodies for lawyers in common law jurisdictions began developing written **codes of conduct** to guide their members. Generally speaking, these codes are not directly enforceable by court action. It is the profession itself, through law societies, that takes disciplinary action against its members who breach the codes of conduct.

The Canadian Bar Association (CBA) is a federal organization, membership in which is voluntary for lawyers in some provinces but mandatory in others. It developed and adopted its first code of conduct in 1920—Canada's first code for lawyers. The Canons of Legal Ethics (CBA Canons), as they were called, borrowed in part from the Canons of Professional Ethics, adopted in 1908 by the American Bar Association. The CBA Canons were revised and replaced in 1974 with the Code of Professional Conduct. This latter code has been revised a number of times, most recently in 2009, but is being discontinued in favour of the FLSC Model Code referred to below.

Almost every law society in Canada has passed its own code of conduct, similar to the CBA Code if not identical to it. (Prince Edward Island, the Northwest Territories, and Nunavut have simply adopted the CBA Code.)

In 2009, the Federation of Law Societies of Canada (FLSC), working with the law societies from all Canadian provinces and territories, adopted the Model Code of Professional Conduct (FLSC Model Code). It is drawn in part from the CBA Code. Membership in provincial/territorial law societies is mandatory for lawyers practising in a particular jurisdiction, as is following the law society's particular code. One of the consequences of living in a federal state is a multiplicity of rules. Uniformity is valuable in this context, however—hence the move to create the FLSC Model Code. New rules dealing with conflicts of interest and confidentiality were added to the FLSC Model Code in 2011. (See Box 16.1.) Since then the Model Code has been adopted by all law societies, in whole or in part, in Canada, except the *Chambre des notaires* in Quebec.[4]

---

4   See Federation of Law Societies of Canada, "Implementation of the Model Code," online: <https://flsc.ca/resources/implementation-of-the-model-code/>.

BOX 16.1

The FLSC Model Code

The preface to the FLSC Model Code emphasizes the importance of legal ethics in relation to the public interest. It includes the following provision:

> Rules of conduct should assist, not hinder, lawyers in providing legal services to the public in a way that ensures the public interest is protected. This calls for a framework based on ethical principles that, at the highest level, are immutable, and a profession that dedicates itself to practise according to the standards of competence, honesty and loyalty.

The seven chapters of the FLSC Model Code are as follows:

- chapter 1: Interpretation and Definitions;
- chapter 2: Standards of the Legal Profession;
- chapter 3: Relationship to Clients;
- chapter 4: Marketing of Legal Services;
- chapter 5: Relationship to the Administration of Justice;
- chapter 6: Relationship to Students, Employees, and Others; and
- chapter 7: Relationship to the Society and Other Lawyers.

Professionalism and Integrity

Underlying all the more specific ethical obligations imposed on lawyers is the general obligation to act honourably, in good faith, and with integrity when dealing with others.

The preface to the CBA Code stated the following:

> The essence of professional responsibility is that the lawyer must act at all times *uberrimae fidei*, meaning with utmost good faith to the court, to the client, to other lawyers, and to members of the public.

Chapter I of the CBA Code, entitled "Integrity," stated the following:

> The lawyer must discharge with integrity all duties owed to clients, the court or tribunal or other members of the profession and the public.

Rule 2.1 of chapter 2 of the FLSC Model Code, also entitled "Integrity," provides as follows:

> 2.1-1 A lawyer has a duty to carry on the practice of law and discharge all responsibilities to clients, tribunals, the public and other members of the profession honourably and with integrity.
>
> 2.1-2 A lawyer has a duty to uphold the standards and reputation of the legal profession and to assist in the advancement of its goals, organizations and institutions.

The commentary following these provisions states that integrity is the "fundamental quality of any person who seeks to practise as a member of the legal profession." The commentary goes on to state that while dishonourable conduct in a lawyer's private life can be so serious as to call into question the lawyer's professional integrity, law societies will not, generally speaking, be concerned with a lawyer's purely private activities.

A Question of Integrity

Michael Ryan was a lawyer hired by clients to pursue a possible wrongful dismissal claim against their employer. For over six years, he did nothing to further their claim. In response to their inquiries about the progress of the claim, he "spun an elaborate web of deceit." He told them that others were responsible for the delays, including other members of the bar; that discoveries had been cancelled; that he was pursuing a contempt motion against the defendants for failing to appear; and that a new precedent would require them to start the entire process over again. He even went so far as to forge a decision of the Court of Appeal. Finally, he admitted to his clients that he had done nothing and that all of his excuses were lies.

His clients filed a complaint with the Law Society of New Brunswick. Ryan was "apologetic and contrite and admitted his fault." In his defence, he argued that he was suffering from physical and emotional problems after separating from his wife and that he was abusing alcohol and taking medication for panic attacks. Ryan had been disciplined twice before for failing to carry out services for his clients. The decision of the Discipline Committee was that Ryan should be disbarred. They reasoned that, given all the circumstances, his "unethical behaviour" was very serious and that "his honesty, trustworthiness, and fitness as a lawyer were irreparably compromised." When the case finally made it to the Supreme Court of Canada, the decision of the Discipline Committee was affirmed.*

Do you think that Ryan's excuses for failing to pursue his clients' claim mitigate the lack of integrity demonstrated by his lies and by the forged court document? Was his lack of integrity so serious as to justify disbarment?

* *Law Society of New Brunswick v Ryan*, 2003 SCC 20.

Ethical Duties

Lawyers owe ethical obligations to the state, the court (and others when engaged in an advocacy role), the profession, the public, and their clients.

Duty to the State

The old CBA Canons and some older provincial codes provided that a "lawyer owes a duty to the State, to maintain its integrity and its law." The notions of "duty to the state" and "integrity" are flexible ones, changing with the times (see Box 16.3). The modern codes do not expressly refer to a duty to the state, but they do cite an obligation to "encourage public respect for and try to improve the administration of justice."[5]

It might seem common sense that lawyers must not break the law or promote its breach. That is the ideal, of course, but the reality is bound to be different. Numerous *practising* lawyers have broken the law. Their offences have ranged from impaired driving to possession of narcotics to theft to violent crimes. The disciplinary consequences have varied depending on the circumstances, from reprimands, to fines, to disbarment. There is a difference, of course, between, on the one hand, breaking the law or advocating that it should be broken and, on the other hand, using legal means to argue that the law should be changed or challenged. Unjust or unconstitutional laws can be questioned by appropriate methods, such as court challenges or fighting for political or legislative change.

---

5 See CBA Code, ch XIII, and FLSC Model Code, ch 5, r 5.6-1. The provincial and territorial codes all contain similar provisions. See Mark M Orkin, "Duty to the State" in *Legal Ethics*, 2nd ed (Toronto: Canada Law Book, 2011) ch 2.

Advising or assisting in the violation of the law—aiding and abetting—can be illegal in itself. Just as breaking the law directly will attract disciplinary consequences, so too will advising or assisting in the violation of the law.

BOX 16.3

A Person of Good Repute

In the mid-20th century, WJ Gordon Martin, a Canadian citizen who happened to be a communist, was not allowed to become a lawyer in British Columbia. Despite his successful completion of the educational requirements for practising law, Martin's support for communist doctrine, which prescribes the abolition of private property and the forcible overthrow of the existing social order, led the benchers of the law society to conclude that he was not a person of good repute. They refused to call him to the bar or admit him to the province's Supreme Court. Their decision was upheld on appeal, first to the BC Supreme Court and then to the Court of Appeal.* The case arose at the height of the Cold War and against the backdrop of McCarthyism—that is, the campaign against alleged communists in the US government and other institutions carried out under Senator Joseph McCarthy. It is unlikely that the Martin case would be decided the same way today.

* *Martin v Law Society of British Columbia*, 1950 CanLII 242, [1950] 3 DLR 173 (BCCA).

Duty to the Court

Lawyers are "officers of the court" in Canada, a status now confirmed by legislation in most provinces and territories.[6] As officers of the court, lawyers are subject to the summary jurisdiction of the court and can be held liable for civil or criminal contempt for misconduct.

COURTESY AND RESPECT

As noted earlier, the preface to the CBA Code states that the lawyer must act "with utmost good faith to the court." Chapter IX states the following:

> When acting as an advocate, the lawyer must treat the court or tribunal with
> courtesy and respect and must represent the client resolutely, honourably and
> within the limits of the law.

Rule 5.1 of chapter 5 of the FLSC Model Code is entitled "The Lawyer as Advocate." Rule 5.1-1 is similar to the CBA Code rule regarding courtesy and respect. It provides as follows:

> 5.1-1 When acting as an advocate, a lawyer must represent the client resolutely
> and honourably within the limits of the law, while treating the tribunal with
> candour, fairness, courtesy and respect.

The commentary following this last provision states that maintaining decorum and dignity in the courtroom is not an "empty formality." This statement is based on the principle that "unless order is maintained, rights cannot be protected." This requirement that lawyers

---

6   See, for example, *Legal Profession Act*, RSA 2000, c L-8, s 102(2); *Legal Profession Act*, SBC 1998, c 9, s 14(2); *Legal Profession Act*, RSNWT (Nu) 1988, c L-2, s 64; and *Law Society Act*, RSO 1990, c L.8, s 29.

behave with courtesy and respect extends beyond court proceedings to "proceedings before boards, administrative tribunals, arbitrators, mediators and others who resolve disputes, regardless of their function or the informality of their procedures."

ABUSE OF PROCESS

Rule 5.1-2(a) of chapter 5 of the FLSC Model Code states the following:

> 5.1-2(a) When acting as an advocate, a lawyer must not abuse the process of the tribunal by instituting or prosecuting proceedings that, although legal in themselves, are clearly motivated by malice on the part of the client and are brought solely for the purpose of injuring the other party.

A lawyer has two strong reasons not to abuse the process in the way prohibited by this provision. First, the lawyer would be potentially liable for misconduct. Second, the client would be at risk of facing a later tort claim by the defendant for abuse of process or for malicious prosecution.

OTHER OBLIGATIONS TO THE COURT

Lawyers' responsibility to act in good faith and with courtesy and respect when appearing before the courts involves a number of specific obligations. Among them are the following:

- they must not knowingly mislead the tribunal by using false evidence (such as a false affidavit), and they must not misstate the facts;
- they must not fail to inform the court of binding authority that is directly on point, if that binding authority is not otherwise before the court; and
- they must not publicly criticize the tribunal or the adjudicator if they are on the wrong end of a ruling.

Ethics of Advocacy

The ethics of advocacy overlap with lawyers' duty to the court. We may distinguish the two on the following grounds: the duty to the court deals with responsibilities that affect the court process, whereas the ethics of advocacy are more concerned with lawyers' need to balance their obligations to the court and their obligations to others.

CONFLICTING OBLIGATIONS TO THE COURT, TO THE CLIENT, AND TO OTHERS

Lawyers are required to treat tribunals with "candour, fairness, courtesy and respect," but at the same time to represent their clients "resolutely." As an advocate, a lawyer "has a duty to the client to raise fearlessly every issue, advance every argument, and ask every question, however distasteful, that the lawyer thinks will help the client's case."[7] It is hardly surprising, then, that lawyers sometimes have difficulty knowing when the pursuit of one objective infringes the other. The line between decorum and the pursuit of justice can become blurred. For example, a lawyer who aggressively cross-examines a witness—attempting to elicit

---

7 See the commentary following FLSC Model Code, ch 5, r 5.1-1.

favourable evidence for her client—may be seen as failing in her responsibility to be "courteous and civil and act in good faith" with others.[8] Conflicting loyalties of this kind can give rise to complicated ethical issues for lawyers.

PROBLEMS THAT ARISE IN LITIGATION

Lawyers face many situations during the litigation process that give rise to ethical questions. A few of the more common ones are discussed below.

Particular Clients: Organizations and Accused Persons

Generally, a lawyer should conduct litigation the same way for all clients. Special considerations can apply when lawyers are dealing with organizations or when defending accused persons.

When representing an organization, the lawyer may discover that the organization has perpetrated a fraud—has falsified evidence, for example. The lawyer must disclose the fraudulent or illegal activity not only to the person in the organization from whom the lawyer is taking instructions but also to the chief legal officer and, in some cases, to the chief executive officer. The lawyer must also advise that the activity should be stopped. If this advice is not followed, the lawyer must withdraw from representing the client. This requirement applies when the lawyer is providing any kind of legal service, not just services related to litigation.

When representing an accused person, the lawyer must do his utmost to ensure that his client is not convicted unless it is on sound legal evidence before a competent tribunal. In his efforts to ensure this, he should rely on technicalities, so long as he knows them not to be false or groundless. The lawyer must do this regardless of what he believes about his client's credibility or the merits of the case. However, if the accused is competent and clearly admits to committing the crime, there will be limitations on what the lawyer can do. The lawyer will not be able to "set up an affirmative case inconsistent with the admission."[9] The client should be made aware of this restriction at the outset.

Particular Cases: Criminal Prosecutions and Family Law Matters

Criminal cases tend to give rise to particular ethical problems for lawyers. Defence counsel face special problems (as described above), but so do prosecutors. Crown attorneys (also referred to as Crown prosecutors) in criminal cases are in a unique position compared with other advocates. Because they represent the public interest and the administration of justice, their primary duty is not to convict but to see that justice is done. This means that the Crown attorney cannot do anything to hinder the accused's ability to obtain representation or to communicate with counsel. Also, the Crown attorney must make timely disclosure to defence counsel (or to the accused directly, if she is unrepresented) of relevant facts and witnesses, regardless of whether these facts and witnesses support the accused's guilt or her innocence.

Family law cases also pose particular ethical problems for lawyers. In these cases, the adversarial process will not always lead to the best outcome. This is particularly so if the custody and support of children are involved. Representing a client "resolutely" in these cases will most often mean *not* pursuing every litigation tactic available to win a judgment

---

8 See, for example, FLSC Model Code, ch 7, r 7.2-1.

9 *Supra* note 7.

for the client. For example, in divorce proceedings a client may instruct his legal representative to argue for exclusive custody of his child. Such an outcome, however, may not be in the best interests of the child. In family law cases, negotiation and mediation have been shown to result in better long-term outcomes than the adversarial system does (see the discussion of alternative dispute resolution more generally in Chapter 17 and in Chapter 14).

Withdrawing from Cases

Lawyers must not withdraw from representing a client without good reason. This applies whether or not the client's file is before the courts. During litigation, however, withdrawal can be particularly damaging to the client's interests. If there is a serious breakdown in the relationship—for example, if the client is not paying her fees or is engaging in criminal behaviour that is affecting the litigation—the lawyer can withdraw his services. If the lawyer is withdrawing from a criminal defence case and the trial date is close, he must try to obtain an adjournment.

In all cases, the lawyer must withdraw her services if she has been discharged by the client, if the client continually requests that she violate professional ethics, or if the lawyer finds herself not competent to handle the file.

Delaying Tactics

Lawyers may use the rules of the court—for example, by taking full advantage of all the time available—to advance their clients' interests. However, tactics that are designed solely to delay or to embarrass the other side and are not directly related to the client's case are considered unethical.

Duty to Settle

Most cases that begin as lawsuits settle out of court. There is no guarantee of winning a large judgment by going to court. There is always the risk of winning nothing. If a fair and reasonable result is possible through agreement, the lawyers on both sides should encourage the parties to take that route.

Rule 3.2-4 of chapter 3 of the FLSC Model Code states the following in this regard:

> 3.2-4 A lawyer must advise and encourage a client to compromise or settle a dispute whenever it is possible to do so on a reasonable basis and must discourage the client from commencing or continuing useless legal proceedings.[10]

Use of Evidence

Lawyers must not mislead the court with false evidence, no matter how strongly they believe in the overall merits of a client's case and want the client to win. This line must never be crossed. Lying to the court directly is wrong, and so is failing to enlighten the court about any falsehood with respect to evidence in the case. For a lawyer knowingly to allow false evidence to go before the court is clearly a breach of this obligation. So is not correcting a mistake or falsehood discovered after evidence has been entered.

Where witnesses are concerned, a number of rules apply. For example, supporting witnesses can be interviewed and prepared for proceedings, but they must not be counselled

---

10   See also CBA Code, ch III, commentary 6.

to give false evidence or to suppress evidence. Similarly, lawyers cannot, without the leave of the court, communicate with their supporting witnesses while the opposing side is cross-examining them. And lawyers must not unduly harass or abuse adverse witnesses during examination.

BOX 16.4

What Would You Do?

Assume you are a lawyer. The client you are representing in a case is a young child who has been seriously and permanently disabled by the negligence of a doctor—the defendant in the case. The claim is centred on the cost of future care for the child. At the time your firm was retained, the child was in an expensive facility that cares 24 hours a day for patients with your client's type of disability.

You win a favourable award at trial, an award that will cover the cost of the care facility for the rest of the child's life. The case is appealed. During argument on appeal, a judge asks you if the child is still in the facility. You answer truthfully that, as far as you are aware, the child is still in the facility. On a break in the proceedings, you contact the parents of the child,

who tell you that they couldn't stand being apart from their child and that he is now back at home with them and that they are caring for him at a much reduced cost.

What would you do? When the proceedings resume, will you inform the court of this new information, knowing that it could affect the quantum (that is, amount) of the award for your client's future care?

Now assume that you are a paralegal assisting the lawyer in this case and that it is you who phones the parents during the break and becomes aware of this new information. Do you tell the lawyer—your employer? What if you tell the lawyer and she fails to pass this information on to the court? What do you do then?

Other Issues

During the pretrial discovery process, no adjudicator is present, and there is a potential for lawyers to abuse the opposition. They must not do this. Lawyers at this early stage in the process should not engage in, for instance, "the dogged pursuit of irrelevant details, and questioning that is calculated to exhaust or intimidate the opponent."[11]

In jury trials, lawyers can evaluate potential jurors but must not communicate with them during or after trials.[12]

In the heat of battle, lawyers may be tempted to publicly criticize opposing counsel. This is unprofessional and encourages disrespect for the system.

Duties to the Profession and to the General Public

Along with the duties they owe to the state and to the court, lawyers owe duties to their governing bodies, to other legal professionals, and to members of the public.

---

11 Gavin MacKenzie, "Advocacy" in *Lawyers & Ethics: Professional Responsibility and Discipline* (Toronto: Carswell, 1993) (loose-leaf updated 2018, release 3), ch 4 at 4-10.

12 See CBA Code, ch IX, commentary 21, and FLSC Model Code, ch 5, r 5.5.

DUTY TO THE LEGAL PROFESSION: INTEGRITY

Chapter XV of the CBA Code, entitled "Responsibility to the Profession Generally," states the following: "The lawyer should assist in maintaining the integrity of the profession and should participate in its activities." The commentary on this provision gives some specific examples of what is being referred to. Lawyers must respond promptly to communications from the governing body (that is, the law society), and they must report ethical breaches by other lawyers, particularly if these breaches involve serious matters such as misappropriation of client funds or criminal activity related to the lawyer's practice.

Rule 7.1 of chapter 7 of the FLSC Model Code has the following heading: "Responsibility to the Society and the Profession Generally." It is similar to the CBA Code requirement regarding integrity except that it takes what is commentary in the CBA Code and makes it part of the rule.

Both codes emphasize the importance of effectively communicating with the law society and of reporting malpractice. These things are important because of the potentially serious consequences to clients and to the public if professional misconduct is left unchecked.

DUTY TO LEGAL PROFESSIONALS AND TO OTHERS: COURTESY AND GOOD FAITH

Chapter XVI of the CBA Code, entitled "Responsibility to the Profession Generally," states the following:

> The lawyer's conduct toward all persons with whom the lawyer comes into contact in practice should be characterized by courtesy and good faith.

Rule 7.2-1 of chapter 7 of the FLSC Model Code is similar in what it prescribes:

> 7.2-1 A lawyer must be courteous and civil and act in good faith with all persons with whom the lawyer has dealings in the course of his or her practice.

These rules provide that everyone with whom a lawyer has dealings—other legal professionals, clients, and the public—should be treated fairly and with deference. The rationale for these rules is that the legal profession plays an important role in society and that its representatives must positively reflect the system of justice they serve.

SPECIFIC ISSUES IN PRACTICE

Lawyers have a number of specific obligations based on these general duties regarding integrity, courtesy, and good faith. Among the more important of these obligations are those concerned with undertakings and advertising.

Undertakings

undertaking
clear statement of intention by one person, usually a lawyer, that is reasonably relied on by another, amounting to a solemn promise that must be kept or the person who has given the undertaking will be liable for misconduct

Practising lawyers are frequently called upon to give undertakings. An **undertaking** is a clear statement of intention by one person that another person may reasonably rely on. Most lawyers' undertakings are made to further clients' interests. For instance, a lawyer representing a purchaser in a real estate transaction might receive a title transfer document from the seller on an undertaking by the lawyer to the seller not to register the transfer until the lawyer's client, the purchaser, has paid the lawyer the purchase price so that the lawyer can in turn pay the seller.

Undertakings by lawyers are solemn promises and are crucial to many legal transactions. Any lawyer who fails to live up to an undertaking has committed a serious ethical breach and will be liable for professional misconduct.

Advertising

Historically, advertising by lawyers was considered undignified or worse. Governing bodies treated it as conduct that warranted disciplinary action. In 1982, for example, just before the Charter came into effect, the Supreme Court of Canada (SCC) affirmed a law society ruling disciplining a lawyer for advertising her services, which the law society held to be "conduct unbecoming" a lawyer.[13]

Times have changed. The Charter in effect guarantees "freedom of expression" under section 2. In consequence, there is general acceptance by the profession and by the public that advertising legal services is acceptable if done within reasonable bounds (that is, if it is not misleading or untruthful, meets a public need, and is done with integrity).[14] Television ads and full-page listings in directories promoting legal services are now common.

Other Matters: Sharp Practice and Public Criticism

Engaging in so-called sharp practices—issuing misleading statements to opposing counsel or to the court, breaking agreements with other lawyers, issuing threats, making improper use of process, or using tricky means that are barely within the law—and taking advantage of "slips, irregularities or mistakes" by other lawyers are not considered fair play.[15] Public criticism by lawyers of other lawyers is unacceptable. Soliciting clients in order to take them away from other lawyers is also regarded as unethical. The practice of law is not like other businesses, which have fewer restrictions on competition.

Duty to the Client

Of all their ethical obligations, the duty to the client is the one that concerns most lawyers in their day-to-day practice. Lawyers have a general right to refuse to take on a particular client or case if they don't want to.[16] But once a lawyer takes on a client, a special relationship is created.

The relationship between lawyer and client is based on contract, but it is a special kind of contractual relationship. It is one of confidence and one that has attached to it certain **fiduciary obligations** that require the lawyer to be open and honest, to be loyal, and to treat the client with good faith. The contractual relationship also involves an implied term that the lawyer must be competent and must exercise reasonable care in the delivery of the agreed-upon services.

fiduciary obligations
trust-like obligations, such as loyalty and good faith, that apply in certain contexts, including lawyer–client dealings

As well as having contractual obligations, lawyers are subject to a duty in negligence. In other words, a lawyer can be liable for his negligent performance of services and for his careless words if the client's reliance on them results in damage to the client. In such a case, the degree of the lawyer's liability depends on the closeness of the lawyer–client relationship and on the neighbour principle—that is, every person's obligation to take reasonable care to avoid acts or omissions that might injure his or her neighbour. (For more in-depth discussion of this principle and of torts generally, see Chapters 1 and 8.)

In addition to these contractual and tortious obligations where their clients are concerned, lawyers have related *ethical* duties, the most important of which are duties of competence,

---

13 *AG Can v Law Society of BC*, [1982] 2 SCR 307, 1982 CanLII 29.

14 See CBA Code, ch XIV (and the 2009 supplement, "Guidelines for Ethical Marketing Practices Using New Information Technologies"), and FLSC Model Code, ch 4, r 4.2.

15 See Orkin, *supra* note 5 at 131.

16 The right to refuse a client is subject to a few exceptions. For instance, lawyers can't refuse a client assigned to them by the court, and they must not refuse a client on discriminatory grounds.

confidence, and loyalty. What distinguishes these ethical duties from most others is that they coincide with legal or fiduciary obligations in contract and tort, as described above. Clients can clearly sue for the breach of such obligations. For example, if a lawyer represents a purchaser in a real estate transaction and stands to profit from the sale because of her relationship with the seller, she has to disclose this conflict of interest to her client—the purchaser. If she fails to do so, she will be in breach of not only her ethical obligations to her client but also her contractual and fiduciary obligations and can be sued.[17]

In the following sections, we examine the following duties that lawyers owe to their clients: the duty of competence, the duty of confidentiality, and the duty of loyalty.

DUTY OF COMPETENCE

duty of competence
lawyer's obligation to provide services that meet the standard of a reasonably skilled lawyer

Lawyers have an obligation to provide services competently. The **duty of competence** does not require the lawyer to meet a standard of perfection, but it does require him to meet the standard of a reasonably skilled lawyer. If a matter is outside a lawyer's competence, the lawyer has a number of options: he may decline to act, he may request permission to bring in skilled co-counsel, or he may seek extra time to become competent in the matter (so long as this does not involve added risk or expense for the client).

DUTY OF CONFIDENTIALITY

Lawyers have an obligation not to divulge information concerning a client's affairs that is acquired in the course of the professional relationship, unless they are authorized to do so by the client. However, information acquired in informal settings, outside of a professional relationship, is not protected.

duty of confidentiality
lawyer's obligation not to divulge information concerning a client's affairs that has been acquired in the course of the professional relationship, unless the client authorizes the lawyer to divulge this information

The rationale for this **duty of confidentiality** is that it is required for the proper administration of justice. If clients had no assurance of the full confidentiality of their communications, many would only partially disclose relevant information to their lawyers, and this would hinder the lawyer's ability to provide appropriate and effective legal services.

This duty of confidentiality applies to all information concerning a client, subject to a few exceptions. One notable exception is a case where the lawyer reasonably believes, on the basis of information disclosed by the client, that there is an imminent risk of serious harm to someone. Also, while the codes are silent on this point, we may assume that the duty of confidentiality doesn't apply to criminal communications—in other words, to communications that are criminal in themselves (for example, a threat of physical harm to the lawyer or to her employees) or to communications made with a view to furthering a criminal scheme.[18]

The duty of confidentiality survives the professional relationship. The lawyer cannot subsequently use information about the client for personal benefit or for the benefit of others. This duty also applies to the lawyer's colleagues (for example, articling students and other lawyers) and staff (for example, paralegals, legal administrative assistants, and human resources personnel).

---

17 Lawyers are permitted to structure their law practices so as to limit liability for ordinary operational risks (see the discussion of limited liability partnerships [LLPs] and corporations in Chapter 10). However, legislation prevents lawyers from using LLPs or the corporate shield to avoid personal liability for failing to satisfy contractual, tortious, or other private law obligations. See, for example, *Legal Profession Act*, SBC 1998, c 9, s 84; *Legal Profession Act*, CCSM c L107, s 36(1); *Legal Profession Act*, SNS 2004, c 28, s 23(1); *Law Society Act*, RSO 1990, c L.8, s 61.0.5(1).

18 Alice Woolley, *Understanding Lawyers' Ethics in Canada*, 2nd ed (Toronto: LexisNexis, 2016) at 183.

The duty of confidentiality is distinguishable from the related rule concerning **lawyer–client privilege**, also known as solicitor–client privilege. The latter is a rule of evidence and is slightly narrower in application than the duty of confidentiality. Lawyer–client privilege applies to confidential information that meets the following two criteria:

1. it is connected to the giving or receiving of legal advice, and
2. it is in the form of a communication between lawyer and client.

The duty of confidentiality applies to all client information regardless of whether it is connected with legal advice and regardless of the source of the information. The difference between the duty of confidentiality and lawyer–client privilege is not important to most clients. What is not covered by the privilege is covered by the duty.

DUTY OF LOYALTY: AVOIDING CONFLICTS OF INTEREST

A lawyer's **duty of loyalty** applies both to conflicts of interest between clients and to conflicts of interest between the lawyer and his client.

Conflicts of Interest between Clients

Lawyers must avoid conflicts of interest between clients so that one client's interests are not advanced at the expense of another client's interests. For instance, lawyers cannot represent two clients who are opposing each other in a dispute or who are on opposite sides of certain kinds of transactions (such as a real estate purchase or sale of a business). Advancing one client's interest in these situations may come at the expense of the other client's interest. Where the conflict of interest is minimal, however, a lawyer might be permitted to represent both clients. In order to do so, and as a general rule, both parties must be informed of the conflict and give their consent.

Conflicts of interest between clients are especially a problem for large law firms that have many lawyers and many clients (with the rise of megafirms and multinational mergers, clients of one firm could number in the thousands). Difficulties in this regard also arise from the fact that lawyers are very mobile, often moving from one firm to another. For example, a lawyer may work for a period of time in a firm that represents a client on one side of a dispute. Then, subsequently, this lawyer may leave that firm and go to work for the firm that represents the other party in the dispute. Law firms are required to be diligent in this regard and to have systems in place to ensure that any conflicts are discovered and dealt with appropriately.

With respect to *former clients*, the SCC has recognized that, even without client disclosure and consent, it might be possible for members of a law firm to represent a client in a dispute despite the fact that another member of the firm has formerly represented the *other* party (a former client) and has confidential information that could be used against that former client. In order for this to happen, two conditions must be satisfied:

1. the members of the law firm representing the client must not have received any confidential information about the other side from the colleague who formerly represented the other side; and
2. the firm must have measures in place to ensure that this cannot happen (such measures preventing the disclosure of confidential information are sometimes called **cones of silence**—the expression *Chinese wall* is also used, referring to the Great Wall of China and an institutional barrier to the sharing of confidential information).

lawyer–client privilege
lawyer's obligation not to divulge confidential information concerning a client's affairs that has been communicated to the lawyer by the client and is connected to the giving or receiving of legal advice

duty of loyalty
lawyer's obligation to avoid conflicts of interest between clients and between lawyer and client

cones of silence
institutional mechanisms used by law firms to secure confidential information so that lawyers working at the same law firm are prevented from accessing information that could prejudice a former client; sometimes also called Chinese walls

bright line rule

strict rule that a lawyer
or law firm cannot
represent two current
clients whose interests
are directly adverse to
each other unless both
clients consent after
receiving full disclosure
from the lawyer

Concerning *current clients*, the SCC has set out a **bright line rule** that provides that a lawyer cannot represent two current clients whose interests are directly adverse to each other unless both clients consent after receiving full disclosure from the lawyer. And it is not only the individual lawyer who is subject to this rule, but the lawyer's *firm* as well.[19] See Box 16.5.

Conflicts of Interest Between Lawyer and Client

Regarding conflicts of interest between lawyers and clients, they must be avoided for the obvious reason that the lawyer might be tempted to advance her own interests at the expense of the client's interests. This kind of conflict can arise not only where a lawyer (or an associate or relative of the lawyer) has direct business dealings with a client, but also where the dealings are with others and they might prejudice the client's interests.

BOX 16.5

Bright Line Rule

In *R v Neil*,* the accused was a paralegal in Alberta who had been working independently and providing legal advice. In doing so, he was acting contrary to the province's *Legal Profession Act*.† After an investigation, he faced criminal charges on two grounds:

- advising a client in a divorce case to forge documents, and
- scheming to defraud a financial institution.

Neil was represented by a law firm under a general retainer, advising him on legal matters generally. The firm gave Neil some initial advice relating to the charges but did not go on to represent him before the courts in these criminal matters. (It is not clear who represented Neil before the courts; he may have represented himself.) It turned out that one of the lawyers working at the firm was currently representing other clients whose interests were opposed to Neil's. One of these clients was a co-accused in the fraud indictment. No confidential information was in fact used against Neil in the criminal proceedings. Nonetheless, Neil argued that his criminal charges should be stayed because his law firm had a conflict of interest representing two clients opposed in interest.

The SCC held that the criminal proceedings were not tainted by the conflict and that there was no reason to stay the charges. However, concerning the law firm's ethical obligations, the court stated the following:

> [I]t is the firm, not just the individual lawyer, that owes a fiduciary duty to its clients, and a bright line is required. The bright line is provided by the general rule that a lawyer may not represent one client whose interests are directly adverse to the immediate interests of another current client—*even if the two mandates are unrelated*—unless both clients consent after receiving full disclosure (and preferably independent legal advice), and the lawyer reasonably believes that he or she is able to represent each client without adversely affecting the other.‡

Therefore, although Neil was unsuccessful in having his criminal charges stayed, he had the option of suing his law firm civilly for breach of their duty of loyalty. And the law firm representing Neil was answerable to the law society for professional misconduct.

*   2002 SCC 70.

†   RSA 2000, c L-8.

‡   2002 SCC 70 at para 29.

---

19   For recent applications of the bright line rule, see *Strother v 3464920 Canada Inc*, 2007 SCC 24; and *Wallace v Canadian Pacific Railway*, 2011 SKCA 108.

Lawyers who are faced with such a conflict must decline to enter into the transaction or must obtain the client's consent after full disclosure (and, preferably, after the client has received independent legal advice). A lawyer who proceeds with the transaction after disclosure and consent should also ensure that doing so is fair and reasonable in the circumstances.

OTHER OBLIGATIONS

Other ethical obligations lawyers owe their clients are the obligations

1. to maintain client property entrusted to the lawyer,[20]
2. not to withdraw services without good cause, and
3. to avoid close personal or sexual relationships with clients.

These other ethical obligations may or may not coincide with legal or fiduciary obligations in contract or tort. For example, the second and third obligations listed will in most cases not. The lawyer's facing civil liability for breaching them is unlikely, although he may face discipline for professional misconduct. Regarding the last obligation—to avoid close personal or sexual relationships with clients—there is no absolute rule in this regard where lawyers are concerned.[21] However, there is a risk that such relationships may affect the lawyer's ability to act with integrity and good faith, to maintain confidences, and to avoid conflicts of interest. (See FLSC Model Code and the commentary following chapter 3, rule 3.4-2.) Codes of ethics for some other professions, particularly in the medical field, are stricter in this area and absolutely ban sexual relationships.

Disciplinary Proceedings

As mentioned, law societies and their discipline committees are charged with disciplining lawyers in cases of malpractice. The governing legislation or the law society rules will determine the composition of the committee (which is typically made up of benchers, non-elected lawyers, and at least one non-lawyer). The legislation or rules will also set out thresholds that will trigger disciplinary action. These thresholds are usually defined as conduct that amounts to

1. professional misconduct,
2. conduct unbecoming a lawyer,
3. professional incompetence, or
4. breach of the governing legislation itself.

Lawyers' misconduct generally comes to the attention of the discipline committee through complaints from the public, from other lawyers, or from the courts. Occasionally,

---

20 Typically, this will involve money held by the lawyer in a trust account. See CBA Code, ch VIII and commentaries, and FLSC Model Code, ch 3, r 3.5 and commentaries.

21 In the United States, the situation is divided. Approximately one-third of state law societies have a strict "no sex with clients" ethics rule, while the others have no such rule. California's law society, the largest in the US, adopted a complete sex ban in 2017 with limited exceptions (such as when the sexual relationship between the lawyer and client preceded the professional relationship).

the committee is alerted by media reports or by a lawyer admitting her own misconduct. To qualify as misconduct, the lawyer's actions must have breached the profession's ethical code of conduct. In some cases, these actions may amount to more than professional misconduct: they may amount to civil or criminal wrongdoing.

After an investigation and a hearing (if the process moves to that stage), the discipline committee will determine whether the lawyer's action qualifies as misconduct on one of the grounds identified above. If the committee concludes that discipline is appropriate, a number of sanctions are possible. These include one or more of the following: reprimands, fines, practice conditions, suspension, retraining, and disbarment. Misconduct that is isolated and not on the serious end of the scale might result in only a reprimand (for example, lack of civility in dealing with a particular client or lawyer), whereas misconduct that is far-reaching and with serious consequences will often result in disbarment (see, for example, the *Ryan* case, described in Box 16.2).

Figure 16.1 shows how complaints are typically processed. The majority of complaints turn out to be unsubstantiated and are closed.

FIGURE 16.1 General Complaint Process for Malpractice by Lawyers

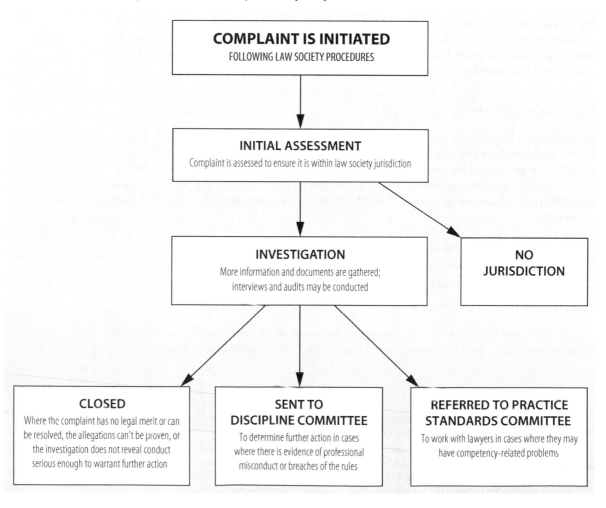

Paralegals, Law Clerks (Ontario), and Legal Assistants

Law society rules and ethical codes address the relationship between lawyers and their employees, including paralegals, Ontario law clerks, and others (including legal assistants, legal administrative assistants, and articling students). For example, rule 6.1-1 of chapter 6 of the FLSC Model Code provides as follows:

> 6.1-1 A lawyer has complete professional responsibility for all business entrusted to him or her and must directly supervise staff and assistants to whom the lawyer delegates particular tasks and functions.

By implication, therefore, lawyers' ethical obligations with respect to their work apply to the employees to whom they delegate that work. Lawyers have complete professional responsibility for all business entrusted to them, so their employees' ethical lapses could subject the supervising lawyers to discipline. It is the lawyers' responsibility to ensure that their employees are aware of the high ethical standards that must guide them in their work. Employees who fall below those standards will likely suffer employment consequences, including being let go from their positions in cases of serious breaches.

Employees of lawyers may also belong to voluntary associations—for example, Ontario law clerks and Institute of Law Clerks of Ontario (ILCO), Alberta paralegals and the Alberta Association of Professional Paralegals (AAPP), and BC paralegals and the BC Paralegal Association (BCPA)—that publish their own codes of ethics. Membership in these associations requires adherence to these codes, which mirror in short form some of the obligations set out in the lawyers' codes.

Paralegals in Ontario, because of their special status (that is, their ability to practise independently and their licensure by the Law Society of Ontario [LSO]), are in a different position. In 2007, the LSO approved an ethical code of conduct for paralegals practising in Ontario: the Paralegal Rules of Conduct. The LSO is responsible for handling complaints against Ontario paralegals and for disciplinary decisions concerning their professional misconduct.

Notaries

For notaries who are non-lawyers and who do not practise independently, but practise as government appointees, the ethical rules of conduct governing their behaviour are the same as those imposed on public servants generally in their jurisdiction. British Columbia is an exception in this regard. Notaries in British Columbia have their own legislation and governing body, the Society of Notaries Public of British Columbia.[22] This body has adopted its own ethical code, the Principles for Ethical & Professional Conduct Guideline, and it is responsible for disciplining its members for professional misconduct.

Other Legal Professionals

Other legal professionals may or may not be required to follow specific codes of conduct and be subject to disciplinary action under legislative mandate in the event of malpractice.

---

22 See the *Notaries Act*, RSBC 1996, c 334.

Immigration consultants, for instance, are formally regulated. They must follow the Immigration Consultants of Canada Regulatory Council's ethical guidelines as set out in their Code of Ethical Conduct, and they are subject to discipline for professional misconduct. Similarly, patent and trademark agents are federally licensed and must adhere to a specific code of ethics or face disciplinary proceedings.

Some legal positions are more limited in scope—for example, marriage commissioners and commissioners for taking affidavits—and there are no separate ethical codes of conduct applicable to them. They may be bound to general codes connected with their status as government appointees or with other sources of employment.

Although there are no separate codes applicable to court agents, they are nonetheless held to a high standard of behaviour. In British Columbia, for example, the legislation provides that the court has the right to refuse audience to a court agent and "has the same control over an unprofessional person practising in the court or before the justice as the court or justice would have over a qualified practitioner practising in there."[23]

Others working in law-related careers, such as insurance and policing, will have governing bodies, codes of ethics, and disciplinary processes specific to their professions.

---

23 *Court Agent Act*, RSBC 1996, c 76, s 2.

CHAPTER SUMMARY

High ethical standards have always been expected of the legal profession. An effective system of justice needs such high standards, which help protect the public. Historically, these high standards were taken for granted, at least within the profession itself. In the modern era, codes of conduct are the main ethical guides for lawyers and other legal professionals. For lawyers in particular, these codes define various duties, including their duties to the state (or administration of justice), to the courts, to the profession and public, and to clients.

Integrity and good faith underlie the notion of professional responsibility. A lawyer's duty to the state involves, at the very least, his upholding the law and not advising or assisting in its violation. A lawyer's duty to the court involves showing courtesy and respect, respecting the established process, and not misleading the court or unfairly criticizing judges. The ethics of advocacy, which overlap with the duty to the court, often involve balancing obligations to the client with obligations to others. Lawyers sometimes find it difficult to pursue a client's case resolutely, as they are obliged to do, while maintaining courtesy to the courts and witnesses.

Lawyers' duties to the profession include providing prompt and accurate communications to the law society and reporting malpractice. Duties that lawyers owe to others are courtesy and good faith. Lawyers observe these duties through the absolute reliability of their undertakings and through professionalism in advertising. The lawyer's ethical duty to the client has three main aspects: (1) providing competent services, (2) keeping client information confidential, and (3) avoiding conflicts of interest between clients and between lawyer and client. Frequently, breaches of ethics in this area will also involve civil liability based on contractual, fiduciary, or tortious duties.

Law societies are responsible for disciplining lawyers. Discipline committees treat complaints against lawyers seriously, and they investigate these complaints. A finding of professional misconduct and conduct unbecoming a lawyer, based on breaches of ethical and other duties, can result in fines, suspension, or disbarment, among other sanctions. Lawyers are also responsible for the ethical lapses of their employees, including paralegals and legal assistants; depending on the nature and severity, such lapses will have employment consequences for the employee. Other legal professionals who are regulated—such as paralegals in Ontario, notaries in British Columbia, and immigration consultants—will be subject to disciplinary sanctions for ethical breaches by the regulatory bodies that govern their profession.

KEY TERMS

bright line rule, 434

codes of conduct, 422

cones of silence, 433

duty of competence, 432

duty of confidentiality, 432

duty of loyalty, 433

fiduciary obligations, 431

lawyer–client privilege, 433

legal ethics, 420

undertaking, 430

FURTHER READING

BOOKS

Cockfield, Arthur. *Introduction to Legal Ethics*, 2nd ed (Toronto: LexisNexis, 2016).

Graham, Randal NM. *Legal Ethics: Theories, Cases, and Professional Regulation*, 3rd ed (Toronto: Emond Montgomery, 2014).

Hutchinson, Allan. *Legal Ethics and Professional Responsibility*, 2nd ed (Toronto: Irwin Law, 2006).

Knight, S Patricia. *Ethics and Professional Practice for Paralegals*, 4th ed (Toronto: Emond, 2018).

MacKenzie, Gavin. *Lawyers & Ethics: Professional Responsibility and Discipline*, 6th ed (Toronto: Carswell, 2018) (loose-leaf updated 2018, release 3).

MacNair, M Deborah. *Conflicts of Interest: Principles for the Legal Profession* (Toronto: Canada Law Book, 2005) (loose-leaf updated 2018, release 31).

Orkin, Mark M. *Legal Ethics*, 2nd ed (Toronto: Canada Law Book, 2011).

Woolley, Alice. *Understanding Lawyers' Ethics in Canada*, 2nd ed (Toronto: LexisNexis, 2016).

Woolley, Alice et al. *Lawyers' Ethics and Professional Regulation*, 3rd ed (Toronto: LexisNexis, 2017).

CODES OF CONDUCT

Judges

Canadian Judicial Council, Ethical Principles for Judges: <http://www.cjc-ccm.gc.ca/cmslib/general/news_pub_judicialconduct_Principles_en.pdf>.

Lawyers

Model Code of Professional Conduct (FLSC Model Code), Federation of Law Societies of Canada: <http://www.flsc.ca/en/model-code-of-professional-conduct>.

Notaries

BC Notaries, Principles for Ethical & Professional Conduct Guideline: <http://www.notaries.bc.ca/resources> (see under Society Standards).

Paralegals and Law Clerks

Alberta Association of Professional Paralegals (AAPP), Code of Ethics: <http://alberta-paralegal.com/coe.html>.

BC Paralegal Association (BCPA), Code of Ethics: <http://www.bcparalegalassociation.com/cpages/code-of-ethics>.

Institute of Law Clerks of Ontario (ILCO), Code of Ethics: <http://www.ilco.on.ca/about-ilco/about-us/our-code-of-ethics>.

[Ontario] Paralegal Rules of Conduct, Law Society of Ontario: <http://lso.ca/about-lso/legislation-rules/paralegal-rules-of-conduct>.

Patent and Trademark Agents

Intellectual Property Institute of Canada Code of Ethics: <http://www.ipic.ca> (search for Code of Ethics).

REVIEW QUESTIONS

1. Name the body that is responsible for investigating complaints against federally appointed judges. Under what legislation was it created?

2. Name two ethical codes of conduct for Canadian lawyers that are national in scope.

3. In the practice of law, what core ethical principle underlies professional responsibility?

4. Define the duty of lawyers in relation to the administration of justice.

5. Describe three specific obligations involved in a lawyer's duty to the court.

6. How is a Crown attorney's duty in a criminal case different from a lawyer's duty in a civil case?

7. What is an undertaking by a lawyer?

8. Explain the difference between a lawyer's duty of confidentiality and lawyer–client privilege.

9. What are cones of silence?

10. What is the bright line rule?

11. Name three grounds for disciplinary action against a lawyer.

12. A number of legal paraprofessional groups are permitted to practise independently in Canada. Name three that have their own ethical codes of conduct.

EXERCISES

1. Imagine a Canadian justice system in which legal professionals are no longer held to any particular ethical standards and the legal profession is treated like any other business. Using specific arguments and examples, describe how you think these altered expectations and standards would change the Canadian justice system as we know it.

2. Research the law society website for your province or territory and find the code of conduct for lawyers. Identify and record the specific rule that deals with a lawyer's duty of competence.

3. A lawyer has recently received a judgment in a court action in which a piece of real property was sold. The court ordered that the proceeds of the sale be paid out by the lawyer to various parties in specified amounts. A paralegal (or a law clerk, in Ontario), working under the supervision of the lawyer, was delegated the task of arranging payment to the various parties. By mistake, the paralegal neglected to pay one of the parties. When the party contacted the lawyer's firm, the paralegal was asked to deal with the inquiry. She realized her mistake but refused to admit what had happened. It was not until the supervising lawyer reviewed the whole affair that the mistake was discovered and the money paid out as required.

   Name and describe at least two specific ethical rules that have been breached here.

4. A husband and wife are both practising lawyers who do not work together and who specialize in different areas of the law. When either one has a legal problem that relates to the other's expertise, they employ each other as counsel. What ethical problems arise, if any, when they provide each other with advice in this way?

5. Research the law society website for your province or territory and locate the record of disciplinary hearings. Find cases involving lawyers who have been cited for professional misconduct that involved criminal activity (for example, impaired driving, possession of illegal drugs, domestic violence, or fraud). From among these cases, choose one that interests you and describe which ethical obligations were violated in the case.

6. Do you think the bright line rule goes too far, especially in an age of megafirms that have offices around the world and thousands of clients? Assuming that confidential information is being adequately protected by the lawyers involved, should a law firm always be prohibited from representing two clients with opposing interests at the same time unless the clients give the firm their consent? Why or why not?

17 Access to Justice and Law Reform

Protest march against the Kinder Morgan oil pipeline expansion project led by Indigenous Coast Salish Elders and Chiefs (Burnaby BC, 2018).

After reading this chapter, you will understand:

- What lawyers in Canada have accomplished to provide affordable legal services to the public.
- How alternative dispute resolution mechanisms function in comparison with courts.
- Important steps taken to make the law and legal knowledge more accessible to the public.

- Key law reform initiatives that governments have introduced.
- How public interest groups and their legal strategies influence law reform.

We are fortunate to live in a country with a robust justice system buttressed by an independent judiciary. Yet access to justice in Canada remains a serious problem that imperils the public's confidence in the justice system. ... While progress has been made, there is still much to do. Rules and processes are still more complicated than they should be, causing unnecessary delays. Financial barriers continue to thwart access to justice. The low level of funding for legal aid leads litigants to appear in courtrooms without the support of counsel, placing unfair burdens on courts, the litigants, the bar and, ultimately, the public purse. And finally, some may hold attitudes of mistrust or fear toward the justice system, refusing to engage with it or acknowledge its legitimacy.

The Right Honourable Beverley McLachlin, PC, Chief Justice of Canada, *Remarks to the Council of the Canadian Bar Association at the Canadian Legal Conference* (Ottawa: Canadian Bar Association, 11 August 2016)

Introduction

As described in earlier chapters, Canadian law has seen many changes since colonial times, when French civil law and English common law were first received into this country. For example, with Confederation in 1867 came significant changes to our legal system, and with our country's growth and development came parallel changes in our laws.

We have seen how a heightened awareness of human rights in the aftermath of the Second World War, in combination with the influence of the American civil rights movement in the 1950s and 1960s, helped motivate the provinces and territories to introduce human rights codes. And these forces joined with others to bring about the patriation of our Constitution and passage of the *Canadian Charter of Rights and Freedoms* in 1982 (see Chapter 7). We have also seen a movement for greater consumer protection in today's marketplace (see Chapter 10).

This chapter looks at elements of the multifaceted access-to-justice movement and discusses some modern law reform initiatives undertaken by governments, lawyers, courts, and the public that are helping change (and improve) Canadian law.

Access to Legal Services

A general legal trend in Canada, beginning prior to the Second World War, has been toward increased access to legal services for *all* Canadians, regardless of their socio-economic level or their status as a minority or person with a disability. A number of developments in the criminal justice system and the legal profession illustrate this trend.

Legal Aid Plans

It has been an increasing concern of lawyers and the public in Canada that lower-income and otherwise disadvantaged individuals have better access to legal services. A movement based on this concern began in the decades before the Second World War and continued to grow after the war. Lawyers in Ontario and lawyers belonging to the national Canadian Bar Association began to acknowledge a social responsibility as a group regarding the legal needs of *all* Canadians, especially those who could not afford to pay for the services of a lawyer.[1] Lawyers also became aware that the legal needs of indigent persons were different from those of wealthier clients capable of paying lawyers' fees. People living on a lower income—including those living on a pension or on social assistance—were more likely to need legal help with matters such as rental accommodation, welfare, employment assistance, discrimination, debt, workers' compensation, education expenses, and accessing government services in general.[2] Increasingly conscious of the barriers faced by lower-income Canadians, lawyers all across Canada began working with their respective law societies and provincial governments to effect change. Their efforts resulted in formalized publicly funded **legal aid** programs that began in the 1960s.

Today, legal aid services for designated matters, criminal and non-criminal, are provided to lower-income Canadians across Canada either free of charge or for a modest fee. Legal aid plans vary from province to province. Generally speaking, they help those in need in the following ways:

legal aid
government funding of lawyers who provide legal assistance to persons with low income

- Lawyers in private practice can do legal aid work based on a judicare, or fee-for-service, delivery system. The process works in the following way: a person who needs legal help attends his local legal aid office, which determines whether he is qualified to receive legal aid on the basis of his particular legal need and a financial means test. If qualified, this person takes a legal aid certificate to a lawyer of his choice who is on a legal aid panel. The lawyer then performs the legal work and bills for it in accordance with the rates set by the legal aid tariff. The lawyer is paid by legal aid, not by the client.
- Many people coming to court for the first time do so without legal representation, and many lack an understanding of the courtroom process. Legal aid plans help

---

1   Mary P Reilly, "The Origins and Development of Legal Aid in Ontario" (1988) 8 Windsor YB Access Just 81; N Larsen, "Legal Aid in Manitoba" in C Harvey, ed, *The Law Society of Manitoba, 1877-1977* (Winnipeg: Peguis, 1977) at 158.

2   James E Lockyer, QC, "The Roles and Responsibilities of the Legal Profession in Furthering Access to Justice" (1992) 12 Windsor YB Access Just 356; I Cotler & H Marx, eds, *The Law and the Poor in Canada* (Montreal: Black Rose Books, 1977).

these individuals by directing them to a lawyer known as *duty counsel*, who typically can help with criminal, immigration, or family law matters (exact eligibility rules vary depending on the province or territory). Duty counsel lawyers in criminal court might, for example, speak to the judge on an individual's behalf and arrange an adjournment so that the accused can apply for legal aid.

- Legal aid plans in some jurisdictions have also established community legal clinics. These are an alternative form of delivering legal services. Their salaried staff— lawyers and community legal workers—help low-income Canadians with legal matters concerning such areas as landlord and tenant obligations, social welfare assistance, job search, immigration, debt collection, and human rights.[3]
  In Ontario, for example, specialty legal clinics help Canadians from ethnically diverse communities, as well as people with disabilities, with their unique needs. These legal clinics also tend to have offices that are easily accessible.

In addition to provincial legal aid plans, other measures that lawyers in Canada have taken to help make this country's justice system less costly and more accessible to the public are as follows:[4]

- offering pro bono legal services,
- increasing the use of paralegals,
- offering prepaid legal services plans, and
- producing legal scholarship on access-to-justice matters.

Pro Bono Legal Services

Many lawyers may not be involved with legal aid work but may still want to help lower-income Canadians, charities, and disadvantaged persons with their legal needs. These lawyers can choose to offer assistance to the public **pro bono**, or without charge (from the Latin *pro bono publico*, meaning "for the public good"). They can do this, for example, by

pro bono
term applied to legal work that lawyers do at no charge to help the public (from the Latin *pro bono publico*: "for the public good")

- providing justice education in high schools and participating in school "law days";
- providing legal talks at neighbourhood community centres on selected topics, such as making a will;
- helping people on social assistance; or
- giving free legal advice to new immigrants to Canada.

Pro bono organizations have been established in many provinces (see Box 17.1).

---

3 Mary Jane Mossman, "Community Legal Clinics in Ontario" (1983) 3 Windsor YB Access Just 375.

4 See Roderick A Macdonald, "Access to Justice in Canada Today: Scope, Scale and Ambitions" in Julia Bass, WA Bogart & Frederick Zemans, eds, *Access to Justice for a New Century: The Way Forward* (Toronto: Law Society of Upper Canada, 2004) at 19.

Pro Bono Ontario

Pro Bono Ontario (PBO) is a charity founded in 2001 to bridge the justice gap between lawyers who want to give back and the many Ontarians who can't afford legal services and have a legal problem not covered by government funding. PBO creates and manages volunteer programs that connect these lawyers with low-income Ontarians—either directly or in partnership with charitable organizations working in the local community. Through this work, PBO has emerged as the legal profession's only organized volunteer response to unmet legal needs. The result is that PBO serves over 13,000 clients each year who have nowhere else to turn. The demand for these services increases each year.

Programs for the Public

PBO manages a variety of programs in-house and creates several others that are managed externally. PBO's in-house programs focus on:

- people suing or being sued in the civil courts and who are unable to afford a lawyer;
- children who face barriers to their health, wellbeing, and educational progress and who might benefit from assistance of a lawyer; and
- charities and nonprofits that do not have the resources to address their legal needs.

As much as possible we "go to where our clients are," embedding programs in court houses, children's hospitals, and community organizations. This means that individuals trying to navigate the court system, children and families with legal issues that affect health outcomes, and other individuals in the community have access to legal help at the very time and place they need it.

Source: Reproduced from Pro Bono Ontario, online: <https://www.probonoontario.org>.

Increased Use of Paralegals

Legal services are becoming increasingly expensive. Another way that lawyers in law firms have sought to reduce expenses and make their legal services more affordable to the public is by using more paralegals.[5] Lawyers can assign work that they would otherwise do to paralegals, billing for this work at a lower rate and passing the cost savings on to their clients.

As discussed in Chapter 15, paralegals are not lawyers, but they are trained to do procedural and substantive legal work under the supervision of a lawyer (in Ontario, such paraprofessionals are called *law clerks*). Many paralegals nowadays are responsible for work that, previously, would have been done by lawyers. And paralegals in Ontario have a special status allowing them to represent clients in some lower-level courts and before administrative bodies (Ontario paralegals are formally regulated by the Law Society of Ontario). Other jurisdictions are considering moving in the direction of the Ontario model as they try to improve access to justice. Implementing the necessary changes will depend on rules set by provincial or territorial legislation for the jurisdiction in question, by the relevant courts and tribunals, and by the province's or territory's law society. In British Columbia, for example, "designated paralegals" may be given increased responsibilities when dealing with clients; however, they still work under the supervision of a lawyer.

---

5   Frederick H Zemans, "The Non-Lawyer as a Means of Providing Legal Services" in Robert G Evans & Michael J Trebilcock, eds, *Lawyers and the Consumer Interest: Regulating the Market for Legal Services* (Toronto: Butterworths, 1982) at 263.

Prepaid Legal Services Plans

Another new delivery method for legal services—and a model that is particularly attractive to middle-income Canadians—is a prepaid legal services benefits plan. Such plans arose in Canada in the 1980s, under the leadership of the Canadian Auto Workers. Members of this union make individual contributions to the plan, which helps pay for a lawyer who does prescribed legal services under the plan for members at a reasonable cost.[6]

Legal Scholarship

Canada's legal community includes many legal academics who support law reform. They write books and articles on this subject, and such scholarship can be influential in effecting changes in the law. The *Windsor Yearbook of Access to Justice* is an example of a specialized law journal that publishes learned articles in this area.

Courts and Alternative Dispute Resolution Mechanisms

The traditional adjudicative process of resolving legal disputes in courts has come under increasing criticism in Canada. Many people worry about the cost of a lawyer. Long trial delays, complex legal procedures, lack of privacy, unfamiliar legal terminology and rules of evidence, and an expensive appeal process are further concerns about the court process held by many middle-income Canadians. Many are also intimidated by the adversarial system used in civil court, whereby one side tries to win outright, with the loser paying the winner's costs.

As a result, a growing number of people are favouring **alternative dispute resolution (ADR)** mechanisms instead of courts. There are three main ADR mechanisms: (1) negotiation, (2) mediation, and (3) arbitration.

alternative dispute resolution (ADR) process used instead of a court trial to help settle a dispute

Negotiation

Negotiation is the simplest method of resolving disputes and is conducted by the parties themselves (either directly or using representatives). Both sides talk to each other, usually informally, to determine the possibility of finding a mutually acceptable solution to their dispute. Because both sides must agree to the solution for it to be binding, both parties need to cooperate, be flexible, and be willing to compromise for a negotiation to be successful.

negotiation dispute resolution process whereby the parties talk to each other directly and seek a mutually acceptable solution to their problem

Mediation

Mediation takes negotiation one step further. A neutral and impartial third party, called a mediator, assists the parties in their efforts to resolve their dispute. It may be a dispute, for example, between two neighbours over pets in the backyard. Or it could involve a dispute

mediation dispute resolution process whereby the parties try to reach a settlement with the assistance of a third party

---

6 C Wydrzynski, K Hildebrandt & D Blonde, "The CAW Prepaid Legal Services Plan: A Case Study of an Alternative Funding and Delivery Method for Legal Services" (1990) 10 Windsor YB Access Just 22 at 72.

between two tenants over loud noise, between spouses going through a marriage breakdown and dealing with financial arrangements and custody matters, or between business partners (for example, a franchisor and franchisee) arguing about their contractual obligations. The mediator, who is chosen by the parties beforehand, helps both sides find a solution to their problem. This person does not necessarily have to be a lawyer. The mediator's role is to keep both sides talking, clarify issues, help uncover sources behind the conflict, and suggest compromises and solutions that both sides can accept. The mediator meets often with both sides, individually as well as together, and can do so at their own homes. Sessions are confidential and informal, and they may be flexible in terms of timing. For example, the meetings might take place in the evenings or on weekends. However, as with negotiation, a mediator can only *recommend* a solution, which is not binding on the parties unless both sides agree to it.

When we compare the traditional court process of resolving disputes with this alternative approach, we can see why many people are attracted to mediation. In the court system, the parties cannot pick their judge. The judge will not come to the parties' home or meet with them on weekends. Nor will a judge meet with one side in the absence of the other. In the traditional court system, the judge's decision must be obeyed, even if one side does not like it, and the costs for legal representation there can be expensive.

With respect to certain kinds of disputes, however, legislation may make mediation mandatory. Examples of these kinds of disputes include family law conflicts, small claims actions, and various administrative tribunal matters. And while in these situations the mediator's recommendations are still not binding, the parties may have less flexibility in terms of the choice of the mediator (for instance, a judge or tribunal adjudicator may be assigned to the parties) and the time and place of the mediation.

Arbitration

In the case of **arbitration**, as with mediation, the parties consent beforehand to the appointment of an impartial third party, here called an arbitrator, to help resolve their dispute. They also agree to assume the costs involved. However, unlike mediation, the parties can also decide beforehand to accept binding or non-binding arbitration. In binding arbitration, the decision of the arbitrator must be followed. In non-binding arbitration, the arbitrator's decision is only advisory. The parties may submit to an arbitration arrangement by way of an arbitration agreement reached after a dispute arises, or in advance of the dispute pursuant to an arbitration clause in an existing contract between the parties.

The advantages of using arbitration are the following:

- the parties can pick their own arbitrator, often someone with experience in the area;
- sessions can be informal and confidential; and
- the process can proceed at the parties' own pace.

One difficulty with arbitration is that the process can become quite legalistic and formal, particularly if the arbitrator is a lawyer and both sides are represented by a lawyer as well.[7]

arbitration
dispute resolution process whereby the parties agree beforehand on an arbitrator to assist them, and they agree on whether the arbitrator's decision will be advisory or binding

---

7   Cheryl Picard et al, *The Art and Science of Mediation* (Toronto: Emond Montgomery, 2004); EG Tannis, *Alternative Dispute Resolution That Works* (Toronto: Captus Press, 1989); W Estey, "Who Needs Courts?" (1981) 1 Windsor YB Access Just 263.

TABLE 17.1   Comparison of the Three Main Forms of ADR with Litigation

	NEGOTIATION	MEDIATION	ARBITRATION	LITIGATION
Third-party intervention	No	Yes	Yes	Yes
Choice of third party	n/a	Usually parties select on agreement	Usually parties select on agreement	No, assigned by court
Role of third party	n/a	Helps facilitate a settlement	Assesses evidence and arguments and makes binding or non-binding decision	Assesses evidence and arguments and makes binding decision
Decision outcome	Not binding	Not binding	Usually binding	Binding on parties
Confidentiality	Yes, private	Yes, private	Usually private but may be public	No, public court process
Participation of parties	Voluntary	Usually voluntary	Usually voluntary	Coercive
Style of participation of parties	Collaborative	Collaborative	Adversarial	Adversarial
Process and rules of procedure	Informal, flexible	Informal, flexible	More formal, somewhat flexible	Formal, inflexible

As with mediation, and as an exception to the generally consensual nature of ADR, legislation may make arbitration compulsory in certain contexts, such as for some labour disputes and residential tenancy matters.

Table 17.1, above, shows a comparison of the three main forms of ADR with litigation.

Public Access to Legal Information

Even if ADR mechanisms become more widely used, courts are still central to the administration of justice and are not likely to be replaced anytime soon. Canadians who are unable to afford a lawyer or who do not qualify for legal aid face some difficult problems when going to court. Among their most pressing concerns are how and where they can obtain legal information about

- how the formal legal system works,
- what the law is concerning their legal matter, and
- what their rights are in court.

Many such people have to be self-reliant and find answers to these questions on their own. For this reason, they want the law demystified and they want technology to help them gain knowledge about the law.

This topic—public access to legal information—was examined by professor Martin Friedland in a groundbreaking 1975 study he conducted for the Law Reform Commission of Canada.[8] Friedland noted that many people did not know where to go for accurate and

---

8   ML Friedland, *Access to the Law: A Study Conducted for the Law Reform Commission of Canada* (Toronto: Carswell/Methuen, 1975).

complete legal information and had trouble using and understanding legal materials such as cases, statutes, and regulations. He identified four ways of providing the public with better access to law:

1. improving the clarity of existing legal materials;
2. doing more to educate the public about law;
3. improving the quality of legal information that intermediary facilities, such as community information centres and public libraries, provide to the public; and
4. developing a new reference source, such as an encyclopedia of law for non-lawyers, that could be regularly updated and made available in public libraries, schools, and government offices.

Many technological measures for improving public access to legal information have been taken since Friedland's 1975 study. These measures include, for example, telephone access to legal information providers such as the Legal Information Society of Nova Scotia; a lawyer referral service administered by provincial law societies; dial-a-law programs for taped legal information; online legal research websites such as that created by the Canadian Legal Information Institute (CanLII); and having federal, provincial, and territorial governments place government statutes, regulations, and other legal information online on official government websites.[9]

Government Measures to Enhance Access to Justice

The access-to-justice movement has influenced federal and provincial governments to make further reforms that increase public access to government institutions and policies. The use of collaborative law models is being encouraged in some jurisdictions, particularly in the resolution of family law matters. Other reforms introduced by federal and provincial governments to make the court process more accessible include the following:

- unified family courts, where family matters—which are under the jurisdiction of both the federal and provincial governments—are heard in one convenient place;
- raising the monetary limits of small claims courts (where non-lawyers can appear) so that matters need not go to a higher court where only lawyers can appear;
- creating specialized courts, such as domestic violence and drug treatment courts, which aim to achieve better long-term outcomes for some types of offenders and for society as a whole (see the discussion of criminal courts in Chapter 12);
- case management, where a designated court official, such as a judge or a master, is responsible for supervising the flow of cases going through the courts, so that delays are minimized; and
- the establishment of administrative bodies to address areas of law that are more efficiently dealt with outside of the court process. (See the discussion of administrative agencies in Chapter 11.)

---

9 T Gregory Kane & Edward R Myers, "The Role of Self-Help in the Provision of Legal Services" in Evans & Trebilcock, *supra* note 5 at 439.

Public access to government records is another area related to access to justice. In the 1960s, a determined campaign began in Canada for greater public access to information contained in government records. Influenced by a similar movement in the United States and led by lawyers, academics, the press, and some members of Parliament, proponents argued that increased access would make governments more accountable to the public.

Today, access-to-information legislation exists at the provincial, territorial, and federal levels. The Supreme Court of Canada (SCC) has characterized the overarching purpose of this legislation as facilitating democracy "by helping to ensure that citizens have the information to participate meaningfully in the democratic process and that politicians and bureaucrats remain accountable to the citizenry."[10] The federal *Access to Information Act*[11] came into effect in July 1983, making Canada one of the first countries in the world to protect this right. The Act gives Canadian citizens and permanent residents the right to access information contained in government records. Section 2(1) sets out the three principles that underpin the Act:

1. government information should be available to the public,
2. necessary exceptions to the right of access should be limited and specific, and
3. decisions on the disclosure of government information should be reviewed independently of government.

Although the Act requires the head of a government institution to make reasonable efforts to assist individuals with their requests and to respond to requests accurately, completely, and in a timely way, in reality insufficient resources and a large increase in the volume of requests create barriers to access; between 2002 and 2003, and 2011 and 2012, the number of requests increased by 88 percent.[12] Many have expressed concerns that the Act, which has changed little in the three decades since its passage, has not kept pace with technological advances and other developments, and that the right to access is being undermined in critical ways.

In addition to information acts, in many provinces the office of the ombudsman has helped improve access to justice for Canadians by drawing public attention and scrutiny to problems people have with the government—for example, government waste or inaction. The ombudsman (called an *ombudsperson* in certain provinces, such as British Columbia) is an official with powers to investigate alleged government abuses or maladministration at the request of citizens. The ombudsman acts independently of the legislature and reports to it. Alberta was the first province to introduce this office, in 1967, and other provinces and territories have followed suit. The ombudsman does not have unlimited jurisdiction to investigate maladministration in all government departments, ministries, agencies, and institutions. It is also an office whose powers vary from province to province. In all cases, the ombudsperson's services are provided free of charge. (See Box 17.2.)

---

10   *Dagg v Canada (Minister of Finance)*, [1997] 2 SCR 403, 1997 CanLII 358.

11   RSC 1985, c A-1.

12   Office of the Information Commissioner of Canada, "The Access to Information Act in Canada: Taking Stock of 30 Years" (Presentation to the Library of Parliament, 5 December 2013), online: <http://www.oic-ci.gc.ca/eng/media-room-salle-media_speeches-discours_2013_9.aspx>.

BOX 17.2

What Kinds of Matters Can an Ombudsperson Help Resolve?

A provincial or territorial ombudsperson may help resolve a range of problems or misunderstandings, subject to certain exceptions. Ombudspersons oversee provincial or territorial ministries; Crown corporations; and administrative tribunals, agencies, boards, and commissions—for example, in Ontario, the Ministry of Indigenous Relations and Reconciliation, the Ministry of the Attorney General, the Ministry of Community Safety and Correctional Services, the Liquor Control Board of Ontario, and the Ministry of Government and Consumer Services. They may deal with thousands of complaints each year. Ombudspersons *cannot* investigate matters between individuals and private companies, individuals and other individuals (for example, judges, doctors, or lawyers), or individuals and the federal government.

The case summaries below illustrate just a few of the many situations an ombudsperson may help resolve.

BC Ombudsperson Case Summary

Jolene, Jolene

Having carefully inputted all the information online, Jolene was surprised to see her daughter's birth certificate arrive with a glaring error: "Jolene" was repeated twice as the mother's name.

When Jolene contacted Vital Statistics to correct the error, she was told to pay the $71 fee for the correction of online registration user errors. Jolene grudgingly paid the fee and happily received a correct birth certificate for her newborn.

Still, Jolene did not like paying for someone else's mistake and wanted a refund. Vital Statistics declined to investigate or refund the fee. Unhappy with this response, Jolene came to us.

We agreed to investigate, concerned that Vital Statistics might have dismissed Jolene's request for a refund without first taking reasonable steps to identify the source of the error on her daughter's birth certificate.

Vital Statistics' electronic files showed that the mistake was indeed not Jolene's fault. Because of our investigation, Vital Statistics agreed to amend its internal procedures. Now, when a customer calls about an error on their baby's birth certificate, Vital Statistics will review the customer's file to determine the cause—before deciding whether to request a fee. Vital Statistics also agreed to provide a refund to Jolene and a letter of apology.[*]

Ontario Ombudsperson Case Summaries

Hits the Spot

When a woman hit a pothole on a county road that damaged her vehicle, she tried to seek reimbursement. The county told her it was the Ministry of Transportation's jurisdiction, but the Ministry told her the opposite. After our staff contacted both levels of government, Ministry officials determined it was indeed in their jurisdiction, and the woman was compensated the more than $1,100 it cost to repair her vehicle.[†]

Just Missed the Mark

A mother of three who was enrolled in a combined college and university nursing program was not allowed to progress to the university portion of the program because her grade in a college course was 1.5 percent below the required threshold. She appealed the mark but complained to us that the college's appeal decision did not address an in-course evaluation that had a major impact on her grade. Our Office referred her to the college's ombudsman, who was able to help her get a new evaluation by a different professor. This resulted in a high enough grade to allow her to enrol in the university portion of the program.[‡]

---

[*]   Office of the Ombudsperson, Province of British Columbia, "Jolene, Jolene" (2015), online: <http://bcombudsperson.ca/documents/jolene-jolene>.

[†]   Ombudsman Ontario, "Hits the Spot" (26 June 2018), online: <http://www.ombudsman.on.ca/resources/reports-and-case-summaries/selected-cases/2018/hits-the-spot>.

[‡]   Ombudsman Ontario, "Just Missed the Mark" (26 June 2018), online: <http://www.ombudsman.on.ca/resources/reports-and-case-summaries/selected-cases/2018/just-missed-the-mark-en>.

Law Reform

Both the federal and provincial governments, as well as citizens working alone or in organized groups, can try to change laws. Law reform may be initiated by law reform commissions, public inquiries, political demonstrations, lobbying by national organizations, or public interest groups appearing as interveners before the Supreme Court of Canada.

Law Reform Commissions

Law reform commissions are independent bodies set up by either the provincial or federal government to study selected areas of law and recommend ways to improve, modernize, and reform them. Members of the commission publish reports recommending how laws in that area could be improved. (Martin Friedland's 1975 report on access to justice, mentioned above, was one of these reports.) Though the government is not bound to accept and implement all (or any) of the commission's recommendations, its reports are considered important contributions to legal scholarship and can be cited in courts.

The Law Reform Commission of Canada, which existed from 1971 to 1993 and again from 1997 to 2006 (as the Law Commission of Canada), was set up to make recommendations regarding areas of law under federal jurisdiction—for example, criminal law and criminal procedure. It also considered bijural aspects regarding our law, which, as we have seen, use both the common law and civil law legal systems.

At the provincial level, most of Canada's provinces have established provincial law reform commissions at one time or another (though most have now ceased operation as a result of funding cuts). Law reform commissions recommend measures to improve and reform laws under provincial jurisdiction, such as the administration of justice in a province. They generally operate with a small number of lawyers, academics, and judges on their board of governors and utilize research staff to conduct research into areas considered in need of reform. This scholarly analysis of the law found in background and discussion papers, and in final reports published by commissions, provides an excellent source of well-researched information about many areas of law.

Canada-wide, the Federation of Law Reform Agencies of Canada is also involved in promoting cooperation between Canada's law reform agencies on the broad topic of law reform. As well, the Uniform Law Conference of Canada, in existence since 1918, works to improve harmony between laws of the provinces and territories across Canada.

Public Inquiries

Public inquiries into matters of national and public concern, formerly known as royal commissions, have played an important role in the development of law and policy in Canada. They may be tasked with finding facts and reporting on those facts, with making recommendations aimed at developing public policy, or with a combination of these two functions.[13] Either the federal government or a provincial government may call an inquiry; legislation provides the executive with the authority to appoint a commission and provides the commission with the authority it needs to carry out its mandate.[14]

---

13   Hon Associate Chief Justice Dennis R O'Connor & Freya Kristjanson, "Some Observations on Public Inquiries" (Canadian Institute for the Administration of Justice, Annual Conference, 10 October 2007, Halifax), online: <http://www.ontariocourts.ca/coa/en/ps/speeches/publicinquiries.htm>.

14   The federal legislation is the *Inquiries Act*, RSC 1985, c I-11; an example of provincial legislation is Ontario's *Public Inquiries Act, 2009*, SO 2009, c 33, Schedule 6.

Fact-finding inquiries (and inquiries that combine fact-finding and policy recommendations) are often established in response to an event, such as a high-profile scandal or a tragedy, that negatively affects the public's trust in or perception of public institutions—for example, miscarriages of justice such as wrongful convictions, suspicious deaths in hospitals, and tainted water scandals. The goal of such inquiries is often to address failings and restore the public's confidence in the system. High-profile inquiries include the Air India Inquiry into the terrorist bombing of Air India Flight 182; the Braidwood Inquiry into the tasering death of Robert Dziekański; and the Missing Women Commission of Inquiry into the disappearance of women from Vancouver's Downtown Eastside.

Inquiries with a focus on policy analyze issues and make recommendations for policies in the future. For example, an inquiry conducted by Justice Emmett Hall in the 1960s was instrumental in the creation of the national Medicare system, and the *Official Languages Act*[15]—which was passed in 1969 and declares French and English to be the official languages of Canada, and requires all federal institutions to provide their services in both languages—was one of the most important legacies of the Royal Commission on Bilingualism and Biculturalism.

Political Demonstrations

People upset with a particular government law or policy, and who also want laws reformed, have traditionally participated in public protest marches and political demonstrations, which might end up before a city hall, a provincial legislature, or before Parliament Hill in Ottawa. The widespread use of social media today has made it easier for people to organize and coordinate such events. The problem with demonstrations as a political tactic is that not all Canadians support them, and they can also attract negative publicity, depending on the tactics used. Another disadvantage is that they tend to be one-off events, with momentum and publicity often—though not always—subsiding at their conclusion. As well, the government may not support the change requested.

National Organizations and Lobbying

Many professional and occupational groups across Canada have established national organizations that meet annually to discuss issues important to their members. Examples of such national organizations are

- the Canadian Bar Association,
- the Assembly of First Nations, and
- the Canadian Labour Congress.

These associations also try to influence governments to introduce law reforms or policies that favour their group's interests. Many of these national organizations have full-time staff and offices in provincial capitals or in Ottawa. They submit briefs to the government and meet with members of Parliament and with key bureaucrats in the civil service to further their association's goals. Many also seek to influence government action by **lobbying**. Lobbying is an organized effort to influence legislators and bureaucrats with respect to laws and government policies. For example, lobbying can be done to obtain material benefits from the government such as favourable tax breaks, research grants, subsidies, or government supply contracts. Lobbying may not result in as high a public profile as demonstrating in the

lobbying
organized effort to influence legislators on behalf of a particular interest

15   RSC 1985, c 31 (4th Supp).

streets. It is perhaps more effective, however; lobby groups can retain a law firm or the services of skilled public relations professionals and former politicians who have direct knowledge of the political process and previous familiarity with the legislators.[16]

Public Interest Groups as Interveners

intervener
a party, other than the original parties to a court proceeding, who does not have a substantial and direct interest in the proceeding but has interests and perspectives helpful to the judicial determination and whose input is accepted by the court

Another way public interest groups can try to influence and change Canadian law or government policy is to participate as **interveners** in cases before the SCC.[17] (See also Chapter 6.) If granted intervener status, which is given at the court's discretion, an interest group may be entitled to give further evidence to supplement the record or be authorized to present an oral argument at the hearing.[18] They have to demonstrate sufficient interest in the court case, have submissions that are useful and different from the other parties' submissions, and be a credible organization. Examples of public interest groups who have participated as interveners this way are LEAF (the Women's Legal Education and Action Fund) and the Canadian Civil Liberties Association. The SCC is now increasingly receptive to hearing from public interest interveners; the judges on the court realize that many matters facing them are complex and that their decisions will have far-reaching implications for Canadian law. An interest group may influence the court to take a broader perspective on a matter under consideration and increase its awareness of the issues, or change, it is intervening to support.

---

16 Rand Dyck, *Canadian Politics: Critical Approaches* (Toronto: Nelson, 2012) at 425; Keith Archer et al, *Parameters of Power: Canada's Political Institutions*, 3rd ed (Toronto: Nelson, 2002).

17 See Sharon Lavine, "Advocating Values: Public Interest Intervention in Charter Litigation" (1993) 2 NJCL 27; Ian Brodie, *Friends of the Court: The Privileging of Interest Group Litigants in Canada* (Albany, NY: State University of New York Press, 2002).

18 Under the Rules of the Supreme Court of Canada (SOR/2002-156), a Motion for Intervention is rule 55. Adding, Substituting and Removing Parties is rule 18. See also Ian Brodie, "Lobbying the Supreme Court" in H Mellon & M Westmacott, eds, *Political Dispute and Judicial Review: Assessing the Work of the Supreme Court of Canada* (Toronto: Nelson, 2000) at 195.

CHAPTER SUMMARY

The issue of access to justice has become increasingly important to Canadians as court costs rise, court delays grow longer, and the court process becomes harder for many low- and middle-income Canadians to navigate. A multifaceted reform movement exploring alternative dispute resolution mechanisms, such as mediation and arbitration, is gaining acceptance. The benefits of these alternative forms of dispute resolution are many. They offer reduced court costs, less time in court, and more personal control over the process. Other benefits of ADR are confidentiality and the opportunity for the parties to craft solutions they feel are best suited to their problem.

Canadian law has changed over time in response to broad shifts in our society. As outlined in this chapter, one desire for change is increasingly focused on making the law more accessible and affordable to the public. Many people today want or need to access legal information on their own and want this legal information to be understandable. As for specific initiatives to reform the law, law reform commissions and institutes have researched various areas of the law and made recommendations for improvement (and some of these recommendations have been implemented through legislative change). Sometimes, individual Canadians try to change the law on their own, while others pursue collective action. Such action can take a variety of forms, including political demonstrations, national organizations, lobbying, and applying to participate as interveners in court cases.

KEY TERMS

alternative dispute
  resolution (ADR), 448
arbitration, 449

intervener, 456
legal aid, 445
lobbying, 455

mediation, 448
negotiation, 448
pro bono, 446

FURTHER READING

BOOKS

Brodie, Ian. *Friends of the Court: The Privileging of Interest Group Litigants in Canada* (Albany, NY: State University of New York, 2002).

Hanycz, Colleen M, Trevor CW Farrow & Frederick H Zemans. *The Theory and Practice of Representative Negotiation* (Toronto: Emond Montgomery, 2008).

Jhappen, Radha ed. *Women's Legal Strategies in Canada* (Toronto: University of Toronto Press, 2002).

Rowat, Donald Cameron ed. *The Making of the Federal Access Act: A Case Study of Policy-Making in Canada* (Ottawa: Carleton University, 1985).

Trebilcock, Michael, Anthony J Duggan & Lorne Sossin. *Middle Income Access to Justice* (Toronto: University of Toronto Press, 2012).

Young, Margot et al, eds. *Poverty: Rights, Social Citizenship, and Legal Activism* (Vancouver: University of British Columbia Press, 2007).

Zubick, Jennifer & Samantha Callow. *ADR for Legal Professionals* (Toronto: Emond, 2017).

JOURNALS AND ARTICLES

Morton, FL & Avril Allen. "Feminists and the Courts: Measuring Success in Interest Group Litigation in Canada" (2001) 34 Can J Poli Sci 55.

Windsor Yearbook of Access to Justice (Windsor, Ont: University of Windsor Faculty of Law), online: <http://www.uwindsor.ca/law/wyaj>.

REVIEW QUESTIONS

1. How do legal aid plans help lower-income people in need of legal services? List three main ways.

2. List three measures that lawyers in Canada have taken to increase access to justice for disadvantaged Canadians.

3. List five common criticisms of the traditional court process of resolving disputes.

4. What is the main difference between negotiation and mediation?

5. How does arbitration differ from mediation?

6. When two parties are using arbitration to resolve their disputes, what can they decide beforehand regarding the arbitrator's decision?

7. What four measures did Martin Friedland propose for improving Canadians' access to legal information?

8. List three measures the government has taken to increase the Canadian public's access to justice.

EXERCISES

1. Do you think enough is being done in this country to increase access to justice for lower-income and disadvantaged Canadians? Explain. Suggest another measure that you think might be introduced.

2. Look up the legal term *in forma pauperis*. Would the Canadian legal system be improved by lawyers adopting this concept? Why or why not?

3. Using the Internet, look up the website for the Canadian Federation of Students. List and discuss ways that this association tries to help post-secondary students.

4. Describe the qualities you think a good mediator would possess. Give reasons for your choices.

Appendixes

Note: To view the complete versions of the *Constitution Act, 1867* and the *Constitution Act, 1982*, with full explanatory footnotes, visit www.emond.ca/ILC2.

A Constitution Act, 1867

30 & 31 Victoria, c 3 (UK)

TABLE OF CONTENTS

An Act for the Union of Canada, Nova Scotia, and New Bruns-wick, and the Government thereof; and for Purposes connected therewith

(29th March 1867)

WHEREAS the Provinces of Canada, Nova Scotia, and New Brunswick have expressed their Desire to be federally united into One Dominion under the Crown of the United Kingdom of Great Britain and Ireland, with a Constitution similar in Principle to that of the United Kingdom:

And whereas such a Union would conduce to the Welfare of the Provinces and promote the Interests of the British Empire:

And whereas on the Establishment of the Union by Authority of Parliament it is expedient, not only that the Constitution of the Legislative Authority in the Dominion be provided for, but also that the Nature of the Executive Government therein be declared:

And whereas it is expedient that Provision be made for the eventual Admission into the Union of other Parts of British North America:

I. PRELIMINARY

Short title

1. This Act may be cited as the *Constitution Act, 1867.*

2. Repealed.

II. UNION

Declaration of Union

3. It shall be lawful for the Queen, by and with the Advice of Her Majesty's Most Honourable Privy Council, to declare by Proclamation that, on and after a Day therein appointed, not being more than Six Months after the passing of this Act, the Provinces of Canada, Nova Scotia, and New Brunswick shall form and be One Dominion under the Name of Canada; and on and after that Day those Three Provinces shall form and be One Dominion under that Name accordingly.

Construction of subsequent Provisions of Act

4. Unless it is otherwise expressed or implied, the Name Canada shall be taken to mean Canada as constituted under this Act.

Four Provinces

5. Canada shall be divided into Four Provinces, named Ontario, Quebec, Nova Scotia, and New Brunswick.

Provinces of Ontario and Quebec

6. The Parts of the Province of Canada (as it exists at the passing of this Act) which formerly constituted respectively the Provinces of Upper Canada and Lower Canada shall be deemed to be severed, and shall form Two separate Provinces. The Part which formerly constituted the Province of Upper Canada shall constitute the Province of Ontario; and the Part which formerly constituted the Province of Lower Canada shall constitute the Province of Quebec.

Provinces of Nova Scotia and New Brunswick

7. The Provinces of Nova Scotia and New Brunswick shall have the same Limits as at the passing of this Act.

Decennial Census

8. In the general Census of the Population of Canada which is hereby required to be taken in the Year One thousand eight hundred and seventy-one, and in every Tenth Year thereafter, the respective Populations of the Four Provinces shall be distinguished.

III. EXECUTIVE POWER

Declaration of Executive Power in the Queen

9. The Executive Government and Authority of and over Canada is hereby declared to continue and be vested in the Queen.

Application of Provisions referring to Governor General

10. The Provisions of this Act referring to the Governor General extend and apply to the Governor General for the Time being of Canada, or other the Chief Executive Officer or Administrator for the Time being carrying on the Government of Canada on behalf and in the Name of the Queen, by whatever Title he is designated.

Constitution of Privy Council for Canada

11. There shall be a Council to aid and advise in the Government of Canada, to be styled the Queen's Privy Council for Canada; and the Persons who are to be Members of that Council shall be from Time to Time chosen and summoned by the Governor General and sworn in as Privy Councillors, and Members thereof may be from Time to Time removed by the Governor General.

All Powers under Acts to be exercised by Governor General with Advice of Privy Council, or alone

12. All Powers, Authorities, and Functions which under any Act of the Parliament of Great Britain, or of the Parliament of the United Kingdom of Great Britain and Ireland, or of the

Legislature of Upper Canada, Lower Canada, Canada, Nova Scotia, or New Brunswick, are at the Union vested in or exerciseable by the respective Governors or Lieutenant Governors of those Provinces, with the Advice, or with the Advice and Consent, of the respective Executive Councils thereof, or in conjunction with those Councils, or with any Number of Members thereof, or by those Governors or Lieutenant Governors individually, shall, as far as the same continue in existence and capable of being exercised after the Union in relation to the Government of Canada, be vested in and exerciseable by the Governor General, with the Advice or with the Advice and Consent of or in conjunction with the Queen's Privy Council for Canada, or any Members thereof, or by the Governor General individually, as the Case requires, subject nevertheless (except with respect to such as exist under Acts of the Parliament of Great Britain or of the Parliament of the United Kingdom of Great Britain and Ireland) to be abolished or altered by the Parliament of Canada.

Application of Provisions referring to Governor General in Council

13. The Provisions of this Act referring to the Governor General in Council shall be construed as referring to the Governor General acting by and with the Advice of the Queen's Privy Council for Canada.

Power to Her Majesty to authorize Governor General to appoint Deputies

14. It shall be lawful for the Queen, if Her Majesty thinks fit, to authorize the Governor General from Time to Time to appoint any Person or any Persons jointly or severally to be his Deputy or Deputies within any Part or Parts of Canada, and in that Capacity to exercise during the Pleasure of the Governor General such of the Powers, Authorities, and Functions of the Governor General as the Governor General deems it necessary or expedient to assign to him or them, subject to any Limitations or Directions expressed or given by the Queen; but the Appointment of such a Deputy or Deputies shall not affect the Exercise by the Governor General himself of any Power, Authority, or Function.

Command of Armed Forces to continue to be vested in the Queen

15. The Command-in-Chief of the Land and Naval Militia, and of all Naval and Military Forces, of and in Canada, is hereby declared to continue and be vested in the Queen.

Seat of Government of Canada

16. Until the Queen otherwise directs, the Seat of Government of Canada shall be Ottawa.

IV. LEGISLATIVE POWER

Constitution of Parliament of Canada

17. There shall be One Parliament for Canada, consisting of the Queen, an Upper House styled the Senate, and the House of Commons.

Privileges, etc., of Houses

18. The privileges, immunities, and powers to be held, enjoyed, and exercised by the Senate and by the House of Commons, and by the members thereof respectively, shall be such as are from time to time defined by Act of the Parliament of Canada, but so that any Act of the Parliament of Canada defining such privileges, immunities, and powers shall not confer any privileges, immunities, or powers exceeding those at the passing of such Act held, enjoyed, and exercised by the Commons House of Parliament of the United Kingdom of Great Britain and Ireland, and by the members thereof.

First Session of the Parliament of Canada

19. The Parliament of Canada shall be called together not later than Six Months after the Union.

20. Repealed.

THE SENATE

Number of Senators

21. The Senate shall, subject to the Provisions of this Act, consist of One Hundred and five Members, who shall be styled Senators.

Representation of Provinces in Senate

22. In relation to the Constitution of the Senate Canada shall be deemed to consist of Four Divisions:
1. Ontario;
2. Quebec;
3. The Maritime Provinces, Nova Scotia and New Brunswick, and Prince Edward Island;
4. The Western Provinces of Manitoba, British Columbia, Saskatchewan, and Alberta;

which Four Divisions shall (subject to the Provisions of this Act) be equally represented in the Senate as follows: Ontario by twenty-four senators; Quebec by twenty-four senators; the Maritime Provinces and Prince Edward Island by twenty-four senators, ten thereof representing Nova Scotia, ten thereof representing New Brunswick, and four thereof representing Prince Edward Island; the Western Provinces by twenty-four senators, six thereof representing Manitoba, six thereof representing British Columbia, six thereof representing Saskatchewan, and six thereof representing Alberta; Newfoundland shall be entitled to be represented in the Senate by six members; the Yukon Territory, the Northwest Territories and Nunavut shall be entitled to be represented in the Senate by one member each.

In the Case of Quebec each of the Twenty-four Senators representing that Province shall be appointed for One of the Twenty-four Electoral Divisions of Lower Canada specified in Schedule A. to Chapter One of the Consolidated Statutes of Canada.

Qualifications of Senator

23. The Qualifications of a Senator shall be as follows:

(1) He shall be of the full age of Thirty Years;

(2) He shall be either a natural-born Subject of the Queen, or a Subject of the Queen naturalized by an Act of the Parliament of Great Britain, or of the Parliament of the United Kingdom of Great Britain and Ireland, or of the Legislature of One of the Provinces of Upper Canada, Lower Canada, Canada, Nova Scotia, or New Brunswick, before the Union, or of the Parliament of Canada after the Union;

(3) He shall be legally or equitably seised as of Freehold for his own Use and Benefit of Lands or Tenements held in Free and Common Socage, or seised or possessed for his own Use and Benefit of Lands or Tenements held in Franc-alleu or in Roture, within the Province for which he is appointed, of the Value of Four thousand Dollars, over and above all Rents, Dues, Debts, Charges, Mortgages, and Incumbrances due or payable out of or charged on or affecting the same;

(4) His Real and Personal Property shall be together worth Four thousand Dollars over and above his Debts and Liabilities;

(5) He shall be resident in the Province for which he is appointed;

(6) In the Case of Quebec he shall have his Real Property Qualification in the Electoral Division for which he is appointed, or shall be resident in that Division.

Summons of Senator

24. The Governor General shall from Time to Time, in the Queen's Name, by Instrument under the Great Seal of Canada, summon qualified Persons to the Senate; and, subject to the Provisions of this Act, every Person so summoned shall become and be a Member of the Senate and a Senator.

25. Repealed.

Addition of Senators in certain cases

26. If at any Time on the Recommendation of the Governor General the Queen thinks fit to direct that Four or Eight Members be added to the Senate, the Governor General may by Summons to Four or Eight qualified Persons (as the Case may be), representing equally the Four Divisions of Canada, add to the Senate accordingly.

Reduction of Senate to normal Number

27. In case of such Addition being at any Time made, the Governor General shall not summon any Person to the Senate, except on a further like Direction by the Queen on the like Recommendation, to represent one of the Four Divisions until such Division is represented by Twenty-four Senators and no more.

Maximum Number of Senators

28. The Number of Senators shall not at any Time exceed One Hundred and thirteen.

Tenure of Place in Senate

29(1) Subject to subsection (2), a Senator shall, subject to the provisions of this Act, hold his place in the Senate for life.

Retirement upon attaining age of seventy-five years

(2) A Senator who is summoned to the Senate after the coming into force of this subsection shall, subject to this Act, hold his place in the Senate until he attains the age of seventy-five years.

[Sections 30–36 omitted.]

THE HOUSE OF COMMONS

Constitution of House of Commons in Canada

37. The House of Commons shall, subject to the Provisions of this Act, consist of three hundred and eight members of whom one hundred and six shall be elected for Ontario, seventy-five for Quebec, eleven for Nova Scotia, ten for New Brunswick, fourteen for Manitoba, thirty-six for British Columbia, four for Prince Edward Island, twenty-eight for Alberta, fourteen for Saskatchewan, seven for Newfoundland, one for the Yukon Territory, one for the Northwest Territories and one for Nunavut.

Summoning of House of Commons

38. The Governor General shall from Time to Time, in the Queen's Name, by Instrument under the Great Seal of Canada, summon and call together the House of Commons.

Senators not to sit in House of Commons

39. A Senator shall not be capable of being elected or of sitting or voting as a Member of the House of Commons.

[Sections 40–49 omitted.]

Duration of House of Commons

50. Every House of Commons shall continue for Five Years from the Day of the Return of the Writs for choosing the House (subject to be sooner dissolved by the Governor General), and no longer.

[Section 51 omitted.]

Constitution of House of Commons

51A. Notwithstanding anything in this Act a province shall always be entitled to a number of members in the House of Commons not less than the number of senators representing such province.

Increase of Number of House of Commons

52. The Number of Members of the House of Commons may be from Time to Time increased by the Parliament of Canada, provided the proportionate Representation of the Provinces prescribed by this Act is not thereby disturbed.

MONEY VOTES; ROYAL ASSENT

Appropriation and Tax Bills

53. Bills for appropriating any Part of the Public Revenue, or for imposing any Tax or Impost, shall originate in the House of Commons.

Recommendation of Money Votes

54. It shall not be lawful for the House of Commons to adopt or pass any Vote, Resolution, Address, or Bill for the Appropriation of any Part of the Public Revenue, or of any Tax or Impost, to any Purpose that has not been first recommended to that House by Message of the Governor General in the Session in which such Vote, Resolution, Address, or Bill is proposed.

Royal Assent to Bills, etc.

55. Where a Bill passed by the Houses of the Parliament is presented to the Governor General for the Queen's Assent, he shall declare, according to his Discretion, but subject to the Provisions of this Act and to Her Majesty's Instructions, either that he assents thereto in the Queen's Name, or that he withholds the Queen's Assent, or that he reserves the Bill for the Signification of the Queen's Pleasure.

Disallowance by Order in Council of Act assented to by Governor General

56. Where the Governor General assents to a Bill in the Queen's Name, he shall by the first convenient Opportunity send an authentic Copy of the Act to One of Her Majesty's Principal Secretaries of State, and if the Queen in Council within Two Years after Receipt thereof by the Secretary of State thinks fit to disallow the Act, such Disallowance (with a Certificate of the Secretary of State of the Day on which the Act was received by him) being signified by the Governor General, by Speech or Message to each of the Houses of the Parliament or by Proclamation, shall annul the Act from and after the Day of such Signification.

Signification of Queen's Pleasure on Bill reserved

57. A Bill reserved for the Signification of the Queen's Pleasure shall not have any Force unless and until, within Two Years from the Day on which it was presented to the Governor General for the Queen's Assent, the Governor General signifies, by Speech or Message to each of the Houses of the Parliament or by Proclamation, that it has received the Assent of the Queen in Council.

An Entry of every such Speech, Message, or Proclamation shall be made in the Journal of each House, and a Duplicate thereof duly attested shall be delivered to the proper Officer to be kept among the Records of Canada.

V. PROVINCIAL CONSTITUTIONS

EXECUTIVE POWER

Appointment of Lieutenant Governors of Provinces

58. For each Province there shall be an Officer, styled the Lieutenant Governor, appointed by the Governor General in Council by Instrument under the Great Seal of Canada.

Tenure of Office of Lieutenant Governor

59. A Lieutenant Governor shall hold Office during the Pleasure of the Governor General; but any Lieutenant Governor appointed after the Commencement of the First Session of the Parliament of Canada shall not be removeable within Five Years from his Appointment, except for Cause assigned, which shall be communicated to him in Writing within One Month after the Order for his Removal is made, and shall be communicated by Message to the Senate and to the House of Commons within One Week thereafter if the Parliament is then sitting, and if not then within One Week after the Commencement of the next Session of the Parliament.

Salaries of Lieutenant Governors

60. The Salaries of the Lieutenant Governors shall be fixed and provided by the Parliament of Canada.

Oaths, etc., of Lieutenant Governor

61. Every Lieutenant Governor shall, before assuming the Duties of his Office, make and subscribe before the Governor General or some Person authorized by him Oaths of Allegiance and Office similar to those taken by the Governor General.

Application of Provisions referring to Lieutenant Governor

62. The Provisions of this Act referring to the Lieutenant Governor extend and apply to the Lieutenant Governor for the Time being of each Province, or other the Chief Executive Officer or Administrator for the Time being carrying on the Government of the Province, by whatever Title he is designated.

Appointment of Executive Officers for Ontario and Quebec

63. The Executive Council of Ontario and of Quebec shall be composed of such Persons as the Lieutenant Governor from Time to Time thinks fit, and in the first instance of the following Officers, namely,—the Attorney General, the Secretary and Registrar of the Province, the Treasurer of the Province, the Commissioner of Crown Lands, and the Commissioner of Agriculture and Public Works, with in Quebec the Speaker of the Legislative Council and the Solicitor General.

Executive Government of Nova Scotia and New Brunswick

64. The Constitution of the Executive Authority in each of the Provinces of Nova Scotia and New Brunswick shall, subject to the Provisions of this Act, continue as it exists at the Union until altered under the Authority of this Act.

Powers to be exercised by Lieutenant Governor of Ontario or Quebec with Advice, or alone

65. All Powers, Authorities, and Functions which under any Act of the Parliament of Great Britain, or of the Parliament of the United Kingdom of Great Britain and Ireland, or of the Legislature of Upper Canada, Lower Canada, or Canada, were or are before or at the Union vested in or exerciseable by the respective Governors or Lieutenant Governors of those Provinces, with the Advice or with the Advice and Consent of the respective Executive Councils thereof, or in conjunction with those Councils, or with any Number of Members thereof, or by those Governors or Lieutenant Governors individually, shall, as far as the same are capable of being exercised after the Union in relation to the Government of Ontario and Quebec respectively, be vested in and shall or may be exercised by the Lieutenant Governor of Ontario and Quebec respectively, with the Advice or with the Advice and Consent of or in conjunction with the respective Executive Councils, or any Members thereof, or by the Lieutenant Governor individually, as the Case requires, subject nevertheless (except with respect to such as exist under Acts of the Parliament of Great Britain, or of the Parliament of the United Kingdom of Great Britain and Ireland,) to be abolished or altered by the respective Legislatures of Ontario and Quebec.

Application of Provisions referring to Lieutenant Governor in Council

66. The Provisions of this Act referring to the Lieutenant Governor in Council shall be construed as referring to the Lieutenant Governor of the Province acting by and with the Advice of the Executive Council thereof.

Administration in Absence, etc., of Lieutenant Governor

67. The Governor General in Council may from Time to Time appoint an Administrator to execute the Office and Functions of Lieutenant Governor during his Absence, Illness, or other Inability.

Seats of Provincial Governments

68. Unless and until the Executive Government of any Province otherwise directs with respect to that Province, the Seats of Government of the Provinces shall be as follows, namely,—of Ontario, the City of Toronto; of Quebec, the City of Quebec; of Nova Scotia, the City of Halifax; and of New Brunswick, the City of Fredericton.

LEGISLATIVE POWER

1. Ontario

Legislature for Ontario

69. There shall be a Legislature for Ontario consisting of the Lieutenant Governor and of One House, styled the Legislative Assembly of Ontario.

[Section 70 omitted.]

2. Quebec

Legislature for Quebec

71. There shall be a Legislature for Quebec consisting of the Lieutenant Governor and of Two Houses, styled the Legislative Council of Quebec and the Legislative Assembly of Quebec.

[Sections 72–80 omitted.]

3. Ontario and Quebec

[Sections 81–85 omitted.]

Yearly Session of Legislature

86. There shall be a Session of the Legislature of Ontario and of that of Quebec once at least in every Year, so that Twelve Months shall not intervene between the last Sitting of the Legislature in each Province in one Session and its first Sitting in the next Session.

[Section 87 omitted.]

4. Nova Scotia and New Brunswick

Constitutions of Legislatures of Nova Scotia and New Brunswick

88. The Constitution of the Legislature of each of the Provinces of Nova Scotia and New Brunswick shall, subject to the Provisions of this Act, continue as it exists at the Union until altered under the Authority of this Act.

5. Ontario, Quebec, and Nova Scotia

89. Repealed.

6. The Four Provinces

Application to Legislatures of Provisions respecting Money Votes, etc.

90. The following Provisions of this Act respecting the Parliament of Canada, namely,—the Provisions relating to Appropriation and Tax Bills, the Recommendation of Money Votes, the Assent to Bills, the Disallowance of Acts, and the Signification of Pleasure on Bills reserved,—shall extend and apply to the Legislatures of the several Provinces as if those Provisions were here re-enacted and made applicable in Terms to the respective Provinces and the Legislatures thereof, with the Substitution of the Lieutenant Governor of the Province for the Governor General, of the Governor General for the Queen and for a Secretary of State, of One Year for Two Years, and of the Province for Canada.

VI. DISTRIBUTION OF LEGISLATIVE POWERS

POWERS OF THE PARLIAMENT

Legislative Authority of Parliament of Canada

91. It shall be lawful for the Queen, by and with the Advice and Consent of the Senate and House of Commons, to make Laws for the Peace, Order, and good Government of Canada, in relation to all Matters not coming within the Classes of Subjects by this Act assigned exclusively to the Legislatures of the Provinces; and for greater Certainty, but not so as to restrict the Generality of the foregoing Terms of this Section, it is hereby declared that (notwithstanding anything in this Act) the exclusive Legislative Authority of the Parliament of Canada extends to all Matters coming within the Classes of Subjects next hereinafter enumerated; that is to say,

1. Repealed.
1A. The Public Debt and Property.
2. The Regulation of Trade and Commerce.
2A. Unemployment insurance.
3. The raising of Money by any Mode or System of Taxation.
4. The borrowing of Money on the Public Credit.
5. Postal Service.
6. The Census and Statistics.
7. Militia, Military and Naval Service, and Defence.
8. The fixing of and providing for the Salaries and Allowances of Civil and other Officers of the Government of Canada.
9. Beacons, Buoys, Lighthouses, and Sable Island.
10. Navigation and Shipping.
11. Quarantine and the Establishment and Maintenance of Marine Hospitals.
12. Sea Coast and Inland Fisheries.
13. Ferries between a Province and any British or Foreign Country or between Two Provinces.
14. Currency and Coinage.
15. Banking, Incorporation of Banks, and the Issue of Paper Money.
16. Savings Banks.
17. Weights and Measures.
18. Bills of Exchange and Promissory Notes.
19. Interest.
20. Legal Tender.
21. Bankruptcy and Insolvency.
22. Patents of Invention and Discovery.
23. Copyrights.
24. Indians, and Lands reserved for the Indians.
25. Naturalization and Aliens.
26. Marriage and Divorce.

27. The Criminal Law, except the Constitution of Courts of Criminal Jurisdiction, but including the Procedure in Criminal Matters.
28. The Establishment, Maintenance, and Management of Penitentiaries.
29. Such Classes of Subjects as are expressly excepted in the Enumeration of the Classes of Subjects by this Act assigned exclusively to the Legislatures of the Provinces.

And any Matter coming within any of the Classes of Subjects enumerated in this Section shall not be deemed to come within the Class of Matters of a local or private Nature comprised in the Enumeration of the Classes of Subjects by this Act assigned exclusively to the Legislatures of the Provinces.

EXCLUSIVE POWERS OF PROVINCIAL LEGISLATURES

Subjects of exclusive Provincial Legislation

92. In each Province the Legislature may exclusively make Laws in relation to Matters coming within the Classes of Subjects next hereinafter enumerated; that is to say,

1. Repealed.
2. Direct Taxation within the Province in order to the raising of a Revenue for Provincial Purposes.
3. The borrowing of Money on the sole Credit of the Province.
4. The Establishment and Tenure of Provincial Offices and the Appointment and Payment of Provincial Officers.
5. The Management and Sale of the Public Lands belonging to the Province and of the Timber and Wood thereon.
6. The Establishment, Maintenance, and Management of Public and Reformatory Prisons in and for the Province.
7. The Establishment, Maintenance, and Management of Hospitals, Asylums, Charities, and Eleemosynary Institutions in and for the Province, other than Marine Hospitals.
8. Municipal Institutions in the Province.
9. Shop, Saloon, Tavern, Auctioneer, and other Licences in order to the raising of a Revenue for Provincial, Local, or Municipal Purposes.
10. Local Works and Undertakings other than such as are of the following Classes:
    (a) Lines of Steam or other Ships, Railways, Canals, Telegraphs, and other Works and Undertakings connecting the Province with any other or others of the Provinces, or extending beyond the Limits of the Province:
    (b) Lines of Steam Ships between the Province and any British or Foreign Country:
    (c) Such Works as, although wholly situate within the Province, are before or after their Execution declared by the Parliament of Canada to be for the general Advantage of Canada or for the Advantage of Two or more of the Provinces.
11. The Incorporation of Companies with Provincial Objects.
12. The Solemnization of Marriage in the Province.
13. Property and Civil Rights in the Province.
14. The Administration of Justice in the Province, including the Constitution, Maintenance, and Organization of Provincial Courts, both of Civil and of Criminal Jurisdiction, and including Procedure in Civil Matters in those Courts.
15. The Imposition of Punishment by Fine, Penalty, or Imprisonment for enforcing any Law of the Province made in relation to any Matter coming within any of the Classes of Subjects enumerated in this Section.
16. Generally all Matters of a merely local or private Nature in the Province.

NON-RENEWABLE NATURAL RESOURCES, FORESTRY RESOURCES AND ELECTRICAL ENERGY

Laws respecting non-renewable natural resources, forestry resources and electrical energy

92A(1) In each province, the legislature may exclusively make laws in relation to

(a) exploration for non-renewable natural resources in the province;

(b) development, conservation and management of non-renewable natural resources and forestry resources in the province, including laws in relation to the rate of primary production therefrom; and

(c) development, conservation and management of sites and facilities in the province for the generation and production of electrical energy.

Export from provinces of resources

(2) In each province, the legislature may make laws in relation to the export from the province to another part of Canada of the primary production from non-renewable natural resources and forestry resources in the province and the production from facilities in the province for the generation of electrical energy, but such laws may not authorize or provide for discrimination in prices or in supplies exported to another part of Canada.

Authority of Parliament

(3) Nothing in subsection (2) derogates from the authority of Parliament to enact laws in relation to the matters referred to in that subsection and, where such a law of Parliament and a law of a province conflict, the law of Parliament prevails to the extent of the conflict.

Taxation of resources

(4) In each province, the legislature may make laws in relation to the raising of money by any mode or system of taxation in respect of

(a) non-renewable natural resources and forestry resources in the province and the primary production therefrom, and

(b) sites and facilities in the province for the generation of electrical energy and the production therefrom,

whether or not such production is exported in whole or in part from the province, but such laws may not authorize or provide for taxation that differentiates between production exported to another part of Canada and production not exported from the province.

"Primary production"

(5) The expression "primary production" has the meaning assigned by the Sixth Schedule.

Existing powers or rights

(6) Nothing in subsections (1) to (5) derogates from any powers or rights that a legislature or government of a province had immediately before the coming into force of this section.

EDUCATION

Legislation respecting Education

93. In and for each Province the Legislature may exclusively make Laws in relation to Education, subject and according to the following Provisions:

(1) Nothing in any such Law shall prejudicially affect any Right or Privilege with respect to Denominational Schools which any Class of Persons have by Law in the Province at the Union;

(2) All the Powers, Privileges, and Duties at the Union by Law conferred and imposed in Upper Canada on the Separate Schools and School Trustees of the Queen's Roman Catholic Subjects shall be and the same are hereby extended to the Dissentient Schools of the Queen's Protestant and Roman Catholic Subjects in Quebec;

(3) Where in any Province a System of Separate or Dissentient Schools exists by Law at the Union or is thereafter established by the Legislature of the Province, an Appeal shall lie to the Governor General in Council from any Act or Decision of any Provincial Authority affecting any Right or Privilege of the Protestant or Roman Catholic Minority of the Queen's Subjects in relation to Education;

(4) In case any such Provincial Law as from Time to Time seems to the Governor General in Council requisite for the due Execution of the Provisions of this Section is not made, or in case any Decision of the Governor General in Council on any Appeal under this Section is not duly executed by the proper Provincial Authority in that Behalf, then and in every such Case, and as far only as the Circumstances of each Case require, the Parliament of Canada may make remedial Laws for the due Execution of the Provisions of this Section and of any Decision of the Governor General in Council under this Section.

Quebec

93A. Paragraphs (1) to (4) of section 93 do not apply to Quebec.

UNIFORMITY OF LAWS IN ONTARIO, NOVA SCOTIA, AND NEW BRUNSWICK

Legislation for Uniformity of Laws in Three Provinces

94. Notwithstanding anything in this Act, the Parliament of Canada may make Provision for the Uniformity of all or any of the Laws relative to Property and Civil Rights in Ontario, Nova Scotia, and New Brunswick, and of the Procedure of all or any of the Courts in those Three Provinces, and from and after the passing of any Act in that Behalf the Power of the Parliament of Canada to make Laws in relation to any Matter comprised in any such Act shall, notwithstanding anything in this Act, be unrestricted; but any Act of the Parliament of Canada making Provision for such Uniformity shall not have effect in any Province unless and until it is adopted and enacted as Law by the Legislature thereof.

OLD AGE PENSIONS

Legislation respecting old age pensions and supplementary benefits

94A. The Parliament of Canada may make laws in relation to old age pensions and supplementary benefits, including survivors' and disability benefits irrespective of age, but no such law shall affect the operation of any law present or future of a provincial legislature in relation to any such matter.

AGRICULTURE AND IMMIGRATION

Concurrent Powers of Legislation respecting Agriculture, etc.

95. In each Province the Legislature may make Laws in relation to Agriculture in the Province, and to Immigration into the Province; and it is hereby declared that the Parliament of Canada may from Time to Time make Laws in relation to Agriculture in all or any of the Provinces, and to Immigration into all or any of the Provinces; and any Law of the Legislature of a Province relative to Agriculture or to Immigration shall have effect in and for the Province as long and as far only as it is not repugnant to any Act of the Parliament of Canada.

VII. JUDICATURE

Appointment of Judges

96. The Governor General shall appoint the Judges of the Superior, District, and County Courts in each Province, except those of the Courts of Probate in Nova Scotia and New Brunswick.

Selection of Judges in Ontario, etc.

97. Until the Laws relative to Property and Civil Rights in Ontario, Nova Scotia, and New Brunswick, and the Procedure of the Courts in those Provinces, are made uniform, the Judges of the Courts of those Provinces appointed by the Governor General shall be selected from the respective Bars of those Provinces.

Selection of Judges in Quebec

98. The Judges of the Courts of Quebec shall be selected from the Bar of that Province.

Tenure of office of Judges

99(1) Subject to subsection (2) of this section, the judges of the superior courts shall hold office during good behaviour, but shall be removable by the Governor General on address of the Senate and House of Commons.

Termination at age 75

(2) A judge of a superior court, whether appointed before or after the coming into force of this section, shall cease to hold office upon attaining the age of seventy-five years, or upon the coming into force of this section if at that time he has already attained that age.

Salaries, etc., of Judges

100. The Salaries, Allowances, and Pensions of the Judges of the Superior, District, and County Courts (except the Courts of Probate in Nova Scotia and New Brunswick), and of the Admiralty Courts in Cases where the Judges thereof are for the Time being paid by Salary, shall be fixed and provided by the Parliament of Canada.

General Court of Appeal, etc.

101. The Parliament of Canada may, notwithstanding anything in this Act, from Time to Time provide for the Constitution, Maintenance, and Organization of a General Court of Appeal for Canada, and for the Establishment of any additional Courts for the better Administration of the Laws of Canada.

VIII. REVENUES; DEBTS; ASSETS; TAXATION

[Sections 102–104 omitted.]

Salary of Governor General

105. Unless altered by the Parliament of Canada, the Salary of the Governor General shall be Ten thousand Pounds Sterling Money of the United Kingdom of Great Britain and Ireland, payable out of the Consolidated Revenue Fund of Canada, and the same shall form the Third Charge thereon.

[Sections 106–107 omitted.]

Transfer of Property in Schedule

108. The Public Works and Property of each Province, enumerated in the Third Schedule to this Act, shall be the Property of Canada.

Property in Lands, Mines, etc.

109. All Lands, Mines, Minerals, and Royalties belonging to the several Provinces of Canada, Nova Scotia, and New Brunswick at the Union, and all Sums then due or payable for such Lands, Mines, Minerals, or Royalties, shall belong to the several Provinces of Ontario, Quebec, Nova Scotia, and New Brunswick in which the same are situate or arise, subject to any Trusts existing in respect thereof, and to any Interest other than that of the Province in the same.

[Sections 110–116 omitted.]

Provincial Public Property

117. The several Provinces shall retain all their respective Public Property not otherwise disposed of in this Act, subject to the Right of Canada to assume any Lands or Public Property required for Fortifications or for the Defence of the Country.

[Sections 118–120 omitted.]

Canadian Manufactures, etc.

121. All Articles of the Growth, Produce, or Manufacture of any one of the Provinces shall, from and after the Union, be admitted free into each of the other Provinces.

Continuance of Customs and Excise Laws

122. The Customs and Excise Laws of each Province shall, subject to the Provisions of this Act, continue in force until altered by the Parliament of Canada.

[Sections 123–124 omitted.]

Exemption of Public Lands, etc.

125. No Lands or Property belonging to Canada or any Province shall be liable to Taxation.

[Section 126 omitted.]

IX. MISCELLANEOUS PROVISIONS

GENERAL

127. Repealed.

Oath of Allegiance, etc.

128. Every Member of the Senate or House of Commons of Canada shall before taking his Seat therein take and subscribe before the Governor General or some Person authorized by him, and every Member of a Legislative Council or Legislative Assembly of any Province shall before taking his Seat therein take and subscribe before the Lieutenant Governor of the Province or some Person authorized by him, the Oath of Allegiance contained in the Fifth Schedule to this Act; and every Member of the Senate of Canada and every Member of the Legislative Council of Quebec shall also, before taking his Seat therein, take and subscribe before the Governor General, or some Person authorized by him, the Declaration of Qualification contained in the same Schedule.

Continuance of existing Laws, Courts, Officers, etc.

129. Except as otherwise provided by this Act, all Laws in force in Canada, Nova Scotia, or New Brunswick at the Union, and all Courts of Civil and Criminal Jurisdiction, and all legal Commissions, Powers, and Authorities, and all Officers, Judicial, Administrative, and Ministerial, existing therein at the Union, shall continue in Ontario, Quebec, Nova Scotia, and

New Brunswick respectively, as if the Union had not been made; subject nevertheless (except with respect to such as are enacted by or exist under Acts of the Parliament of Great Britain or of the Parliament of the United Kingdom of Great Britain and Ireland,) to be repealed, abolished, or altered by the Parliament of Canada, or by the Legislature of the respective Province, according to the Authority of the Parliament or of that Legislature under this Act.

[Sections 130–131 omitted.]

Treaty Obligations

132. The Parliament and Government of Canada shall have all Powers necessary or proper for performing the Obligations of Canada or of any Province thereof, as Part of the British Empire, towards Foreign Countries, arising under Treaties between the Empire and such Foreign Countries.

Use of English and French Languages

133. Either the English or the French Language may be used by any Person in the Debates of the Houses of the Parliament of Canada and of the Houses of the Legislature of Quebec; and both those Languages shall be used in the respective Records and Journals of those Houses; and either of those Languages may be used by any Person or in any Pleading or Process in or issuing from any Court of Canada established under this Act, and in or from all or any of the Courts of Quebec.

The Acts of the Parliament of Canada and of the Legislature of Quebec shall be printed and published in both those Languages.

[Sections 134–144 omitted.]

[Part X omitted.]

XI. ADMISSION OF OTHER COLONIES

Power to admit Newfoundland, etc., into the Union

146. It shall be lawful for the Queen, by and with the Advice of Her Majesty's Most Honourable Privy Council, on Addresses from the Houses of the Parliament of Canada, and from the Houses of the respective Legislatures of the Colonies or Provinces of Newfoundland, Prince Edward Island, and British Columbia, to admit those Colonies or Provinces, or any of them, into the Union, and on Address from the Houses of the Parliament of Canada to admit Rupert's Land and the Northwestern Territory, or either of them, into the Union, on such Terms and Conditions in each Case as are in the Addresses expressed and as the Queen thinks fit to approve, subject to the Provisions of this Act; and the Provisions of any Order in

Council in that Behalf shall have effect as if they had been enacted by the Parliament of the United Kingdom of Great Britain and Ireland.

[Section 147 omitted.]

[The First and Second Schedules omitted.]

THE THIRD SCHEDULE

PROVINCIAL PUBLIC WORKS AND PROPERTY TO BE THE PROPERTY OF CANADA

1. Canals, with Lands and Water Power connected therewith.
2. Public Harbours.
3. Lighthouses and Piers, and Sable Island.
4. Steamboats, Dredges, and public Vessels.
5. Rivers and Lake Improvements.
6. Railways and Railway Stocks, Mortgages, and other Debts due by Railway Companies.
7. Military Roads.
8. Custom Houses, Post Offices, and all other Public Buildings, except such as the Government of Canada appropriate for the Use of the Provincial Legislatures and Governments.
9. Property transferred by the Imperial Government, and known as Ordnance Property.
10. Armouries, Drill Sheds, Military Clothing, and Munitions of War, and Lands set apart for general Public Purposes.

[The Fourth Schedule omitted.]

THE FIFTH SCHEDULE

OATH OF ALLEGIANCE

I *A.B.* do swear, That I will be faithful and bear true Allegiance to Her Majesty Queen Victoria.

Note.—The Name of the King or Queen of the United Kingdom of Great Britain and Ireland for the Time being is to be substituted from Time to Time, with proper Terms of Reference thereto.

DECLARATION OF QUALIFICATION

I *A.B.* do declare and testify, That I am by Law duly qualified to be appointed a Member of the Senate of Canada [*or as the Case may be*], and that I am legally or equitably seised as of Freehold for my own Use and Benefit of Lands or Tenements held in Free and Common Socage [*or seised or possessed for my own Use and Benefit of Lands or Tenements* held in Franc-alleu or in Roture (*as the Case may be*),] in the Province of Nova Scotia [*or as the Case may be*] of the Value of Four thousand Dollars over and above all Rents, Dues, Debts, Mortgages, Charges, and Incumbrances due or payable out of or charged on or affecting the same, and that I have not collusively or colourably obtained a Title to or become possessed of the said Lands and Tenements or any Part thereof for the Purpose of enabling me to become a Member of the Senate of Canada [*or as the Case may be*], and that my Real and Personal Property are together worth Four thousand Dollars over and above my Debts and Liabilities

THE SIXTH SCHEDULE

PRIMARY PRODUCTION FROM NON-RENEWABLE NATURAL RESOURCES AND FORESTRY RESOURCES

1. For the purposes of section 92A of this Act,

   (*a*) production from a non-renewable natural resource is primary production therefrom if

   (i) it is in the form in which it exists upon its recovery or severance from its natural state, or

   (ii) it is a product resulting from processing or refining the resource, and is not a manufactured product or a product resulting from refining crude oil, refining upgraded heavy crude oil, refining gases or liquids derived from coal or refining a synthetic equivalent of crude oil; and

   (*b*) production from a forestry resource is primary production therefrom if it consists of sawlogs, poles, lumber, wood chips, sawdust or any other primary wood product, or wood pulp, and is not a product manufactured from wood.

B   Constitution Act, 1982

TABLE OF CONTENTS

PART I

CANADIAN CHARTER OF RIGHTS AND FREEDOMS

Whereas Canada is founded upon principles that recognize the supremacy of God and the rule of law:

GUARANTEE OF RIGHTS AND FREEDOMS

Rights and freedoms in Canada

1. The *Canadian Charter of Rights and Freedoms* guarantees the rights and freedoms set out in it subject only to such reasonable limits prescribed by law as can be demonstrably justified in a free and democratic society.

FUNDAMENTAL FREEDOMS

Fundamental freedoms

2. Everyone has the following fundamental freedoms:
  (*a*) freedom of conscience and religion;
  (*b*) freedom of thought, belief, opinion and expression, including freedom of the press and other media of communication;
  (*c*) freedom of peaceful assembly; and
  (*d*) freedom of association.

DEMOCRATIC RIGHTS

Democratic rights of citizens

3. Every citizen of Canada has the right to vote in an election of members of the House of Commons or of a legislative assembly and to be qualified for membership therein.

Maximum duration of legislative bodies

4(1) No House of Commons and no legislative assembly shall continue for longer than five years from the date fixed for the return of the writs at a general election of its members.

Continuation in special circumstances

(2) In time of real or apprehended war, invasion or insurrection, a House of Commons may be continued by Parliament and a legislative assembly may be continued by the legislature beyond five years if such continuation is not opposed by the votes of more than one-third of the members of the House of Commons or the legislative assembly, as the case may be.

Annual sitting of legislative bodies

5. There shall be a sitting of Parliament and of each legislature at least once every twelve months.

MOBILITY RIGHTS

Mobility of citizens

6(1) Every citizen of Canada has the right to enter, remain in and leave Canada.

Rights to move and gain livelihood

(2) Every citizen of Canada and every person who has the status of a permanent resident of Canada has the right
  (*a*) to move to and take up residence in any province; and
  (*b*) to pursue the gaining of a livelihood in any province.

Limitation

(3) The rights specified in subsection (2) are subject to
  (*a*) any laws or practices of general application in force in a province other than those that discriminate among persons primarily on the basis of province of present or previous residence; and
  (*b*) any laws providing for reasonable residency requirements as a qualification for the receipt of publicly provided social services.

Affirmative action programs

(4) Subsections (2) and (3) do not preclude any law, program or activity that has as its object the amelioration in a province of conditions of individuals in that province who are socially or economically disadvantaged if the rate of employment in that province is below the rate of employment in Canada.

LEGAL RIGHTS

Life, liberty and security of person

7. Everyone has the right to life, liberty and security of the person and the right not to be deprived thereof except in accordance with the principles of fundamental justice.

Search or seizure

8. Everyone has the right to be secure against unreasonable search or seizure.

Detention or imprisonment

9. Everyone has the right not to be arbitrarily detained or imprisoned.

Arrest or detention

10. Everyone has the right on arrest or detention
  (*a*) to be informed promptly of the reasons therefor;

(*b*) to retain and instruct counsel without delay and to be informed of that right; and

(*c*) to have the validity of the detention determined by way of *habeas corpus* and to be released if the detention is not lawful.

Proceedings in criminal and penal matters

11. Any person charged with an offence has the right

(*a*) to be informed without unreasonable delay of the specific offence;

(*b*) to be tried within a reasonable time;

(*c*) not to be compelled to be a witness in proceedings against that person in respect of the offence;

(*d*) to be presumed innocent until proven guilty according to law in a fair and public hearing by an independent and impartial tribunal;

(*e*) not to be denied reasonable bail without just cause;

(*f*) except in the case of an offence under military law tried before a military tribunal, to the benefit of trial by jury where the maximum punishment for the offence is imprisonment for five years or a more severe punishment;

(*g*) not to be found guilty on account of any act or omission unless, at the time of the act or omission, it constituted an offence under Canadian or international law or was criminal according to the general principles of law recognized by the community of nations;

(*h*) if finally acquitted of the offence, not to be tried for it again and, if finally found guilty and punished for the offence, not to be tried or punished for it again; and

(*i*) if found guilty of the offence and if the punishment for the offence has been varied between the time of commission and the time of sentencing, to the benefit of the lesser punishment.

Treatment or punishment

12. Everyone has the right not to be subjected to any cruel and unusual treatment or punishment.

Self-crimination

13. A witness who testifies in any proceedings has the right not to have any incriminating evidence so given used to incriminate that witness in any other proceedings, except in a prosecution for perjury or for the giving of contradictory evidence.

Interpreter

14. A party or witness in any proceedings who does not understand or speak the language in which the proceedings are conducted or who is deaf has the right to the assistance of an interpreter.

EQUALITY RIGHTS

Equality before and under law and equal protection and benefit of law

15(1) Every individual is equal before and under the law and has the right to the equal protection and equal benefit of the law without discrimination and, in particular, without discrimination based on race, national or ethnic origin, colour, religion, sex, age or mental or physical disability.

Affirmative action programs

(2) Subsection (1) does not preclude any law, program or activity that has as its object the amelioration of conditions of disadvantaged individuals or groups including those that are disadvantaged because of race, national or ethnic origin, colour, religion, sex, age or mental or physical disability.

OFFICIAL LANGUAGES OF CANADA

Official languages of Canada

16(1) English and French are the official languages of Canada and have equality of status and equal rights and privileges as to their use in all institutions of the Parliament and government of Canada.

Official languages of New Brunswick

(2) English and French are the official languages of New Brunswick and have equality of status and equal rights and privileges as to their use in all institutions of the legislature and government of New Brunswick.

Advancement of status and use

(3) Nothing in this Charter limits the authority of Parliament or a legislature to advance the equality of status or use of English and French.

English and French linguistic communities in New Brunswick

16.1(1) The English linguistic community and the French linguistic community in New Brunswick have equality of status and equal rights and privileges, including the right to distinct educational institutions and such distinct cultural institutions as are necessary for the preservation and promotion of those communities.

Role of the legislature and government of New Brunswick

(2) The role of the legislature and government of New Brunswick to preserve and promote the status, rights and privileges referred to in subsection (1) is affirmed.

Proceedings of Parliament

17(1) Everyone has the right to use English or French in any debates and other proceedings of Parliament.

Proceedings of New Brunswick legislature

(2) Everyone has the right to use English or French in any debates and other proceedings of the legislature of New Brunswick.

Parliamentary statutes and records

18(1) The statutes, records and journals of Parliament shall be printed and published in English and French and both language versions are equally authoritative.

New Brunswick statutes and records

(2) The statutes, records and journals of the legislature of New Brunswick shall be printed and published in English and French and both language versions are equally authoritative.

Proceedings in courts established by Parliament

19(1) Either English or French may be used by any person in, or in any pleading in or process issuing from, any court established by Parliament.

Proceedings in New Brunswick courts

(2) Either English or French may be used by any person in, or in any pleading in or process issuing from, any court of New Brunswick.

Communications by public with federal institutions

20(1) Any member of the public in Canada has the right to communicate with, and to receive available services from, any head or central office of an institution of the Parliament or government of Canada in English or French, and has the same right with respect to any other office of any such institution where

    (*a*) there is a significant demand for communications with and services from that office in such language; or

    (*b*) due to the nature of the office, it is reasonable that communications with and services from that office be available in both English and French.

Communications by public with New Brunswick institutions

(2) Any member of the public in New Brunswick has the right to communicate with, and to receive available services from, any office of an institution of the legislature or government of New Brunswick in English or French.

Continuation of existing constitutional provisions

21. Nothing in sections 16 to 20 abrogates or derogates from any right, privilege or obligation with respect to the English and French languages, or either of them, that exists or is continued by virtue of any other provision of the Constitution of Canada.

Rights and privileges preserved

22. Nothing in sections 16 to 20 abrogates or derogates from any legal or customary right or privilege acquired or enjoyed either before or after the coming into force of this Charter with respect to any language that is not English or French.

Minority Language Educational Rights

Language of instruction

23(1) Citizens of Canada

    (*a*) whose first language learned and still understood is that of the English or French linguistic minority population of the province in which they reside, or

    (*b*) who have received their primary school instruction in Canada in English or French and reside in a province where the language in which they received that instruction is the language of the English or French linguistic minority population of the province,

have the right to have their children receive primary and secondary school instruction in that language in that province.

Continuity of language instruction

(2) Citizens of Canada of whom any child has received or is receiving primary or secondary school instruction in English or French in Canada, have the right to have all their children receive primary and secondary school instruction in the same language.

Application where numbers warrant

(3) The right of citizens of Canada under subsections (1) and (2) to have their children receive primary and secondary school instruction in the language of the English or French linguistic minority population of a province

(*a*) applies wherever in the province the number of children of citizens who have such a right is sufficient to warrant the provision to them out of public funds of minority language instruction; and

(*b*) includes, where the number of those children so warrants, the right to have them receive that instruction in minority language educational facilities provided out of public funds.

ENFORCEMENT

Enforcement of guaranteed rights and freedoms

24(1) Anyone whose rights or freedoms, as guaranteed by this Charter, have been infringed or denied may apply to a court of competent jurisdiction to obtain such remedy as the court considers appropriate and just in the circumstances.

Exclusion of evidence bringing administration of justice into disrepute

(2) Where, in proceedings under subsection (1), a court concludes that evidence was obtained in a manner that infringed or denied any rights or freedoms guaranteed by this Charter, the evidence shall be excluded if it is established that, having regard to all the circumstances, the admission of it in the proceedings would bring the administration of justice into disrepute.

GENERAL

Aboriginal rights and freedoms not affected by Charter

25. The guarantee in this Charter of certain rights and freedoms shall not be construed so as to abrogate or derogate from any aboriginal, treaty or other rights or freedoms that pertain to the aboriginal peoples of Canada including

(*a*) any rights or freedoms that have been recognized by the Royal Proclamation of October 7, 1763; and

(*b*) any rights or freedoms that now exist by way of land claims agreements or may be so acquired.

Other rights and freedoms not affected by Charter

26. The guarantee in this Charter of certain rights and freedoms shall not be construed as denying the existence of any other rights or freedoms that exist in Canada.

Multicultural heritage

27. This Charter shall be interpreted in a manner consistent with the preservation and enhancement of the multicultural heritage of Canadians.

Rights guaranteed equally to both sexes

28. Notwithstanding anything in this Charter, the rights and freedoms referred to in it are guaranteed equally to male and female persons.

Rights respecting certain schools preserved

29. Nothing in this Charter abrogates or derogates from any rights or privileges guaranteed by or under the Constitution of Canada in respect of denominational, separate or dissentient schools.

Application to territories and territorial authorities

30. A reference in this Charter to a province or to the legislative assembly or legislature of a province shall be deemed to include a reference to the Yukon Territory and the Northwest Territories, or to the appropriate legislative authority thereof, as the case may be.

Legislative powers not extended

31. Nothing in this Charter extends the legislative powers of any body or authority.

APPLICATION OF CHARTER

Application of Charter

32(1) This Charter applies

(*a*) to the Parliament and government of Canada in respect of all matters within the authority of Parliament including all matters relating to the Yukon Territory and Northwest Territories; and

(*b*) to the legislature and government of each province in respect of all matters within the authority of the legislature of each province.

Exception

(2) Notwithstanding subsection (1), section 15 shall not have effect until three years after this section comes into force.

Exception where express declaration

33(1) Parliament or the legislature of a province may expressly declare in an Act of Parliament or of the legislature, as the case may be, that the Act or a provision thereof shall operate notwithstanding a provision included in section 2 or sections 7 to 15 of this Charter.

Operation of exception

(2) An Act or a provision of an Act in respect of which a declaration made under this section is in effect shall have such operation as it would have but for the provision of this Charter referred to in the declaration.

Five year limitation

(3) A declaration made under subsection (1) shall cease to have effect five years after it comes into force or on such earlier date as may be specified in the declaration.

Re-enactment

(4) Parliament or the legislature of a province may re-enact a declaration made under subsection (1).

Five year limitation

(5) Subsection (3) applies in respect of a re-enactment made under subsection (4).

CITATION

Citation

34. This Part may be cited as the *Canadian Charter of Rights and Freedoms.*

PART II

RIGHTS OF THE ABORIGINAL PEOPLES OF CANADA

Recognition of existing aboriginal and treaty rights

35(1) The existing aboriginal and treaty rights of the aboriginal peoples of Canada are hereby recognized and affirmed.

Definition of "aboriginal peoples of Canada"

(2) In this Act, "aboriginal peoples of Canada" includes the Indian, Inuit and Métis peoples of Canada.

Land claims agreements

(3) For greater certainty, in subsection (1) "treaty rights" includes rights that now exist by way of land claims agreements or may be so acquired.

Aboriginal and treaty rights are guaranteed equally to both sexes

(4) Notwithstanding any other provision of this Act, the aboriginal and treaty rights referred to in subsection (1) are guaranteed equally to male and female persons.

Commitment to participation in constitutional conference

35.1 The government of Canada and the provincial governments are committed to the principle that, before any amendment is made to Class 24 of section 91 of the "*Constitution Act, 1867*," to section 25 of this Act or to this Part,

(*a*) a constitutional conference that includes in its agenda an item relating to the proposed amendment, composed of the Prime Minister of Canada and the first ministers of the provinces, will be convened by the Prime Minister of Canada; and

(*b*) the Prime Minister of Canada will invite representatives of the aboriginal peoples of Canada to participate in the discussions on that item.

PART III

EQUALIZATION AND REGIONAL DISPARITIES

Commitment to promote equal opportunities

36(1) Without altering the legislative authority of Parliament or of the provincial legislatures, or the rights of any of them with respect to the exercise of their legislative authority, Parliament and the legislatures, together with the government of Canada and the provincial governments, are committed to

(*a*) promoting equal opportunities for the well-being of Canadians;

(*b*) furthering economic development to reduce disparity in opportunities; and

(*c*) providing essential public services of reasonable quality to all Canadians.

Commitment respecting public services

(2) Parliament and the government of Canada are committed to the principle of making equalization payments to ensure that provincial governments have sufficient revenues to provide reasonably comparable levels of public services at reasonably comparable levels of taxation.

[Parts IV and IV.1 omitted.]

PART V

PROCEDURE FOR AMENDING CONSTITUTION OF CANADA

General procedure for amending Constitution of Canada

38(1) An amendment to the Constitution of Canada may be made by proclamation issued by the Governor General under the Great Seal of Canada where so authorized by

(*a*) resolutions of the Senate and House of Commons; and

(*b*) resolutions of the legislative assemblies of at least two-thirds of the provinces that have, in the aggregate, according to the then latest general census, at least fifty per cent of the population of all the provinces.

Majority of members

(2) An amendment made under subsection (1) that derogates from the legislative powers, the proprietary rights or any other rights or privileges of the legislature or government of a province shall require a resolution supported by a majority of the members of each of the Senate, the House of Commons and the legislative assemblies required under subsection (1).

Expression of dissent

(3) An amendment referred to in subsection (2) shall not have effect in a province the legislative assembly of which has expressed its dissent thereto by resolution supported by a majority of its members prior to the issue of the proclamation to which the amendment relates unless that legislative assembly, subsequently, by resolution supported by a majority of its members, revokes its dissent and authorizes the amendment.

Revocation of dissent

(4) A resolution of dissent made for the purposes of subsection (3) may be revoked at any time before or after the issue of the proclamation to which it relates.

Restriction on proclamation

39(1) A proclamation shall not be issued under subsection 38(1) before the expiration of one year from the adoption of the resolution initiating the amendment procedure thereunder, unless the legislative assembly of each province has previously adopted a resolution of assent or dissent.

Idem

(2) A proclamation shall not be issued under subsection 38(1) after the expiration of three years from the adoption of the resolution initiating the amendment procedure thereunder.

Compensation

40. Where an amendment is made under subsection 38(1) that transfers provincial legislative powers relating to education or other cultural matters from provincial legislatures to Parliament, Canada shall provide reasonable compensation to any province to which the amendment does not apply.

Amendment by unanimous consent

41. An amendment to the Constitution of Canada in relation to the following matters may be made by proclamation issued by the Governor General under the Great Seal of Canada only where authorized by resolutions of the Senate and House of Commons and of the legislative assembly of each province:

(a) the office of the Queen, the Governor General and the Lieutenant Governor of a province;

(b) the right of a province to a number of members in the House of Commons not less than the number of Senators by which the province is entitled to be represented at the time this Part comes into force;

(c) subject to section 43, the use of the English or the French language;

(d) the composition of the Supreme Court of Canada; and

(e) an amendment to this Part.

Amendment by general procedure

42(1) An amendment to the Constitution of Canada in relation to the following matters may be made only in accordance with subsection 38(1):

(a) the principle of proportionate representation of the provinces in the House of Commons prescribed by the Constitution of Canada;

(b) the powers of the Senate and the method of selecting Senators;

(c) the number of members by which a province is entitled to be represented in the Senate and the residence qualifications of Senators;

(d) subject to paragraph 41(d), the Supreme Court of Canada;

(e) the extension of existing provinces into the territories; and

(f) notwithstanding any other law or practice, the establishment of new provinces.

Exception

(2) Subsections 38(2) to (4) do not apply in respect of amendments in relation to matters referred to in subsection (1).

Amendment of provisions relating to some but not all provinces

43. An amendment to the Constitution of Canada in relation to any provision that applies to one or more, but not all, provinces, including

(a) any alteration to boundaries between provinces, and

(b) any amendment to any provision that relates to the use of the English or the French language within a province,

may be made by proclamation issued by the Governor General under the Great Seal of Canada only where so authorized by resolutions of the Senate and House of Commons and of the legislative assembly of each province to which the amendment applies.

Amendments by Parliament

44. Subject to sections 41 and 42, Parliament may exclusively make laws amending the Constitution of Canada in relation to the executive government of Canada or the Senate and House of Commons.

Amendments by provincial legislatures

45. Subject to section 41, the legislature of each province may exclusively make laws amending the constitution of the province.

Initiation of amendment procedures

46(1) The procedures for amendment under sections 38, 41, 42 and 43 may be initiated either by the Senate or the House of Commons or by the legislative assembly of a province.

Revocation of authorization

(2) A resolution of assent made for the purposes of this Part may be revoked at any time before the issue of a proclamation authorized by it.

Amendments without Senate resolution

47(1) An amendment to the Constitution of Canada made by proclamation under section 38, 41, 42 or 43 may be made without a resolution of the Senate authorizing the issue of the proclamation if, within one hundred and eighty days after the adoption by the House of Commons of a resolution authorizing its issue, the Senate has not adopted such a resolution and if, at any time after the expiration of that period, the House of Commons again adopts the resolution.

Computation of period

(2) Any period when Parliament is prorogued or dissolved shall not be counted in computing the one hundred and eighty day period referred to in subsection (1).

Advice to issue proclamation

48. The Queen's Privy Council for Canada shall advise the Governor General to issue a proclamation under this Part forthwith on the adoption of the resolutions required for an amendment made by proclamation under this Part.

Constitutional conference

49. A constitutional conference composed of the Prime Minister of Canada and the first ministers of the provinces shall be convened by the Prime Minister of Canada within fifteen years after this Part comes into force to review the provisions of this Part.

[Part VI omitted.]

PART VII

GENERAL

Primacy of Constitution of Canada

52(1) The Constitution of Canada is the supreme law of Canada, and any law that is inconsistent with the provisions of the Constitution is, to the extent of the inconsistency, of no force or effect.

Constitution of Canada

(2) The Constitution of Canada includes

(*a*) the *Canada Act 1982*, including this Act;

(*b*) the Acts and orders referred to in the schedule; and

(*c*) any amendment to any Act or order referred to in paragraph (*a*) or (*b*).

Amendments to Constitution of Canada

(3) Amendments to the Constitution of Canada shall be made only in accordance with the authority contained in the Constitution of Canada.

Repeals and new names

53(1) The enactments referred to in Column I of the schedule are hereby repealed or amended to the extent indicated in Column II thereof and, unless repealed, shall continue as law in Canada under the names set out in Column III thereof.

Consequential amendments

(2) Every enactment, except the *Canada Act 1982*, that refers to an enactment referred to in the schedule by the name in Column I thereof is hereby amended by substituting for that name the corresponding name in Column III thereof, and any British North America Act not referred to in the schedule may be cited as the *Constitution Act* followed by the year and number, if any, of its enactment.

Repeal and consequential amendments

54. Part IV is repealed on the day that is one year after this Part comes into force and this section may be repealed and this Act renumbered, consequentially upon the repeal of Part IV and this section, by proclamation issued by the Governor General under the Great Seal of Canada.

54.1 Repealed.

French version of Constitution of Canada

55. A French version of the portions of the Constitution of Canada referred to in the schedule shall be prepared by the Minister of Justice of Canada as expeditiously as possible and, when any portion thereof sufficient to warrant action being taken has been so prepared, it shall be put forward for enactment by proclamation issued by the Governor General under the Great Seal of Canada pursuant to the procedure then applicable to an amendment of the same provisions of the Constitution of Canada.

English and French versions of certain constitutional texts

56. Where any portion of the Constitution of Canada has been or is enacted in English and French or where a French version of any portion of the Constitution is enacted pursuant to section 55, the English and French versions of that portion of the Constitution are equally authoritative.

English and French versions of this Act

57. The English and French versions of this Act are equally authoritative.

Commencement

58. Subject to section 59, this Act shall come into force on a day to be fixed by proclamation issued by the Queen or the Governor General under the Great Seal of Canada.

Commencement of paragraph 23(1)(*a*) in respect of Quebec

59(1) Paragraph 23(1)(*a*) shall come into force in respect of Quebec on a day to be fixed by proclamation issued by the Queen or the Governor General under the Great Seal of Canada.

Authorization of Quebec

(2) A proclamation under subsection (1) shall be issued only where authorized by the legislative assembly or government of Quebec.

Repeal of this section

(3) This section may be repealed on the day paragraph 23(1)(*a*) comes into force in respect of Quebec and this Act amended and renumbered, consequentially upon the repeal of this section, by proclamation issued by the Queen or the Governor General under the Great Seal of Canada.

Short title and citations

60. This Act may be cited as the *Constitution Act, 1982*, and the Constitution Acts 1867 to 1975 (No. 2) and this Act may be cited together as the *Constitution Acts, 1867 to 1982*.

References

61. A reference to the "*Constitution Acts, 1867 to 1982*" shall be deemed to include a reference to the "*Constitution Amendment Proclamation, 1983.*"

SCHEDULE TO THE CONSTITUTION ACT, 1982

(Section 53)

MODERNIZATION OF THE CONSTITUTION

Item	Column I Act Affected	Column II Amendment	Column III New Name
1.	British North America Act, 1867, 30-31 Vict., c. 3 (U.K.)	(1) Section 1 is repealed and the following substituted therefor: "1. This Act may be cited as the *Constitution Act, 1867.*" (2) Section 20 is repealed. (3) Class 1 of section 91 is repealed. (4) Class 1 of section 92 is repealed.	Constitution Act, 1867
2.	An Act to amend and continue the Act 32-33 Victoria chapter 3; and to establish and provide for the Government of the Province of Manitoba, 1870, 33 Vict., c. 3 (Can.)	(1) The long title is repealed and the following substituted therefor: "*Manitoba Act, 1870.*" (2) Section 20 is repealed.	Manitoba Act, 1870
3.	Order of Her Majesty in Council admitting Rupert's Land and the North-Western Territory into the union, dated the 23rd day of June, 1870		Rupert's Land and North-Western Territory Order
4.	Order of Her Majesty in Council admitting British Columbia into the Union, dated the 16th day of May, 1871.		British Columbia Terms of Union
5.	British North America Act, 1871, 34-35 Vict., c. 28 (U.K.)	Section 1 is repealed and the following substituted therefor: "1. This Act may be cited as the *Constitution Act, 1871.*"	Constitution Act, 1871
6.	Order of Her Majesty in Council admitting Prince Edward Island into the Union, dated the 26th day of June, 1873.		Prince Edward Island Terms of Union
7.	Parliament of Canada Act, 1875, 38-39 Vict., c. 38 (U.K.)		Parliament of Canada Act, 1875
8.	Order of Her Majesty in Council admitting all British possessions and Territories in North America and islands adjacent thereto into the Union, dated the 31st day of July, 1880.		Adjacent Territories Order

Item	Column I Act Affected	Column II Amendment	Column III New Name
9.	British North America Act, 1886, 49-50 Vict., c. 35 (U.K.)	Section 3 is repealed and the following substituted therefor: "3. This Act may be cited as the *Constitution Act, 1886.*"	Constitution Act, 1886
10.	Canada (Ontario Boundary) Act, 1889, 52-53 Vict., c. 28 (U.K.)		Canada (Ontario Boundary) Act, 1889
11.	Canadian Speaker (Appointment of Deputy) Act, 1895, 2nd Sess., 59 Vict., c. 3 (U.K.)	The Act is repealed.	
12.	The Alberta Act, 1905, 4-5 Edw. VII, c. 3 (Can.)		Alberta Act
13.	The Saskatchewan Act, 1905, 4-5 Edw. VII, c. 42 (Can.)		Saskatchewan Act
14.	British North America Act, 1907, 7 Edw. VII, c. 11 (U.K.)	Section 2 is repealed and the following substituted therefor: "2. This Act may be cited as the *Constitution Act, 1907.*"	Constitution Act, 1907
15.	British North America Act, 1915, 5-6 Geo. V, c. 45 (U.K.)	Section 3 is repealed and the following substituted therefor: "3. This Act may be cited as the *Constitution Act, 1915.*"	Constitution Act, 1915
16.	British North America Act, 1930, 20-21 Geo. V, c. 26 (U.K.)	Section 3 is repealed and the following substituted therefor: "3. This Act may be cited as the *Constitution Act, 1930.*"	Constitution Act, 1930
17.	Statute of Westminster, 1931, 22 Geo. V, c. 4 (U.K.)	In so far as they apply to Canada, (*a*) section 4 is repealed; and (*b*) subsection 7(1) is repealed.	Statute of Westminster, 1931
18.	British North America Act, 1940, 3-4 Geo. VI, c. 36 (U.K.)	Section 2 is repealed and the following substituted therefor: "2. This Act may be cited as the *Constitution Act, 1940.*"	Constitution Act, 1940
19.	British North America Act, 1943, 6-7 Geo. VI, c. 30 (U.K.)	The Act is repealed.	
20.	British North America Act, 1946, 9-10 Geo. VI, c. 63 (U.K.)	The Act is repealed.	
21.	British North America Act, 1949, 12-13 Geo. VI, c. 22 (U.K.)	Section 3 is repealed and the following substituted therefor: "3. This Act may be cited as the *Newfoundland Act.*"	Newfoundland Act
22.	British North America (No. 2) Act, 1949, 13 Geo. VI, c. 81 (U.K.)	The Act is repealed.	
23.	British North America Act, 1951, 14-15 Geo. VI, c. 32 (U.K.)	The Act is repealed.	

Item	Column I Act Affected	Column II Amendment	Column III New Name
24.	British North America Act, 1952, 1 Eliz. II, c. 15 (Can.)	The Act is repealed.	
25.	British North America Act, 1960, 9 Eliz. II, c. 2 (U.K.)	Section 2 is repealed and the following substituted therefor: "2. This Act may be cited as the *Constitution Act, 1960.*"	Constitution Act, 1960
26.	British North America Act, 1964, 12-13 Eliz. II, c. 73 (U.K.)	Section 2 is repealed and the following substituted therefor: "2. This Act may be cited as the *Constitution Act, 1964.*"	Constitution Act, 1964
27.	British North America Act, 1965, 14 Eliz. II, c. 4, Part I (Can.)	Section 2 is repealed and the following substituted therefor: "2. This Part may be cited as the *Constitution Act, 1965.*"	Constitution Act, 1965
28.	British North America Act, 1974, 23 Eliz. II, c. 13, Part I (Can.)	Section 3, as amended by 25-26 Eliz. II, c. 28, s. 38(1) (Can.), is repealed and the following substituted therefor: "3. This Part may be cited as the *Constitution Act, 1974.*"	Constitution Act, 1974
29.	British North America Act, 1975, 23-24 Eliz. II, c. 28, Part I (Can.)	Section 3, as amended by 25-26 Eliz. II, c. 28, s. 31 (Can.), is repealed and the following substituted therefor: "3. This Part may be cited as the *Constitution Act (No. 1), 1975.*"	Constitution Act (No. 1), 1975
30.	British North America Act (No. 2), 1975, 23-24 Eliz. II, c. 53 (Can.)	Section 3 is repealed and the following substituted therefor: "3. This Act may be cited as the *Constitution Act (No. 2), 1975.*"	Constitution Act (No. 2), 1975

Glossary

administrative agency   government bodies created under various federal, provincial, and territorial statutes with the purpose of administering particular statutory regimes *(p. 319)*

administrative tribunal   administrative agency that fulfills quasi-judicial functions as part of its mandate *(p. 324)*

admiralty (or maritime) law   area of law that concerns maritime trade and commerce and that has a private international law component *(p. 397)*

adversarial system   system, used in common law courts, whereby the primary responsibility for the presentation of cases lies with the opposing litigants and their counsel, not with the judge presiding over the case *(p. 39)*

affinity   the relationship that a person has to the blood relatives of his or her spouse *(p. 288)*

affirmative action   policy, particularly in relation to education or employment, intended to assist groups who have suffered past discrimination *(p. 213)*

aggravating circumstance   a factor in the case that causes the judge to impose a harsher sentence on the convicted person than he or she would otherwise *(p. 355)*

agreement for sale   agreement by which a person selling his property agrees to finance the purchase himself, keeping the title to the property while allowing the purchaser to take possession of it, and then transferring the title to the purchaser once the balance of the purchase price is paid *(p. 277)*

alternative dispute resolution (ADR)   process used instead of a court trial to help settle a dispute *(p. 448)*

annulment   the legal cancellation or invalidation of a marriage *(p. 287)*

appearance notice   a document given to a person, usually at the scene of the crime, requiring that person to come to court on a certain date and time to answer to a charge *(p. 350)*

appellant   individual, corporation, or other entity who lost at trial and who initiates an appeal to a higher court *(p. 181)*

arbitration   dispute resolution process whereby the parties agree beforehand on an arbitrator to assist them, and they agree on whether the arbitrator's decision will be advisory or binding *(p. 449)*

arraignment   procedure by which the charge is read to the accused in open court and the accused is asked how she wishes to plead *(p. 352)*

arrest   detaining or holding a person by legal authority *(p. 346)*

articles   an apprenticeship under a practising lawyer *(p. 410)*

assault   psychological tort involving one person's apprehension of harmful physical contact from another person *(p. 233)*

banns of marriage   the public announcement in church of an impending marriage *(p. 289)*

battery   tort requiring actual occurrence of harmful or offensive physical contact *(p. 233)*

benchers   lawyers (and some non-lawyers) who are responsible for administering and governing a provincial or territorial law society *(p. 408)*

beneficial owner   also called an *equitable owner*, the person on whose behalf and for whose benefit the trustee holds and manages the property *(p. 278)*

bicameral   legislature with two houses involved in the passage of legislation *(p. 92)*

bijural   term describing the operation of two legal systems in one jurisdiction, such as the common law and civil law systems in Canada *(p. 32)*

bilateral contract   contracts in the form of a "promise for a promise" whereby the offeror promises something in exchange for a reciprocal promise *(p. 255)*

bill   the draft version of a proposed new statute *(p. 104)*

Bill of Rights (1689)   English statute that formally ended the power of the Crown to legislate without the consent of Parliament *(p. 40)*

binding   term used to describe a higher court decision that a lower court in the same jurisdiction must follow according to the principle of *stare decisis* *(pp. 37, 173)*

bona fide occupational requirement   in the context of employment, a bona fide (Latin for "in good faith") requirement is one that exists for a legitimate reason—for example, safety—and that cannot be removed without undue hardship on the employer *(p. 213)*

bright line rule   strict rule that a lawyer or law firm cannot represent two current clients whose interests are directly adverse to each other unless both clients consent after receiving full disclosure from the lawyer *(p. 434)*

builders' (or construction) lien   charge against land that builders use to secure amounts owed them for work done on landowners' property *(p. 307)*

called to the bar   formal ceremony whereby a law student becomes entitled to practise law *(p. 411)*

case   depending on context, refers to the reasons for judgment (where the court provides them), to the court process more generally, or to the entire dispute from beginning to end *(p. 180)*

case brief   summary of a case, with the constituent parts of the court's reasons for judgment arranged in a set order *(p. 184)*

cattle trespass   a strict liability tort involving damage caused by straying cattle or other farm animals *(p. 245)*

cession   the transfer of a colony from one country to another *(p. 62)*

Chancery   department of state established by English monarchs to assist with legal matters and to issue writs *(p. 34)*

chapter number   the number assigned to a statute when it is first passed or when it is republished in a statutory revision—refers to the chronological position of the statute within a particular legislative session, year, or revision *(p. 117)*

charges and encumbrances   any claim on a parcel of real property—for example, mortgages, property taxes, or water rights *(p. 276)*

chattels   tangible, movable objects such as furniture, equipment, and cars *(p. 282)*

chose in action   the right to sue someone for an unpaid debt or liability; an intangible personal property right *(p. 283)*

civil code   authoritative legislative encoding of a country's private law *(p. 41)*

Civil Code of Quebec (Code Civil du Québec)   Quebec's current civil code, which came into effect on January 1, 1994, and which replaced the *Civil Code of Lower Canada* that had been in force since 1866 *(pp. 53, 67)*

civil law   system of law based on codified rules; may also refer to private law *(p. 32)*

civil liberties   rights and freedoms protected by the Charter *(p. 206)*

civil wrong   a wrong that occurs in the context of relationships between persons and is addressed by one of the areas of private law *(p. 232)*

codes of conduct   written sets of rules regulating the ethical behaviour of professionals *(p. 422)*

commencement (or coming-into-force) section   section that details when or how a statute comes into effect *(p. 118)*

commissioner   federally appointed official who is the formal head of the territorial executive government *(p. 141)*

Commissioner in Executive Council   official name for a territorial Cabinet *(p. 141)*

common law   system of law, based on the English legal tradition, that relies on precedent rather than on codified rules; may also refer to (1) decisions by courts exercising their common law jurisdiction as opposed to their equitable jurisdiction based on broad principles of fairness, or (2) case law generally as opposed to legislation *(p. 32)*

compensatory damages   damages in a tort claim that compensate the plaintiff for proven and recognized types of losses *(p. 249)*

cones of silence   institutional mechanisms used by law firms to secure confidential information so that lawyers working at the same law firm are prevented from accessing information that could prejudice a former client; sometimes also called Chinese walls *(p. 433)*

Confederation   the coming together of the three British North American colonies of Nova Scotia, New Brunswick, and the Province of Canada (Ontario and Quebec) to form the Dominion of Canada in 1867. The term later included all the provinces and territories that have joined Canada since that date *(p. 63)*

confidence convention   convention requiring the government to resign if it loses the support of the majority of the elected representatives in the House of Commons and, if a new government cannot be formed, to call an election *(p. 141)*

conflict of laws   area of law—also referred to as *private international law*—that covers private law disputes that have an interprovincial or international component *(p. 396)*

consanguinity   a blood relationship between relatives *(p. 288)*

consent (defence of)   a defence against a variety of tort claims that is based on the idea that the plaintiff was aware of the risks associated with the activity that led to damages and agreed to participate in the activity anyway *(p. 243)*

consequential amendment section   section in a new statute that amends existing legislation to make it consistent with the new statute *(p. 118)*

constitutional law   law dealing with the distribution of governmental powers under Canada's Constitution *(p. 84)*

constitutionally entrenched   describes a statute that falls within the definition of the Constitution of Canada as set out in section 52 of the *Constitution Act, 1982 (p. 94)*

contributory negligence (defence of)   a defence against negligent tort claims that is based on the idea that the plaintiff negligently contributed to her losses *(p. 243)*

convention   established and traditional "rules" on which our system of responsible government is based and which qualify many of the rules of government set out in constitutional legislation such as the *Constitution Act, 1867*, but which are not, technically, legally binding *(p. 137)*

conveyancing   the part of the real estate transaction that begins after the contract is entered into and that involves the actual transfer of title, or conveyance *(p. 281)*

conviction   a judge or jury's finding an accused person guilty of an offence *(p. 352)*

corporation   company or group of people authorized by statute to act as a single entity (legally a person) and recognized as such in law *(p. 304)*

Corpus Juris Civilis   comprehensive codification of Roman civil law, compiled by the emperor Justinian (483-565 CE) *(p. 42)*

corrective justice   theory of justice according to which (1) a person has a moral responsibility for harm caused to another, and (2) the latter's loss must be rectified or corrected *(p. 8)*

court   state-sanctioned forum where disputes between opposing litigants are formally adjudicated *(p. 156)*

Court of Chancery   English court, existing separate from common law courts, established to provide equity *(p. 35)*

Court of King's (or Queen's) Bench   English court that decided criminal matters *(p. 34)*

creditors' remedies   procedural law area that governs techniques available to creditors to collect their debts, including pre-judgment garnishment of bank accounts, post-judgment garnishment of wages, seizure and sales of motor vehicles, and the registration of judgments against real property *(p. 392)*

critical legal studies   theory of law largely concerned with exposing law as an instrument of the rich and powerful *(p. 18)*

critical race theory   theory of law that focuses on race-based inequities; an offshoot of critical legal studies *(p. 18)*

Crown   the sovereign (currently the Queen), whose authority in Canada has been formally delegated to the governor general (federally) and to the lieutenant governor (provincially), but is actually exercised by the executive branch of government *(p. 137)*

Crown attorney   a lawyer, also known as a Crown prosecutor, who is an agent of the attorney general and who represents the Crown in court, particularly in criminal matters *(p. 336)*

Crown immunity   covering term for the various protections afforded the Crown, including Crown privilege, the presumptions of legislation not applying to the Crown, and (formerly) immunity from tortious liability *(p. 145)*

Crown privilege   aspect of Crown immunity that permits the Crown to claim that evidence is privileged on the ground that its disclosure would adversely affect some matter of public interest *(p. 146)*

customary law   system of law based on rules of conduct considered binding either at a local or an international level, with no formalized process in place for making, changing, or recording them *(p. 50)*

decision   depending on context, refers to the outcome or disposition of a case, to the holding in the case, or (where the court provides them) to the entire set of reasons the court gives for its judgment *(p. 180)*

deeds   formal documents showing ownership of property *(p. 280)*

defamation   a tort involving allegations of impropriety that injure a person's reputation *(p. 247)*

defeasible   term used for life estates that can be terminated by the fee simple owner if certain conditions are not met or certain defined events occur *(p. 276)*

defendant   individual, corporation, or other entity who defends a non-criminal lawsuit initiated by the plaintiff *(p. 181)*

definition section   a statute section that defines words that have a specific meaning in the statute *(p. 118)*

delegates non potest delegare   principle that a person or body to whom power is delegated cannot subdelegate that power (Latin: "one to whom power is delegated cannot himself further delegate that power") *(p. 113)*

deontological   theories that focus on the inherent rightness or wrongness of behaviour, without regard to the behaviour's consequences or outcomes *(p. 8)*

devolution   the legislative arrangement whereby a central authority grants power to regional authorities that are subordinate to the central authority *(p. 111)*

discrimination   prejudicial treatment of people on the ground of race, age, sex, disability, or other recognized ground; prohibited by human rights legislation *(p. 210)*

dissent   refers (in the context of a split decision on appeal) to the judgment of one or more justices in the minority *(p. 166)*

distinguishable   term given to a precedent from a higher court that a lower court decides not to follow, usually on the grounds that the facts in the cases differ *(p. 37)*

distributive justice   theory of justice concerned with appropriate distributions of entitlements, such as wealth and power, in a society *(p. 11)*

division of powers   refers to the divided jurisdiction—between Parliament, on one hand, and the provinces, on the other hand—to make legislation in a federal state such as Canada *(p. 97)*

domestic law   the law of a particular state or society *(p. 24)*

double-aspect law   a law whose subject matter falls within a federal subject area *and* a provincial one *(p. 104)*

duty of competence   lawyer's obligation to provide services that meet the standard of a reasonably skilled lawyer *(p. 432)*

duty of confidentiality   lawyer's obligation not to divulge information concerning a client's affairs that has been acquired in the course of the professional relationship, unless the client authorizes the lawyer to divulge this information *(p. 432)*

duty of disclosure   the Crown's mandatory disclosure to the accused, before the trial, of the evidence against him or her *(p. 347)*

duty of loyalty   lawyer's obligation to avoid conflicts of interest between clients and between lawyer and client *(p. 433)*

elder law   area of private law that covers the various legal issues facing the elderly *(p. 388)*

enabling section   section that delegates authority to make regulations to another person or body *(p. 118)*

environmental law   hybrid area of law with public law and private law aspects involving land, air, and water pollution, and that has a large regulatory component *(p. 395)*

equity   discretionary legal decisions offered by judges in the Court of Chancery, based on fairness and providing relief from the rigid procedures that had evolved under common law courts *(p. 35)*

essential validity   concerns a person's capacity to marry and the substantive requirements of a valid marriage *(p. 285)*

ethics   standards of right and wrong often applied to specific groups—for example, professions *(p. 7)*

evidence (law of)   procedural law area detailing rules relevant in all matters of proof, including non-litigious situations (such as applying for licences) but more commonly in court and tribunal proceedings *(p. 391)*

executive   the branch of government that is responsible for administering or implementing the laws in Canada and whose authority, in this country, is divided between the federal, provincial, and territorial governments based on the division of legislative authority under the Constitution *(p. 136)*

expectation damages   a remedy for contract disputes that attempts to place the innocent party in the position she would have been in if the contract had been performed as promised and all the contractual representations had been true *(p. 264)*

express terms   contract terms that the parties have considered and deliberately included in the contract *(p. 258)*

facta (sing. *factum*)   written legal arguments to be presented on an appeal *(p. 165)*

fairness (also procedural fairness or natural justice)   principle that fairness requires that certain "rights" be accorded to persons engaged with an administrative process, such as the right to notice, the right to be heard and to respond, the right to representation, and the right to an adjudicator who is free from bias or an appearance of bias *(p. 330)*

false imprisonment   tort whereby one person totally restrains the movement of another person *(p. 233)*

federalism   in Canada, the division of state powers between the federal Parliament in Ottawa and the legislatures of the provinces and territories *(p. 73)*

federal paramountcy doctrine   doctrine according to which, in the event of conflict between a federal law and a provincial law in an area over which both levels of government have jurisdiction, the federal law governs and overrides the provincial one *(p. 104)*

federal superior courts (or federal courts)   the Federal Court, the Federal Court of Appeal, the Tax Court of Canada, and the Court Martial Appeal Court *(p. 160)*

fee simple ownership   the most absolute form of private ownership, entitling the owner to possess the property, to build on it, and to transfer it to others during her lifetime or in a will at her death *(p. 274)*

feminist theories of law   theories of law that generally concern the legal, social, and economic rights of and improving opportunities for women *(p. 18)*

feudalism   socio-political system in medieval Europe based on relationships of obligation and allegiance among king, nobles, and subjects, with land given to subordinates in return for loyalty and military support *(p. 33)*

fiduciary duty   in the context of a partnership, the responsibility to act carefully and reasonably in the best interest of the firm *(p. 302)*

fiduciary obligations   trust-like obligations, such as loyalty and good faith, that apply in certain contexts, including lawyer–client dealings *(p. 431)*

fixtures   things that are attached to the land *(p. 282)*

foreclosure proceedings   proceedings that the mortgagee (the lender) brings against the defaulting mortgagor (borrower) in order to foreclose the mortgagor's right to redeem her property *(p. 277)*

formal validity   concerns the formalities or ceremonial requirements of a marriage (p. 286)

freehold interests   form of property ownership that does not imply an obligation to pay rent (p. 276)

general partnership   business structure in which two or more persons carry on business in common with a view to profit (p. 302)

governor general   Queen's representative in Canada, formally authorized to exercise her powers as head of the executive government in Canada, but who, by convention, exercises these powers only on the advice of the prime minister and federal Cabinet (p. 139)

Governor in Council   official name for the federal Cabinet (p. 139)

headnote   concise summary of reasons for judgment, located near the beginning of a reported version of the case (p. 182)

headnotes   notes immediately above a section briefly summarizing its contents, serving the same purpose as marginal notes (p. 119)

human rights   rights that respect the dignity and worth of an individual (p. 210)

hybrid offence   a dual procedure offence, meaning that the Crown attorney has the option of choosing whether to prosecute it as a summary conviction offence or as an indictable offence (p. 345)

illegality (defence of)   a defence to negligence claims that used to be applied when the plaintiff and defendant were involved in criminal or immoral activity at the time of the injury, but is now applied mainly when the plaintiff is trying to use the negligence action to avoid a criminal penalty (p. 243)

imperial statute   law passed by the English Parliament applying specifically to an overseas English colony (p. 62)

implied terms   contract terms that the parties have not explicitly included in the contract but that are nonetheless part of the agreement (p. 258)

indefeasible   not able to be annulled, made void, or overturned (p. 280)

indictable offence   the most serious type of offence in the *Criminal Code* (for example, murder), carrying the most serious sentences (p. 344)

indictment   written document, used in superior court, describing the offences with which the accused is charged (p. 352)

inferior courts   provincial and territorial courts whose jurisdiction is limited to the less serious criminal matters, family and youth matters, and small claims disputes; the federal courts martial, part of the military court system, are also inferior courts (p. 158)

information   written document, used in provincial court, describing the offences with which the accused is charged (p. 352)

Inns of Court   professional associations for lawyers in England and Wales, with supervisory and disciplinary functions over their members and authority to call law students to the bar; the four Inns of Court today are Inner Temple, Middle Temple, Lincoln's Inn, and Gray's Inn (p. 36)

inquisitorial system   feature of civil law proceedings whereby trial judges actively assist lawyers in presenting their cases and are free to call and question witnesses and to order investigations into other evidentiary matters; contrasts with the adversarial system used in common law courts (p. 44)

instrumentalist   theories that focus on something— for example, justice or the law—as a means to an end (p. 8)

insurance law   area of private law based on a contract between an insured person and an insurer (usually a large insurance company); covers many topics, including risk planning for businesses and individuals, handling of claims, interpretation of contract clauses, and fiduciary obligations (p. 387)

intellectual property   property derived from the intellect, or mind—works of art, inventions, and designs (p. 284)

interest   any right, claim, or privilege that an individual has with respect to real or personal property (p. 273)

intervener   a party, other than the original parties to a court proceeding, who does not have a substantial and direct interest in the proceeding but has interests and perspectives helpful to the judicial determination and whose input is accepted by the court (p. 456)

joint tenancy   a form of co-ownership that features the right of survivorship as well as the "four unities" of *possession* (each co-owner has an equal right to possess the entire property), *interest* (each co-owner has an identical interest in the property), *time* (the co-owners receive their interests at the same time), and *title* (the co-owners receive their interests under the same instrument, such as a will) (p. 278)

judgment   final outcome or disposition of the dispute heard before the court, or, when the court provides reasons for its judgment, the entire set of reasons (p. 180)

Judicial Committee of the Privy Council   the highest appeal authority for colonies in the British Empire; exercised final appeal for Canada until 1949 (p. 76)

judicial independence   principle that judges should be free to make decisions based on the law and free from outside interference (p. 178)

judicial interim release   formal name for bail; the release of an accused prior to his or her trial (p. 350)

judicial review (of decisions by administrative bodies)   process by which a superior court can review the decision of an administrative body or inferior court on a number of grounds, including substantive review (review of the merits of the decision), review of discretionary decisions, and procedural review (review of the *process* followed in making the decision)   *(p. 327)*

judicial review on Charter grounds (or Charter challenge)   process by which a court reviews the constitutionality of legislation on the basis that it infringes the Charter   *(p. 97)*

judicial review on federalism grounds   process by which a court reviews the constitutionality of legislation based on a division-of-powers analysis, that is, by determining whether one level of government has attempted to enact legislation in an area assigned to the other level under the Constitution   *(p. 76)*

jurisdiction   refers (in the context of legislative power under the Constitution) to the specific subject areas over which the federal Parliament and the provincial legislatures have been assigned authority   *(p. 95)*

jurisprudence   also known as *philosophy of law* or *science of law*; concerns theories that are used to describe, explain, or criticize the law   *(p. 12)*

jus cogens   principles of international law, based on custom, that are overriding or peremptory and that cannot be changed by treaty   *(p. 371)*

king's peace   the ideal peace and well-being of a nation that the English monarch was obliged to uphold and protect   *(p. 34)*

law and society   a kind of legal study that looks at law from a broadly social, interdisciplinary perspective   *(p. 18)*

law society   the governing body of lawyers in a province or territory   *(p. 408)*

lawyer–client privilege   lawyer's obligation not to divulge confidential information concerning a client's affairs that has been communicated to the lawyer by the client and is connected to the giving or receiving of legal advice   *(p. 433)*

leasehold interests   form of property ownership that implies an obligation to pay rent   *(p. 276)*

legal aid   government funding of lawyers who provide legal assistance to persons with low income   *(p. 445)*

legal ethics   legal ethics involve the rules of conduct that govern the legal profession, and their primary purpose is the protection of the public   *(p. 420)*

legal positivism   theory that the only valid source of law is the principles, rules, and regulations expressly enacted by the institutions or persons within a society that are generally recognized as having the power to enact them   *(p. 15)*

legal realism   a theory, developed in the US and Scandinavian countries, that encouraged a more thoroughly empirical study of the process by which laws are made and applied   *(p. 16)*

legislation   written laws made by legislative assemblies   *(p. 93)*

legislative intent   a legislature's express or implied intent in passing a statute   *(p. 121)*

legislature   representative assembly charged under a constitution with making laws for a particular region or state   *(p. 92)*

letters patent   orders, based on royal prerogative, that establish rights, titles, or offices of particular persons or corporations   *(p. 143)*

libel   a kind of defamation that involves defamatory language in writing, such as in a newspaper article or book, whether in print or online   *(p. 247)*

lieutenant governor   formal head of the provincial executive government who, by convention, exercises executive power on the advice of the provincial premier and Cabinet   *(p. 139)*

Lieutenant Governor in Council   official name for a provincial Cabinet   *(p. 141)*

life estate   type of ownership whereby the fee simple owner grants a person (the life tenant) exclusive possession of a property for that person's lifetime, with the condition that the estate reverts to the fee simple owner at the life tenant's death   *(p. 275)*

limitation period   the period in which a legal action must be taken or the ability to do so is lost   *(p. 344)*

limited liability partnership   partnership structure used by certain professions in Canada (accountants and lawyers, for the most part) whereby partners are not liable for the professional negligence of other partners   *(p. 303)*

limited partnership   partnership structure involving at least one general partner, who operates the partnership and is liable for any partnership debts, and at least one limited partner, who invests in the partnership but does not operate it or take part in managing its business and is not personally liable for its debts and obligations   *(p. 302)*

litigation procedures   procedural law area involving court and tribunal procedures in civil proceedings and including such matters as the steps involved in commencing actions, notice requirements, and time limitations   *(p. 390)*

lobbying   organized effort to influence legislators on behalf of a particular interest   *(p. 455)*

majority   refers (in the context of a split decision on appeal) to the group of justices who form the majority and whose decision becomes the decision of the court   *(p. 166)*

marginal notes   notes in the margin beside a section briefly summarizing its contents *(p. 119)*

Marxist theories of law   legal theories, based on the writing of the communist philosopher Karl Marx, that are concerned with the distribution of wealth in a society; related to distributive justice theories *(p. 18)*

mediation   dispute resolution process whereby the parties try to reach a settlement with the assistance of a third party *(p. 448)*

military law   a constitutionally separate and relatively self-contained system of law regulating the Canadian Forces *(p. 27)*

misfeasance   negligent tort that involves doing something carelessly (as opposed to omitting to do something) *(p. 241)*

misrepresentation   a false representation made during contract negotiations *(p. 261)*

mitigating circumstance   a factor in the case that causes the judge to impose a milder sentence on the convicted person than she would otherwise *(p. 355)*

morality   standards of right and wrong, often associated with personal character *(p. 6)*

mortgage   a kind of charge against land that secures a debt owed by the landowner *(p. 276)*

municipal by-laws   form of subordinate legislation passed by municipalities *(p. 114)*

natural law   theory that there is a source of law that is higher than man-made law, with which man-made law must try to comply *(p. 13)*

negligence   area of tort law that addresses harm caused by *carelessness*, not intentional harm *(p. 237)*

negotiable instrument   a document that promises the payment of a specific amount of money to the payee, on demand or at a set time, and that can be transferred to a third party *(p. 306)*

negotiation   dispute resolution process whereby the parties talk to each other directly and seek a mutually acceptable solution to their problem *(p. 448)*

neutral citation   unique citation protocol, recognized internationally and in all Canadian courts, according to which courts number each of their judgments consecutively for the year in question, as well as the paragraphs within judgments *(p. 198)*

nominal damages   damages in a tort claim that reflect the breach of a plaintiff's right where no actual loss has been sustained *(p. 249)*

non-refoulement   the internationally acknowledged principle that refugees will not be returned to countries where they would face serious threats to their life or freedom *(p. 376)*

nonfeasance   negligent tort that involves omitting to do something the law requires you to do *(p. 241)*

nuisance   in law, either public or private nuisance *(p. 246)*

***obiter dicta* or *obiter* (sing. *obiter dictum*)**   statements made by the court in its reasons for judgment that may be of interest but that are inessential to the decision and therefore have no binding authority *(p. 182)*

occupiers' liability   the liability of occupiers of land for injuries that visitors sustain while on the occupiers' property *(p. 244)*

open court principle   principle that judicial proceedings should be administered in public *(p. 177)*

parliamentary sovereignty   doctrine that Parliament has ultimate and complete power to pass any law *(p. 115)*

patriate   remove a nation's legislation or constitution from the control of the mother country and bring it under the control of the nation itself *(p. 78)*

personal property   tangible, movable objects as well as intangible interests such as shares in a company *(p. 281)*

personal property security   creditor's security based on the debtor's personal property *(p. 283)*

persuasive   describes a precedent that a court is persuaded to give some weight to but is not bound to follow, because the precedent is from another jurisdiction or is otherwise not binding *(pp. 37, 173)*

plaintiff   individual, corporation, or other entity who initiates a non-criminal lawsuit *(p. 181)*

plea bargain   agreement between the Crown and the defence on how the accused will plead in court and on the sentence he will receive *(p. 351)*

plead   to answer to a criminal charge in ways permitted by the *Criminal Code* *(p. 351)*

POGG power   the general *residuary power* given to Parliament—in other words, the power to fill in the gaps left by the specifically enumerated areas of jurisdiction assigned to the two levels of government *(p. 99)*

positive law   man-made law, as opposed to a higher law (natural law) that transcends persons or institutions *(p. 15)*

practice norms   ethical standards and legal skills that legal practitioners must follow and possess to deliver legal services effectively *(p. 24)*

pre-sentence report   a report, prepared by a probation officer that provides information about the background and character of the offender, to assist a judge in sentencing *(p. 355)*

preamble   an introductory sentence or two at the beginning of a statute that succinctly states the statute's key philosophical aspect or purpose *(p. 118)*

precedent   court decision that, under the doctrine of *stare decisis*, is binding on lower courts in the same jurisdiction *(pp. 36, 172)*

preliminary inquiry   hearing before a provincial court judge to determine whether the Crown has sufficient evidence for the accused to stand trial for the offence *(p. 351)*

premier   the political head of a provincial or territorial government who leads the party with control of the majority in the Legislative Assembly (in Nunavut, there are no political parties, but the premier must command the support of the majority in the Assembly) *(p. 141)*

prerogative writs   special common law remedies for administrative infractions *(p. 332)*

prime minister   the political head of state in Canada who leads the party with control of the majority in the House of Commons *(p. 140)*

principle of non-interference   the convention prohibiting direct interference by politicians with court proceedings *(p. 149)*

private bill   a bill dealing with a private matter that relates, for example, to a particular individual, corporation, or charity *(p. 105)*

private law   law that concerns the relationships between persons *(p. 26)*

private nuisance   a tort that involves one person's using her property in such a way as to substantially interfere with another person's enjoyment or use of his property, but without any actual trespass occurring *(p. 246)*

pro bono   term applied to legal work that lawyers do at no charge to help the public (from the Latin *pro bono publico*: "for the public good") *(p. 446)*

procedural law   law relating to the process by which core rights and obligations are determined and enforced *(p. 24)*

proclamation   a special government order bringing a statute into force *(p. 106)*

prorogued   the formal closing of a legislative session *(p. 99)*

provincial superior courts   provincially constituted courts with inherent jurisdiction to hear all matters (unless taken away by legislation); two levels—a trial level and an appeal level; sometimes refers just to the trial level *(p. 159)*

public bill   a bill dealing with a matter of public policy *(p. 105)*

public international law (or international law)   law relating primarily to international treaties and customs and to inter-state relationships *(p. 364)*

public international law (or international law)   the law relating to international treaties and customs, to inter-state relationships, and to the relationship between states and non-nationals *(p. 24)*

public law   law dealing with the legal relationship between a state and individual members of the state *(p. 26)*

public nuisance   occurs when a public interest is interfered with—for example, when a highway is obstructed or a river is polluted through the defendant's actions *(p. 246)*

puisne   term applied to describe judges who rank below another judge or judges on the same court—for example, the judges below the chief justice on an appeal court *(p. 162)*

punitive damages   damages in a tort claim that are granted in situations where the court wishes to punish the defendant for socially objectionable behaviour *(p. 250)*

quasi-criminal offences   less serious offences, such as pollution or traffic offences, that do not fall under the federal criminal law power—they may be passed by all levels of government but are frequently created under provincial legislation *(p. 340)*

quasi-legislative materials   non-legislated written rules that relate to and affect a legal process *(p. 115)*

Queen's Privy Council for Canada   formal advisory council of the governor general, the active portion of which is the federal Cabinet *(p. 141)*

ratio or ratio decidendi   Latin phrase ("the reason for the decision") referring to the governing rule in a case or the way it was applied to the facts *(p. 37)*

reading   a bill's formal presentation to the legislature before it becomes a statute *(p. 105)*

real property (or real estate)   land and anything attached to the land, such as buildings and resources *(p. 272)*

rectification   for contract disputes based on errors in the written contract, a remedy whereby the court orders that the contract be rewritten to correct the mistake *(p. 266)*

reference   special case in which the executive branch of government refers a question of law to a court of appeal, usually a question concerning the constitutionality of a statute or course of action the government is considering *(p. 164)*

regulations   form of subordinate legislation passed by a person or body (frequently the government Cabinet) to expand on or fill out a statute's legislative scheme *(p. 113)*

reliance damages   a remedy for contract disputes that compensates the innocent party for expenses he incurred preparing for the performance of contractual obligations *(p. 265)*

rescission   a remedy for contract disputes whereby the contract is cancelled and the parties are returned to the positions they were in just before the contract was entered into *(p. 266)*

reserve   postpone rendering its decision, after a hearing has concluded, so the court can carefully prepare the reasons for its judgment *(p. 166)*

respondent   individual, corporation, or other entity who won at trial and who is responding to the appellant on an appeal to a higher court *(p. 181)*

responsible government   system of government in which the members of the executive branch are drawn from the elected members of the legislative branch and in which their power continues only so long as they enjoy the support of the majority in the legislature *(p. 136)*

restitution damages   a remedy for contract disputes that compensates the innocent party for moneys usually paid over to the other party (deposits and part payments, for example) *(p. 265)*

retributive justice   theory of justice based on *lex talionis*, or the law of retaliation *(p. 9)*

revised statutes   republished, revised collection of all public statutes for a jurisdiction, providing a comprehensive statutory "snapshot" as of the revision date *(p. 128)*

right of survivorship   a main condition of joint tenancy whereby the surviving co-owners automatically inherit a deceased owner's share *(p. 278)*

riparian rights   rights that are attached to property fronting lakes or rivers and that include the right to make use of the water for certain activities and the obligation not to interfere with the riparian rights of others *(p. 279)*

royal assent   formal approval of a bill by the Queen's representative *(p. 105)*

royal prerogative   powers and privileges given by the common law to the Crown; a source of limited executive power *(p. 142)*

royal proclamation   public announcement of a formal order concerning some executive action based on royal prerogative, such as a declaration of war *(p. 142)*

rule in *Rylands v Fletcher*   the strict liability rule that the person who brings a dangerous substance onto his property is answerable for the damage it causes if it should escape *(p. 244)*

rule of law   a key legal concept whose central tenets are that everyone is equal before the law and that power under the law should not be used arbitrarily *(p. 19)*

***scienter* action**   a strict liability tort claim concerning damage caused by a domestic animal; based on the idea that the defendant (the owner) had knowledge the animal was dangerous *(p. 245)*

search warrant   a warrant, issued by a justice of the peace or a provincial court judge, authorizing police to conduct a search *(p. 348)*

section   the basic unit of a statute *(p. 118)*

section 96 courts   provincial superior courts, so called because their judges are federally appointed under section 96 of the *Constitution Act, 1867* *(p. 159)*

sentence   the punishment the judge imposes on a person convicted of a criminal offence *(p. 354)*

separation-of-powers doctrine   doctrine according to which separate powers are assigned to the legislative, executive, and judicial branches of government *(p. 92)*

short title   abbreviated version of the full statute title *(p. 117)*

slander   a kind of defamation transmitted via oral or other transitory forms of communication *(p. 247)*

sociology of law   a kind of sociological study that looks at law from a broadly social, interdisciplinary perspective *(p. 18)*

sole proprietorship   business that is owned and operated by an individual and that is not a legal entity separate from the owner *(p. 301)*

specific performance   a remedy for contract disputes whereby the court orders the party in breach to perform his obligations as promised *(p. 266)*

standard of review   defines the level of deference the court pays to the tribunal when conducting a judicial review *(p. 329)*

stare decisis   Latin phrase ("to stand by decided matters") referring to the common law principle that a precedent is binding on lower courts in the same jurisdiction *(p. 36)*

state immunity   immunity that a state or its officials have in the event they become the subject of judicial proceedings in another state *(p. 367)*

state jurisdiction   area of control within which a state's sovereignty can be exercised *(p. 366)*

state responsibility   principle that a state should be held accountable for breaches of international obligations *(p. 367)*

state sovereignty   principle that a state has exclusive power in certain areas, such as the power to make, administer, and adjudicate its own laws in relation to itself and its own citizens and residents *(p. 366)*

statutes   the primary form of legislation *(pp. 93, 128)*

statutory interpretation   process of interpreting legislation to resolve any ambiguities regarding its meaning or effect *(p. 121)*

strict liability tort   a tort for which the defendant is held responsible even if the damaging action was neither intentional nor a result of negligence *(p. 243)*

style of cause   the name of the case or title of the proceeding, consisting of the names of the parties to the dispute *(p. 198)*

subject of international law   usually a state that has as an "international legal personality" and is capable of possessing international rights and obligations *(p. 366)*

subordinate (or delegated) legislation   legislation passed pursuant to a statute whereby the principal lawmaking power has *delegated* authority to another body to make laws *(p. 112)*

substantive laws   laws that deal with core rights and obligations *(p. 24)*

substantive review   review of an administrative decision's merits that considers both the legal and factual bases of the tribunal's analysis *(p. 329)*

succession law   area of private law that covers issues concerning wills and estates and the transmission of property upon death *(p. 388)*

summary conviction offence   the least serious type of offence in the *Criminal Code* (for example, trespassing or disturbing the peace), tried only in provincial court and subject to the lightest sentences *(p. 344)*

summons   a document served personally on an accused person requiring her to be in court at a certain date and time *(p. 350)*

superior court of criminal jurisdiction   the highest court in each province and territory to hear criminal matters, sometimes with a jury, its designation varying by province and territory *(p. 345)*

support   property owner's obligation to consider how changes made to his property may affect his neighbour's property *(p. 279)*

supremacy clause   section 52(1) of the *Constitution Act, 1982*, which provides that the Constitution is the supreme law of Canada and empowers the courts to find that laws that are inconsistent with the Constitution are of no force and effect *(p. 96)*

Supreme Court of Canada   Canada's highest court and final court of appeal *(p. 160)*

taxation law   complex, wide-ranging area of public law encompassing federal, provincial, and municipal taxation laws applicable to personal, property, and business income; capital gains; property ownership; and sales transactions *(p. 386)*

tenancy in common   a form of co-ownership that does not involve the four unities or the right of survivorship, meaning that a co-owner can transfer her interest to others during her lifetime or leave it to others in her will *(p. 278)*

territorial superior courts   federally constituted superior courts with jurisdiction in the territories *(p. 160)*

Torrens system (or land titles system)   system for registering property ownership that eliminates the transfer of title by deeds and replaces them with statutory transfer forms, meaning that the title is guaranteed (or *indefeasible*) *(p. 280)*

tort   a type of civil wrong for which damages can be obtained by the person wronged *(p. 232)*

trespass to goods (or trespass to chattels)   a tort whereby one person intentionally interferes with another's rightful possession of movable property *(p. 234)*

trespass to land   tort involving the physical intrusion by one person onto land occupied by another *(p. 234)*

trespass to person   an intentional tort encompassing three subcategories of tort: assault, battery, and false imprisonment *(p. 233)*

trustee   someone who has legal title to the property but holds it for another and has the fiduciary responsibility to make decisions for the benefit of the other party *(p. 278)*

trusts (law of)   private law area dealing with how trusts are created, the relationship between the legal owner of property (the trustee) and the equitable owner (or beneficiary), the regulation of trust relationships by legislation, and the remedies for breach of trust *(p. 389)*

undertaking   clear statement of intention by one person, usually a lawyer, that is reasonably relied on by another, amounting to a solemn promise that must be kept or the person who has given the undertaking will be liable for misconduct *(pp. 351, 430)*

unicameral   legislature with one house involved in the passage of legislation *(p. 92)*

unified family courts   special divisions of the trial level of a provincial superior court with complete jurisdiction over family law matters, including matters that would otherwise be heard in a provincial inferior court *(p. 168)*

unilateral contract   contracts that are in the form of a "promise for an action," the offeror promising something (usually payment) if the offeree accepts by performing a requested action *(p. 255)*

unitary government   a form of government whereby one supreme authority governs the whole country *(p. 73)*

verdict   the finding of a jury on the matter before it—for example, whether the accused is guilty or not guilty *(p. 352)*

vicarious liability   the strict liability of one party for the fault of another due to the special relationship between them (typically, an employer–employee relationship) *(p. 245)*

writ   court document, obtained by a plaintiff, by which the defendant was informed that a particular type of action had been started against him *(p. 35)*

Index

Credits

CHAPTER 1

Page 3: xstock/Shutterstock.com

Page 9: duncan1890/iStock.com

Page 11: Chiloa/Wikipedia Commons

Page 14: *Jean-Jacques Rosseau*, 1766, Allan Ramsay, 1713–1784, oil on canvas, 84.9 x 64.8 cm. Scottish National Gallery (no. NG 820).

Page 20: Photos.com/Thinkstock.com

CHAPTER 2

Page 31: North Wind Picture Archives/Alamy Stock Photo

Page 41: EmmePi Images/Alamy Stock Photo

CHAPTER 3

Page 59: Canadian Charter of Rights and Freedoms, © Government of Canada. Reproduced with the permission of the Minister of Public Works and Government Services Canada (2013). Library and Archives Canada/Robert Stacey fonds/e010758222.

Page 64: Collections of the Nova Scotia Historical Society. Volume XVIII. Printed for the Society by WM MacNab & Son, Halifax, NS, 1914.

Page 66: *The Death of General Wolfe*, 1770, Benjamin West. American, British, 1738–1820, oil on canvas, 152.6 x 214.5 cm. Transfer from the Canadian War Memorials, 1921 (Gift of the 2nd Duke of Westminster, England, 1918). National Gallery of Canada (no. 8007).

Page 68: MP-0000.1815.2 | Photograph | Commission to codify the laws of Lower Canada in civil matters, Quebec City, QC, about 1865 ©McCord Museum.

Page 69-70: Canadian Geographic

Page 71: M993X.5.1010 | Print | The East welcomes the West. Presentation to BC representatives by Sir John A. ©McCord Museum.

Page 72: GP Roberts/Library and Archives Canada, C-000733

Page 75: John McNeill/*The Globe and Mail*/CP Photo

CHAPTER 4

Page 91: achinthamb/Shutterstock.com

Page 99: World Stock/Shutterstock.com

Page 100: David J. Mitchell/Shutterstock.com

CHAPTER 5

Page 135: Library and Archives Canada/C-9060

Page 137: Andrew Milligan/CP Photo

CHAPTER 6

Page 155: Wangkun Jia/Shutterstock.com

Page 165: Dennis MacDonald/Alamy Stock Photo

Page 173: Michael Bedford, Ottawa

Page 175: Credit: Roy Grogan, photographer. Supreme Court of Canada Collection.

CHAPTER 7

Page 205: Rawpixel.com/Shutterstock.com

Page 208: Photo by © Hulton-Deutsch Collection/CORBIS/ Corbis via Getty Images

Page 212: Martin Perreault/Shutterstock.com

Page 217: Trevor Florence, The Invermere Soaring Centre

Page 220: Tom Hansom/CP Photo

CHAPTER 8

Page 229: tommaso79/Shutterstock.com

Page 238: Ray Delgado/Artizans.com

Page 244: Paul Mahoney/Cartoonstock.com. No. pmnn52.

CHAPTER 9

Page 271: HQuality/Shutterstock.com

Page 287: Ric Ernst/*The Province*/PNG

CHAPTER 10

Page 299: Pop Tika/Shutterstock.com

Page 303: Table 10.1: "Comparison Three Types of Partnership": Tamra Alexander & Pat Papadeas, *Canadian Business Law*, 3rd ed (Toronto: Emond, 2018) at 225-226.

CHAPTER 11

Page 317: Sophie James/Shutterstock.com

CHAPTER 12

Page 335: Sirtravelalot/Shutterstock.com

Page 338: Figure 12.1: "Overview of Canada's Criminal Justice System": Karla O'Regan & Susan Reid, *Thinking About Criminal Justice in Canada*, 2nd ed (Toronto: Emond, 2017) at xii.

Page 359: Table 12.1: "Euro–Canadian Versus Traditional Indigenous Justice": James S Frideres & René R Gadacz, *Aboriginal Peoples in Canada*, 9th ed (Toronto: Pearson, 2012) at 119.

CHAPTER 13

Page 363: United Nations General Assembly Hall in the UN Headquarters, New York. Photo by Basil D. Soufi, Creative Commons, Wikipedia.

Page 378: Courtesy of Johnson Space Center of the United States, NASA #AS11-40-5874. Public domain.

CHAPTER 14

Page 383: Osgoode Hall, Great Library, Toronto, Ontario, #DSC00432. Creative Commons, Public Domain, Wikipedia.

CHAPTER 15

Page 403: Law Society of Ontario Archives, Archives Department collection, "Toronto: Osgoode Hall," S1156.

Page 407: Library and Archives Canada/ PA-12848

CHAPTER 16

Page 419: stoatphoto/Shutterstock.com

CHAPTER 17

Page 443: Michael Wheatley/Alamy Stock Photo